AQA PSYCHOLOGY For A Level Year 1 & AS

2nd Ed

Cara Flanagan
Matt Jarvis
Rob Liddle

Illuminate Publishing

Published in 2020 by Illuminate Publishing Limited, an imprint of Hodder Education, an Hachette UK Company, Carmelite House, 50 Victoria Embankment, London EC4Y 0DZ

Orders: Please visit www.illuminatepublishing.com or email sales@illuminatepublishing.com

British Library Cataloguing in Publication Data

A catalogue record for this book is available from the British Library

ISBN 978-1-912820-42-9

Printed in Wales by Cambrian Printers Ltd

10.21

Editor: Nic Watson

Design: Nigel Harriss

Layout: Sarah Clifford (Kamae Design)

The Year 1 course: A level and AS

Co-teachability

Students doing the AS or Year 1 of the A level cover exactly the same topics during their course of study. A level students have a few additional topics for Paper 2 (see bottom of this page). This means that the AS and Year 1 of the A level are co-teachable.

In the A level exams questions are worth a maximum of 16 marks and AS questions a maximum of 12 marks (see page 213 for more on this).

If you are an A level student, you can take the AS exam at the end of your first year but this will not count towards your A level. A level students must take all three A level papers at the end of their final year of study.

AS level

- There are two papers.
- Each paper is 1½ hours and 72 marks in total.
- Each paper is worth 50% of the final AS level mark.

Paper 1 Introductory Topics in Psychology

Each section is worth 24 marks. All questions are compulsory.

Section A: Social influence
Section B: Memory
Section C: Attachment

Paper 2 Psychology in Context

Each section is worth 24 marks. All questions are compulsory.

Section A: Approaches in Psychology
Section B: Psychopathology
Section C: Research methods

Research methods

About 25% of the overall assessment will assess skills in relation to research methods.

A minimum of 10% of the overall assessment will assess mathematical skills (see page 217) for both AS and A level.

A level

- There are three papers.
- Each paper is 2 hours and 96 marks in total.
- Each paper is worth 33.3% of the final A level mark.

Paper 1 Introductory Topics in Psychology

Each section is worth 24 marks. All questions are compulsory.
Section A: Social influence
Section B: Memory
Section C: Attachment
Section D: Psychopathology

Paper 2 Psychology in Context

Sections A and B are worth 24 marks, Section C is worth 48 marks.
All questions are compulsory.
Section A: Approaches in Psychology
Section B: Biopsychology
Section C: Research methods

Paper 3 Issues and Options in Psychology

Each section is worth 24 marks. Section A is compulsory, Sections B, C and D contain three topics each and students select one topic from each.
Section A: Issues and debates in Psychology
Section B: Relationships, Gender or Cognition and Development
Section C: Schizophrenia, Eating Behaviour or Stress
Section D: Aggression, Forensic Psychology or Addiction

Paper 2: Extra topics for A level (covered in our Year 2 book)

If you are doing A level rather than AS, then you will need to study Paper 3 topics plus the following additional topics for Paper 2:

Approaches: The psychodynamic and humanistic approaches, plus a comparison of all approaches.

Biopsychology: Localisation of function in the brain, ways of studying the brain, biological rhythms.

Research methods: Content analysis, case studies, reliability, validity, features of science, reporting psychological investigations, levels of measurement, probability and significance, choosing inferential tests.

Contents

How to use this book

Psychology assessment consists of three skills: describing what you know, applying your knowledge and analysing/evaluating this knowledge. This applies to all students – AS students and A level students.

On pages 213–223 we look at the skills needed for AS/A level Psychology, which will help you see why we have designed our spreads as they are.

What is an 'assessment objective' (AO)?

It is something that is used to assess your ability.

You can demonstrate what you know by describing it (AO1) but there is more to knowledge than that. There is the further skill of being able to use your knowledge in new situations (applying your knowledge, AO2). And a further skill is to be able to judge the value of your knowledge (evaluation, AO3).

All three of these skills are what you are examined on.

Describing what you know

Assessment objective 1 (AO1) is concerned with your ability to report *detailed* descriptions of psychological knowledge and demonstrate your *understanding* of this knowledge.

We have presented all the AO1 material on the left-hand side of each spread.

We have divided the text up with subheadings to help you organise your understanding. Each heading should act as a cue for material to recall and matches the material in the summary at the end of each chapter.

Applying your knowledge

Assessment objective 2 (AO2) is concerned with being able to apply your psychological knowledge.

It is a really good way to assess whether you do understand the psychological knowledge.

On every spread we usually have two or three '**Apply it**' questions which give you a chance to practise this AO2 skill of application in relation to both concepts and research methods.

Research methods topics are covered in Chapter 6 but we have given you a chance to apply this knowledge throughout the book.

Analysing and evaluating

Assessment objective 3 (AO3) is concerned with your ability to evaluate the theories, concepts and studies you have learned about.

We have presented the AO3 material on the right-hand side of each spread.

Generally we have provided:

- Two or three **evaluation points**. Each of these is divided into three paragraphs to help you understand how to structure evaluation using PET. →
- One **counterpoint** – to help you develop the skill of *discussion*. Extended writing questions may say 'Discuss' which means you should present your evaluation points as a two-sided discussion (point and counterpoint).
- One **evaluation extra** – for those who want a bit more evaluation we offer a debate to consider. It is always preferable to include fewer points but really elaborate the ones you do, rather than trying to cover many poorly explained points. So this really is an 'extra'.

P – Identify the POINT to be made.

E – ELABORATE the point. Which can be done with an EXAMPLE, or some EVIDENCE from a research study or an EXPLANATION.

T – End with a link back to the essay title and/or give a conclusion: 'THIS suggests ...' 'THEREFORE ...' 'THIS means ...'.

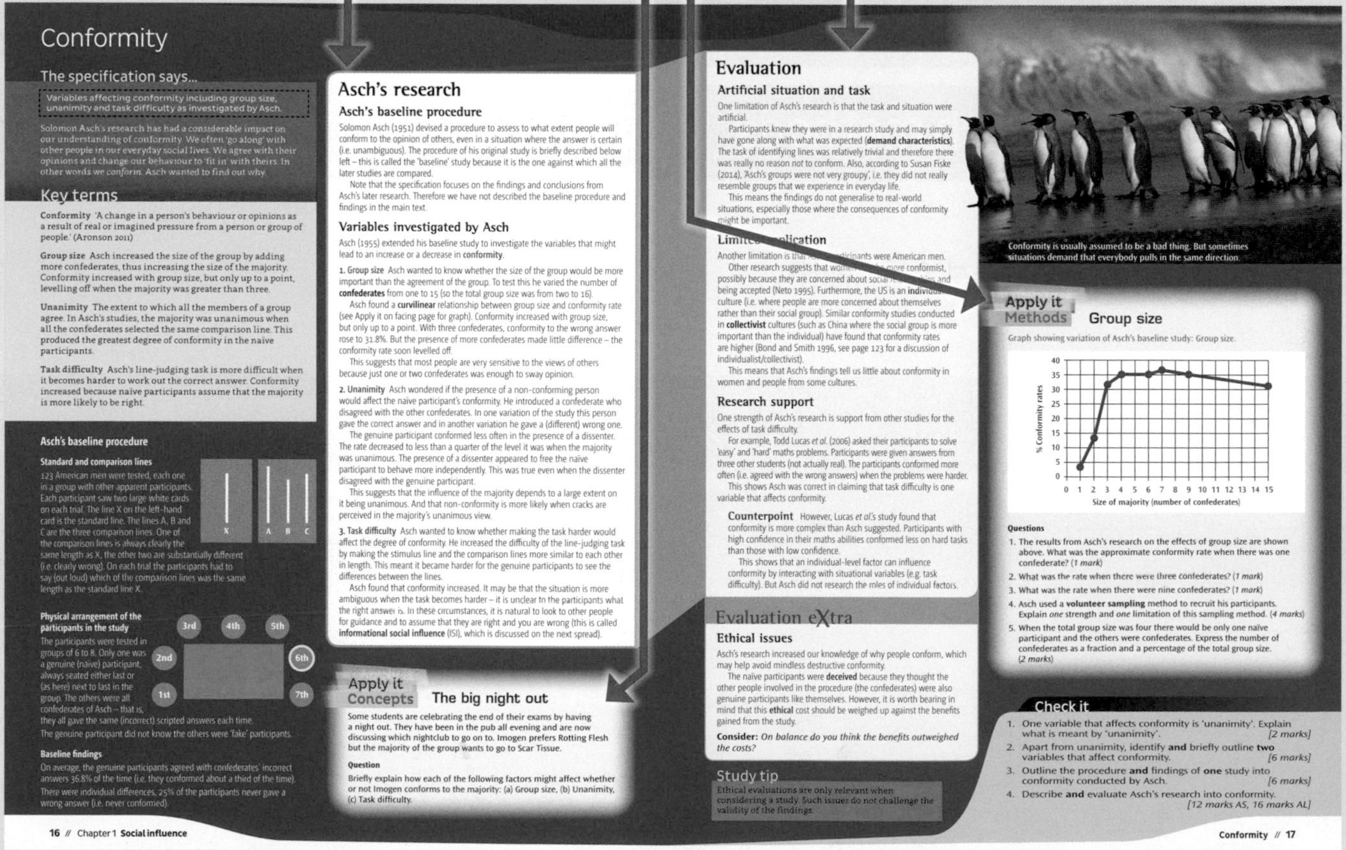

Conformity
The specification says...
Key terms
Asch's research
Asch's baseline procedure
Variables investigated by Asch
Asch's baseline procedure
Apply it Concepts The big night out
Evaluation
Artificial situation and task
Research support
Evaluation eXtra
Ethical issues
Study tip
Apply it Methods Group size
Check it
16 // Chapter 1 Social influence
Conformity // 17

Extra features on each spread

he specification says

he spread begins (top left) with an excerpt from the specification showing what ; covered on the spread. There is also a brief analysis of what the specification ntry means.

ey terms

he specification terms are explained, mirroring what you might be expected to now if you were asked to explain the terms. These key terms are emboldened 1 blue in the text.

Other important words are emboldened in the text and explained in the **lossary**, which forms part of the index.

tudy tips

his book has been written by very experienced teachers and subject experts. Vhen there is room they give you some of their top tips about the skills ecessary to demonstrate your understanding of psychology. The study tips nay also include pointers about typical misunderstandings.

heck it

sample of practice questions to help you focus on how you will be using the naterial on the spread.

The final question is an extended writing question. AS students should aim o answer a 12-mark version whereas A level students will need to practise a 6-mark version. Extended writing skills are discussed on pages 220–221.

Student digital book (SDB)

A digital version of this student book is also available if your school has access to our Digital Book Bundle of student and teacher resources. You can view this digital version via a tablet or computer at school, home or on the bus – wherever it suits you.

There are extra features in the student digital book that support your studies. For every spread in this book there are:

- **Lifelines**: Very straightforward, easy-to-digest key descriptive points for the spread topic.
- **Extensions**: Extra information, studies or activities to challenge and stretch you further.
- **Weblinks** to useful YouTube videos or other sites.
- **Answers** to the **Apply It** and **Evaluation extra** questions in this book (invaluable!).
- **Quizzes**: Interactive, self-marking quizzes that help to check and reinforce your understanding of a topic.
- **Practice questions**: Extra questions to help you practise your skills.

Need a lifeline?
The SDB is your answer.

Extra features in each chapter

Chapter introduction

Each chapter begins with discussion points that might help you start thinking about the topic.

Practical corner

Questions on research methods account for about 25% of the assessment, therefore you should devote a lot of time to understanding how psychologists conduct research. There is no better way to do this than being a researcher yourself. We offer some ideas for research activities and provide additional opportunities to practise mathematical skills.

Chapter summary

Each chapter ends with a useful spread summarising the key points from each main content spread.

These summaries should help you revise. Look at each key point and see what you can remember. Look back at the spread to remind yourself. Each time you do this you should remember more.

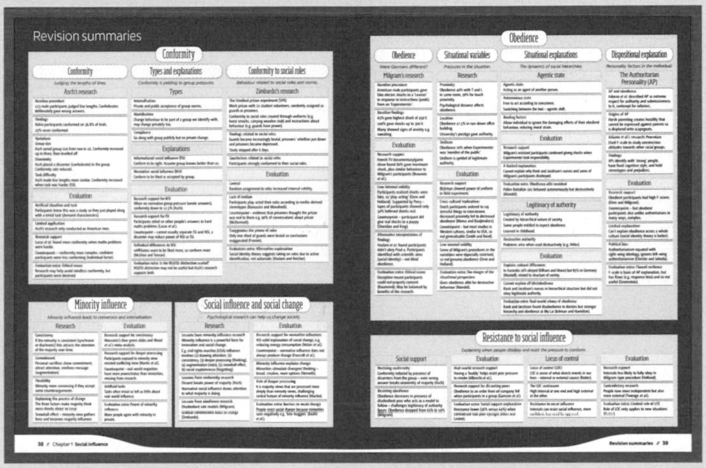
Revision summaries

Practice questions, answers and feedback

Learning how to produce effective question answers is a SKILL. On this spread in each chapter we look at some typical student answers to practice questions. The comments provided indicate what is good and bad in each answer.

Multiple-choice questions (MCQs)

Here's a chance to test your new-found knowledge. Questions are given for each main content spread in the chapter, with answers at the bottom right of the multiple-choice questions spread. Keep trying until you get 100%.

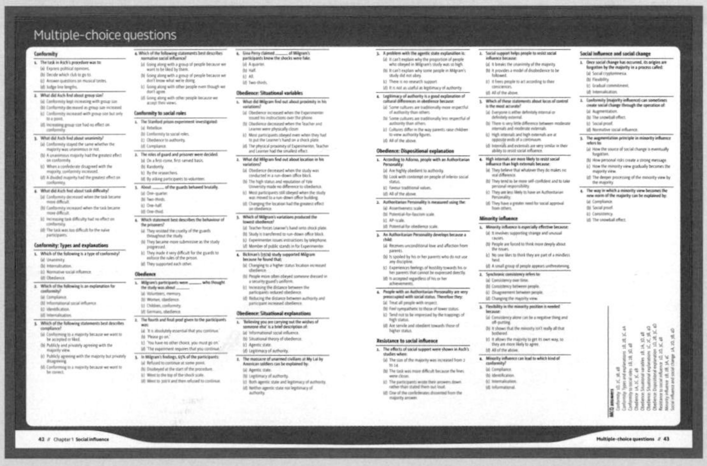
Multiple-choice questions

What is Psychology?

Some people think that psychology is just common sense – but it isn't. In some ways, psychology can be seen as a *test* of common sense. Psychology has shown that what we have always strongly believed to be true often turns out to be wrong. And sometimes things that sound like wild ideas turn out to be true.

Psychology specialises in what are called counter-intuitive findings. These are the results from psychological research studies that you just didn't expect, which pleasingly and surprisingly contradict common sense. You read them, and you think, 'Well, how about that then?'.

The philosopher Voltaire said, 'Common sense is not so common'. He could well have added, 'and doesn't often make a lot of sense either'.

Decisions, decisions, decisions

You have probably had many experiences of having to make a decision about something important and agonising over it. Should I or shouldn't I?

For example, Cara's daughter recently couldn't decide whether or not she should break up with her boyfriend. I won't list the things he had done wrong but she really wasn't sure that he was the one. On the other hand she loved him.

She eventually decided to stay with the relationship but kept asking herself, 'Did I do the right thing, or would I be better off without him?'

Psychologists have explained Cara's daughter's confusion. Let's begin with a study they carried out.

They told students in their study: I am going to pay you £50 to spend an hour to turn the pegs on a board 90 degrees at a time.

(So far, this sounds like a good deal. But there is a little more to it.)

When you have finished I wonder if you would mind telling some other students that you actually really enjoyed the task.

The two psychologists who did this study – Leon Festinger and James Carlsmith (1959) – demonstrated something quite surprising. What do you think the students said when they had to describe the task to another student? Those students who were paid a lot (it was actually $20 but the study *was* done in 1959) were a bit negative. But students who were paid a measly $1 gave a glowing account of what fun they had!

If there is a budding psychologist inside you, you should be asking 'That's odd – I wonder why?'

Festinger and Carlsmith came up with a theory called *cognitive dissonance*. If you do a boring task for a lot of money and then have to tell someone it was fun, this produces *no* conflict in your mind ('I did it because I was paid a lot'). If you do a boring task and have to say it was fun but get very little money, you may be asking yourself, 'why did I do that?' – there is some conflict in your mind.

12
3
9
6
TODAY'S SCHEDULE
TURN PEGS
WATCH PAINT DRY
GO CARPET SHOPPING
SNOOKER

Turning pegs for an hour. Would you do it?

The students with conflict had to find an excuse for themselves about why they did such a boring task and lied, so they convinced themselves it wasn't actually that boring – and that meant they could justify their behaviour to themselves.

The theory of cognitive dissonance says that when we are faced with a decision that produces conflict (dissonance), we want to reduce the conflict. One way to do this is to increase or decrease the desirability of one of the options, and then the anxiety vapourises.

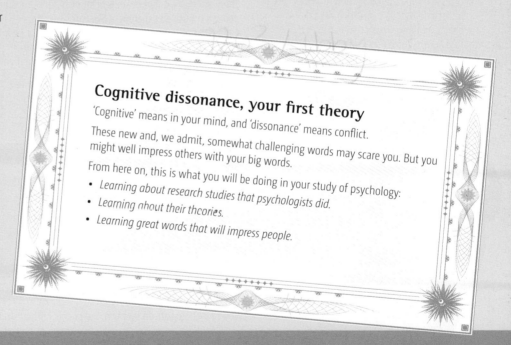

Cognitive dissonance, your first theory

'Cognitive' means in your mind, and 'dissonance' means conflict.

These new and, we admit, somewhat challenging words may scare you. But you might well impress others with your big words.

From here on, this is what you will be doing in your study of psychology:

- *Learning about research studies that psychologists did.*
- *Learning about their theories.*
- *Learning great words that will impress people.*

And what does this have to do with Cara's daughter and her boyfriend?

Her distress is a state of *cognitive dissonance* – holding two conflicting thoughts – should I have finished the relationship or should I have continued? That creates discomfort and we naturally seek to reduce it. Cara's daughter spoke to a friend, Alison, who was in a similar situation. Alison ended her relationship and says she has regretted it ever since. Alison's ex has now found someone else. This makes Cara's daughter feel better – she made the right choice. Her dissonance is reduced.

Psychology is great!

Psychology is the science of behaviour and experience

Armchair psychology

People like to offer their own explanations for why people do what they do.

Psychologists go beyond common sense and beyond personal opinions. The single thing that matters most in psychology is evidence. Real psychologists, as opposed to armchair ones, are expected to provide evidence for their every utterance (well, almost every one).

Evidence doesn't come from personal experience, or subjective opinion. It comes from what we call **empirical** data, which is what research studies are all about.

Research studies are crucially important, and form the foundations of psychology. Psychologists do research studies – they write down what they did (**procedures**) and what they found (**findings**). Then other psychologists can read about the studies and criticise them or design a new study.

But let's not be too dismissive of that armchair theorising. That's the starting point of our psychological knowledge. We then use the evidence from studies to evaluate our theories, to change and develop them, to get as close to the truth about behaviour as we scientifically can.

The key word is **science**.

We think science is the best thing since sliced bread – but actually it isn't a 'thing', it's a *process*. It is a wonderful process that enables us to get closer and closer to understanding the world. This is the process:

Step 1: Identify a research question or issue. This usually stems from observing an interesting behaviour, or from a broader psychological theory.

For example (and lets take a simple example), have you ever heard the saying 'familiarity breeds contempt' or 'absence makes the heart grow fonder'? So which is true?

Step 2: Decide on a topic to study (your **aim**). Your observations lead you to decide on a topic to study. In some kinds of scientific research a formal statement is made – a **hypothesis**. This is a statement of what you believe is true. You state this so that you can test to see whether it is supported by evidence and thus may reflect reality.

In order to test our idea we need to go with one of the views – familiarity leads to increased liking rather than contempt.

So here's our hypothesis 'You feel more positive about a word you hear ten times than a word you hear just once'.

Step 3: Design a study to test your hypothesis. This is where it gets remarkable. The key feature of science (as you should know from GCSE) is that it is controlled. There are many different kinds of study but let's consider doing a controlled experiment like Festinger and Carlsmith's (previous page) – we get one group of people to do a task in one way and we get another group of people to do a task differently so we can compare them.

Step 4: Carry out the study. It's very important to take due account of **ethical issues** when conducting the study (see facing page).

In fact Robert Zajonc (a well-known psychologist whose name just happens to be pronounced as 'Science' – yes, really) tested just such a hypothesis. He made up a list of words such as ZABULON and ENANWAL.

Participants were asked to listen to a list of words. One group of participants heard the word ZABULON 10 times in the list and a second group heard it once. The opposite was true for ENANWAL.*

At the end participants were asked to rate how much they liked all the words in the list.

Step 5: Analyse the results and draw conclusions. You may present your results in a bar chart or may do a statistical test to see if your hypothesis is supported.

Step 6: Evaluate and feed back. If the hypothesis has been rejected by the analysis, then it needs to be revised and retested. So we form a revised hypothesis ...

Even if your hypothesis is supported, you might come up with further ideas to refine your original hypothesis ...

Zajonc found that participants did rate the words heard more frequently as more likeable. So we can conclude that familiarity does not breed contempt.

However, there are strengths and limitations of this study. Can you think of any?

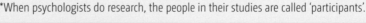

*When psychologists do research, the people in their studies are called 'participants'.

The even better news is that psychologists don't have all the answers. The truly great thing about psychology, the thing that really gets thousands of researchers and practitioners up in the mornings, is that there is still so much to learn and understand. There is still a lot of room for discussion and debate. And now you can join in.

Validity

If you think about the study by Zajonc on the facing page, something might have occurred to you – participants would have realised that some of the words were repeated a lot. This may have led at least some participants to try to guess what the study was about and alter their behaviour.

Therefore the results of the study might not actually represent anything real. This is an issue of **validity** – which refers to whether something is real or just an outcome of a research study that actually doesn't represent reality. Validity is a difficult topic to understand so don't expect to get it all at once. But it is an issue of central importance in psychological research so you will need to get it eventually.

Internal validity

Internal validity concerns things *inside* a research study. It may be the question of whether we are testing what we actually intend to test. **In our familiarity example, do you think we were actually testing whether familiarity makes something more likeable?**

Internal validity also concerns the question of 'control'. It might be that other factors affected our findings. For example, some people might have heard the words ZABULON and ENANWAL before (not likely – that's why they were chosen). But if they had, that would have spoiled everything. Researchers need to try to control everything that could cause the findings to be due to anything other than what was intended. This is something discussed in Chapter 6.

External validity

External validity is concerned with things *outside* the research study. To what extent can we generalise our research findings to other situations? **Do you think Zajonc's study could be used to explain why repeated adverts are very successful on TV?**

A mysterious student has been attending a class at Oregon State University for the past two months enveloped in a big black bag. Only his bare feet show. Each Monday, Wednesday and Friday at 11.00 am the Black Bag sits on a small table near the back of the classroom. The class is Speech 113 – basic persuasion ... Charles Goetzinger, professor of the class, knows the identity of the person inside. None of his students in the class do. Goetzinger said the students' attitude changed from hostility toward the Black Bag to curiosity and finally to friendship.

Taken from the Associated Press (27 February 1967)

When Zajonc (1968) wrote a report of his study described on the facing page he began with the story above. It was the starting point for his study. This event in the basic persuasion class suggests that familiarity doesn't breed contempt – it actually breeds liking for something. At least in some situations...

He called this the *mere exposure effect*.

Research methods in Psychology

Psychologists use a variety of methods in their research – all of them aim to be scientific because they seek to be objective and controlled and repeatable. Often psychologists conduct **experiments**, which means they can draw conclusions about cause and effect. The main issue with experiments is they can be quite trivial, just looking at a few variables doesn't always represent real life (you might feel that about Zajonc's study).

One alternative is to simply **observe** what people do in their everyday lives – psychologists watch people through two-way mirrors or from behind a bush in a park (not very often). The problem here is that, frequently, there is just too much going on to allow us to draw useful conclusions. Other methods include **questionnaires**, **interviews**, **case studies** and also performing **correlational analysis**.

The key is using all kinds of different methods to study one aspect of behaviour and considering how the findings from the different kinds of study inform us.

As research methods are so important to psychology, they feature very prominently throughout this book.

Ethics in Psychology

Ethics refers to standards of behaviour, behaving with due respect for the people (or animals) you are studying. Ethical issues matter in psychology because the potential for causing damage is so much greater in psychology than it is in, say, chemistry. The subject matter of psychology is alive and can get upset. It is all too easy to carry out studies that could expose people to embarrassment, anxiety, stress or even worse forms of **psychological harm**.

So psychologists are always very careful to include steps to reduce this possibility, to make sure that the dignity and welfare of participants are protected. Ethical guidance is issued by professional psychological associations such as the British Psychological Society (BPS) or the American Psychological Association (APA). These organisations publish codes of conduct that psychologists and researchers have to follow in their research and professional practice.

Statistical analysis in Psychology

We've seen that conducting empirical research is a fundamental activity of psychology, but it would all be wasted effort if we didn't have a way of knowing what our results mean. This is where statistics come in.

There are two types of statistics in widespread use in psychology – ***descriptive*** **statistics** and ***statistical tests***. Descriptive statistics summarise data. They include measures such as the **mean** and drawing **graphs**. Such methods allow us to get a quick snapshot of the patterns in our data. Statistical tests are based on **probability** (see Chapter 6). The key thing for you to know is they tell us if any pattern in our results is just due to chance.

Approaches

In Chapter 4 we discuss approaches in psychology, so this is a very brief introduction to support you until you get to that chapter.

The idea of an 'approach' is that psychologists tend to have a general view of what causes behaviour. Some psychologists think that the way we behave is largely inherited (that's one approach), others believe it is largely learned through your life experience (another approach to understanding behaviour).

For example – think about football.

What is it that makes someone interested in football or good at it? Did they inherit some kind of football gene from their parents or did they learn to love it perhaps because their family enjoyed kicking a ball around?

Psychologists call this **nature** (what you are born with) or **nurture** (your life experiences).

Aside from views on nature–nurture, there are other key differences between the main approaches described on this page.

Nature or nurture? *Or nappies?*

Biological approach

The biological approach explains behaviour in terms of physical causes in our brains and bodies, and this includes our **genes**.

The most likely biological source of causes of behaviour is the brain, which produces chemicals called **neurotransmitters** (such as **serotonin**, which plays an important role in regulating our moods).

The **endocrine system** is also significant because it produces **hormones** (for example **adrenaline**) that have a big impact on our behaviour.

The methods used by this approach to investigate behaviour are physical too. **Brain scans** can show us the structure and functioning of the brain. Researchers then try to relate these to normal as well as abnormal behaviours. In the last 20 years the development of brain scanning techniques has led to a massive increase in understanding how the brain relates to behaviour.

Research on animals can be helpful too, because we can't deliberately make changes to the human brain to observe the effect on behaviour (no really, we can't, not for research purposes).

This approach to understanding behaviour is largely 'nature' – though many aspects of the brain and body and even your genes (surprisingly) can be changed by nurture.

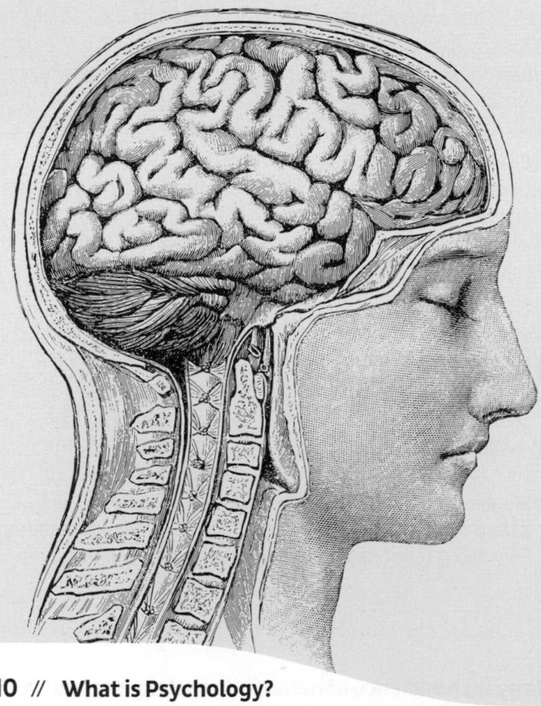

Behaviourist approach

The central concept of this approach is the influence of experience on our behaviour, and how we *learn* behaviours. Basically we are born as 'blank slates' and what we become is shaped by experience (sometimes termed 'the environment').

Basically we either learn through association (**classical conditioning**) or **reinforcement** (**operant conditioning**).

If you have cats you will know that they come running as soon as they hear a cupboard door being opened. They have learned to *associate* that noise with food.

You probably also know the usefulness of treats with animals – a small reward *reinforces* a behaviour and makes it more likely to happen in the future.

These are examples of classical and operant conditioning. Whatever characteristics we might be born with, these take second place to the crucial roles of our experience and the environment.

Because this approach is most closely associated with scientific psychology, it's no surprise that **behaviourists** are cheerleaders for the **laboratory** research in psychology because it involves precise and objective measurement of behaviour in controlled conditions. The approach also uses research with animals, because it sees no significant qualitative differences between human and animal behaviour.

PS: There is also **social learning theory**, an extension of the behaviourist approach that incorporates indirect learning.

AS level students only need to study the biological, behaviourist and cognitive approaches. A level students go on to study the psychodynamic and humanistic approaches. We have covered all these approaches in Chapter 4.

The unconscious mind lies beneath.

Psychodynamic approach

This is the approach that originated with Sigmund Freud, possibly the most well-known psychologist ever. He believed that the causes of behaviour lie within the **unconscious** mind, the part of the mind that is normally inaccessible but is extremely active. The iceberg metaphor has been used to represent this 'invisible' unconscious mind that has powerful effects (think Titanic).

There is constant dynamic conflict between parts of the unconscious and the conscious mind. We can get a brief glimpse of this conflict when we dream, which is why Freud advocated the use of dream interpretation to help us understand what's in the unconscious and why it affects us.

The approach also emphasises the importance of childhood experiences, which have a major impact on our personality development and our behaviour as adults.

Humanistic approach

The **humanistic approach** is firmly based on the concept of the self. This concerns issues to do with your self-concept (how you see yourself), and your **self-esteem** (how you feel about yourself).

The humanistic approach also emphasises the importance of being able to make our own rational choices. All of the other approaches suggest that our behaviour is, to a large extent, **determined** by other forces not always under our control – genes, the environment, our thought patterns, or our unconscious mind. Humanistic psychologists believe the goal of psychology is not prediction or control but to understand the whole person.

Cognitive approach

This approach focuses on thinking – our feelings, beliefs, attitudes and expectations and the effects they have on our behaviour.

The approach employs the 'computer metaphor' to explain how our minds work. Like computers, we process information.

The approach has been used to explain many things including mental disorders such as **depression**. According to the cognitive approach depression occurs because people *think* negatively – they put the worst possible interpretation on events and play down the good things that happen to them. They think it will never get better. This leads to despair.

Like behaviourist psychologists, cognitive psychologists use laboratory research as a key research method. But a big difference is that while behaviourists have no interest in what goes on inside the mind, cognitive psychologists are the opposite. The processes inside the mind are precisely what they are interested in and have an important link to the behaviours we observe.

Whatever works best

The distance from the biological approach to the humanistic perspective represents the huge range that is psychology.

Although researchers working in these two approaches may call themselves psychologists, they have very little in common in terms of their assumptions about behaviour, their preferred explanations, their philosophical viewpoints, the methods they use to investigate behaviour, or even the research questions they are interested in answering.

That's how broad a subject psychology is – and that's one reason why it's so exciting. These different approaches also reflect the undoubted truth that human behaviour is complex and is probably not going to be fully understood from just one approach.

Because of this, in recent years, there has been a growth of the eclectic approach. This is preferred by psychologists who aren't committed to any one particular approach. The eclectic approach uses the assumptions, explanations and methods from many different approaches. Their slogan could well be: 'Whatever works best'.

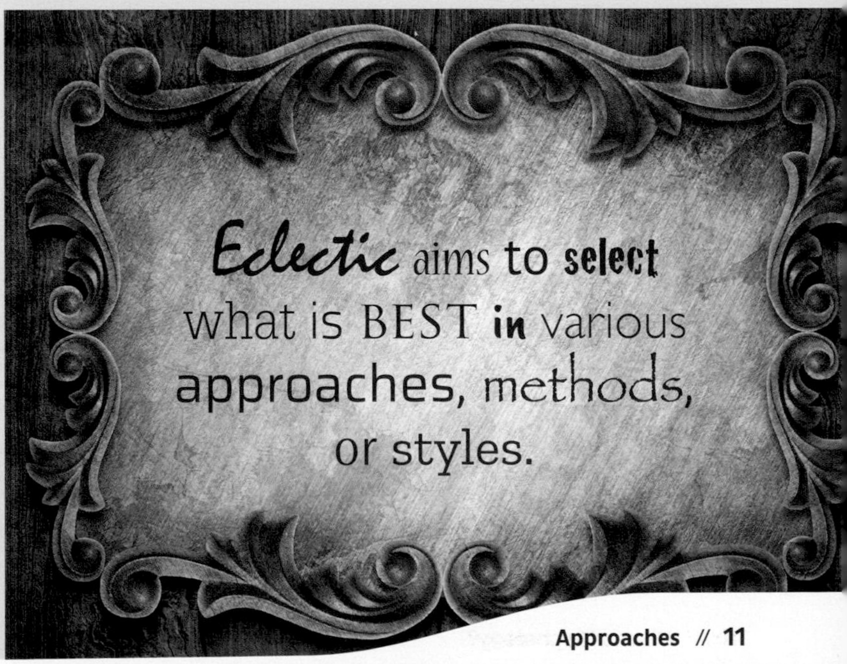
Eclectic aims to select
what is BEST in various
approaches, methods,
or styles.

Psychology in the real world

The goals of Psychology

Consider one of the really important health issues of our times – the obesity crisis in Britain. Here's a disturbing statistic to be getting on with – over half of the men and women in Britain are overweight or clinically obese. Can psychology do anything to help? In the Apply it on the right we use obesity as an example to illustrate the goals of psychology below.

Describing behaviour

Psychologists want to be able to describe what is happening when people 'behave'. This is mostly a matter of observation. Psychologists observe how behaviours are related to each other. They might, for example, notice that certain behaviours occur together quite often and form a pattern. They might even begin to get an indication of which behaviours are 'normal' and which 'abnormal'. Eventually, after enough studies have been conducted, possible explanations of the behaviour emerge, which takes us on to the next goal of psychology.

Explaining behaviour

Describing behaviour is just a starting point. Psychologists really want to go beyond merely describing the behaviour that is happening and try to *explain* where it comes from, the reasons for it, what causes it. To do this, they formulate theories of behaviour and then use the **scientific method** (see page 8) to test them. This of course is where disagreements emerge. There are many competing theories about the causes of behaviour, which often reflect the general **approach** psychologists adopt within psychology. Can psychologists do more than explain behaviour? Yes, they can predict behaviour.

Predicting behaviour

This is the logical next step. Once we are confident that certain behaviours consistently occur under certain conditions, we can use that knowledge to predict how a person's behaviour (including their thoughts) might change in the future. These predictions (known as **hypotheses**) can be turned into statements that can be tested in studies to see if the explanation was right.

Controlling behaviour

The idea that psychology should be in the business of controlling behaviour may have sinister overtones for some people. But what if we changed the language a little? What if we said that the ultimate goal of psychology is to *change* behaviour? This is unquestionably something that many branches of psychology attempt to do. For example, psychological therapies for mental disorders are not just about trying to understand or explain behaviours such as phobias or depression. The intention is to change people's behaviour, from **maladaptive**, 'abnormal' behaviours that cause pain and suffering to adaptive, 'normal' behaviours that bring happiness (or less pain, at least).

Apply it
Concepts

Obesity and the goals of Psychology

Describing obesity

Researchers use various research methods to work out what obesity is and how it relates to other factors. For example, they may use questionnaires or interviews to learn about attitudes towards eating in obese people. Psychologists might observe people's eating behaviour and measure how much people actually do eat. They might do **brain scans** to see if obese and thin people differ in thinking patterns.

Explaining obesity

The descriptions that are collected enable psychologists to develop explanations. There are several current explanations drawn from the whole range of approaches in psychology. There's a **biological explanation** that explains obesity in terms of the activity of **hormones** and other chemicals within the body. There's a **behaviourist explanation** that focuses on past learning experiences of rewards and punishments involving food. There's also a **cognitive explanation** that emphasises the ways that we think about, interpret and perceive the meaning of food and eating.

Predicting obesity

If obesity is associated with inactivity, it is a short step to make the prediction that less active people are more likely to be overweight.

If we identify **depression** as one of the causes of obesity, then again it is a simple matter to predict that depressed people are more likely to be obese.

Controlling obesity

There may even be a political dimension to behavioural control (see 'The Nudge Unit' on the facing page). The obesity crisis is a good example. Because the costs of obesity are so high (especially Type 2 diabetes) the government employs psychologists to devise programmes to change eating and exercise behaviours in people who are overweight.

Psychologists conduct research studies and develop theories so they might be in a position to predict behaviours that lead to obesity. Ultimately this would allow people to better control their eating behaviour.

Why did you do Psychology?

Some people think it will help them read other people's minds. Some people, when they find out you're doing psychology, really do say things like, 'I'd better watch what I say then,' or, 'Does that mean you're trying to analyse me?' They might even say, 'I had this really interesting dream last night. What happened was...' At which point, you might be wishing you'd said you were doing English Lit instead.

Apply it Concepts: The science of self-talk

Motivating self-talk refers to the things we say to ourselves to get us moving or motivated to do something. We probably all do this from time to time but sportsmen and sportswomen use this technique more than most.

Sanda Dolcos and Dolores Albarracin (2014) noticed that there are two ways of using such self-talk – first person and second person. For instance, we can say to ourselves '*I* can do it' (first-person) or '*you* can do it' (second-person). But does this actually make a difference to performance? Dolcos and Albarracin suspected it does because it reminds us of our childhood experiences of encouragement, with people such as parents and teachers (hopefully) saying 'you can do it'.

The researchers got the participants to imagine themselves to be a character in a story. Participants had to write down the advice that they would give themselves to motivate themselves to complete a task (solving a set of anagrams). Half of the participants had to write their advice down in the first person and the other half in the second person. So the hypothesis they tested was: 'There is a difference in the number of anagrams solved by the participants who used first-person self-talk and those who used second-person self-talk'.

Dolcos and Albarracin found that more anagrams were solved when second person self-talk was used (17.53 on average) than with the first-person variety (15.96 on average). This does not look like a big difference, but statistical analysis showed that it was unlikely to be a chance result.

They concluded that second-person self-talk is more motivating than first person. However, whether this is really due to reminders of encouragement in childhood can't be conclusively decided by this one study. So more research is needed to test further hypotheses in order to narrow down the range of alternative explanations.

Questions

1. Briefly outline what behaviour is being described.
2. What explanation do the researchers propose for the behaviour?
3. How could this research be used to predict and control behaviour?

YOU CAN DO IT

Change behaviour

The Nudge Unit

This is the popular name for the *Behavioural Insights Team*, an organisation that used to be part of the UK government. It was formed to change behaviour one small step at a time (that is, to 'nudge' people into making small changes, because such changes are more achievable).

For example, the Nudge Unit has devised projects to get more people to sign up to organ donation or to give blood, to encourage people to pay their taxes on time, to give more time and money to charity, reduce food waste, and so on.

They even tried to offer some advice to the England team at the World Cup in 2014, by applying psychological research to taking better penalties (ironically, the team never had the chance to put this advice to the test).

Here's another example of behavioural control:

The people at Schiphol Airport in Amsterdam wanted to know how you might stop men from missing the urinals and making a mess on the floor of the airport toilets. You could put up signs telling them to be more careful, or warn them of dire consequences if they don't get their aim straightened out.

But here's a better idea. Men (OK, *some* men) like nothing more than having something to aim at. So men's urinals at Schiphol Airport were given a small but significant redesign. A tiny black spot, in the shape of a fly, was inlaid into the middle of the pristine white porcelain urinal. It stood out like... well, like a fly on a white urinal.

Although no truly scientific studies have been conducted into the effectiveness of this method, apparently Schiphol's cleaning costs were reduced by 8%.

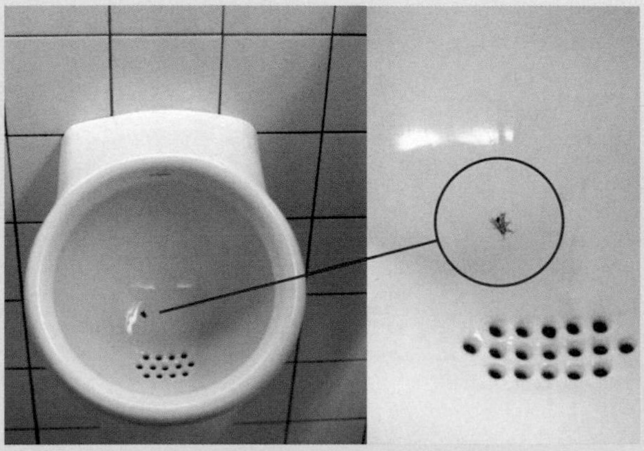

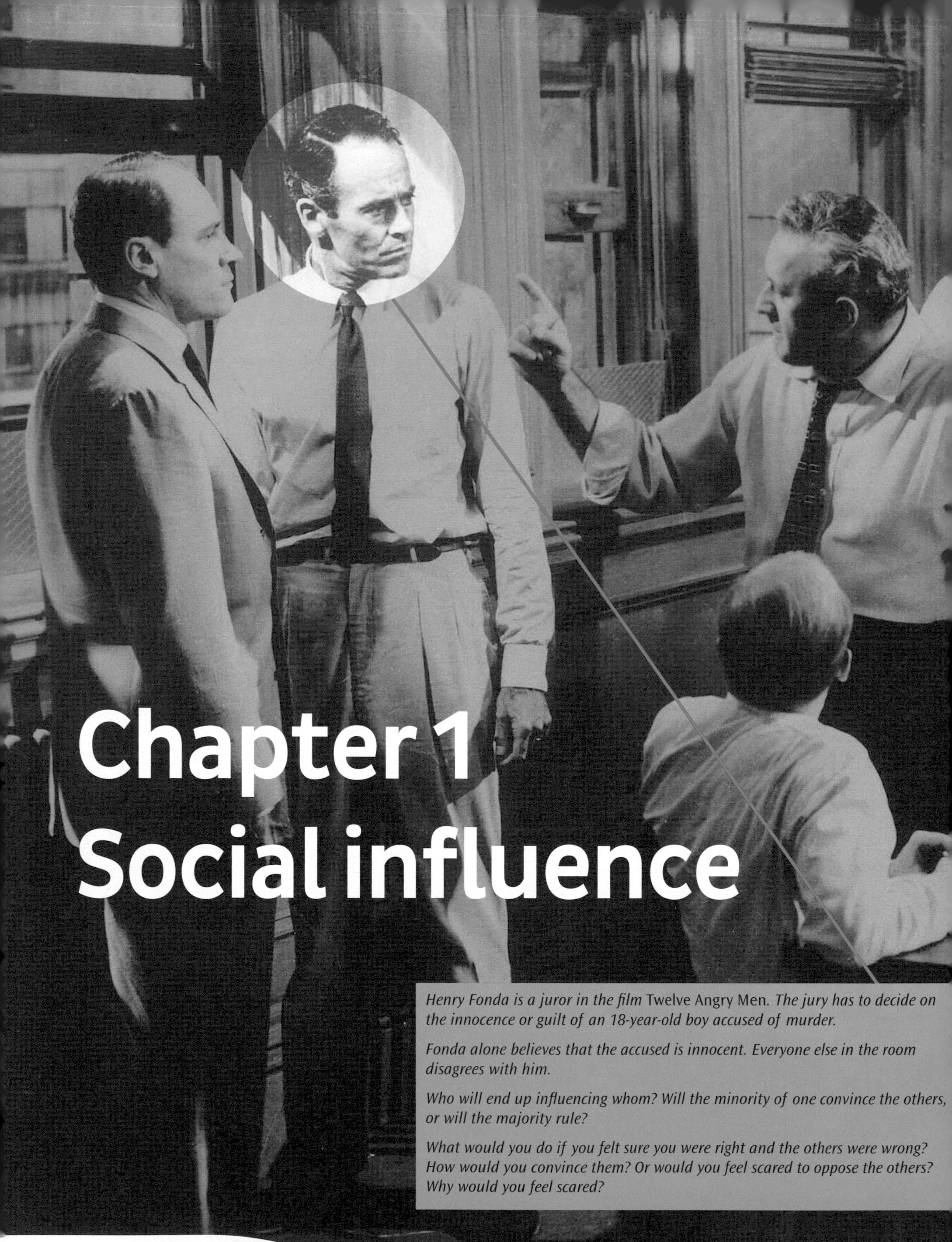

Chapter 1 Social influence

Henry Fonda is a juror in the film Twelve Angry Men. *The jury has to decide on the innocence or guilt of an 18-year-old boy accused of murder.*

Fonda alone believes that the accused is innocent. Everyone else in the room disagrees with him.

Who will end up influencing whom? Will the minority of one convince the others, or will the majority rule?

What would you do if you felt sure you were right and the others were wrong? How would you convince them? Or would you feel scared to oppose the others? Why would you feel scared?

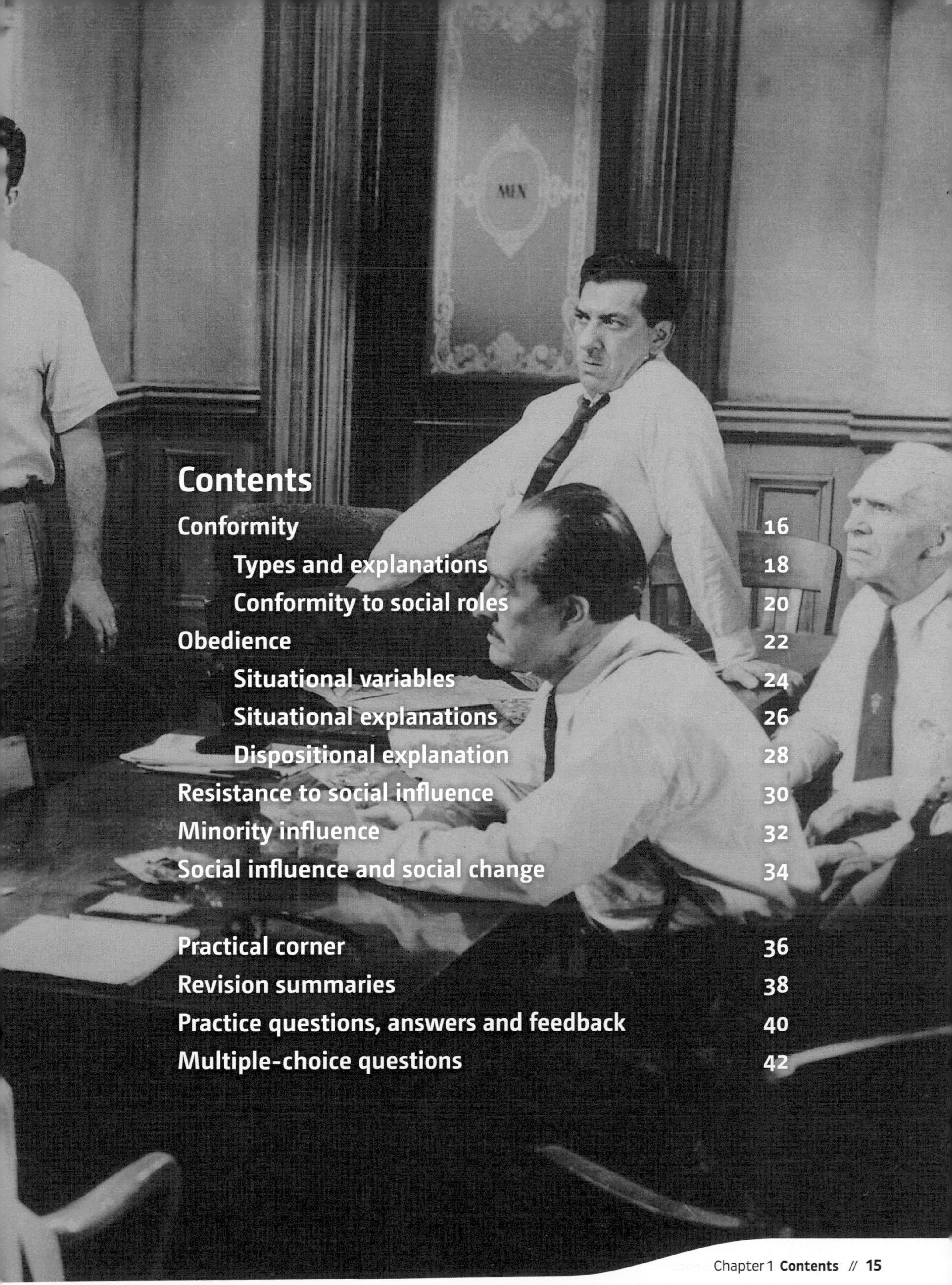
MEN

Contents

Conformity

The specification says...

Variables affecting conformity including group size, unanimity and task difficulty as investigated by Asch.

Solomon Asch's research has had a considerable impact on our understanding of conformity. We often 'go along' with other people in our everyday social lives. We agree with their opinions and change our behaviour to 'fit in' with theirs. In other words we *conform*. Asch wanted to find out why.

Key terms

Conformity 'A change in a person's behaviour or opinions as a result of real or imagined pressure from a person or group of people.' (Aronson 2011)

Group size Asch increased the size of the group by adding more confederates, thus increasing the size of the majority. Conformity increased with group size, but only up to a point, levelling off when the majority was greater than three.

Unanimity The extent to which all the members of a group agree. In Asch's studies, the majority was unanimous when all the confederates selected the same comparison line. This produced the greatest degree of conformity in the naïve participants.

Task difficulty Asch's line-judging task is more difficult when it becomes harder to work out the correct answer. Conformity increased because naïve participants assume that the majority is more likely to be right.

Asch's baseline procedure

Standard and comparison lines

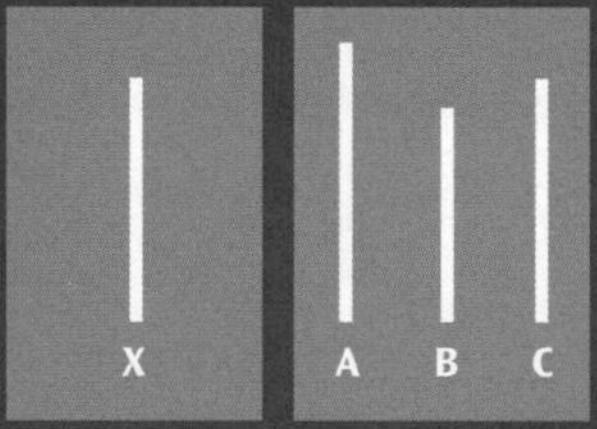

X
A
B
C

123 American men were tested, each one in a group with other apparent participants. Each participant saw two large white cards on each trial. The line X on the left-hand card is the standard line. The lines A, B and C are the three comparison lines. One of the comparison lines is always clearly the same length as X, the other two are substantially different (i.e. clearly wrong). On each trial the participants had to say (out loud) which of the comparison lines was the same length as the standard line X.

Physical arrangement of the participants in the study

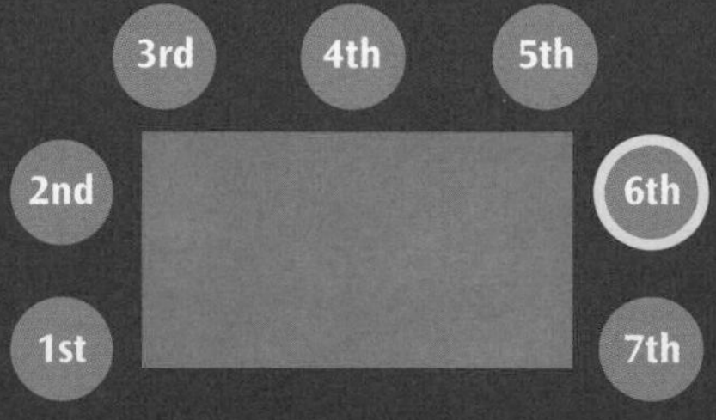

3rd
4th
5th
2nd
6th
1st
7th

The participants were tested in groups of 6 to 8. Only one was a genuine (naïve) participant, always seated either last or (as here) next to last in the group. The others were all confederates of Asch – that is, they all gave the same (incorrect) scripted answers each time.

The genuine participant did not know the others were 'fake' participants.

Baseline findings

On average, the genuine participants agreed with confederates' incorrect answers 36.8% of the time (i.e. they conformed about a third of the time).

There were individual differences, 25% of the participants never gave a wrong answer (i.e. never conformed).

Asch's research

Asch's baseline procedure

Solomon Asch (1951) devised a procedure to assess to what extent people will conform to the opinion of others, even in a situation where the answer is certain (i.e. unambiguous). The procedure of his original study is briefly described below left – this is called the 'baseline' study because it is the one against which all the later studies are compared.

Note that the specification focuses on the findings and conclusions from Asch's later research. Therefore we have not described the baseline procedure and findings in the main text.

Variables investigated by Asch

Asch (1955) extended his baseline study to investigate the variables that might lead to an increase or a decrease in **conformity**.

1. Group size Asch wanted to know whether the size of the group would be more important than the agreement of the group. To test this he varied the number of **confederates** from one to 15 (so the total group size was from two to 16).

Asch found a **curvilinear** relationship between group size and conformity rate (see Apply it on facing page for graph). Conformity increased with group size, but only up to a point. With three confederates, conformity to the wrong answer rose to 31.8%. But the presence of more confederates made little difference – the conformity rate soon levelled off.

This suggests that most people are very sensitive to the views of others because just one or two confederates was enough to sway opinion.

2. Unanimity Asch wondered if the presence of a non-conforming person would affect the naïve participant's conformity. He introduced a confederate who disagreed with the other confederates. In one variation of the study this person gave the correct answer and in another variation he gave a (different) wrong one.

The genuine participant conformed less often in the presence of a dissenter. The rate decreased to less than a quarter of the level it was when the majority was unanimous. The presence of a dissenter appeared to free the naïve participant to behave more independently. This was true even when the dissenter disagreed with the genuine participant.

This suggests that the influence of the majority depends to a large extent on it being unanimous. And that non-conformity is more likely when cracks are perceived in the majority's unanimous view.

3. Task difficulty Asch wanted to know whether making the task harder would affect the degree of conformity. He increased the difficulty of the line-judging task by making the stimulus line and the comparison lines more similar to each other in length. This meant it became harder for the genuine participants to see the differences between the lines.

Asch found that conformity increased. It may be that the situation is more ambiguous when the task becomes harder – it is unclear to the participants what the right answer is. In these circumstances, it is natural to look to other people for guidance and to assume that they are right and you are wrong (this is called **informational social influence** (ISI), which is discussed on the next spread).

Apply it Concepts — The big night out

Some students are celebrating the end of their exams by having a night out. They have been in the pub all evening and are now discussing which nightclub to go on to. Imogen prefers Rotting Flesh but the majority of the group wants to go to Scar Tissue.

Question

Briefly explain how each of the following factors might affect whether or not Imogen conforms to the majority: (a) Group size, (b) Unanimity, (c) Task difficulty.

Evaluation

Artificial situation and task

One limitation of Asch's research is that the task and situation were artificial.

Participants knew they were in a research study and may simply have gone along with what was expected (**demand characteristics**). The task of identifying lines was relatively trivial and therefore there was really no reason *not* to conform. Also, according to Susan Fiske (2014), 'Asch's groups were not very groupy', i.e. they did not really resemble groups that we experience in everyday life.

This means the findings do not generalise to real-world situations, especially those where the consequences of conformity might be important.

Limited application

Another limitation is that Asch's participants were American men.

Other research suggests that women may be more conformist, possibly because they are concerned about social relationships and being accepted (Neto 1995). Furthermore, the US is an **individualist** culture (i.e. where people are more concerned about themselves rather than their social group). Similar conformity studies conducted in **collectivist** cultures (such as China where the social group is more important than the individual) have found that conformity rates are higher (Bond and Smith 1996, see page 123 for a discussion of individualist/collectivist).

This means that Asch's findings tell us little about conformity in women and people from some cultures.

Research support

One strength of Asch's research is support from other studies for the effects of task difficulty.

For example, Todd Lucas *et al.* (2006) asked their participants to solve 'easy' and 'hard' maths problems. Participants were given answers from three other students (not actually real). The participants conformed more often (i.e. agreed with the wrong answers) when the problems were harder.

This shows Asch was correct in claiming that task difficulty is one variable that affects conformity.

Counterpoint However, Lucas *et al.*'s study found that conformity is more complex than Asch suggested. Participants with high confidence in their maths abilities conformed less on hard tasks than those with low confidence.

This shows that an individual-level factor can influence conformity by interacting with situational variables (e.g. task difficulty). But Asch did not research the roles of individual factors.

Evaluation eXtra

Ethical issues

Asch's research increased our knowledge of why people conform, which may help avoid mindless destructive conformity.

The naïve participants were **deceived** because they thought the other people involved in the procedure (the confederates) were also genuine participants like themselves. However, it is worth bearing in mind that this **ethical** cost should be weighed up against the benefits gained from the study.

Consider: *On balance do you think the benefits outweighed the costs?*

Study tip

Ethical evaluations are only relevant when considering a study. Such issues do not challenge the validity of the findings.

Conformity is usually assumed to be a bad thing. But sometimes situations demand that everybody pulls in the same direction.

Apply it Methods: Group size

Graph showing variation of Asch's baseline study: Group size.

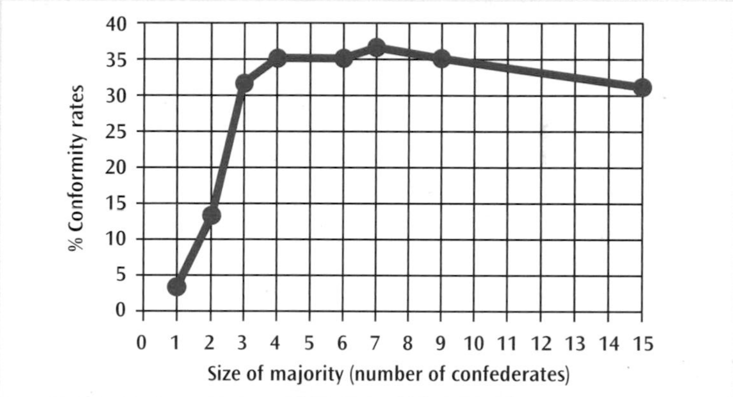
% Conformity rates
0
5
10
15
20
25
30
35
40
0 1 2 3 4 5 6 7 8 9 10 11 12 13 14 15
Size of majority (number of confederates)

Questions

1. The results from Asch's research on the effects of group size are shown above. What was the approximate conformity rate when there was one confederate? (*1 mark*)
2. What was the rate when there were three confederates? (*1 mark*)
3. What was the rate when there were nine confederates? (*1 mark*)
4. Asch used a **volunteer sampling** method to recruit his participants. Explain *one* strength and *one* limitation of this sampling method. (*4 marks*)
5. When the total group size was four there would be only one naïve participant and the others were confederates. Express the number of confederates as a fraction and a percentage of the total group size. (*2 marks*)

Check it

1. One variable that affects conformity is 'unanimity'. Explain what is meant by 'unanimity'. *[2 marks]*
2. Apart from unanimity, identify **and** briefly outline **two** variables that affect conformity. *[6 marks]*
3. Outline the procedure **and** findings of **one** study into conformity conducted by Asch. *[6 marks]*
4. Describe **and** evaluate Asch's research into conformity. *[12 marks AS, 16 marks AL]*

Conformity: Types and explanations

The specification says...

Types of conformity: internalisation, identification and compliance.

Explanations for conformity: informational social influence and normative social influence.

You learned about conformity on the previous spread. Asch looked at a number of different factors that affect how much we conform. These are *explanations* for conformity.

On this spread we will look at some more explanations for why people conform. We will start by looking at different levels or types of conformity.

Key terms

Internalisation A deep type of conformity where we take on the majority view because we accept it as correct. It leads to a far-reaching and permanent change in behaviour, even when the group is absent.

Identification A moderate type of conformity where we act in the same way as the group because we value it and want to be part of it. But we don't necessarily agree with everything the group/majority believes.

Compliance A superficial and temporary type of conformity where we outwardly go along with the majority view, but privately disagree with it. The change in our behaviour only lasts as long as the group is monitoring us.

Informational social influence (ISI) An explanation of conformity that says we agree with the opinion of the majority because we believe it is correct. We accept it because we want to be correct as well. This may lead to internalisation (see above).

Normative social influence (NSI) An explanation of conformity that says we agree with the opinion of the majority because we want to gain social approval and be liked. This may lead to compliance (see above).

Types of conformity

Herbert Kelman (1958) suggested that there are three ways in which people **conform** to the opinion of a majority:

Internalisation

Internalisation occurs when a person genuinely accepts the group norms. This results in a private as well as a public change of opinions/behaviour. This change is usually permanent because attitudes have been internalised, i.e. become part of the way the person thinks. The change in opinions/behaviour persists even in the absence of other group members.

Identification

Sometimes we conform to the opinions/behaviour of a group because there is something about that group we value. We identify with the group, so we want to be part of it. This **identification** may mean we publicly change our opinions/behaviour to be accepted by the group, even if we don't privately agree with everything the group stands for.

Compliance

This type of conformity involves simply 'going along with others' in public, but privately not changing personal opinions and/or behaviour. **Compliance** results in only a superficial change. It also means that a particular behaviour or opinion stops as soon as group pressure stops.

Explanations for conformity

Morton Deutsch and Harold Gerard (1955) developed a **two-process theory**, arguing that there are two main reasons people conform. They are based on two central human needs: the need to be *right* (ISI), and the need to be *liked* (NSI).

Informational social influence

Informational social influence (ISI) is about who has the better information – you or the rest of the group. Often we are uncertain about what behaviours or beliefs are right or wrong. For example, you may not know the answer to a question in class. But if most of your class gives one answer, you accept it because you feel they are likely to be right. We follow the behaviour of the group (the majority) because we want to be right. ISI is a **cognitive** process because it is to do with what you think. It leads to a permanent change in opinion/behaviour (internalisation).

ISI is most likely to happen in situations that are new to a person (so you don't know what is right) or where there is some ambiguity (so it isn't clear what is right). It also occurs in crisis situations where decisions have to be made quickly and we assume that the group is more likely to be right.

Normative social influence

Normative social influence (NSI) is about norms, i.e. what is 'normal' or typical behaviour for a social group. Norms regulate the behaviour of groups and individuals so it is not surprising that we pay attention to them. People do not like to appear foolish and prefer to gain social approval rather than be rejected. So NSI is an *emotional* rather than a cognitive process. It leads to a temporary change in opinions/behaviour (compliance).

NSI is likely to occur in situations with strangers where you may feel concerned about rejection. It may also occur with people you know because we are most concerned about the social approval of our friends. It may be more pronounced in stressful situations (than non-stressful situations) where people have a greater need for social support.

Apply it Concepts — Social influence at college

It is Oliver's and Lola's first day at college and they are keen to make a good impression. Oliver pretends to be interested in the other students' conversations even though he really finds them boring. Lola watches other students very carefully because she wants to complete her work just like they do, to avoid making any mistakes.

Question

Whose behaviour is being influenced by informational social influence, Oliver's or Lola's? Whose is being influenced by normative social influence? Explain both of your answers.

There are many reasons for going along with the other people in a group. Often, it's so we can be accepted and liked by them, even if we don't really share their values and opinions.

Practical activity on page 37

Evaluation

Research support for NSI

One strength of NSI is that evidence supports it as an explanation of conformity.

For example, when Asch (1951, see previous spread) interviewed his participants, some said they conformed because they felt self-conscious giving the correct answer and they were afraid of disapproval. When participants wrote their answers down, conformity fell to 12.5%. This is because giving answers privately meant there was no normative group pressure.

This shows that at least some conformity is due to a desire not to be rejected by the group for disagreeing with them (i.e. NSI).

Research support for ISI

Another strength is that there is research evidence to support ISI from the study by Todd Lucas *et al.* (2006, see previous spread).

Lucas *et al.* found that participants conformed more often to incorrect answers they were given when the maths problems were difficult. This is because when the problems were easy the participants 'knew their own minds' but when the problems were hard the situation became ambiguous (unclear). The participants did not want to be wrong, so they relied on the answers they were given.

This shows that ISI is a valid explanation of conformity because the results are what ISI would predict.

Counterpoint However, it is often unclear whether it is NSI or ISI at work in research studies (or in real life). For example, Asch (1955) found that conformity is reduced when there is one other dissenting participant (see previous spread). The dissenter may reduce the power of NSI (because they provide social support) or they may reduce the power of ISI (because they provide an alternative source of social information). Both interpretations are possible.

Therefore, it is hard to separate ISI and NSI and both processes probably operate together in most real-world conformity situations.

Individual differences in NSI

One limitation is that NSI does not predict conformity in every case.

Some people are greatly concerned with being liked by others. Such people are called **nAffiliators** – they have a strong need for 'affiliation' (i.e. they want to relate to other people). Paul McGhee and Richard Teevan (1967) found that students who were nAffiliators were more likely to conform.

This shows that NSI underlies conformity for some people more than it does for others. There are individual differences in conformity that cannot be fully explained by one general theory of situational pressures.

Evaluation eXtra

Is the NSI/ISI distinction useful?

The counterpoint (above) suggests the distinction is not useful because it is impossible to work out which is operating. Lucas *et al.*'s findings could be due to NSI, ISI or both.

However, Asch's research from the previous spread clearly demonstrates both NSI and ISI as reasons for conformity. For instance in terms of group unanimity, a unanimous group is a powerful source of disapproval. The possibility of rejection is a strong reason for conforming (NSI). But it is also true that a unanimous group conveys the impression that everyone is 'in the know' apart from you (ISI).

Consider: *Using Asch's research, is the distinction between ISI and NSI useful?*

Apply it Concepts

Real-life application

Wesley Schultz *et al.* (2008) found they were able to change the behaviour of hotel guests by using printed messages encouraging them to save energy. The messages that suggested other guests were using fewer bath towels were the most successful.

Question

Does this demonstrate ISI or NSI? Explain your answer.

Apply it Methods

Conformity at work

A psychologist studied conformity by observing five people starting new jobs in an office of a major British retail company.

Questions

1. Explain why this could be considered to be a **naturalistic observation**. (*2 marks*)
2. Explain *one* strength and *one* limitation of naturalistic observation. (*2 marks + 2 marks*)
3. The psychologist needed to devise some **behavioural categories**. So she had to decide which behaviours could be considered examples of conformity. Explain what is meant by behavioural categories. (*2 marks*)
4. Give *three* examples of possible behavioural categories in the context of this study. (*3 marks*)
5. The psychologist used **event sampling** to observe conforming behaviours over a two-week period during break-times and lunchtimes. Explain what is meant by *event sampling*. (*2 marks*)
6. When the psychologist analysed her results, she found high levels of conforming behaviour by people starting new jobs.
   Use your knowledge of informational social influence and normative social influence to explain why people might conform in this situation. (*4 marks*)

Study tip

There are two other relevant explanations for conformity in this chapter – the influence of social roles (see next spread) and having an external locus of control (see page 30).

Check it

1. Explain internalisation as a type of conformity. *[2 marks]*
2. Explain what is meant by 'informational social influence' in relation to conformity. *[2 marks]*
3. Outline normative social influence as an explanation for conformity. *[4 marks]*
4. Describe **and** evaluate informational social influence **and** normative social influence as explanations for conformity. *[12 marks AS, 16 marks AL]*

Conformity to social roles

The specification says...

Conformity to social roles as investigated by Zimbardo.

We turn our attention on this spread to a special kind of conformity. Previously, we've looked at our tendency to conform to the behaviours or opinions of other people when they form the majority of a group. But to what extent do we conform to the *expectations* that people have of us? These expectations arise out of the roles we play in society and are powerful influences on our behaviour.

Key term

Social roles The 'parts' people play as members of various social groups. Everyday examples include parent, child, student, passenger and so on. These are accompanied by expectations we and others have of what is appropriate behaviour in each role, for example caring, obedient, industrious, etc.

In the Stanford prison experiment both prisoners and guards were given uniforms that would help dictate their social roles.

Apply it Concepts

A mock psychiatric ward

This scenario is based on an actual study by Norma Jean Orlando (1973).

A researcher decided to investigate how conformity to social roles can influence people to behave in extreme ways. She selected staff at a psychiatric hospital to play the roles of patients on a ward for one week. After two days, several mock patients experienced symptoms of psychological disturbance, some cried uncontrollably, others became extremely withdrawn, and a few tried to escape. As time went on, most of the participants became more anxious and depressed, and felt very strongly that they were trapped and isolated. The study had to be ended early because some 'patients' were losing their sense of self-identity.

Question

Use your knowledge of Zimbardo's research into conformity to social roles to explain why the mock patients behaved as they did.

Zimbardo's research

In the 1970s Philip Zimbardo and colleagues conducted one of the most memorable studies in psychology. There had been many prison riots in America and Zimbardo wanted to know why prison guards behave brutally – was it because they have sadistic personalities or was it their **social role** (as a prison guard) that created such behaviour?

The Stanford prison experiment (SPE)

Zimbardo *et al.* (1973) set up a mock prison in the basement of the psychology department at Stanford University. They selected 21 men (student volunteers) who tested as 'emotionally stable'. The students were **randomly assigned** to play the role of prison guard or prisoner.

Prisoners and guards were encouraged to **conform** to social roles both through the uniforms they wore and also instructions about their behaviour.

Uniforms The prisoners were given a loose smock to wear and a cap to cover their hair, and they were identified by number (their names were never used). The guards had their own uniform reflecting the status of their role, with wooden club, handcuffs and mirror shades.

These uniforms created a loss of personal identity (called **de-individuation**), and meant they would be more likely to conform to the perceived social role.

Instructions about behaviour The prisoners were further encouraged to identify with their role by several procedures. For example rather than leaving the study early, prisoners could 'apply for parole'. The guards were encouraged to play their role by being reminded that they had complete power over the prisoners.

Findings related to social roles

The guards took up their roles with enthusiasm, treating the prisoners harshly. Within two days, the prisoners rebelled. They ripped their uniforms and shouted and swore at the guards, who retaliated with fire extinguishers.

The guards used 'divide-and-rule' tactics by playing the prisoners off against each other. They harassed the prisoners constantly, to remind them of the powerlessness of their role. For example they conducted frequent headcounts, sometimes at night, when the prisoners would stand in line and call out their numbers. The guards highlighted the differences in social roles by creating opportunities to enforce the rules and administer punishments.

After their rebellion was put down, the prisoners became subdued, depressed and anxious. One was released because he showed symptoms of psychological disturbance. Two more were released on the fourth day. One prisoner went on a hunger strike. The guards tried to force-feed him and then punished him by putting him in 'the hole', a tiny dark closet.

The guards identified more and more closely with their role. Their behaviour became increasingly brutal and aggressive, with some of them appearing to enjoy the power they had over the prisoners. Zimbardo ended the study after six days instead of the intended 14.

Conclusions related to social roles

Social roles appear to have a strong influence on individuals' behaviour. The guards became brutal and the prisoners became submissive.

Such roles were very easily taken on by all participants. Even volunteers who came in to perform specific functions (such as the 'prison chaplain') found themselves behaving as if they were in a prison rather than in a psychological study.

Apply it Concepts

Abu Ghraib

From 2003 to 2004, United States Army Military Police personnel committed serious human rights violations against Iraqi prisoners at Abu Ghraib prison in Baghdad. The prisoners were tortured, physically and sexually abused, routinely humiliated and some were murdered. Zimbardo noticed some remarkable similarities between the behaviour of the personnel at Abu Ghraib and the guards in the Stanford prison experiment.

Question

Using your knowledge of Zimbardo's research, explain what happened at Abu Ghraib in terms of conformity to social roles.

Evaluation

Control

One strength of the SPE is that Zimbardo and his colleagues had control over key variables.

The most obvious example of this was the selection of participants. Emotionally-stable individuals were chosen and randomly assigned to the roles of guard and prisoner. This was one way in which the researchers ruled out individual personality differences as an explanation of the findings. If guards and prisoners behaved very differently, but were in those roles only by chance, then their behaviour must have been due to the role itself.

This degree of control over variables increased the **internal validity** of the study, so we can be much more confident in drawing conclusions about the influence of roles on conformity.

Lack of realism

One limitation of the SPE is that it did not have the realism of a true prison.

Ali Banuazizi and Siamak Movahedi (1975) argued the participants were merely play-acting rather than genuinely conforming to a role. Participants' performances were based on their **stereotypes** of how prisoners and guards are supposed to behave. For example, one of the guards claimed he had based his role on a brutal character from the film *Cool Hand Luke*. This would also explain why the prisoners rioted – they thought that was what real prisoners did.

This suggests that the findings of the SPE tell us little about conformity to social roles in actual prisons.

Counterpoint However, Mark McDermott (2019) argues that the participants did behave as if the prison was real to them. For example, 90% of the prisoners' conversations were about prison life. Amongst themselves, they discussed how it was impossible to leave the SPE before their 'sentences' were over. 'Prisoner 416' later explained how he believed the prison was a real one, but run by psychologists rather than the government.

This suggests that the SPE did **replicate** the social roles of prisoners and guards in a real prison, giving the study a high degree of internal validity.

Exaggerates the power of roles

Another limitation is that Zimbardo may have exaggerated the power of social roles to influence behaviour (Fromm 1973).

For example, only one-third of the guards actually behaved in a brutal manner. Another third tried to apply the rules fairly. The rest actively tried to help and support the prisoners. They sympathised, offered cigarettes and reinstated privileges (Zimbardo 2007). Most guards were able to resist situational pressures to conform to a brutal role.

This suggests that Zimbardo overstated his view that SPE participants were conforming to social roles and minimised the influence of dispositional factors (e.g. personality).

Evaluation eXtra

Alternative explanation

Zimbardo's explanation for the guards' (and prisoners') behaviour was that conforming to a social role comes 'naturally' and easily. Being given the role of guard means that these participants will inevitably behave brutally because that is the behaviour expected of someone with that role.

However, Steve Reicher and Alex Haslam (2006) criticise Zimbardo's explanation because it does not account for the behaviour of the non-brutal guards. They used **social identity theory** (SIT) instead to argue that the 'guards' had to actively identify with their social roles to act as they did.

Consider: *Explain how SIT may be a better explanation of the prison guards' behaviour.*

Apply it – Methods: Gender roles

In our society there are many social roles in which men and women are portrayed as behaving differently, such as parenting behaviour. A psychologist was interested in studying conformity to gender roles in parenting. She decided to conduct an observational study of parents of one-year-old children.

Her hypothesis was that the parenting behaviour of mothers and fathers would conform to stereotypical gender roles – mothers would behave in stereotypically 'feminine' ways and fathers in stereotypically 'masculine' ways. More specifically, she predicted that mothers would show more 'caring' behaviours and fathers more 'aggressive' behaviours.

Questions

1. Identify *one* **behavioural category** to record 'caring' behaviour and *one* to record 'aggressive' behaviour. (*2 marks*)
2. The psychologist decided to use **time sampling** to record her observations. Explain what is meant by time sampling. (*2 marks*)
3. Explain why the psychologist might carry out a **pilot study** before the main observation. (*3 marks*)
4. Identify *two* **ethical issues** the psychologist should consider before conducting her investigation. (*2 marks*)
5. Explain how she could deal with *one* of these issues. (*2 marks*)
6. The psychologist's hypothesis was supported by her findings. Use your knowledge of conformity to social roles to explain this outcome. (*3 marks*)

The abuses at Abu Ghraib prison (described on the facing page) woke up the whole world to how the power of the situation and of social roles can make apparently ordinary people (i.e. people with no apparent antisocial attitudes) do evil things.

Check it

1. Using an example, explain what is meant by 'social roles'. *[2 marks]*
2. Explain what Zimbardo's study tells us about conformity to social roles. *[6 marks]*
3. Discuss research into conformity to social roles. *[12 marks AS, 16 marks AL]*

Obedience

The specification says...

Obedience, as investigated by Milgram.

Stanley Milgram sought an answer to the question of why such a high proportion of the German population obeyed Hitler's commands to murder over 6 million Jews in the Holocaust as well as 5 million Romani, homosexuals, black Germans, Poles and members of other social groups during the Second World War.

He thought one possible explanation was that Germans were different from people from other countries – perhaps they were more obedient. In order to determine this he needed a procedure which could assess how obedient people are.

Key term

Obedience A form of social influence in which an individual follows a direct order. The person issuing the order is usually a figure of authority, who has the power to punish when obedient behaviour is not forthcoming.

Apply it Concepts — Ethical guidance

Milgram was not breaking any official ethical guidance at the time because none existed. It was because of his research (and that of Zimbardo a few years later) that ethical issues became an urgent priority for psychology.

All professional psychological associations publish and frequently update ethical guidance for practising psychologists and researchers. In Britain, the British Psychological Society (BPS) produces a *Code of Ethics and Conduct* that is described and discussed on pages 178–179. It addresses several issues, including:

- A participant's right to withdraw from the research.
- The need to get fully informed consent from the participants.
- The use of deception.
- The importance of protecting participants from the risk of psychological and physical harm.

Questions

1. For each of these ethical issues, identify how they arose in Milgram's study.
2. What steps did Milgram take to address these issues?
3. To what extent do you think he was successful?

Milgram's research

Stanley Milgram (1963) designed a baseline procedure that could be used to assess **obedience** levels. This procedure was adapted in later variations by Milgram (discussed on the next spread) and the baseline findings were used to make comparisons.

The specification focuses on the findings and conclusions from Milgram's research. However, you do also need some knowledge of the baseline procedure. The fuller details are at the bottom of the page for background reading.

Baseline procedure

40 American men volunteered to take part in a study, supposedly on memory. When each volunteer arrived at Milgram's lab he was introduced to another participant (a **confederate** of Milgram's). They drew lots to see who would be the 'Teacher' (T) and who would be the 'Learner' (L). The draw was fixed so that the participant was always the Teacher. An 'Experimenter' (E) was also involved (also a confederate, dressed in a grey lab coat).

The detailed procedure is explained below left and the diagram illustrates the layout of the study. The study aimed to assess obedience in a situation where an authority figure (Experimenter) ordered the participant (Teacher) to give an increasingly strong shock to a Learner located in a different room (in 15-volt steps up to 450 volts). The shocks were fake but the Teacher did not know this.

Baseline findings

Every participant delivered all the shocks up to 300 volts. 12.5% (five participants) stopped at 300 volts ('intense shock') and 65% continued to the highest level of 450 volts, i.e. they were fully obedient.

Milgram also collected **qualitative data** including **observations** such as: the participants showed signs of extreme tension; many of them were seen to 'sweat, tremble, stutter, bite their lips, groan and dig their fingernails into their hands'; three even had 'full-blown uncontrollable seizures'.

Other data

Before the study, Milgram asked 14 psychology students to predict the participants' behaviour. The students estimated that no more than 3% of the participants would continue to 450 volts. This shows that the findings were unexpected – the students underestimated how obedient people actually are.

All participants in the baseline study were **debriefed** and assured that their behaviour was entirely normal. They were also sent a follow-up questionnaire – 84% said they were glad to have participated.

Conclusions

Milgram concluded that German people are not 'different'. The American participants in his study were willing to obey orders even when they might harm another person. He suspected there were certain factors in the situation that encouraged obedience, so decided to conduct further studies to investigate these (see next spread).

Further procedural detail of Milgram's research

Milgram's participants were men (aged 20–50 years) who came from the area around New Haven, Connecticut, USA. They were volunteers recruited through a newspaper advert or mailshot, and were paid $4.50 for participating. The Learner (called 'Mr Wallace') was strapped into a chair and wired up with electrodes. The Teacher (the real participant) was given a small shock to experience for themselves. This was the only genuine shock in the procedure.

The Learner had to remember pairs of words. Each time he made an error, the Teacher delivered a stronger (fake) 'electric shock' by pressing switches on a 'shock machine'. The switches were labelled from 'slight shock' through 'intense shock' to 'danger – severe shock'. When the Teacher got to 300 volts the Learner pounded on the wall and then gave no response to the next question. At 315 volts he again pounded on the wall but was then silent for the rest of the procedure.

The four standard 'prods' the Experimenter used to order the Teacher to continue were:

Prod 1 – 'Please continue' or 'Please go on.'

Prod 2 – 'The experiment requires that you continue.'

Prod 3 – 'It is absolutely essential that you continue.'

Prod 4 – 'You have no other choice, you must go on.'

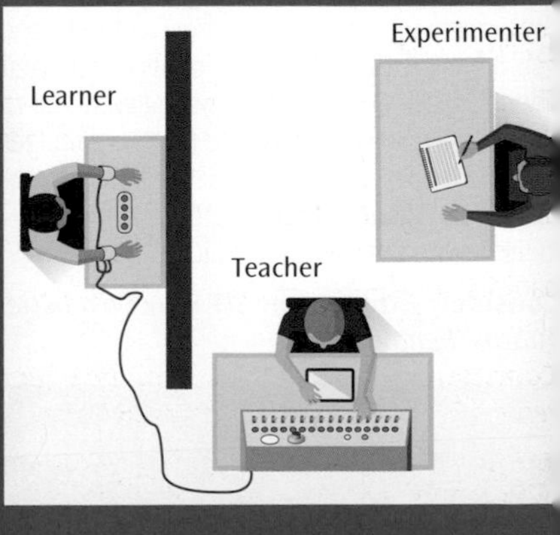
Experimenter
Learner
Teacher

Evaluation

Practical activity on page 204

Research support

One strength is that Milgram's findings were replicated in a French documentary that was made about reality TV.

This documentary (Beauvois *et al.* 2012) focused on a game show made especially for the programme. The participants in the 'game' believed they were contestants in a pilot episode for a new show called *Le Jeu de la Mort* (*The Game of Death*). They were paid to give (fake) electric shocks (ordered by the presenter) to other participants (who were actually actors) in front of a studio audience. 80% of the participants delivered the maximum shock of 460 volts to an apparently unconscious man. Their behaviour was almost identical to that of Milgram's participants – nervous laughter, nail-biting and other signs of anxiety.

This supports Milgram's original findings about obedience to authority, and demonstrates that the findings were not just due to special circumstances.

Low internal validity

One limitation is that Milgram's procedure may not have been testing what he intended to test.

Milgram reported that 75% of his participants said they believed the shocks were genuine. However Martin Orne and Charles Holland (1968) argued that participants behaved as they did because they didn't really believe in the set up, so they were 'play-acting'. Gina Perry's (2013) research confirms this. She listened to tapes of Milgram's participants and reported that only about half of them believed the shocks were real. Two-thirds of these participants were disobedient.

This suggests that participants may have been responding to **demand characteristics**, trying to fulfil the aims of the study.

Counterpoint However, Charles Sheridan and Richard King (1972) conducted a study using a procedure like Milgram's. Participants (all students) gave real shocks to a puppy in response to orders from an experimenter. Despite the real distress of the animal, 54% of the men and 100% of the women gave what they thought was a fatal shock.

This suggests that the effects in Milgram's study were genuine because people behaved obediently even when the shocks were real.

Alternative interpretation of findings

Another limitation is that Milgram's conclusions about blind obedience may not be justified.

Alex Haslam *et al.* (2014) showed that Milgram's participants obeyed when the Experimenter delivered the first three verbal prods (see facing page). However, every participant who was given the fourth prod ('You have no other choice, you must go on') without exception disobeyed. According to **social identity theory** (SIT), participants in Milgram's study only obeyed when they identified with the scientific aims of the research ('The experiment requires that you continue'). When they were ordered to blindly obey an authority figure, they refused.

This shows that SIT may provide a more valid interpretation of Milgram's findings, especially as Milgram himself suggested that 'identifying with the science' is a reason for obedience.

Evaluation eXtra

Ethical issues

The participants in this study were deceived. For example, the participants thought that the allocation of roles (Teacher and Learner) was random, but in fact it was fixed. They also thought the shocks were real. Milgram dealt with this by debriefing participants.

However, Diana Baumrind (1964) criticised Milgram for deceiving his participants. She objected because she believed that deception in psychological studies can have serious consequences for participants and researchers.

Consider: *How might deception be a limitation of Milgram's research? Do the benefits outweigh the costs?*

Apply it Methods — Milgram's debriefing

At the end of the procedure, Milgram carried out a debriefing session with each of his participants. This was an opportunity for him to explain the true purpose of the study and what had really happened. It was also intended to make the participants feel better about their role in the study, especially if they had been completely obedient throughout.

Part of the debriefing was a structured interview to ask participants questions about their experiences in the study. Milgram also wanted to collect qualitative data about the reasons why participants obeyed or disobeyed the Experimenter.

Questions

1. Explain *one* strength and *one* limitation of a **structured interview**. (*2 + 2 marks*)
2. Explain *one* difference between a structured interview *and* an **unstructured interview**. (*2 marks*)
3. Explain what is meant by **qualitative data** and give an example from Milgram's study. (*2 marks*)
4. Write *one* suitable question Milgram could have asked in the interviews to collect qualitative data. (*1 mark*)
5. Explain what is meant by **quantitative data**. (*1 mark*)
6. Write *one* suitable question Milgram could have asked in the interviews to collect quantitative data. (*1 mark*)

Apply it Concepts — When nurses disobey

Charles Hofling *et al.* (1966) arranged for an unknown doctor to telephone 22 nurses and ask each of them (alone) to administer an overdose of a drug that was not on their ward list ('Astroten'). A startling 95% of nurses (21 out of 22) started to administer the drug (they were prevented from continuing). The nurses obeyed without question.

Steven Rank and Cardell Jacobson (1977) replicated Hofling *et al.*'s study but altered some aspects of the original procedure that might have maximised obedience.

For instance, being given an order over the telephone was unusual. It was also unusual to be asked to administer an unknown drug. In the Rank and Jacobson study the nurses were told by a doctor to administer an overdose of *valium*, a real drug that the nurses would have been familiar with. The doctor's name was also known to the nurses and they all had the chance to discuss the order with each other.

In these more realistic circumstances, only two out of 18 nurses obeyed the doctor's order (before they were prevented from carrying it out).

Question

What would you conclude about obedience to authority from these studies?

Check it

1. Explain what is meant by 'obedience'. *[2 marks]*
2. Describe the procedure **and** findings of **one** study investigating obedience. *[6 marks]*
3. Describe **and** evaluate Milgram's research into obedience. *[12 marks AS, 16 marks AL]*

Obedience: Situational variables

The specification says...

Explanations for obedience: situational variables affecting obedience including proximity and location, as investigated by Milgram, and uniform.

Milgram's 'baseline study', described on the previous spread, established a method he could repeat and vary, and use to place a numerical value on obedience. Milgram began his research with the belief that obedience might be due to personality – were the Germans different? However, he found that situational factors might explain obedience better. He continued to explore this in further studies.

Key terms

Situational variables Features of the immediate physical and social environment which may influence a person's behaviour (such as proximity, location and uniform). The alternative is dispositional variables where behaviour is explained in terms of personality.

Proximity The physical closeness or distance of an authority figure to the person they are giving an order to. Also refers to the physical closeness of the Teacher to the victim (Learner) in Milgram's studies.

Location The place where an order is issued. The relevant factor that influences obedience is the status or prestige associated with the location.

Uniform People in positions of authority often have a specific outfit that is symbolic of their authority, for example police officers and judges. This indicates that they are entitled to expect our obedience.

Situational variables

After Stanley Milgram conducted his first study on obedience (described on the previous spread), he carried out a large number of variations in order to consider the **situational variables** that might lead to more or less obedience.

Proximity

In Milgram's baseline study, the Teacher could hear the Learner but not see him. In the **proximity** variation, Teacher and Learner were in the same room. The obedience rate dropped from the original 65% to 40% (see graph below).

In the *touch proximity* variation, the Teacher had to force the Learner's hand onto an 'electroshock plate' if he refused to place it there himself after giving a wrong answer. Obedience dropped further to 30%.

In the *remote instruction* variation, the Experimenter left the room and gave instructions to the Teacher by telephone. Obedience reduced to 20.5%. The participants also frequently pretended to give shocks.

Explanation Decreased proximity allows people to psychologically distance themselves from the consequences of their actions. For example, when the Teacher and Learner were physically separated (as in the baseline study), the Teacher was less aware of the harm they were causing to another person so they were more obedient.

Graph showing obedience levels in Milgram's variations of his baseline study. The graph shows how proximity, location and uniform all affected obedience.

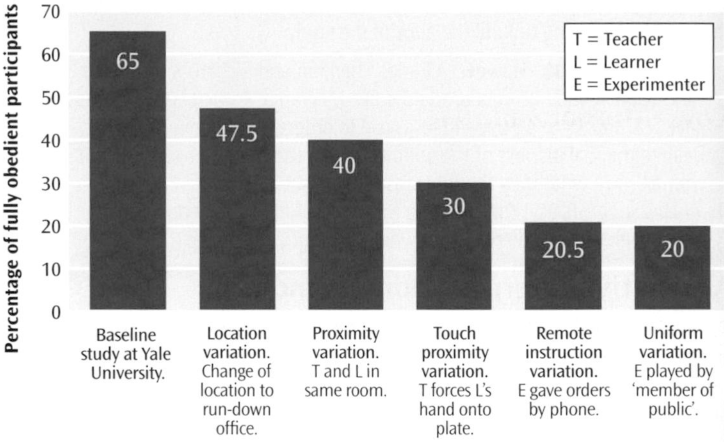

Percentage of fully obedient participants
70
60
50
40
30
20
10
0
65
47.5
40
30
20.5
20
T = Teacher
L = Learner
E = Experimenter
Baseline study at Yale University.
Location variation. Change of location to run-down office.
Proximity variation. T and L in same room.
Touch proximity variation. T forces L's hand onto plate.
Remote instruction variation. E gave orders by phone.
Uniform variation. E played by 'member of public'.

Location

Milgram conducted a variation in a run-down office block rather than in the prestigious Yale University setting of the baseline study. In this **location**, obedience fell to 47.5%.

Explanation The prestigious university environment gave Milgram's study legitimacy and authority. Participants were more obedient in this location because they perceived that the Experimenter shared this legitimacy and that obedience was expected. However, obedience was still quite high in the office block because the participants perceived the 'scientific' nature of the procedure.

Uniform

In the baseline study, the Experimenter wore a grey lab coat as a symbol of his authority (a kind of **uniform**). In one variation, the Experimenter was called away because of an inconvenient telephone call at the start of the procedure. The role of the Experimenter was taken over by an 'ordinary member of the public' (a **confederate**) in everyday clothes rather than a lab coat. The obedience rate dropped to 20%, the lowest of these variations.

Explanation Uniforms 'encourage' obedience because they are widely recognised symbols of authority. We accept that someone in a uniform is entitled to expect obedience because their authority is legitimate (i.e. it is granted by society). Someone without a uniform has less right to expect our obedience.

Apply it
Concepts

The power of a uniform

A psychologist conducted an investigation into obedience. He used two confederates – one was dressed as a firefighter and the other was dressed in everyday smart-but-casual clothes. The confederates stood on different streets and instructed people to pick up a piece of litter and put it into a bin. A record was kept of how many people obeyed the instruction.

Questions

1. From what you know about obedience research, what is the likely outcome of this study? Explain your answer.
2. Are there any **ethical issues** that might arise in this study?

Evaluation

Research support

One strength is that other studies have demonstrated the influence of situational variables on obedience.

In a **field experiment** in New York City, Leonard Bickman (1974) had three confederates dress in different outfits – jacket and tie, a milkman's outfit and a security guard's uniform. The confederates individually stood in the street and asked passers-by to perform tasks such as picking up litter or handing over a coin for the parking meter. People were twice as likely to obey the assistant dressed as a security guard than the one dressed in jacket and tie.

This supports the view that a situational variable, such as a uniform, does have a powerful effect on obedience.

Cross-cultural replications

Another strength of Milgram's research is that his findings have been **replicated** in other cultures.

For instance, Wim Meeus and Quintin Raaijmakers (1986) used a more realistic procedure than Milgram's to study obedience in Dutch participants. The participants were ordered to say stressful things in an interview to someone (a confederate) desperate for a job. 90% of the participants obeyed. The researchers also replicated Milgram's findings concerning proximity. When the person giving the orders was not present, obedience decreased dramatically.

This suggests that Milgram's findings about obedience are not just limited to Americans or men, but are valid across cultures and apply to women too.

Counterpoint However, replications of Milgram's research are not very 'cross-cultural'. Peter Smith and Michael Bond (1998) identified just two replications between 1968 and 1985 that took place in India and Jordan – both countries culturally quite different from the US. Whereas the other countries involved (e.g. Spain, Australia, Scotland) are culturally quite similar to the US (e.g. they have similar notions about the role of authority).

Therefore, it may not be appropriate to conclude that Milgram's findings (including those about proximity, location and uniform) apply to people in all or most cultures.

Low internal validity

One limitation is that participants may have been aware the procedure was faked.

Martin Orne and Charles Holland (1968) made this criticism of Milgram's baseline study. They point out that it is even more likely in his variations because of the extra manipulation of variables. A good example is the variation where the Experimenter is replaced by a 'member of the public'. Even Milgram recognised that this situation was so contrived that some participants may well have worked out the truth.

Therefore, in all of Milgram's studies it is unclear whether the findings are genuinely due to the operation of obedience or because the participants saw through the **deception** and just 'play-acted' (i.e. responded to **demand characteristics**).

Evaluation eXtra

The danger of the situational perspective

Milgram's research findings support a situational explanation of obedience (proximity, location and uniform are all aspects of the situation).

But this perspective has been criticised by David Mandel (1998) who argues that it offers an excuse or 'alibi' for evil behaviour. In his view, it is offensive to survivors of the Holocaust to suggest that the Nazis were simply obeying orders. Milgram's explanation also ignores the role of dispositional factors (such as personality), implying that the Nazis were victims of situational factors beyond their control.

Consider: *Is the situational perspective justified?*

Apply it Concepts — Obedience in the supermarket

As everyone knows, teachers have lives outside work. Students might even be lucky enough to see a teacher they recognise at the weekend, shopping or suchlike. One day, in the college canteen, a teacher asked a student to pick up a piece of litter and put it in the bin. The student duly obliged. A few days later, outside a local supermarket, another teacher asked the same student to pick up some litter and bin it. This time the student refused.

Question

Using your knowledge of Milgram's variations, explain this difference in the student's behaviour.

Not all uniforms are symbols of authority. Perhaps sometimes a uniform is just about being smartly dressed.

Apply it Methods — Milgram and proximity

The graph of results from Milgram's variations on the facing page of this spread gives obedience rates relating to proximity, location and uniform, plus the original baseline result. Use that information to answer the following questions.

Questions

1. Draw up a table to present the results provided in the graph. Make sure you label the table accurately and clearly. (*3 marks*)
2. Use your knowledge of research to explain what these results tell us about the effect of situational variables on obedience. (*3 marks*)
3. There were 50 participants in the 'Teacher and Learner in the same room' variation. Calculate the number of participants who obeyed. (*2 marks*)
4. Milgram carried out several **pilot studies** of his procedure. Explain what is meant by a pilot study. (*1 mark*)
5. Explain *two* strengths of carrying out a pilot study. (*2 marks + 2 marks*)
6. One limitation of Milgram's studies is that the findings were influenced by **demand characteristics**. What is meant by demand characteristics? (*1 mark*)
7. Explain how demand characteristics might have influenced the results of Milgram's studies. (*3 marks*)

Check it

1. Milgram investigated situational variables affecting obedience to authority. Identify **two** of these variables **and** explain how **each** of them affects obedience. *[3 marks + 3 marks]*
2. Explain how Milgram investigated proximity. In your answer include the procedure **and** what he concluded. *[4 marks]*
3. Describe **and** evaluate **two** situational variables that have been shown by Milgram to affect obedience to authority. *[12 marks AS, 16 marks AL]*

Obedience: Situational explanations

The specification says...

Explanations for obedience: agentic state and legitimacy of authority.

On the previous spread we explored situational variables that influence levels of obedience – proximity, location and uniform. This is one way to explain why people obey – because of characteristics of people around you. Now we turn to two further explanations which are situational but this time concern the dynamics of social hierarchies.

Key terms

Agentic state A mental state where we feel no personal responsibility for our behaviour because we believe ourselves to be acting for an authority figure, i.e. as their agent. This frees us from the demands of our consciences and allows us to obey even a destructive authority figure.

Legitimacy of authority An explanation for obedience which suggests that we are more likely to obey people who we perceive to have authority over us. This authority is justified (legitimate) by the individual's position of power within a social hierarchy.

Agentic state

Stanley Milgram's initial interest in **obedience** was sparked by the trial of Adolf Eichmann in 1961 for war crimes. Eichmann had been in charge of the Nazi death camps and his defence was that he was only obeying orders. This led Milgram to propose that obedience to destructive authority occurs because a person does not take responsibility. Instead they believe they are acting for someone else, i.e. that they are an 'agent'. An 'agent' is someone who acts for or in place of another.

An agent is not an unfeeling puppet – they experience high anxiety ('moral strain') when they realise that what they are doing is wrong, but feel powerless to disobey.

Autonomous state

The opposite of being in an **agentic state** is being in an **autonomous state**. 'Autonomy' means to be independent or free. So a person in an autonomous state is free to behave according to their own principles and feels a sense of responsibility for their own actions.

The shift from autonomy to 'agency' is called the **agentic shift**. Milgram (1974) suggested that this occurs when a person perceives someone else as an authority figure. The authority figure has greater power because they have a higher position in a **social hierarchy**. In most social groups, when one person is in charge others defer to the legitimate authority (see below) of this person and shift from autonomy to agency.

Binding factors

Milgram observed that many of his participants said they wanted to stop but seemed powerless to do so. He wondered why they remained in an agentic state. The answer is **binding factors** – aspects of the situation that allow the person to ignore or minimise the damaging effect of their behaviour and thus reduce the 'moral strain' they are feeling. Milgram proposed a number of strategies that the individual uses, such as shifting the responsibility to the victim ('he was foolish to volunteer') or denying the damage they were doing to the victims.

Apply it Concepts I will obey

Max's younger sister finds out that he has a bag of sweets. 'Give me one of those sweets,' she demands, trying to snatch the bag from his hand. But Max refuses. Just then, Max's dad comes into the room. He has finally had enough, so he tells Max: 'Your room is a complete disgrace, go and tidy it up immediately. And when you've done that, you can go to the shops and get me a loaf of bread.' Max replies, 'Certainly dad, I'll go and do that right now.'

Question

Use your knowledge of why people obey to explain Max's behaviour. Refer to both the agentic state and legitimacy of authority explanations.

Legitimacy of authority

Most societies are structured in a hierarchical way. This means that people in certain positions hold authority over the rest of us. For example, parents, teachers, police officers, nightclub bouncers... all have authority over us at times. The authority they wield is legitimate in the sense that it is agreed by society. Most of us accept that authority figures have to be allowed to exercise social power over others because this allows society to function smoothly.

One of the consequences of this **legitimacy of authority** is that some people are granted the power to punish others. We generally agree that the police and courts have the power to punish wrongdoers. So we are willing to give up some of our independence and to hand control of our behaviour over to people we trust to exercise their authority appropriately. We learn acceptance of legitimate authority from childhood, from parents initially and then teachers and adults generally.

Destructive authority

Problems arise when legitimate authority becomes destructive. History has too often shown that charismatic and powerful leaders (such as Hitler, Stalin and Pol Pot) can use their legitimate powers for destructive purposes, ordering people to behave in ways that are cruel and dangerous. Destructive authority was obvious in Milgram's study, when the Experimenter used prods to order participants to behave in ways that went against their consciences.

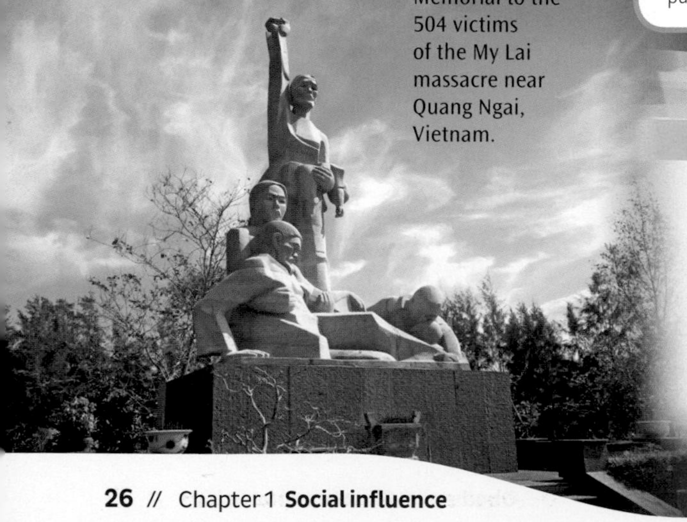

Memorial to the 504 victims of the My Lai massacre near Quang Ngai, Vietnam.

Apply it Concepts Massacre at My Lai

Milgram's findings have been used to explain the notorious war crime at My Lai in 1968 during the Vietnam War. As many as 504 unarmed civilians were killed by American soldiers. Women were gang-raped and people were shot down as they emerged from their homes with their hands in the air. The soldiers blew up buildings, burned the village to the ground and killed all the animals. Only one soldier faced charges and was found guilty, Lt William Calley. His defence was the same as the Nazi officers at the Nuremberg trials, that he was only doing his duty by following orders.

Question

Explain the behaviour of the soldiers in terms of agentic state and legitimacy of authority.

'If yer name's not on the list...' Most people accept that a nightclub doorperson's authority is worth respecting because we trust him or her to exercise it responsibly.

Evaluation

Research support

One strength is that Milgram's own studies support the role of the agentic state in obedience.

Most of Milgram's participants resisted giving the shocks at some point, and often asked the Experimenter questions about the procedure. One of these was 'Who is responsible if Mr Wallace (the Learner) is harmed?' When the Experimenter replied 'I'm responsible', the participants often went through the procedure quickly with no further objections.

This shows that once participants perceived they were no longer responsible for their own behaviour, they acted more easily as the Experimenter's agent, as Milgram suggested.

A limited explanation

One limitation is that the agentic shift doesn't explain many research findings about obedience.

For example, it does not explain the findings of Steven Rank and Cardell Jacobson's (1977) study. They found that 16 out of 18 hospital nurses disobeyed orders from a doctor to administer an excessive drug dose to a patient. The doctor was an obvious authority figure. But almost all the nurses remained autonomous, as did many of Milgram's participants.

This suggests that, at best, the agentic shift can only account for some situations of obedience.

Evaluation eXtra

Obedience alibi revisited

David Mandel (1998) described one incident in the Second World War involving German Reserve Police Battalion 101. These men shot many civilians in a small town in Poland, despite not having direct orders to do so (they were told they could be assigned to other duties if they preferred), i.e. they behaved autonomously.

Consider: *As the men of Battalion 101 were not ordered to murder civilians, how does their behaviour challenge the agentic state explanation?*

Evaluation

Explains cultural differences

One strength of the legitimacy explanation is that it is a useful account of cultural differences in obedience.

Many studies show that countries differ in the degree to which people are obedient to authority. For example, Wesley Kilham and Leon Mann (1974) found that only 16% of Australian women went all the way up to 450 volts in a Milgram-style study. However, David Mantell (1971) found a very different figure for German participants – 85%.

This shows that, in some cultures, authority is more likely to be accepted as legitimate and entitled to demand obedience from individuals. This reflects the ways that different societies are structured and how children are raised to perceive authority figures.

Cannot explain all (dis)obedience

One limitation is that legitimacy cannot explain instances of disobedience in a hierarchy where the legitimacy of authority is clear and accepted.

This includes the nurses in Rank and Jacobson's study (above). Most of them were disobedient despite working in a rigidly hierarchical authority structure. Also, a significant minority of Milgram's participants disobeyed despite recognising the Experimenter's scientific authority.

This suggests that some people may just be more (or less) obedient than others (see next spread). It is possible that innate tendencies to obey or disobey have a greater influence on behaviour than the legitimacy of an authority figure.

Evaluation eXtra

Real-world crimes of obedience

Rank and Jacobson (see above) found that nurses were prepared to disobey a legitimate authority (a doctor).

But Herbert Kelman and Lee Hamilton (1989) argue that a real-world crime of obedience (the My Lai massacre, see Apply it on the facing page) can be understood in terms of the power hierarchy of the US Army. Commanding officers (COs) operate within a clearer legitimate hierarchy than hospital doctors and have a greater power to punish.

Consider: *How does this support the legitimacy of authority explanation?*

Apply it Methods

An obedience survey

A psychologist was interested in the attitudes students have towards obedience. He wanted to know whether the students thought that obeying the orders of an authority figure was desirable or not. He also wanted to know what factors influenced the students' decisions to obey authority figures.

He produced a questionnaire and distributed it to 200 students at a local sixth-form college. When he returned the next day to collect the questionnaires, he found that 160 students had completed it.

Questions

1. Identify *two* methods the psychologist could have used to select a **sample** of participants. Explain *one* strength and *one* limitation of *one* of these methods. (*2 marks + 2 marks + 2 marks*)
2. Explain *one* strength and *one* limitation of using a questionnaire. (*2 marks + 2 marks*)
3. In terms of questionnaires, explain what is meant by **closed questions** and **open questions**. (*2 marks + 2 marks*)
4. Give *one* example of a closed question and *one* example of an open question the psychologist could have used in his study. (*2 marks + 2 marks*)
5. Calculate the number of completed questionnaires as a percentage of the total distributed. (*1 mark*)

Study tip

A great way to evaluate an explanation is to consider the research evidence that supports or contradicts it. But make sure you use the evidence effectively. Focus on explaining how the evidence supports or challenges the theory. Don't get sidetracked into describing the evidence at length.

You can go even further with your evaluation. Are there any limitations with the evidence itself? Are there any problems with the research method, for example? Make sure you also show how this supports (or otherwise) the explanation.

Check it

1. Explain what is meant by 'agentic state' and 'legitimacy of authority'. *[2 marks + 2 marks]*
2. Explain **one** limitation of the agentic state explanation for obedience. Refer to Milgram's research in your answer. *[4 marks]*
3. Outline **and** evaluate **one or more** explanations of obedience. *[12 marks AS, 16 marks AL]*

Obedience: Dispositional explanation

The specification says...

Dispositional explanation for obedience: the Authoritarian Personality.

Not all psychologists accept that obedience can be fully explained by factors in the situation or the social structure. They reason that there must be at least some role for the personality or *disposition* of the individual. After all, not all of Milgram's participants fully obeyed, and some actively rebelled, despite them experiencing identical situational and social pressures.

There are several dispositional explanations of obedience, but the most influential concerns the Authoritarian Personality.

Key terms

Dispositional explanation Any explanation of behaviour that highlights the importance of the individual's personality (i.e. their disposition). Such explanations are often contrasted with situational explanations.

Authoritarian Personality (AP) A type of personality that Adorno argued was especially susceptible to obeying people in authority. Such individuals are also thought to be submissive to those of higher status and dismissive of inferiors.

Consistently harsh and critical parenting can lead to the development of an Authoritarian Personality when the child becomes an adult.

Apply it Concepts: Trouble with the boss

Leon works in the Head Office of a big national company. His boss is always shouting at people and telling them what to do in no uncertain terms. The floor Leon works on is open-plan so his boss can easily see what everyone is doing. Leon has noticed that his boss is always sucking up to the senior managers at every opportunity.

Question

Explain the behaviour of Leon's boss in terms of (a) situational variables, (b) social structures/hierarchies, (c) dispositional factors.

The Authoritarian Personality

Like Milgram, Theodor Adorno and his colleagues wanted to understand the **anti-Semitism** of the Holocaust. Their research led them to draw very different conclusions from Milgram's. They believed that a high level of **obedience** was basically a psychological disorder (i.e. pathological). They believed that the causes of such a disorder lie in the personality of the individual rather than in the situation, i.e. it is a **dispositional explanation**.

Authoritarian Personality and obedience

Adorno *et al.* argued that people with an **Authoritarian Personality** (AP) first of all show an extreme respect for (and submissiveness to) authority. Second, such people view society as 'weaker' than it once was, so believe we need strong and powerful leaders to enforce traditional values such as love of country and family. Both of these characteristics make people with an Authoritarian Personality more likely to obey orders from a source of authority.

People with Authoritarian Personalities also show contempt for those of inferior social status. This is fuelled by their inflexible outlook on the world – for them there are no 'grey areas'. Everything is either righ or wrong and they are very uncomfortable with uncertainty. Therefore people who are 'other' (e.g. belong to a different ethnic group) are responsible for the ills of society. 'Other' people are a convenient target for authoritarians who are likely to obey orders from authority figures even when such orders are destructive (as in Nazi Germany).

Origins of the Authoritarian Personality

Adorno *et al.* believed the Authoritarian Personality type forms in childhood, mostly as a result of harsh parenting. This parenting style typically features extremely strict discipline, an expectation of absolute loyalty, impossibly high standards and severe criticism of perceived failings. Parents give conditional love – that is, their love and affection for their child depends entirely on how he or she behaves ('I will love you *if* ...').

Adorno *et al.* argued that these childhood experiences create resentment and hostility in a child. But the child cannot express these feelings directly against their parents because they fear punishment. So their fears are **displaced** onto others who they perceive to be weaker, in a process known as *scapegoating*. This explains the hatred towards people considered to be socially inferior or who belong to other social groups, a central feature of obedience to a higher authority. This is a **psychodynamic explanation**.

Adorno *et al.*'s research

Adorno *et al.* (1950) based their theory on research data.

Procedure Adorno *et al.* (1950) studied more than 2000 middle-class, white Americans and their **unconscious** attitudes towards other ethnic groups. The researchers developed several measurement scales, including the potential-for-fascism scale (F-scale). This scale is still used to measure Authoritarian Personality.

Two examples of items from the F-scale are: 'Obedience and respect for authority are the most important virtues for children to learn', and 'There is hardly anything lower than a person who does not feel great love, gratitude and respect for his parents'. Other examples are given on the facing page.

Findings People with authoritarian leanings (i.e. those who scored high on the F-scale and other measures) identified with 'strong' people and were generally contemptuous of the 'weak'. They were very conscious of status (their own and others') and showed extreme respect, deference and servility to those of higher status – these traits are the basis of obedience.

Adorno *et al.* also found that authoritarian people had a certain **cognitive style** (way of perceiving others) in which there was no 'fuzziness' between categories of people (i.e. 'black and white' thinking). They had fixed and distinctive **stereotypes** about other groups. Adorno *et al.* found a strong **positive correlation** between authoritarianism and prejudice.

Apply it Concepts: Caleb's grandad

Caleb's grandad is the old-fashioned type. As far as he's concerned, there are good Zombies and there are bad Zombies and that's all there is to it. He thinks the youth of today are a bunch of wasters and what they all need is a spell in the Zombie Army. He longs for the days when we had strong leaders who knew how to get things done. Caleb has also noticed that his grandad talks with a lot of respect about his old bosses from work: 'They don't make them like that anymore – you'd do anything for them.' Caleb often wonders why his grandad thinks like this.

Question

From what you know about obedience, how would you explain to Caleb why his grandad has these attitudes?

Evaluation

Research support

One strength is evidence from Milgram supporting the Authoritarian Personality.

Milgram, together with Alan Elms (Elms and Milgram 1966), **interviewed** a small sample of people who had participated in the original obedience studies and been fully obedient. They all completed the F-scale (and other measures) as part of the interview. These 20 obedient participants scored significantly higher on the overall F-scale than a comparison group of 20 disobedient participants. The two groups were clearly quite different in terms of authoritarianism.

This finding supports Adorno *et al.*'s view that obedient people may well show similar characteristics to people who have an Authoritarian Personality.

Counterpoint However, when the researchers analysed the individual subscales of the F-scale, they found that the obedient participants had a number of characteristics that were unusual for authoritarians. For example unlike authoritarians, Milgram's obedient participants generally did not glorify their fathers, did not experience unusual levels of punishment in childhood and did not have particularly hostile attitudes towards their mothers.

This means that the link between obedience and authoritarianism is complex. The obedient participants were unlike authoritarians in so many ways that authoritarianism is unlikely to be a useful predictor of obedience.

Limited explanation

One limitation is that authoritarianism cannot explain obedient behaviour in the majority of a country's population.

For example, in pre-war Germany, millions of individuals displayed obedient and anti-Semitic behaviour. This was despite the fact that they must have differed in their personalities in all sorts of ways. It seems extremely unlikely that they could all possess an Authoritarian Personality. An alternative view is that the majority of the German people *identified* with the anti-Semitic Nazi state, and scapegoated the 'outgroup' of Jews, a **social identity theory** approach.

Therefore Adorno's theory is limited because an alternative explanation is much more realistic.

Political bias

Another limitation is that the F-scale only measures the tendency towards an extreme form of right-wing ideology.

Richard Christie and Marie Jahoda (1954) argued that the F-scale is a politically-biased interpretation of Authoritarian Personality. They point out the reality of left-wing authoritarianism in the shape of Russian Bolshevism or Chinese Maoism. In fact, extreme right-wing and left-wing ideologies have a lot in common. For example they both emphasise the importance of complete obedience to political authority.

This means Adorno's theory is not a comprehensive dispositional explanation that accounts for obedience to authority across the whole political spectrum.

Evaluation eXtra

Flawed evidence

On the positive side, research with the F-scale has provided the basis of an explanation of obedience based on Authoritarian Personality. On the other hand, Fred Greenstein (1969) calls the F-scale 'a comedy of methodological errors' because it is a seriously flawed scale. For instance, it is possible to get a high score just by selecting 'agree' answers. This means that anyone with this response bias is assessed as having an Authoritarian Personality.

Consider: *On balance, how useful is the F-scale in helping us understand obedience?*

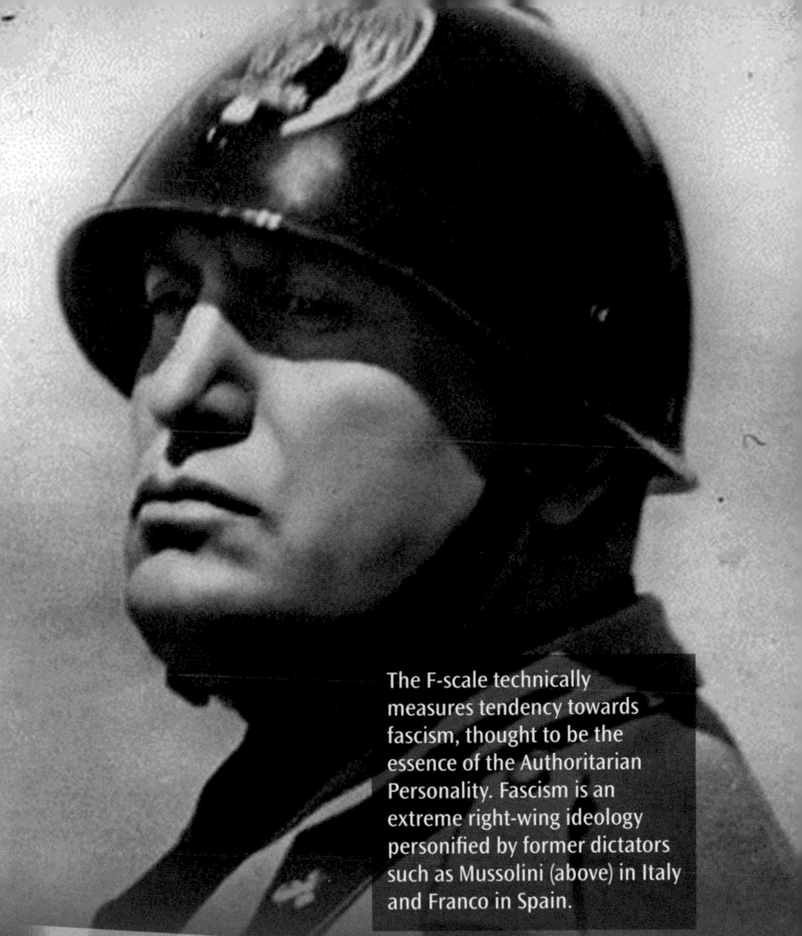

The F-scale technically measures tendency towards fascism, thought to be the essence of the Authoritarian Personality. Fascism is an extreme right-wing ideology personified by former dictators such as Mussolini (above) in Italy and Franco in Spain.

Apply it Concepts — The F-scale

Here are some more items from the F-scale created by Adorno and his colleagues to measure the nine dimensions of the Authoritarian Personality. Participants had to rate their agreement with each item on a 6-point scale ranging from 1 (disagree strongly) to 6 (agree strongly).

- The businessman and the manufacturer are much more important to society than the artist and the professor.
- Science has its place, but there are many important things that can never be understood by the human mind.
- Every person should have complete faith in some supernatural power whose decisions he obeys without question.
- Nobody ever learned anything really important except through suffering.
- Homosexuals are hardly better than criminals and ought to be severely punished.

Question

Use your knowledge of Adorno's theory to explain how each of these items relates to the features of the Authoritarian Personality.

Check it

1. Explain 'dispositional explanation' in relation to explanations of obedience. *[2 marks]*
2. Explain what is meant by the 'Authoritarian Personality'. *[2 marks]*
3. Outline the Authoritarian Personality explanation of obedience. *[6 marks]*
4. Discuss the Authoritarian Personality as an explanation for obedience. *[12 marks AS, 16 marks AL]*

Resistance to social influence

The specification says...

Explanations of resistance to social influence, including social support and locus of control.

Based on research covered in the previous spreads, you'd be forgiven for thinking that people are mostly puppets easily swayed by the forces of social pressure to conform or obey. But this is far from the truth. Even in Milgram's studies, a healthy minority of participants refused to fully obey (35%). In Asch's studies the most common behaviour was not conformity (most people did not conform most of the time).

Key terms

Resistance to social influence Refers to the ability of people to withstand the social pressure to conform to the majority or to obey authority. This ability to withstand social pressure is influenced by both situational and dispositional factors.

Social support The presence of people who resist pressures to conform or obey can help others to do the same. These people act as models to show others that resistance to social influence is possible.

Locus of control (LOC) Refers to the sense we each have about what directs events in our lives. Internals believe they are mostly responsible for what happens to them (internal locus of control). Externals believe it is mainly a matter of luck or other outside forces (external locus of control).

Social support

Resisting conformity

The pressure to **conform** can be resisted if there are other people present who are not conforming. As we saw in Solomon Asch's research (see page 16), the **confederate** who is not conforming may not be giving the 'right' answer.

Simply the fact that someone else is not following the majority is **social support**. It enables the naïve participant to be free to follow their own conscience. The confederate acts as a 'model' of independent behaviour. Their dissent gives rise to more dissent because it shows that the majority is no longer unanimous.

Resisting obedience

The pressure to obey can be resisted if there is another person who is seen to disobey. In one of Milgram's variations, the rate of **obedience** dropped from 65% to 10% when the genuine participant was joined by a disobedient confederate. The participant may not follow the disobedient person's behaviour but the point is the other person's disobedience acts as a 'model' of dissent for the participant to copy and this frees him to act from his own conscience. The disobedient model challenges the legitimacy of the authority figure, making it easier for others to disobey.

Locus of control

Julian Rotter (1966) proposed **locus of control** (LOC) as a concept concerned with internal control versus external control. Some people have an internal LOC (internals) – they believe that the things that happen to them are largely controlled by themselves. For example, if you do well in an exam it is because you worked hard, if you don't do well it is because you didn't work hard.

Some people have an external LOC (externals) – they tend to believe the things that happen are outside their control. So if they did well in an exam it was because they used an excellent textbook (ours, obviously). If they failed they might blame it on the textbook (not ours) or they had bad luck because the questions were hard.

The LOC continuum

People are not just either internal or external. LOC is a scale and individuals vary in their position on it. So, high internal LOC is at one end of the continuum and high external at the other. Low internal and low external lie in-between.

Resistance to social influence

People with a high internal LOC are more able to resist pressures to conform or obey. If a person takes personal responsibility for their actions and experiences (as internals do), they tend to base their decisions on their own beliefs rather than depending on the opinions of others.

Another explanation is that people with a high internal LOC tend to be more self-confident, more achievement-oriented and have higher intelligence. These traits lead to greater **resistance to social influence**. These are also characteristics of leaders, who have much less need for social approval than followers.

Apply it Concepts — Under pressure

You are a member of the student council at a sixth-form college. You are all meeting to elect a chairperson. The three candidates have all addressed the meeting and have now left. It's decision time. But you begin to get a bit worried because the teacher who liaises with the student council is asking a lot of questions about one of the candidates. After a while, it becomes clear that he is trying to influence the students to vote for this person.

Question

What factors might make it difficult for you to resist the pressure from the teacher to vote a certain way?

Apply it Concepts — Locus of control in action

Asgarth and Hyacinth are students at Rydell High. They have very different outlooks on life. Asgarth believes you have to grasp opportunities with both hands because your fate is under your own control. That is why he has put his name forward to be his tutor group's representative on the school council. Hyacinth, on the other hand, thinks that 'what will be will be' and there's very little she can do to change that. She is also standing as tutor group rep, but she thinks it's just down to luck whether she wins or loses.

Questions

1. Identify Asgarth's and Hyacinth's locus of control.
2. Whoever wins the election is likely to come under pressure to conform or obey. Will Asgarth or Hyacinth be better able to resist social influence? Explain your choice.

Practical activity on page 36

Evaluation

Real-world research support

One strength is research evidence for the positive effects of social support.

For example, Susan Albrecht *et al.* (2006) evaluated Teen Fresh Start USA, an eight-week programme to help pregnant adolescents aged 14–19 resist peer pressure to smoke. Social support was provided by a slightly older mentor or 'buddy'. At the end of the programme adolescents who had a 'buddy' were significantly less likely to smoke than a control group of participants who did not have a 'buddy'.

This shows that social support can help young people resist social influence as part of an intervention in the real world.

Research support for dissenting peers

Another strength is research evidence to support the role of dissenting peers in resisting obedience.

William Gamson *et al.*'s (1982) participants were told to produce evidence that would be used to help an oil company run a smear campaign. The researchers found higher levels of resistance in their study than Milgram did in his. This was probably because the participants were in groups so could discuss what they were told to do. 29 out of 33 groups of participants (88%) rebelled against their orders.

This shows that peer support can lead to disobedience by undermining the legitimacy of an authority figure.

Evaluation eXtra

Social support explanation

A study by Vernon Allen and John Levine (1971) showed that social support can help individuals to resist the influence of a group. In an Asch-type task, when the dissenter was someone with apparently good eyesight, 64% of genuine participants refused to conform. When there was no supporter at all only 3% of participants resisted.

However, the study also showed that social support does not always help. This is because when the dissenter had obviously poor eyesight (thick glasses) resistance was only 36%.

Consider: *On balance, what does this suggest about the validity of the social support explanation in the context of resisting social influence?*

Evaluation

Research support

One strength is research evidence to support the link between LOC and resistance to obedience.

Charles Holland (1967) repeated Milgram's baseline study and measured whether participants were internals or externals. He found that 37% of internals did not continue to the highest shock level (i.e. they showed some resistance), whereas only 23% of externals did not continue. In other words, internals showed greater resistance to authority in a Milgram-type situation.

This shows that resistance is at least partly related to LOC, which increases the validity of LOC as an explanation of disobedience.

Contradictory research

One limitation is evidence that challenges the link between LOC and resistance.

For example, Jean Twenge *et al.* (2004) analysed data from American locus of control studies conducted over a 40-year period (from 1960 to 2002). The data showed that, over this time span, people became more resistant to obedience but also more external. This is a surprising outcome. If resistance is linked to an internal locus of control, we would expect people to have become more internal.

This suggests that locus of control is not a valid explanation of how people resist social influence.

Evaluation eXtra

Limited role of LOC

As we have seen, many studies (e.g. Holland 1967) show that having an internal LOC is linked with being able to resist social influence. However, Rotter (1982) points out that LOC is not necessarily the most important factor in determining whether someone resists social influence. LOC's role depends on the situation. A person's LOC only significantly affects their behaviour in new situations. If you have conformed or obeyed in a specific situation in the past, the chances are you will do so again in that situation regardless of whether you have a high internal or high external LOC.

Consider: *To what extent is the LOC explanation of resistance valid?*

NO!

What is the effect of one dissenter?

Apply it Methods — Social support

A researcher wanted to investigate the effect of having a supporter on the level of conformity. She used an Asch-type task where participants had to judge the lengths of lines. On each trial, only one participant was genuine – the others were confederates of the researcher. One of these confederates was instructed to give the correct answer every time, even when this disagreed with the majority. The procedure was repeated, but this time the majority was unanimous and there was no dissenter.

Table showing conforming responses.

	Total trials	Conforming responses
One dissenter	150	30
No dissenter	120	30

Questions

1. Identify the **independent** and **dependent variable** in this study. (*2 marks*)
2. Write a suitable **directional hypothesis** for this study. (*2 marks*)
3. Identify the **experimental design** used in this study. (*1 mark*)
4. Explain *one* strength and *one* limitation of this design. (*2 marks + 2 marks*)
5. Calculate *both* results as percentages of the total number of trials. (*2 marks*)
6. What do the results of this study tell us about the role of social support in resisting social influence? (*3 marks*)

Study tip

When answering questions it helps to use specialist terms – it provides detail. So make a point, on every spread, of identifying such specialist terms (they are often emboldened) and don't be afraid to use them.

Check it

1. In the context of resistance to social influence, explain what is meant by 'social support'. *[2 marks]*
2. Using an example, explain how social support could lead to resistance to social influence. *[4 marks]*
3. Outline locus of control as an explanation of resistance to social influence. *[4 marks]*
4. Describe **and** evaluate **two** explanations of resistance to social influence. *[12 marks AS, 16 marks AL]*

Minority influence

The specification says...

Minority influence including reference to consistency, commitment and flexibility.

We've said quite a lot so far about how *majorities* apply (real or imagined) pressure to others in their group. But if this is the only pressure that is felt, how does change come about? Where do new ideas come from? Serge Moscovici was the first to identify the process of minority influence as a contrast to majority influence. He introduced the idea of minority influence to explain innovation – new ways of doing things.

Key terms

Minority influence A form of social influence in which a minority of people (sometimes just one person) persuades others to adopt their beliefs, attitudes or behaviours. Leads to internalisation or conversion, in which private attitudes are changed as well as public behaviours.

Consistency Minority influence is most effective if the minority keeps the same beliefs, both over time and between all the individuals that form the minority. Consistency is effective because it draws attention to the minority view.

Commitment Minority influence is more powerful if the minority demonstrates dedication to their position, for example, by making personal sacrifices. This is effective because it shows the minority is not acting out of self-interest.

Flexibility Relentless consistency could be counter-productive if it is seen by the majority as unbending and unreasonable. Therefore minority influence is more effective if the minority show flexibility by accepting the possibility of compromise.

Minority influence

Minority influence refers to situations where one person or a small group of people (i.e. a minority) influences the beliefs and behaviour of other people. This is distinct from **conformity** where the majority is doing the influencing (and thus conformity is sometimes called **majority influence**). In both cases the people being influenced may be just one person, or a small group or a large group of people. Minority influence is most likely to lead to **internalisation** – both public behaviour and private beliefs are changed by the process.

Serge Moscovici first studied this process in his 'blue slide, green slide' study (see below left). This study and other research have drawn attention to three main processes in minority influence.

Consistency

The minority must be consistent in their views. Over time, this **consistency** increases the amount of interest from other people. Consistency can take the form of agreement between people in the minority group (**synchronic consistency** – they're all saying the same thing), and/or consistency over time (**diachronic consistency** – they've been saying the same thing for some time now). A consistent minority makes other people start to rethink their own views ('Maybe they've got a point if they all think this way' or 'Maybe they've got a point if they have kept saying it').

Commitment

The minority must demonstrate **commitment** to their cause or views. Sometimes minorities engage in quite extreme activities to draw attention to their views. It is important that these extreme activities present some risk to the minority because this shows greater commitment. Majority group members then pay even more attention ('Wow, she must really believe in what she's saying so perhaps I ought to consider her view'). This is called the **augmentation principle.**

Flexibility

Charlan Nemeth (1986) argued that consistency is not the only important factor in minority influence because it can be off-putting. Someone who is extremely consistent, who simply repeats the same old arguments and behaviours again and again may be seen as rigid, unbending and dogmatic. This approach on its own is unlikely to gain many converts to the minority position. Instead, members of the minority need to be prepared to adapt their point of view and accept reasonable and valid counterarguments. The key is to strike a balance between consistency and **flexibility**.

Explaining the process of change

All of the three factors outlined above make people think about the minority's view or cause. Hearing something you already agree with doesn't usually make you stop and think. But if you hear something new, then you might think more deeply about it, especially if the source of this other view is consistent, committed and flexible.

It is this deeper processing which is important in the process of *conversion* to a different, minority viewpoint. Over time, increasing numbers of people switch from the majority position to the minority position. They have become 'converted'.

The more this happens, the faster the rate of conversion. This is called the **snowball effect** (like a snowball gathering more snow as it rolls along). Gradually the minority view has become the majority view and change has occurred.

Apply it Methods — The blue-green slides

Moscovici *et al.* (1969) demonstrated minority influence in a study where a group of six people was asked to view a set of 36 blue-coloured slides that varied in intensity and then state whether the slides were blue or green. In each group there were two confederates who consistently said the slides were green. The true participants gave the same wrong answer (green) on 8.42% of the trials, i.e. agreed with the confederates.

A second group of participants was exposed to an inconsistent minority (the confederates said 'green' 24 times and 'blue' 12 times). In this case, agreement with the answer 'green' fell to 1.25%. For a third control group there were no confederates and all participants had to do was identify the colour of each slide. They got this wrong on just 0.25% of the trials.

Questions

1. What is meant by **control group** and why was one used in this study? (*3 marks*)
2. Present the findings in the form of a properly-labelled table. (*2 marks*)
3. Present the findings in the form of a **bar chart**. Make sure you label the axes. (*3 marks*)
4. State *two* conclusions that you could draw from this study. (*4 marks*)
5. The findings are given to two decimal places. What does this mean? (*2 marks*)

Calling a blue slide green is not as silly as you might think. Some blues do look quite green.

Evaluation

Research support for consistency

One strength is research evidence demonstrating the importance of consistency.

Moscovici *et al.*'s blue/green slide study (see facing page) showed that a consistent minority opinion had a greater effect on changing the views of other people than an inconsistent opinion. Wendy Wood *et al.* (1994) carried out a **meta-analysis** of almost 100 similar studies and found that minorities who were seen as being consistent were most influential.

This suggests that presenting a consistent view is a minimum requirement for a minority trying to influence a majority.

Research support for deeper processing

Another strength is evidence showing that a change in the majority's position does involve deeper processing of the minority's ideas.

Robin Martin *et al.* (2003) presented a message supporting a particular viewpoint and measured participants' agreement. One group of participants then heard a minority group agree with the initial view while another group heard a majority group agree with it. Participants were finally exposed to a conflicting view and attitudes were measured again. People were less willing to change their opinions if they had listened to a minority group than if they had listened to a majority group.

This suggests that the minority message had been more deeply processed and had a more enduring effect, supporting the central argument about how minority influence works.

Counterpoint Research studies such as Martin *et al.*'s make clear distinctions between the majority and the minority. Doing this in a controlled way is a strength of minority influence research. But real-world social influence situations are much more complicated. For example, majorities usually have a lot more power and status than minorities. Minorities are very committed to their causes – they have to be because they often face very hostile opposition. These features are usually absent from minority influence research – the minority is simply the smallest group.

Therefore Martin *et al.*'s findings are very limited in what they can tell us about minority influence in real-world situations.

Artificial tasks

One limitation of minority influence research is that the tasks involved are often just as artificial as Asch's line judgement task.

This includes Moscovici *et al.*'s task of identifying the colour of a slide. Research is therefore far removed from how minorities attempt to change the behaviour of majorities in real life. In cases such as jury decision-making and political campaigning, the outcomes are vastly more important, sometimes even literally a matter of life or death.

This means findings of minority influence studies are lacking in **external validity** and are limited in what they can tell us about how minority influence works in real-world social situations.

Evaluation eXtra

Power of minority influence

In Moscovici *et al.*'s study, the figure for agreement with a consistent minority was very low, on average only 8%. This suggests that minority influence is quite rare and not a useful concept.

But when participants wrote down their answers privately, they were more likely to agree with the minority view. This suggests that the view expressed by people in public was just the 'tip of the iceberg'.

Consider: *On the basis of these two findings, is minority influence a valid form of social influence?*

Being in a minority in the real world can be dangerous. But even a minority of one can be persuasive if he or she is consistent, committed to the cause and flexible. Maybe it wouldn't work in a tug-of-war, though?

Apply it Concepts: Recycling

There was a time in this country when very few people recycled cans, bottles, newspapers and the like. In fact, people who did were viewed by the majority with suspicion, as anyone who carried out such 'green' activities was often considered 'a bit strange'.

Question

How did the minority activity of recycling become so widely accepted by the majority? (Include all of the features of minority influence in your answer.)

Apply it Concepts: A jury decides

Psychologists have discovered that minority influence can be an important social influence process in jury decision-making. Let's say that a jury of 12 people has to decide on the guilt or innocence of a defendant charged with murder. A vote is taken at the start of the jury's deliberations – 11 believe the defendant is guilty. Only one person is convinced of his innocence. Because the jury has to reach a unanimous decision, the discussion begins. After several hours, another vote is taken. This time, all 12 jurors believe the defendant is not guilty.

Question

Using what you know about minority influence, explain how this change of opinion could have happened.

Study tip

Research studies can serve two purposes. You can use them when asked to describe research or you can use them as part of any evaluation/discussion.

The key issue is the description of what the researchers did (the procedure). This is creditworthy material in a descriptive question but not when using the study for evaluation – in this case you should just focus on what the study has demonstrated, i.e. what it 'shows' (the findings and/or conclusions).

Check it

1. Explain what is meant by 'minority influence'. *[2 marks]*
2. Briefly explain what is meant by 'consistency, commitment and flexibility' as factors that enable a minority to influence a majority. *[3 marks]*
3. Describe **and** evaluate research into minority influence. *[12 marks AS, 16 marks AL]*

Social influence and social change

The specification says...

The role of social influence processes in social change.

Serge Moscovici's research into minority influence rejuvenated the study of social influence because it gave psychologists a new and exciting direction. They started investigating how major changes in behaviour occurred on the level of whole societies, and not just as a result of minority influence but other forms of social influence as well. This spread presents the ultimate practical application of such psychological knowledge.

Key terms

Social influence The process by which individuals and groups change each other's attitudes and behaviours. Includes conformity, obedience and minority influence.

Social change This occurs when whole societies, rather than just individuals, adopt new attitudes, beliefs and ways of doing things. Examples include accepting that the Earth orbits the Sun, women's suffrage, gay rights and environmental issues.

YOU CAN DO IT!

Apply it Concepts — Tackling obesity

Everyone agrees that Britain is in an obesity crisis – 65% of men and 58% of women are now overweight or obese. Heart disease, certain cancers and especially type 2 diabetes are all on the increase, costing the NHS billions of pounds every year.

Experts agree that any improvement in the situation is going to require significant changes in attitudes and behaviours across the whole of society.

Question

You have been asked to advise a government department worried about the developing obesity crisis. Using your knowledge of how both (a) conformity and (b) obedience processes can influence social change, explain what advice you would give the government. Make sure you refer to social influence research in your advice.

Social change

Lessons from minority influence research

Let's consider the steps in how minority **social influence** creates **social change** by looking at a real-world example – the African-American civil rights movement of the 1950s and 60s.

(1) **Drawing attention** through social proof – In the 1950s, black and white segregation applied to all parts of America. There were black neighbourhoods and, in the southern states of America, places such as certain schools and restaurants were exclusive to whites. The civil rights marches of this period *drew attention* to this situation, providing *social proof* of the problem.

(2) **Consistency** – Civil rights activists represented a minority of the American population, but their position remained *consistent*. Millions of people took part in many marches over several years, always presenting the same non-aggressive messages.

(3) **Deeper processing** of the issue – The activism meant that many people who had simply accepted the status quo began to think *deeply* about the unjustness of it.

(4) The **augmentation principle** – Individuals risked their lives numerous times. For example the 'freedom riders' were mixed ethnic groups who boarded buses in the south, challenging racial segregation of transport. Many freedom riders were beaten. This personal risk indicates a strong belief and reinforces (or augments) their message.

(5) The **snowball effect** – Activists (e.g. Martin Luther King) gradually got the attention of the US government. More and more people backed the minority position. In 1964 the US Civil Rights Act prohibited discrimination, marking a change from minority to majority support for civil rights.

(6) **Social cryptomnesia** (people have a memory that change has occurred but don't remember how it happened) – Social change clearly did come about so the south is quite a different place now. But some people have no memory (*cryptoamnesia*) of the events that led to that change.

Lessons from conformity research

Earlier in this chapter you read about Solomon Asch's research. He highlighted the importance of dissent in one of his variations in which one **confederate** gave correct answers throughout the procedure. This broke the power of the majority, encouraging others to do likewise. Such dissent has the potential to ultimately lead to social change.

A different approach is one used by environmental and health campaigns which exploit conformity processes by appealing to **normative social influence**. They do this by providing information about what other people are doing. Examples include reducing litter by printing normative messages on litter bins ('Bin it – others do'), and preventing young people from taking up smoking (telling them that most other young people do not smoke). In other words social change is encouraged by drawing attention to what the majority are actually doing.

Lessons from obedience research

Stanley Milgram's research clearly demonstrates the importance of disobedient role models. In the variation where a confederate Teacher refuses to give shocks to the Learner, the rate of obedience in the genuine participants plummeted.

Philip Zimbardo (2007) suggested how obedience can be used to create social change through the process of **gradual commitment**. Once a small instruction is obeyed, it becomes much more difficult to resist a bigger one. People essentially 'drift' into a new kind of behaviour.

Apply it Concepts — Minority influence and social change

There are many examples of how minority influence has led to social change. Just a few are: how opinion changed from believing the world is flat to accepting it is round, suffragists and suffragettes campaigning for the vote for women, changing attitudes towards waste disposal (the green movement) and changing attitudes about smoking.

Question

Choose *one* (*or more*) of these examples. Describe how the six-step process of minority influence (outlined above) can explain the social change you have selected.

Evaluation

Research support for normative influences

One strength is that research has shown that social influence processes based on psychological research do work.

Jessica Nolan *et al.* (2008) aimed to see if they could change people's energy-use habits. The researchers hung messages on the front doors of houses in San Diego, California every week for one month. The key message was that most residents were trying to reduce their energy usage. As a control, some residents had a different message that just asked them to save energy but made no reference to other people's behaviour. There were significant decreases in energy usage in the first group compared to the second.

This shows that conformity (majority influence) can lead to social change through the operation of normative social influence, i.e. it is a **valid** explanation.

Counterpoint However some studies show that people's behaviour is not always changed through exposing them to social norms. David Foxcroft *et al.* (2015) reviewed social norms interventions as part of the 'gold standard' *Cochrane Collaboration*. This review included 70 studies where the social norms approach was used to reduce student alcohol use. The researchers found only a small reduction in drinking quantity and no effect on drinking frequency.

Therefore it seems that using normative influence does not always produce long-term social change.

Minority influence explains change

Another strength is that psychologists can explain how minority influence brings about social change.

Charlan Nemeth (2009) claims social change is due to the type of thinking that minorities inspire. When people consider minority arguments, they engage in divergent thinking. This type of thinking is broad rather than narrow, in which the thinker actively searches for information and weighs up more options. Nemeth argues this leads to better decisions and more creative solutions to social issues.

This shows why dissenting minorities are valuable – they stimulate new ideas and open minds in a way that majorities cannot.

Role of deeper processing

One limitation is that deeper processing may not play a role in how minorities bring about social change.

Some people are supposedly converted because they think more deeply about the minority's views. Diane Mackie (1987) disagrees and presents evidence that it is majority influence that may create deeper processing if you do not share their views. This is because we like to believe that other people share our views and think in the same ways as us. When we find that a majority believes something different, then we are forced to think long and hard about their arguments and reasoning.

This means that a central element of minority influence has been challenged, casting doubt on its validity as an explanation of social change.

Evaluation eXtra

Barriers to social change

The research on this spread provides a lot of practical advice useful to a minority wanting to influence majority opinion or behaviour (e.g. the importance of consistency).

However, according to Nadia Bashir *et al.* (2013), the fact is that people still resist social change. For example, Bashir *et al.* found that their participants were less likely to behave in environmentally-friendly ways because they did not want to be associated with stereotypical and minority 'environmentalists'. They described environmental activists in negative ways (e.g. 'tree-huggers'). Despite this resistance, the researchers were still able to suggest ways in which minorities can overcome barriers to social change.

Consider: *On balance, does minority influence research help to produce social change?*

DEEDS
NOT
WORDS
VOTES FOR WOMEN
Millennium 1999/24
Equal rights/N.Kerr
19

Women who actively campaigned for the vote were seen as deviant (and worse). Seventy years later, they were celebrated as social reformers on British postage stamps.

Apply it — Methods: Normative influence and social change

One morning a group of five volunteers went knocking on doors to ask residents of an inner-city housing estate to spend one hour helping a local charity to construct a small garden.

At 20 of the flats the volunteers gave a *normative message* – they described the project and included the information that the majority of neighbours agreed to help out. At another 20 flats they gave a *control message* – they simply described the project before asking the residents to commit one hour of their time.

Questions

1. What research method was used in this study? Explain your answer. (*1 mark*)
2. Explain *one* strength and *one* limitation of this research method. (*2 marks + 2 marks*)
3. The **sampling method** was not a **volunteer sample**. What was it? (*1 mark*)
4. Explain *one* limitation of this sampling method. (*2 marks*)
5. Using your knowledge of the role of social influence processes in social change, explain the likely outcome of this study. (*2 marks*)

Check it

1. Explain what is meant by 'social change'. *[2 marks]*
2. For many years, people regarded smoking as quite acceptable behaviour but today fewer and fewer people smoke. Smoking is illegal in enclosed public spaces but even in private, people tend not to smoke without asking permission of people around them.

   Using your knowledge of social influence, explain how this social change came about. *[4 marks]*
3. Describe how social influence processes contribute to social change. Use an example in your answer. *[6 marks]*
4. Discuss the role of social influence processes in social change. *[12 marks AS, 16 marks AL]*

Practical corner

The specification says...

Knowledge and understanding of ... research methods, practical research skills and maths skills. These should be developed through ... ethical practical research activities.

This means that you should conduct practical investigations wherever possible. On this spread you have an opportunity to try a correlational study as well as collecting data by using questionnaires and by using interviews.

Ethics check

Ethics are discussed in detail on pages 178–179. We suggest strongly that you complete this checklist before collecting data.

1. Do participants know participation is voluntary?
2. Do participants know what to expect?
3. Do participants know they can withdraw at any time?
4. Are individuals' results anonymous?
5. Have I minimised the risk of distress to participants?
6. Have I avoided asking sensitive questions?
7. Will I avoid bringing my school/teacher/psychology into disrepute?
8. Have I considered all other ethical issues?
9. Has my teacher approved this?

This is where all your friends want to go next. But you don't. Will you be susceptible to their persuasion?

Practical idea 1: Susceptibility to social influence

In this chapter you learned that **internals** are more likely to resist **social influence** (see page 30). In contrast **externals** are more susceptible to social influence because they believe that what happens to them is down to luck. Is this true?

This practical investigates the **correlation** between **locus of control** and resisting social influence. You will use **questionnaires** to measure the **co-variables**.

The practical bit

Locus of control scale

You could create your own scale to measure **locus of control** (**LOC**). You will need items that tap into internality and externality. You could produce a scale that is tailored to your likely participants and their daily experiences.

Alternatively, you could use Rotter's LOC scale, which has the benefit of being a well-established instrument that has been used in literally thousands of research studies. Plus it's already done for you. Use the term 'Rotter locus of control scale' in the search engine of your choice. Note that a low score indicates an internal locus of control, a high score is external.

Susceptibility to social influence scale

This one you will have to create yourself. Think of social influence scenarios that your participants might find familiar. For example, *'You are on a night out with a group of friends. Most of them want to go on to a nightclub that you hate. Will you go along with them?'* Devise ten items that cover situations of conformity and obedience.

Your participants' responses need to be quantifiable, so use a **Likert scale** to rate each answer (see page 188). If 5 means 'very likely' then the higher a participant's score, the more susceptible to social influence they are.

Response bias

People sometimes give the same responses to all the items on a questionnaire just out of habit. This is a particular problem in this practical because people who are susceptible to social influence will probably just agree with all the items. The solution is to mix up the 'directions' of the items – half of them should be worded 'negatively' so that when scoring for these items 1 becomes 'very likely', 2 becomes 'quite likely', and so on.

Ethical issues

It's tempting to believe that **ethical issues** don't matter a great deal in studies like this. But using questionnaires to measure personal variables does involve asking sensitive questions. So you should be aware of the importance of **anonymity** and **confidentiality**. Make sure the items on your scales are not going to cause any degree of psychological harm (anxiety, humiliation, embarrassment, and so on). You should also, as always, consider the issues of **informed consent** and the **right to withdraw**.

Selecting your participants

The most convenient sampling method to use is **opportunity sampling.** It might be useful to ask participants to complete the questionnaires in a quiet place so they can give the task their full attention.

Analysing your data

A correlational relationship can be positive or negative (see page 190). The clearest way to assess this is by drawing a **scattergram**. You will have two scores for each participant, and will need to present your results in a table as well as a graph.

Table 1 A set of example data.

Participant	LOC score	Social influence score
1	21	38
2	12	20
3	17	32
4	3	14
5	7	19
6	19	47
7	15	27
8	23	42
9	16	15
10	2	12

A high LOC score is external.
A high social influence score reflects high obedience/conformity.

Apply it Methods — The maths bit 1

1. A sample set of data is given in Table 1. Draw a **scattergram** of the results. Remember to plot the pairs of scores precisely and label your axes carefully. (*3 marks*)
2. What kind of **correlation** does this scattergram show? Explain your answer. (*2 marks*)
3. Explain why the **median** would be the most suitable measure of central tendency. (*2 marks*)
4. Calculate the median for each variable. (*1 mark*)
5. Calculate the **range** for each variable. (*1 mark*)
6. Based on your analysis, what conclusion could you draw about the relationship between locus of control and susceptibility to social influence? (*2 marks*)
7. Do these findings support previous research into this relationship? Explain your answer. (*2 marks*)

Practical idea 2: Social influence and lifestyle choices

Social psychologists are interested in the lifestyle choices that people make from the perspective of social influence. Is it possible that people's choices are affected by the attitudes and behaviours of others?

The purpose of this practical is to find out why people engage in positive or negative lifestyle-related behaviours, and to see if any of them are linked to social influence processes.

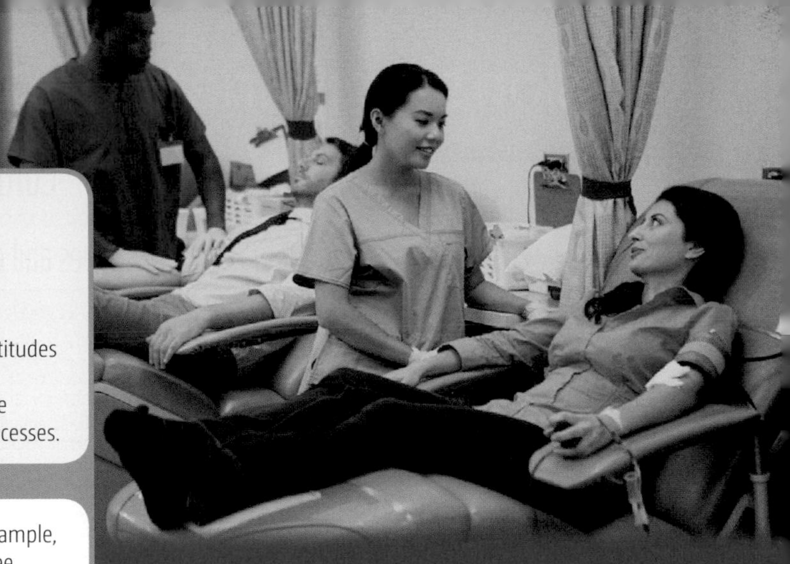

Lives depend on people donating blood and coming back again and again to give more. But are some people put off by social pressures to conform or obey? Interviews are an ideal method to research this question.

The practical bit

This practical uses an **interview** as the research method to collect **qualitative data**. You need to choose a socially relevant topic that interests you and involves social influences such as **conformity** and **obedience**. Here are some examples for you to think about: giving blood, donating organs, getting involved in sporting activities, leading a healthier and more active lifestyle, reducing alcohol intake, giving up smoking, volunteering for good causes or getting your baby vaccinated.

Designing the interview

The first decision you need to make concerns the type of interview you'll conduct. A good choice is a **semi-structured interview**. You have questions that you want to ask but are willing to follow up the interviewee's responses where necessary, especially if they highlight a social influence process.

Next, what type of questions will you ask? **Closed questions** are possible, but a more useful option is **open questions**. This gives your interviewees the opportunity to respond in their own words, but this does make it more difficult to record their responses as you go along. So you should consider using a device to record the whole interview for analysis later.

You should create some questions around the four social influence processes of conformity (**compliance**, **internalisation**, **identification**) and obedience. For example, take blood donation. If the interviewee donates blood on a regular basis, you could ask them *'Have you ever talked about giving blood with any of your friends or family? What happened?'* Or, *'Has anybody ever told you that you should give blood? What were their reasons?'* Or even, *'Would you still give blood even if nobody else you knew did? Why is that?'*

Finally, you should think about rapport between yourself and the interviewee. What can you do to put them at ease so they are relaxed and more willing to respond to questions truthfully?

Selecting your participants

Once again, opportunity sampling should be suitable as it's convenient. But because you are interviewing people face-to-face, you need to give some thought to location. Somewhere quiet and relaxing would be ideal. You should aim to interview no more than eight participants on the same topic.

Ethical considerations

When getting consent, make sure participants are fully informed, for example by making them aware that you will ask questions about your chosen issue. Give due consideration to **privacy**, confidentiality and the right to withdraw. Avoid questions that are intrusive, or might cause offence or **psychological harm** (including embarrassment).

Analysing your data

The challenge you face is turning your answers into **quantitative data**.

For each answer decide what kind of social influence was being assessed and then decide whether or not the participant was showing this behaviour (e.g. being compliant or identifying).

It may be more reliable to ask a second person to also score the data and compare the outcome.

Apply it
Methods

The maths bit 2

Table 2 below summarises the reasons people gave for donating blood in a hypothetical sample.

Calculate all of the following:

1. The total number of responses for each type of social influence. (*1 mark*)
2. The total number of responses for each participant. (*1 mark*)
3. The total number of responses for each type as a percentage of the overall number of responses (that is, calculate four percentages). (*1 mark*)
4. The **mean** number of compliance, identification, internalisation and obedience responses per participant (that is, calculate four means). (*1 mark*)

Also:

5. Draw a suitable **bar chart** to represent the data in Table 2 for each type of influence. Label your axes carefully. (*3 marks*)
6. Do any of the participants stand out as especially vulnerable to social influence or resistant to it? Explain your answer. (*2 marks*)
7. Explain what the **qualitative data** tells us about the reasons the interviewees gave for donating blood. (*2 marks*)

Table 2 A set of example data.

Participant	Compliance	Identification	Internalisation	Obedience
1	2	3	2	0
2	4	1	2	2
3	1	0	3	0
4	0	2	0	3
5	0	3	2	0
6	2	1	1	0
7	5	4	4	3
8	1	2	3	1

Revision summaries

Conformity

Conformity

Judging the lengths of lines.

Asch's research

Baseline procedure
123 men judged line lengths. Confederates deliberately gave wrong answers.

Findings
Naïve participants conformed on 36.8% of trials.

25% never conformed.

Variations

Group size
Asch varied group size from two to 16. Conformity increased up to three, then levelled off.

Unanimity
Asch placed a dissenter (confederate) in the group. Conformity rate reduced.

Task difficulty
Asch made line lengths more similar. Conformity increased when task was harder (ISI).

Evaluation

Artificial situation and task
Participants knew this was a study so they just played along with a trivial task (demand characteristics).

Limited application
Asch's research only conducted on American men.

Research support
Lucas *et al*. found more conformity when maths problems were harder.

Counterpoint – conformity more complex, confident participants were less conforming (individual factor).

Evaluation extra: Ethical issues
Research may help avoid mindless conformity, but participants were deceived.

Types and explanations

Conformity is yielding to group pressures.

Types

Internalisation
Private and public acceptance of group norms.

Identification
Change behaviour to be part of a group we identify with, may change privately too.

Compliance
Go along with group publicly but no private change.

Explanations

Informational social influence (ISI)
Conform to be right. Assume group knows better than us.

Normative social influence (NSI)
Conform to be liked or accepted by group.

Evaluation

Research support for NSI
When no normative group pressure (wrote answers), conformity down to 12.5% (Asch).

Research support for ISI
Participants relied on other people's answers to hard maths problems (Lucas *et al.*).

Counterpoint – cannot usually separate ISI and NSI, a dissenter may reduce power of NSI or ISI.

Individual differences in NSI
nAffiliators want to be liked more, so conform more (McGhee and Teevan).

Evaluation extra: Is the NSI/ISI distinction useful?
NSI/ISI *distinction* may not be useful but Asch's research supports both.

Conformity to social roles

Behaviour related to social roles and norms.

Zimbardo's research

The Stanford prison experiment (SPE)
Mock prison with 21 student volunteers, randomly assigned as guards or prisoners.

Conformity to social roles created through uniforms (e.g. loose smocks, carrying wooden club) and instructions about behaviour (e.g. guards have power).

Findings related to social roles
Guards became increasingly brutal, prisoners' rebellion put down and prisoners became depressed.

Study stopped after 6 days.

Conclusions related to social roles
Participants strongly conformed to their social roles.

Evaluation

Control
Random assignment to roles increased internal validity.

Lack of realism
Participants play-acted their roles according to media-derived stereotypes (Banuazizi and Movahedi).

Counterpoint – evidence that prisoners thought the prison was real to them e.g. 90% of conversations about prison (McDermott).

Exaggerates the power of roles
Only one-third of guards were brutal so conclusions exaggerated (Fromm).

Evaluation extra: Alternative explanation
Social identity theory suggests taking on roles due to active identification, not automatic (Haslam and Reicher).

Minority influence

Minority influence leads to conversion and internalisation.

Research

Consistency
If the minority is consistent (synchronic or diachronic) this attracts the attention of the majority over time.

Commitment
Personal sacrifices show commitment, attract attention, reinforce message (augmentation).

Flexibility
Minority more convincing if they accept some counterarguments.

Explaining the process of change
The three factors make majority think more deeply about an issue.

Snowball effect – minority view gathers force and becomes majority influence.

Evaluation

Research support for consistency
Moscovici's blue-green slides and Wood *et al.*'s meta-analysis.

Research support for deeper processing
Participants exposed to minority view resisted conflicting view (Martin *et al.*).

Counterpoint – real-world majorities have more power/status than minorities, missing from research.

Artificial tasks
Tasks often trivial so tell us little about real-world influence.

Evaluation extra: Power of minority influence
More people agree with minority in private.

Social influence and social change

Psychological research can help us change society.

Research

Lessons from minority influence research
Minority influence is a powerful force for innovation and social change.

E.g. civil rights marches (US): influence involves (1) drawing attention, (2) consistency, (3) deeper processing (thinking), (4) augmentation (risks), (5) snowball effect, (6) social cryptomnesia (forgetting).

Lessons from conformity research
Dissent breaks power of majority (Asch).

Normative social influence draws attention to what majority is doing.

Lessons from obedience research
Disobedient role models (Milgram).

Gradual commitment leads to change (Zimbardo).

Evaluation

Research support for normative influences
NSI valid explanation of social change, e.g. reducing energy consumption (Nolan *et al.*).

Counterpoint – normative influence does not always produce change (Foxcroft *et al.*).

Minority influence explains change
Minorities stimulate divergent thinking – broad, creative, more options (Nemeth).

Role of deeper processing
It is majority views that are processed more deeply than minority views, challenging central feature of minority influence (Mackie).

Evaluation extra: Barriers to social change
People resist social change because minorities seen negatively e.g. 'tree-huggers' (Bashir *et al.*).

Obedience

Obedience

Were Germans different?

Milgram's research

Baseline procedure
American men gave fake electric shocks to a 'Learner' in response to instructions (prods) from an 'Experimenter'.

Baseline findings
65% gave highest shock of 450 V.

100% gave shocks up to 300 V.

Many showed signs of anxiety e.g. sweating.

Evaluation

Research support
French TV documentary/game show found 80% gave maximum shock, plus similar behaviour to Milgram's participants (Beauvois *et al.*).

Low internal validity
Participants realised shocks were fake, so 'play-acting' (Orne and Holland). Supported by Perry – tapes of participants showed only 50% believed shocks real.

Counterpoint – participants did give real shocks to a puppy (Sheridan and King).

Alternative interpretation of findings
Haslam *et al.* found participants didn't obey Prod 4. Participants identified with scientific aims (social identity) – not blind obedience.

Evaluation extra: Ethical issues
Deception meant participants could not properly consent (Baumrind). May be balanced by benefits of the research.

Situational variables

Pressures in the situation.

Research

Proximity
Obedience 40% with T and L in same room, 30% for touch proximity.

Psychological distance affects obedience.

Location
Obedience 47.5% in run-down office building.

University's prestige gave authority.

Uniform
Obedience 20% when Experimenter was 'member of the public'.

Uniform is symbol of legitimate authority.

Evaluation

Research support
Bickman showed power of uniform in field experiment.

Cross-cultural replications
Dutch participants ordered to say stressful things to interviewee, decreased proximity led to decreased obedience (Meeus and Raaijmakers).

Counterpoint – but most studies in countries similar to US, so not generalisable (Smith and Bond).

Low internal validity
Some of Milgram's procedures in the variations were especially contrived, so not genuine obedience (Orne and Holland).

Evaluation extra: The danger of the situational perspective
Gives obedience alibi for destructive behaviour (Mandel).

Situational explanations

The dynamics of social hierarchies.

Agentic state

Agentic state
Acting as an agent of another person.

Autonomous state
Free to act according to conscience.

Switching between the two – agentic shift.

Binding factors
Allow individual to ignore the damaging effects of their obedient behaviour, reducing moral strain.

Evaluation

Research support
Milgram's resistant participants continued giving shocks when Experimenter took responsibility.

A limited explanation
Cannot explain why Rank and Jacobson's nurses and some of Milgram's participants disobeyed.

Evaluation extra: Obedience alibi revisited
Police Battalion 101 behaved autonomously but destructively (Mandel).

Legitimacy of authority

Legitimacy of authority
Created by hierarchical nature of society.

Some people entitled to expect obedience.

Learned in childhood.

Destructive authority
Problems arise when used destructively (e.g. Hitler).

Evaluation

Explains cultural differences
In Australia 16% obeyed (Kilham and Mann) but 85% in Germany (Mantell), related to structure of society.

Cannot explain all (dis)obedience
Rank and Jacobson's nurses in hierarchical structure but did not obey legitimate authority.

Evaluation extra: Real-world crimes of obedience
Rank and Jacobson found disobedience to doctors but stronger hierarchy and obedience at My Lai (Kelman and Hamilton).

Dispositional explanation

Personality factors in the individual.

The Authoritarian Personality (AP)

AP and obedience
Adorno *et al.* described AP as extreme respect for authority and submissiveness to it, contempt for inferiors.

Origins of AP
Harsh parenting creates hostility that cannot be expressed against parents so is displaced onto scapegoats.

Adorno *et al.*'s research: Procedure
Used F-scale to study unconscious attitudes towards other ethnic groups.

Findings
APs identify with 'strong' people, have fixed cognitive style, and hold stereotypes and prejudices.

Evaluation

Research support
Obedient participants had high F-scores (Elms and Milgram).

Counterpoint – but obedient participants also unlike authoritarians in many ways, complex.

Limited explanation
Can't explain obedience across a whole culture (social identity theory is better).

Political bias
Authoritarianism equated with right-wing ideology, ignores left-wing authoritarianism (Christie and Jahoda).

Evaluation extra: Flawed evidence
F-scale is basis of AP explanation, but has flaws (e.g. response bias) and so not useful (Greenstein).

Resistance to social influence

Explaining when people disobey and resist the pressure to conform.

Social support

Resisting conformity
Conformity reduced by presence of dissenters from the group – even wrong answer breaks unanimity of majority (Asch).

Resisting obedience
Obedience decreases in presence of disobedient peer who acts as a model to follow – challenges legitimacy of authority figure. Obedience dropped from 65% to 10% (Milgram).

Evaluation

Real-world research support
Having a 'buddy' helps resist peer pressure to smoke (Albrecht *et al.*).

Research support for dissenting peers
Obedience to an order from oil company fell when participants in a group (Gamson *et al.*).

Evaluation extra: Social support explanation
Resistance lower (36% versus 64%) when confederate had poor eyesight (Allen and Levine).

Locus of control

Locus of control (LOC)
LOC is sense of what directs events in our lives – internal or external source (Rotter).

The LOC continuum
High internal at one end and high external at the other.

Resistance to social influence
Internals can resist social influence, more confident, less need for approval.

Evaluation

Research support
Internals less likely to fully obey in Milgram-type procedure (Holland).

Contradictory research
People now more independent but also more external (Twenge *et al.*).

Evaluation extra: Limited role of LOC
Role of LOC only applies to new situations (Rotter).

Practice questions, answers and feedback

Question 1 Using an example, explain what is meant by 'social roles'. (*2 marks*)

Answer	Feedback
Morticia's answer *A social role is something that people do when they are with others. For example, being a mother or teacher. That is a social role.*	**Morticia's definition is weak but there is a discernible example.**
Luke's answer *They are the parts that people play when they are in social situations, i.e. with other people. They create expectations of what we have to do. For example, being a doctor or a mother has expectations attached.*	**In contrast Luke's definition here is much better than Morticia's and there are relevant examples too, a great answer.**
Vladimir's answer *A role is something you do, social is being with other people. So a social role is what you do as affected by other people.*	**Vladimir has missed the point. His definition lacks clarity and is a little too much like common sense to be of any value. There is no example either, which was required in the question.**

Question 2 Proximity is one situational variable affecting obedience. Outline **one** other situational variable affecting obedience. (*3 marks*)

Answer	Feedback
Morticia's answer *One other situational variable is location. This refers to the place you are when being ordered to do something. In Milgram's study when people were in a run-down office they were less obedient.*	**Morticia has provided sufficient detail for a question of this kind. A situational variable is identified and explained. Detail of a Milgram variation is further elaboration.**
Luke's answer *Location is a situational variable. It's where you are and it affects how much people will obey an order. It relates to the situation, that's why it is a situational variable.*	**The boys didn't do as well. Luke has identified a variable but the elaboration is not strong. There is also no account of the effect of this factor on obedience levels. Vladimir just says 'proximity' which is ambiguous – it does make sense because there is further clarification. However, the question asks for a situational variable *other* than proximity. So he won't get any credit.**
Vladimir's answer *Proximity is a situational variable. It is how close you are physically to the person giving the orders or the person you may be harming. Closer proximity reduces willingness to obey.*	

Question 3 Asch conducted research on conformity. Describe what conclusions can be drawn from this research. (*4 marks*)

Answer	Feedback
Morticia's answer *Asch studied group size by changing the number of confederates between one and 15. Conformity was 32% when there were three confederates but it did not increase much when the group got bigger. He also investigated unanimity. Conformity reduced when a dissenter was present. Asch argued this meant that the influence of a group depends a lot on it being unanimous.*	**Morticia's answer correctly focuses on the variables investigated by Asch. But most of the answer focuses on findings, with just passing reference to a conclusion. So this answer is mostly irrelevant to the question.**
Luke's answer *Asch concluded that a group causes more conformity when it is unanimous. If there are divisions in the group, then an individual feels free to disagree with the majority and behave independently. He also concluded that informational social influence operates when the task is hard. This is because the situation is more ambiguous (unclear), so the individual looks to other people for guidance.*	**Luke also writes about two of the variables studied by Asch. But his answer is almost fully focused on conclusions with very little irrelevant material on findings or procedure. A strong answer.**
Vladimir's answer *Participants had to judge the length of a line. There were confederates giving the wrong answers on some of the trials. The participant always went last and was quite anxious when he saw that the others were giving the wrong answer. Nevertheless they conformed most of the time to the wrong answer. All the participants were men and were American.*	**Vladimir gives some accurate description of Asch's baseline procedure but that is irrelevant to this question. He avoids writing about conclusions at all and the evaluative comment gets no credit.**

Question 4 Briefly outline **and** evaluate the Authoritarian Personality as an explanation for obedience. (*4 marks*)

Answer	Feedback
Morticia's answer *The Authoritarian Personality is an explanation for why some people are more obedient than others. It may be because they are born like that or it may be because they are brought up that way. Such people tend to be quite conformist as well and right-wing in their politics. People were measured using an F-scale to see how authoritarian they were and this matched up with how obedient they were.* *One limitation with this explanation is that there isn't much other research evidence to support the explanation. It might not really be an Authoritarian Personality but it could be situational factors that make people obey.*	**Morticia's answer is inaccurate ('born like that' is wrong) and the description focuses a little too much on method rather than theory. There is relevant content though (reference to upbringing and right-wing views). The limitation is relevant though the first sentence is generic. Overall a reasonable but not good answer.**
Luke's answer *This is a dispositional explanation for why some people obey. Essentially some people have high respect for authority figures and are more dismissive of inferiors, which is why they obey. There was support for this from Milgram's research where participants who had been most obedient were found to be high in Authoritarianism, thus demonstrating the link.*	**Luke summarises the explanation very well in the first two sentences and there is a clear link to obedience (which answers to this question often lack). The use of evidence as evaluation is good too but there is room for a little more of this.**
Vladimir's answer *People with Authoritarian Personality have a strict upbringing and look to authority figures. They are afraid of being the odd one out so they think they have to listen to being told. They are afraid of punishment and concerned with norms and values.*	**Vladimir is correct in mentioning 'strict upbringing' but that's about all that is relevant in his answer. There is some relevance further on in the answer but also confusion with conformity. Although Authoritarian Personality has been used to explain conformist attitudes the focus of the question is on obedience.**

On this spread we look at some typical student answers to questions. The comments provided indicate what is good and bad in each answer. Learning how to produce effective question answers is a SKILL. Read pages 213–223 for guidance.

Question 5 Betty and Sue are two newly qualified teachers who are discussing their decision to support a recent one-day strike.

'I wasn't sure at first,' said Betty, 'but having spoken to the other teachers, they really convinced me it was a good idea. And I would do it again in similar circumstances.'

'Oh dear,' replied Sue. 'I'm a bit embarrassed really. I'm afraid I only did it because everyone else did.'

Discuss normative social influence and informational social influence as explanations of conformity. Refer to Betty and Sue in your answer. (*12 marks AS, 16 marks AL*)

Morticia's answer *Normative social influence is when people go along with the group to avoid rejection and not stand out and to fit in with others. Although the person may do one thing in public, in private their opinion doesn't change, e.g. smoking in front of friends. This kind of influence is most likely in unfamiliar situations.*

Informational social influence is when we look to others for information on how to behave in a new situation when we are unsure. We take the group's views into account and change both private and public opinion, e.g. we follow our friend's answer in class when we don't know the answer. This kind of influence is most likely in situations where there is uncertainty such as something that is new or something that is contradictory.

So in the example of Betty and Sue, Betty is an example of informational social influence (ISI) and Sue is an example of normative social influence (NSI).

This understanding was demonstrated by Asch's study. When Asch arranged for the number of confederates to be reduced, conformity also fell because there was reduced NSI on the participant. When the conformity task was made harder, conformity went up because participants were unsure of the answer and therefore they looked to others which was a result of ISI. When participants wrote their answer down there was no conformity because there was then no normative pressure because no one knew about it.

In Asch's original study there was NSI because participants went along with the majority view so they didn't stand out and to avoid rejection. They didn't really believe they were right but went along with the group answer.

Some people conform more than others. These are nAffiliators because they want to be accepted by the group. Also there might be other reasons for conformity such as identification where someone actually identifies with the people in the group and changes their views both publicly but not privately. **(324 words)**

Morticia's essay is an AS response whereas Luke's is an A level response.

Morticia presents a concise and well-focused answer. The description of the two explanations is clear and accurate.

In terms of evaluation and analysis, Morticia has used the Asch variation effectively and linked these to the two explanations in each case. This is something that students rarely do well in this type of question. There is relevant evaluative comment at the end of the answer also.

The weakest part of the answer is the application to the question stem. Although Morticia has successfully matched the two characters with the two explanations, there is little engagement with the stem beyond that. The lack of engagement with the stem would cost proportionately more in an A level answer than an AS one.

This is an excellent answer because there is a lot of knowledge and understanding shown.

Luke's answer *Normative social influence is the desire to be liked and accepted into a group and could also be from fear of ridicule. Normative influence leads to compliance which is where a person changes their public behaviour whilst maintaining their private views. In the example, Sue is behaving in this way because she changed her behaviour to fit in with the others because she wanted to be liked – she did it because everyone else did (the majority). But she didn't necessarily believe in what she was doing.*

In contrast Betty clearly changed her private views. So in this case it would be an example of informational social influence where someone changes what they think and they do this both publicly and privately. This is often done out of a desire to be right. A person may feel uncertain about the right thing to do and turns to the majority as a way of establishing what is right. This leads to internalisation where a person changes their private opinion along with public behaviour.

Evidence for normative social influence was demonstrated by Asch in a variation of his classic study. The participant wrote their answers down rather than give them out loud, so the pressure to conform was removed. In this condition the conformity rate fell from the baseline of about 35% to 12.5%. This shows that conformity decreases when there is no fear of rejection, which demonstrates the influence of normative social influence.

One strength of normative social influence is that it is the only explanation for conformity in unambiguous situations. How else can you explain the levels of conformity in Asch's study where the answers were clearly wrong? The participants showed they were confused and yet they conformed. This is a situation where they didn't know the other people so it might not have mattered but they still clearly didn't want to look foolish.

Support for informational social influence comes from Lucas et al. who asked students to give answers to easy and difficult maths problems. They found that conformity increased when the problems were more difficult. This is because people feel less sure and therefore look to the majority to find the answer. The increased conformity was especially high in those students who were not confident about their maths skills, supporting the idea of informational social influence when there is uncertainty or ambiguity. **(392 words)**

Luke's answer is also excellent, in fact marginally better than Morticia's. The description of both explanations is clear and accurate. There is also description of relevant evidence (Asch, Lucas) in support of the explanations.

Notice how engagement with the stem is much more effective here than in the answer above. Luke 'embeds' his application points within the description of the explanations. The answer would be improved if the application continued as part of the evaluation.

There is effective analysis and evaluation too. Normative social influence is analysed in the context of the Asch study and informational social influence in relation to Lucas. There is also good use of examples.

Multiple-choice questions

Conformity

1. The task in Asch's procedure was to:
   (a) Express political opinions.
   (b) Decide which club to go to.
   (c) Answer questions on musical tastes.
   (d) Judge line lengths.

2. What did Asch find about group size?
   (a) Conformity kept increasing with group size.
   (b) Conformity decreased as group size increased.
   (c) Conformity increased with group size but only to a point.
   (d) Increasing group size had no effect on conformity.

3. What did Asch find about unanimity?
   (a) Conformity stayed the same whether the majority was unanimous or not.
   (b) A unanimous majority had the greatest effect on conformity.
   (c) When a confederate disagreed with the majority, conformity increased.
   (d) A divided majority had the greatest effect on conformity.

4. What did Asch find about task difficulty?
   (a) Conformity decreased when the task became more difficult.
   (b) Conformity increased when the task became more difficult.
   (c) Increasing task difficulty had no effect on conformity.
   (d) The task was too difficult for the naïve participants.

Conformity: Types and explanations

1. Which of the following is a type of conformity?
   (a) Unanimity.
   (b) Internalisation.
   (c) Normative social influence.
   (d) Obedience.

2. Which of the following is an explanation for conformity?
   (a) Compliance.
   (b) Informational social influence.
   (c) Identification.
   (d) Internalisation.

3. Which of the following statements best describes compliance?
   (a) Conforming to a majority because we want to be accepted or liked.
   (b) Publicly and privately agreeing with the majority view.
   (c) Publicly agreeing with the majority but privately disagreeing.
   (d) Conforming to a majority because we want to be correct.

4. Which of the following statements best describes normative social influence?
   (a) Going along with a group of people because we want to be liked by them.
   (b) Going along with a group of people because we don't know what we're doing.
   (c) Going along with other people even though we don't agree.
   (d) Going along with other people because we accept their views.

Conformity to social roles

1. The Stanford prison experiment investigated:
   (a) Rebellion.
   (b) Conformity to social roles.
   (c) Obedience to authority.
   (d) Compliance.

2. The roles of guard and prisoner were decided:
   (a) On a first-come, first-served basis.
   (b) Randomly.
   (c) By the researchers.
   (d) By asking participants to volunteer.

3. About ______ of the guards behaved brutally.
   (a) One-quarter.
   (b) Two-thirds.
   (c) One-half.
   (d) One-third.

4. Which statement best describes the behaviour of the prisoners?
   (a) They resisted the cruelty of the guards throughout the study.
   (b) They became more submissive as the study progressed.
   (c) They made it very difficult for the guards to enforce the rules of the prison.
   (d) They supported each other.

Obedience

1. Milgram's participants were ______ who thought the study was about ______.
   (a) Volunteers, memory.
   (b) Women, obedience.
   (c) Children, conformity.
   (d) Germans, obedience.

2. The fourth and final prod given to the participants was:
   (a) 'It is absolutely essential that you continue.'
   (b) 'Please go on.'
   (c) 'You have no other choice, you must go on.'
   (d) 'The experiment requires that you continue.'

3. In Milgram's findings, 65% of the participants:
   (a) Refused to continue at some point.
   (b) Disobeyed at the start of the procedure.
   (c) Went to the top of the shock scale.
   (d) Went to 300 V and then refused to continue.

4. Gina Perry claimed ______ of Milgram's participants knew the shocks were fake.
   (a) A quarter.
   (b) Half.
   (c) All.
   (d) Two-thirds.

Obedience: Situational variables

1. What did Milgram find out about proximity in his variations?
   (a) Obedience increased when the Experimenter issued his instructions over the phone.
   (b) Obedience decreased when the Teacher and Learner were physically closer.
   (c) Most participants obeyed even when they had to put the Learner's hand on a shock plate.
   (d) The physical proximity of Experimenter, Teacher and Learner had the smallest effect.

2. What did Milgram find out about location in his variations?
   (a) Obedience decreased when the study was conducted in a run-down office block.
   (b) The high status and reputation of Yale University made no difference to obedience.
   (c) Most participants still obeyed when the study was moved to a run-down office building.
   (d) Changing the location had the greatest effect on obedience.

3. Which of Milgram's variations produced the lowest obedience?
   (a) Teacher forces Learner's hand onto shock plate.
   (b) Study is transferred to run-down office block.
   (c) Experimenter issues instructions by telephone.
   (d) Member of public stands in for Experimenter.

4. Bickman's (1974) study supported Milgram because he found that:
   (a) Changing to a higher status location increased obedience.
   (b) People more often obeyed someone dressed in a security guard's uniform.
   (c) Increasing the distance between the participants reduced obedience.
   (d) Reducing the distance between authority and participant increased obedience.

Obedience: Situational explanations

1. 'Believing you are carrying out the wishes of someone else' is a brief description of:
   (a) Informational social influence.
   (b) Situational theory of obedience.
   (c) Agentic state.
   (d) Legitimacy of authority.

2. The massacre of unarmed civilians at My Lai by American soldiers can be explained by:
   (a) Agentic state.
   (b) Legitimacy of authority.
   (c) Both agentic state and legitimacy of authority.
   (d) Neither agentic state nor legitimacy of authority.

3. A problem with the agentic state explanation is:
   (a) It can't explain why the proportion of people who obeyed in Milgram's study was so high.
   (b) It can't explain why some people in Milgram's study did not obey.
   (c) There is no research support.
   (d) It is not as useful as legitimacy of authority.

4. Legitimacy of authority is a good explanation of cultural differences in obedience because:
   (a) Some cultures are traditionally more respectful of authority than others.
   (b) Some cultures are traditionally less respectful of authority than others.
   (c) Cultures differ in the way parents raise children to view authority figures.
   (d) All of the above.

Obedience: Dispositional explanation

1. According to Adorno, people with an Authoritarian Personality:
   (a) Are highly obedient to authority.
   (b) Look with contempt on people of inferior social status.
   (c) Favour traditional values.
   (d) All of the above.

2. Authoritarian Personality is measured using the:
   (a) Assertiveness scale.
   (b) Potential-for-fascism scale.
   (c) AP-scale.
   (d) Potential for obedience scale.

3. An Authoritarian Personality develops because a child:
   (a) Receives unconditional love and affection from parents.
   (b) Is spoiled by his or her parents who do not use any discipline.
   (c) Experiences feelings of hostility towards his or her parents that cannot be expressed directly.
   (d) Is accepted regardless of his or her achievements.

4. People with an Authoritarian Personality are very preoccupied with social status. Therefore they:
   (a) Treat all people with respect.
   (b) Feel sympathetic to those of lower status.
   (c) Tend not to be impressed by the trappings of high status.
   (d) Are servile and obedient towards those of higher status.

Resistance to social influence

1. The effects of social support were shown in Asch's studies when:
   (a) The size of the majority was increased from 2 to 14.
   (b) The task was more difficult because the lines were closer.
   (c) The participants wrote their answers down rather than stated them out loud.
   (d) One of the confederates dissented from the majority answer.

2. Social support helps people to resist social influence because:
   (a) It breaks the unanimity of the majority.
   (b) It provides a model of disobedience to be followed.
   (c) It frees people to act according to their consciences.
   (d) All of the above.

3. Which of these statements about locus of control is the most accurate?
   (a) Everyone is either definitely internal or definitely external.
   (b) There is very little difference between moderate internals and moderate externals.
   (c) High internals and high externals are at opposite ends of a continuum.
   (d) Internals and externals are very similar in their ability to resist social influence.

4. High internals are more likely to resist social influence than high externals because:
   (a) They believe that whatever they do makes no real difference.
   (b) They tend to be more self-confident and to take personal responsibility.
   (c) They are less likely to have an Authoritarian Personality.
   (d) They have a greater need for social approval from others.

Minority influence

1. Minority influence is especially effective because:
   (a) It involves supporting strange and unusual causes.
   (b) People are forced to think more deeply about the issues.
   (c) No one likes to think they are part of a mindless herd.
   (d) A small group of people appears unthreatening.

2. Synchronic consistency refers to:
   (a) Consistency over time.
   (b) Consistency between people.
   (c) Disagreement between people.
   (d) Changing the majority view.

3. Flexibility in the minority position is needed because:
   (a) Consistency alone can be a negative thing and off-putting.
   (b) It shows that the minority isn't really all that bothered.
   (c) It allows the majority to get its own way, so they are more likely to agree.
   (d) All of the above.

4. Minority influence can lead to which kind of conformity?
   (a) Compliance.
   (b) Identification.
   (c) Internalisation.
   (d) Informational.

Social influence and social change

1. Once social change has occurred, its origins are forgotten by the majority in a process called:
   (a) Social cryptomnesia.
   (b) Flexibility.
   (c) Gradual commitment.
   (d) Internalisation.

2. Conformity (majority influence) can sometimes create social change through the operation of:
   (a) Augmentation.
   (b) The snowball effect.
   (c) Social proof.
   (d) Normative social influence.

3. The augmentation principle in minority influence refers to:
   (a) How the source of social change is eventually forgotten.
   (b) How personal risks create a strong message.
   (c) How the minority view gradually becomes the majority view.
   (d) The deeper processing of the minority view by the majority.

4. The way in which a minority view becomes the new norm of the majority can be explained by:
   (a) Compliance.
   (b) Social proof.
   (c) Consistency.
   (d) The snowball effect.

MCQ answers

Conformity 1D, 2C, 3B, 4B
Conformity: Types and explanations 1B, 2B, 3C, 4A
Conformity to social roles 1B, 2B, 3D, 4B
Obedience 1A, 2C, 3C, 4B
Obedience: Situational variables 1B, 2A, 3D, 4B
Obedience: Situational explanations 1C, 2C, 3B, 4D
Obedience: Dispositional explanation 1D, 2B, 3C, 4D
Resistance to social influence 1D, 2D, 3C, 4B
Minority influence 1B, 2B, 3A, 4C
Social influence and social change 1A, 2D, 3B, 4D

Chapter 2 Memory

Can you remember…

… what this feels like?

… what this smells like?

… what this tastes like?

… your first day at school?

Contents

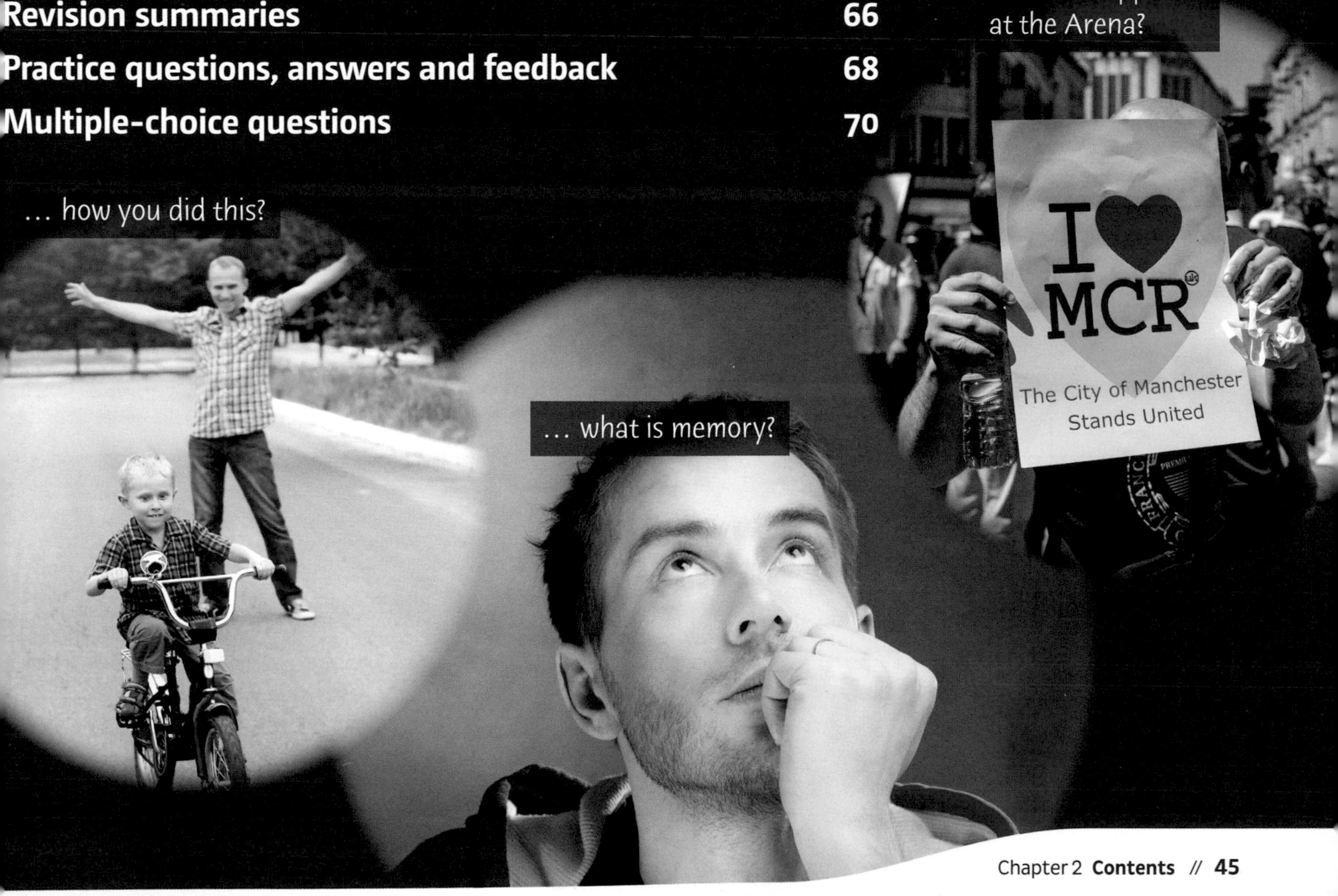

... what happened at the Arena?
... how you did this?
... what is memory?
I ♥ MCR
The City of Manchester Stands United

Coding, capacity and duration of memory

The specification says...

Short-term memory and long-term memory. Features of each store: coding, capacity and duration.

Our everyday experience of memory is that there are two main types. Some are brief and quickly forgotten, but others can last a very long time indeed. Psychologists broadly agree, and have investigated in great detail three main features of what they call short-term memory (STM) and long-term memory (LTM).

Key terms

Short-term memory (STM) The limited-capacity memory store. In STM, coding is mainly acoustic (sounds), capacity is between 5 and 9 items on average, duration is about 18 seconds.

Long-term memory (LTM) The permanent memory store. In LTM, coding is mainly semantic (meaning), it has unlimited capacity and can store memories for up to a lifetime.

Coding The format in which information is stored in the various memory stores.

Capacity The amount of information that can be held in a memory store.

Duration The length of time information can be held in memory.

Apply it Methods — Peterson and Peterson

Some psychology students tried the technique used by Peterson and Peterson to assess the duration of short-term memory. Their results are shown in the graph below.

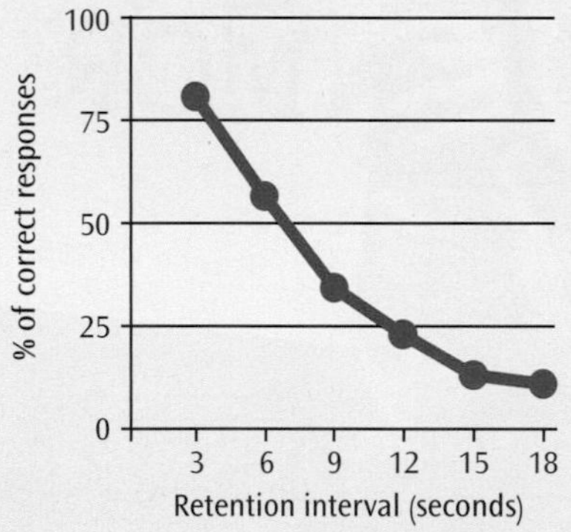

100
75
50
25
0
% of correct responses
3
6
9
12
15
18
Retention interval (seconds)

Questions

1. Estimate the percentage of correct responses at each retention interval using the graph above. Place your answers in a table. (*3 marks*)
2. The results shown above are almost identical to Peterson and Peterson's results. What can you conclude about the duration of STM from this graph? (*3 marks*)

Research on coding

Information is stored in memory in different forms, depending on the memory store. The process of converting information between different forms is called **coding**.

Alan Baddeley (1966a, 1966b) gave different lists of words to four groups of participants to remember:

- Group 1 (*acoustically similar*): words sounded similar (e.g. cat, cab, can).
- Group 2 (*acoustically dissimilar*): words sounded different (e.g. pit, few, cow).
- Group 3 (*semantically similar*): words with similar meanings (e.g. great, large, big).
- Group 4 (*semantically dissimilar*): words with different meanings (e.g. good, huge, hot).

Participants were shown the original words and asked to recall them in the correct order. When they did this task immediately, recalling from **short-term memory** (STM), they tended to do worse with **acoustically** similar words. When they recalled the word list after a time interval of 20 minutes, recalling from **long-term memory** (LTM), they did worse with the **semantically** similar words.

These findings suggest that information is coded acoustically in STM and semantically in LTM.

Research on capacity

Digit span

How much information can STM hold at one time – what is its **capacity**? Joseph Jacobs (1887) found out by measuring **digit span**. For example, the researcher reads out four digits and the participant recalls these out loud in the correct order. If this is correct the researcher reads out five digits and so on until the participant cannot recall the order correctly. This indicates the individual's digit span.

Jacobs found that the **mean** span for digits across all participants was 9.3 items. The mean span for letters was 7.3.

Span of memory and chunking

George Miller (1956) made observations of everyday practice. For example, he noted that things come in sevens: seven notes on the musical scale, seven days of the week, seven deadly sins, etc. Miller thought that the span (i.e. capacity) of STM is about 7 items, plus or minus 2. But he also noted that people can recall five words as easily as they can recall five letters. We do this by **chunking** – grouping sets of digits or letters into units or chunks.

Research on duration

Research on the duration of the sensory register is described on the next spread.

Duration of STM

How short is the **duration** of STM? Margaret and Lloyd Peterson (1959) tested 24 students in eight trials each (a 'trial' is one test). On each trial the student was given a **consonant syllable** (such as YCG) to remember. They were also given a 3-digit number. The student counted backwards from this number until told to stop. The counting backwards was to prevent any mental rehearsal of the consonant syllable (which would increase the duration of STM memory for the syllable).

On each trial they were told to stop after varying periods of time: 3, 6, 9, 12, 15 or 18 seconds (the retention interval). The findings were similar to the student data on the left. After 3 seconds, average recall was about 80%, after 18 seconds it was about 3%. Peterson and Peterson's findings suggested that STM duration may be about 18 seconds, unless we repeat the information over and over (i.e. verbal rehearsal).

Duration of LTM

Harry Bahrick *et al.* (1975) studied 392 American participants aged between 17 and 74. High school yearbooks were obtained from the participants or directly from some schools. Recall was tested in various ways, including: (1) photo-recognition test consisting of 50 photos, some from the participants' high school yearbooks, (2) free recall test where participants recalled all the names of their graduating class.

Participants tested within 15 years of graduation were about 90% accurate in photo recognition. After 48 years, recall declined to about 70% for photo recognition. Free recall was less accurate than recognition – about 60% after 15 years, dropping to 30% after 48 years.

This shows that LTM may last up to a lifetime for some material.

Evaluation

Separate memory stores

One strength of Baddeley's study is that it identified a clear difference between two memory stores.

Later research showed that there are some exceptions to Baddeley's findings. But the idea that STM uses mostly acoustic coding and LTM mostly semantic has stood the test of time.

This was an important step in our understanding of the memory system, which led to the **multi-store model** (see next spread).

Artificial stimuli

One limitation of Baddeley's study was that it used quite artificial stimuli rather than meaningful material.

For example, the word lists had no personal meaning to participants. So Baddeley's findings may not tell us much about coding in different kinds of memory tasks, especially in everyday life. When processing more meaningful information, people may use semantic coding even for STM tasks.

This suggests that the findings from this study have limited application.

Evaluation

A valid study

One strength of Jacobs' study is that it has been **replicated**.

The study is a very old one and early research in psychology often lacked adequate controls. For example, some participants' digit spans might have been underestimated because they were distracted during testing (**confounding variable**). Despite this, Jacobs' findings have been confirmed by other, better controlled studies since (e.g. Bopp and Verhaeghen 2005).

This suggests that Jacobs' study is a valid test of digit span in STM.

Not so many chunks

One limitation of Miller's research is that he may have overestimated STM capacity.

Nelson Cowan (2001) reviewed other research and concluded that the capacity of STM is only about 4 (plus or minus 1) chunks.

This suggests that the lower end of Miller's estimate (five items) is more appropriate than seven items.

Evaluation

Meaningless stimuli in STM study

One limitation of Peterson and Peterson's study is that the stimulus material was artificial.

The study is not completely irrelevant because we do sometimes try to remember fairly meaningless material (e.g. phone numbers). Even so, recalling consonant syllables does not reflect most everyday memory activities where what we are trying to remember is meaningful.

This means the study lacked **external validity**.

High external validity

One strength of Bahrick *et al.*'s study is that it has high external validity.

This is because the researchers investigated meaningful memories (i.e. of people's names and faces). When studies on LTM were conducted with meaningless pictures to be remembered, recall rates were lower (e.g. Shepard 1967).

This suggests that Bahrick *et al.*'s findings reflect a more 'real' estimate of the duration of LTM.

Apply it Concepts: Chunking in STM

Have a quick read of the following letters, look away and try to recall them in the same order:

Y E B N O I P D T A L G R C U

Try the same thing with this list:

D A T N O L P I B R E Y C U G

And, finally, try again with this list:

C A R D O G L I T P E N B U Y

Question

Use your knowledge of the capacity of STM to explain why one of these lists is easier to recall than the others.

Pelmanism

A great card game – try it! You shuffle the cards and put them face down on the table. The first player turns two cards over. If the cards match, the player keeps them and has another go. If the cards don't match, they are turned back over and both players have to try to remember where they are for their next turn. It is a test of STM capacity and duration.

Study tip

If asked to describe a study, always try to include information about what the researchers did (the procedure) and what they found (the findings or results). You can also include conclusions as part of the findings. BUT, if you are asked to describe what a researcher did then only describe the procedure, and if you are asked what a study showed, then only include findings/conclusions.

Check it

1. Explain what is meant by 'duration' of short-term memory. *[1 mark]*
2. Explain what is meant by 'coding' in long-term memory. *[1 mark]*
3. Outline the difference between the duration of short-term memory and the duration of long-term memory. *[4 marks]*
4. Outline **and** evaluate research related to the features of short-term memory (coding, capacity **and** duration). *[12 marks AS, 16 marks AL]*

The multi-store model of memory

The specification says...

The multi-store model of memory: sensory register, short-term memory and long-term memory. Features of each store: coding, capacity and duration.

Psychologists have produced many theories/models of memory to represent and explain how our memories work. The specification includes two of these models of memory. On this spread we look at the first of these, the multi-store model.

This model is based on the features of STM and LTM as well as a third store, the sensory register.

Key terms

Multi-store model (MSM) A representation of how memory works in terms of three stores called the sensory register, short-term memory (STM) and long-term memory (LTM). It also describes how information is transferred from one store to another, what makes some memories last and what makes some memories disappear.

Sensory register The memory stores for each of our five senses, such as vision (iconic store) and hearing (echoic store). Coding in the iconic sensory register is visual and in the echoic sensory register it is acoustic (sounds). The capacity of sensory registers is huge (millions of receptors) and information lasts for a very short time (less than half a second).

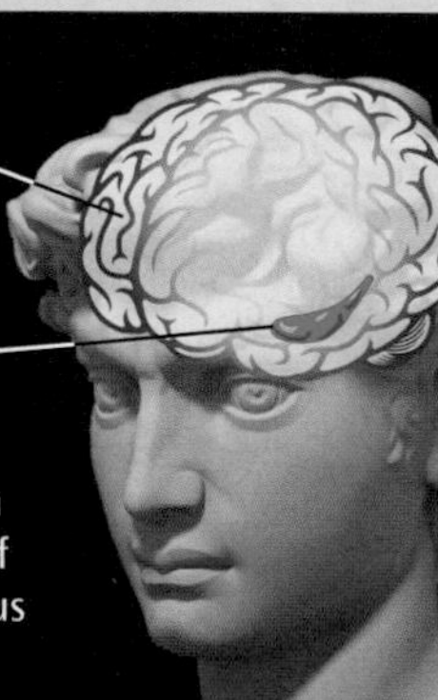

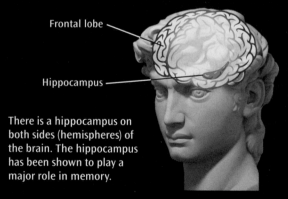

Frontal lobe
Hippocampus

There is a hippocampus on both sides (hemispheres) of the brain. The hippocampus has been shown to play a major role in memory.

Study tip

You can use the case study of HM as a point of evaluation for the MSM – it provides supporting evidence.

You can also evaluate the methodology used (it was a unique case study of a brain-damaged individual). However, such methodological evaluations are only creditworthy if they are explicitly linked to the MSM, e.g. you say 'therefore this case study does not offer good support for the MSM'.

The multi-store model

Richard Atkinson and Richard Shiffrin's (1968, 1971) **multi-store model** (MSM) describes how information flows through the memory system (see diagram below). The model suggests that memory is made up of three stores linked by processing.

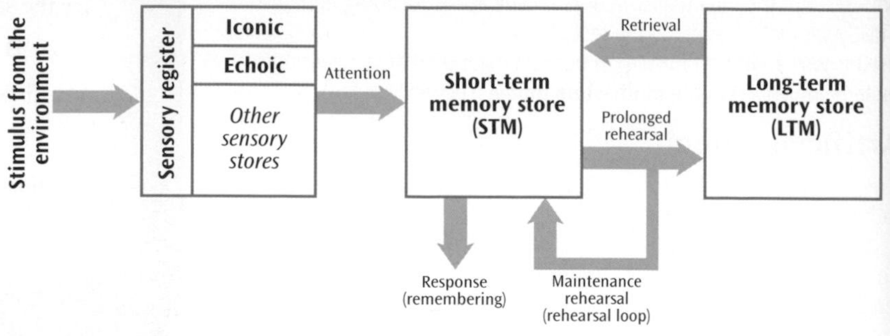

Stimulus from the environment
Sensory register
Iconic
Echoic
Other sensory stores
Attention
Short-term memory store (STM)
Retrieval
Prolonged rehearsal
Long-term memory store (LTM)
Response (remembering)
Maintenance rehearsal (rehearsal loop)

Sensory register

All stimuli from the environment (e.g. the sound of someone talking) pass into the **sensory register** (SR). This part of memory comprises several registers (sensory memory stores), one for each of our five senses. **Coding** in each store is modality-specific (i.e. it depends on the sense). For example, the store coding for visual information is **iconic memory** and the store coding acoustically (i.e. for sound) is **echoic memory**. There are other sensory stores for touch, taste and smell information.

Duration of material in the SRs is very brief – less than half a second (see Apply it at top of facing page). The SRs have a very high **capacity**, for example over one hundred million cells in one eye, each storing data.

Information passes further into the memory system only if you pay attention to it (so *attention* is the key process).

Short-term memory

Information in **short-term memory** (STM) is coded mainly acoustically and lasts about 18 seconds unless it is rehearsed, so STM is more of a temporary store. STM is a limited-capacity store, because it can only contain a certain number of 'things' before forgetting occurs. On the previous spread we noted that the capacity of STM is between five and nine items of information ('the magical number 7 ± 2'), though Cowan's research suggests it might be more like five rather than nine.

Maintenance rehearsal occurs when we repeat (rehearse) material to ourselves over and over again. We can keep the information in our STMs as long as we rehearse it. If we rehearse it long enough, it passes into **long-term memory** (LTM).

Long-term memory

This is the potentially permanent memory store for information that has been rehearsed for a prolonged time. We have already seen that LTMs are coded mostly **semantically** (i.e. in terms of meaning). Psychologists believe that its duration may be up to a lifetime. For example, as we saw in the previous spread, Bahrick *et al.* (1975) found that many of their participants were able to recognise the names and faces of their school classmates almost 50 years after graduating. The capacity of LTM is thought to be practically unlimited.

According to the MSM, when we want to recall information from LTM, it has to be transferred back into STM by a process called **retrieval**.

Apply it Concepts: The case of HM

Case studies of individuals with memory disorders have provided some useful evidence relating to the multi-store model. One of them has become especially well known – the case of a man referred to by his initials, HM (Henry Molaison).

HM underwent brain surgery to relieve his epilepsy. Unfortunately for him, the procedure used was in its infancy and not fully understood. Crucially, a part of his brain known as the hippocampus was removed from both sides of his brain. We now know this to be central to memory function. When his memory was assessed in 1955, he thought the year was 1953, and that he was 27 years old (he was actually 31). He had very little recall of the operation.

He could not form new long-term memories. For example, he would read the same magazine repeatedly without remembering it. He couldn't recall what he had eaten earlier the same day. However, despite all this, he performed well on tests of immediate memory span, a measure of STM.

Question

The case of HM is usually taken to support the multi-store model. Can you explain why?

Evaluation

Research support

One strength of the MSM is support from studies showing that STM and LTM are different.

For example, Alan Baddeley (1966, see previous spread) found that we tend to mix up words that sound similar when we are using our STMs. But we mix up words that have similar meanings when we use our LTMs. Further support comes from the studies of capacity and duration we encountered in the previous spread.

These studies clearly show that STM and LTM are separate and independent memory stores, as claimed by the MSM.

Counterpoint Despite such apparent support, in everyday life we form memories related to all sorts of useful things – people's faces, their names, facts, places, etc. But many of the studies that support the MSM used none of these materials. Instead, they used digits, letters (Jacobs), and sometimes words (Baddeley). They even used what are known as **consonant syllables** that have no meaning (Peterson and Peterson).

This means that the MSM may not be a valid model of how memory works in our everyday lives where we have to remember much more meaningful information.

More than one STM store

One limitation of the MSM is evidence of more than one STM store.

Tim Shallice and Elizabeth Warrington (1970) studied a client they referred to as KF who had a clinical memory disorder called **amnesia**. KF's STM for digits was very poor when they were read out loud to him. But his recall was much better when he read the digits to himself. Further studies of KF (and others) showed that there could even be another short-term store for non-verbal sounds (e.g. noises).

This evidence suggests that the MSM is wrong in claiming that there is just one STM store processing different types of information (e.g. visual, auditory, etc.).

Elaborative rehearsal

Another limitation of the MSM is that prolonged rehearsal is not needed for transfer to LTM.

According to the MSM, what matters about rehearsal is the amount of it – the more you rehearse something, the more likely it is to transfer to LTM. This is prolonged rehearsal. But Fergus Craik and Michael Watkins (1973) found that the *type* of rehearsal is more important than the amount. **Elaborative rehearsal** is needed for long-term storage. This occurs when you link the information to your existing knowledge, or you think about what it means. This means that information can be transferred to LTM without prolonged rehearsal.

This suggests that the MSM does not fully explain how long-term storage is achieved.

Evaluation eXtra

Bygone model

Atkinson and Shiffrin based the MSM on the research evidence available at the time that showed STM and LTM to be single memory stores, separate and independent from each other.

However, there is a lot of research evidence that LTM, like STM, is not a single memory store. For example, we have one long-term store for our memories of facts about the world, and we have a different one for our memories of how to ride a bicycle. Combined with research showing there is more than one type of STM and more than one type of rehearsal, the MSM is an oversimplified model of memory.

Consider: *Does this mean the MSM is worthless and should be abandoned?*

Apply it Concepts — Duration of the sensory register

Evidence to support the limited duration of the sensory registers (SRs) was collected in a study by George Sperling (1960), testing the iconic sensory register (memory store). Participants saw a grid of digits and letters (see below) for 50 milliseconds.

They were either asked to write down all 12 items or they were told they would hear a tone immediately after the exposure and they should just write down the row indicated (top, middle, bottom). When asked to report the whole thing their recall was poorer (five items recalled, about 42%) than when asked to give one row only (three items recalled, 75%).

Table showing stimulus material used by Sperling.

7	1	V	F
X	L	5	3
B	4	W	7

Questions

1. Explain why the findings of Sperling's study show that information decays rapidly in the iconic sensory register.
2. Explain why the sensory registers have such a very large capacity and brief duration.

This well-known effect from Bonfire Night depends on your iconic memory store, one of the memory stores of the multi-store model. You can write your name in the air with one sparkler because an afterimage persists on the retina for approximately one twenty-fifth of a second after the stimulus has moved on. This is called persistence of vision.

SAM

Apply it Methods — Duration of STM

An experiment was carried out to investigate the duration of STM. Two groups of participants were given a list of words to learn. Both groups were given 30 seconds to do this. One group (Group A) then had to recall as many words as they could after a 6-second delay. The other group (Group B) was given a 20-second delay.

Questions

1. Identify the **independent** and **dependent variables** in this study. (*2 marks*)
2. Identify the **experimental design** used in this study. (*1 mark*)
3. Explain *one* limitation of this type of design in this study. (*2 marks*)
4. The researcher wanted to find the average number of words recalled for each group. What would be the most appropriate measure to use? Justify your answer. (*2 marks*)
5. The experimenter found that Group B recalled fewer words than Group A. Does this support the MSM? Explain why or why not. (*3 marks*)

Check it

1. Outline what research has shown about long-term memory according to the multi-store model of memory. *[6 marks]*
2. Outline **two** limitations of the multi-store model of memory. *[4 marks]*
3. Discuss the multi-store model of memory. *[12 marks AS, 16 marks AL]*

Types of long-term memory

The specification says...

Types of long-term memory: episodic, semantic, procedural.

As we have seen, a major limitation of the multi-store model is its description of long-term memory (LTM) as a single, unitary store.

On the basis of hundreds of research studies, psychologists now know that there are potentially many different long-term stores. This is perhaps unsurprising when you consider the vast range of information we can remember, from facts to faces. On this spread, we look at the three types included in the specification.

Key terms

Episodic memory A long-term memory store for personal events. It includes memories of when the events occurred and of the people, objects, places and behaviours involved. Memories from this store have to be retrieved consciously and with effort.

Semantic memory A long-term memory store for our knowledge of the world. This includes facts and our knowledge of what words and concepts mean. These memories usually also need to be recalled deliberately.

Procedural memory A long-term memory store for our knowledge of how to do things. This includes our memories of learned skills. We usually recall these memories without making a conscious or deliberate effort.

I'll meet you at the top of Memory Lane

And we'll be fine if you recall my name.

Top of Memory Lane by Lenka

Types of long-term memory

Endel Tulving (1985) was one of the first **cognitive** psychologists to realise that the **multi-store model's** view of **long-term memory** (LTM) was too simplistic and inflexible. Tulving proposed that there are in fact three LTM stores, containing quite different types of information. He called them **episodic memory**, **semantic memory** and **procedural memory**.

Episodic memory

Episodic memory refers to our ability to recall events (episodes) from our lives. This has been likened to a diary, a record of daily personal experiences. Some examples are: your most recent visit to the dentist, a gig you went to last week, the psychology class you had yesterday, the breakfast you ate this morning, and so on. These memories are complex.

First of all, they are 'time-stamped' – in other words you remember when they happened as well as what happened. Episodic memories also store information about how events relate to each other in time.

Second, your memory of a single episode will include several elements, such as people and places, objects and behaviours. All of these memories are interwoven to produce a single memory.

Third, you have to make a conscious effort to recall episodic memories. You do this quickly, but you are still aware that you are searching for your memory of what happened when you went to the dentist.

Semantic memory

This store contains our shared knowledge of the world. It has been likened to a combination of an encyclopaedia and a dictionary. So it includes knowledge of such things as: how to apply to university, what an orange tastes like, what zombies like for dinner and the meaning of words. This last one is important. Your semantic memory contains your knowledge of an impressive number of concepts such as 'animals', 'love' and '*Frozen*'.

These memories are not 'time-stamped'. We don't usually remember when we first heard about the new *Frozen* film, for example. Semantic knowledge is less personal and more about facts we all share. It contains an immense collection of material which, given its nature, is constantly being added to. According to Tulving, it is less vulnerable to distortion and forgetting than episodic memory.

Procedural memory

This is our memory for actions or skills, or basically how we do things. We can recall these memories without conscious awareness or much effort (eventually). A good example is driving a car. Our ability to do this becomes automatic through practice. We change gear without having to recall how. We indicate left or right without even realising we've done so.

These are the sorts of skills we might even find quite hard to explain to someone else. If you try to describe what you are doing as you drive the car, the task may well become more difficult.

A child learns to swim. What kind of LTM is this?

Apply it Methods — Amnesia

As part of a clinical study, five people with amnesia are given tests of long-term memory. Their scores for two of these tests are shown in the table below. The higher the score, the better the recall.

Participant	Episodic memory score	Semantic memory score
1	6	9
2	3	7
3	5	7
4	6	8
5	4	10

Questions

1. Calculate the **mean** score for each test. (*2 marks*)
2. Draw a **bar chart** of the mean scores you calculated in Question 1. (*3 marks*)
3. Explain how a bar chart differs from a histogram. (*2 marks*)
4. Explain what the findings tell us about long-term memory. (*2 marks*)

Evaluation

Clinical evidence

One strength is evidence from the famous case studies of HM (Henry Molaison) and Clive Wearing.

Episodic memory in both men was severely impaired due to brain damage (caused by an operation and infection respectively). But their semantic memories were relatively unaffected. They still understood the meaning of words. For example, HM could not recall stroking a dog half an hour earlier but he did not need to have the concept of 'dog' explained to him. Their procedural memories were also intact. They both still knew how to walk and speak, and Clive Wearing (a professional musician) knew how to read music, sing and play the piano.

This evidence supports Tulving's view that there are different memory stores in LTM – one store can be damaged but other stores are unaffected.

Counterpoint Studying people with brain injuries can help researchers to understand how memory is supposed to work normally. But clinical studies are not perfect. A major limitation is that they lack control of variables. The brain injuries experienced by participants were usually unexpected. The researcher had no way of controlling what happened to the participant before or during the injury. The researcher has no knowledge of the individual's memory before the damage. Without this, it is difficult to judge exactly how much worse it is afterwards.

This lack of control limits what clinical studies can tell us about different types of LTM.

Conflicting neuroimaging evidence

One limitation is that there are conflicting research findings linking types of LTM to areas of the brain.

For example, Randy Buckner and Steven Petersen (1996) reviewed evidence regarding the location of semantic and episodic memory. They concluded that semantic memory is located in the left side of the **prefrontal cortex** and episodic memory on the right. However, other research links the left prefrontal cortex with *encoding* of episodic memories and the right prefrontal cortex with episodic *retrieval* (Tulving *et al.* 1994).

This challenges any neurophysiological evidence to support types of memory as there is poor agreement on where each type might be located.

Real-world application

Another strength is that understanding types of LTM allows psychologists to help people with memory problems.

For example, as people age, they experience memory loss. But research has shown this seems to be specific to episodic memory – it becomes harder to recall memories of personal events/experiences that occurred relatively recently though past episodic memories remain intact. Sylvie Belleville *et al.* (2006) devised an intervention to improve episodic memories in older people. The trained participants performed better on a test of episodic memory after training than a control group.

This shows that distinguishing between types of LTM enables specific treatments to be developed.

Evaluation eXtra

Same or different?

More recently Tulving (2002) has taken the view that episodic memory is a 'specialised subcategory' of semantic memory (so essentially the same store). His research showed that some people with amnesia have a functioning semantic memory alongside a damaged episodic memory. But he also concluded it is not possible to have a functioning episodic memory with a damaged semantic memory.

However, John Hodges and Karalyn Patterson (2007) found that some people with Alzheimer's disease (a type of dementia) could form new episodic memories but not semantic memories.

Consider: *Does this evidence suggest that episodic and semantic memory are different or the same?*

Clive Wearing lost access to many of his memories because of a viral infection in his brain.

Apply it Concepts — Clive Wearing

Clive Wearing has a severe form of amnesia that resulted from a viral infection that attacked his brain, damaging the hippocampus and associated areas. Before this infection Clive was a world-class musician and he can still play the piano brilliantly and conduct a choir but he can't remember his musical education. He can remember some other aspects of his life before the infection, but not others. For example, he knows that he has children from an earlier marriage, but cannot remember their names. He recognises his second wife, Deborah, and greets her joyously every time they meet, believing he has not seen her in years, even though she may have just left the room for a few minutes.

Questions

1. Can you explain why Clive will play the same piece of music over and over again?
2. Imagine you have been asked to test Clive Wearing's memory to see which of Tulving's three types of LTM are intact. Explain how you might do this.

Study tip

You may need to explain a difference between the types of LTM (see Check it below). A common mistake is to describe one type of LTM, and then describe a second type of LTM. If you do this there is no connection between the two definitions. You must identify a difference.

A good way of doing this is to choose a feature of memory that one type of LTM has but another type does not. For example, if we were contrasting episodic and semantic memory we might say 'One difference between them is the extent to which we are taught them – no one teaches you your episodic memories but many semantic ones are taught'.

Check it

1. Explain what is meant by 'episodic memory', 'semantic memory' **and** 'procedural memory'. *[6 marks]*
2. Explain **one** difference between semantic memory and procedural memory. *[2 marks]*
3. Briefly evaluate research into episodic memory. *[4 marks]*
4. Discuss different types of long-term memory. *[12 marks AS, 16 marks AL]*

The working memory model

The specification says...

The working memory model: central executive, phonological loop, visuo-spatial sketchpad and episodic buffer. Features of the model: coding and capacity.

One of the limitations of the multi-store model (see page 48) is the fact that the stores were described as single units. On the previous spread we saw that long-term memory can be subdivided. Research has also shown that short-term (working) memory has qualitatively different subdivisions. Alan Baddeley and Graham Hitch (1974) developed a model of short-term memory to account for this research.

Key terms

Working memory model (WMM) A representation of short-term memory (STM). It suggests that STM is a dynamic processor of different types of information using subunits co-ordinated by a central decision-making system.

Central executive (CE) The component of the WMM that co-ordinates the activities of the three subsystems in memory. It also allocates processing resources to those activities.

Phonological loop (PL) The component of the WMM that processes information in terms of sound. This includes both written and spoken material. It's divided into the phonological store and the articulatory process.

Visuo-spatial sketchpad (VSS) The component of the WMM that processes visual and spatial information in a mental space often called our 'inner eye'.

Episodic buffer (EB) The component of the WMM that brings together material from the other subsystems into a single memory rather than separate strands. It also provides a bridge between working memory and long-term memory.

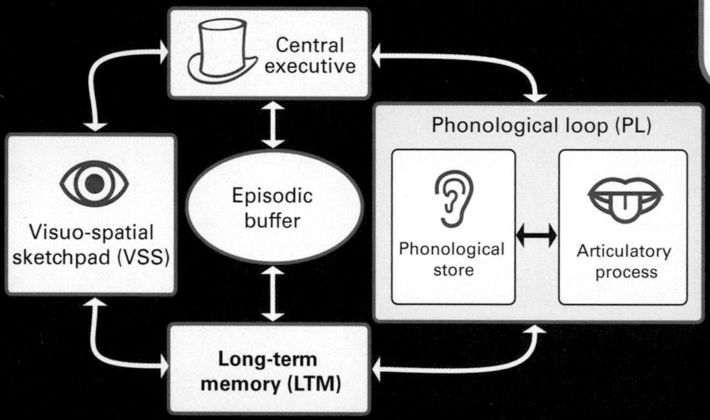
Central executive
Phonological loop (PL)
Episodic buffer
Visuo-spatial sketchpad (VSS)
Phonological store
Articulatory process
Long-term memory (LTM)

The PL contributes to our learning of the sounds of language (phonology). It accesses long-term memory to store and retrieve information about language sounds. This allows us to develop our vocabulary as children and, in a foreign language, as adults.

The VSS contributes to our understanding of 'visual semantics' – the meanings of objects in our visual environment. It can access LTM to store and retrieve visuo-spatial information. For example, if someone says to us, 'Think of something you sit on', we can easily retrieve an image of a chair or a sofa from LTM.

The working memory model

The **working memory model** (WMM, Baddeley and Hitch 1974) is an explanation of how one aspect of memory (**short-term memory**) is organised and how it functions.

The WMM is concerned with the 'mental space' that is active when we are temporarily storing and manipulating information, for example when working on an arithmetic problem or playing chess or comprehending language, etc.

The model consists of four main components, each of which is qualitatively different especially in terms of **coding** and **capacity**.

Central executive

The **central executive** (CE) has a 'supervisory' role. It monitors incoming data, focuses and divides our limited attention and allocates subsystems to tasks (see below). The CE has a very limited processing capacity and does not store information.

Phonological loop

One of the subsystems is the **phonological loop** (PL). It deals with auditory information (i.e. coding is **acoustic**) and preserves the order in which the information arrives. The PL is subdivided into:

- The **phonological store**, which stores the words you hear.
- The **articulatory process**, which allows **maintenance rehearsal** (repeating sounds or words in a 'loop' to keep them in working memory while they are needed). The capacity of this 'loop' is believed to be two seconds' worth of what you can say.

Visuo-spatial sketchpad

The second subsystem is the **visuo-spatial sketchpad** (VSS). The VSS stores visual and/or spatial information when required. For example, if you are asked to work out how many windows there are on your house you visualise it. It also has a limited capacity, which according to Baddeley (2003) is about three or four objects (see Apply it below). Robert Logie (1995) subdivided the VSS into:

- The **visual cache**, which stores visual data.
- The **inner scribe**, which records the arrangement of objects in the visual field.

Episodic buffer

The third subsystem is the **episodic buffer** (EB). This was added to the model by Baddeley in 2000. It is a temporary store for information, integrating the visual, spatial, and verbal information processed by other stores and maintaining a sense of time sequencing – basically recording events (episodes) that are happening. It can be seen as the storage component of the central executive and has a limited capacity of about four chunks (Baddeley 2012). The episodic buffer links working memory to **long-term memory** and wider cognitive processes such as perception.

Apply it Concepts — Using working memory

Picture in your mind the capital letters J and D, side-by-side. At the moment they are the same size and colour. Now manipulate your images of these letters to form an object, let's say an umbrella. You can change their size and orientation but not the letters themselves; they have to be capital J and capital D. You can colour them in mentally if you wish.

Let's try that again, this time with different elements. Imagine a square, a triangle and the capital letter H. Try and arrange these into an object, your choice this time.

One more go: how about an oval, a triangle, the capital letter K and the lower case letter b? Oh, and a question mark? You might have noticed that it very soon becomes quite difficult and eventually impossible to mentally hold onto that much information.

Question

What do you think this tells us about working memory? What were you doing when you performed this task?

Practical activity on page 64

Evaluation

Clinical evidence

One strength is support from Tim Shallice and Elizabeth Warrington's (1970) case study of patient KF (see also page 49).

After his brain injury, KF had poor STM ability for auditory (sound) information but could process visual information normally. For instance his immediate recall of letters and digits was better when he read them (visual) than when they were read to him (acoustic). KF's phonological loop was damaged but his visuo-spatial sketchpad was intact.

This finding strongly supports the existence of separate visual and acoustic memory stores.

Counterpoint However, it is unclear whether KF had other cognitive impairments (apart from damage to his phonological loop) which might have affected his performance on memory tasks. For example, his injury was caused by a motorcycle accident. The trauma involved may have affected his cognitive performance quite apart from any brain injury.

This challenges evidence that comes from clinical studies of people with brain injuries that may have affected many different systems.

Dual-task performance

Another strength is that studies of dual-task performance support the separate existence of the visuo-spatial sketchpad.

When Baddeley *et al.*'s (1975) participants carried out a visual and verbal task at the same time (dual task), their performance on each was similar to when they carried out the tasks separately. But when both tasks were visual (or both were verbal), performance on both declined substantially. This is because both visual tasks compete for the same subsystem (VSS), whereas there is no competition when performing a verbal and visual task together.

This shows there must be a separate subsystem (the VSS) that processes visual input (and one for verbal processing, the PL).

Nature of the central executive

One limitation is that there is a lack of clarity over the nature of the central executive.

Baddeley (2003) himself recognised this when he said, 'The central executive is the most important but the least understood component of working memory'. The CE needs to be more clearly specified than just being simply 'attention'. For example, some psychologists believe the CE may consist of separate subcomponents.

This means that the CE is an unsatisfactory component and this challenges the integrity of the WMM.

Evaluation eXtra

Validity of the model

We have seen that dual-task studies support the WMM because two tasks that share a subsystem are much harder to perform together than tasks that involve separate subsystems. Therefore, there must be separate components in working memory (e.g. VSS and PL).

However, these studies use tasks that are very unlike the tasks we perform in our everyday lives (e.g. identifying the correct order of letters such as A and B, recalling random sequences of letters). They are also carried out in highly-controlled lab conditions (e.g. where presentation of stimuli is precisely timed).

Consider: *On balance, do dual-task studies support or challenge the working memory model?*

There is a very good reason why it is against the law to use your mobile phone and drive at the same time. Carrying out two tasks that use the same components of working memory can lead to poor performance on one or both of them.

Apply it Concepts — Dual-task performance

Think about performing the following two tasks at the same time. You have to repeat a phone number over and over to yourself (maintenance rehearsal) while also answering a true or false quiz in a magazine.

It turns out that most people can do this quite successfully. The multi-store model cannot explain this, but the working memory model can.

Question

How can you use the working memory model to explain what is happening?

Apply it Methods — The word length effect

A cognitive psychologist presented one group of participants with a list of short words to learn (e.g. torch, ear, sun). Other participants were given a list of longer words to learn (e.g. caravan, elephant, celery). She found that participants in the first group were able to recall more words than participants in the second group.

Questions

1. Write a suitable **hypothesis** for this experiment. (*2 marks*)
2. Is your hypothesis **directional** or **non-directional**? (*1 mark*)
3. Identify *one* possible **confounding variable** and explain how it might affect the findings of this study. (*2 marks*)
4. Use your knowledge of the working memory model to explain the finding from this study. (*2 marks*)

Check it

1. Outline the central executive **and** episodic buffer components of the working memory model. *[2 marks + 2 marks]*
2. Briefly outline the working memory model. *[4 marks]*
3. Outline **one** limitation of the working memory model. *[2 marks]*
4. Describe **and** evaluate the working memory model. *[12 marks AS, 16 marks AL]*

Explanations for forgetting: Interference

The specification says...

Explanations for forgetting: proactive and retroactive interference.

Forgetting is the other side of the coin to remembering. Psychologists have tried to understand and explain it by carrying out research studies and formulating theories about why we forget. The specification focuses on two explanations. On this spread we consider the first of these: interference.

Key terms

Interference Forgetting because one memory blocks another, causing one or both memories to be distorted or forgotten.

Proactive interference (PI) Forgetting occurs when older memories, already stored, disrupt the recall of newer memories. The degree of forgetting is greater when the memories are similar.

Retroactive interference (RI) Forgetting occurs when newer memories disrupt the recall of older memories already stored. The degree of forgetting is again greater when the memories are similar.

Graph showing findings from the study by McGeoch and McDonald.

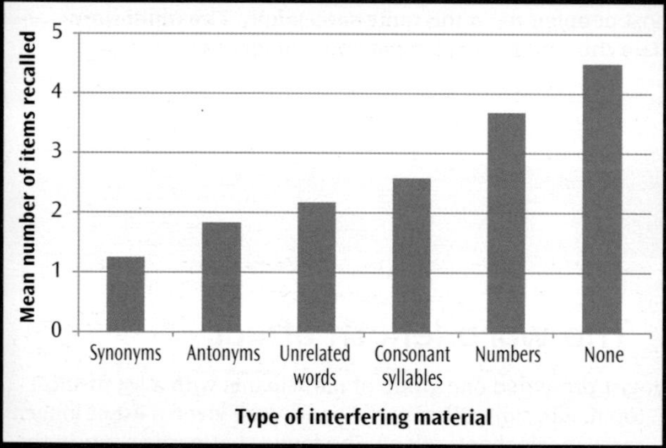

Mean number of items recalled
0
1
2
3
4
5
Synonyms
Antonyms
Unrelated words
Consonant syllables
Numbers
None
Type of interfering material

Interference theory

Some forgetting takes place because of **interference**. This occurs when two pieces of information disrupt each other, resulting in forgetting of one or both, or in some distortion of memory.

Interference has been proposed mainly as an explanation for forgetting in **long-term memory** (LTM). Once information has reached LTM it is more-or-less permanent. Therefore, any forgetting of LTMs is most likely because we can't get *access* to them even though they are *available*. Interference between memories makes it harder for us to locate them, and this is experienced as 'forgetting'.

Types of interference

It is very likely that the two (or more) memories that are interfering with each other were stored at different times. So psychologists recognise that there are two types of interference

- **Proactive interference** (PI) occurs when an older memory interferes with a newer one (*pro* in this context means working *forwards*, from old to new). For example, your teacher has learned so many names in the past that she has difficulty remembering the names of her current class.
- **Retroactive interference** (RI) happens when a newer memory interferes with an older one (*retro* meaning working *backwards*). For example, your teacher has learned so many new names this year that she has difficulty remembering the names of the students last year.

Research on effects of similarity

In both PI and RI, the interference is worse when the memories (or learning) are similar, as discovered by John McGeoch and William McDonald (1931).

Procedure McGeoch and McDonald studied retroactive interference by changing the amount of similarity between two sets of materials. Participants had to learn a list of 10 words until they could remember them with 100% accuracy. They then learned a new list. There were six groups of participants who had to learn different types of new lists:

- Group 1: synonyms – words with the same meanings as the originals.
- Group 2: antonyms – words with the opposite meanings to the originals.
- Group 3: words unrelated to the original ones.
- Group 4: **consonant syllables**.
- Group 5: three-digit numbers.
- Group 6: no new list – these participants just rested (**control condition**).

Findings and conclusions When the participants were asked to recall the original list of words, the most similar material (synonyms) produced the worst recall. This shows that interference is strongest when the memories are similar. The findings are shown in the graph on the left.

Explanation of the effects of similarity

The reason similarity affects recall may be for one of two reasons. It could be due to PI – previously stored information makes new similar information more difficult to store. Or it could be due to RI – new information overwrites previous similar memories because of the similarity.

Apply it Concepts: Forgetting adverts

Raymond Burke and Thomas Skrull (1988) presented a series of magazine adverts to their participants, who had to recall the details of what they had seen (for example, the brand names).

In some cases, they had more difficulty in recalling earlier adverts. In other cases, they had problems remembering the later ones. The effect was greater when the adverts were similar (that is, the adverts were for identical products by different brands).

Question

Use your knowledge of interference theory to explain the findings of this study.

Apply it Concepts: Caleb

Caleb saw a film about zombies a while ago, and went to see a different one recently. A friend, Ashton, asked him some questions about the first film but Caleb found he had trouble recalling the details accurately. A second friend, Anais, then joined in and wanted to know about the recent film Caleb went to see. But, again, Caleb seemed to forget some parts of it.

Question

Outline the interference theory of forgetting, referring to Caleb's experience in your answer.

Evaluation

Real-world interference

One strength is that there is evidence of interference effects in more everyday situations.

Alan Baddeley and Graham Hitch (1977) asked rugby players to recall the names of the teams they had played against during a rugby season. The players all played for the same time interval (over one season) but the number of intervening games varied because some players missed matches due to injury. Players who played the most games (most interference for memory) had the poorest recall.

This study shows that interference can operate in at least some real-world situations, increasing the **validity** of the theory.

Counterpoint Interference may cause some forgetting in everyday situations but it is unusual. This is because the conditions necessary for interference to occur are relatively rare. This is very unlike lab studies, where the high degree of control means a researcher can create ideal conditions for interference. For instance, as we have seen on this spread, two memories (or sets of learning) have to be fairly similar in order to interfere with each other. This may happen occasionally in everyday life (e.g. if you were to revise similar subjects close in time), but not often.

This suggests that most forgetting may be better explained by other theories such as retrieval failure due to a lack of cues (see 'Interference and cues' below and next spread).

Interference and cues

One limitation is that interference is temporary and can be overcome by using cues (hints or clues to help us remember something).

Endel Tulving and Joseph Psotka (1971) gave participants lists of words organised into categories, one list at a time (participants were not told what the categories were). Recall averaged about 70% for the first list, but became progressively worse as participants learned each additional list (proactive interference). But had the words really disappeared from LTM or were they still available? At the end of the procedure the participants were given a cued recall test – they were told the names of the categories. Recall rose again to about 70%.

This shows that interference causes a *temporary* loss of accessibility to material that is still in LTM, a finding not predicted by interference theory.

Support from drug studies

Another strength comes from evidence of *retrograde facilitation*.

Anton Coenen and Gilles van Luijtelaar (1997) gave participants a list of words and later asked them to recall the list, assuming the intervening experiences would act as interference. They found that when a list of words was learned under the influence of the drug *diazepam*, recall one week later was poor (compared with a **placebo** control group). But when a list was learned *before* the drug was taken, later recall was better than placebo. So the drug actually improved (facilitated) recall of material learned beforehand. John Wixted (2004) suggests that the drug prevents new information (i.e. experienced after taking the drug) reaching parts of the brain involved in processing memories, so it cannot interfere retroactively with information already stored.

This finding shows that forgetting can be due to interference – reduce the interference and you reduce the forgetting.

Evaluation eXtra

Validity issues

Most studies supporting interference theory are lab-based, so researchers can control variables (e.g. the time between learning the material and recalling it). Control over confounding variables also means studies show a clear link between interference and forgetting.

But these studies use artificial materials and unrealistic procedures. In everyday life we often learn something and recall it much later (e.g. revising for exams).

Consider: *On balance, is interference a valid explanation for forgetting?*

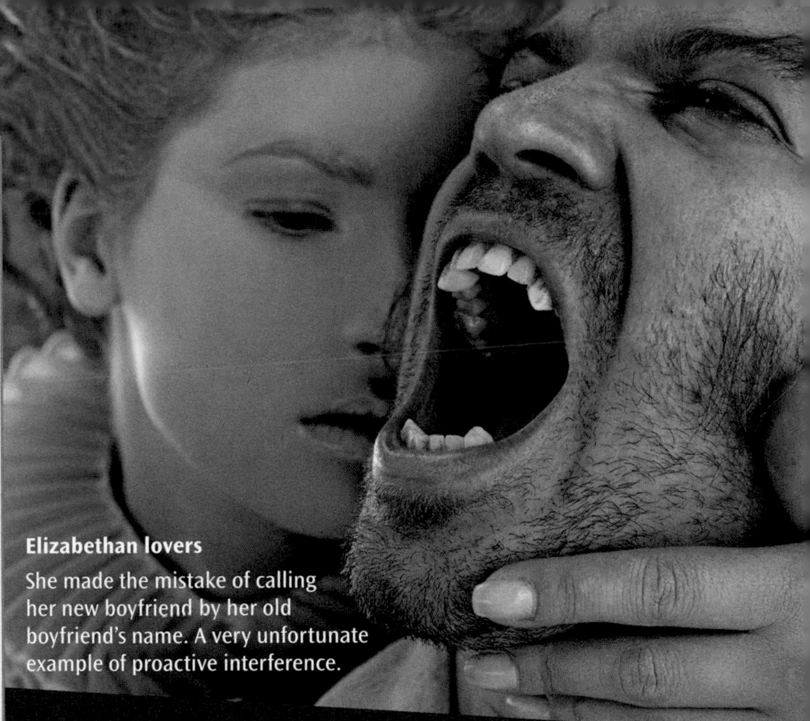

Elizabethan lovers

She made the mistake of calling her new boyfriend by her old boyfriend's name. A very unfortunate example of proactive interference.

Apply it Concepts — Driving

To illustrate the difference between the two types of interference, imagine you have learned to drive a car in the UK (you may not need to imagine this, of course). You will have learned to drive on the left side of the road.

You then fly to Spain for your holidays and hire a car. Driving out of the airport, you narrowly avoid causing an accident because you failed to drive on the right. This is one example of interference.

You return to the UK and, driving out of the car park, you find yourself in the right-hand lane. This is another example of interference. (One of our authors lives in Spain and has clearly had problems – ed.)

Question

Can you identify which is proactive interference and which is retroactive interference? Explain why you made this choice.

Study tip

Don't confuse evaluation and description. Students often think they are doing evaluation but they aren't evaluating at all – they're just describing. You might evaluate the interference explanation by pointing to the supporting evidence. But if all you do is say what the evidence is, that's description. To evaluate, you need to use the evidence effectively. Don't focus on what the evidence is (a brief description is sufficient) – focus instead on what it tells us about interference. Does it support the explanation? How? Why is this a good thing? That is the road to effective evaluation.

Check it

1. Briefly outline proactive interference as an explanation for forgetting. *[2 marks]*
2. Briefly outline retroactive interference as an explanation for forgetting. *[2 marks]*
3. Outline interference as an explanation for forgetting. *[6 marks]*
4. Describe **and** evaluate interference as an explanation for forgetting. *[12 marks AS, 16 marks AL]*

Explanations for forgetting: Retrieval failure

The specification says…

Explanations for forgetting: retrieval failure due to absence of cues.

There is a difference between accessibility and availability of information in memory. The main reason we forget material from our vast long-term memory store is because the material is not accessible (we can't get at it) even though it is available (it is actually present). This is likely to be due to a lack of the right 'triggers' or cues.

Key terms

Retrieval failure A form of forgetting. It occurs when we don't have the necessary cues to access memory. The memory is available but not accessible unless a suitable cue is provided.

Cue A 'trigger' of information that allows us to access a memory. Such cues may be meaningful or may be indirectly linked by being encoded at the time of learning. Indirect cues may be external (environmental context) or internal (mood or degree of drunkenness).

Retrieval-failure theory argues that forgetting will occur when the contexts of learning and recall are different.

Retrieval failure due to the absence of cues

The reason people forget information may be because of insufficient **cues**. When information is initially placed in memory, associated cues are stored at the same time. If these cues are not available at the time of recall, it may appear as if you have forgotten the information but, in fact, this is due to **retrieval failure** – not being able to access memories that are there (i.e. available).

Encoding specificity principle

Endel Tulving (1983) reviewed research into retrieval failure and discovered a consistent pattern to the findings. He summarised this pattern in what he called the **encoding specificity principle** (ESP). This states that a cue (if it is going to be helpful) has to be both (1) present at encoding (when we learn the material) and (2) present at retrieval (when we are recalling it). It follows from this that if the cues available at encoding and retrieval are different (or if cues are entirely absent at retrieval) there will be some forgetting.

Some cues are encoded at the time of learning in a meaningful way. For example, the cue 'STM' may lead you to recall all sorts of information about short-term memory. Such cues are used in many **mnemonic techniques** (see page 223).

Other cues are also encoded at the time of learning but not in a meaningful way. We will consider two examples of non-meaningful cues:

- **Context-dependent forgetting** – recall depends on external cue (e.g. weather or a place).
- **State-dependent forgetting** – recall depends on internal cue (e.g. feeling upset, being drunk).

Research on context-dependent forgetting

Procedure Duncan Godden and Alan Baddeley (1975) studied deep-sea divers who work underwater to see if training on land helped or hindered their work underwater. The divers learned a list of words either underwater or on land and then were asked to recall the words either underwater or on land. This created four conditions:

- Learn on land – recall on land.
- Learn on land – recall underwater.
- Learn underwater – recall on land.
- Learn underwater – recall underwater.

Findings and conclusions In two of these conditions the environmental contexts of learning and recall matched, whereas in the other two they did not. Accurate recall was 40% lower in the non-matching conditions. They concluded that the external cues available at learning were different from the ones available at recall and this led to retrieval failure.

Research on state-dependent forgetting

Procedure Sara Carter and Helen Cassaday (1998) gave antihistamine drugs (for treating hay fever) to their participants. The antihistamines had a mild sedative effect making the participants slightly drowsy. This creates an internal physiological state different from the 'normal' state of being awake and alert. The participants had to learn lists of words and passages of prose and then recall the information, again creating four conditions:

- Learn on drug – recall when on drug.
- Learn on drug – recall when not on drug.
- Learn not on drug – recall when on drug.
- Learn not on drug – recall when not on drug.

Findings In the conditions where there was a mismatch between internal state at learning and recall, performance on the memory test was significantly worse. So when the cues are absent (for example, you are drowsy when recalling information but had been alert learning it) then there is more forgetting.

Apply it Concepts: Paul

Paul drove his friends out to the countryside for an evening meal. Just as they got to the restaurant car park he suddenly realised he had forgotten his wallet. 'I keep my wallet and jacket in different places, but always pick them up together,' Paul said. 'But because it's such a lovely evening, I decided not to bother with the jacket.'

Question

Can you explain how Paul leaving his jacket meant that he also forgot his wallet?

Apply it Concepts: That stinks!

Smell can act as a context-related cue to memory as shown in a study by John Aggleton and Louise Waskett (1999). They conducted their study at the Jorvik Museum in the city of York. In Viking times, 1000 years ago, York was called Jorvik and the ruins still exist under today's city. At the museum, the town has been reconstructed so you can travel back in time and experience what Jorvik was like – including the smells.

The researchers found that recreating these smells helped people to recall the details of their trip to the museum more accurately, even after several years.

Questions

1. Explain this finding in terms of cues.
2. Can you think of a way in which findings like these could be used to help elderly people who are having memory difficulties?

Evaluation

Real-world application

One strength is that retrieval cues can help to overcome some forgetting in everyday situations.

Although cues may not have a very strong effect on forgetting, Baddeley uggests they are still worth paying attention to. For instance, we have robably all had the experience of being in one room and thinking 'I must o and get such-and-such item from another room.' You go to the other oom only to forget what it was you wanted. But the moment you go back o the first room, you remember again. When we have trouble remembering omething, it is probably worth making the effort to recall the environment n which you learned it first.

This shows how research can remind us of strategies we use in the real world to improve our recall.

Research support

Another strength is the impressive range of research that supports the retrieval failure explanation.

The studies by Godden and Baddeley and Carter and Cassaday (facing page) re just two examples because they show that a lack of relevant cues at recall an lead to context-dependent and state-dependent forgetting in everyday fe. Memory researchers Michael Eysenck and Mark Keane (2010) argue that etrieval failure is perhaps the main reason for forgetting from LTM.

This evidence shows that retrieval failure occurs in real-world situations as well as in the highly controlled conditions of the lab.

Counterpoint Baddeley (1997) argues that context effects are actually not very strong, especially in everyday life. Different contexts have to be very different indeed before an effect is seen. For example, it would be hard to find an environment as different from land as underwater (Godden and Baddeley). In contrast, learning something in one room and recalling it in another is unlikely to result in much forgetting because these environments are generally not different enough.

This means that retrieval failure due to lack of contextual cues may not actually explain much everyday forgetting.

Recall versus recognition

One limitation is that context effects may depend substantially on the *type* of memory being tested.

Godden and Baddeley (1980) **replicated** their underwater experiment but used a recognition test instead of recall – participants had to say whether hey recognised a word read to them from a list, instead of retrieving it for hemselves. When recognition was tested there was no context-dependent effect, performance was the same in all four conditions.

This suggests that retrieval failure is a limited explanation for forgetting because it only applies when a person has to recall information rather than ecognise it.

Evaluation eXtra

Problems with the ESP

There is a lot of evidence that forgetting takes place when there is a mismatch (or absence) of encoding and retrieval cues (Tulving's encoding pecificity principle).

However, is it possible to independently establish whether a cue has been encoded or not? The reasoning is circular and based on assumptions. In an experiment, if a cue did not produce recall we assume it cannot have been encoded. If the cue did produce recall, we assume it must have been encoded.

Consider: *How does this affect the validity of the retrieval failure theory?*

Apply it Methods — A sticky problem

Can chewing gum enhance memory? Jess Baker *et al.* (2004) investigated this question.

Students were randomly placed into one of four groups, which were:

- *Gum–gum* (chewing gum when learning a list of words and when recalling it).
- *Gum–no gum* (chewing gum when learning but not when recalling).
- *No gum–gum* (not chewing gum when learning, but doing so when recalling).
- *No gum–no gum* (not chewing gum when learning or recalling).

All of the participants had to learn a list of 15 words in two minutes. They then had to recall the words straight away and again 24 hours later. Immediate recall showed only small differences between the groups. But after 24 hours, the average number of words correctly recalled was 11 for the gum–gum, 8 for gum–no gum, 7 for the no gum–gum group and 8.5 for the no gum–no gum group.

Questions

1. Explain how **demand characteristics** might have operated in this study. (*2 marks*)
2. The procedures were **standardised**. Explain what this means and give *one* example. (*3 marks*)
3. A **measure of dispersion** was used to summarise the findings. Identify which one might be the most appropriate to use and explain why. (*2 marks*)
4. Sketch a **bar chart** to display the four findings given. Remember to label axes clearly. (*3 marks*)
5. Use your knowledge of retrieval failure to explain the findings of this study. (*3 marks*)

Check it

1. Briefly explain retrieval failure as an explanation for forgetting. *[2 marks]*
2. Explain what a cue is in the context of forgetting. *[2 marks]*
3. Briefly outline **two** explanations for forgetting. *[2 marks + 2 marks]*
4. Describe **and** evaluate retrieval failure as an explanation for forgetting. *[12 marks AS, 16 marks AL]*

Factors affecting the accuracy of eyewitness testimony: Misleading information

The specification says...

Factors affecting the accuracy of eyewitness testimony: misleading information, including leading questions and post-event discussion.

The next three spreads consider how memory research can be applied to a very important topic – the dependability of eyewitness testimony. We begin by looking at the effects of misleading information on what eyewitnesses can recall after an incident.

Key terms

Eyewitness testimony (EWT) The ability of people to remember the details of events, such as accidents and crimes, which they themselves have observed. Accuracy of EWT can be affected by factors such as misleading information and anxiety.

Misleading information Incorrect information given to an eyewitness usually after the event (hence often called '*post*-event information'). It can take many forms, such as leading questions and post-event discussion between co-witnesses and/or other people.

Leading question A question which, because of the way it is phrased, suggests a certain answer. For example: 'Was the knife in his left hand?' leads a person to think that's where the knife was.

Post-event discussion (PED) occurs when there is more than one witness to an event. Witnesses may discuss what they have seen with co-witnesses or with other people. This may influence the accuracy of each witness's recall of the event.

Misleading information research

Research on leading questions

When you are asked a question, the wording of the question may lead (or mislead) you to give a certain answer. This is a particular issue for **eyewitness testimony** (EWT) because police questions may 'direct' a witness to give a particular answer. In the experiment below words such as *smashed* or *bumped* were used to suggest the speed of the car.

Procedure Elizabeth Loftus and John Palmer (1974) arranged for 45 participants (students) to watch film clips of car accidents and then asked them questions about the accident. In the *critical question* (a **leading question** or also called **misleading information**) participants were asked to describe how fast the cars were travelling: *'About how fast were the cars going when they hit each other?'*

There were five groups of participants and each group was given a different verb in the critical question. One group had the verb *hit*, the others had *contacted, bumped, collided, smashed*.

Findings The **mean** estimated speed was calculated for each participant group. The verb *contacted* resulted in a mean estimated speed of 31.8 mph. For the verb *smashed*, the mean was 40.5 mph (full findings on facing page). The leading question biased the eyewitness's recall of an event.

Why do leading questions affect EWT?

The *response-bias explanation* suggests that the wording of the question has no real effect on the participants' memories, but just influences how they decide to answer. When a participant gets a leading question using the word *smashed*, this encourages them to choose a higher speed estimate.

Loftus and Palmer (1974) conducted a second experiment that supported the *substitution explanation*, which proposes that the wording of a leading question changes the participant's memory of the film clip. This was shown because participants who originally heard *smashed* were later more likely to report seeing broken glass (there was none) than those who heard *hit*. The critical verb altered their memory of the incident.

Research on post-event discussion

Eyewitnesses to a crime may sometimes discuss their experiences and memories with each other. The following experiment explores the effects of such **post-event discussion** (PED).

Procedure Fiona Gabbert *et al.* (2003) studied participants in pairs. Each participant watched a video of the same crime, but filmed from different points of view. This meant that each participant could see elements in the event that the other could not. For example, only one of the participants could see the title of a book being carried by a young woman.

Both participants then discussed what they had seen before individually completing a test of recall.

Findings The researchers found that 71% of the participants mistakenly recalled aspects of the event that they did not see in the video but had picked up in the discussion. The corresponding figure in a **control group**, where there was no discussion, was 0%. This was evidence of memory conformity.

Why does post-event discussion affect EWT?

One explanation is *memory contamination*. When co-witnesses to a crime discuss it with each other, their eyewitness testimonies may become altered or distorted. This is because they combine (mis)information from other witnesses with their own memories.

Another explanation is *memory conformity*. Gabbert *et al.* concluded that witnesses often go along with each other, either to win social approval or because they believe the other witnesses are right and they are wrong. Unlike with memory contamination, the actual memory is unchanged.

Apply it Concepts False memory

Seema Clifasefi and colleagues (2013) attempted to use leading questions to implant a memory of an event that never happened (called a false memory). They did this by giving their participants a document that claimed to be a personalised food and drink profile. This was supposedly put together by powerful computer software based on the participants' earlier responses to a questionnaire. For one group, their profiles included the false information that they had once, many years earlier, drunk so much alcohol that they were sick.

Later, the participants completed a memory test in which a leading question asked when they had become sick from drinking too much alcohol. The researchers found that a significant number of the participants 'recalled' being sick due to drinking too much alcohol when they were younger. But even more surprisingly, a proportion of these participants also claimed that they now disliked certain alcoholic drinks because of this (non-existent) experience.

Question

Using your knowledge of the effects of misleading information, explain the findings from this study.

Practical activity on page 65

Evaluation

Real-world application

One strength of research into misleading information is that it has important practical uses in the criminal justice system.

The consequences of inaccurate EWT can be very serious. Loftus (1975) believes that leading questions can have such a distorting effect on memory that police officers need to be very careful about how they phrase their questions when interviewing eyewitnesses. Psychologists are sometimes asked to act as expert witnesses in court trials and explain the limits of EWT to juries.

This shows that psychologists can help to improve the way the legal system works, especially by protecting innocent people from faulty convictions based on unreliable EWT.

Counterpoint However, the practical applications of EWT may be affected by issues with research. For instance, Loftus and Palmer's participants watched film clips in a lab, a very different experience from witnessing a real event (e.g. less stressful). Also, Rachel Foster *et al.* (1994) point out that what eyewitnesses remember has important consequences in the real world, but participants' responses in research do not matter in the same way (so research participants are less motivated to be accurate).

This suggests that researchers such as Loftus are too pessimistic about the effects of misleading information – EWT may be more dependable than many studies suggest.

Evidence against substitution

One limitation of the substitution explanation is that EWT is more accurate for some aspects of an event than for others.

For example, Rachel Sutherland and Harlene Hayne (2001) showed participants a video clip. When participants were later asked misleading questions, their recall was more accurate for central details of the event than for peripheral ones. Presumably the participants' attention was focused on central features of the event and these memories were relatively resistant to misleading information.

This suggests that the original memories for central details survived and were not distorted, an outcome that is not predicted by the substitution explanation.

Evidence challenging memory conformity

Another limitation of the memory conformity explanation is evidence that post-event discussion actually alters EWT.

Elin Skagerberg and Daniel Wright (2008) showed their participants film clips. There were two versions, e.g. a mugger's hair was dark brown in one but light brown in the other. Participants discussed the clips in pairs, each having seen different versions. They often did not report what they had seen in the clips or what they had heard from the co-witness, but a 'blend' of the two (e.g. a common answer to the hair question was not 'light brown' or 'dark brown' but 'medium brown').

This suggests that the memory itself is distorted through contamination by misleading post-event discussion, rather than the result of memory conformity.

Evaluation eXtra

Demand characteristics

Lab studies have identified misleading information as a cause of inaccurate EWT, partly by being able to control variables.

But Maria Zaragoza and Michael McCloskey (1989) argue that many answers given by participants in lab studies are due to demand characteristics. Participants usually want to be helpful and not let the researcher down. So they guess when they are asked a question they don't know the answer to.

Consider: *How can researchers maximise the internal validity of EWT research?*

Witnesses in court trials swear an oath to tell the truth. They may think they are telling the truth but psychological research shows this could be an illusion.

Apply it Methods: Loftus and Palmer

We described Loftus and Palmer's study on the facing page. The findings from this study are shown in the table on the right.

Verb	Mean estimate (mph)
Contacted	31.8
Hit	34.0
Bumped	38.1
Collided	39.3
Smashed	40.5

Questions

1. Write a suitable **aim** for this study. (*2 marks*)
2. There were five groups of participants in this study. Explain why it would have been necessary to **randomly allocate** participants to each of the five groups. (*2 marks*)
3. **Questionnaires** were used to collect the data. Explain *one* strength and *one* limitation of using questionnaires in this study. (*4 marks*)
4. Identify and explain *one* **ethical issue** that arose in this study. (*3 marks*)
5. Use your knowledge of how misleading information affects EWT to explain the findings of this study. (*3 marks*)

Apply it Concepts: Disentangling post-event discussion

Hartmut Bodner *et al.* (2009) found that the effects of post-event discussion can be reduced if participants are warned of their impact. Recall was more accurate for those participants who were warned that anything they hear from a co-witness is second-hand information (or 'hearsay') and that they should forget it and recall only their own memory of the event.

This finding can help us decide if Gabbert *et al.*'s explanation of PED on the facing page is correct.

Question

If a warning can negate the effects of post-event discussion, does this show that memory conformity is occurring? Explain your answer.

Check it

1. Explain what is meant by 'post-event discussion'. *[2 marks]*
2. Give an example of a leading question **and** explain how this might affect the accuracy of eyewitness testimony. *[3 marks]*
3. Explain how post-event discussion may affect the accuracy of eyewitness testimony. *[3 marks]*
4. Describe **and** evaluate research into the influence of misleading information on the accuracy of eyewitness testimony. *[12 marks AS, 16 marks AL]*

Factors affecting the accuracy of eyewitness testimony: Anxiety

The specification says...

Factors affecting the accuracy of eyewitness testimony: anxiety.

Stressful situations create anxiety. Crimes and accidents are no exception. When we witness such events, we experience physiological and psychological changes that could affect what we later remember. So now we turn our attention to the second major factor that can affect the accuracy of EWT – anxiety.

Key term

Anxiety A state of emotional and physical arousal. The emotions include having worried thoughts and feelings of tension. Physical changes include an increased heart rate and sweatiness. Anxiety is a normal reaction to stressful situations, but it can affect the accuracy and detail of eyewitness testimony.

Tunnel theory

Anxiety narrows your attention onto one aspect of a scene (e.g. a weapon in Johnson and Scott's study), like tunnel vision, and this means you won't be able to recall much else.

The effects of anxiety

Anxiety has strong emotional and physical effects. But it is not clear whether these effects make eyewitness recall better or worse. Research supports both possibilities.

Anxiety has a negative effect on recall (weapon focus)

Anxiety creates physiological arousal in the body which prevents us paying attention to important cues, so recall is worse. One approach to studying anxiety and **eyewitness testimony** (EWT) is to look at the effect of the presence of a weapon which creates anxiety. This leads to a focus on the weapon, reducing a witness's recall for other details of the event.

Procedure Craig Johnson and William Scott (1976) did research on this. Their participants believed they were taking part in a **lab study**. While seated in a waiting room participants in the low-anxiety condition heard a casual conversation in the next room and then saw a man walk past them carrying a pen and with grease on his hands. Other participants overheard a heated argument, accompanied by the sound of breaking glass. A man walked out of the room, holding a knife covered in blood. This was the high-anxiety condition.

Findings and conclusion The participants later picked out the man from a set of 50 photos, 49% who had seen the man carrying the pen were able to identify him. The corresponding figure for the participants who had seen the man holding the blood-covered knife was 33%. The **tunnel theory** of memory argues that people have enhanced memory for central events. Weapon focus as a result of anxiety can have this effect.

Anxiety has a positive effect on recall

Witnessing a stressful event creates anxiety through physiological arousal within the body. The **fight or flight response** is triggered, increasing alertness. This may improve memory for the event as we become more aware of cues in the situation.

Procedure John Yuille and Judith Cutshall (1986) conducted a study of an actual shooting in a gun shop in Vancouver, Canada. The shop owner shot a thief dead. There were 21 witnesses – 13 took part in the study. They were interviewed four to five months after the incident and these interviews were compared with the original police interviews at the time of the shooting. Accuracy was determined by the number of details reported in each account. The witnesses were also asked to rate how stressed they had felt at the time of the incident (on a 7-point scale) and whether they had any emotional problems since the event (e.g. sleeplessness).

Findings and conclusion The witnesses were very accurate in their accounts and there was little change in the amount recalled or accuracy after five months – though some details were less accurate, such as recollection of the colour of items and age/height/weight estimates. Those participants who reported the highest levels of stress were most accurate (about 88% compared to 75% for the less-stressed group). This suggests that anxiety does not have a detrimental effect on the accuracy of eyewitness memory in a real-world context and may even enhance it.

Explaining the contradictory findings

According to Robert Yerkes and John Dodson (1908) the relationship between emotional arousal and performance looks like an 'inverted U' (see graph below).

Kenneth Deffenbacher (1983) reviewed 21 studies of EWT and noted contradictory findings on the effects of anxiety. He used the **Yerkes-Dodson Law** to explain the findings. When we witness a crime/accident we become emotionally and physiologically aroused. That is, we experience anxiety (emotional) as well as physiological changes in our body (the fight or flight response). Lower levels of anxiety/arousal produce lower levels of recall accuracy, and then memory becomes more accurate as the level of anxiety/arousal increases. However, there is an optimal level of anxiety, which is the point of maximum accuracy. If a person (or eyewitness) experiences any more arousal, then their recall suffers a drastic decline.

Apply it Concepts — Natural disasters

One problem with many lab-based and real-world studies of anxiety is that they only compare *high* and *low* anxiety groups. The inverted-U theory cannot be properly tested unless there is a *moderate* anxiety group as well.

Janat Parker *et al.* (2006) overcame this problem by interviewing people who had been affected by the destruction wrought by Hurricane Andrew in the United States in 1992. The researchers defined anxiety in terms of the amount of damage the participants suffered to their homes.

The researchers found that there was a link between the level of recall and the amount of damage/anxiety experienced.

Questions

1. Based on the inverted-U theory, can you predict which group showed the most accurate recall? Explain why you chose this group.
2. Do you think the method used to **operationalise** anxiety is a valid way of measuring anxiety?

Yerkes-Dodson Law

The inverted-U theory states that performance will increase with stress, but only to a certain point, where it decreases drastically.

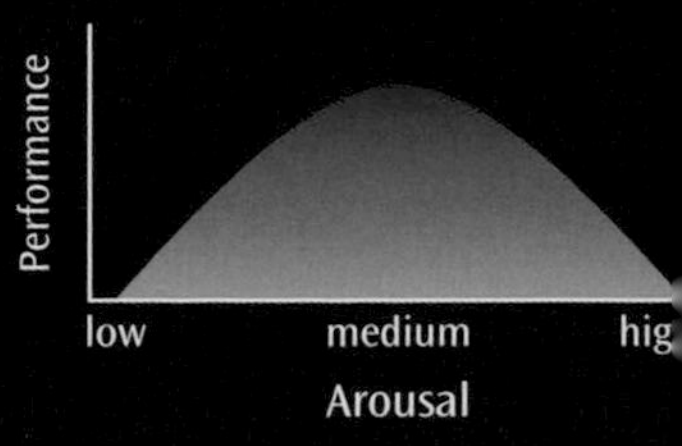
Performance
low
medium
hig
Arousal

Evaluation

Unusualness not anxiety

One limitation of the study by Johnson and Scott (facing page) is that it may not have tested anxiety.

The reason participants focused on the weapon may be because they were surprised at what they saw rather than scared. Kerri Pickel (1998) conducted an experiment using scissors, a handgun, a wallet or a raw chicken as the hand-held items in a hairdressing salon video (where scissors would be high anxiety, low unusualness). Eyewitness accuracy was significantly poorer in the high unusualness conditions (chicken and handgun).

This suggests that the weapon focus effect is due to unusualness rather than anxiety/threat and therefore tells us nothing specifically about the effects of anxiety on EWT.

Support for negative effects

One strength is evidence supporting the view that anxiety has a negative effect on the accuracy of recall.

The study by Tim Valentine and Jan Mesout (2009, see right) supports the research on weapon focus, finding negative effects on recall. The researchers used an objective measure (heart rate) to divide participants into high- and low-anxiety groups. In this study anxiety clearly disrupted the participants' ability to recall details about the actor in the London Dungeon's Labyrinth.

This suggests that a high level of anxiety does have a negative effect on the immediate eyewitness recall of a stressful event.

Support for positive effects

Another strength is evidence showing that anxiety can have positive effects on the accuracy of recall.

Sven-Åke Christianson and Birgitta Hübinette (1993) interviewed 58 witnesses to actual bank robberies in Sweden. Some of the witnesses were directly involved (e.g. bank workers) and some were indirectly involved (e.g. bystanders). The researchers assumed that those directly involved would experience the most anxiety. It was found that recall was more than 75% accurate across all witnesses. The direct victims (most anxious) were even more accurate.

These findings from actual crimes confirm that anxiety does not reduce the accuracy of recall for eyewitnesses and may even enhance it.

Counterpoint Christianson and Hübinette interviewed their participants several months after the event (four to 15 months). The researchers therefore had no control over what happened to their participants in the intervening time (e.g. post-event discussions). The effects of anxiety may have been overwhelmed by these other factors and impossible to assess by the time the participants were interviewed.

Therefore it is possible that a lack of control over **confounding variables** may be responsible for these findings, invalidating their support.

Evaluation eXtra

Problems with inverted-U theory

The inverted-U theory appears to be a reasonable explanation of the contradictory findings linking anxiety with both increased and decreased eyewitness recall.

On the other hand it ignores the fact that anxiety has many elements – cognitive, behavioural, emotional and physical. It focuses on just the last of these (physical arousal) and assumes this is the only aspect linked to EWT. But the way we think about the stressful situation (i.e. cognitive) may also be important.

Consider: *Does this mean that the inverted-U explanation is too simplistic?*

Death statue outside the London Dungeon, a good place for a psychology experiment.

Apply it Methods: Labyrinth of Horror

Valentine and Mesout (2009) carried out a study in the real-world setting of the Horror Labyrinth at the London Dungeon. It is designed to be frightening with many 'scares' such as darkness, screams, gory models and sudden movements. Visitors to the Labyrinth were offered a reduced entrance fee if they agreed to complete questionnaires at the end of their visit to assess their level of self-reported anxiety. They wore wireless heart monitors to confirm that they were experiencing anxiety. On the basis of these two measures participants were divided into two groups: high anxiety and low anxiety.

The participants' task was to describe a person encountered in the Labyrinth (played by an actor). The researchers found that the high-anxiety participants recalled the fewest correct details of the actor and made more mistakes. The researchers also found that 17% of the high-anxiety group correctly identified the actor in a line-up compared to 75% correct identification by those in the low-anxiety group.

Questions

1. Explain why this study is an example of a **quasi-experiment**. (*2 marks*)
2. Explain *one* limitation of a quasi-experiment. Refer to the study above in your answer. (*2 marks*)
3. Identify the **sampling method** used in this study and explain *one* strength of this method. (*3 marks*)
4. **Questionnaires** were used to collect the data. Write *one* **closed question** and *one* **open question** that could have been used in this study. (*4 marks*)
5. Select *one* other study of the effect of anxiety on the accuracy of EWT. How do the findings compare with the findings in the London Dungeon study? (*3 marks*)

Check it

1. Explain what is meant by 'anxiety' in the context of eyewitness testimony. *[2 marks]*
2. Briefly describe **two** factors that affect the accuracy of eyewitness testimony. *[6 marks]*
3. Describe the effect of anxiety on the accuracy of eyewitness testimony. *[4 marks]*
4. Discuss what research has shown about the influence of anxiety on the accuracy of eyewitness testimony. *[12 marks AS, 16 marks AL]*

Improving the accuracy of eyewitness testimony: Cognitive interview

The specification says...

Improving the accuracy of eyewitness testimony, including the use of the cognitive interview.

We have seen that eyewitness testimony may lack accuracy, yet such accuracy is vital to the police and the courts. So psychologists have turned their attention to finding ways of improving the accuracy of EWT based on sound psychological evidence, such as the cognitive interview.

Key term

Cognitive interview (CI) A method of interviewing eyewitnesses to help them retrieve more accurate memories. It uses four main techniques, all based on evidence-based psychological knowledge of human memory – report everything, reinstate the context, reverse the order and change perspective.

Study tip

It is worth thinking about how the cognitive interview might be used in a real-world scenario. Think about how a police officer would ask questions and how this would affect the responses from witnesses. Always consider the effects on characters in any scenario.

Apply it Concepts

Try it yourself

A great strength of the cognitive interview is that its techniques are based on sound psychological research into how human memory works. For example, *report everything* and *reinstate the context* are both based on Tulving's encoding specificity hypothesis (see page 56).

These techniques aren't just useful in recalling crimes. You can use them to try and recall any event you have been part of or witnessed and want to remember more about. Try it for yourself.

Think of any fairly recent situation. Picture the setting in your mind. What is the weather like? What time of day is it? What can you see? Think about the internal context as well. How do you feel? Happy? Sad? Can't remember? It's worth persisting – you might be surprised how much you recall that you thought you'd forgotten.

Now change your perspective. Is there someone else there? Picture the situation as they see it. What can you see now? Anything different?

Questions

1. What did you discover?
2. What do you think the techniques of the cognitive interview tell us about the difference between the availability and accessibility of memories?

The cognitive interview

Ronald Fisher and Edward Geiselman (1992) argued that **eyewitness testimony** could be improved if the police used better techniques when interviewing witnesses. Fisher and Geiselman recommended that such techniques should be based on psychological insights into how memory works, and called these techniques collectively the **cognitive interview** (CI) to indicate its foundation in *cognitive* psychology. There are four main techniques that are used.

1. Report everything

Witnesses are encouraged to include every single detail of the event, even though it may seem irrelevant or the witness doesn't feel confident about it. Seemingly trivial details may be important and, moreover, they may trigger other important memories.

2. Reinstate the context

The witness should return to the original crime scene 'in their mind' and imagine the environment (such as what the weather was like, what they could see) and their emotions (such as whether they were happy or bored). This is related to **context-dependent forgetting** discussed on page 56.

3. Reverse the order

Events should be recalled in a different order from the original sequence, for example, from the final point back to the beginning, or from the middle to the beginning.

This is done to prevent people reporting their *expectations* of how the event must have happened rather than reporting the actual events. It also prevents dishonesty (it's harder for people to produce an untruthful account if they have to reverse it).

4. Change perspective

Witnesses should recall the incident from other people's perspectives. For example, how it would have appeared to other witnesses or to the perpetrator. This again is done to disrupt the effect of expectations and also the effect of **schema** on recall. The schema you have for a particular setting (such as going into a shop) generate expectations of what would have happened and it is the schema that is recalled rather than what actually happened.

The enhanced cognitive interview (ECI)

Fisher *et al.* (1987) developed some additional elements of the CI to focus on the social dynamics of the interaction. For example, the interviewer needs to know when to establish eye contact and when to relinquish it. The enhanced CI also includes ideas such as reducing eyewitness anxiety, minimising distractions, getting the witness to speak slowly and asking open-ended questions.

Friendly, relaxed, business-like. In the enhanced CI the interviewer takes time to establish rapport with the witness, to encourage them to recall more information about what they have seen.

Evaluation

Support for the effectiveness of the CI

One strength of the cognitive interview is evidence that it works.

For example, a **meta-analysis** by Günter Köhnken *et al.* (1999) combined data from 55 studies comparing the CI (and the ECI) with the standard police interview. The CI gave an average 41% increase in accurate information compared with the standard interview. Only four studies in the analysis showed no difference between the types of interview.

This shows that the CI is an effective technique in helping witnesses to recall information that is stored in memory (available) but not immediately accessible.

Counterpoint Köhnken *et al.* also found an increase in the amount of *in*accurate information recalled by participants. This was a particular issue in the ECI, which produced more incorrect details than the CI. Cognitive interviews may sacrifice quality of EWT (i.e. accuracy) in favour of quantity (amount of details).

This means that police officers should treat eyewitness evidence from CIs/ECIs with caution.

Some elements may be more useful

One limitation of the original CI is that not all of its elements are equally effective or useful.

Rebecca Milne and Ray Bull (2002) found that each of the four techniques used alone produced more information than the standard police interview. But they also found that using a combination of *report everything* and *reinstate the context* produced better recall than any of the other elements or combination of them. This confirmed police officers' suspicions that some aspects of the CI are more useful than others.

This casts some doubt on the credibility of the overall cognitive interview.

The CI is time-consuming

Another limitation is that police officers may be reluctant to use the CI because it takes more time and training than the standard police interview.

For example, more time is needed to establish rapport with a witness and allow them to relax. The CI also requires special training and many forces do not have the resources to provide more than a few hours (Kebbell and Wagstaff 1997).

This suggests that the complete CI as it exists is not a realistic method for police officers to use and (as in the point above) it might be better to focus on just a few key elements.

Evaluation eXtra

Variations of the CI

Police forces have taken a 'pick and mix' approach to the various techniques in the CI. This means it is hard to compare the effectiveness of different approaches in research studies.

On the other hand, this 'pick and mix' approach is more flexible. It means that individuals can develop their own approach according to what works best for them.

Consider: *On balance, is this variation between police forces a strength or limitation of the CI?*

Apply it Methods: Assessing the cognitive interview

A psychologist carried out an experiment to find out if a cognitive interview was more effective than a standard police interview (no fancy cognitive techniques) in helping witnesses to recall more information. She placed an advert in local newspapers asking for people to participate. The advert indicated that participants would be shown a short film of a knifepoint mugging, and that they would be interviewed by a police officer.

Once all the data was collected, the psychologist compared the **mean** number of items correctly recalled in the cognitive interview with the mean number of items correctly recalled in the standard police interview.

Questions

1. Explain what **experimental design** might be used in this study. Outline what you would do to conduct the study. (*3 marks*)
2. Explain *one* strength and *one* limitation of this experimental design. Refer to the study described above in your answer. (*2 marks + 2 marks*)
3. Identify the **sampling method** used in this study. (*1 mark*)
4. Explain how **investigator effects** might have operated in this study. (*3 marks*)
5. Explain how a **pilot study** might have been conducted in the context of this study. (*3 marks*)

Apply it Concepts: Write your own

A police officer trained in using the cognitive interview is helping a witness to recall more information about a mugging. Eventually, she gives the witness the following instruction: 'Please tell me as much as you can remember about what you saw. Please do not leave anything out, even if you think they are just unimportant small details.'

Questions

1. Which of the four main techniques of the cognitive interview is being used in the above statement?
2. For the three other techniques, write down the exact wording of the instructions the police officer might give to the witness.

Check it

1. Explain what is meant by 'cognitive interview'. [2 marks]
2. Outline how the cognitive interview can improve the accuracy of EWT. [4 marks]
3. Cognitive interviews have been developed to improve EWT. Identify **and** explain **two** techniques used in the cognitive interview. [6 marks]
4. Describe **and** evaluate the cognitive interview as a way of improving the accuracy of EWT. [12 marks AS, 16 marks AL]

Practical corner

The specification says...

Knowledge and understanding of ... research methods, practical research skills and maths skills. These should be developed through ... ethical practical research activities.

This means that you should conduct practical investigations wherever possible. The topic of memory is ideally suited to experimental research. Questionnaires are also frequently used to gather data for analysis. The two practical activities on this spread give you an opportunity to use both of these methods.

Ethics check

Ethics are discussed in detail on pages 178–179. We strongly suggest that you complete this checklist before collecting data.

1. Do participants know participation is voluntary?
2. Do participants know what to expect?
3. Do participants know they can withdraw at any time?
4. Are individuals' results anonymous?
5. Have I minimised the risk of distress to participants?
6. Have I avoided asking sensitive questions?
7. Will I avoid bringing my school/teacher/psychology into disrepute?
8. Have I considered all other ethical issues?
9. Has my teacher approved this?

Creating your materials

For all groups you need a reasoning task (Task 1). You should construct a table for this. It should include ten sentences about the relationship between the letters A and B, plus space for the participants to record a response. You can use these five sentences to start you off:

Letters	Statement	TRUE	FALSE
AB	A follows B.		
BA	B is followed by A.		
BA	A does not come before B.		
AB	B is followed by A.		
BA	A follows B.		

Practical idea 1: Dual-task performance

Hitch and Baddeley (1976) tested their working memory model by considering the prediction that people can perform two tasks at the same time as long as the tasks use different components of the working memory system, for example the tasks use the **phonological loop** and the **central executive**. If the task uses the same component, performance should be slowed down.

This practical is a **laboratory experiment** to investigate **dual-task performance**.

The practical bit

Designing your experiment

Your participants have to perform two tasks at the same time – a verbal task and a reasoning task. For some participants the two tasks will use the same component of working memory.

All participants do Task 1, a reasoning task that uses the central executive. They are shown two letters, such as 'AB' and a statement 'B is followed by A', and asked to indicate if the statement is true or false (see 'Creating your materials', below left).

Simultaneously participants do Task 2, either:

- Condition A: Participants say 'the the the' repeatedly – this involves just the phonological loop.
- Condition B: Participants generate random digits (i.e. just say any digits) – this involves both the central executive and the phonological loop.
- Condition C: No additional task – this is a **control condition**.

The hypothesis is that participants in Condition B perform Task 1 more slowly than participants in Condition A or C because they will be performing two tasks that involve the central executive.

You will use an **independent groups design** with three groups of participants (one each for Conditions A, B and C – though you don't have to include Condition C).

Ethical issues

You can tackle ethical issues by writing a **consent** form and a **debriefing** script. One issue you should address is **confidentiality**. Your participants will probably not want their results to be made public or to risk being identified. Another issue is the **right to withdraw** at any point, which includes the right for participants to withdraw their data. Finally, you should consider **protection from psychological harm**. Some participants may feel that their performance is being evaluated. They may be worried that their memories are poor. For some other issues, see the 'Ethics check' box (left).

Choosing your sample

You could use an **opportunity sampling** method. You're going to have to test participants individually, so you could just approach people in your school/college canteen or wherever, as long as you have somewhere quiet to go to.

Analysing your data

You want to see if there are any differences between the groups of participants in the time taken to complete the reasoning task (the **dependent variable**). You could also consider the number of errors made.

Apply it Methods

The maths bit 1

1. Redo Table 1 on the right, giving all data to the nearest whole number. (*2 marks*)
2. Calculate the **mean** and the **range** for each group/condition. (*3 marks*)
3. Which type of **graphical** display would be appropriate to present the results in Table 1? (*1 mark*)
4. Sketch the graphical display you have identified in your previous answer. Remember to label your axes carefully. (*3 marks*)
5. Based on the **descriptive statistics**, what conclusion could you draw about the effect of the verbal task on performance of the reasoning task? (*2 marks*)
6. Do these findings support the working memory model? Explain your answer. (*2 marks*)

Table 1 Time taken to complete reasoning task (secs).

Condition A	Condition B
32.38	42.73
28.93	50.21
34.27	43.63
30.41	46.25
36.84	44.37
34.28	45.81
37.11	67.32
29.79	48.91
37.46	41.63
35.58	47.79

Practical idea 2: EWT and leading questions

Research has shown that various factors can affect the accuracy of eyewitness testimony. One of these factors is **misleading information** in the form of **leading questions**.

The aim of this study is to use a video clip to find out if leading questions affect eyewitness recall of an event. This is a laboratory experiment using a **questionnaire** to assess the **dependent variable**.

The justice system recognises that leading questions can influence an eyewitness's testimony, which is why they are officially banned. But that doesn't stop most barristers from trying!

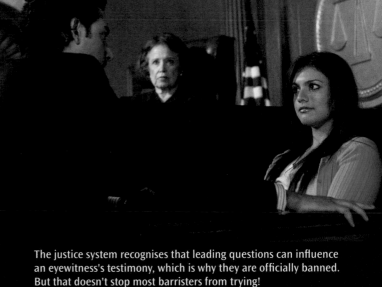

The practical bit

You will need two groups of participants in order to analyse the impact of a leading question on accuracy of recall. The wording of a single question should vary between the two groups.

Selecting and constructing your materials

You will need to find a suitable video clip, most likely from YouTube. You are looking for something brief, an incident of some kind about which you can ask questions concerning what happened, who was involved and so on. You need to take ethical issues into account when choosing the clip (see below).

You will also need to construct a **questionnaire**. A crucial design element of this concerns the types of questions that you might use. These are likely to be a combination of **closed** and **open questions**. The open questions could ask your participants to describe in their own words the incident they have seen. The closed questions will be specific and offer a yes/no or true/false response.

One of these closed questions should be your leading question. The answers to this question will be the only ones you are interested in and will analyse. This question should differ for the two groups in your study, so that you can make a comparison. This means that you will have two questionnaires (A and B), but the only difference between them will be in this one question. It is probably worth running a **pilot study** to see if the questionnaire works.

Choosing your sample

Individual testing would be time-consuming and inconvenient. A better approach would be to show the clip to a whole class at once. You could **randomly** select a class from your school **population**. The two forms of the questionnaire should be randomly distributed to class members, thus participants are **randomly allocated** to **experimental conditions**. Note this does not mean just handing the questionnaires out in any order – you should number participants and then use a random selection method to select which participants get questionnaire A.

Ethical considerations

It is unlikely in a study like this that you are going to ask anything that invades your participants' **privacy**. But, even so, it is advisable to steer clear of any questions that might be considered sensitive. Your choice of clip needs to be carefully thought through. Avoid anything that may cause offence or anxiety. So choose something fairly mundane and everyday, rather than an accident or violent crime.

When people have their memories tested, in any form, they may feel that they are being evaluated on their performance. So you should reassure participants that this is not the case in any debriefing that you carry out at the end of the procedure. This will help to protect participants from possible psychological harm. You should also take steps to secure your participants' consent, and respect their right to withdraw from the study.

Analysing your data

You will want to be able to show your results so that someone will instantly be able to see what impact a leading question has had on the accuracy of eyewitness recall. So you should present your data using appropriately selected tables and graphs.

I'm outta here!
Don't forget, your participants have a right to withdraw from your experiment.

Apply it
Methods

The maths bit 2

1. Table 2 below shows the results of an experiment like the one on the left. How many participants were there in the leading question group? (*1 mark*)
2. How many participants were there in the non-leading question group? (*1 mark*)
3. Calculate the number of participants in the leading question group as a percentage of the total number of participants. (*1 mark*)
4. Is the data in Table 2 **quantitative** or **qualitative**? Explain your answer. (*2 marks*)
5. Explain *one* strength and *one* limitation of this type of data. (*2 marks + 2 marks*)
6. Draw a **bar chart** of the results in Table 2. Remember to label your axes accurately. (*3 marks*)
7. Explain what conclusions you can draw from the bar chart about the impact of leading questions on eyewitness testimony. (*2 marks*)

Table 2 Impact of leading question on accuracy of eyewitness recall.

Condition A: participants answered a leading question		Condition B: participants answered a non-leading question	
Yes	No	Yes	No
8	2	4	6

Revision summaries

Coding, capacity and duration of memory

Features of short-term memory and long-term memory.

Research on coding

Word recall of similar/dissimilar words
Baddeley: acoustic in STM, semantic in LTM.

Evaluation

Separate memory stores
Identified STM and LTM, supporting multi-store model.

Artificial stimuli
Word lists had no personal meaning.

Research on capacity

Digit span
Jacobs: 9.3 digits, 7.3 letters.

Span of memory and chunking
Miller: 7 ± 2 span, putting items together extends STM capacity.

Evaluation

A valid study
Later studies replicated findings (e.g. Bopp and Verhaeghen), so valid test of digit span.

Not so many chunks
Miller overestimated STM, only four chunks (Cowan).

Research on duration

Duration of STM
Peterson and Peterson: about 18 seconds without rehearsal.

Duration of LTM
Bahrick *et al.* (yearbooks): face recognition 90%, free recall 60% (15 years). Face recognition 70%, free recall 30% (48 years).

Evaluation

Meaningless stimuli in STM study
Petersons used consonant syllables, lacks external validity.

High external validity
Bahrick *et al.* used meaningful materials, better recall than studies with meaningless stimuli (Shepard).

The multi-store model of memory (MSM)

A representation of memory with three stores.

The theory

Sensory register
Modality-specific coding. Very brief duration (Sperling's study, less than 50 ms). High capacity.
Transfer to STM by attention.

Short-term memory (STM)
Mainly acoustic coding. Limited duration and capacity.
Transfer to LTM by rehearsal.

Long-term memory (LTM)
Mainly semantic coding. Unlimited duration and capacity.
Created through maintenance rehearsal.
Retrieval from LTM via STM.

Evaluation

Research support
Research shows STM and LTM use different coding and have different capacity.
Counterpoint – studies do not use everyday materials (e.g. consonant syllables), low validity.

More than one STM store
Studies of amnesia (e.g. KF) show different STMs for visual and auditory material.

Elaborative rehearsal
Transfer to LTM more about elaboration (meaningful processing) than maintenance rehearsal (Craik and Watkins).

Evaluation extra: Bygone model
Supporting evidence but also e.g. evidence of more than one type of STM and LTM.

Types of long-term memory

Three different long-term memory stores.

The theory

Episodic memory
Memory for events in our lives ('diary'). Time-stamped.

Semantic memory
Memory for knowledge of the world, like an encyclopaedia and dictionary (knowledge of words).

Procedural memory
Memory for automatic and often skilled behaviours. Unconscious recall.

Evaluation

Clinical evidence
Clive Wearing and HM had damaged episodic memories but semantic and procedural memories were relatively fine.
Counterpoint – clinical studies lack control of variables (e.g. memory before injury).

Conflicting neuroimaging evidence
Research links semantic to left prefrontal cortex and episodic to right (Buckner and Petersen), different in other studies (Tulving *et al.*).

Real-world application
Old-age memory loss improved by intervention to target episodic memory (Belleville *et al.*).

Evaluation extra: Same or different?
Tulving now suggests episodic may be specialised subcategory of semantic but Alzheimer's patients could form episodic not semantic memories (Hodges and Patterson).

The working memory model (WMM)

Dynamic processing in short-term memory.

The theory

Central executive (CE)
Supervisory, allocates subsystems to tasks, very limited capacity.

Phonological loop (PL)
Auditory information – phonological store and articulatory process (maintenance rehearsal). Coding = acoustic, capacity = 2 seconds of speech.

Visuo-spatial sketchpad (VSS)
Visual information – visual cache (store) and inner scribe (spatial arrangement). Coding = visual, capacity = 3 or 4 objects.

Episodic buffer (EB)
Integrates data from subsystems and records the order of events. Linked to LTM. Coding = flexible, capacity = 4 chunks.

Evaluation

Clinical evidence
KF had poor auditory memory but good visual memory. Damaged PL but VSS fine.
Counterpoint – KF may have had other impairments that affected his WM.

Dual-task performance
Difficult to do two visual tasks (or two verbal) at same time, but one visual and one verbal is OK (Baddeley *et al.*).

Nature of the central executive
Not well specified, needs to be more than 'attention'.

Evaluation extra: Validity of the model
Dual-task studies support WMM but are highly controlled, using artificial tasks (e.g. letter sequences).

Explanations for forgetting

One memory disrupts another.

Interference

Types of interference
Proactive – old memories disrupt new ones.
Retroactive – new memories disrupt old ones.

Effects of similarity
McGeoch and McDonald – six groups learned lists, similar words (synonyms) created more interference.

Explanation of the effects of similarity
PI (makes new information difficult to store) or RI (old information overwritten).

Evaluation

Real-world interference
Rugby players remembered less if played more games over a season (Baddeley and Hitch).
Counterpoint – interference unusual in everyday situations (e.g. similarity unusual).

Interference and cues
Interference effects are overcome using cues (Tulving and Psotka).

Support from drug studies
Taking *diazepam* after learning reduces interference and forgetting = retrograde facilitation (Coenen and van Luijtelaar).

Evaluation extra: Validity issues
Lab studies have high control but use artificial materials and unrealistic procedures.

Forgetting because of a lack of cues.

Retrieval failure

Encoding specificity principle
Tulving: cues most effective if present at coding and at retrieval.
Link between cues and material may be meaningful (e.g. 'STM') or meaningless (context and state).

Context-dependent forgetting
Godden and Baddeley (deep-sea divers) – recall better when external contexts matched.

State-dependent forgetting
Carter and Cassaday (antihistamine) – recall better when internal states matched.

Evaluation

Real-world application
Cues are weak but worth paying attention to as strategy for improving recall.

Research support
Wide range of support suggests this is main reason for forgetting (Eysenck and Keane).
Counterpoint – no forgetting unless contexts are very different, e.g. on land versus underwater (Baddeley).

Recall versus recognition
No context effects when memory assessed using recognition test (Godden and Baddeley).

Evaluation extra: Problems with the ESP
Research support for the principle but no independent measure of cue encoding.

Factors affecting eyewitness testimony

Post-event information and high arousal affect EWT.

Misleading information

Leading questions
Speed estimates affected by leading question e.g. smashed, contacted (Loftus and Palmer).

Why do leading questions affect EWT?
Response bias – no change to memory.
Substitution explanation – supported by report of seeing broken glass.

Post-event discussion (PED)
Co-witness discussion affects memories of event (Gabbert *et al.*).

Why does PED affect EWT?
Memory contamination – mix (mis)information from others.
Memory conformity – responses given for social approval.

Evaluation

Real-world application
Insights applied to police interviewing and expert witnesses.
Counterpoint – film clips in lab are less stressful than everyday life, no consequences. EWT more reliable.

Evidence against substitution
Central details not much affected by misleading information (Sutherland and Hayne).

Evidence challenging memory conformity
Post-event information on hair colour blended, supporting contamination (Skagerberg and Wright).

Evaluation extra: Demand characteristics
Lab environment enables control but answers in lab studies influenced by desire to be helpful (demand characteristics).

The effects of anxiety

Anxiety has a negative effect on recall
Johnson and Scott (weapon focus) – high-anxiety knife condition led to poorer recall.
Tunnel theory of memory.

Anxiety has a positive effect on recall
Yuille and Cutshall (shooting in gun shop) – high anxiety associated with better recall when witnessing real crime.

Explaining the contradictory findings
Deffenbacher reviewed 21 studies, Yerkes-Dodson inverted-U theory suggests both low and high anxiety lead to poor recall.

Evaluation

Unusualness not anxiety
Poor recall due to unusualness (chicken and handgun), not anxiety (Pickel).

Support for negative effects
London Dungeon – anxiety reduced accurate recall of an individual (Valentine and Mesout).

Support for positive effects
The most anxious eyewitness at bank robbery had the most accurate recall (Christianson and Hübinette).
Counterpoint – interviews were long after event, lacks control of confounding variables.

Evaluation extra: Problems with inverted-U theory
Explains contradictory findings but focuses just on physical arousal, ignores cognitive aspects of anxiety.

Improving the accuracy of eyewitness testimony

Fisher and Geiselman's method is based on psychological evidence.

The cognitive interview (CI)

1. Report everything
Include even unimportant details.

2. Reinstate the context
Picture the scene and recall how you felt.
Avoids context-dependent forgetting.

3. Reverse the order
Recall from the end and work backwards.
Disrupts expectations.

4. Change perspective
Put yourself in the shoes of someone else present.
Disrupts schema.

5. The enhanced cognitive interview (ECI)
Adds social dynamics, e.g. establishing eye contact.

Evaluation

Support for the effectiveness of the CI
CI produce 41% more accurate recall than standard interview (Köhnken *et al.*).
Counterpoint – CI also increases inaccurate information (Köhnken *et al.*), even more true for ECI.

Some elements may be more useful
Report everything and *reinstate the context* used together produced best recall (Milne and Bull).

The CI is time-consuming
It takes longer and needs special training (Kebbell and Wagstaff), full CI not realistic for police.

Evaluation extra: Variations of the CI
'Pick and mix' approach makes it hard to compare effectiveness but gives more flexibility.

Practice questions, answers and feedback

Question 1 Outline the procedure **and** findings of **one** study that has investigated the working memory model. (*4 marks*)

Morticia's answer *Baddeley et al. looked at dual-task performance. Participants had to do a verbal task and a visual task together. Their performance was the same as when they did the tasks separately. But when they did two visual tasks together, performance on both was poor. This shows there are separate subsystems processing verbal and visual information.*	Morticia has produced a detailed and accurate description of a relevant study. The procedure and findings are all well-explained as required by the question.
Luke's answer *The working memory model was investigated where participants were given two tasks, one task was a visual task and one was a verbal task. The results showed that these could be done because there are different parts to short-term memory. However, the study lacked ecological validity.*	Luke describes a study that is not identifiable without more detail/explanation of the tasks involved. There might have been some value in the answer if the subcomponents that would be needed to perform these tasks were mentioned. The last sentence does not add anything.
Vladimir's answer *There was a case study of KF who had brain damage. KF had some problems with his short-term memory but not his long-term memory. In fact it was only some aspects of STM that were damaged. KF could deal with visual input and remember this in the short term but could not deal with numbers. This supports the working memory model.*	Vladimir includes some relevant information – the idea that parts of STM can remain intact whilst others are damaged. However, there again are no named components of working memory here and the reference to KF not being able to 'deal with numbers' is vague. A weak answer.

Question 2 Briefly explain **one** strength of the working memory model. (*2 marks*)

Morticia's answer *One strength is that it is unlike the multi-store model which suggests short-term memory is a unitary store whereas the WMM shows how STM is divided into different subsystems such as the phonological loop and visuo-spatial sketchpad.*	Morticia gives an accurate and sufficiently detailed answer for a 2-mark question. She uses a reasoned comparison with the multi-store model.
Luke's answer *One strength is it goes into more complex detail on how short-term memory works than the multi-store model.*	Luke also makes a comparison with the multi-store model but his point needs further elaboration for the second mark (how is working memory 'more complex'?).
Vladimir's answer *It is a more detailed explanation than the multi-store model as it begins to show processes that may occur.*	Vladimir says nothing of any value. The first half of the sentence is not strong enough to earn credit and the second half is vague.

Question 3 What is meant by 'procedural memory'? Give an example. (*2 marks*)

Morticia's answer *Procedural memory is a type of long-term memory that stores actions and skills, such as riding a bike.*	Morticia provides a clear definition and a relevant example – just a perfect student!
Luke's answer *Procedural memory is a type of long-term memory that holds unlimited information and has knowledge of sequences, events, personal memories, lists and can be retrieved at a later date.*	Luke provides an inaccurate definition and there is no example.
Vladimir's answer *Procedural memory is a type of long-term memory which remembers how to do something such as how to ride a bike.*	Vladimir's example is fine but the definition that comes before it is not strong enough to be worth including. Vladimir should have referred to 'memory for actions/motor skills' rather than 'how to do something' which is a little vague.

Question 4 A woman is being questioned by a police officer about a heated argument she witnessed on an evening out with friends. The argument took place in a bar and ended with a violent assault. The police officer later discovered a knife behind the bar.
'Did you see the knife the attacker was holding?' asked the police officer.
'I'm not sure there was a knife – yes, there probably was,' replied the woman. 'I was so scared at the time it's hard to remember, and my friends and I have talked about what happened so many times since I'm almost not sure what I did see.'

Explain **two** factors that affect the accuracy of eyewitness testimony. Refer to the information above in your answer. (*4 marks*)

Morticia's answer *One factor is leading questions, which suggest a particular event/detail and change how a person remembers an experience. In the police officer's question, the use of the phrase 'the knife' is leading and suggests there was a knife. The second factor was the post-event discussion, so the woman has been affected by what her friends have been saying (they have talked about the incident 'many times') and this may change her memory.*	Morticia's answer is excellent (again). Both factors are clearly identified and explained, and there is good application/engagement with the stem.
Luke's answer *It was a violent assault so the woman probably felt anxious. Studies like Johnson and Scott show that such anxiety reduces the accuracy of a person's recall. Another factor that might affect accuracy would be the way the police officer put the question ('the knife' suggests there was a knife) – it was a leading question. Loftus and Palmer showed that such questions suggest an answer to a witness and also alter the person's memory, thus reducing accuracy.*	Luke starts well, with reference to anxiety as something that would affect accuracy, and provides support from psychological research. The second factor mentioned is the leading question, again supported with research. Both factors are clearly contextualised.
Vladimir's answer *The accuracy of EWT can be affected by misleading information and also by anxiety. Misleading information is information that may confuse a witness and anxiety can have a negative effect. The woman wasn't sure what she had seen so the police officer's question may have had a big effect.*	Vladimir has identified two factors (misleading information and anxiety) and tried to explain them but there is very little of value here. The attempted application is too weak to be considered (Vladimir would have to make it clear *how* the question was leading).

On this spread we look at some typical student answers to questions. The comments provided indicate what is good and bad in each answer. Learning how to produce effective question answers is a SKILL. Read pages 213–223 for guidance.

Question 5 Discuss interference and retrieval failure as explanations for forgetting. Refer to research studies in your answer. (*12 marks AS, 16 marks AL*)

Morticia's answer *Interference theory considers how forgetting in LTM occurs because one memory blocks another memory. The result may be a distortion of what you recall or a complete inability to recall the information.*

There are two types of interference. With proactive interference an older memory interferes with a newer one. For example, your teacher may find it difficult to recall the names of all the students in your class because she has learned so many names in the past.

The second kind of interference is retroactive interference, where a newer memory interferes with past learning. Taking the same example it could be that your teacher has difficulty remembering the names of some of her past students because she has learned many more student names.

In both cases the problem is that the memory is actually available (it is there in memory) it has just become inaccessible. This was demonstrated in a study by Tulving and Psotka who showed that the more word lists people had to remember the lower their recall rate fell. But at the end they were given cues to help them and they could remember many more words – this shows that the words were there but interference was preventing recall.

Research studies, especially lab experiments have demonstrated interference effects. For example, McGeoch and McDonald's study showing that the more similar two word lists were the more retroactive interference was created. Such support is good because lab studies are well controlled. However, such studies tend to use stimuli (such as word lists), which are not like what people do with their memories in everyday life. This means that lab studies make it look like interference is a more important explanation for forgetting than it really is in everyday life.

Nevertheless there are studies of interference in everyday life which show that interference does happen. Baddeley and Hitch studied recall in rugby players. They compared what the players could recall of their match scores over a season. Those players who played in more games had a lower percentage of scores, showing that interference was affecting what they could recall.

The other explanation of forgetting is retrieval failure which is also about accessibility rather than availability but is about cues – context or state-dependent. **(372 words)**

Morticia's essay is an AS response whereas Vladimir's is an A level response.

Morticia starts very well with a clear definition of interference, including the two types, and these are clarified through the use of examples. There is a really good description of relevant evidence here, too. Three studies are clear, accurate and concisely presented. There is a very limited descriptive account of retrieval failure at the end of the essay.

There is effective use of evidence. The findings from all three studies are clearly linked/related to the relevant explanation in each case, which is something that many students fail to do.

There are some methodological evaluations of the McGeoch and McDonald study and some attempt to relate these evaluations to the explanation more generally. That said, Morticia might have been better advised to focus her evaluation on the explanation itself rather than criticising the supporting evidence.

The description in this answer is slightly better than the evaluation which is OK for an AS response. This is a reasonable answer but not a good one because of the poor coverage of cue retrieval.

Vladimir's answer *There are several explanations for forgetting such as trace decay, displacement, interference and retrieval failure.*

Interference theory suggests that the reason why people forget things is because two memories interfere with each other. There is proactive interference and retroactive interference. In the case of proactive interference something you learned first interferes with something you learned later. In retroactive it is the opposite. A study to support the interference theory was done by McGeoch. He gave participants word lists to be learned and showed that the new lists had an effect on being able to recall the older lists. This supports retroactive interference.

Another explanation for forgetting is retrieval failure. What happens is that a memory that is in your memory can't be recalled because you don't have the cues to help you recall it. There are two types of retrieval failure of forgetting. These are context-dependent and state-dependent. In the case of context-dependent forgetting this means that people recall things better if they learn and recall them in the same place. In mood-dependent forgetting this means mood rather than context is important, for example if you are sad or drunk. A study that supports this is the study of underwater divers who learned word lists on land or underwater and then recalled them on land or underwater. The divers had the best recall if they learned them underwater and later recalled them underwater or if they learned them on land and later recalled them on land.

There are several issues surrounding studies into memory and forgetting. One issue is the lack of validity as the studies often use artificial stimuli. This means the findings cannot be generalised because they are not like everyday life. Also the studies often had small samples and this makes the studies difficult to generalise to other people. In some studies only men were involved so that makes generalisation difficult. **(315 words)**

Vladimir's answer does not start too promisingly – the explanation of interference is not very clear (note the use of 'interfere' in the definition – don't define a term using the same word) and neither is the explanation of the two types clear, though it is just about accurate.

The description of retrieval failure is better with reference to absence of cues as well as context-dependent and state-dependent forms of forgetting. The point about the influence of mood is not properly developed though. There is some accurate descriptive detail of two studies (the divers study is better explained).

Apart from a brief reference to retroactive interference at the end of the first study, there is very little 'use of evidence' which is an evaluation skill. Similarly, the evaluation points at the end are focused on the studies rather than the explanations and would receive very little evaluation credit.

This is another reasonable answer but less successful than Morticia's. There is a much better attempt to consider both explanations, as required by the question but the evaluation has really let Vladimir down. It is important to practise writing detailed descriptions that are the right length for the time allowed.

Multiple-choice questions

Coding, capacity and duration of memory

1. 'Coding is acoustic, capacity is limited and duration is about 18 seconds.' Which memory store is being described?
   (a) Sensory register.
   (b) Long-term memory.
   (c) Short-term memory.
   (d) Procedural memory.

2. 'Coding' refers to what?
   (a) The form in which information is stored.
   (b) The length of time information is stored for.
   (c) The amount of information that can be stored in memory at any one time.
   (d) The transfer of information from one memory store to another.

3. Which of these statements best describes LTM?
   (a) Memory store with unlimited capacity and acoustic coding.
   (b) Permanent memory store, unlimited capacity, semantic coding.
   (c) Temporary memory store, semantic coding.
   (d) Memory store with semantic coding and limited capacity.

4. Peterson and Peterson investigated:
   (a) The capacity of STM.
   (b) The duration of STM.
   (c) The coding of STM.
   (d) The duration of LTM.

The multi-store model of memory

1. Which of the following are features of the sensory register?
   (a) It has a capacity of seven items, plus or minus two.
   (b) Memories in the register can last up to a lifetime.
   (c) The capacity is very large.
   (d) Coding is semantic.

2. The multi-store model describes which of the following memory stores?
   (a) Short-term memory and long-term memory only.
   (b) Sensory register, long-term memory and short-term memory.
   (c) Episodic memory, semantic memory and procedural memory.
   (d) Good memory and poor memory.

3. 'The process by which information is held in STM by repeating it over and over again'. What is being described here?
   (a) Retrieval.
   (b) Consolidation.
   (c) Elaborative rehearsal.
   (d) Maintenance rehearsal.

4. The case of KF contradicts the MSM because it shows that:
   (a) STM and LTM are separate.
   (b) There is more than one STM.
   (c) There is more than one LTM.
   (d) There is more than one type of rehearsal.

Types of long-term memory

1. Which of the following are most likely to be stored in episodic long-term memory?
   (a) Memories for facts such as '*Frozen* is a film'.
   (b) Memories of events that have happened to us involving other people and places.
   (c) Our knowledge of what words mean.
   (d) Memories of our skilled actions, such as being able to play the guitar.

2. HM and Clive Wearing had problems with:
   (a) Episodic memory.
   (b) Semantic memory.
   (c) Procedural memory.
   (d) Procedural and episodic memory.

3. 'Time-stamped and needs to be consciously searched' is a description of?
   (a) Short-term memory.
   (b) Procedural memory.
   (c) Episodic memory.
   (d) Semantic memory.

4. Which specific area of the brain is important in recalling both semantic and episodic memories?
   (a) The hippocampus.
   (b) The cerebral cortex.
   (c) The prefrontal cortex.
   (d) The amygdala.

The working memory model

1. 'Brings together material from other subsystems into a single memory' is a description of which component of the working memory model?
   (a) Central executive.
   (b) Episodic buffer.
   (c) Phonological loop.
   (d) Visuo-spatial sketchpad.

2. The case study of KF supports the WMM because he had:
   (a) A poor STM but intact LTM.
   (b) Poor STM for verbal material but near-normal STM for visual information.
   (c) A near-normal STM but he could not recall events from long ago.
   (d) No ability to learn new skills.

3. The phonological loop of working memory is divided into two elements. These are:
   (a) The central executive and long-term memory.
   (b) The phonological store and the articulatory process.
   (c) The visuo-spatial sketchpad and the episodic buffer.
   (d) Short-term memory and long-term memory.

4. Which component of the WMM links working memory with LTM?
   (a) Central executive.
   (b) Episodic buffer.
   (c) Phonological loop.
   (d) Visuo-spatial sketchpad.

Explanations for forgetting: Interference

1. Interference is an explanation for forgetting from which memory store?
   (a) Sensory register.
   (b) Iconic memory.
   (c) Echoic memory.
   (d) Long-term memory.

2. Proactive interference occurs when:
   (a) Newer memories cause forgetting of older ones.
   (b) Memories fade over time.
   (c) Older memories cause forgetting of newer ones.
   (d) We don't have the right information to trigger our memory.

3. Which of the following situations makes interference *less* likely?
   (a) When two instances of learning are similar.
   (b) When two instances of learning are meaningful.
   (c) When two instances of learning are different.
   (d) When the time between two instances of learning is short.

4. Which of the following is the best example of retroactive interference?
   (a) A student revises for her Spanish exam, then her French exam and has trouble recalling her Spanish.
   (b) A student revises for her Spanish exam, then her French exam and has trouble recalling her French.
   (c) You have a new mobile phone number but keep telling people your old one.
   (d) You accidentally call your new boyfriend or girlfriend by your old one's name.

Explanations for forgetting: Retrieval failure

1. Retrieval failure occurs when:
   (a) Information disappears from memory and is no longer available.
   (b) Information was never encoded in long-term memory in the first place.
   (c) We don't have the right cues to recall a memory.
   (d) We have a lot of relevant cues and we pay attention to them.

2. Being drunk when you learn something and when you recall it is an example of which kind of cue?
   (a) State-dependent.
   (b) Context-dependent.
   (c) Mood-dependent.
   (d) Memory-dependent.

3. Godden and Baddeley found lower levels of recall when:
   (a) Learning and recall both took place underwater.
   (b) Learning and recall both took place on land.
   (c) Recall took place only a short time after learning.
   (d) Learning took place on land and recall took place underwater.

4. Tulving's encoding specificity principle states that forgetting is likely when:
   (a) A cue present when we learn information is also present when we try to retrieve the information.
   (b) A cue present when we learn information is absent when we try to retrieve the information.
   (c) Retrieving information happens very soon after we learn it.
   (d) Two sets of information are very different.

Factors affecting the accuracy of eyewitness testimony: Misleading information

1. Which of the following statements is the best definition of eyewitness testimony?
   (a) Our ability to remember such things as facts and figures.
   (b) How people remember the details of events they have observed themselves, such as crimes and accidents.
   (c) Our memories for people's names and faces.
   (d) Memories that last for weeks, months or even years.

2. The study by Skagerberg and Wright supported:
   (a) Substitution effect.
   (b) Response-bias.
   (c) Memory contamination.
   (d) Memory conformity.

3. Which of the following sequences of verbs did Loftus and Palmer (1974) use in their study?
   (a) Contacted, pranged, hit, collided, smashed.
   (b) Touched, bumped, hit, collided, smashed.
   (c) Contacted, bumped, hit, collided, smashed.
   (d) Contacted, bumped, hit, walloped, smashed.

4. The study by Gabbert *et al.* provided evidence of:
   (a) Memory conformity.
   (b) Memory contamination.
   (c) Memory substitution.
   (d) The effect of leading questions.

Factors affecting the accuracy of eyewitness testimony: Anxiety

1. What did Johnson and Scott investigate?
   (a) EWT for natural disasters.
   (b) The inverted-U theory.
   (c) The weapon focus effect.
   (d) The Labyrinth of Horror.

2. The tunnel theory of the relationship between EWT and anxiety suggests that:
   (a) We are able to recall the details of many aspects of an event.
   (b) People have enhanced memory for central events such as a weapon.
   (c) A high level of anxiety is related to a high level of recall.
   (d) Most people experience anxiety when witnessing crimes and accidents.

3. The study by Valentine and Mesout found that:
   (a) High levels of anxiety are associated with high levels of accurate recall.
   (b) High levels of anxiety are associated with low levels of accurate recall.
   (c) Anxiety and accurate recall are not related.
   (d) Yuille and Cutshall's findings were correct.

4. A limitation of Christianson and Hübinette's study is:
   (a) It took place in a laboratory.
   (b) They failed to measure anxiety.
   (c) Interviews took place long after the event.
   (d) Recall was only 25% accurate.

Improving the accuracy of eyewitness testimony: Cognitive interview

1. Two of the main techniques of the cognitive interview are:
   (a) Change perspective and reinstate the context.
   (b) Change perspective and change your opinion.
   (c) Report everything and use retrieval cues.
   (d) Reverse the order and answer the interviewer's questions.

2. The enhanced cognitive interview uses the four techniques of the CI. It also:
   (a) Is a lot quicker.
   (b) Is more widely used.
   (c) Gets the witness to speak slowly.
   (d) Is nearly as effective as the CI.

3. One of the main techniques of the CI is based on:
   (a) Research into context-dependent forgetting.
   (b) Miller's research into the capacity of STM.
   (c) The multi-store model of memory.
   (d) Baddeley's research into coding in memory.

4. A significant limitation of the CI is:
   (a) It is time-consuming for the police to use.
   (b) It is less effective than the standard police interview.
   (c) The findings from Köhnken *et al.*'s meta-analysis.
   (d) It is not supported by the bulk of psychological research into how human memory works.

MCQ answers

Coding, capacity and duration of memory 1C, 2A, 3B, 4B
The multi-store model of memory 1C, 2B, 3D, 4B
Types of long-term memory 1B, 2A, 3C, 4C
The working memory model 1B, 2B, 3B, 4B
Explanations for forgetting: Interference 1D, 2C, 3C, 4A
Explanations for forgetting: Retrieval failure 1C, 2A, 3D, 4B
Factors affecting the accuracy of eyewitness testimony: Misleading information 1B, 2C, 3C, 4A
Factors affecting the accuracy of eyewitness testimony: Anxiety 1C, 2B, 3B, 4C
Improving the accuracy of eyewitness testimony: Cognitive interview 1A, 2C, 3A, 4A

Chapter 3 Attachment

From Étude Réaliste *by AC Swinburne*

A baby's eyes, ere speech begin,
Ere lips learn words or sighs,
Bless all things bright enough to win
A baby's eyes.

Love, while the sweet thing laughs and lies,
And sleep flows out and in,
Sees perfect in them Paradise.

Their glance might cast out pain and sin,
Their speech make dumb the wise,
By mute glad godhead felt within
A baby's eyes.

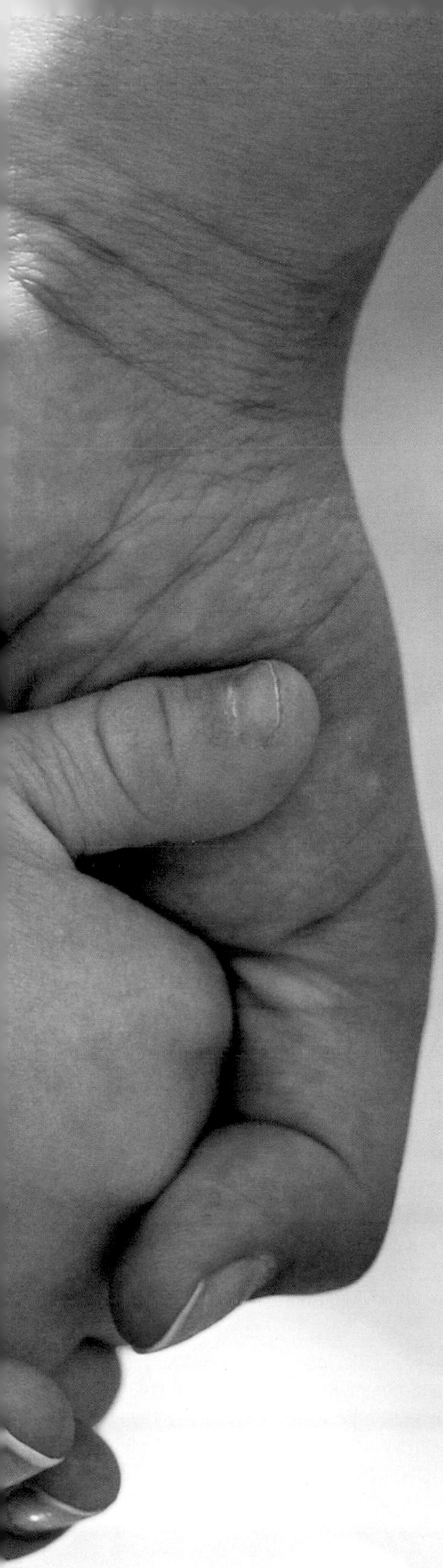

Contents

Caregiver–infant interactions

The specification says...

Caregiver–infant interactions in humans: reciprocity and interactional synchrony.

Attachment begins with the interactions between babies and their caregivers. It is the responsiveness of the caregiver to the baby's signals that has profound effects.

Key terms

Reciprocity A description of how two people interact. Caregiver–infant interaction is reciprocal in that both caregiver and baby respond to each other's signals and each elicits a response from the other.

Interactional synchrony Caregiver and baby reflect both the actions and emotions of the other *and* do this in a co-ordinated (synchronised) way.

What is an attachment?

An **attachment** can be defined as a close two-way emotional bond between two individuals in which each individual sees the other as essential for their own emotional security.

Attachment in humans takes a few months to develop. We can recognise an attachment when people display the following behaviours:

- Proximity – people try to stay physically close to their attachment figure.
- Separation distress – people show signs of anxiety when an attachment figure leaves their presence.
- Secure-base behaviour – even when we are independent of our attachment figures we tend to make regular contact with them. Babies display secure-base behaviour when they regularly return to their attachment figure while playing.

The look of love – a two-way emotional bond where both individuals gain emotional security.

Caregiver–infant interactions

From the start babies have meaningful social interactions with their carers. Psychologists believe that these interactions have important functions for the child's social development. In particular good quality early social interactions are associated with the successful development of attachments between babies and their caregiver(s).

Reciprocity

From birth babies and their mothers (or other caregivers) spend a lot of time in intense and highly pleasurable interaction. An interaction is said to show **reciprocity** when each person responds to the other and elicits a response from them. For example, a caregiver might respond to his baby's smile by saying something and then this in turn elicits a response from his baby. This kind of reciprocal interaction is also sometimes called 'turn-taking'. It is an essential part of any conversation, otherwise people talk over each other.

Alert phases Babies have periodic 'alert phases' in which they signal (e.g. making eye contact) that they are ready for a spell of interaction. Research shows that mothers typically pick up on and respond to their baby's alertness around two-thirds of the time (Feldman and Eidelman 2007), although this varies according to the skill of the mother and external factors such as stress (Finegood *et al.* 2016).

From around three months this interaction tends to become increasingly frequent and involves both mother and baby paying close attention to each other's verbal signals and facial expressions (Feldman 2007).

Active involvement Traditional views of childhood have portrayed babies in a passive role, receiving care from an adult. However, it seems that babies as well as caregivers actually take quite an active role. Both caregiver and baby can initiate interactions and they appear to take turns in doing so. T. Berry Brazelton *et al.* (1975) described this interaction as a 'dance' because it is just like a couple's dance where each partner responds to the other person's moves.

Interactional synchrony

You might have watched the sport of synchronised swimming in which pairs of swimmers perform the same actions in unison (see picture on facing page). Two people are said to be 'synchronised' when they carry out the same action simultaneously. **Interactional synchrony** can thus be defined as 'the temporal co-ordination of micro-level social behaviour' (Feldman 2007). It takes place when caregiver and baby interact in such a way that their actions and emotions mirror the other.

Synchrony begins Andrew Meltzoff and Keith Moore (1977) observed the beginnings of interactional synchrony in babies as young as two weeks old. An adult displayed one of three facial expressions or one of three distinctive gestures. The baby's response was filmed and labelled by independent observers. Babies' expression and gestures were more likely to mirror those of the adults more than chance would predict i.e. there was a significant association.

Importance for attachment It is believed that interactional synchrony is important for the development of caregiver–infant attachment. Russell Isabella *et al.* (1989) observed 30 mothers and babies together and assessed the degree of synchrony. The researchers also assessed the quality of mother–baby attachment. They found that high levels of synchrony were associated with better quality mother–baby attachment (e.g. the emotional intensity of the relationship).

Apply it Concepts — Reciprocity with Rudy

Psychologists John and Mary are relaxing with their baby son, Rudy. One day John asks Mary a question but she is focused on Rudy. Mary replies, 'Sorry darling, give me a minute. Rudy's just entered an alert phase and I want to establish some reciprocity.'

Question

Explain what Mary means by this and why it might be important to respond to Rudy's signals.

Practical activity on page 96

Evaluation

Filmed observations

One strength of the research on this topic is that caregiver–infant interactions are usually filmed in a laboratory.

This means that other activity, that might distract a baby, can be controlled. Also, using films means that observations can be recorded and analysed later. Therefore it is unlikely that researchers will miss seeing key behaviours. Furthermore having filmed interactions means that more than one observer can record data and establish the **inter-rater reliability** of observations. Finally, babies don't know they are being observed, so their behaviour does not change in response to observation (this is generally the main problem for **overt observations**).

Therefore the data collected in such research should have good **reliability** and **validity**.

Difficulty observing babies

One limitation of research into caregiver–infant interaction is that it is hard to interpret a baby's behaviour.

Young babies lack co-ordination and much of their bodies are almost immobile. The movements being observed are just small hand movements or subtle changes in expression. It is difficult to be sure, for example, whether a baby is smiling or just passing wind. It is also difficult to determine what is taking place from the baby's perspective. For example, we cannot know whether a movement such as a hand twitch is random or triggered by something the caregiver has done.

This means we cannot be certain that the behaviours seen in caregiver–infant interactions have a special meaning.

Developmental importance

A further limitation is that simply observing a behaviour does not tell us its developmental importance.

Ruth Feldman (2012) points out that ideas like synchrony (and by implication reciprocity) simply give names to patterns of observable caregiver and baby behaviours. These are robust phenomena in the sense that they can be reliably observed, but they still may not be particularly useful in understanding child development as it does not tell us the purpose of these behaviours.

This means that we cannot be certain from observational research alone that reciprocity and synchrony are important for a child's development.

Counterpoint There is evidence from other lines of research to suggest that early interactions are important. For example Isabella *et al.* (1989) found that achievement of interactional synchrony predicted the development of a good quality attachment.

This means that, on balance, caregiver–infant interaction is probably important in development.

Evaluation eXtra

Practical value versus ethics

Research into early caregiver–infant interaction has practical applications in parenting skills training. For example, Rebecca Crotwell *et al.* (2013) found that a 10-minute Parent–Child Interaction Therapy (PCIT) improved interactional synchrony in 20 low-income mothers and their pre-school children.

On the other hand research into caregiver–infant interaction is **socially sensitive** because it can be used to argue that when a mother returns to work soon after having a baby this may risk damaging their baby's development.

Consider: *Does the practical value outweigh the social sensitivity of the research? How valuable is this research?*

Sports such as diving and swimming can involve synchronisation.

Interactional synchrony involves a bit more than just performing in unison – each partner is responding to the other's cues.

Apply it Methods — Observations

Much of the research into caregiver–infant interaction has been carried out by observation. For example Meltzoff and Moore observed caregiver–infant interaction in very young babies.

Questions

1. Observations are often recorded. Explain why this could increase the validity of the research. (*2 marks*)
2. Explain how the reliability of the observations could be checked. (*2 marks*)
3. What would be the benefit of conducting this research in a laboratory? (*2 marks*)

Apply it Concepts — Helping Helga

Research into caregiver–infant interaction has therapeutic applications. Helga is a first-time mother who is unemployed and without permanent accommodation. She is struggling to bond with her three-month-old baby, Wilma. Helga attends a clinic where a psychologist notices that Helga is experiencing severe stress. The psychologist explores the reason for this.

Question

Referring to research into caregiver–infant interaction, suggest how Helga's psychologist might explain her difficulties.

Check it

1. Explain what is meant by 'interactional synchrony'. *[2 marks]*
2. Outline research into caregiver–infant interactions. *[4 marks]*
3. Outline **one** strength **and one** limitation of research into caregiver–infant interactions. *[6 marks]*
4. Describe **and** evaluate research into caregiver–infant interactions. *[12 marks AS, 16 marks A4]*

S[redacted]haffer'[redacted]stages[redacted]f a[redacted]ta[redacted]hment

The specification says...

Stages of attachment as identified by Schaffer. Multiple attachments.

Various theorists have identified stages in the development of attachments, but we are concerned with those that emerged from a study by Schaffer and Emerson carried out in the 1960s in Glasgow, and the stages they identified.

Key terms

Stages of attachment Many developmental theories identify a sequence of qualitatively different behaviours linked to specific ages. In the case of 'stages of attachment' qualitatively different infant (baby) behaviours are linked to specific ages, and all babies go through them in the same order.

Multiple attachments Attachments to two or more people. Most babies appear to develop multiple attachments once they have formed one strong attachment to one of their carers.

Multiple attachments.

Age at onset of specific attachments, of attachment-to-mother, and fear-of-strangers

Age in weeks	Specific attachments *N*	Attachment-to-mother *N*	Fear-of-strangers *N*
21–24	4	3	0
25–28	15	13	10
29–32	17	18	15
33–36	7	8	19
37–40	7	8	7
41–44	4	4	4
45–48	3	3	2
49–52	1	1	0
53–78	2	2	3
Total	60	60	60

Age of onset of first specific attachment (Schaffer and Emerson 1964).

Stages of attachment

Rudolf Schaffer and Peggy Emerson (1964) studied the **attachment** behaviours of babies (see details of the study in the second box on this page). Their findings led them to develop an account of how attachment behaviours change as a baby gets older. They proposed that there were four identifiable **stages of attachment**, a sequence which is observed in all babies.

Stage 1: Asocial stage

In a baby's first few weeks of life its observable behaviour towards humans and inanimate objects is fairly similar – hence the term 'asocial'. However, Schaffer and Emerson did not believe that it is entirely asocial because even at this stage babies show signs that they prefer to be with other people. Babies also tend to show a preference for the company of familiar people and are more easily comforted by them. At this stage the baby is forming bonds with certain people and these form the basis of later attachments.

Stage 2: Indiscriminate attachment

From 2 to 7 months babies start to display more obvious and observable social behaviours. They now show a clear preference for being with other humans rather than inanimate objects. They also recognise and prefer the company of familiar people. However, at this stage babies usually accept cuddles and comfort from any person – hence the term 'indiscriminate'. They do not usually show **separation anxiety** when caregivers leave their presence or **stranger anxiety** in the presence of unfamiliar people.

Stage 3: Specific attachment

From around 7 months the majority of babies start to display the classic signs of attachment towards one particular person. These signs include **anxiety** directed towards strangers (stranger anxiety), especially when their attachment figure is absent, and anxiety when separated from their attachment figure (separation anxiety).

At this point the baby is said to have formed a specific attachment. This person with whom the attachment is formed is called the **primary attachment figure**. This person is not necessarily the individual the child spends most time with but the one who offers the most interaction and responds to the baby's 'signals' with the most skill. This is the baby's mother in 65% of cases.

Stage 4: Multiple attachments

Shortly after babies start to show attachment behaviour (e.g. stranger anxiety and separation anxiety) towards one person they usually extend this behaviour to **multiple attachments** with other people with whom they regularly spend time. These relationships are called **secondary attachments**. Schaffer and Emerson observed that 29% of the children formed secondary attachments within a month of forming a primary (specific) attachment. By the age of one year the majority of babies had developed multiple attachments.

Schaffer and Emerson's research

Schaffer and Emerson (1964) based their stage theory (above) on an observational study of the formation of early infant–adult attachments. The specification does not require that you know the procedural details of the study but they are useful background which may help your understanding.

Procedure The study involved 60 babies – 31 boys and 29 girls. All were from Glasgow and the majority were from skilled working-class families. Researchers visited babies and mothers in their own homes every month for the first year and again at 18 months.

The researchers asked the mothers questions about the kind of protest their babies showed in seven everyday separations, e.g. adult leaving the room (a measure of separation anxiety). This was designed to measure the babies' attachment. The researchers also assessed stranger anxiety – the babies' anxiety response to unfamiliar people.

Findings The data about attachments is shown in the table on the left. Schaffer and Emerson identified four distinct stages in the development of infant attachment behaviour. These make up their stage theory (above).

Evaluation

Good external validity

One strength of Schaffer and Emerson's research is that it has good **external validity**.

Most of the observations (though not stranger anxiety) were made by parents during ordinary activities and reported to the researchers. The alternative would have been to have researchers present to record observations. This might have distracted the babies or made them feel more anxious.

This means it is highly likely that the participants behaved naturally while being observed.

Counterpoint On the other hand there are issues with asking the mothers to be the 'observers'. They were unlikely to be objective observers. They might have been biased in terms of what they noticed and what they reported, for example they might not have noticed when their baby was showing signs of anxiety or they may have misremembered it.

This means that even if babies behaved naturally their behaviour may not have been accurately recorded.

Poor evidence for the asocial stage

One limitation of Schaffer and Emerson's stages is the validity of the measures they used to assess attachment in the asocial stage.

Young babies have poor co-ordination and are fairly immobile. If babies less than two months old felt anxiety in everyday situations they might have displayed this in quite subtle, hard-to-observe ways. This made it difficult for mothers to observe and report back to researchers on signs of anxiety and attachment in this age group.

This means that the babies may actually be quite social but, because of flawed methods, they appear to be asocial.

Real-world application

Another strength of Schaffer and Emerson's stages is that they have practical application in day care (where babies are cared for outside of their home by a non-family adult).

In the asocial and indiscriminate attachment stages day care is likely to be straightforward as babies can be comforted by any skilled adult. However, Schaffer and Emerson's research tells us that day care, especially *starting* day care with an unfamiliar adult, may be problematic during the specific attachment stage.

This means that parents' use of day care can be planned using Schaffer and Emerson's stages.

Evaluation eXtra

Generalisability

On the positive side Schaffer and Emerson based their stage account on a large-scale study with some good design features.

On the other hand, they only looked at one sample which had unique features in terms of the cultural and historical context – 1960s working-class Glasgow. In other cultures, for example **collectivist cultures**, multiple attachments from a very early age are more the norm (van IJzendoorn 1993).

Consider: *On balance, how likely is it that Schaffer and Emerson's stages generalise to other populations?*

Study tip

Note how, throughout this book, we have endeavoured to close each evaluation with a summary sentence 'This means that ...' or 'This shows that ...' It is important to make your critical point crystal clear.

Babies and their carers behave more naturally when observed in their own homes.

Apply it Concepts: Tam's separation anxiety

Jock and Morag live with their son Tam and Morag's mother, who looks after little Tam while Jock and Morag both work. Despite the fact that Morag works, she makes a special effort to sit and play with Tam when she gets home.

When Tam got to the age of 7 months old he began to get quite upset when his parents left for work. His grandmother tried to distract him and give him lots of attention.

Questions

1. Referring to Schaffer and Emerson's stages of attachment, how would you explain to Jock and Morag why Tam's behaviour has changed?
2. Based on Schaffer and Emerson's stages, what could you advise them to expect from Tam's attachment behaviour in the future?

Apply it Methods: Observations

Schaffer and Emerson used a mix of self-report and observation in their study. The observations took place in babies' own homes – observers noted how the babies responded to their presence (stranger anxiety).

Questions

1. In what way is this study a **naturalistic observation**? (*2 marks*)
2. In what way could this study be described as an **overt observation**? (*2 marks*)
3. In what way could this study be described as a **participant observation**? (*2 marks*)
4. Data on separation anxiety was collected from the mothers themselves. In what way may this have challenged the **validity** of the data collected? (*2 marks*)

Check it

1. Outline stages of attachment as identified by Schaffer. *[4 marks]*
2. Outline **one** strength of Schaffer's stages of attachment. *[4 marks]*
3. Explain what is meant by 'multiple attachments'. *[3 marks]*
4. Evaluate research into multiple attachments. *[4 marks]*
5. Describe **and** evaluate Schaffer's stages of attachment. *[12 marks AS, 16 marks AL]*

The role of the father

The specification says...

The role of the father.

Fathers may be important attachment figures. Furthermore it has been suggested that they have distinctive roles in parenting.

Key term

Father In attachment research the father is anyone who takes on the role of the main male caregiver. This can be but is not necessarily the biological father.

Caregiver versus attachment figure

There is a difference between a primary caregiver and a primary attachment figure. A primary caregiver is the person who spends most time with a baby, caring for its needs. A primary attachment figure is the person to whom the baby has the strongest attachment. Often the same person fulfils the two roles but not always.

Apply it
Concepts — A lifestyle choice

Jacob and Kalwant have a decision to make. Their baby is four weeks old. Kalwant would really like to be a full-time mother but she earns a lot more than Jacob and they fear they will not manage financially if she is the stay-at-home parent. The alternative is for Jacob to take on the role of primary caregiver.

Question

Referring to research into fathers' attachment, what could you tell Jacob and Kalwant about Jacob's suitability as primary caregiver?

Attachment to a father may be more about play than 'nurturing' (emotional care) but this makes an important contribution to development.

The role of the father

Most attachment research has focused on mother and baby **attachment**, and the role of the **father** in the development of attachment has often been neglected. However, there is research on the specific roles that fathers play in development. (Note that a 'father' does not specially refer to a baby's biological male parent – it refers to a child's closest male caregiver. So this is about what men may contribute as caregivers.)

Attachment to fathers

Perhaps the most basic question about the role of fathers is whether babies actually attach to them and, if so, when. Available evidence suggests that fathers are much less likely to become babies' first attachment figure compared to mothers.

For example, on the previous spread we looked at stages of attachment based on research by Rudolf Schaffer and Peggy Emerson (1964). They found that the majority of babies first became attached to their mother at around 7 months. In only 3% of cases the father was the first sole object of attachment. In 27% of cases the father was the joint first object of attachment with the mother.

However, it appears that most fathers go on to become important attachment figures. 75% of the babies studied by Schaffer and Emerson formed an attachment with their father by the age of 18 months. This was determined by the fact that the babies protested when their father walked away – a sign of attachment.

Distinctive role for fathers

A different research question is whether attachment to fathers holds some specific value in a child's development and, if so, whether it plays a different role in a child's development from attachment to the mother. In other words, do caregiving men make a unique contribution to early development?

Klaus Grossmann *et al.* (2002) carried out a **longitudinal study** where babies' attachments were studied until they were into their teens. The researchers looked at both parents' behaviour and its relationship to the quality of their baby's later attachments to other people. Quality of a baby's attachment with mothers but not fathers was related to attachments in adolescence. This suggests that attachment to fathers is less important than attachment to mothers.

However, Grossmann *et al.* also found that the quality of fathers' play with babies was related to the quality of adolescent attachments. This suggests that fathers have a different role from mothers – one that is more to do with play and stimulation, and less to do with emotional development.

Fathers as primary attachment figures

A distinction is made between primary and secondary attachment figures. On the previous spread we described the first specific attachment as a **primary attachment** and later attachments (in stage 4) as **secondary attachments**. But there is more to primary attachment than being first – a baby's primary attachment has special emotional significance. A baby's relationship with their primary attachment figure forms the basis of all later close emotional relationships.

Interestingly there is some evidence to suggest that when fathers do take on the role of primary caregiver they are able to adopt the emotional role more typically associated with mothers.

For example, in one study Tiffany Field (1978) filmed 4-month-old babies in face-to-face interaction with primary caregiver mothers, secondary caregiver fathers and primary caregiver fathers. Primary caregiver fathers, like primary caregiver mothers, spent more time smiling, imitating and holding babies than the secondary caregiver fathers. Smiling, imitating and holding babies are all part of reciprocity and interactional synchrony which, as we saw on page 75, are part of the process of attachment formation (see research by Isabella *et al.* 1989).

So it seems that fathers have the potential to be the more emotion-focused primary attachment figure – they can provide the responsiveness required for a close emotional attachment but perhaps only express this when given the role of primary caregiver.

Heteronormativity

This line of research focusing on the role of the father in infant development is based on the assumption that babies have two opposite-gender parents. This is of course not always the case. Although the research reported here concerns fathers in two-parent heterosexual partnerships there is no suggestion from respectable psychologists that having a single parent or two san gender parents has any negative impact on children's developmer

:valuation

:onfusion over research questions

ne limitation of research into the role of fathers is lack of clarity over the uestion being asked.

The question, 'What is the role of the father?' in the context of attachment ; much more complicated than it sounds. Some researchers attempting to nswer this question actually want to understand the role of fathers as secondary ttachment figures. But others are more concerned with fathers as a rimary attachment figure. The former have tended to see fathers s behaving differently from mothers and having a distinct role. The atter have found that fathers can take on a 'maternal' role.

This makes it difficult to offer a simple answer as to the 'role of the ather'. It really depends what specific role is being discussed.

:onflicting evidence

further limitation of research into the role of fathers is that findings vary ccording to the methodology used.

Longitudinal studies such as that of Grossmann *et al.* (see facing page) have uggested that fathers as secondary attachment figures have an important and istinct role in their children's development, involving play and stimulation. owever, if fathers have a distinctive and important role we would expect that hildren growing up in single-mother and lesbian-parent families would turn ut in some way different from those in two-parent heterosexual families. In act studies (e.g. McCallum and Golombok 2004) consistently show that these hildren do not develop differently from children in two-parent heterosexual amilies.

This means that the question as to whether fathers have a distinctive role emains unanswered.

Counterpoint These lines of research may not in fact be in conflict. It could be that fathers typically take on distinctive roles in two-parent heterosexual families, but that parents in single-mother and lesbian-parent families simply adapt to accommodate the role played by fathers.

This means that the question of a distinctive role for fathers is clear after all. When present, fathers tend to adopt a distinctive role, but families can adapt to not having a father.

?eal-world application

ne strength of research into the role of the father is that it can be used to offer dvice to parents.

Parents and prospective parents sometimes agonise over decisions like vho should take on the primary caregiver role. For some this can even mean orrying about whether to have children at all. Mothers may feel pressured) stay at home because of stereotypical views of mothers' and fathers' roles. qually, fathers may be pressured to focus on work rather than parenting. In ome families this may not be economically the best solution. Research into ie role of the father can be used to offer reassuring advice to parents. For xample, heterosexual parents can be informed that fathers are quite capable of ecoming **primary attachment figures**. Also lesbian-parent and single-mother amilies can be informed that not having a father around does not affect a child's evelopment.

This means that parental anxiety about the role of fathers can be reduced.

:valuation eXtra

?ias in this research

reconceptions about how fathers do or should behave can be created y stereotypical accounts and images of parenting roles and behaviour, ›r example those used in advertising. These stereotypes (e.g. fathers are ot primary caregivers, fathers are stricter, etc.) may cause unintentional bserver bias whereby observers 'see' what they expect to see rather ıan recording objective reality.

onsider: *To what extent do you think this might have been a roblem for the studies discussed on this spread?*

Who says fathers can't be primary caregivers?

Apply it Methods — Observational research

A group of students decide they would like to conduct some research on the differences between mothers and fathers as attachment figures. They decide to go to a soft-play centre near where they live and observe mothers and fathers with their babies.

Questions

1. Name *two* **behavioural categories** the students might use to record parental behaviour. Explain how each category might be relevant to assessing attachment behaviour (e.g. emotional responses). (*2 marks + 2 marks*)
2. Identify and explain *two* ethical issues that the students should think about in relation to their planned research. (*2 marks + 2 marks*)

Apply it Concepts — Cheering up Jasper

Research into the role of the father in attachment has allowed psychologists to advise parents about their children's development. Jasper is the father of a 9-month-old girl, Emily. Jasper has noticed that recently when Emily is distressed she only accepts comfort from her mother. This upsets him and leaves him feeling unimportant as a parent.

Question

Referring to research into the role of fathers, what could you tell Jasper about his role in Emily's developing attachments?

Check it

1. Research has shown that mothers and fathers may play different roles in attachment. Outline **one** difference that has been found in the roles of mothers and fathers in attachment. [*2 marks*]
2. Outline **two** limitations of research into the role of the father in attachment. [*4 marks*]
3. Discuss what research has shown about the role of the father in attachment. [*8 marks*]

Animal studies of attachment

The specification says...

Animal studies of attachment: Lorenz and Harlow.

Animal studies have looked at the formation of early bonds between non-human parents and their offspring. This is of interest to psychologists because attachment-like behaviour is common to a range of species and so animal studies can help us understand attachment in humans.

Key term

Animal studies In psychology these are studies carried out on non-human animal species rather than on humans, either for ethical or practical reasons – practical because animals breed faster and researchers are interested in seeing results across more than one generation of animals.

Konrad Lorenz with his imprinted geese.

Apply it Concepts

Poppy's rescue

Spike is a zookeeper who specialises in the care of monkeys. He has just been asked by the police to take charge of a 45-day-old orphan monkey called Poppy who was rescued from a home where she was kept alone in a cage with a soft towel. When Spike first meets the baby monkey, Poppy clings to the towel and screams in fear when she sees she is in a new environment.

Questions

1. Based on Harlow's research how might Poppy's social development have turned out if she had not been rescued?
2. Referring to Harlow's research, suggest how Spike should proceed with Poppy. How good are her chances of healthy development?

Lorenz's research

In the early 20th century a number of **ethologists** conducted **animal studies** of the relationships between newborn animals and their mothers. Their observations informed psychologists' understanding of caregiver–infant attachment in humans. One of the most prominent ethologists was Konrad Lorenz.

Imprinting

Lorenz (1952) first observed the phenomenon of **imprinting** when he was a child and a neighbour gave him a newly hatched duckling that then followed him around.

Procedure As an adult researcher Lorenz set up a classic **experiment** in which he randomly divided a large clutch of goose eggs. Half the eggs were hatched with the mother goose in their natural environment. The other half hatched in an incubator where the first moving object they saw was Lorenz.

Findings The incubator group followed Lorenz everywhere whereas the **control group**, hatched in the presence of their mother, followed her. When the two groups were mixed up the control group continued to follow the mother and the **experimental group** followed Lorenz.

This phenomenon is called imprinting – whereby bird species that are mobile from birth (like geese and ducks) attach to and follow the first moving object they see. Lorenz identified a **critical period** in which imprinting needs to take place. Depending on the species this can be as brief as a few hours after hatching (or birth). If imprinting does *not* occur within that time Lorenz found that chicks did not attach themselves to a mother figure.

Sexual imprinting

Lorenz also investigated the relationship between imprinting and adult mate preferences. He observed that birds that imprinted on a human would often later display courtship behaviour towards humans.

In a **case study** Lorenz (1952) described a peacock that had been reared in the reptile house of a zoo where the first moving objects the peacock saw after hatching were giant tortoises. As an adult this bird would only direct courtship behaviour towards giant tortoises. Lorenz concluded that this meant the peacock had undergone **sexual imprinting**.

Harlow's research

Harry Harlow carried out perhaps the most important animal research in terms of informing our understanding of attachment. Harlow worked with rhesus monkeys, which are much more similar to humans than Lorenz's birds.

The importance of contact comfort

Harlow observed that newborns kept alone in a bare cage often died but that they usually survived if given something soft like a cloth to cuddle.

Procedure Harlow (1958) tested the idea that a soft object serves some of the functions of a mother. In one experiment he reared 16 baby monkeys with two wire model 'mothers' (see picture on facing page). In one condition milk was dispensed by the plain-wire mother whereas in a second condition the milk was dispensed by the cloth-covered mother.

Findings The baby monkeys cuddled the cloth-covered mother in preference to the plain-wire mother and sought comfort from the cloth one when frightened (e.g. by a noisy mechanical teddy bear) regardless of which mother (cloth-covered or plain-wire) dispensed milk. This showed that 'contact comfort' was of more importance to the monkeys than food when it came to attachment behaviour.

Maternally deprived monkeys as adults

Harlow and colleagues also followed the monkeys who had been deprived of a 'real' mother into adulthood to see if this early **maternal deprivation** had a permanent effect. The researchers found severe consequences. The monkeys reared with plain-wire mothers only were the most dysfunctional.

However, even those reared with a cloth-covered mother did not develop normal social behaviour. These deprived monkeys were more aggressive and less sociable than other monkeys and they bred less often than is typical for monkeys, being unskilled at mating. When they became mothers, some of the deprived monkeys neglected their young and others attacked their children, even killing them in some cases.

The critical period for normal development

Like Lorenz, Harlow concluded that there was a critical period for attachment formation – a mother figure had to be introduced to a young monkey within 90 days for an attachment to form. After this time attachment was impossible and the damage done by early deprivation became irreversible.

Apply it Concepts — Farming

Farmers have long been aware of the idea of imprinting. One common practice to ensure the survival of orphan (motherless) lambs is to take the fleece from a dead lamb and wrap it around the orphan lamb. The mother of the dead lamb looks after the orphan as if it were her own offspring, thus ensuring its survival.

Question

How can you use the concept of imprinting to explain this?

Evaluation

Research support

One strength of Lorenz's research is the existence of support for the concept of imprinting.

A study by Lucia Regolin and Giorgio Vallortigara (1995) supports Lorenz's idea of imprinting. Chicks were exposed to simple shape combinations that moved, such as a triangle with a rectangle in front. A range of shape combinations were then moved in front of them and they followed the original most closely.

This supports the view that young animals are born with an innate mechanism to imprint on a moving object present in the critical window of development, as predicted by Lorenz.

Generalisability to humans

One limitation of Lorenz's studies is the ability to generalise findings and conclusions from birds to humans.

The mammalian attachment system is quite different and more complex than that in birds. For example, in mammals attachment is a two-way process, so it is not just the young who become attached to their mothers but also the mammalian mothers show an emotional attachment to their young.

This means that it is probably not appropriate to generalise Lorenz's ideas to humans.

Evaluation eXtra

Applications to understanding human behaviour

Although human attachment is very different from that in birds there have been attempts to use the idea that some kind of 'imprinting' explains human behaviour. For example, Peter Seebach (2005) suggested that computer users exhibit 'baby duck syndrome' – which is the attachment formed to their first computer operating system, leading them to reject others.

Consider: *To what extent is imprinting a useful idea in humans?*

Evaluation

Real-world value

One strength of Harlow's research is its important real-world applications.

For example, it has helped social workers and clinical psychologists understand that a lack of bonding experience may be a risk factor in child development allowing them to intervene to prevent poor outcomes (Howe 1998). We also now understand the importance of attachment figures for baby monkeys in zoos and breeding programmes in the wild.

This means that the value of Harlow's research is not just theoretical but also practical.

Generalisability to humans

One limitation of Harlow's research is the ability to generalise findings and conclusions from monkeys to humans.

Rhesus monkeys are much more similar to humans than Lorenz's birds, and all mammals share some common attachment behaviours. However, the human brain and human behaviour is still more complex than that of monkeys.

This means that it may not be appropriate to generalise Harlow's findings to humans.

Evaluation eXtra

Ethical issues

Harlow's research caused severe and long-term distress to the monkeys. However, his findings and conclusions have important theoretical and practical applications.

Consider: *On balance should Harlow have carried out his research and should we make use of it?*

The plain-wire and cloth-covered mothers used in Harlow's study. In this photo the feeding bottle is attached to the plain-wire mother but for some of the monkeys the bottle was on the cloth-covered mother.

Apply it Methods — Deprivation damages brains

Follow-up studies have replicated Harlow's findings and, in addition, autopsies have been carried out on the deprived monkeys to see whether their deprivation caused any physical changes in their developing brains. A researcher is interested in levels of two brain chemicals (serotonin and oxytocin) in the monkey brains. She measures the levels of each chemical extracted from the brains of deprived and control monkeys.

Questions

1. State the **aim** of this study. (*2 marks*)
2. Write a **non-directional hypothesis** for this study. (*2 marks*)
3. Explain the difference between an aim and a **hypothesis**. (*2 marks*)

Study tip

You need to know about both Harlow's animal research and Lorenz's animal research in a fair amount of detail. It helps to be able to divide your description into the procedures and the findings, as we have done on the facing page. And try to learn specific details.

Check it

1. Outline how Lorenz studied attachment using animals. *[4 marks]*
2. Describe **one** study where Harlow used animals to investigate attachment. *[4 marks]*
3. Briefly evaluate Harlow's animal studies. *[4 marks]*
4. Describe **and** evaluate animal studies of attachment. *[12 marks AS, 16 marks AL]*

Ex[redacted]lanati[redacted]ns [redacted]f attachment: Learning theory

The specification says...

Explanations of attachment: learning theory.

Psychologists seek to explain behaviour. One popular explanation for attachment in the 1950s was learning theory – the view that attachments develop through classical and/or operant conditioning (described on page 108).

Key term

Learning theory A set of theories from the behaviourist approach to psychology, that emphasise the role of learning in the acquisition of behaviour. Explanations for learning of behaviour include classical and operant conditioning.

Classical conditioning of attachment

Unconditioned stimulus → Unconditioned response
Food — Pleasure

Neutral stimulus → No response
Caregiver

Unconditioned + neutral stimulus → Unconditioned response
Food + Caregiver — Pleasure

Conditioned stimulus → Conditioned response
Caregiver — Pleasure

Baby food – is that really all there is to love?

Learning theory and attachment

Learning theorists John Dollard and Neal Miller (1950) proposed that caregiver–infant **attachment** can be explained by **learning theory**. Their approach is sometimes called a 'cupboard love' approach because it emphasises the importance of the **attachment figure** as a provider of food. Put simply they proposed that children learn to love whoever feeds them!

Classical conditioning

Classical conditioning involves learning to associate two stimuli together so that we begin to respond to one in the same way as we already respond to the other. In the case of attachment, food serves as an **unconditioned stimulus**. Being fed gives us pleasure – we don't have to learn that, it is an **unconditioned response**.

A caregiver starts as a **neutral stimulus**, i.e. something that produces no response. However, when the caregiver provides food over time they become associated with food. When the baby then sees this person there is an expectation of food. The neutral stimulus has become a **conditioned stimulus**. Once conditioning has taken place the sight of the caregiver produces a **conditioned response** of pleasure. To a learning theorist this conditioned pleasure response is love, i.e. an attachment is formed and the caregiver becomes an attachment figure.

Operant conditioning

Operant conditioning involves learning from the consequences of behaviour. If a behaviour produces a pleasant consequence, that behaviour is likely to be repeated again. The behaviour is said to be **reinforced**. If a behaviour produces an unpleasant consequence (**punishment**) it is less likely to be repeated.

Operant conditioning can explain why babies cry for comfort – an important behaviour in building attachment. Crying leads to a response from the caregiver, for example feeding. As long as the caregiver provides the correct response, crying is reinforced. The baby then directs crying for comfort towards the caregiver who responds with comforting 'social suppressor' behaviour.

This reinforcement is a two-way process. At the same time as the baby is reinforced for crying, the caregiver receives **negative reinforcement** because the crying stops – escaping from something unpleasant is reinforcing. This interplay of mutual reinforcement strengthens an attachment.

Attachment as a secondary drive

As well as conditioning, learning theory draws on the concept of **drive reduction**. Hunger can be thought of as a **primary drive** – it's an innate, biological motivator. We are motivated to eat in order to reduce the hunger drive.

Robert Sears *et al.* (1957) suggested that, as caregivers provide food, the primary drive of hunger becomes generalised to them. Attachment is thus a **secondary drive** learned by an association between the caregiver and the satisfaction of a primary drive.

Apply it Methods — Sampling

A team of attachment researchers are interested in whether feeding influences attachment. The team believe that mothers and babies who have difficulty breastfeeding are less likely to develop good quality attachments. They ask for volunteers from a hospital where mothers who struggle with breastfeeding attend feeding support groups. At one year from birth these mother–baby pairs are assessed for attachment.

Questions

1. Explain what is meant by a **volunteer sample**. (*2 marks*)
2. Identify *two* strengths of using a volunteer sample in this study. (*2 marks*)
3. Explain *one* limitation of volunteer sampling. (*2 marks*)
4. A better (more representative) sample could be obtained by **random sampling**. Explain how the researchers in the above study might obtain a random sample. (*4 marks*)

Apply it Concepts — Angus's choice

Angus is a baby. His family is very well off and his mother has enlisted the help of a nanny to help with practical care. Angus is bottle-fed and most of his feeds are given by the nanny. Angus's mother works part-time so Angus spends approximately the same number of hours a week with his mother as he does with the nanny. The nanny is mostly interested in practical care whereas when Angus's mother is with him she plays with him and spends a lot of time cuddling.

Questions

1. Angus's mother is concerned that he will get more attached to the nanny because she usually feeds him. Based on your understanding of learning theory should Angus's mother be worried?
2. Now read the evaluations of the learning theory account of attachment. How would you explain to Angus's mother that she might not need to worry? Refer to psychological evidence.

:valuation

:ounter-evidence from animal studies

)ne limitation of learning theory explanations for attachment is lack of support ·om studies conducted on animals.

For example, Lorenz's geese imprinted on the first moving object they saw egardless of whether this object was associated with food. Also, if we consider Iarlow's research with monkeys, there is no support for the importance of food. Vhen given a choice, Harlow's monkeys displayed attachment behaviour towards soft surrogate 'mother' in preference to a wire one which provided milk.

This shows that factors other than association with food are important in the ɔrmation of attachments.

:ounter-evidence from studies on humans

. further limitation of learning theory explanations is lack of support from tudies of human babies.

For example Rudolph Schaffer and Peggy Emerson (1964) found that babies ended to form their main attachment to their mother regardless of whether he was the one who usually fed them. In another study, Russell Isabella *et al.* 1989) found that high levels of interactional synchrony predicted the quality of ttachment (see page 74). These factors are not related to feeding.

This again suggests that food is not the main factor in the formation of uman attachments.

;ome conditioning may be involved

)ne strength of learning theory is that elements of conditioning could be ıvolved in some aspects of attachment.

It seems unlikely that association with food plays a central role in ttachment, but conditioning may still play a role. For example a baby may ssociate feeling warm and comfortable with the presence of a particular adult, nd this may influence the baby's choice of their main attachment figure.

This means that learning theory may still be useful in understanding the evelopment of attachments.

Counterpoint Both classical and operant conditioning explanations see the baby playing a relatively passive role in attachment development, simply responding to associations with comfort or reward. In fact research shows that babies take a very active role in the interactions that produce attachment (e.g. Feldman and Eidelman 2007, see page 74).

This means that conditioning may not be an adequate explanation of any aspect of attachment.

:valuation eXtra

ocial learning theory

ale Hay and Jo Vespo (1988) suggest that parents teach children to love them y demonstrating (modelling) attachment behaviours, for example hugging. arents also reinforce loving behaviour by showing approval when babies isplay their own attachment behaviours (e.g. giving attention or cuddles to ıeir parents).

This social learning perspective has the further advantage that it is based round two-way interaction between baby and adult, so it fits better with esearch into the importance of reciprocity.

:onsider: *To what extent does this theory of attachment get around he problems of earlier learning theory explanations?*

;tudy tip

f you are writing about learning theory as an explanation for ttachment, remember that there is no point in giving general ıformation on conditioning. It absolutely has to be applied to xplaining the development of caregiver–infant attachment.

f there is no mention of attachment, it is not a good answer.

Apply it Methods

Ethical issues in infant research

Psychologists are concerned with ethical issues in their research. Sometimes the obvious way to gather data raises really serious issues.

A group of psychologists are interested in which is more important when it comes to forming attachments with adults – feeding or cuddling babies. The psychologists come up with the following experimental design: they will ask the parent who does most of the feeding to stop cuddling their baby. They will ask the other parent to do no feeding but provide comfort and cuddles. A year later the researchers will assess how strongly attached the baby is to each parent.

Questions

1. Referring to the **British Psychological Society's code of ethics**, explain *two* reasons why this experiment would be ethically unacceptable. (*4 marks*)
2. Explain *one* way in which psychologists deal with ethical issues in their research. (*4 marks*)

A grandmother who regularly cares for a baby may become the baby's primary attachment figure – but not because she fed the baby.

Check it

1. Outline the learning theory explanation of attachment. *[4 marks]*
2. Outline **two** limitations of learning theory as an explanation of attachment. *[2 marks + 2 marks]*
3. Discuss **and** evaluate learning theory as an explanation of attachment. *[12 marks AS, 16 marks AL]*

Explanati[redacted]ns [redacted]f attachment: Bowlby's theory

The specification says...

Explanations of attachment: Bowlby's monotropic theory. The concepts of a critical period and an internal working model.

The specification identifies a second explanation for the formation of attachment – Bowlby's theory, which has become the dominant theory of attachment in psychology.

Key terms

Monotropic A term sometimes used to describe Bowlby's theory. Mono means 'one' and tropic means 'leaning towards'. This indicates that one particular attachment is different from all others and of central importance to a child's development.

Critical period The time within which an attachment must form if it is to form at all. Lorenz and Harlow noted that attachment in birds and monkeys had critical periods. Bowlby extended the idea to humans, proposing that human babies have a sensitive period after which it will be much more difficult to form an attachment.

Internal working model Our mental representations of the world, e.g. the representation we have of our relationship to our primary attachment figure. This model affects our future relationships because it carries our perception of what relationships are like.

Babies' smiles are 'social releasers'. They elicit innate attachment behaviours from adults.

Bowlby's monotropic theory

John Bowlby (1988) rejected learning theory as an explanation for **attachment** because, as he said, 'were it true, an infant of a year or two should take readily to whomever feeds him and this is clearly not the case'. Instead Bowlby looked at the work of Lorenz and Harlow for ideas and proposed an **evolutionary** explanation – that attachment was an **innate** system that gives a survival advantage. So attachment, like imprinting, evolved as a mechanism to keep young animals safe by ensuring they stay close to adult caregivers.

Monotropy

Bowlby's theory (1958, 1969) is described as **monotropic** because he placed great emphasis on a child's attachment to *one* particular caregiver (hence the word mono). He believed that the child's attachment to this one caregiver is different and more important than others. Bowlby called this person the 'mother' but it was clear that it need not be the biological mother (or indeed a woman). Bowlby believed that the more time a baby spent with this mother-figure – or **primary attachment figure** as we usually call them now – the better. He put forward two principles to clarify this:

- The *law of continuity* stated that the more constant and predictable a child's care, the better the quality of their attachment.
- The *law of accumulated separation* stated that the effects of every separation from the mother add up 'and the safest dose is therefore a zero dose' (Bowlby 1975).

Social releasers and the critical period

Bowlby suggested that babies are born with a set of innate 'cute' behaviours like smiling, cooing and gripping that encourage attention from adults. He called these **social releasers** because their purpose is to activate adult social interaction and so make an adult attach to the baby. Bowlby recognised that attachment was a reciprocal process. Both mother and baby are 'hard-wired' to become attached.

The interplay between baby and adult attachment systems gradually builds the relationship between baby and caregiver, beginning in the early weeks of life (as we discussed on page 74). Bowlby proposed that there is a **critical period** around six months when the infant attachment system is active. In fact Bowlby viewed this as more of a **sensitive period**. A child is maximally sensitive at six months and this possibly extends up to the age of two. If an attachment is not formed in this time, a child will find it much harder to form one later.

Internal working model

Bowlby proposed that a child forms a mental representation of their relationship with their primary attachment figure. This is called an **internal working model** because it serves as a model for what relationships are like.

A child whose first experience is of a loving relationship with a reliable caregiver will tend to form an expectation that all relationships are as loving and reliable, and they will bring these qualities to future relationships. However, a child whose first relationship involves poor treatment will tend to form further poor relationships in which they expect such treatment from others and/or treat others in that way.

Most importantly the internal working model affects the child's later ability to be a parent themselves. People tend to base their parenting behaviour on their own experiences of being parented. This explains why children from functional families tend to have similar families themselves.

Apply it Methods

Meta-analysis

Heidi Bailey *et al.* (2007, see facing page) looked at how consistent attachment quality was in three generations of families. Marinus van IJzendoorn (1995) carried out a meta-analysis of the results of 18 similar studies covering a total of 854 parents.

Results strongly supported the idea that well-attached parents tend to have children with good attachments. This suggests that attachment quality is transmitted from one generation to the next.

Questions

1. Explain what is meant by **meta-analysis**. (*2 marks*)
2. Explain the difference between a meta-analysis and a review. (*2 marks*)
3. Explain **one** strength of meta-analysis as a research method. (*2 marks*)
4. Explain how this research supports the internal working model. (*3 marks*)

Apply it Concepts

Bibi and Amir

Bowlby identified a critical period after which human children cannot easily form a secure attachment.

Bibi and Amir are considering adopting a child. They have made contact with a potential adoptee with a troubled past. The boy, Hugo, is now four years old. For his first two years Hugo lived with an abusive family and never formed a proper attachment.

Question

Based on your understanding of the ideas of a critical period, what advice might you give Bibi and Amir?

valuation

alidity of monotropy challenged

ne limitation of Bowlby's theory is that the concept of monotropy lacks **validity**.

Rudolph Schaffer and Peggy Emerson (1964) found that although most abies did attach to one person at first, a significant minority formed multiple ttachments at the same time. Also, although the first attachment does appear o have a particularly strong influence on later behaviour, this may simply nean it is *stronger*, not necessarily *different* in quality from the child's other ttachments. For example other attachments to family members provide all the ame key qualities (emotional support, a safe base etc).

This means that Bowlby may be incorrect that there is a unique quality and nportance to the child's primary attachment.

upport for social releasers

ne strength of Bowlby's theory is the evidence supporting the role of social eleasers.

There is clear evidence that cute baby behaviours are designed to elicit nteraction from caregivers. T. Berry Brazelton *et al.* (1975) observed babies trigger nteractions with adults using social releasers. The researchers then instructed the abies' primary attachment figures to ignore their babies' social releasers. Babies who were previously shown to be normally responsive) became increasingly istressed and some eventually curled up and lay motionless.

This illustrates the role of social releasers in emotional development and uggests that they are important in the process of attachment development.

upport for internal working model

further strength of Bowlby's theory is support for the internal working model.

The idea of the internal working model predicts that patterns of attachment vill be passed from one generation to the next. Heidi Bailey *et al.* (2007) ssessed attachment relationships in 99 mothers and their one-year-old abies. The researchers measured the mothers' attachment to their own rimary attachment figures (i.e. their parents). The researchers also assessed he attachment quality of the babies. They found that mothers with poor ttachment to their own primary attachment figures were more likely to have oorly attached babies.

This supports Bowlby's idea that mothers' ability to form attachments to their abies is influenced by their internal working models (which in turn comes from heir own early attachment experiences).

Counterpoint There are probably other important influences on social development. For example some psychologists believe that genetic differences in anxiety and sociability affect social behaviour in both babies and adults. These differences could also impact on their parenting ability (Kornienko 2016).

This means that Bowlby may have overstated the importance of the internal working model in social behaviour and parenting at the expense of other factors.

valuation eXtra

eminist concerns

he laws of continuity and accumulated separation suggest that mothers vho work may negatively affect their child's emotional development. eminists like Erica Burman (1994) point out that this belief sets up nothers to take the blame for anything that goes wrong for the child in he future. It also gives people an excuse to restrict mothers' activities, for xample returning to work.

On the other hand, prior to Bowlby's time people didn't think the nother's role was important, and, in fact, many custody disputes were ettled in favour of the father because mothers were not regarded as ecessary. Also, Bowlby's ideas have many real-world applications, such as ey workers in day care who build an attachment with particular babies.

onsider: *On balance, has Bowlby's theory done more harm or nore good?*

There is support for the internal working model. This mother (on the left) is likely to have a similar quality of attachment to her mother and her daughter.

Apply it Concepts — Psychology teachers

John and Mary are both teachers of psychology (you may know them). Much to the amusement of their students they recently married and had a baby. They see this as a great opportunity to use their knowledge of child development in bringing up their own child, Ian.

One day Mary walks in to find Ian attempting without success to catch John's eye and initiate interaction while John watches television, ignoring his baby son.

Mary is cross. 'Remember what happened in the Brazelton study!' she says.

Question

With reference to Bowlby's idea of social releasers and the Brazelton *et al.* study (see left), explain what Mary is talking about.

Study tip

Some people feel very passionate about the working mothers debate and how Bowlby's evidence may support stay-at-home mothers. Bowlby himself never suggested this. However, the key point is to ensure that your passions don't get in the way of a reasoned argument. Make sure you research and describe both sides of any debate.

Check it

1. Outline Bowlby's theory of attachment. Refer to the concepts of the critical period **and** the internal working model in your answer. *[6 marks]*
2. Explain what is meant by a 'monotropic theory'. *[2 marks]*
3. Outline **one** strength **and one** limitation of Bowlby's monotropic theory of attachment. *[2 marks + 2 marks]*
4. Describe **and** evaluate Bowlby's monotropic theory of attachment. *[12 marks AS, 16 marks AL]*

Types of attachment

The specification says...

Ainsworth's 'Strange Situation'. Types of attachment: secure, insecure-avoidant and insecure-resistant.

Mary Ainsworth worked with John Bowlby on the development of attachment theory. Her particular contribution was to produce a method, still used today, to assess the quality of attachment between a baby and others. This method of assessment is called the Strange Situation.

Key terms

Strange Situation A controlled observation designed to test attachment security. Babies are assessed on their response to playing in an unfamiliar room, being left alone, left with a stranger and being reunited with a caregiver.

Secure attachment Generally thought of as the most desirable attachment type, associated with psychologically healthy outcomes. In the Strange Situation this is shown by moderate stranger and separation anxiety and ease of comfort at reunion.

Insecure–avoidant attachment An attachment type characterised by low anxiety but weak attachment. In the Strange Situation this is shown by low stranger and separation anxiety and little response to reunion, maybe even an avoidance of the caregiver.

Insecure–resistant attachment An attachment type characterised by strong attachment and high anxiety. In the Strange Situation this is shown by high levels of stranger and separation anxiety and by resistance to being comforted at reunion.

Securely attached children are happy to be reunited with their caregiver. Other children may show avoidance or resistance at reunion and are classified as insecure–avoidant or insecure–resistant respectively because of this.

Ainsworth's 'Strange Situation'

The **Strange Situation** was developed by Mary Ainsworth and Silvia Bell (1970). The aim was to be able to observe key attachment behaviours as a means of assessing the quality of a baby's attachment to a caregiver.

Procedure

The Strange Situation is a **controlled observation** procedure designed to measure the security of attachment a baby displays towards a caregiver. It takes place in a room with quite controlled conditions (i.e. a **laboratory**) with a **two-way mirror** and/or cameras through which psychologists can observe the baby's behaviour.

The behaviours used to judge attachment included:

- **Proximity-seeking** – a baby with a good quality attachment will stay fairly close to a caregiver.
- **Exploration and secure-base behaviour** – good attachment enables a baby to feel confident to explore, using their caregiver as a secure base, i.e. a point of contact that will make them feel safe.
- **Stranger anxiety** – one of the signs of becoming closely attached is a display of anxiety when a stranger approaches.
- **Separation anxiety** – another sign of becoming attached is to protest at separation from the caregiver.
- **Response to reunion** – babies who are securely attached greet the caregiver's return with pleasure and seek comfort.

The procedure has seven episodes, each of which lasts three minutes.

Beginning: Caregiver and baby enter an unfamiliar playroom.	
1. The baby is encouraged to explore.	Tests exploration and secure base.
2. A stranger comes in, talks to the caregiver and approaches the baby.	Tests stranger anxiety.
3. The caregiver leaves the baby and stranger together.	Tests separation and stranger anxiety.
4. The caregiver returns and the stranger leaves.	Tests reunion behaviour and exploration/secure base.
5. The caregiver leaves the baby alone.	Tests separation anxiety.
6. The stranger returns.	Tests stranger anxiety.
7. The caregiver returns and is reunited with the baby.	Tests reunion behaviour.

Findings – types of attachment

Ainsworth *et al.* (1978) found that there were distinct patterns in the way that babies behaved. They identified three main types of attachment:

- **Secure attachment** (Type B). These babies explore happily but regularly go back to their caregiver (proximity-seeking and secure-base behaviour). They usually show moderate separation distress and moderate stranger anxiety. Securely attached babies require and accept comfort from the caregiver in the reunion stage. About 60–75% of British babies are classified as secure.
- **Insecure–avoidant attachment** (Type A). These babies explore freely but do not seek proximity or show secure-base behaviour. They show little or no reaction when their caregiver leaves and little stranger anxiety. They make little effort to make contact when the caregiver returns and may even avoid such contact. About 20–25% of British babies are classified as insecure–avoidant.
- **Insecure–resistant attachment** (Type C). These babies seek greater proximity than others and so explore less. They show high levels of stranger and separation distress but they resist comfort when reunited with their caregiver. Around 3% of British babies are classified as insecure–resistant.

Apply it Concepts

What's the difference?

Rosie is studying Psychology and has just learned about the Strange Situation. She is confused about what behaviours go with each type of attachment. So she creates the table on the right.

Task

Fill in her table using words like 'high' or 'low', 'strong', etc.

	Secure	Insecure–avoidant	Insecure–resistant
Proximity-seeking			
Exploration/secure base			
Stranger anxiety			
Separation anxiety			
Response on reunion			

Evaluation

Practical activity on page 97

Good predictive validity

One strength of the Strange Situation is that its outcome predicts a number of aspects of the baby's later development.

A large body of research has shown that babies and toddlers assessed as Type B (secure) tend to have better outcomes than others, both in later childhood and in adulthood. In childhood this includes better achievement in school and less involvement in bullying (McCormick *et al.* 2016, Kokkinos 2007). Securely attached babies also tend to go on to have better mental health in adulthood (Ward *et al.* 2006). Those babies assessed as having insecure–resistant attachment and those not falling into Types A, B or C tend to have the worst outcomes.

This suggests that the Strange Situation measures something real and meaningful in a baby's development.

Counterpoint The Strange Situation clearly measures something important that is associated with later development. However, not all psychologists believe this something is attachment. For example, Jerome Kagan (1982) suggested that genetically-influenced anxiety levels could account for variations in attachment behaviour in the Strange Situation and later development.

This means that the Strange Situation may not actually measure attachment.

Good reliability

A further strength of the Strange Situation is good **inter-rater reliability** (the agreement between different observers).

Johanna Bick *et al.* (2012) tested inter-rater reliability for the Strange Situation for a team of trained observers and found agreement on attachment type in 94% of cases. This high level of reliability may be because the procedure takes place under controlled conditions and because behaviours (such as proximity-seeking and stranger anxiety) involve large movements and are therefore easy to observe. For example, anxious babies cry and crawl away from strangers.

This means that we can be confident that attachment type as assessed by the Strange Situation does not depend on subjective judgements.

The test may be culture-bound

One limitation of the Strange Situation is that it may not be a valid measure of attachment in different cultural contexts.

The Strange Situation was developed in Britain and the US. It may be culture-bound, i.e. only valid for use in certain cultures (in this case Europe and the US). One reason for this is that babies have different experiences in different cultures and these experiences may affect their responses to the Strange Situation. For example, in one Japanese study by Keiko Takahashi (1986), babies displayed very high levels of separation anxiety and so a disproportionate number were classified as insecure–resistant. Takahashi (1990) suggests that this anxiety response was not due to high rates of attachment insecurity but to the unusual nature of the experience in Japan where mother–baby separation is very rare.

This means that it is very difficult to know what the Strange Situation is measuring when used outside Europe and the US.

Evaluation eXtra

Other attachment types

Mary Main and Judith Solomon (1986) identified a fourth category of attachment – a disorganised or Type D attachment, a mix of resistant and avoidant behaviours.

However, Type D babies are unusual and have generally experienced some form of severe neglect or abuse. Most will go on to develop psychological disorders by adulthood.

Consider: *To what extent does Ainsworth's classification of attachment types hold up in the face of the existence of Type Ds?*

Ainsworth's attachment types have been shown to be good predictors of future behaviour.

Apply it Methods: Sampling

The Strange Situation is a controlled observation procedure. It takes just over 20 minutes and involves time sampling – every 15 seconds observers noted what behaviours were being displayed. The alternative to time sampling is event sampling.

The Strange Situation involves non-participant observation. The alternative is participant observation in which observers infiltrate the situation being observed and take part in the observed activity.

Questions

1. Explain *one* advantage of **time sampling** over **event sampling**. (*2 marks*)
2. Explain why **non-participant observation** is appropriate for the Strange Situation. (*2 marks*)

Apply it Concepts: James's first visit to his childminder

James is a one-year-old boy whose parents are both psychologists. They have decided to send James to a childminder so that his mother, Ruth, can return to work part-time. The first time James meets the childminder Ruth introduces them and encourages James to play in the playroom. James explores a little but regularly comes back to Ruth. Ruth then leaves the room for a few minutes. James is upset when Ruth leaves and is wary of the childminder but he is overjoyed when Ruth comes back in and accepts comfort readily from her. When James's father calls later to ask how the visit went, Ruth says 'Great. He's securely attached!'

Question

Based on your understanding of attachment types, explain what Ruth meant by this and why she judged James to have a secure attachment.

Check it

1. Describe how Ainsworth studied types of attachment. [*6 marks*]
2. Outline what is meant by a 'secure attachment'. [*3 marks*]
3. Explain the difference in behaviours between a baby who is classified as insecure–avoidant and one who is classified as insecure–resistant. [*4 marks*]
4. Describe **and** evaluate the Strange Situation as a method of assessing attachment type. [*12 marks AS, 16 marks AL*]

Cultural variations in attachment

The specification says...

Cultural variations in attachment, including van IJzendoorn.

Child-rearing styles vary across different cultures. The question is how these might impact on the proportions of different attachment types in different countries. It might be that attachment types are the same across the world or they might be different. We look in detail at the classic meta-analysis of cultural differences by van IJzendoorn.

Key term

Cultural variations 'Culture' refers to the norms and values that exist within any group of people. Cultural variations then are the differences in norms and values that exist between people in different groups. In attachment research we are concerned with the differences in the proportion of children of different attachment types.

Proportions of secure, avoidant and resistant babies in van IJzendoorn and Kroonenberg's meta-analysis.

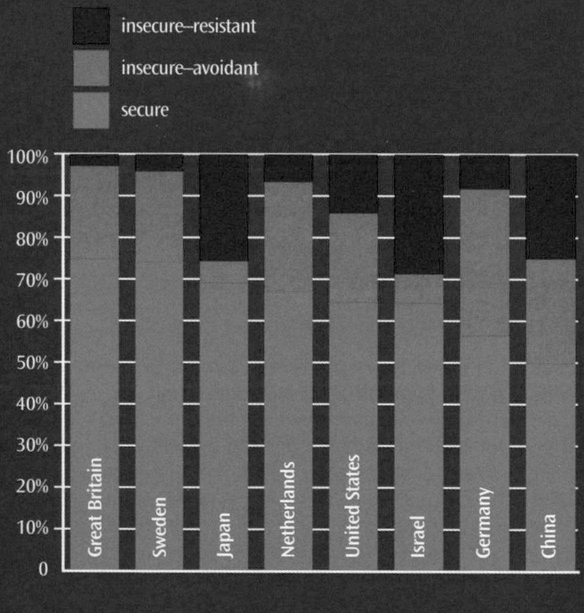

insecure–resistant
insecure–avoidant
secure
100%
90%
80%
70%
60%
50%
40%
30%
20%
10%
0
Great Britain
Sweden
Japan
Netherlands
United States
Israel
Germany
China

Studies of cultural variations

van IJzendoorn and Kroonenberg's research

Marinus van IJzendoorn and Pieter Kroonenberg (1988) conducted a study to look at the proportions of **secure**, **insecure–avoidant** and **insecure–resistant attachments** across a range of countries to assess **cultural variation**. They also looked at the differences within the same countries to get an idea of variations *within* a culture.

Procedure The researchers located 32 studies of attachment where the **Strange Situation** had been used to investigate the proportions of babies with different attachment types. These were conducted in eight countries – 15 were in the US. Overall the studies yielded results for 1,990 children. The data for these 32 studies was **meta-analysed**. This means that the results of the studies were combined and analysed together, weighting each study for its sample size.

Findings The findings are shown in the graph below left. There was wide variation between the proportions of attachment types in different studies. In all countries secure attachment was the most common classification. However the proportion varied from 75% in Britain to 50% in China.

In **individualist** cultures rates of insecure–resistant attachment were similar to Ainsworth's original sample (all under 14%) but this was not true for the **collectivist** samples from China, Japan and Israel where rates were above 25% (and where rates of insecure–avoidant attachment were reduced).

An interesting finding was that variations between results of studies *within* the same country were actually 150% greater than those *between* countries. In the US, for example, one study found only 46% securely attached compared to one sample as high as 90%.

Other studies of cultural variations

An Italian study Alessandra Simonelli *et al.* (2014) conducted a study in Italy to see whether the proportions of babies of different attachment types still matches those found in previous studies. The researchers assessed 76 babies aged 12 months using the Strange Situation.

They found 50% were secure, with 36% insecure–avoidant. This is a lower rate of secure attachment and higher rate of insecure–avoidant attachment than has been found in many studies. The researchers suggest this is because increasing numbers of mothers of very young children work long hours and use professional childcare.

These findings suggest that patterns of attachment types are not static but vary in line with cultural change.

A Korean study Mi Kyoung Jin *et al.* (2012) conducted a study to compare the proportions of attachment types in Korea to other studies. The Strange Situation was used to assess 87 babies.

The overall proportions of insecure and secure babies were similar to those in most countries, with most babies being secure. However, more of those classified as insecurely attached were resistant and only one baby was avoidant. This distribution is similar to the distribution of attachment types found in Japan (van IJzendoorn and Kroonenberg 1988).

Since Japan and Korea have quite similar child-rearing styles this similarity might be explained in terms of child-rearing style.

Conclusions

Secure attachment seems to be the norm in a wide range of cultures, supporting Bowlby's idea that attachment is innate and universal and this type is the universal norm.

However, the research also clearly shows that cultural practices have an influence on attachment type.

Apply it Concepts — Helga's worried

The proportion of babies classified with each attachment type differs between nationalities. Helga and Lars have recently moved to England from Germany with their son Kurt. They take part in some attachment research at their local university and are disturbed to hear that Kurt has an insecure–avoidant attachment.

Question

Should Helga and Lars be concerned by this? Refer to the proportions of German children of each attachment type in the van IJzendoorn study.

Apply it Methods — Pilot studies

A team of psychologists are interested in cultural variations in attachment. They want to see if the Strange Situation works as a test of attachment security in a range of countries including some where attachment type has not been assessed before. They decide to carry out a pilot study in these countries.

Questions

1. Outline what is meant by a **pilot study**. (*2 marks*)
2. Why is it advisable to carry out a pilot study before using a test on a new population? (*2 marks*)

Evaluation

Indigenous researchers

One strength of the research on the facing page is that most of the studies were conducted by indigenous psychologists.

Indigenous psychologists are those from the same cultural background as the participants. For example, van IJzendoorn and Kroonenberg included research by a German team (Grossmann *et al.* 1981) and Keiko Takahashi (1986) who is Japanese. This kind of research means that many of the potential problems in cross-cultural research can be avoided, such as researchers' misunderstandings of the language used by participants or having difficulty communicating instructions to them. Difficulties can also include bias because of one nation's stereotypes of another.

This means there is an excellent chance that researchers and participants communicated successfully – enhancing the **validity** of the data collected.

Counterpoint However this has not been true of all cross-cultural attachment research. For example Gilda Morelli and Edward Tronick (1991) were outsiders from America when they studied child-rearing and patterns of attachment in the Efé of Zaire. Their data might have been affected by difficulties in gathering data from participants outside their own culture.

This means that the data from some countries might have been affected by bias and difficulty in cross-cultural communication.

Confounding variables

One limitation of cross-cultural research, including meta-analyses of patterns of attachment types, is the impact of **confounding variables** on findings.

Studies conducted in different countries are not usually matched for methodology when they are compared in reviews or meta-analyses. Sample characteristics such as poverty, social class and urban/rural make-up can confound results as can the age of participants studied in different countries. Environmental variables might also differ between studies and confound results. For example the size of the room and the availability of interesting toys there – babies might appear to explore more in studies conducted in small rooms with attractive toys compared to large, bare rooms. Less visible proximity-seeking because of room size might make a child more likely to be classified as avoidant.

This means that looking at attachment behaviour in different non-matched studies conducted in different countries may not tell us anything about cross-cultural patterns of attachment.

Imposed etic

A further limitation of cross-cultural research is in trying to impose a test designed for one cultural context to another context.

Cross-cultural psychology includes the ideas of emic (cultural uniqueness) and etic (cross-cultural universality). **Imposed etic** occurs when we assume an idea or technique that works in one cultural context will work in another. An example of this in attachment research is in the use of babies' response to reunion with the caregiver in the Strange Situation. In Britain and the US, lack of affection on reunion may indicate an avoidant attachment. But in Germany such behaviour would be more likely interpreted as independence rather than insecurity. Therefore that part of the Strange Situation may not work in Germany.

This means that the behaviours measured by the Strange Situation may not have the same meanings in different cultural contexts, and comparing them across cultures is meaningless.

Evaluation eXtra

Competing explanations

Cross-cultural research has found very similar attachment types in different countries. Bowlby's theory explains this similarity by identifying attachment as innate and universal.

However, van IJzendoorn and Kroonenberg suggest an alternative explanation. Namely that global media represents a particular view of how parents and babies are meant to behave. This may override traditional cultural differences in the way children are brought up.

Consider: *What is the best way to explain universal behaviours? You could also consider learning theory explanations.*

Apply it Methods: Populations and samples

Studies of cultural variation in attachment make use of samples of babies and their primary attachment figures. These samples are drawn from different populations. For example, the van IJzendoorn and Kroonenberg meta-analysis looked at 32 studies each of which tested attachment in a particular and different population.

The best sampling techniques are those that are likely to produce a representative sample. Two common ways to obtain a representative sample are by systematic and random sampling.

Questions

1. With reference to the van IJzendoorn and Kroonenberg study explain the difference between a **target population** and a **sample**. (*2 marks*)
2. With reference to the populations of the eight countries, explain what is meant by a **representative sample**. (*2 marks*)
3. Explain how both **random** and **systematic sampling** could have been used to obtain a sample of babies in Britain. (*2 marks + 2 marks*)

Recent research on attachment in Korea supports the idea that there are only modest differences in attachment types across countries.

Check it

1. Explain how van IJzendoorn studied cultural variations in attachment. *[4 marks]*
2. Describe findings of research into cultural variations in attachment. *[6 marks]*
3. Explain **one** limitation of research into cultural variation in attachment. *[3 marks]*
4. Describe **and** evaluate research into cultural variations in attachment. *[12 marks AS, 16 marks AL]*

B[redacted]wl[redacted]y's the[redacted]ry [redacted]f maternal [redacted]e[redacted]rivati[redacted]n

The specification says...

Bowlby's theory of maternal deprivation.

We have already looked at Bowlby's monotropic theory of attachment (see page 84). This spread is concerned with his earlier theory of maternal deprivation. This theory focuses on how the effects of early experiences may *interfere* with the usual processes of attachment formation. Bowlby proposed that separation from the mother or mother-substitute has a serious effect on psychological development.

Key term

Maternal deprivation The emotional and intellectual consequences of separation between a child and his/her mother or mother-substitute. Bowlby proposed that continuous care from a mother is essential for normal psychological development, and that prolonged separation from this adult causes serious damage to emotional and intellectual development.

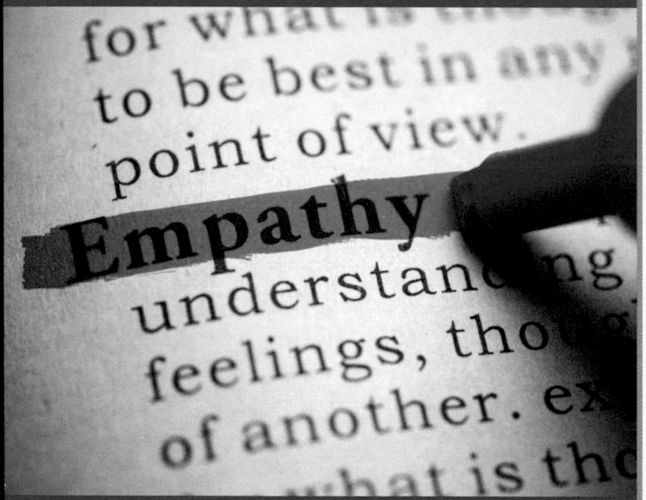
to be best in any
point of view.
Empathy
feelings,
of another.

Psychopaths are often stereotyped as unfeeling murderers but the term refers to people who appear to have no conscience about what they do – they lack empathy for other people's feelings and experience little remorse. They can be very charming. More recently, psychopathy has been called antisocial personality disorder (in the **DSM** classification) and is thus seen as a category of mental disorder.

Theory of maternal deprivation

John Bowlby is known for his **monotropic** theory of **attachment**. However, earlier in his career he also proposed the theory of **maternal deprivation**. This earlier theory focused on the idea that the continual presence of care from a mother or mother-substitute is essential for normal psychological development of babies and toddlers, both emotionally and intellectually. Bowlby (1953) famously said that 'mother-love in infancy and childhood is as important for mental health as are vitamins and proteins for physical health'. Being separated from a mother in early childhood has serious consequences (maternal deprivation).

Separation versus deprivation

There is an important distinction to be made between separation and deprivation. Separation simply means the child not being in the presence of the primary attachment figure. This only becomes a problem if the child becomes *deprived* of emotional care (which can happen even if a mother is present and, say, depressed). Brief separations, particularly where the child is with a substitute caregiver who can provide emotional care, are not significant for development but extended separations can lead to deprivation, which by definition causes harm.

The critical period

Bowlby saw the first two-and-a-half years of life as a **critical period** for psychological development. If a child is separated from their mother in the absence of suitable substitute care and so deprived of her emotional care for an extended duration during this critical period then (Bowlby believed) psychological damage was inevitable. He also believed there was a continuing risk up to the age of five.

Effects on development

Intellectual development One way in which maternal deprivation affects children's development is their intellectual development. Bowlby believed that if children were deprived of maternal care for too long during the critical period they would experience delayed intellectual development, characterised by abnormally low IQ. This has been demonstrated in studies of adoption. For example, William Goldfarb (1947) found lower IQ in children who had remained in institutions as opposed to those who were fostered and thus had a higher standard of emotional care (see facing page for details of study).

Emotional development A second major way in which being deprived of a mother figure's emotional care affects children is in their emotional development. Bowlby identified **affectionless psychopathy** as the inability to experience guilt or strong emotion towards others. This prevents a person developing fulfilling relationships and is associated with criminality. Affectionless psychopaths cannot appreciate the feelings of victims and so lack remorse for their actions.

Bowlby's research

Bowlby's (1944) 44 thieves study examined the link between affectionless psychopathy and maternal deprivation.

Procedure The sample in this study consisted of 44 criminal teenagers accused of stealing. All 'thieves' were interviewed for signs of affectionless psychopathy: characterised as a lack of affection, lack of guilt about their actions and lack of empathy for their victims. Their families were also interviewed in order to establish whether the 'thieves' had prolonged early separations from their mothers. The sample was compared to a **control group** of 44 non-criminal but emotionally-disturbed young people.

Findings Bowlby (1944) found that 14 of the 44 thieves could be described as affectionless psychopaths and 12 of these had experienced prolonged separation from their mothers in the first two years of their lives. In contrast only five of the remaining 30 'thieves' had experienced separations. Only two participants in the control group of 44 had experienced long separations. Bowlby concluded that prolonged early separation/deprivation caused affectionless psychopathy.

Apply it Methods — Natural experiment

Bowlby's 44 thieves study is an example of a natural experiment. He identified an independent variable of maternal separation/deprivation and measured its effects on social development. It was not, however, possible to randomly allocate participants to experimental groups because the independent variable (deprivation and no deprivation) already existed and was assessed retrospectively.

Questions

1. Explain why this study is a **natural experiment**. (*2 marks*)
2. Explain how the **dependent variable** of social development was **operationalised**. (*2 marks*)
3. If the **independent variable** is deprivation in infancy, what are some likely **confounding variables**? In other words what sort of things might co-occur with deprivation that might influence social development? (*2 marks*)

Evaluation

Flawed evidence

One limitation of the theory of maternal deprivation is the poor quality of the evidence it is based on.

Bowlby's 44 thieves study (facing page) is flawed because it was Bowlby himself who carried out both the family interviews and the assessments for affectionless psychopathy. This left him open to bias because he knew in advance which teenagers he expected to show signs of psychopathy. Other sources of evidence were equally flawed. For example, Bowlby was also influenced by the findings of Goldfarb's (1943) research on the development of deprived children in wartime orphanages. This study has problems of **confounding variables** because the children in Goldfarb's study had experienced early trauma and institutional care as well as prolonged separation from their primary caregivers.

This means that Bowlby's original sources of evidence for maternal deprivation had serious flaws and would not be taken seriously as evidence nowadays.

Counterpoint A new line of research has provided some modest support for the idea that maternal deprivation can have long-term effects. Frederic Lévy *et al.* (2003) showed that separating baby rats from their mother for as little as a day had a permanent effect on their social development though not other aspects of development.

This means that, although Bowlby relied on flawed evidence to support the theory of maternal deprivation, there are other sources of evidence for his ideas.

Deprivation and privation

Another limitation of Bowlby's theory of maternal deprivation is his confusion between different types of early experience.

Michael Rutter (1981) drew an important distinction between two types of early negative experience. Deprivation strictly refers to the loss of the primary attachment figure after attachment has developed. On the other hand privation is the failure to form any attachment in the first place – this may take place when children are brought up in institutional care. Rutter pointed out that the severe long-term damage Bowlby associated with deprivation is actually more likely to be the result of privation. So the children studied by Goldfarb may actually have been 'prived' rather than deprived. Similarly, many of the children in the 44 thieves study had disrupted early lives (e.g. spells in hospital) and may never have formed strong attachments.

This means that Bowlby may have overestimated the seriousness of the effects of deprivation in children's development.

Critical versus sensitive periods

A further limitation of the theory is Bowlby's idea of a critical period.

For Bowlby, damage was inevitable if a child had not formed an attachment in the first two-and-a-half years of life. Hence this is a critical period. However, there is evidence to suggest that in many cases good quality aftercare can prevent most or all of this damage. For example Jarmila Koluchová (1976) reported the case of the Czech Twins. The twins experienced very severe physical and emotional abuse from the age of 18 months up until they were seven years old. Although they were severely damaged emotionally by their experience they received excellent care and by their teens they had recovered fully.

This means that lasting harm is not inevitable even in cases of severe privation. The 'critical period' is therefore better seen as a 'sensitive period'.

Evaluation eXtra

Conflicting evidence

Most attempts to replicate the 44 thieves study failed to produce similar results. For example, Hilda Lewis (1954) looked at 500 young people and found no association between early separation and later psychopathy (criminality or relationship difficulties).

On the other hand, more recent research (for example, Gao *et al.* 2010) has partially supported Bowlby by showing that poor quality maternal care was associated with high rates of psychopathy in adults.

Consider: *In the light of this conflicting evidence, how seriously should we take maternal deprivation as an explanation for abnormal development (psychopathy)?*

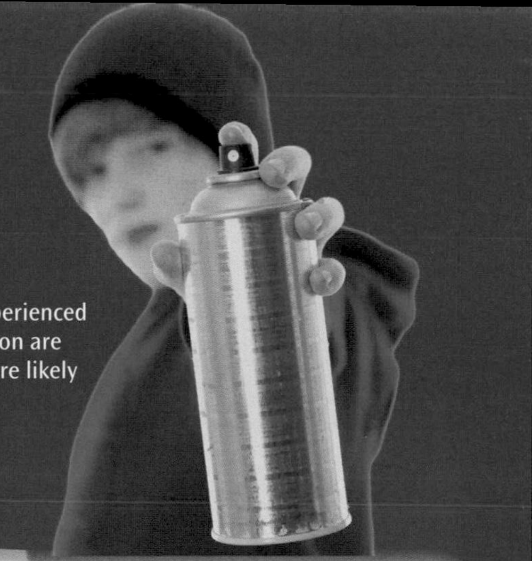

Teenagers who experienced maternal deprivation are not necessarily more likely to be criminals.

Apply it Concepts: Maternal deprivation as a legal defence

Maternal deprivation has been associated with criminality, in particular criminality involving no empathy or guilt.

Simon is a habitual criminal. Since his early teens he has stolen many car stereos and shoplifted. More recently he has turned to burglary and violent crime. Simon is now in court for mugging a 75-year-old woman. Simon studied psychology and as his defence mentions his mother's long spell in hospital when he was a baby.

Questions

1. How could Simon use the theory of maternal deprivation to excuse his actions?
2. Referring to the evaluations of the theory of maternal deprivation, explain why Simon might be unwise to use this defence.

Apply it Concepts: A deprivation study

Goldfarb (1955) followed up 30 orphaned children to the age of 12. Half of the original sample had been fostered by four months of age whilst the other half remained in an orphanage. At 12 their IQs were assessed using a standard IQ test called the Stanford-Binet test. It was found that the fostered group had an average IQ of 96 whereas the group that remained in the orphanage averaged only 68, below the cut-off point used to define intellectual disability.

Question

Using Bowlby's theory of maternal deprivation, explain Goldfarb's results.

Check it

1. Explain what is meant by 'maternal deprivation'. *[3 marks]*
2. According to Bowlby, prolonged separation from the mother or mother-substitute can have serious effects on children's psychological development. Outline **two** effects that maternal deprivation can have on children's psychological development. *[4 marks]*
3. Explain **one** limitation of Bowlby's theory of maternal deprivation. *[4 marks]*
4. Describe **and** evaluate Bowlby's theory of maternal deprivation. *[12 marks AS, 16 marks AL]*

Romanian orphan studies: Instituti[redacted]nalisati[redacted]n

The specification says...

Romanian orphan studies: effects of institutionalisation.

The theory of maternal deprivation predicted that long-term negative effects result from early deprivation. This can be studied in the context of institutional care. Research on emotional deprivation in the 1940s and 1950s showed the harm it caused. This meant that institutional care for young children largely disappeared, and therefore research opportunities ceased to exist.

Key terms

Orphan studies These concern children placed in care because their parents cannot look after them. An orphan is a child whose parents have either died or have abandoned them permanently.

Institutionalisation A term for the effects of living in an institutional setting. The term 'institution' refers to a place like a hospital or an orphanage where people live for long, continuous periods of time. In such places there is often very little emotional care provided. In attachment research we are interested in the effects of institutional care on children's attachment and subsequent development.

Apply it Methods Correlations

In Rutter's research on Romanian orphans it was found that there was a negative correlation between age at adoption and intellectual development (IQ score) at age 4.

Questions

1. Briefly explain the difference between a **correlation** and an **experiment**. (*2 marks*)
2. Explain why you might expect to obtain a **negative correlation** in this study. (*2 marks*)
3. Sketch a **scattergram** showing what the results might look like. (*3 marks*)

Good parenting by adopters made up for the physical and intellectual problems experienced at first by the Romanian adoptees.

Romanian orphan studies

Research on maternal deprivation has turned to **orphan studies** as a means of studying the effects of **deprivation** on emotional and intellectual development. A tragic opportunity to look at the effects of institutional care and the consequent **institutionalisation** arose in Romania in the 1990s. Former President Nicolai Ceauçescu required Romanian women to have five children. Many Romanian parents could not afford to keep their children and the children ended up in huge orphanages in very poor conditions. After the 1989 Romanian revolution many of the children were adopted, some by British parents.

Rutter *et al.*'s research

Procedure Michael Rutter and colleagues (2011) have followed a group of 165 Romanian orphans for many years as part of the English and Romanian adoptee (ERA) study. The orphans had been adopted by families in the UK. The aim of the ERA has been to investigate the extent to which good care could make up for poor early experiences in institutions. Physical, cognitive and emotional development has been assessed at ages 4, 6, 11, 15 and 22–25 years. A group of 52 children from the UK adopted around the same time have served as a **control group**.

Findings When the children first arrived in the UK, half the adoptees showed signs of delayed intellectual development and the majority were severely undernourished. At age 11 the adopted children showed differential rates of recovery that were related to their age of adoption. The **mean** IQ of those children adopted before the age of six months was 102, compared with 86 for those adopted between six months and two years and 77 for those adopted after two years. These differences remained at age 16 (Beckett *et al.* 2010). ADHD was more common in 15- and 22–25-year-old samples (Kennedy *et al.* 2016).

In terms of attachment, there appeared to be a difference in outcome related to whether adoption took place before or after six months. Those children adopted after they were six months showed signs of a particular attachment style called **disinhibited attachment**. Symptoms include attention-seeking, clinginess and social behaviour directed indiscriminately towards all adults, both familiar and unfamiliar.

In contrast those children adopted before the age of six months rarely displayed disinhibited attachment.

Zeanah *et al.*'s research

Procedure Charles Zeanah *et al.* (2005) conducted the Bucharest early intervention (BEI) project, assessing attachment in 95 Romanian children aged 12–31 months who had spent most of their lives in institutional care (90% on average). They were compared to a control group of 50 children who had never lived in an institution. Their attachment type was measured using the **Strange Situation**. In addition carers were asked about unusual social behaviour including clingy, attention-seeking behaviour directed inappropriately at all adults (a measure of disinhibited attachment).

Findings The researchers found that 74% of the control group were classed as **securely attached** in the Strange Situation. However, only 19% of the institutional group were securely attached. In contrast, the description of disinhibited attachment applied to 44% of institutionalised children as opposed to less than 20% of the controls.

Effects of institutionalisation

Disinhibited attachment Children who have spent their early lives in an institution often show signs of disinhibited attachment, being equally friendly and affectionate towards familiar people and strangers. This is highly unusual behaviour – remember that most children in their second year show **stranger anxiety**.

Rutter (2006) has explained disinhibited attachment as an adaptation to living with multiple caregivers during the sensitive period for attachment formation (see Shaffer's stages of attachment, page 76 and Bowlby's critical period for attachment, page 84). In poor quality institutions, like those in Romania, a child might have 50 carers but doesn't spend enough time with any one of them to be able to form a secure attachment.

Intellectual disability In Rutter's study most children showed signs of intellectual disability when they arrived in Britain. However, most of those adopted before they were six months old caught up with the control group by age four.

It appears that, like emotional development, damage to intellectual development as a result of institutionalisation can be recovered provided adoption takes place before the age of six months – the age at which attachments form.

Evaluation

Real-world application

One strength of the Romanian orphanage studies is their application to improve conditions for children growing up outside their family home.

Studying the Romanian orphans has improved psychologists' understanding of the effects of early institutional care and how to prevent the worst of these effects (Langton 2006). This has led to improvements in the conditions experienced by looked-after children, i.e. children growing up in the care system. For example children's homes now avoid having large numbers of caregivers for each child. Instead the children tend to have one or two 'key workers' who play a central role in their emotional care. Also institutional care is now seen as an undesirable option for looked-after children. Considerable effort is made to accommodate such children in foster care or to have them adopted instead.

This means that children in institutional care have a chance to develop normal attachments and disinhibited attachment is avoided.

Fewer confounding variables

Another strength of the Romanian studies is the lack of **confounding variables**.

There were many orphan studies before the Romanian orphans became available to study (e.g. orphans studied during the Second World War). Many of the children studied in orphanages had experienced varying degrees of trauma, and it is difficult to disentangle the effects of neglect, physical abuse and bereavement from those of institutional care. However the children from Romanian orphanages had, in the main, been handed over by loving parents who could not afford to keep them.

This means that results were much less likely to be confounded by other negative early experiences (higher internal validity).

Counterpoint On the other hand, studying children from Romanian orphanages might have introduced different confounding variables. The quality of care in these institutions was remarkably poor, with children receiving very little intellectual stimulation or comfort.

This means that the harmful effects seen in studies of Romanian orphans may represent the effects of *poor* institutional care rather than institutional care *per se*.

Lack of adult data

One limitation of the Romanian orphanage studies is the current lack of data on adult development.

The latest data from the ERA Study looked at the children in their early- to mid-20s. This means that we do not currently have data to answer some of the most interesting research questions about the long-term effects of early institutional care. These research questions include the lifetime prevalence of mental health problems and participants' success in forming and maintaining adult romantic and parental relationships. It will take a long time to gather this data because of the **longitudinal** design of the study, i.e. the same participants are followed over a long period.

This means it will be some time before we know more completely what the long-term effects are for the Romanian orphans. It is possible that late-adopted children may 'catch up'.

Evaluation eXtra

Social sensitivity

The Romanian orphan studies are socially sensitive because the results show that late-adopted children typically have poor developmental outcomes. Results have been published while the children have been growing up, meaning that their parents, teachers and anyone else who knew them might have lowered their expectations and treated the adopted children differently. This might even have created a self-fulfilling prophecy.

On the other hand, much has been learned from the Romanian orphan studies that might benefit future institutionalised or potentially institutionalised children.

Consider: *Should the results of the Romanian orphan studies have been published?*

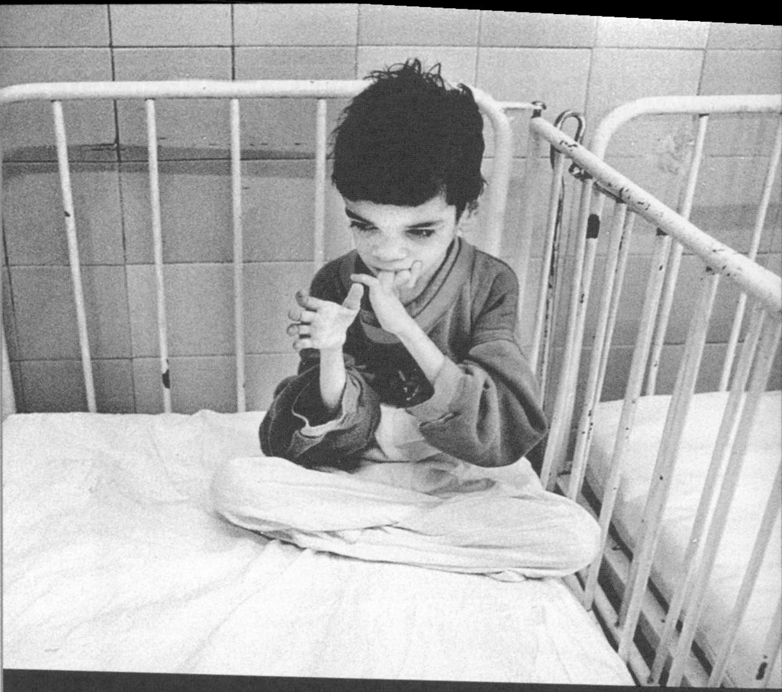

The Romanian orphanages may have been of such bad quality that results cannot be generalised to other institutions.

Apply it Concepts — Nadia

Nadia was adopted when she was two years old. Prior to this she had lived in a home for orphans. Now at the age of 11 she is doing well at school but her parents and teachers have noticed that she has a tendency to be attention-seeking with familiar people and strangers. Her adoptive parents wonder if this could be related to her early experiences before being adopted.

Question

Referring to the effects of institutionalisation, explain why Nadia may be showing this unusual social behaviour.

Apply it Concepts — Irena

Irena was adopted by British parents when she was two months old. She had lived for most of her life prior to this in a poor quality Romanian orphanage. At the age of 16 she did less well in her GCSEs than most of her friends. A family friend (actually a pretty rubbish friend) says to Irena's adoptive mother 'what can you expect with her background?'.

Question

Referring to what you know about the intellectual development of Romanian orphans adopted in Britain, what would you say to the family friend?

Check it

1. Briefly outline what is meant by 'institutionalisation'. *[2 marks]*
2. Outline what research has found about the effects of 'institutionalisation' on attachment. *[6 marks]*
3. Describe **and** evaluate research (theories and/or studies) into Romanian orphans. *[12 marks AS, 16 marks AL]*

Influence of early attachment on later relationships

The specification says...

The influence of early attachment on childhood and adult relationships, including the role of an internal working model.

The major importance of attachment is its role in the ability to form relationships with people other than your primary attachment figure. On this spread we look again at Bowlby's idea of internal working models and at research into the link between attachment type and the quality of later relationships.

Key terms

Childhood relationships Affiliations with other people in childhood, including friends and classmates, and with adults such as teachers.

Adult relationships Those relationships the child goes on to have later in life as an adult. These include friendships and working relationships but most critically relationships with romantic partners and the person's own children.

Internal working model Our mental representations of the world, e.g. the representation we have of our relationship to our primary attachment figure. This model affects our future relationships because it carries our perception of what relationships are like.

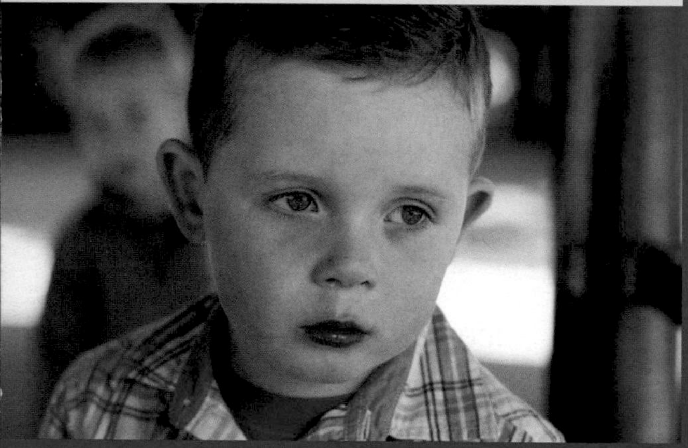

Insecure–resistant babies are the most likely to struggle to get on with friends as they get older.

Attachment and later relationships

Internal working model

Earlier in this chapter we discussed the formation of the **internal working model** (see page 84). John Bowlby (1969) suggested that a baby's first relationship with their primary attachment figure leads to a mental representation of this relationship. This internal working model acts as a template for future **childhood** and **adult relationships**.

The quality of a baby's first attachment is crucial because this template will powerfully affect the nature of their future relationships. A baby whose first experience is of a loving relationship with a reliable attachment figure will tend to assume this is how relationships are meant to be. They will then seek out functional relationships and behave functionally within them, i.e. without being too uninvolved or emotionally close (which would typify **insecure–avoidant attachment**) or being controlling and argumentative (**insecure–resistant attachment**).

A child with bad experiences of their first attachment will bring these bad experiences to bear on later relationships. This may mean they struggle to form relationships in the first place or they may not behave appropriately within relationships, displaying insecure–avoidant or insecure–resistant behaviour towards friends and partners.

Relationships in childhood

Attachment type is associated with the quality of peer relationships in childhood. **Securely attached** babies tend to go on to form the best quality childhood friendships whereas insecurely attached babies later have friendship difficulties (Kerns 1994).

In particular, bullying behaviour can be predicted by attachment type. Rowan Myron-Wilson and Peter Smith (1998) assessed attachment type and bullying involvement using standard questionnaires in 196 children aged 7–11 from London. Secure children were very unlikely to be involved in bullying. Insecure–avoidant children were the most likely to be victims and insecure–resistant children were most likely to be bullies.

Relationships in adulthood

Internal working models affect two major adult experiences – romantic relationships and parental relationships with your own children.

A classic study about romantic relationships and attachment, by Cindy Hazan and Phillip Shaver (1987), is described on the left. In another, Gerard McCarthy (1999) studied 40 adult women who had been assessed when they were babies to establish their early attachment type. Those assessed as securely attached babies had the best adult friendships and romantic relationships. Adults classed as insecure–resistant as babies had particular problems maintaining friendships whilst those classed as insecure–avoidant struggled with intimacy in romantic relationships.

Internal working models also affect the child's ability to parent their own children. People tend to base their parenting style on their internal working model so attachment type tends to be passed on through generations of a family. Recall the study by Heidi Bailey *et al.* (2007, see page 85). They considered the attachments of 99 mothers to their babies and to their own mothers. Mother–baby attachment was assessed using the **Strange Situation** and mother's attachment to their own mother was assessed using an adult attachment interview. The majority of women had the same attachment classification both to their babies and their own mothers.

The love quiz

Hazan and Shaver (1987) conducted a classic study of the association between attachment and adult relationships.

Procedure – They analysed 620 replies to a 'love quiz' printed in an American local newspaper. The quiz had three sections. The first assessed respondents' current or most important relationship. The second part assessed general love experiences such as number of partners. The third section assessed attachment type by asking respondents to choose which of three statements best described their feelings.

Findings and conclusion – 56% of respondents were identified as securely attached, with 25% insecure–avoidant and 19% insecure–resistant. Those reporting secure attachments were the most likely to have good and longer-lasting romantic experiences. The avoidant respondents tended to reveal jealousy and fear of intimacy. These findings suggest that patterns of attachment behaviour are reflected in romantic relationships.

Apply it Methods — Questionnaires and interviews

Research into the quality of peer and romantic relationships and attachment requires self-reporting of attitudes towards and experiences of relationships. This can be done by means of interviews or questionnaires. Interviews can be structured or unstructured. The kinds of interviews used to assess relationship quality are usually structured.

Questions

1. Explain how you might use both a **questionnaire** and an **interview** to assess the quality of peer relationships. (*2 marks*)
2. Why would psychologists usually use a **structured interview** to assess relationship quality? (*2 marks*)
3. Explain why you might use **closed questions** in your interview. (*2 marks*)

Evaluation

Research support

One strength of the research into attachment and later relationships is supporting evidence.

We have looked at studies linking attachment to later development. Reviews of such evidence (e.g. Fearon and Roisman 2017) have concluded that early attachment consistently predicts later attachment, emotional well-being and attachment to own children. How strong the relationship is between early attachment type and later development depends both on the attachment type and the aspect of later development. So whilst insecure–avoidant attachment seems to convey fairly mild disadvantages for any aspect of development, **disorganised attachment** is strongly associated with later mental disorder.

This means that secure attachment as a baby appears to convey advantages for future development while disorganised attachment appears to seriously disadvantage children.

Counterpoint Not all evidence supports the existence of close links between early attachment and later development. For example the Regensburg longitudinal study (Becker-Stoll *et al.* 2008) followed 43 individuals from one year of age. At age 16 attachment was assessed using the adult attachment interview and there was no evidence of continuity.

This means that it is not clear to what extent the quality of early attachment really predicts later development. There may be other important factors.

Validity issues with retrospective studies

One limitation of most research into the influence of attachment is that early attachment is assessed retrospectively.

Most research on the link between early attachment and later development are not longitudinal (i.e. they don't assess attachment in early life and then revisit the same person later in life). Instead researchers usually ask adolescent or adult participants questions about their relationship with parents, and identify attachment type from this. This causes two **validity** problems. First, asking questions relies on the honesty and accurate perception of the participants. Second, it means it is very hard to know whether what is being assessed is early attachment or in fact adult attachment (see evidence from the Regensburg longitudinal study above).

This means that the measures of early attachment used in most studies may be confounded with other factors making them meaningless.

Confounding variables

A further limitation of studies into the influence of early attachment on later development is the existence of **confounding variables**.

Some studies do assess attachment in infancy (e.g. McCarthy on facing page), which means that the assessment of early attachment is valid. However, even these studies may have validity problems because associations between attachment quality and later development may be affected by confounding variables. For example parenting style may influence both attachment quality and later development. Alternatively genetically-influenced personality may be an influence on both factors.

This means that we can never be entirely sure that it is early attachment and not some other factor that is influencing later development.

Evaluation eXtra

Balancing opportunity and risk

It seems likely that the influence of early attachment is probabilistic (Clarke and Clarke 1998). This means that an insecure attachment does not invariably cause increased risk of later developmental problems – no one is inevitably going to have unsuccessful romantic relationships because of their early attachment experiences. It may be more likely but a host of other factors are involved.

By knowing someone's attachment status we have an opportunity to intervene and help their development. However, we may also become too pessimistic and create a self-fulfilling prophecy.

Consider: *Is it better to know that a child is at increased risk of developmental problems as a result of insecure attachment or can this knowledge do more harm than good?*

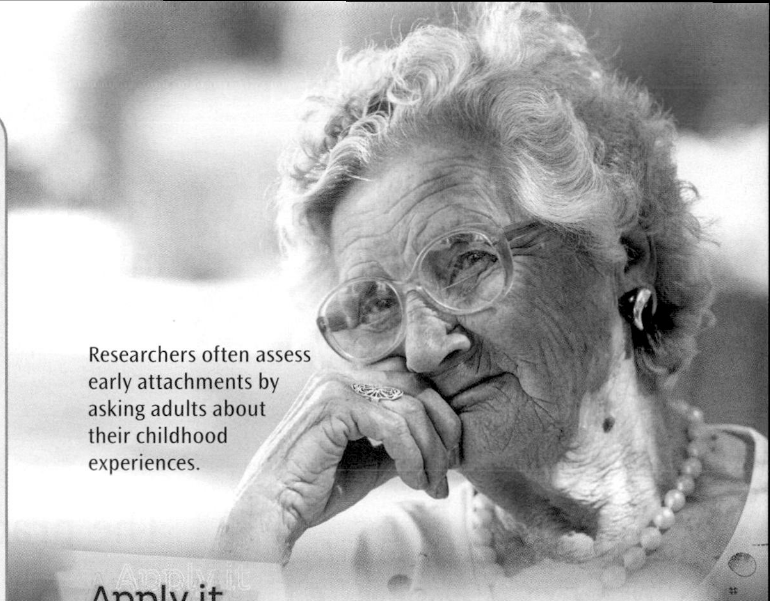

Researchers often assess early attachments by asking adults about their childhood experiences.

Apply it Concepts: Internal working models in social work

Sarah works in Social Services assessing risk to children from parents who have been referred after issues have arisen with the quality of their parenting. Sarah has just received a new case – a neighbour of a family with a 10-year-old girl has complained that the child is being neglected. When Sarah interviews the mother about the family it emerges that the mother was neglected in her own childhood.

Question

Referring to internal working models, explain what Sarah might think about the origins of the alleged neglect.

Apply it Concepts: Internal working models in therapy

Some types of psychological therapy make use of internal working models.

Gary and Carly have just started relationship counselling. They have been together for a year but they have frequent rows. Carly feels that Gary is distant and wants to spend a lot of time alone. Gary says he is not used to intimacy. He also objects to Carly wanting to know where he is and starting rows.

Gary and Carly have very different relationships with their parents. Gary's mother was always fairly uninvolved and they are not close now. Carly says that her mother is argumentative and controlling.

Question

What might their therapist say about Gary's and Carly's internal working models?

Check it

1. Explain what is meant by an 'internal working model'. *[3 marks]*
2. Describe what psychological research has shown about the link between early attachment **and** adult relationships. *[6 marks]*
3. Describe **and** evaluate research into the influence of attachment on childhood **and** adult relationships. *[12 marks AS, 16 marks AL]*

Practical corner

The specification says...

Knowledge and understanding of ... research methods, practical research skills and maths skills. These should be developed through ... ethical practical research activities.

This means that you should conduct practical investigations wherever possible. For both practical and ethical reasons we don't recommend you carry out practical work with young children, but there are relevant things you can do using your peers as participants, as suggested here. One practical activity uses observational techniques, the other involves questionnaires as the means of assessing the dependent variable in a quasi-experiment.

Ethics check

Ethics are discussed in detail on pages 178–179. We strongly suggest that you complete this checklist before collecting data.

1. Do participants know participation is voluntary?
2. Do participants know what to expect?
3. Do participants know they can withdraw at any time?
4. Are individuals' results anonymous?
5. Have I minimised the risk of distress to participants?
6. Have I avoided asking sensitive questions?
7. Will I avoid bringing my school/teacher/psychology into disrepute?
8. Have I considered all other ethical issues?
9. Has my teacher approved this?

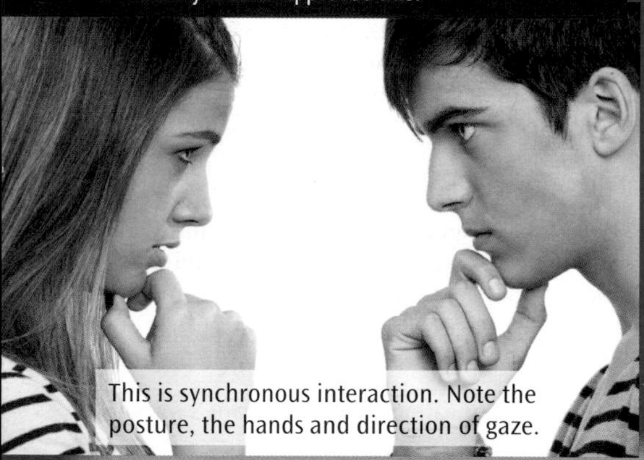

This is synchronous interaction. Note the posture, the hands and direction of gaze.

Practical idea 1: Observing synchronous interactions in adult conversation

It would be great to observe synchronous interactions in a mother and baby but there is the practical issue of having a mother and baby available! However, synchronous interactions can be observed between pairs of adults. We suggest that you can observe synchronous interactions happening in peer-to-peer communication.

The aim of this study is to investigate whether people's non-verbal communication (NVC) synchronises, i.e. becomes more similar during a conversation. This involves the use of **observational techniques**.

The practical bit

You are testing the hypothesis that NVC becomes more synchronised as a conversation progresses. If we want this interaction to mimic what takes place between mother and baby, the communication needs to be friendly – this won't work with an argument!

Choosing your participants

The usual considerations about **sampling** don't really apply in this study. You only need to look at two people, although there is no reason why you shouldn't extend this to a larger sample if you wish. It is, however, critical that interaction between the two participants is friendly and natural, therefore it is more important that the two people you observe already have a reasonable level of intimacy than it is that they are representative of the **population**. Choose two friends or perhaps a romantic couple.

Behavioural categories

You will need to decide what to observe. We suggest looking at facial expression or gestures. You could also look at posture if you wish. You will need to agree specific **behavioural categories** that will capture the kind of NVC you are likely to see. Things like smiling, laughing, frowning, direction of gaze and clasping hands or waving hands should work. Maybe conduct a **pilot study** in which you watch pairs talking and make a note of their NVC. These can form your behavioural categories. Don't have too many categories because you may find it difficult to record what is going on. When you know what you are looking for, draw up a table like the one in the Apply it below.

Time sampling

You are interested in whether NVC synchronise during a conversation so you need to regularly check whether each category is synchronised at an agreed time interval, say every 30 seconds. At exactly that point observe the two participants and record whether each target behaviour is synchronised.

Ethical issues

This study should be ethically acceptable as long as it is conducted well, but there are some issues to be aware of. Make sure you have real consent from your observees. They should know exactly what is going to happen to them and there should be no social pressure to participate. Participants must be aware of their **right to withdraw**. If you film the interactions you must delete the video file once it has been analysed.

Analysing your data

You will need to present your results in the form of tables and graphs (see suggestions in the Apply it below). You will want to be able to show your results so that someone will instantly be able to see whether synchrony increases during the course of a conversation.

Table 1 Synchronisation of NVC at 30-second intervals.
y = synchronised   n = not synchronised

	30s	60s	90s	120s	150s	180s	210s	240s
Smile/frown	n	n	y	y	n	y	y	y
Gaze	n	n	n	y	y	n	y	y
Hands	n	n	n	n	y	y	y	y
Posture	n	n	n	n	n	y	y	y
Total synchronised	0	0	1	2	2	3	4	4

Apply it **Methods**

The maths bit 1

1. Identify *two or more* characteristics of good **behavioural categories**. (*2 marks*)
2. What fraction of the scores in Table 1 are synchronised? (*2 marks*)
3. Explain this statement 'number of synchronised observations > number of not synchronised observations'. (*1 mark*)
4. What conclusion would you reach based on the information in Table 1? (*2 marks*)
5. Draw a **scattergram** to show the **correlation** between time spent in conversation and synchronisation. (*3 marks*)
6. Draw a **bar chart** to represent the data in Table 1. (*3 marks*)

Practical idea 2: Attachment to mobile phones

We love our mobile phones. No really, we actually *love* them! We don't just get attached to people. We also display **attachment** behaviour to fictional characters, places and even technology. Jane Vincent (2006) has identified a range of reasons for our attachment to phones – we use phones frequently, we rely on them, associate them with social relationships and take comfort in the fact that they allow us to interact with loved ones.

The aim of this study is to use **questionnaires** (or **interviews**) to see if people of different phone attachment types respond differently to the loss of their phone. The study is a **quasi-experiment** because the **independent variable** is attachment type.

People really love their mobile phones.

The practical bit

This will require putting together your own **self-report** measures. You will need a measure of attachment to phone type and a way to assess people's distress at losing their phone.

Ethics ethics ethics!!!!!

There are some critical **ethical issues** to get right in this study, mostly around the risks of harm and distress. First, you have no business assessing people's general attachment types. The risk of seriously worrying and upsetting them is just too great. Your attachment measure must purely measure the quality of people's attachment to their mobile phone.

Second, you should not try to assess participants' reaction to a real loss of their phone. In other words you can't steal it – even for a short period – just to see the response! Instead you must ask people to imagine their response to the loss of their phone.

Your measure of attachment to phone

You need to put together a simple way to classify people's attachment to their phone as **secure**, **insecure–avoidant** or **insecure–resistant**. One way is to ask participants to choose which of three statements (on the right) best describes their attachment to their phone. These statements were used by Cindy Hazan and Phillip Shaver to classify romantic attachment type.

A secure attachment to your phone will be indicated by high in affection for it but low dependence. An insecure–avoidant relationship will be more distant and you might not want to be dependent on your phone. Someone with an insecure–resistant attachment may show ambivalent feelings about the phone but not entirely trust it.

Your measure of phone-loss anxiety

You also need a way to measure how anxious people would become if they lost their phone. The simplest way to do this is to ask them to imagine they cannot find their phone and rate their anxiety on a scale, for example 0–10.

Analysing your data

You will need to present your results in the form of tables and graphs. You will want to be able to show your results so that someone will instantly be able to compare the average anxiety rating for each attachment type. These can be presented as tables of averages or bar charts.

Question: Which of the following best describes your feelings?

Secure: I find it relatively easy to get close to others and am comfortable depending on them and having them depend on me. I don't often worry about being abandoned or about someone getting too close to me.

Avoidant: I am somewhat uncomfortable being close to others; I find it difficult to trust them completely, difficult to allow myself to depend on them. I am nervous when anyone gets too close, and often love partners want me to be more intimate than I feel comfortable being.

Anxious/ambivalent: I find that others are reluctant to get as close as I would like. I often worry that my partner doesn't really love me or won't want to stay with me. I want to merge completely with another person, and this desire sometimes scares people away.

A way of classifying romantic attachment into attachment types. From Hazan and Shaver (1987)

Study tip

Sometimes when you read about a practical activity that was thought up by other people it is hard to visualise the study. We find that it can be useful to look first at the exemplar table of results or the graph of similar findings and work backwards from that. So, in this study, if you aren't getting it yet, look at the graph.

Apply it Methods

The maths bit 2

Graph showing anxiety score in participants with avoidant, secure and resistant attachments to phones.

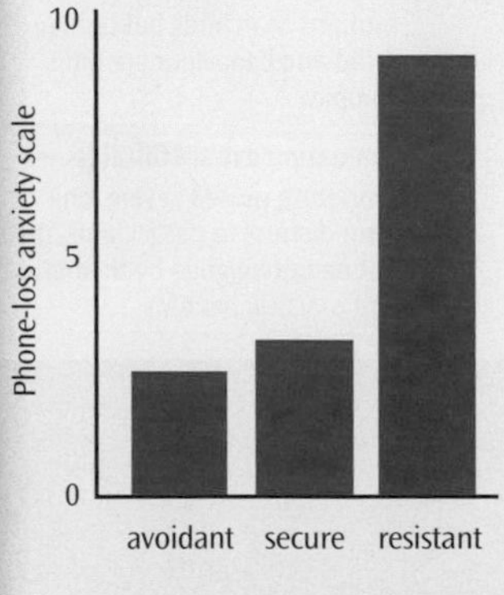

10
5
0
Phone-loss anxiety scale
avoidant
secure
resistant

1. Explain why the data in this **bar chart** could be described as **quantitative**. (*2 marks*)
2. Explain *one* strength and *one* limitation of using this kind of data in this study. (*2 marks + 2 marks*)
3. Estimate the **mean** anxiety score for avoidant, secure and resistant participants from the bar chart. (*3 marks*)
4. Give each of these mean scores as a fraction and a percentage of the total. (*3 marks*)
5. What conclusion would you draw from the bar chart on the left? (*2 marks*)

The maths bit

On page 217 we have given a list of the mathematical skills you will be expected to demonstrate.

Overall, at least 10% of the marks in assessments for Psychology will require the use of mathematical skills.

Revision summaries

Caregiver-infant interactions

Caregiver interactions facilitate attachment.

Research

Interactions
Babies have frequent and important interactions with their caregiver.

Reciprocity
Turn-taking.
Mothers respond when baby is alert.
From 3 months becomes more intense and reciprocal.

Interactional synchrony
Same actions simultaneously.
Interactions co-ordinated from two weeks (Meltzoff and Moore).
Quality of attachment related to synchrony (Isabella *et al.*).

Evaluation

Filmed observations
Capture fine detail, can establish inter-rater reliability and babies not aware of being observed.

Difficulty observing babies
Hard to know meaning of small movements.

Developmental importance
Observation of behaviour does not tell us about its importance in development.
Counterpoint – evidence from e.g. Isabella *et al.* suggests interactional synchrony is important for attachment.

Evaluation extra: Practical value versus ethics
Attachment research has practical value but is controversial (implications for working mothers).

Schaffer's stages of attachment

A classic study of the development of attachment.

The theory

Asocial stage
First few weeks, same response to humans and objects.

Indiscriminate attachment
2–7 months, preference for (familiar) people, no stranger/separation anxiety.

Specific attachments
Stranger and separation anxiety in regard to one particular adult = primary attachment figure (65% were mother).

Multiple attachments
Soon after attachment behaviour directed towards more than one adult (secondary attachments).

Schaffer and Emerson's research
Procedure
Mothers of 60 working-class Glasgow babies reported monthly on separation and stranger anxiety.
Findings
Babies' attachment behaviour progressed as detailed in Schaffer and Emerson's stage theory.

Evaluation

Good external validity
Mothers did the observing so babies not stressed by being observed.
Counterpoint – mothers might not have accurately noted behaviour.

Poor evidence for the asocial stage
Babies have poor co-ordination, so just may seem asocial.

Real-world application
No harm in starting at day care during asocial/indiscriminate stages (any skilled adult adequate), but problematic starting day care in specific attachment stage.

Evaluation extra: Generalisability
Data gathered only in 1960s working-class Glasgow, e.g. multiple attachment may be different in collectivist cultures (van IJzendoorn).

Role of the father

Fathers' contributions should not be overlooked.

Research

Attachment to fathers
Most babies attach to their father, (75% by 18 months) but rarely as the first attachment (only 3% first sole attachment) (Schaffer and Emerson).

Distinctive role for fathers
Fathers may have a distinctive role involving play and stimulation (Grossmann *et al.*).

Fathers as primary attachment figures
Those fathers who were primary caregivers more responsive than secondary caregiver fathers (Field).

Evaluation

Confusion over research questions
Competing research questions prevent a simple answer about the father's role.

Conflicting evidence
Studies have reached different conclusions about a distinctive role for fathers.
Counterpoint – fathers may be predisposed to a role but single mothers and lesbian parents simply take on these roles.

Real-world application
Families can be advised about the father's role in attachment.

Evaluation extra: Bias in this research
Preconceptions lead to observer bias, may affect some studies.

Explanations of attachment: Learning theory

Cupboard love theory (Dollard and Miller).

The theory

Classical conditioning
Caregiver (neutral stimulus) associated with food (unconditioned stimulus).
Caregiver becomes conditioned stimulus.

Operant conditioning
Crying behaviour reinforced positively for baby and negatively for caregiver.

Attachment as a secondary drive
Attachment becomes a secondary drive through association with hunger.

Evaluation

Counter-evidence from animal studies
Lorenz and Harlow showed that feeding is not the key to attachment.

Counter-evidence from studies on humans
Primary attachment figure not always person who does feeding (Schaffer and Emerson), quality of attachment related to interactional synchrony not feeding (Isabella *et al.*).

Some conditioning may be involved
Conditioning (association with comfort) may influence the choice of primary attachment figure.
Counterpoint – babies are more active in attachment than conditioning explanations suggest (Feldman and Eidelman).

Evaluation extra: Social learning theory
Involves modelling attachment behaviours, includes role of active baby (Hay and Vespo).

Animal studies of attachment

Important insights into human behaviour.

Lorenz's research

Procedure
Goslings saw Lorenz when they hatched.

Findings
Newly-hatched chicks attach to the first moving object they see (imprinting).

Sexual imprinting
Adult birds try to mate with whatever species or object they imprint on.

Evaluation

Research support
Regolin and Vallortigara observed chicks imprint on moving shapes.

Generalisability to humans
Attachment systems in birds are less complex and not two-way.

Evaluation extra: Applications to human behaviour
Imprinting explains computer operating system choice (Seebach).

Harlow's research

Procedure
Baby monkeys given cloth-covered or plain-wire 'mother' with feeding bottle attached.

Findings
Monkeys clung to cloth surrogate rather than wire one, regardless of which dispensed milk.

Maternally deprived monkeys as adults
Grew up socially dysfunctional.

The critical period for normal development
After 90 days attachments wouldn't form.

Evaluation

Real-world value
Helps professionals (e.g. social workers) to promote bonding (Howe), also applied to zoos and breeding programmes.

Generalisability to humans
Monkeys more similar to humans than birds but human mind and behaviour are more complex.

Evaluation extra: Ethical issues
Procedure caused severe long-term distress to participants, may not be outweighed by theoretical and practical benefits.

Explanations of attachment: Bowlby's theory

The dominant theory of attachment behaviour.

The theory

Monotropy
One particular attachment is different in quality and importance than others.

Social releasers and the critical period
Innate cute behaviours elicit care.
Critical period up to 6 months, possibly extending to 2 years.

Internal working model
Mental representation of the primary attachment relationship is a template for future relationships.

Evaluation

Validity of monotropy challenged
The primary attachment may be stronger but not different in nature.

Support for social releasers
Babies became upset when attachment figure ignored social releasers (Brazelton *et al.*).

Support for internal working model
Quality of attachment is passed on through generations (Bailey *et al.*).
Counterpoint – ignores other factors (e.g. genetic) in social behaviour and parenting (Kornienko).

Evaluation extra: Feminist concerns
Bowlby's views imply that mothers shouldn't work outside the home (Burman), but Bowlby also gave the mother's role greater credit and the theory had real-world applications.

Types of attachment

Measuring attachment quality.

The Strange Situation

Procedure
7-stage controlled observation.
Assesses proximity-seeking, exploration and secure base, stranger and separation anxiety, response to reunion.

Findings – types of attachment
Babies show consistent patterns of attachment behaviour.
Types of attachment:

- Secure – enthusiastic greeting, generally content, moderate anxiety.
- Avoidant – avoids reunion, generally reduced responses.
- Resistant – resists reunion, generally more distressed.

Evaluation

Good predictive validity
Attachment type predicts later social behaviour e.g. school success, bullying (McCormick *et al.*, Kokkinos).
Counterpoint – Kagan suggests behavioural differences due to genetically-influenced anxiety levels.

Good reliability
94% agreement between trained observers (Bick *et al.*)

The test may be culture-bound
Strange Situation developed in Britain and US, other cultures have different experiences that affect behaviour in the Strange Situation (e.g. in Japan, Takahashi).

Evaluation extra: Other attachment types
Also Type D (Main and Solomon), but related to abnormal experiences and outcomes.

Cultural variations in attachment

Mother–baby relationships differ around the world.

Research

van IJzendoorn and Kroonenberg's research
Compared rates of attachment type in 8 countries.
More variation within than between countries.

Other studies of cultural variations
Simonelli *et al.*: Italian secure attachment rates dropped to 50%, may be due to increased day care.
Jin *et al.*: Korean secure vs insecure attachment rates similar to other studies. But insecure–avoidant similar to Japan, could be due to similar child-rearing styles.

Conclusions
It appears that attachment is innate and universal and secure attachment is the norm.
However cultural practices affect rates of attachment types.

Evaluation

Indigenous researchers
e.g. Grossmann *et al.* (German), reduces bias and miscommunication with participants.
Counterpoint – not true of all cross-cultural studies (e.g. Americans Morelli and Tronick).

Confounding variables
Apparent cultural differences might have been due to sample characteristics or environmental differences (e.g. room size).

Imposed etic
Behaviours in the Strange Situation have different meanings in different cultures (e.g. low affection = independence in Germany).

Evaluation extra: Competing explanations
Cross-cultural similarity may be due to innate system or media influences.

Bowlby's theory of maternal deprivation

Concerns the negative effects of loss of emotional care.

The theory

Separation versus deprivation
Physical separation only leads to deprivation when the child loses emotional care.

The critical period
The first 2½ years are critical and deprivation in that time causes damage.

Effects on development
Goldfarb – deprivation causes low IQ.
Bowlby – deprivation of emotional care leads to affectionless psychopathy.

Bowlby's research
Many more affectionless psychopaths than controls had prolonged early separations.

Evaluation

Flawed evidence
Bowlby may have been a biased observer.
Goldfarb's study had confounding variables.
Counterpoint – research with rats shows deprivation can harm social development (Lévy *et al.*).

Deprivation and privation
Some of the 44 thieves may have been 'prived', deprivation may be less damaging (Rutter).

Critical versus sensitive period
Czech twins' (Koluchová) recovery suggests it is a sensitive period.

Evaluation extra: Conflicting evidence
No evidence for link between deprivation and psychopathy (e.g. Lewis), but other research supports it (e.g. Gao *et al.*).

Romanian orphan studies: Institutionalisation

An example of the effects of (de)privation.

Research

Rutter *et al.*'s research
ERA project studied 165 Romanian orphans adopted in UK later showed low IQ and disinhibited attachment.

Zeanah *et al.*'s research
BEI project found secure attachment in 19% of institutional group (74% in controls), disinhibited attachment in 44% (20% in controls).

Effects of institutionalisation
Disinhibited attachment and delay in intellectual development if institutionalisation continues after sensitive period for attachment.

Evaluation

Real-world application
Both institutional care and adoption practice have been improved using lessons from Romanian orphans.

Fewer confounding variables
Romanian orphans had fewer negative influences before institutionalisation than e.g. war orphans.
Counterpoint – especially poor conditions in Romanian orphanages could be a confounding variable.

Lack of adult data
We don't know the effects of institutional care on adult development.

Evaluation extra: Social sensitivity
Findings report poor outcomes for late-adopted children, might affect self and others' expectations.

Influence of early attachments on later relationships

The effect of the internal working model.

Research

Internal working model
Bowlby's idea that the primary attachment relationship provides a template for later relationships.

Relationships in childhood
Securely attached children have better friendships (Kerns).
Securely attached children less likely to be involved in bullying (Myron-Wilson and Smith).

Relationships in adulthood
Securely attached adults have better relationships with friends and partners (McCarthy).
Secure responders had better and longer-lasting relationships, avoidant responders had fear of intimacy (Hazan and Shaver).
Mothers' attachment type matched that of their mothers and their babies (Bailey *et al.*).

Evaluation

Research support
Review (Fearon and Roisman) showed consistent links e.g. disorganised type and mental disorder.
Counterpoint – Regensburg longitudinal study (Becker-Stoll *et al.*) no continuity in attachment type from 1 to 16 years.

Validity issues with retrospective studies
Self-report answers not always honest, and assumes that attachment type has remained the same into adulthood.

Confounding variables
Associations between attachment type and later development may be due to e.g. parenting style or genes.

Evaluation extra: Balancing opportunity and risk
Knowing early attachment type might cause self-fulfilling prophecies.

Practice questions, answers and feedback

Question 1 Schaffer identified different stages in the development of attachment. Briefly outline **one** of these different stages. (*2 marks*)

Morticia's answer *There are four different stages in Schaffer's theory: asocial stage, indiscriminate, discriminate and multiple attachments. In this last stage a baby forms more than one attachment.*	Morticia correctly identified three of the four stages (and got one wrong), but she only needed to name one. There is a partial outline here of multiple attachments but only a weak answer.
Luke's answer *The first stage is the asocial stage. In this stage a baby doesn't behave differently towards people and objects and has no attachments.*	Luke's is a more focused answer as one stage is identified (as required) and the outline is just about detailed enough for a question of this kind.
Vladimir's answer *One of the stages is when a baby becomes attached. Before that the baby has no especial attachments and after that the baby develops many attachments.*	Vladimir's answer would not gain any credit. He gives a vague and muddled answer that describes the process of attachment in general but not specific stages.

Question 2 Explain how the behaviour of a child who is classified as insecure–avoidant would be different from a child classified as insecure–resistant. (*4 marks*)

Morticia's answer *Insecure-avoidant means a baby avoids its mother on reunion whereas insecure-resistant means the baby resists at reunion. Another difference is in terms of stranger anxiety. Insecure-avoidant babies show little stranger anxiety whereas insecure-resistant babies show a lot.*	Morticia has clearly met the 'distinguish' requirement of the question and made two relevant contrasting points, so top-class answer.
Luke's answer *Stranger anxiety is low in both types of attachment and the same is true for separation anxiety. Avoidant children don't seek proximity but they do explore freely.*	The first part of Luke's answer is inaccurate. The second sentence is correct but there is no distinction made with resistant children so the answer offers nothing of value.
Vladimir's answer *Insecure-avoidant babies explore freely but don't seek proximity. They show little separation or stranger anxiety. Insecure-resistant babies resist comfort on reunion and can get very distressed.*	All the detail in Vladimir's answer is correct; however, his expression is poor. The reader is rather left to make the distinction between the two types themselves rather than being directed by Vladimir (Morticia's answer is much better in this respect). Therefore this constitutes a partial answer.

Question 3 Edgar is an only child. He is one year old. His mother has to work away from home most of the time so he is cared for by his father. Explain the relationship Edgar is likely to have with his father. Refer to psychological evidence in your answer. (*4 marks*)

Morticia's answer *Since he is cared for by his father most of the time then he might be securely attached to his father, though he might not be because research has shown that what matters is the quality of the relationship. So even though he isn't with his mother a lot of the time he still might be more closely attached to her. He would still be attached to his father but not as closely.*	In Morticia's answer the reference to secure attachment is relevant as is the evaluative comment regarding quality. There is very little evidence though so the answer is not really addressing the question.
Luke's answer *The role of the father can be for fun and play. Or children are sometimes most closely attached to their father, more than their mother. There is nothing that says close attachments have to be to mothers. There was a study where some children were more attached to their father than their mothers.*	Luke's answer is too generic and anecdotal (and there is also no application to Edgar). The brief reference to 'a study' at the end of the answer needs additional detail to be regarded as a contribution.
Vladimir's answer *The study by Schaffer and Emerson found that children were occasionally more closely attached to their fathers than their mothers. This means that Edgar might be more closely attached to his father especially as he spends more time with him. Though Schaffer and Emerson didn't find that amount of time was important.*	Vladimir makes reference to evidence here as well as a clear link to Edgar in the context of this. The analytical comment at the end is also relevant. The application and/or use of evidence needs a little bit more development.

Question 4 Briefly evaluate Bowlby's theory of maternal deprivation. (*3 marks*)

Morticia's answer *Bowlby claimed there was a critical period in development, around the age of 2. If attachments don't form at that time it is unlikely they will develop at all. The importance of attachments is that they influence relationships later in life because they are a template from the internal working model.*	Unfortunately Morticia appears to have misinterpreted the question and focused on Bowlby's monotropic theory of attachment instead. There is some marginal relevance in what is written. This reinforces the fact that questions should always be read carefully.
Luke's answer *One limitation of this theory is that Bowlby may have confused deprivation and privation. Another psychologist called Rutter pointed this out – the difference is that privation would refer to a child never having formed an attachment. This might be much more serious than separations and maybe some of Bowlby's 44 thieves experienced privation. So it is all muddled.*	Luke has focused on one limitation only but there is nothing in the question to suggest this is not a legitimate approach. This is a reasonably, well-elaborated point.
Vladimir's answer *There are some problems with the evidence. For example, in Bowlby's 44 thieves it could be that there were other extraneous variables, such as a poor physical environment, that caused the later problems. Other research has shown that children can recover from such experiences. Another issue is that animal studies were used to support this and they can't be generalised to humans.*	Vladimir takes a different approach and provides three separate evaluative points. The emphasis on evaluating the 'evidence' rather than the theory detracts from the overall value of the answer. Not as good an answer as Luke's.

On this spread we look at some typical student answers to questions. The comments provided indicate what is good and bad in each answer. Learning how to produce effective question answers is a SKILL. Read pages 213–223 for guidance.

Question 5 Discuss animal studies of attachment, including research by Lorenz and Harlow. (*12 marks AS, 16 marks AL*)	
Luke's answer *Animal studies of attachment are useful because you can't do the same kinds of things practically or ethically with humans, so they give support to theories like Bowlby's theory. In this essay I am going to describe and evaluate Lorenz's research on imprinting and Harlow's research on contact comfort. Both were important in the development of Bowlby's theory. Before Bowlby's theory there was also learning theory and this research was important in showing that learning theory was wrong.* *Lorenz did research with geese and goslings. He had a group of goose eggs and when one lot hatched the first thing they saw was Lorenz. They followed him around. To test this Lorenz put a whole lot of young geese together, some of them had imprinted on their real mother. As expected the ones that imprinted on Lorenz followed him instead of their real mother. Bowlby based his idea of attachment on imprinting and said that babies become attached like geese imprint – because it makes them more likely to survive as they stick close to an adult and are less likely to be eaten.* *Harlow's study was with baby monkeys. He had observed that baby monkeys often survived better in cages without their mother if you gave them a soft cloth to cuddle. He set up an experiment to test this where there were two wire mothers. One of the mothers was just wire-covered whereas the other was covered in cloth. The monkeys were kept all the time in a cage just with these two wire mothers. The monkeys spent their time with the cloth-covered mother not the other one which shows that contact comfort is important in attachment.* *The big issue with these studies is how much they do tell us about human attachment. In the case of geese they are quite different from humans because the attachment system is much more advanced. Research with monkeys is better because they are mammals too.* **(323 words)**	**Luke's essay is an AS response whereas Vladimir's is an A level response.** Apart from a hint of an evaluative point at the beginning, there is not really anything of value in Luke's first paragraph. Many students waste important time with introductory paragraphs. The second paragraph is better, though elements of the Lorenz description are poorly expressed. There is effective use of evidence at the end of the study though. There is more relevant detail of Harlow's research in the next section followed by another hint of analysis at the end. There is an evaluative comment in the final paragraph too but this should be developed much more. In summary, an overly descriptive essay that includes too little analysis.
Vladimir's answer *The two most important studies are by Lorenz and Harlow. Lorenz studied imprinting in geese. He did this by taking the eggs from a goose and putting some of them in an incubator so when they hatched the first thing they saw was Lorenz. The other eggs hatched with their mother. The goslings with Lorenz continued to follow him around.* *Lorenz also investigated the relationship between imprinting and mate preferences. He observed that a peacock tried to mate with a tortoise because it had been raised in a reptile house.* *Harlow did an experiment with monkeys kept in a cage with two wire mothers. In one condition the feeding bottle was on a wire mother with no covering. In another condition the bottle was on the other wire mother, which was covered in cloth. The monkeys always preferred the mother covered in cloth, which shows that feeding is not important in attachment.* *The research by both Lorenz and Harlow has been very valuable for understanding attachment and how early attachment affects later behaviour. There is support for imprinting from Regolin and Vallortigara who observed that chicks imprint on shapes and follow them when they moved. Later research on attachment supports Harlow's findings about difficulties later in life.* *There is the important issue of ethics. In both these studies the animal's subsequent development was affected by the research. For example the monkeys remained quite disturbed because they were raised in isolation. But it is a question of costs and benefits because, on the other hand, this research has been valuable not only in developing theories but also in the way children are treated. It has helped social workers understand the risk factors in child abuse.* *A major issue is how much these studies can be used in theories of human behaviour. In the case of geese there is much that is different. The mammalian attachment system is quite different from imprinting so it is a mistake to base the idea of attachment on the behaviour of birds. There is a stronger argument for generalising from monkeys to humans, as they are genetically very similar to us but nevertheless differ in important ways. For example, they do not have such prolonged childhoods and may not develop permanent relationships. Their behaviour is less guided by thinking than in the case of humans, which means that their behaviour would be more determined by experiences than their capacity to think about how to conduct a relationship.* **(411 words)**	This is an excellent essay that is extremely well written and clear throughout. The studies at the beginning of the answer are concisely presented but contain all the relevant details. Perhaps Vladimir could have used the evidence in the first paragraphs a little more effectively by adding an implication/conclusion at the end of each paragraph – a bit of analysis. However, this is a minor point. In the 4th paragraph there is effective use of supporting evidence for both Lorenz and Harlow. As this is a 'studies' rather than a 'theories' essay, discussion of ethical issues is perfectly appropriate (ethical issues can't change a theory) and the explanation of the costs and benefits in such research is particularly well considered. The rest of the answer is also impressive and develops the theme of generalisation (or the lack thereof) from animal studies to human behaviour very well.

Multiple-choice questions

Caregiver–infant interactions

1. Which of the following best describes reciprocity?
(a) A walk.
(b) A chat.
(c) A dance.
(d) A fight.

2. During interaction, the mother's and baby's signals are often seen to:
(a) Synchronise.
(b) Differentiate.
(c) Slow down.
(d) Stay the same.

3. Which of the following are associated with good quality caregiver–infant attachment?
(a) Low levels of caregiver skill in responding to signals.
(b) High levels of stress in caregiver(s).
(c) Low levels of interactional synchrony.
(d) High levels of interactional synchrony.

4. Which of these is a strength of research into early interaction?
(a) It is a socially sensitive topic.
(b) It is easy to interpret babies' behaviour.
(c) Controlled observations capture fine detail.
(d) Observations tell us the functions of behaviour.

Schaffer's stages of attachment

1. In which of these stages does a child first display social behaviour towards all adults?
(a) The asocial stage.
(b) The indiscriminate attachment stage.
(c) The specific attachment stage.
(d) The multiple attachment stage.

2. At what age do children usually start to form a specific attachment?
(a) 2 months.
(b) 7 months.
(c) 11 months.
(d) 18 months.

3. In the 1964 study which of the following best describes the participants?
(a) 60 girls aged 18 months from Glasgow.
(b) 60 middle-class children and fathers from Edinburgh.
(c) 30 working-class boys and their families from Glasgow.
(d) 60 working-class children and their families from Glasgow.

4. Schaffer and Emerson assessed what in the babies?
(a) Stranger anxiety.
(b) Separation anxiety.
(c) Separation and stranger anxiety.
(d) Zombie-related anxiety.

The role of the father

1. According to Schaffer and Emerson, what percentage of babies attach to their father before anyone else?
(a) 0%
(b) 3%
(c) 27%
(d) 50%

2. Which of the following statements best describes the importance of attachment to the father?
(a) Not important at all.
(b) The most important attachment.
(c) More important than attachment to the mother.
(d) Less important than attachment to the mother.

3. Which of the following activities is more common in fathers than mothers?
(a) Smiling.
(b) Holding.
(c) Imitating.
(d) Playing.

4. Which of these is a strength of research into the role of the father?
(a) It has real-world applications.
(b) It has good external reliability.
(c) It is subject to bias.
(d) It is socially sensitive.

Animal studies of attachment

1. The term that describes how early contact influences mate preference:
(a) Imprinting.
(b) Contact comfort.
(c) Deprivation.
(d) Sexual imprinting.

2. Which of these behaviours describes Harlow's monkeys that were maternally deprived?
(a) Aggressive.
(b) Sociable.
(c) Socially skilled.
(d) Good parents.

3. In which condition were Harlow's monkeys most damaged by early experience?
(a) Biological mother from birth.
(b) Wire mother with milk bottle.
(c) Wire mother covered in cloth.
(d) Biological mother from two months.

4. Which of the following statements is true of Lorenz's research?
(a) A control group was hatched with a mother goose.
(b) The experimental group was hatched with a mother goose.
(c) Both groups of young geese preferred the mother goose to Lorenz.
(d) Both groups of young geese preferred Lorenz to the mother goose.

Explanations of attachment: Learning theor

1. According to classical conditioning, which of the following best describes the attachment figure:
(a) An unconditioned stimulus.
(b) An unconditioned response.
(c) A conditioned stimulus.
(d) All the above.

2. A parent learning to comfort a crying baby in orde to stop it crying is an example of:
(a) Negative reinforcement.
(b) Positive reinforcement.
(c) Punishment.
(d) A primary drive.

3. In learning theory, which of the following is the focus of a primary drive?
(a) Food.
(b) Love.
(c) Comfort.
(d) Aggression.

4. Which of the following is true of learning theory explanations of attachment?
(a) They make use of classical conditioning only.
(b) There is counter-evidence from human studies.
(c) Attachment is seen as a primary drive.
(d) They focus on the role of interactional synchror

Explanations of attachment: Bowlby's theor

1. Which of the following statements is true of monotropy?
(a) One attachment is seen as different and more important than others.
(b) Children can only attach to one person.
(c) Children must have one caregiver only.
(d) The primary attachment figure must be the biological mother.

2. Which of the following is probably *not* a social releaser?
(a) Smiling.
(b) Cooing.
(c) Gripping.
(d) Projectile vomiting.

3. Internal working models have an influence on whi of the following?
(a) Romantic relationships.
(b) Relationships with children.
(c) Relationships with friends.
(d) All of these.

4. According to Bowlby, the critical period in humans may extend to:
(a) One month.
(b) Twelve months.
(c) Two years.
(d) Sixteen years.

Types of attachment

1. The Strange Situation can be best described as what kind of study?
   (a) Naturalistic observation.
   (b) Controlled observation.
   (c) Laboratory experiment.
   (d) Self-report.

2. How is separation anxiety assessed in the Strange Situation?
   (a) Being spoken to by a stranger.
   (b) Playing in an unfamiliar room.
   (c) Being left alone in the playroom.
   (d) Reunion with the primary attachment figure.

3. Which is true of securely attached babies in the Strange Situation?
   (a) They are clingy.
   (b) They get extremely anxious at separation.
   (c) They are happy at reunion with the primary attachment figure.
   (d) They show little or no anxiety.

4. Which of these is a strength of Ainsworth's attachment types?
   (a) Influence of temperament.
   (b) Inter-rater reliability of the Strange Situation.
   (c) Cross-cultural validity of the Strange Situation.
   (d) Additional attachment types appear to exist.

Cultural variations in attachment

1. In van IJzendoorn and Kroonenberg's study, which country had the highest rate of secure attachment?
   (a) Israel.
   (b) US.
   (c) Great Britain.
   (d) China.

2. In van IJzendoorn and Kroonenberg's study, which country had the highest rate of insecure–avoidant attachment?
   (a) Germany.
   (b) Sweden.
   (c) Great Britain.
   (d) Japan.

3. In their Italian study, Simonelli *et al.* found an unusually high level of:
   (a) Insecure–resistant attachment.
   (b) Secure attachment.
   (c) Insecure–avoidant attachment.
   (d) Atypical attachment.

4. Which is *not* true of cross-cultural attachment comparisons?
   (a) Secure attachment is the most common type in every country.
   (b) There is more variation within countries than between them.
   (c) Some attachment behaviours seem to have different meanings in different countries.
   (d) Some countries have particularly bad parents.

Bowlby's theory of maternal deprivation

1. Which of the following best describes maternal deprivation?
   (a) Separation from the primary attachment figure.
   (b) Failure to attach to a primary attachment figure.
   (c) Failure of attachment figures to feed the baby.
   (d) Loss of emotional care of the primary attachment figure without a substitute.

2. The critical period in which prolonged separation can lead to deprivation is within the first:
   (a) 6 months.
   (b) 1 year.
   (c) 2½ years.
   (d) 5 years.

3. Which of the following is true of the 44 thieves study?
   (a) There was no association between maternal deprivation and affectionless psychopathy.
   (b) Partial replications, e.g. Lewis (1954) have found similar results.
   (c) Goldfarb was part of the team investigating the 44 thieves.
   (d) There may be bias because Bowlby assessed affectionless psychopathy and deprivation.

4. Which of the following is *not* usually a symptom of affectionless psychopathy?
   (a) Lack of empathy.
   (b) Lack of guilt.
   (c) Inability to form close relationships.
   (d) Serial murder.

Romanian orphan studies: Institutionalisation

1. Which of the following best describes the aim of the ERA study?
   (a) A follow-up of Polish orphans looking at social and intellectual development.
   (b) A follow-up of Romanian orphans fostered in Romania.
   (c) A follow-up of Romanian orphans looking at social and intellectual development.
   (d) A follow-up testing the quality of adoptees available from Romania.

2. At four years:
   (a) A negative correlation was found between age at adoption and intellectual development.
   (b) A positive correlation was found between age at adoption and social-emotional development.
   (c) A positive correlation was found between age at adoption and intellectual development.
   (d) No correlations of any sort.

3. Which of the following is a symptom of disinhibited attachment?
   (a) Avoidant attachment behaviour.
   (b) Indiscriminate attachment behaviour.
   (c) Secure attachment behaviour.
   (d) Resistant attachment behaviour.

4. Why are the Romanian orphanage studies socially sensitive?
   (a) They involve adoption.
   (b) They involve immigration.
   (c) They risk self-fulfilling prophecies.
   (d) They risk breaking international law.

Influence of early attachment on later relationships

1. Which of these is a true statement concerning internal working models?
   (a) They serve as templates for future relationships.
   (b) They are the result of temperament.
   (c) They predict perfectly what sort of relationships people will have.
   (d) They determine social development and are unalterable.

2. According to Wilson and Smith (1998), which attachment type is likely to be linked with being a bully?
   (a) Securely attached.
   (b) Insecure–resistant.
   (c) Insecure–avoidant.
   (d) Disinhibited.

3. Which attachment type did McCarthy find had problems maintaining friendships in adulthood?
   (a) Securely attached.
   (b) Insecure–resistant.
   (c) Insecure–avoidant.
   (d) Disinhibited.

4. Which study found no evidence of continuity between infant and adult attachment?
   (a) Rutherford cross-cultural study.
   (b) Regensburg longitudinal study.
   (c) Romanian adoption project.
   (d) Rotterdam university project.

MCQ answers

Caregiver–infant interactions 1C, 2A, 3D, 4C
Schaffer's stages of attachment 1B, 2B, 3D, 4C
The role of the father 1B, 2D, 3D, 4A
Animal studies of attachment 1D, 2A, 3B, 4A
Explanations of attachment: Learning theory 1C, 2A, 3A, 4B
Explanations of attachment: Bowlby's theory 1A, 2D, 3D, 4C
Types of attachment 1B, 2C, 3C, 4B
Cultural variations in attachment 1C, 2A, 3B, 4D
Bowlby's theory of maternal deprivation 1D, 2C, 3D, 4D
Romanian orphan studies 1C, 2A, 3B, 4C
The influence of early attachment on later relationships 1A, 2B, 3B, 4B

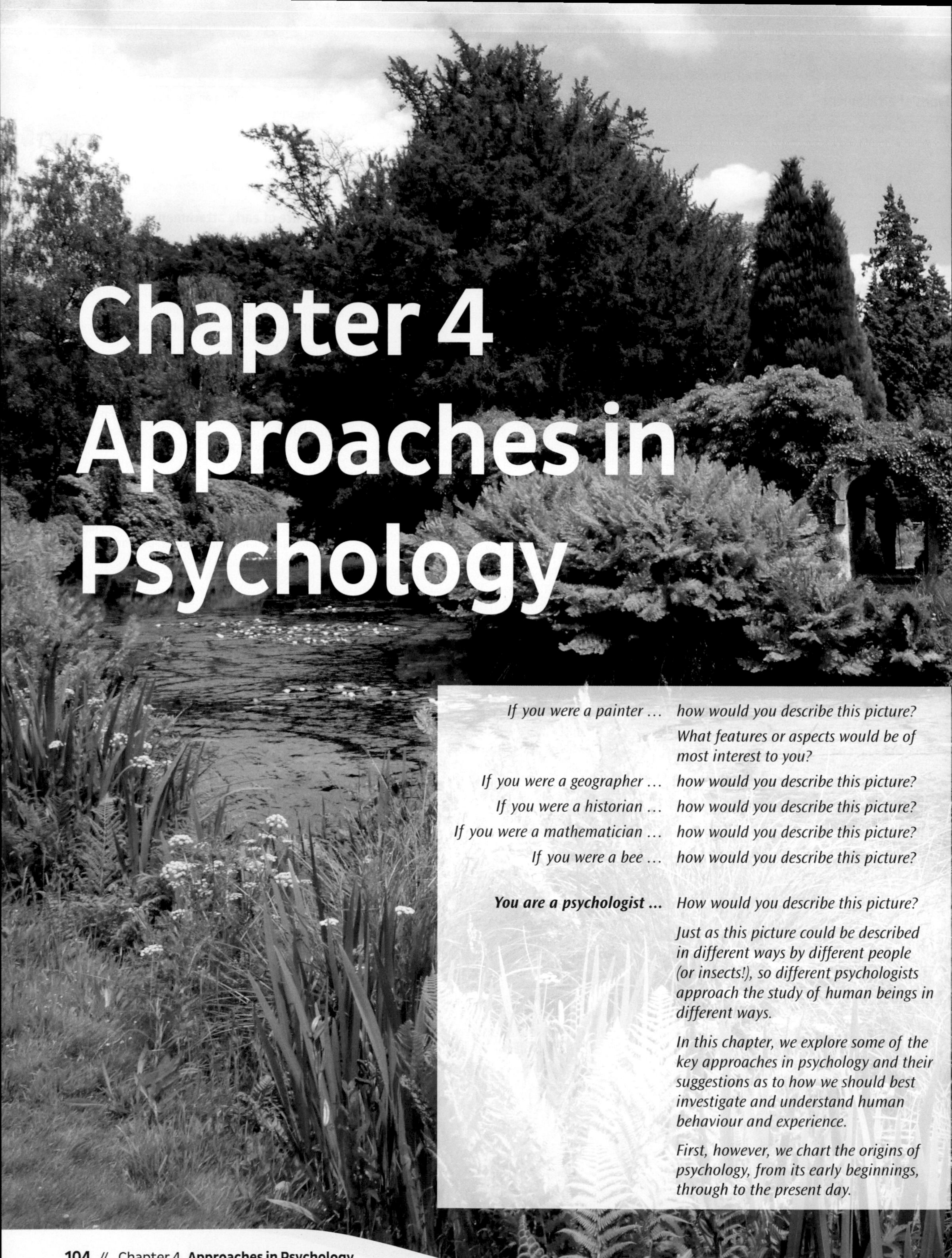

Chapter 4 Approaches in Psychology

If you were a painter ... *how would you describe this picture?*

What features or aspects would be of most interest to you?

If you were a geographer ... *how would you describe this picture?*

If you were a historian ... *how would you describe this picture?*

If you were a mathematician ... *how would you describe this picture?*

If you were a bee ... *how would you describe this picture?*

You are a psychologist ... *How would you describe this picture?*

Just as this picture could be described in different ways by different people (or insects!), so different psychologists approach the study of human beings in different ways.

In this chapter, we explore some of the key approaches in psychology and their suggestions as to how we should best investigate and understand human behaviour and experience.

First, however, we chart the origins of psychology, from its early beginnings, through to the present day.

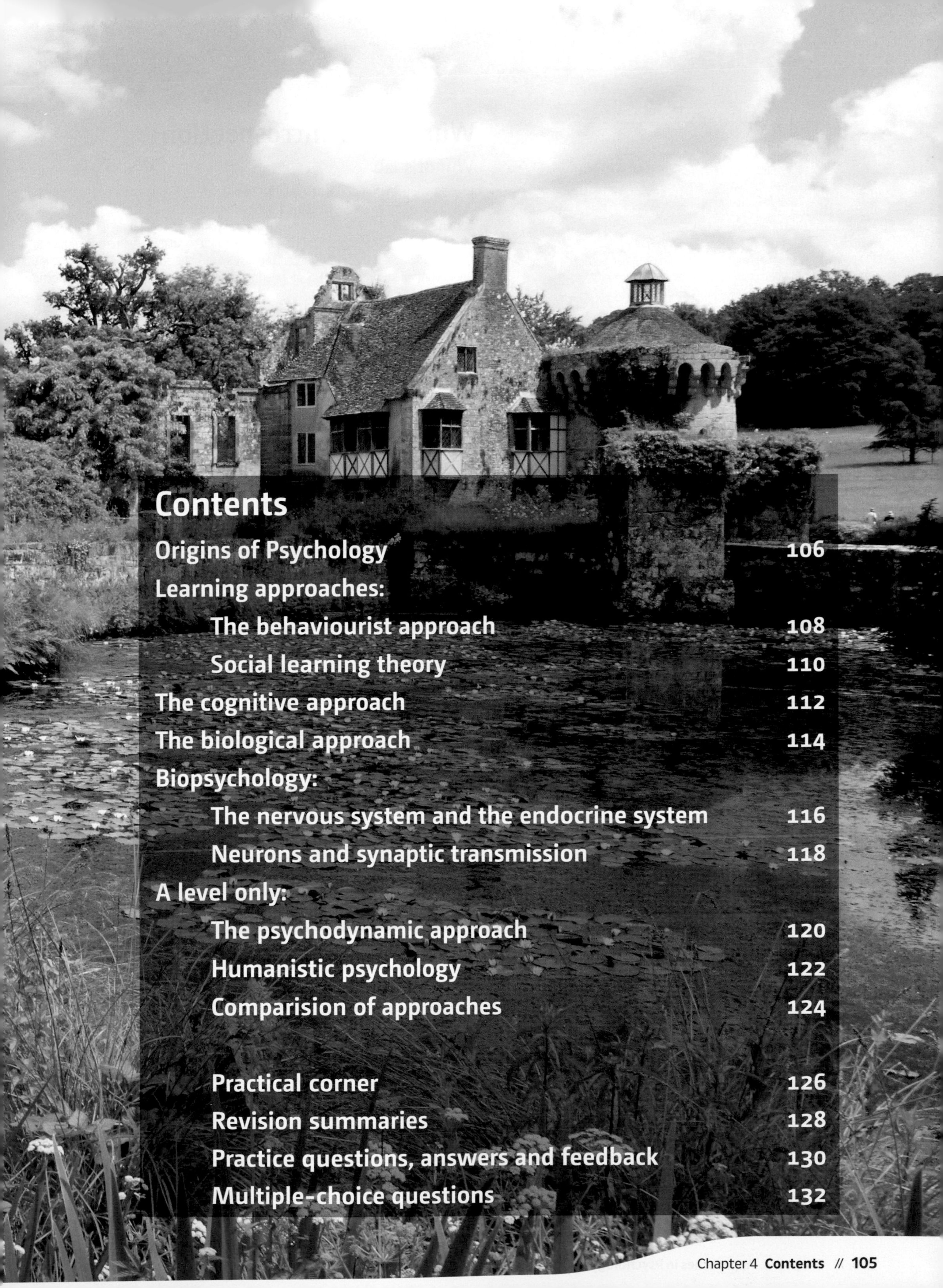

Contents

Origins of Psychology

The specification says...

Origins of Psychology: Wundt, introspection and the emergence of Psychology as a science.

The idea of psychology as a distinct branch of study is generally dated at around 1880 when the first experimental lab was established.

That said, the philosophical roots of psychology stretch back much earlier than this. On this spread, we shall describe the work of the first ever experimental psychologist, as well as chart the emergence of psychology as a scientific discipline.

Key terms

Introspection The first systematic experimental attempt to study the mind by breaking up conscious awareness into basic structures of thoughts, images and sensations.

Psychology The scientific study of the mind, behaviour and experience.

Science A means of acquiring knowledge through systematic and objective investigation. The aim is to discover general laws.

Wundt and introspection

Wundt's lab

In 1879 Wilhelm Wundt opened the first ever lab dedicated entirely to psychological enquiry in a little town called Leipzig in Germany. Wundt's work is significant because it marked the beginning of *scientific* **psychology**, separating it from its broader philosophical roots. Wundt's aim was to try to analyse the nature of human consciousness, and thus represented the first systematic attempt to study the mind under controlled conditions. His pioneering method became known as **introspection**.

Standardised procedures

One of Wundt's main objectives was to try and develop theories about mental processes, such as language and perception. He and his co-workers recorded their experiences of various stimuli they were presented with, such as different objects or sounds. They would divide their observations into three categories: thoughts, images and sensations. For instance, participants might be given a ticking metronome and they would report their thoughts, images and sensations.

Structuralism

Isolating the *structure* of consciousness in this way is called **structuralism**. The stimuli that Wundt and his co-workers experienced were always presented in the same order and the same instructions were issued to all participants.

What we're gonna do right now is go back... back in time.

17th century – 19th century

Psychology is a branch of the broader discipline of philosophy. If psychology has a definition during this time it is as **experimental philosophy**.

1879

Wilhelm Wundt opens the first experimental psychology lab in Germany, and psychology emerges as a distinct discipline in its own right.

1900s

Sigmund Freud emphasises the influence of the unconscious mind on behaviour (the **psychodynamic approach**). He also develops his person-centred therapy, **psychoanalysis**, and shows that physical problems can be explained in terms of conflicts within the mind.

1913

John B. Watson writes *Psychology as the Behaviourist views it* and, later with **B.F. Skinner**, establishes the **behaviourist approach**. The psychodynamic and behaviourist approaches dominate psychology for the first half of the 20th century.

1950s

Carl Rogers and **Abraham Maslow** develop the **humanisti approach**, the so-called 'third force' in psychology, rejecting the behaviourist and the psychodynamic view that human behaviour is determined by outside factors. Humanistic psychologists emphasise the importance of self-determination and free will.

The emergence of Psychology as a science

What is **science**? Science involves building knowledge through systematic and objective (unbiased) measurement. The aim is to discover general laws. If psychology is a science (and most modern commentators would probably agree that it is), what has made psychology the science it is today?

1900s Behaviourists

By the beginning of the 20th century, the value of introspection was questioned by many, most notably the behaviourist John B. Watson. The problem was that introspection produced subjective data (rather than objective), so that it was very difficult to establish general laws. Watson, and later B.F. Skinner, proposed that a truly scientific psychology should only study phenomena that can be observed objectively and measured. For this reason, behaviourists focused on behaviours that they could see, and used carefully controlled experiments. The behaviourist approach would go on to dominate scientific psychology for the next 50 years.

1950s Cognitive approach

The digital revolution of the 1950s gave a new generation of psychologists a metaphor for studying the mind. Cognitive psychologists likened the mind to a computer (e.g. the **multi-store model**) and tested their predictions about memory and attention using experiments. The cognitive approach ensured that the study of the mind was, once again, a legitimate and highly scientific aspect of the discipline.

1980s Biological approach

In more recent times, the biological approach has taken scientific psychology to new levels. Researchers within this area have taken advantage of advances in technology to investigate physiological processes as they happen. An example of this is the use of sophisticated scanning techniques such as **fMRI** and **EEG** to study live activity in the brain. New methods (e.g. **genetic** testing) have also allowed us to better understand the relationship between genes and behaviour.

:valuation

;cientific

)ne strength of Wundt's work is that some of his methods were systematic and well-controlled (i.e. scientific).

All introspections were recorded in the controlled environment of the lab, ensuring that possible **xtraneous variables** were not a factor. As described on the left, procedures and instructions were carefully **tandardised** so that all participants received the same information and were tested in the same way.

This suggests that Wundt's research can be considered a forerunner to later scientific approaches in sychology, such as the behaviourist approach.

;ubjective data

)ne limitation is that other aspects of Wundt's research would be considered unscientific today.

Wundt relied on participants self-reporting their mental processes. Such data is subjective (influenced y a personal perspective). Also participants may have hidden some of their thoughts. It is difficult to stablish meaningful 'laws of behaviour' from such data. And general laws are useful to predict future ehaviour, one of the aims of science.

This suggests that some of Wundt's early efforts to study the mind were flawed and would not meet the riteria of scientific enquiry.

Evaluation eXtra

Wundt's contribution

Wundt produced the first academic journal for psychological research and wrote the first textbook! He is often referred to as the founder of modern psychology. It is even suggested that Wundt's pioneering research set the foundation for approaches that were to come, particularly the behaviourist approach and cognitive psychology.

Consider: *Does this justify the fact that his methods may have been unscientific?*

1950s

The introduction of the digital computer gives psychologists a metaphor for the operations of the human mind. The **cognitive approach** reintroduces the study of mental processes to psychology but in a much more scientific way than Wundt's earlier investigations.

1960s

Albert Bandura proposes the **social learning theory**. This approach draws attention to the role of cognitive factors in learning, providing a bridge between the newly established cognitive approach and traditional behaviourism.

1980s onwards

The **biological approach** begins to establish itself as the dominant scientific perspective in psychology. This is due to advances in technology that have increased understanding of the brain and biological processes.

Eve of the 21st century

Towards the end of the last century, **cognitive neuroscience** emerges as a distinct discipline bringing together the cognitive and biological approaches. Cognitive neuroscience investigates how biological structures influence mental states.

onwards

POLICE PUBLIC CALL BOX
POLICE PUBLIC CALL BOX

:valuation

Modern Psychology

)ne strength is that research in modern psychology can claim to be scientific.

Psychology has the same aims as the natural sciences – to describe, ınderstand, predict and control behaviour. The learning approaches, cognitive pproach and biological approach all rely on the use of scientific methods, for xample, lab studies to investigate theories in a controlled and unbiased way.

This suggests that throughout the 20th century and beyond, psychology has stablished itself as a scientific discipline.

;ubjective data

)ne limitation with psychology is that not all approaches use objective methods.

The humanistic approach rejects the scientific approach, preferring to focus n individual experiences and subjective experience. The psychodynamic pproach makes use of the case study method which does not use epresentative samples. Finally, the subject of study – human beings – are active articipants in research, responding for example to **demand characteristics**.

Therefore a scientific approach to the study of human thought and xperience may not always be desirable or possible.

Evaluation eXtra

Paradigm

The philosopher Thomas Kuhn said that any science must have a paradigm: a set of principles, assumptions and methods that all people who work within that subject agree on. He went on to say that psychology is not a science because it does not have a paradigm as there is so much internal disagreement at its core.

Consider: *Do psychologists generally 'disagree' with each other? What do you conclude about psychology as a science?*

Check it

1. Explain what Wundt meant by 'introspection'. *[3 marks]*
2. Briefly explain Wundt's role in the emergence of psychology as a science. *[4 marks]*
3. Discuss Wundt's contribution to psychology. *[8 marks]*
4. Outline **and** evaluate the emergence of psychology as a science. *[8 marks]*

Learning approaches: The behaviourist approach

The specification says...

Learning approaches: i) The behaviourist approach, including classical conditioning and Pavlov's research, operant conditioning, types of reinforcement and Skinner's research.

The behaviourist approach emerged at the beginning of the 20th century and became the dominant approach in psychology for half of that century.

It is also credited as being the driving force in the development of psychology as a scientific discipline.

Key terms

Behaviourist (behavioural) approach A way of explaining behaviour in terms of what is observable and in terms of learning.

Classical conditioning Learning by association. Occurs when two stimuli are repeatedly paired together – an unconditioned (unlearned) stimulus (UCS) and a new 'neutral' stimulus (NS). The neutral stimulus eventually produces the same response that was first produced by the unconditioned (unlearned) stimulus alone.

Operant conditioning A form of learning in which behaviour is shaped and maintained by its consequences. Possible consequences of behaviour include reinforcement (positive or negative) and punishment.

Reinforcement A consequence of behaviour that increases the likelihood of that behaviour being repeated. Can be positive or negative.

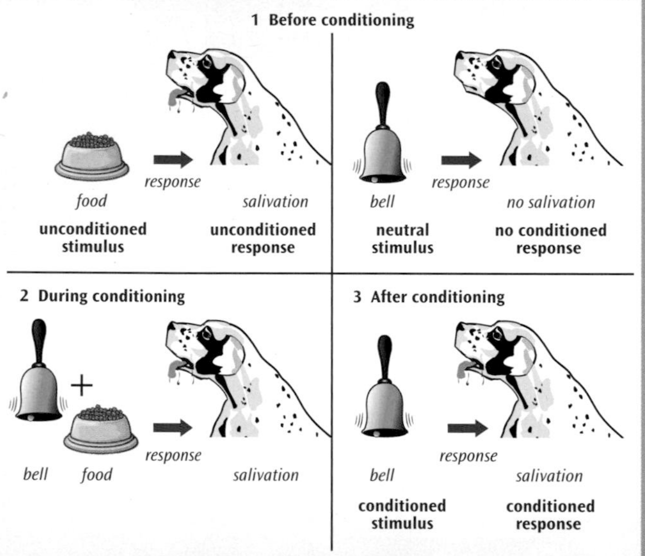
1 Before conditioning
response
food
salivation
unconditioned stimulus
unconditioned response
response
bell
no salivation
neutral stimulus
no conditioned response
2 During conditioning
+
response
bell
food
salivation
3 After conditioning
response
bell
salivation
conditioned stimulus
conditioned response

Study tip

Often, students have difficulty explaining the distinction between negative reinforcement and punishment. Remember that negative reinforcement *increases* the likelihood of a behaviour being repeated (because it avoids an unpleasant consequence). In contrast, punishment *decreases* the likelihood of a behaviour being repeated (because of its unpleasant consequence).

The behaviourist approach

Assumptions

The **behaviourist approach** is only interested in studying behaviour that can be observed and measured. It is not concerned with investigating mental processes of the mind because these were seen as irrelevant. Early behaviourists such as John B. Watson (1913) rejected **introspection** as it involved too many concepts that were vague and difficult to measure. As a result, behaviourists tried to maintain more control and objectivity within their research and relied on **lab studies** as the best way to achieve this.

Behaviourists believe that all behaviour is learned. They describe a baby's mind as a 'blank slate' and this is written on by experience. Following Darwin, behaviourists suggested that the basic processes that govern learning are the same in all species. This meant that in behaviourist research, animals replace humans as experimental subjects. Behaviourists identified two important forms of learning: **classical conditioning** and **operant conditioning**.

Classical conditioning – Pavlov's research

Classical conditioning is learning through *association* and was first demonstrated by Ivan Pavlov (1927). Pavlov showed how dogs could be conditioned to salivate to the sound of a bell if that sound was repeatedly presented at the same time as they were given food. Gradually, Pavlov's dogs learned to *associate* the sound of the bell (a stimulus) with the food (another stimulus) and would produce the salivation response every time they heard the sound.

Thus, Pavlov was able to show how a **neutral stimulus**, in this case a bell, can come to elicit a new learned response (**conditioned response**) through association (see diagram left).

Operant conditioning – Skinner's research

B.F. Skinner (1953) suggested that learning is an active process whereby humans and animals *operate* on their environment. In operant conditioning behaviour is shaped by its *consequences*:

- **Positive reinforcement** is receiving a reward when a certain behaviour is performed, for example, praise from a teacher for answering a question correctly in class.
- **Negative reinforcement** occurs when an animal (or human) avoids something unpleasant. The outcome is a positive experience. For example, when a student hands in an essay so as not to be told off, the avoidance of something unpleasant is the negative reinforcement. Similarly, a rat may learn through negative reinforcement that pressing a lever leads to avoidance of an electric shock (below).
- **Punishment** is an unpleasant consequence of behaviour, for example being shouted at by the teacher for talking during a lesson. (Finding a way to avoid that would be negative reinforcement.)

Positive and negative reinforcement increase the likelihood that behaviour will be repeated. Punishment decreases the likelihood that behaviour will be repeated.

Apply it Concepts: The Skinner box

(A) Skinner conducted experiments with rats, and sometimes pigeons, in specially designed cages called *Skinner boxes*. Every time the rat activated a lever (or pecked a disc in the case of the pigeon) within the box it was rewarded with a food pellet. From then on the animal would continue to perform the behaviour.

(B) Skinner also showed how rats and pigeons could be conditioned to perform the same behaviour to avoid an unpleasant stimulus, for example an electric shock.

Questions

1. Which aspect of operant conditioning does paragraph A illustrate?
2. Which aspect of operant conditioning does paragraph B illustrate?

:valuation

Vell-controlled research

ne strength of the behaviourist approach is that it is based on vell-controlled research.

Behaviourists focused on the measurement of observable ehaviour within highly controlled lab settings. By breaking down ehaviour into basic stimulus–response units, all other possible xtraneous variables were removed, allowing cause-and-effect elationships to be established. For instance, Skinner was able to early demonstrate how reinforcement influenced an animal's ehaviour.

This suggests that behaviourist experiments have scientific redibility.

Counterpoint However, the problem with this is that behaviourists may have oversimplified the learning process. By reducing behaviour to such simple components, behaviourists may have ignored an important influence on learning – that of human thought. Other approaches, such as **social learning theory** (next spread) and the **cognitive approach** (page 112) have drawn attention to the mental processes involved in learning.

This suggests that learning is more complex than observable behaviour alone, and that private mental processes are also essential.

Real-world application

nother strength of the behaviourist approach is that the principles f conditioning have been applied to real-world behaviours and roblems.

For example, operant conditioning is the basis of **token conomy systems** that have been used successfully in institutions, uch as prisons and psychiatric wards. These work by rewarding ppropriate behaviour with tokens that can be exchanged for rivileges. For an example of how classical conditioning has been pplied to the treatment of phobias, see page 148.

This increases the value of the behaviourist approach because it as widespread application.

:nvironmental determinism

)ne limitation of the behaviourist approach is that it sees all ehaviour as conditioned by past conditioning experiences.

Skinner suggested that everything we do is the sum total of our einforcement history. When something happens we may think 'I nade the decision to do that' but, according to Skinner, our past onditioning history determined the outcome. This ignores any ossible influence that **free will** may have on behaviour (Skinner imself said that free will is an illusion).

This is an extreme position and ignores the influence of onscious decision-making processes on behaviour (as suggested y the cognitive approach).

:valuation eXtra

:thical issues

lthough procedures such as the Skinner box allowed ehaviourists to maintain a high degree of control over their xperimental 'subjects', many have questioned the ethics of onducting such investigations. Animals were housed in harsh, ramped conditions and deliberately kept below their natural veight so they were always hungry.

:onsider: *Does what we learn from studies such as the Skinner box justify the way the animals were treated?*

Apply it Concepts: Behaviourism and gambling

Skinner discovered that if an animal was rewarded every time it activated the lever or pecked the disc, the conditioned behaviour would quickly die out (become extinct) as the animal was *satiated* (full of food pellets!).

It was revealed that a variable ratio schedule would prolong the behaviour and was most resistant to extinction. Here, reinforcement is given after an unpredictable (variable) number of responses are produced, for example, every 10, 15, 12, etc., times the lever is pressed.

This has been applied to a number of forms of human behaviour, including gambling addiction.

Question

Explain how addiction to gambling could be explained by the principles above.

How could the urge to shoot zombies in a video game be explained by operant conditioning?

Apply it Concepts: Behaviourism and gaming

David Wong (2008) has used Skinnerian principles to explain addiction to video games in his article *5 creepy ways video games are trying to get you addicted*. His argument is that the video game environment is a form of Skinner box providing reinforcement that is dependent on certain behaviours. For instance, shooting zombies in the example above leads to successful completion of a level, a high score, etc.

The use of the lever or joystick in many video games, it is argued, is analogous to the behaviour exhibited by the rat in the Skinner box, and the success and addictive nature of many early video games, such as Pac-Man, is explained by the fact that the central character navigates its way around the screen literally munching on food pellets!

Question

How could video game addiction be explained using behaviourist principles?

Check it

1. Briefly outline what the behaviourist approach means by 'classical conditioning'. *[2 marks]*
2. Outline **two** types of reinforcement as suggested by the behaviourist approach. *[4 marks]*
3. Outline **and** evaluate the behaviourist approach in psychology. *[12 marks AS, 16 marks AL]*

Learning approaches: Social learning theory

The specification says...

Learning approaches: ii) Social learning theory including imitation, identification, modelling, vicarious reinforcement, the role of mediational processes and Bandura's research.

Albert Bandura proposed social learning theory as a development of the behaviourist approach. He argued that classical and operant conditioning could not account for all human learning – there are important mental processes that mediate between stimulus and response.

Key terms

Social learning theory A way of explaining behaviour that includes both direct and indirect reinforcement, combining learning theory with the role of cognitive factors.

Imitation Copying the behaviour of others.

Identification When an observer associates themselves with a role model and wants to be like the role model.

Modelling From the observer's perspective, modelling is imitating the behaviour of a role model. From the role model's perspective, modelling is the precise demonstration of a specific behaviour that may be imitated by an observer.

Vicarious reinforcement Reinforcement which is not directly experienced but occurs through observing someone else being reinforced for a behaviour. This is a key factor in imitation.

Mediational processes Cognitive factors (i.e. thinking) that influence learning and come between stimulus and response.

CHEVROLET
6

A child may want to imitate the dribbling skills of Paul Pogba (pictured), but may lack the necessary ability required to reproduce the behaviour.

Social learning theory

Assumptions

Albert Bandura agreed with the **behaviourists** that behaviour is learned from experience. However, his **social learning theory** (SLT) proposed a different way in which people learn – through observation and **imitation** of others (i.e. it is *social* – involving others). SLT suggested that learning occurs directly, through **classical** and **operant conditioning**, but also *indirectly*.

Vicarious reinforcement

For indirect learning to take place an individual observes the behaviour of others. The learner may imitate this behaviour but, in general, **imitation** only occurs if the behaviour is seen to be rewarded (reinforced) rather than punished, i.e. **vicarious reinforcement** occurs (see study by Bandura and Walters in Apply it below). Thus, the learner observes a behaviour but most importantly also observes the consequences of a behaviour.

The role of mediational processes

SLT is often described as the 'bridge' between behaviourist **learning theory** (previous spread) and the **cognitive approach** (next spread) because it focuses on how mental (cognitive) factors are involved in learning. These mental factors mediate (i.e. intervene) in the learning process to determine whether a new response is acquired. Four mental or **mediational processes** in learning were identified by Bandura:

1. *Attention* – the extent to which we notice certain behaviours.
2. *Retention* – how well the behaviour is remembered.
3. *Motor reproduction* – the ability of the observer to perform the behaviour.
4. *Motivation* – the will to perform the behaviour, which is often determined by whether the behaviour was rewarded or punished.

The first two of these relate to the *learning* of behaviour and the last two to the *performance* of behaviour. Unlike traditional behaviourism, the learning and performance of behaviour need not occur together. Observed behaviours may be stored by the observer and reproduced at a later time.

Identification

People (especially children) are more likely to imitate people they identify with, a process called **identification**. The person they identify with is called a *role model* and the process of imitating a role model is called **modelling** (note: the behaviour of a role model is also called *modelling*).

A person becomes a role model if they are seen to possess similar characteristics to the observer and/or are attractive and have high status. Role models may not necessarily be physically present in the environment, and this has important implications for the influence of the media on behaviour (see facing page).

Apply it Concepts — Bandura's research

Study A: Bandura *et al.* (1961) recorded the behaviour of young children who watched an adult behave in an aggressive way towards a Bobo doll (see right). The adult hit the doll with a hammer and shouted abuse at it.

When these children were later observed playing with various toys, including a Bobo doll, they behaved much more aggressively towards the doll and the other toys than those who had observed a non-aggressive adult.

Question: Which aspect of SLT does study A illustrate?

Study B: Bandura, together with Richard Walters (Bandura and Walters 1963), showed videos to children where an adult behaved aggressively towards the Bobo doll. One group of children saw the adult praised for their behaviour (being told 'Well done'). A second group saw the adult punished for their aggression towards the doll, by being told off. The third group (**control group**) saw the aggression without any consequence.

When given their own Bobo doll to play with, the first group showed much more aggression, followed by the third group, and then the second.

Question: Which aspect of SLT does study B illustrate?

Evaluation

Practical activity on page 127

Cognitive factors

One strength of the social learning theory approach is that it recognises the importance of **cognitive** factors in learning.

Neither classical nor operant conditioning can offer an adequate account of learning on their own. Humans and animals store information about the behaviour of others and use this to make judgements about when it is appropriate to perform certain actions. As Bandura observed:

'Learning would be exceedingly laborious, not to mention hazardous, if people had to rely solely on the effects of their own actions to inform them what they do. From observing others one forms an idea of how new behaviours are performed, and on later occasions this coded information serves as a guide to action' (Bandura 1977).

This suggests that SLT provides a more comprehensive explanation of human learning by recognising the role of mediational processes.

Counterpoint Despite this, SLT has been criticised for making too little reference to the influence of biological factors on social learning. Although Bandura claimed natural biological differences influenced our learning potential, he thought that learning itself was determined by the environment. However, recent research suggests that observational learning, of the kind Bandura was talking about, may be the result of **mirror neurons** in the brain, which allow us to empathise with and imitate other people.

This suggests that biological influences on social learning were under-emphasised in SLT.

Contrived lab studies

One limitation of social learning theory is that the evidence on which it is based was gathered through lab studies.

Many of Bandura's ideas were developed through observation of young children's behaviour in the lab. Lab studies are often criticised for their contrived nature where participants may respond to **demand characteristics**. It has been suggested, in relation to the Bobo doll research (bottom of facing page) that, because the main purpose of the doll is to strike it, the children were simply behaving in a way that they thought was expected.

This suggests that the research may tell us little about how children actually learn aggression in everyday life.

Real-world application

Another strength is that SLT principles have been applied to a range of real-world behaviours.

Social learning theory has the advantage of being able to explain cultural differences in behaviour. SLT principles, such as modelling, imitation and reinforcement, can account for how children learn from others around them, including the media, and this can explain how cultural norms are transmitted through particular societies. This has proved useful in understanding a range of behaviours, such as how children come to understand their gender role.

This increases the value of the approach as it can account for real-world behaviour.

Evaluation eXtra

Reciprocal determinism

Bandura emphasised **reciprocal determinism**, in the sense that we are not merely influenced by our external environment, but we also exert an influence upon it, through the behaviours we choose to perform. This element of choice suggests that there is some free will in the way we behave.

This contrasts with the behaviourist approach which denies the possibility of free will (see previous spread).

Consider: *Why is a less determinist position preferable?*

Apply it Concepts — Video nasties

Bandura's Bobo doll experiments have implications for the media – are children, and indeed some adults, influenced by the violence and aggression they see on television, in movies and video games?

This debate was brought into sharp focus in 1990 following the death of James Bulger, a toddler from Liverpool murdered by two ten-year-old boys. At the time it was argued by many UK newspapers that the child killers were inspired by the horror film *Child's Play 3*, and there were calls for rules and censorship on such 'video nasties' to be tightened.

However, many researchers dispute the link between the media and real-world violence. For example, Guy Cumberbatch *et al.* (2001) argues that supposed 'video nasties', of the type cited in the Bulger case, are much more likely to frighten children than to make them frightening (aggressive) towards others. He argues that isolated incidents such as these are better explained by other factors such as social deprivation, child abuse and early exposure to violence in the home.

Questions

1. Using social learning principles, explain why media (such as violent videos) may potentially have a negative impact on children's behaviour.
2. How might the media vicariously reinforce violence and aggression?

A CLOCKWORK ORANGE
DIRECTOR.
STANLEY KUBRICK
CAMERAMAN.
JOHN ALCOTT
SLATE

Stanley Kubrick withdrew his controversial 1971 film *A Clockwork Orange* from British cinemas after a series of 'copycat' incidents based on scenes from the film.

Study tip

If you need to evaluate social learning theory you might, for example, use the Bobo doll studies (or other studies) to illustrate key points. However, you should keep descriptions of the procedures and findings within these studies to a minimum and instead make it clear how the implications/conclusions from these studies support (or contradict) key SLT concepts.

Check it

1. Outline what social learning theorists mean by 'identification'. *[2 marks]*
2. Explain **one** strength of social learning theory. *[3 marks]*
3. Outline **and** evaluate social learning theory. *[12 marks AS, 16 marks AL]*

The cognitive approach

The specification says...

The cognitive approach: the study of internal mental processes, the role of schema, the use of theoretical and computer models to explain and make inferences about mental processes. The emergence of cognitive neuroscience.

The cognitive approach developed in the 1950s as a response to the behaviourists' failure to acknowledge mental processes. The development of the first computers gave cognitive psychologists a metaphor for describing mental processes.

Key terms

Cognitive approach The term 'cognitive' has come to mean 'mental processes', so this approach is focused on how our mental processes (e.g. thoughts, perceptions, attention) affect behaviour.

Internal mental processes 'Private' operations of the mind such as perception and attention that mediate between stimulus and response.

Schema A mental framework of beliefs and expectations that influence cognitive processing. They are developed from experience.

Inference The process whereby cognitive psychologists draw conclusions about the way mental processes operate on the basis of observed behaviour.

Cognitive neuroscience The scientific study of those biological structures that underpin cognitive processes.

Apply it Methods — Problem-solving

A cognitive psychologist carried out an experiment into the effects of other people on problem-solving. An independent groups design was used. In Condition A, 15 children were given 30 problems each to solve in two hours. The children completed the task in the same room and were allowed to talk to each other. In Condition B, a different group of 15 children were given the same problems and the same time to solve them but worked in silence.

The number of problems solved in Condition A was 204; the number of problems solved in Condition B was 324.

Questions

1. What percentage of the total number of problems solved were solved in Condition B? (*2 marks*)
2. Calculate the **mean** number of problems solved per child in Condition A and Condition B. (*2 marks*)
3. Sketch a suitable graphical display to represent the mean number of problems solved per child in Condition A and Condition B. (*3 marks*)
4. Explain *one* conclusion that can be drawn from the mean number of problems solved per child in Condition A and Condition B. (*2 marks*)

The cognitive approach

Assumptions

In direct contrast to the **behaviourist approach**, the **cognitive approach** argues that **internal mental processes** can, and should, be studied scientifically. As a result, the cognitive approach has investigated those areas of human behaviour that were neglected by behaviourists, such as memory, perception and thinking. These processes are 'private' and cannot be observed, so cognitive psychologists study them *indirectly* by making **inferences** about what is going on inside people's minds on the basis of their behaviour.

The role of schema

Cognitive processing can often be affected by a person's beliefs or expectations, which are often referred to as **schema**. Schema are 'packages' of ideas and information developed through experience. They act as a mental framework for the interpretation of incoming information received by the cognitive system. For example, you have a schema for a chair – something with legs that you can sit on. That's a package of information learned through experience that helps you to respond to the object appropriately.

Babies are born with simple motor schema for innate behaviours such as sucking and grasping. For example, the grasping schema consists of moving a hand towards an object and shaping the hand around the object in co-ordination with visual input.

As we get older, our schema become more detailed and sophisticated. Adults have developed mental representations for everything from the concept of psychology to a schema for what happens in a restaurant or what a typical zombie looks like.

Schema enable us to process lots of information quickly and this is useful as a sort of mental shortcut that prevents us from being overwhelmed by environmental stimuli. However, schema may also distort our interpretations of sensory information, leading to perceptual errors (see examples on facing page).

Theoretical and computer models

Cognitive psychologists use both **theoretical** and **computer models** to help them understand internal mental processes. In reality there are overlaps between these two models but basically theoretical models are abstract whereas computer models are concrete things.

One important theoretical model is the **information processing approach**, which suggests that information flows through the cognitive system in a sequence of stages. These include input, storage and retrieval, as in the **multi-store model** (see page 48). This information processing approach is based on the way that computers function but a computer model would involve actually programming a computer to see if such instructions produce a similar output to humans. If they do then we can suggest that similar processes are going on in the human mind. Such computational models of the mind have proved useful in the development of 'thinking machines' or **artificial intelligence** (e.g. machines that can have a conversation with you).

The emergence of cognitive neuroscience

Cognitive neuroscience is the scientific study of the influence of brain structures on mental processes. Mapping brain areas to specific cognitive functions has a long history in psychology. As early as the 1860s Paul Broca had identified how damage to an area of the **frontal lobe** (which came to be known as **Broca's Area**) could permanently impair speech production.

It is only in the last twenty-five years, however, with advances in brain imaging techniques such as **fMRI** and **PET** scans, that scientists have been able to systematically observe and describe the **neurological** basis of mental processes. For example, in research involving tasks that required the use of **episodic** and **semantic memory**, Buckner and Peterson (1996, see page 51) were able to show how these different types of **long-term memory** may be located on opposite sides of the **prefrontal cortex**. As well as this, the system in overall charge of **working memory** – the **central executive** – is thought to reside in a similar area (Braver *et al.* 1997).

Scanning techniques have also proved useful in establishing the neurological basis of some mental disorders. On page 154 the link between the **parahippocampal gyrus** and **OCD** is discussed. It appears to play a role in processing unpleasant emotions.

The focus of cognitive neuroscience has expanded recently to include the use of computer-generated models that are designed to 'read' the brain. This has led to the development of mind-mapping techniques known as 'brain fingerprinting'. One possible future application of this could be to analyse the brain wave patterns of **eyewitnesses** to determine whether they are lying in court!

:valuation

;cientific methods

ne strength of the cognitive approach is that it uses objective, cientific methods.

Cognitive psychologists employ highly controlled and rigorous ıethods of study so researchers are able to *infer* cognitive processes t work. This has involved the use of **lab studies** to produce reliable, bjective data. In addition, the emergence of **cognitive neuroscience** as enabled the two fields of biology and cognitive psychology to ome together to enhance the scientific basis of study.

This means that the study of the mind has a credible scientific asis.

Counterpoint As cognitive psychology relies on the inference of mental processes, rather than direct observation of behaviour, it can occasionally suffer from being too abstract and theoretical in nature. Similarly, research studies of mental processes are often carried out using artificial stimuli (such as tests of memory involving word lists) that may not represent everyday experience.

Therefore, research on cognitive processes may lack **external validity**.

?eal-world application

nother strength of the cognitive approach is that it has practical pplication.

The cognitive approach is probably the dominant approach in sychology today and has been applied to a wide range of practical nd theoretical contexts. For example, cognitive psychology has made n important contribution in the field of artificial intelligence (AI) and ıe development of 'thinking machines' (robots). These are exciting dvances that may revolutionise how we live in the future. Cognitive rinciples have also been applied to the treatment of depression (see ages 152–153) and improved the **reliability** of eyewitness testimony ages 58–63).

This supports the value of the cognitive approach.

/lachine reductionism

ne limitation of the cognitive approach is that it is based on **ıachine reductionism**.

There are similarities between the human mind and the perations of a 'thinking machine' such as a computer (inputs nd outputs, storage systems, the use of a central processor). owever, the computer analogy has been criticised. Such machine ductionism ignores the influence of human emotion and otivation on the cognitive system, and how this may affect our bility to process information. For instance, research has found that ıman memory may be affected by emotional factors, such as the fluence of anxiety on eyewitnesses (see pages 60–61).

This suggests that machine reductionism may weaken the alidity of the cognitive approach.

:valuation eXtra

oft determinism

ıe cognitive approach is founded on **soft determinism**, i.e. the ew that human behaviour may be determined by internal and cternal factors but we also can exert our free will at times. The **ırd determinism** view says all our behaviour is determined by ctors other than our will, such as conditioning and genes.

onsider: *Why is the cognitive approach a more flexible osition than the behaviourist approach?*

Plump and Juicy
HotDogs
Always
HOT & FRESH

Misperceived song lyrics
Did Celine Dion really sing 'The hot dogs go on' on the 1997 *Titanic* movie soundtrack? A case of schema distorting our interpretations of sensory information, leading to perceptual errors.

Apply it Concepts — The influence of schema on perception

1. Read the following paragraph: *The Pschyology of Zombeis*

Evrey gneration gtes the mosnter it deserevs as the reprsenetaiton of its depeest faers. Tdoay's zombeis, who are usulaly infetced in thier thuosands, repersent our modren faer of contaiguos disesaes, uncnotrolled medcial techonolgoy and socail colalpse. Zombeis are lniked, in our cutlure, with daeth and we probalby evovled to aviod daed and disesaed bodeis to aviod infcetoin', accrodnig to Lynn Alden, a profsesor of pschyology at the Univesrity of Britsih Colmobia. 'But its one thnig to aviod a corspe that ins't movnig and qiute anotehr wehn tehy strat chasnig you!'

Question

Explain the role of schema in helping you make sense of the information above.

2. Many people misread the following sentences.

PARIS
IN THE
THE SPRING
ONCE
IN A
A LIFETIME
BIRD
IN THE
THE HAND

Question

Explain the role of schema in the misperception of the sentences above.

3. Bugelski and Alampay (1962) The rat-man

Two groups of participants were shown a sequence of pictures, either a number of different faces or a number of different animals. They were then shown the ambiguous figure of the 'rat-man' (below).

Participants who saw a sequence of faces were more likely to perceive the figure as a man, whereas participants who saw a sequence of animals were more likely to perceive the figure as a rat.

Question

Explain how the influence of schema may account for this.

Check it

1. Outline the emergence of cognitive neuroscience. *[4 marks]*
2. Briefly explain how theoretical **and** computer models are used in cognitive psychology to make inferences about mental processes. *[4 marks]*
3. Outline **and** evaluate the cognitive approach. *[12 marks AS, 16 marks AL]*

The biological approach

The specification says...

The biological approach: the influence of genes, biological structures and neurochemistry on behaviour. Genotype and phenotype, genetic basis of behaviour, evolution and behaviour.

The biological approach has always been important in psychology but in recent years has gained prominence due to advances in technology such as the development of brain scanning techniques and increased understanding of the genetic basis of behaviour.

Key terms

Biological approach A perspective that emphasises the importance of physical processes in the body such as genetic inheritance and neural function.

Genes They make up chromosomes and consist of DNA which codes the physical features of an organism (such as eye colour, height) and psychological features (such as mental disorder, intelligence). Genes are transmitted from parents to offspring, i.e. inherited.

Biological structure An arrangement or organisation of parts to form an organ, system or living thing.

Neurochemistry Relating to chemicals in the brain that regulate psychological functioning.

Genotype The particular set of genes that a person possesses.

Phenotype The characteristics of an individual determined by both genes *and* the environment.

Evolution The changes in inherited characteristics in a biological population over successive generations.

The biological approach

Assumptions

The **biological approach** suggests that everything psychological is at first biological, so to fully understand human behaviour, we must look to **biological structures** and processes within the body. From a biological perspective, the mind lives in the brain – meaning that all thoughts, feelings and behaviour ultimately have a physical basis. This is in contrast to, say, the **cognitive approach** that sees mental processes of the mind as being separate from the physical brain.

The neurochemical basis of behaviour

Neurochemistry refers to the action of chemicals in the brain ('neural' refers to the brain). Much of our thought and behaviour relies on chemical transmission in the brain. This occurs using **neurotransmitters** (see synaptic transmission on page 119). An imbalance of neurochemicals in the brain has been implicated as a possible cause of mental disorder, for example low levels of the neurotransmitter **serotonin** in **OCD** and overproduction of **dopamine** in **schizophrenia**.

The genetic basis of behaviour

Psychological characteristics, such as intelligence, are inherited in the same way as height or eye colour. **Twin studies** are used to investigate whether certain psychological characteristics have a **genetic** basis. This is achieved by analysing **concordance rates** – the extent to which twins share the same characteristic. If a characteristic (musical ability, schizophrenia or whatever) is genetic we would expect all identical (**monozygotic**) twins to be concordant (they share 100% of the same genes). Whereas the same would not be true for non-identical (**dizygotic**) twins who share about 50% of the same genes. In both cases the environment is assumed to be constant.

Genotype and phenotype

A person's **genotype** is their actual genetic make-up, whereas **phenotype** is the way that genes are expressed through physical, behavioural and psychological characteristics. Despite having the same genes, the way identical twins' genes are expressed (the phenotype) is different – see also the example of **PKU** (see facing page). This illustrates what many biological psychologists would accept, that much of human behaviour depends upon an interaction between inherited factors (**nature**) and the environment (**nurture**).

Evolution and behaviour

The **evolution** of animals and plants is a fact. In the 19th century, Charles Darwin proposed a theory to explain this fact – the theory of **natural selection**. The main principle of this theory is that any genetically determined behaviour that enhances an individual's survival (and reproduction) will continue in future generations, i.e. be naturally selected. This happens in a similar way to a farmer deciding which animals to use for breeding – the farmer *selects* the ones who possess desirable characteristics. For example, if one of a farmer's cows has a high milk yield the farmer chooses this cow for further breeding so his stock of cows become progressively better milk producers.

In nature this selection takes place 'naturally' – no one 'decides', the selection occurs simply because some traits give the possessor certain advantages. The possessor is more likely to survive, reproduce and pass on these traits. If the individual survives but does not reproduce, the traits do not remain in the gene pool for successive generations.

Apply it Concepts: Giraffes, long necks and Bowlby

When considering the long neck of the giraffe, the evolutionary argument (put forward by Darwin himself) is that its extra height gives the giraffe an advantage in obtaining food that would not be available to shorter-necked rivals. This advantage means that over millions of years longer-necked giraffes become more common. This is an example of how an animal has adapted *physically* in response to its environment. However, what psychologists are really interested in is the evolution of *behaviour*. Some examples of behaviours that are seen in humans and animals are:

- Memory – human memory evolved because it provided advantages.
- Attachment – Bowlby argued that attachment to a primary caregiver is adaptive.
- Mental disorder – some mental disorders, such as OCD, may have a genetic basis. Psychologists argue, therefore, that these genes must have some adaptive advantage.

Question

In each of the above examples, can you suggest what the adaptive advantages might be?

.valuation

eal-world application

ıe strength of the biological approach is that it has real-world application.

Increased understanding of neurochemical processes in the brain is sociated with the use of psychoactive drugs to treat serious mental sorders. For example, the biological approach has promoted the treatment **clinical depression** using **antidepressant** drugs that increase levels of the ɪurotransmitter serotonin at **synapses** in the brain. Such drugs have been sociated with the reduction of depressive symptoms.

This means that people with depression may be better able to manage their ndition and live their lives in the community, rather than remain in hospital.

Counterpoint Although antidepressant drugs are successful for many patients, they do not work for everyone. For instance, a recent study by Andrea Cipriani *et al.* (2018) compared 21 antidepressant drugs and found wide variations in their effectiveness. Although most of the drugs were more effective than **placebos** in comparative trials, the researchers concluded that the effects of antidepressants, in general, were 'mainly modest'.

This challenges the value of the biological approach because it suggests that brain chemistry alone may not account for all cases of, for example, depression.

cientific methods

ıother strength of the approach is that it uses scientific methods of vestigation.

In order to investigate the genetic and biological basis of behaviour, the ological approach makes use of a range of precise and highly objective ethods. These include scanning techniques, such as **fMRIs** and **EEGs**. With vances in technology, it is possible to accurately measure physiological and ural processes in ways that are not open to bias.

This means that much of the biological approach is based on objective and iable data.

iological determinism

ıe limitation of the biological approach is that it is **determinist**.

The biological approach is determinist in that it sees human behaviour governed by internal, genetic causes over which we have no control. owever, we have already seen that the way in which an individual's notype is expressed (phenotype – see facing page) is heavily influenced the environment. Not even identical twins who share the same genes ok the same and think the same. Also, a purely genetic argument comes problematic when we consider things such as crime. Could a olent criminal, for instance, really excuse their actions by claiming their haviour was controlled by a 'crime gene'?

This suggests that the biological view is often too simplistic and ignores e mediating effects of the environment.

valuation eXtra

atural selection

tics of Darwin's work, such as Karl Popper, claim that it is not possible falsify the theory of natural selection (a key criterion of science) as cannot show evolution happening, we can only deduce it has taken ace. However, others claim that the basic principles are supported by ssil records (e.g. showing dinosaurs changing into birds).

nsider: *To what extent is natural selection a substantiated eory?*

udy tip

ou are writing an essay on the biological approach, make sure do not include too much description of biological structures processes. An essay should be a concise overview of the roach itself.

Apply it Methods — Twin study

In a study of depression, a researcher investigated the genetic basis of the disorder. One way to do this is to compare concordance rates for identical twins (monozygotic) who have exactly the same genes with non-identical (dizygotic) twins who share about 50% of the same genes. Both kinds of twins grow up in similar environments. Concordance rates express the likelihood that a trait present in one twin is also found in the other twin.

The following mean concordance rates found by the researcher were:

Monozygotic (MZ) twins – 49%

Dizygotic (DZ) twins – 17%

Ordinary siblings – 9%

Questions

1. Is this a **lab**, **field**, **natural** or **quasi-experiment**? Explain your choice. (*2 marks*)
2. What type of **experimental design** has been used? Explain your answer. (*2 marks*)
3. Identify the **independent** and **dependent variables** within this experiment. (*2 marks*)
4. Explain what the findings above tell us about the genetic basis of depression. Refer to all *three* findings in your answer. (*3 marks*)

105-31198
4HDH 4/11
POLICE DEPT.

My genes made me do it.

Apply it Concepts — PKU

Phenylketonuria (PKU) is a rare genetic disorder that can be detected in babies using a heel prick test. If left unchecked, PKU causes severe learning difficulties in those who carry the genotype. If detected early enough, however, the child can be placed on a restricted diet and will not go on to develop learning difficulties.

Questions

1. Explain how PKU illustrates the relationship between genotype and phenotype.
2. Do some further research yourself and identify another genetic condition that illustrates the relationship between genotype and phenotype.

Check it

1. Explain what is meant by 'evolution' in psychology. *[3 marks]*
2. Using an example, explain the difference between 'genotype' and 'phenotype'. *[4 marks]*
3. Outline **two** features of the biological approach. Explain **two** limitations of the biological approach. *[8 marks]*
4. Discuss the contribution of the biological approach to our understanding of human behaviour. *[12 marks AS, 16 marks AL]*

Biopsychology: The nervous system and the endocrine system

The specification says...

The divisions of the nervous system: central and peripheral (somatic and autonomic).

The function of the endocrine system: glands and hormones.

The fight or flight response including the role of adrenaline.

Humans, like all animals, have two major physiological systems that regulate behaviour in response to the environment. These are the nervous system and the endocrine system.

Key terms

Nervous system Consists of the central nervous system and the peripheral nervous system. Communicates using electrical signals.

Central nervous system (CNS) Consists of the brain and the spinal cord and is the origin of all complex commands and decisions.

Peripheral nervous system (PNS) Sends information to the CNS from the outside world, and transmits messages *from* the CNS to muscles and glands in the body.

Somatic nervous system (SNS) Transmits information from receptor cells in the sense organs to the CNS. It also receives information from the CNS that directs muscles to act.

Autonomic nervous system (ANS) Transmits information to and from internal bodily organs. It is 'autonomic' as the system operates involuntarily (i.e. automatic). It has two main divisions: the *sympathetic* and *parasympathetic* nervous systems.

The nervous system acts more rapidly than the endocrine system but they are both very fast. The nervous system's average response time is 0.25 seconds but may be as quick as 100 milliseconds. The endocrine responses are slower because hormones have to travel through the bloodstream (about 2 or 3 seconds) but last longer.

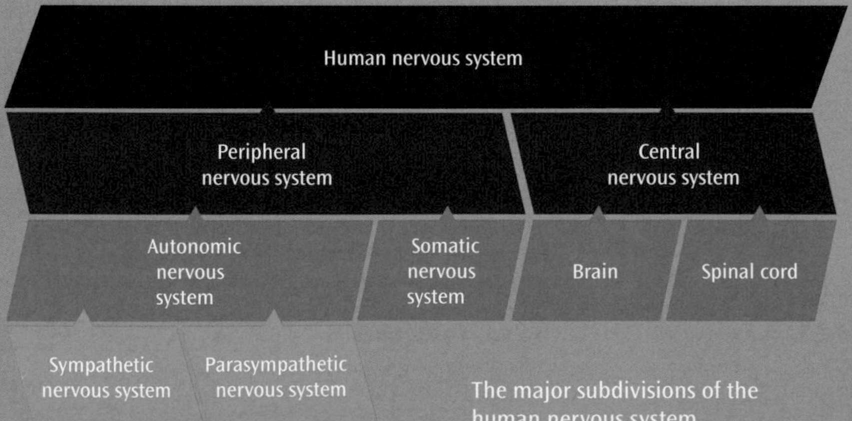
Human nervous system
Peripheral nervous system
Central nervous system
Autonomic nervous system
Somatic nervous system
Brain
Spinal cord
Sympathetic nervous system
Parasympathetic nervous system

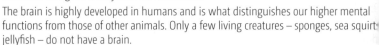

The major subdivisions of the human nervous system.

The nervous system

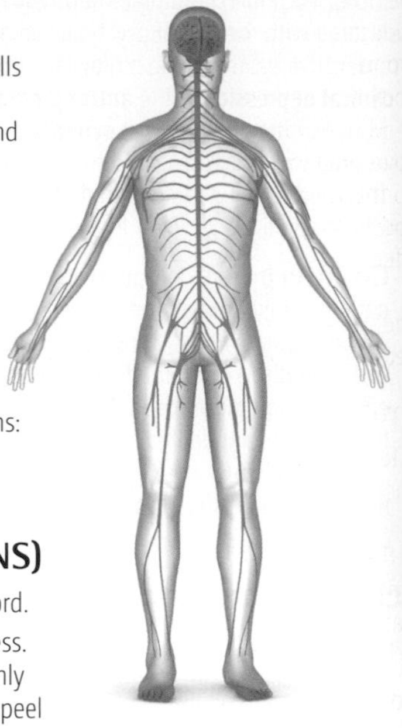

The **nervous system** is a specialised network of cells in the human body and is our primary internal communication system. It is based on electrical and chemical signals whereas the endocrine system (facing page) is based on hormones.

The nervous system has two main functions:

- To collect, process and respond to information in the environment.
- To co-ordinate the working of different organs and cells in the body.

The nervous system is divided into two subsystems:

- **Central nervous system** (CNS).
- **Peripheral nervous system** (PNS).

The central nervous system (CNS)

The CNS is made up of the brain and the spinal cord.

- The **brain** is the centre of all conscious awareness. The brain's outer layer, the **cerebral cortex**, is only 3 mm thick and covers the brain like an orange peel covers an orange. It is only found in mammals.

  The brain is highly developed in humans and is what distinguishes our higher mental functions from those of other animals. Only a few living creatures – sponges, sea squirt jellyfish – do not have a brain.

  The brain is divided into two **hemispheres**.
- The **spinal cord** is an extension of the brain. It passes messages to and from the brain and connects nerves to the PNS. It is also responsible for reflex actions such as pulling your hand away from a hot plate.

The peripheral nervous system (PNS)

The PNS transmits messages, via millions of **neurons** (nerve cells), to and from the centra nervous system. The peripheral nervous system is further subdivided into the:

- **Autonomic nervous system** (ANS) governs vital functions in the body such as breathing, heart rate, digestion, sexual arousal and stress responses.
- **Somatic nervous system** (SNS) governs muscle movement and receives information from sensory receptors.

Apply it Concepts

A frightening experience

Jim Bob was telling his friend Sue Ellen about his recent frightening experience.

'I was walking home by myself in the dark. Suddenly, I heard a shuffling noise behind me and the faint smell of rotting flesh. I realised it was coming closer. I saw a bus at the bus stop and decided to run. I could hear the footsteps getting closer. I don't think I've ever moved so quickly. I leapt on the bus – shaking, sweating and my heart was beating fast. I turned to see an empty street as the bus pulled away from the stop. Had I imagined it?'

Question

Outline the role of the central nervous system and autonomic nervous system in behaviour. Refer to Jim Bob's experience in your answer.

Practical activity on page 126

'he endocrine system

ilands and hormones

ıe **endocrine system** works alongside the nervous system to control vital functions in e body. The endocrine system acts more slowly than the nervous system but has very idespread and powerful effects. Various **glands** in the body, such as the **thyroid gland**, oduce **hormones**. Hormones are secreted into the bloodstream and affect any cell in the ɔdy that has a receptor for that particular hormone.

Most hormones affect cells in more than one body organ, leading to many diverse and ɔwerful responses. For example, the thyroid gland produces the hormone **thyroxine**. This ɔrmone affects cells in the heart (increases heart rate). It also affects cells throughout the ɔdy increasing metabolic rates (the chemical processes taking place in the cells). This in turn fects growth rates.

The main glands of the endocrine system are shown in the diagram on the right. The key ıdocrine gland is the **pituitary gland**, located in the brain. It is often called the 'master gland' ecause it controls the release of hormones from all the other endocrine glands in the body.

ndocrine and ANS working together: Fight or flight

ften the endocrine system and the autonomic nervous system (ANS) work in parallel with one ıother, for instance during a stressful event. When a stressor is perceived (your friend jumps out frighten you or you think about your upcoming exams) the first thing that happens is a part the brain called the **hypothalamus** activates the pituitary gland and this triggers activity in the mpathetic branch of the autonomic nervous system. The ANS changes from its normal resting ate (the **parasympathetic state**) to the physiologically aroused **sympathetic state** (try it – think having to learn all this for your exams and your sympathetic nervous system will kick in).

drenaline The stress hormone **adrenaline** is released from the *adrenal medulla* (a part the adrenal gland lying near your kidneys) into the bloodstream. Adrenaline triggers ıysiological changes in the body (e.g. increased heart rate) which creates the physiological ousal necessary for the **fight or flight response**.

nmediate and automatic All of this happens in an instant as soon as the threat is etected (for example your heart starts beating faster almost as soon as you experience a ght). This is an acute response and an automatic reaction in the body. The physiological ıanges associated with this sympathetic response are listed in the table below right. These ıanges explain why stress, panic, or even excitement, are often experienced as a 'sick' feeling utterflies' in your stomach – does that describe what you were feeling?).

ırasympathetic action Finally, once the threat has passed, the parasympathetic nervous stem returns the body to its resting state. The parasympathetic branch of the ANS works in ɔposition to the sympathetic nervous system – its actions are *antagonistic* to the sympathetic stem. The parasympathetic system acts as a 'brake' and reduces the activities of the body at were increased by the actions of the sympathetic branch. This is sometimes referred to as e *rest and digest* response.

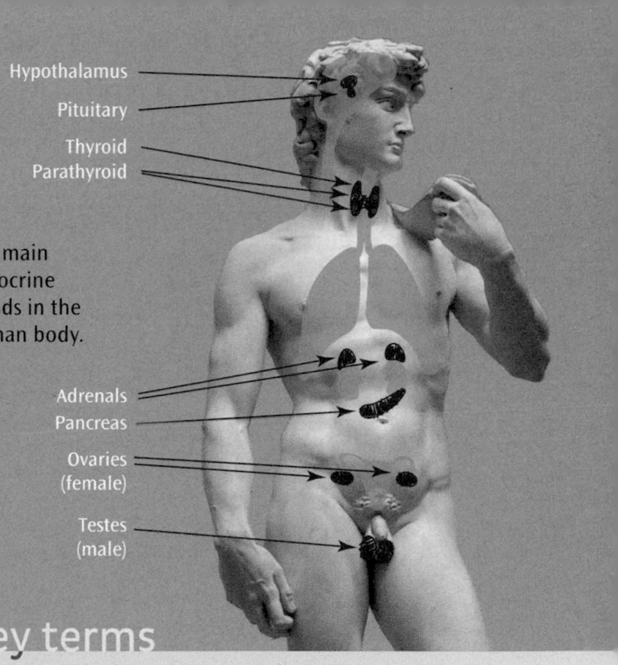

Hypothalamus
Pituitary
Thyroid
Parathyroid
Adrenals
Pancreas
Ovaries (female)
Testes (male)

The main endocrine glands in the human body.

Key terms

Endocrine system One of the body's major information systems that instructs glands to release hormones directly into the bloodstream. These hormones are carried towards target organs in the body. Communicates via chemicals.

Gland An organ in the body that synthesises substances such as hormones.

Hormones Chemical substances that circulate in the bloodstream and only affect target organs. They are produced in large quantities but disappear quickly. Their effects are very powerful.

Fight or flight response The way an animal responds when stressed. The body becomes physiologically aroused in readiness to fight an aggressor or, in some cases, flee.

Adrenaline A hormone produced by the adrenal glands which is part of the human body's immediate stress response system. Adrenaline has a strong effect on the cells of the cardiovascular system – stimulating heart rate, contracting blood vessels and dilating air passages.

Apply it Methods: Stress and illness

Research has shown that people who get ill have often experienced major stressful life events in the previous few months and years, such as getting married, divorce, death of a loved one, etc. A researcher investigated this relationship between illness and life events. She gave 150 participants a questionnaire in which they had to indicate the number of major life events (from a list of 20) they had experienced over the past three years. This was compared with the number of days off work through illness the participants had had over the same period.

The researcher found a positive correlation between the two co-variables.

Questions

1. In the context of the investigation above, what is meant by 'a positive correlation between the two co-variables'? (*2 marks*)
2. Suggest a suitable graphical display that the researcher could have used to show the relationship between the two co-variables. (*1 mark*)
3. Explain *one* advantage of **correlational studies**. Refer to the investigation above in your answer. (*2 marks*)
4. Explain the difference between correlations and experiments. (*3 marks*)

Biological changes associated with the sympathetic and parasympathetic response.

Sympathetic state	*Parasympathetic state*
Increases heart rate	Decreases heart rate
Increases breathing rate	Decreases breathing rate
Dilates pupils	Constricts pupils
Inhibits digestion	Stimulates digestion
Inhibits saliva production	Stimulates saliva production
Contracts rectum	Relaxes rectum

Check it

1. Name **and** briefly outline **two** divisions of the human nervous system. *[4 marks]*
2. Identify **and** describe **two** glands of the endocrine system. *[2 marks + 2 marks]*
3. Briefly outline **two** hormones and explain the function of each of these. *[2 marks + 2 marks]*
4. Explain what is meant by the 'fight or flight response'. *[3 marks]*

Biopsychology: Neurons and synaptic transmission

The specification says...

The structure and function of sensory, relay and motor neurons.

The process of synaptic transmission including reference to neurotransmitters, excitation and inhibition.

On the previous spread we considered the major biological structures and systems. Now we will delve a little deeper and, in so doing, get a good deal smaller! We will investigate how the nervous system transmits signals via the billions of nerve cells (neurons) it houses.

We will also consider how these nerve cells communicate with each other, through electrical and chemical messages, within the body and the brain.

Key terms

Neuron The basic building blocks of the nervous system, neurons are nerve cells that process and transmit messages through electrical and chemical signals.

Sensory neurons These carry messages from the PNS (peripheral nervous system) to the CNS. They have long dendrites and short axons.

Relay neurons These connect the sensory neurons to the motor or other relay neurons. They have short dendrites and short axons.

Motor neurons These connect the CNS (central nervous system) to effectors such as muscles and glands. They have short dendrites and long axons.

Apply it Concepts — Function of neurons

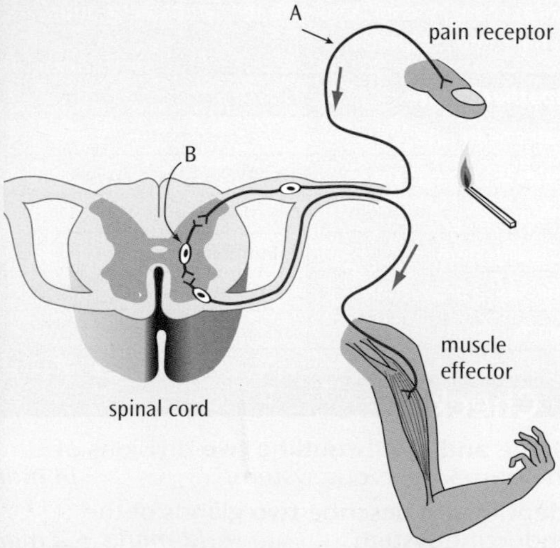
A
pain receptor
B
muscle effector
spinal cord

Question

Identify the type of neuron labelled A and B.

The structure and function of neurons

There are 100 billion **neurons** (nerve cells) in the human nervous system, 80% of which are located in the brain. By transmitting signals *electrically* and *chemically*, these neurons provide the nervous system with its primary means of communication.

Types of neurons

There are three types of neurons: **sensory neurons**, **relay neurons** and **motor neurons**. The features of each are summarised in the key terms on the left and illustrated in the diagram below.

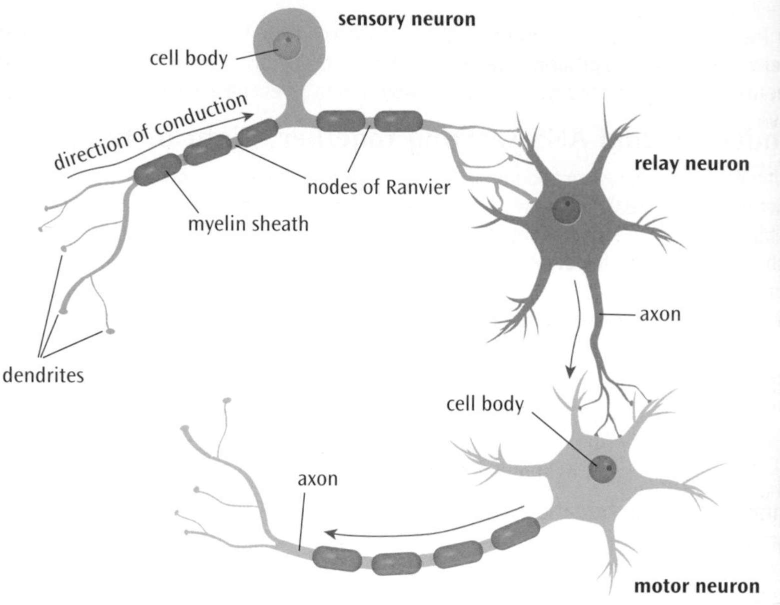
sensory neuron
cell body
direction of conduction
nodes of Ranvier
myelin sheath
relay neuron
axon
dendrites
cell body
axon
motor neuron

The structure of a neuron

Neurons vary in size from less than a millimetre to up to a metre long, but all share the same basic structure.

The **cell body** (or soma) includes a **nucleus**, which contains the **genetic** material of the cell. Branchlike structures called **dendrites** protrude from the cell body. These carry nerve impulses from neighbouring neurons towards the cell body.

The **axon** carries the impulses away from the cell body down the length of the neuron. The axon is covered in a fatty layer of **myelin sheath** that protects the axon and speeds up electrical transmission of the impulse.

If the myelin sheath was continuous this would have the reverse effect and slow down the electrical impulse. Thus, the myelin sheath is segmented by gaps called **nodes of Ranvier**. These speed up the transmission of the impulse by forcing it to 'jump' across the gaps along the axon.

Finally, at the end of the axon are **terminal buttons** that communicate with the next neuron in the chain across a gap known as the **synapse** (see facing page).

Location of neurons

The cell bodies of motor neurons may be in the **central nervous system** (CNS) but they have long axons which form part of the **peripheral nervous system** (PNS). Sensory neurons are located outside of the CNS, in the PNS in clusters known as **ganglia**. Relay neurons make up 97% of all neurons and most are found within the brain and the visual system.

Electrical transmission – the firing of a neuron

When a neuron is in a resting state the inside of the cell is negatively charged compared to the outside. When a neuron is activated by a stimulus, the inside of the cell becomes positively charged for a split second causing an **action potential** to occur. This creates an electrical impulse that travels down the axon towards the end of the neuron.

Synaptic transmission

Chemical transmission

Neurons communicate with each other within groups known as **neural networks**. Each neuron is separated from the next by an extremely tiny gap called the synapse. Signals *within* neurons are transmitted electrically. However, signals *between* neurons are transmitted chemically across the synapse.

When the electrical impulse reaches the end of the neuron (the **presynaptic terminal**) it triggers the release of **neurotransmitter** from tiny sacs called **synaptic vesicles**.

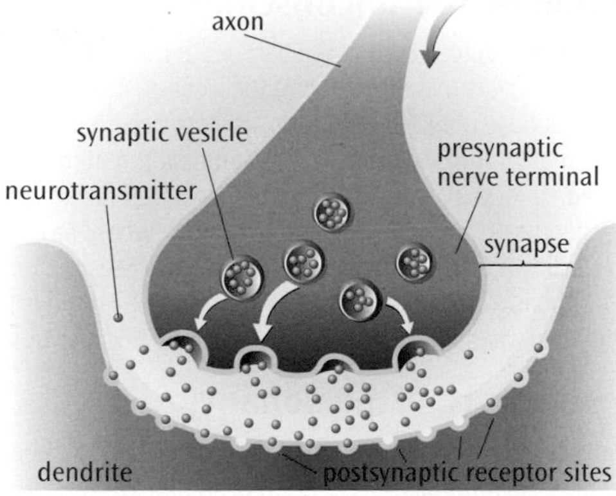
axon
synaptic vesicle
presynaptic nerve terminal
neurotransmitter
synapse
dendrite
postsynaptic receptor sites

Neurotransmitters

Neurotransmitters are chemicals that diffuse across the synapse to the next neuron in the chain. Once a neurotransmitter crosses the gap, it is taken up by a **postsynaptic receptor site** on the dendrites of the next neuron (axons take signals to the synapse, dendrites take signals away). Here, the chemical message is converted back into an electrical impulse and the process of transmission begins again in this other neuron.

It is worth noting that the direction of travel can only be one-way. This is because neurotransmitters are released from the presynaptic neuron terminal and received by the postsynaptic neuron (at the receptor sites).

Several dozen types of neurotransmitter have been identified in the brain (as well as in the spinal cord and some **glands**). Each neurotransmitter has its own specific molecular structure that fits perfectly into a postsynaptic receptor site, similar to a lock and a key. Neurotransmitters also have specialist functions. For instance, **acetylcholine** (ACh) is found at each point where a motor neuron meets a muscle, and upon its release, it will cause muscles to contract.

Excitation and inhibition

Neurotransmitters have either an **excitatory** or **inhibitory** effect on the neighbouring neuron. For instance, the neurotransmitter **serotonin** causes inhibition in the receiving neuron, resulting in the neuron becoming more negatively charged and less likely to fire. In contrast, **adrenaline** (an element of the stress response which is both a **hormone** and a neurotransmitter) causes excitation of the postsynaptic neuron by increasing its positive charge and making it more likely to fire.

Summation

Whether a postsynaptic neuron fires is decided by the process of **summation**. The excitatory and inhibitory influences are summed: if the net effect on the postsynaptic neuron is inhibitory then the postsynaptic neuron is less likely to fire. If the net effect is excitatory it is more likely to fire, i.e. the inside of the postsynaptic neuron momentarily becomes positively charged. Once the electrical impulse is created it travels down the neuron.

Therefore, the action potential of the postsynaptic neuron is only triggered if the sum of the excitatory and inhibitory signals at any one time reaches the threshold.

Apply it Concepts: Psychoactive drugs

Increased understanding of the mode of action of neurotransmitters in the brain has led to the development of psychoactive drugs to treat mental disorders. For instance, depression has been linked to low levels of serotonin, which is thought to play an important role in stabilising mood.

A category of drugs known as SSRIs (selective serotonin reuptake inhibitors) such as Prozac, slow down the reuptake of serotonin after it has crossed the synapse, ensuring it stays active for longer in the synapse.

Question

Use your knowledge of synaptic transmission to explain what is happening at the synapse.

Key terms

Synaptic transmission The process by which neighbouring neurons communicate with each other by sending chemical messages across the gap (the synapse) that separates them.

Neurotransmitter Brain chemicals released from synaptic vesicles that relay signals across the synapse from one neuron to another. Neurotransmitters can be broadly divided into those that perform an excitatory function and those that perform an inhibitory function.

Excitation When a neurotransmitter, such as adrenaline, increases the positive charge of the postsynaptic neuron. This *increases* the likelihood that the postsynaptic neuron will pass on the electrical impulse.

Inhibition When a neurotransmitter, such as serotonin, increases the negative charge of the postsynaptic neuron. This *decreases* the likelihood that the postsynaptic neuron will pass on the electrical impulse.

Apply it Concepts: The reflex arc

Fill in the gaps using the terms provided at the bottom of the box.

The knee-jerk reflex is an example of a reflex arc:

A stimulus, such as a hammer, hits the knee. This is detected by sense organs in the ________________, which convey a message along a ________________.

The message reaches the ________________, where it connects with a ________________. This then transfers the message to a ________________. This then carries the message to an ________________, such as a muscle, which causes the muscle to contract and, hence, causes the knee to move or jerk.

Missing words:

effector	*CNS (central nervous system)*
sensory neuron	*PNS (peripheral nervous system)*
motor neuron	*relay neuron*

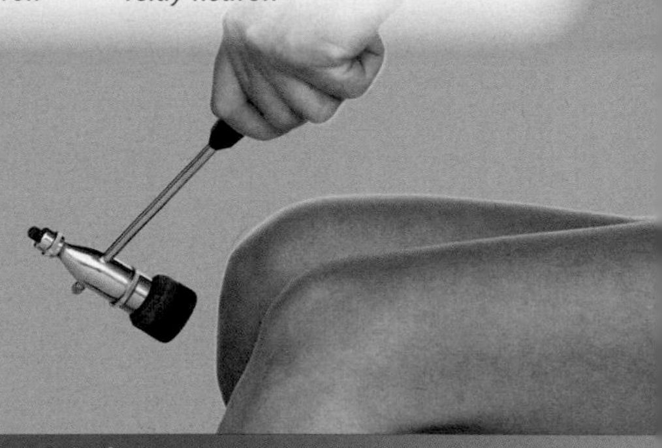

Check it

1. Explain the process of synaptic transmission. *[4 marks]*
2. With reference to neurotransmitters, explain what is meant by both 'excitation' **and** 'inhibition'. *[4 marks]*
3. Explain the difference between a sensory neuron and a relay neuron. *[2 marks]*

The psychodynamic approach A level only

The specification says...

The psychodynamic approach: the role of the unconscious, the structure of personality, that is Id, Ego and Superego, defence mechanisms including repression, denial and displacement, psychosexual stages.

The psychodynamic approach is most closely associated with the work of Sigmund Freud (though several post-Freudians were influenced by and expanded upon many of Freud's ideas).

Key terms

Psychodynamic approach A perspective that describes the different forces (dynamics), most of which are unconscious, that operate on the mind and direct human behaviour and experience.

The unconscious The part of the mind that we are unaware of but which directs much of our behaviour.

Id Entirely unconscious, the Id is made up of selfish aggressive instincts that demand immediate gratification.

Ego The 'reality check' that balances the conflicting demands of the Id and the Superego.

Superego The moralistic part of our personality which represents the ideal self – how we ought to be.

Defence mechanisms Unconscious strategies that the Ego uses to manage the conflict between the Id and the Superego.

Psychosexual stages Five developmental stages that all children pass through. At each stage there is a different conflict, the outcome of which determines future development.

The psychodynamic approach

The role of the unconscious

Sigmund Freud suggested that the part of our mind that we know about and are aware of – the *conscious* mind – is merely the 'tip of the iceberg'. Most of our mind is made up of **the unconscious** – a vast storehouse of biological drives and instincts that has a significant influence on our behaviour and personality. The unconscious also contains threatening and disturbing memories that have been **repressed**, or locked away and forgotten (see 'Defence mechanisms' below). These can be accessed during dreams or through 'slips of the tongue' (what Freud referred to as **parapraxes**). An example of such a slip is calling a female teacher 'mum' instead of 'miss'.

Just bubbling under the surface of our conscious mind is the **preconscious** which contains thoughts and memories which are not currently in conscious awareness but we can access if desired.

The structure of personality

Freud described personality as 'tripartite', composed of three parts:

- The **Id** is the primitive part of our personality. It operates on the **pleasure principle** – the Id gets what it wants. It is a seething mass of unconscious drives and instincts. Only the Id is present at birth (Freud described babies as being 'bundles of Id'). Throughout life the Id is entirely selfish and demands instant gratification of its needs.
- The **Ego** works on the **reality principle** and is the mediator between the other two parts of the personality. The Ego develops around the age of two years and its role is to reduce the conflict between the demands of the Id and the Superego. It manages this by employing a number of **defence mechanisms** (see below).
- The **Superego** is formed at the end of the **phallic stage**, around the age of five. It is our internalised sense of right and wrong. Based on the **morality principle** it represents the moral standards of the child's same-gender parent and punishes the Ego for wrongdoing (through guilt).

Psychosexual stages

Freud claimed that child development occurred in five stages, see table below left. Each stage (apart from *latency*) is marked by a different conflict that the child must resolve in order to progress successfully to the next stage (see the 'Oedipus conflict' on the facing page). Any psychosexual conflict that is unresolved leads to **fixation** where the child becomes 'stuck' and carries certain behaviours and conflicts associated with that stage through to adult life.

Defence mechanisms

The Ego has a difficult job balancing the conflicting demands of the Id and the Superego but it does have help in the form of defence mechanisms. These are unconscious and ensure that the Ego is able to prevent us from being overwhelmed by temporary threats or traumas. However, they often involve some form of distortion of reality and as a long-term solution they are regarded as psychologically unhealthy and undesirable.

Psychosexual stages

Stage	*Description*	*Consequence of unresolved conflict*
Oral 0–1 years	Focus of pleasure is the mouth, mother's breast can be the object of desire.	Oral fixation – smoking, biting nails, sarcastic, critical.
Anal 1–3 years	Focus of pleasure is the anus. Child gains pleasure from withholding and expelling faeces.	Anal retentive – perfectionist, obsessive. Anal expulsive – thoughtless, messy.
Phallic 3–6 years	Focus of pleasure is the genital area.	Phallic personality – narcissistic, reckless.
Latency	Earlier conflicts are repressed.	
Genital	Sexual desires become conscious alongside the onset of puberty.	Difficulty forming heterosexual relationships.

There are many aspects of this stage theory that are clearly outdated.

Apply it Concepts: Examples of defence mechanisms

Three defence mechanisms are listed in the table below with their definitions.

Repression	Forcing a distressing memory out of the conscious mind.
Denial	Refusing to acknowledge some aspect of reality.
Displacement	Transferring feelings from true source of distressing emotion onto a substitute target.

Question

Three examples of defence mechanisms in action are given below. Match each example to one defence mechanism listed in the table above.

A. Continuing to turn up for work even though you have been sacked.

B. An individual forgetting the trauma of their favourite pet dying.

C. Slamming the door after a row with your girlfriend/boyfriend.

:valuation

ɛeal-world application

ne strength of the psychodynamic approach is that it introduced the idea of *sycho*therapy (as opposed to physical treatments).

Freud brought to the world a new form of therapy – psychoanalysis. This ʻas the first attempt to treat mental disorders psychologically rather than hysically. The new therapy employed a range of techniques designed to ccess the unconscious, such as dream analysis. Psychoanalysis claims to elp clients by bringing their repressed emotions into their conscious mind ɔ they can be dealt with. Psychoanalysis is the forerunner to many modern-ay 'talking therapies', such as **counselling**, that have since been established.

This shows the value of the psychodynamic approach in creating a new pproach to treatment.

Counterpoint Although Freudian therapists have claimed success for many clients with mild **neuroses**, psychoanalysis is regarded as inappropriate, even harmful, for people experiencing more serious mental disorders (such as **schizophrenia**). Many of the symptoms of schizophrenia, such as paranoia and delusional thinking, mean that those with the disorder have lost their grip on reality and cannot articulate their thoughts in the way required by psychoanalysis.

This suggests that Freudian therapy (and theory) may not apply to all mental disorders.

:xplanatory power

nother strength of Freud's theory is its ability to explain human behaviour.

Freud's theory is controversial in many ways, and occasionally bizarre, but has nevertheless had a huge influence on psychology and contemporary ıought. Alongside behaviourism, the psychodynamic approach remained key force in psychology for the first half of the 20th century and has een used to explain a wide range of phenomena including personality evelopment, the origins of psychological disorders, moral development and ender identity. The approach is also significant in drawing attention to the ɔnnection between experiences in childhood, such as our relationship with ur parents, and our later development.

This suggests that, overall, the psychodynamic approach has had a ositive impact on psychology – and also on literature, art and other human ndeavours.

Jntestable concepts

ne limitation of the psychodynamic approach is that much of it is untestable.

The philosopher of science Karl Popper argued that the psychodynamic pproach does not meet the scientific criterion of **falsification**. It is not pen to **empirical** testing (and the possibility of being disproved). Many f Freud's concepts (such as the Id and the **Oedipus complex**) are said to ccur at an unconscious level, making them difficult, if not impossible, to ɜst. Furthermore, his ideas were based on the subjective study of single ıdividuals, such as Little Hans, which makes it difficult to make universal aims about human behaviour.

This suggests that Freud's theory was pseudoscientific (not a real science) ather than established fact.

:valuation eXtra

ʼsychic determinism

he psychodynamic approach suggests that much of our behaviour is etermined by unconscious conflicts rooted in childhood. Freud believed ıere is no such thing as an 'accident'. Even something as random as a lip of the tongue' is driven by unconscious forces and has deep meaning.

Critics claim this is an extreme view because it dismisses any possible ıfluence of free will on behaviour.

:onsider: *Do you agree that Freud's psychic determinism is too xtreme?*

Apply it Concepts: Freud's case study of Little Hans and the Oedipus complex

In the phallic stage, Freud claimed that little boys develop incestuous feelings towards their mother and a murderous hatred for their rival in love – their father (the Oedipus complex). Fearing that their father will castrate them, boys repress their feelings for their mother and identify with their father, taking on his gender role and moral values.

Freud also suggested that girls of the same age experience penis envy: they desire their father – as the penis is the primary love object – and hate their mother (the Electra complex). Although Freud was less clear on the process in girls, they are thought to give up the desire for their father over time and replace this with a desire for a baby (identifying with their mother in the process).

Freud supported his concept of the Oedipus complex with his case study of Little Hans. Hans was a five-year-old boy who developed a phobia of horses after seeing one collapse in the street. Freud suggested that Hans's phobia was a form of displacement in which his repressed fear of his father was transferred (displaced) onto horses. Thus, horses were merely a symbolic representation of Hans's real unconscious fear – the fear of castration experienced during the Oedipus complex.

Questions

1. Is the Little Hans case study good evidence for the Oedipus conflict? Explain your answer.
2. Is this a scientific way of investigating phobias? Explain your answer.
3. How might a behaviourist explain Hans's phobia of horses?

Apply it Concepts: Id, Ego and Superego

EGO
I need to do a bit of planning to get it.
ID
I WANT IT NOW!
SUPER EGO
You can't have it– it's not right

What would the Id, Ego and Superego suggest you do in the following situations?

1. You have missed lunch and are walking past a cake shop.
2. You are just leaving work and your boss asks you to stay an extra hour.
3. You are sitting on a bus and notice someone has left a wallet full of £50 notes.
4. You are driving home and another car pulls out in front of you nearly causing a collision.

Check it

1. Using an example, explain the 'role of the unconscious'. *[3 marks]*
2. Identify **one** Freudian defence mechanism **and** explain how it would affect behaviour. *[3 marks]*
3. Discuss the psychodynamic approach. Compare the psychodynamic approach with the cognitive approach. *[16 marks AL]*

Humanistic psychology A level only

The specification says...

Humanistic psychology: free will, self-actualisation and Maslow's hierarchy of needs, focus on the self, congruence, the role of conditions of worth. The influence on counselling psychology.

Humanistic psychology emerged in the United States in the 1950s largely as a result of the work of Carl Rogers and Abraham Maslow. It became known as the 'third force' in psychology – alongside **behaviourist** and **psychodynamic** approaches – and represented a challenge to both. Rogers felt that Freud had dealt with the 'sick half' of psychology, so the humanistic approach concerned itself with explanations of 'healthy' growth in individuals.

Key terms

Humanistic psychology An approach to understanding behaviour that emphasises the importance of subjective experience and each person's capacity for self-determination.

Free will The notion that humans can make choices and are not determined by internal biological or external forces.

Self-actualisation The desire to grow psychologically and fulfil one's full potential – becoming what you are capable of.

Hierarchy of needs A five-levelled hierarchical sequence in which basic physiological needs (such as hunger) must be satisfied before higher psychological needs (such as self-esteem and self-actualisation) can be achieved.

Self The ideas and values that characterise 'I' and 'me' and includes perception and valuing of 'what I am' and 'what I can do'.

Congruence The aim of Rogerian therapy, when the self-concept and ideal self are seen to broadly accord or match.

Conditions of worth When a parent places limits or boundaries on their love of their children. For instance, a parent saying to a child, 'I will only love you if...you study medicine' or 'if you split up with that boy'.

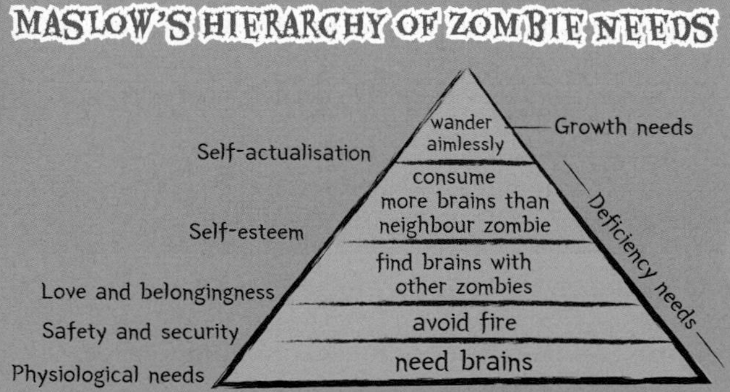
MASLOW'S HIERARCHY OF ZOMBIE NEEDS
wander aimlessly
Growth needs
Self-actualisation
consume more brains than neighbour zombie
Deficiency needs
Self-esteem
find brains with other zombies
Love and belongingness
avoid fire
Safety and security
need brains
Physiological needs

Although it might be possible to apply the hierarchy of needs to zombies, Maslow argued that the need for self-actualisation is uniquely human.

Humanistic psychology

Free will

All the approaches we have considered so far are **determinist** to some degree in their suggestion that behaviour is entirely, or at least partly, shaped by forces over which we have no control. Even the **cognitive approach**, which claims we are free to choose our own thoughts, would still argue that such choice is constrained by the limits of our cognitive system. **Humanistic psychology** is quite different in this respect, claiming that human beings are essentially *self-determining* and have **free will**. People are still affected by external and internal influences, but are also active agents who can determine their own development.

For this reason, humanistic psychologists such as Rogers and Maslow, reject more scientific models that attempt to establish general principles of human behaviour. As active agents we are all unique, and psychology should concern itself with the study of subjective experience rather than general laws. This is often referred to as a *person-centred approach* in psychology.

Maslow's hierarchy of needs

Abraham Maslow was one of the founders of the humanistic movement in psychology. One of his main interests was in what motivates people. He described a **hierachy of needs** that motivate our behaviour. In order to achieve our primary goal of **self-actualisation**, a number of other deficiency needs must first be met. At the bottom (see diagram below left) are physiological needs such as food and water. Imagine you wanted to produce the best psychology essay you had ever written, this would be very difficult if you were hungry or tired.

Moving up the hierarchy, the next deficiency need is safety and security followed by love and belongingness and then **self-esteem**. A person is only able to progress through the hierarchy once the current need in the sequence has been met. At the top is self-actualisation.

Self-actualisation

Most people have an innate desire to achieve their full potential – to become the best they can possibly be. Self-actualisation represents the uppermost level of Maslow's hierarchy of needs. All four lower levels of the hierarchy ('deficiency needs') must be met before the individual can work towards self-actualisation (a 'growth need') and fulfil their potential. This applies to early development when a baby is first focused on physiological needs and applies throughout life.

Humanistic psychologists regard *personal growth* as an essential part of what it is to be human. Personal growth is concerned with developing and changing as a person to become fulfilled, satisfied and goal-orientated. Not everyone will manage this, however, and there are important psychological barriers that may prevent a person from reaching their potential.

The self, congruence and conditions of worth

Carl Rogers argued that for personal growth to be achieved an individual's concept of **self** (the way they see themselves) must be broadly equivalent to, or have **congruence** with, their **ideal self** (the person they want to be). If too big a gap exists between the two 'selves' the person will experience a state of incongruence and self-actualisation will not be possible due to the negative feelings of self-worth that arise from incongruence.

In order to reduce the gap between the self-concept and the ideal self, Rogers developed **client-centred therapy** – also called 'counselling' (see facing page) to help people cope with the problems of everyday living. Rogers claimed that many of the issues we experience as adults, such as worthlessness and low self-esteem, have their roots in childhood and can often be explained by a lack of **unconditional positive regard** (or lack of *unconditional love*) from our parents. A parent who sets boundaries or limits on their love for their child (**conditions of worth**) by claiming *'I will only love you if...'* is storing up psychological problems for that child in the future. Thus, Rogers saw one of his roles as an effective therapist as being able to provide his clients with the unconditional positive regard that they had failed to receive as children.

Apply it Concepts Self-actualisers

Maslow characterised life as a series of peak experiences – moments of great achievement, ecstasy or elation when all deficiency needs are satisfied. He also identified and researched a number of self-actualisers – people who, for whatever reason, were fulfilled in life and had used their abilities to the fullest.

Question

Can you think of any people, in the media or who you know, who could be described as self-actualisers? Explain your choices in each case.

Evaluation

Not reductionist

One strength of the humanistic approach is that it rejects attempts to break up behaviour and experience into smaller components (**reductionism**).

Behaviourists explain human and animal learning in terms of simple stimulus–response connections. Supporters of the cognitive approach see human beings as little more than information-processing machines'. Biological psychologists reduce behaviour to its basic physiological processes. Freud described the whole of personality as a conflict between three things: Id, Ego and Superego. In contrast, humanistic psychologists advocate **holism**, the idea that subjective experience can only be understood by considering the whole person.

This approach may have more validity than its alternatives by considering meaningful human behaviour within its real-world context.

Counterpoint Having said that, reductionist approaches may be more scientific. This is because the ideal of science is the **experiment**, and experiments reduce behaviour to **independent** and **dependent variables**. One issue with humanistic psychology is that, unlike behaviourism, there are relatively few concepts that can be broken down to single variables and measured.

This means that humanistic psychology in general is short on **empirical** evidence to support its claims.

Positive approach

Another strength of the humanistic approach is that it is optimistic.

Humanistic psychologists have been praised for bringing the person back into psychology and promoting a positive image of the human condition. Freud saw human beings as prisoners of their past and claimed all of us existed somewhere between 'common unhappiness and absolute despair'. In contrast, humanistic psychologists see all people as basically good, free to work towards the achievement of their potential and in control of their lives.

This suggests that humanistic psychology offers a refreshing and optimistic alternative to other approaches.

Cultural bias

One limitation of the approach is that it may be culturally-biased.

Many of the ideas that are central to humanistic psychology, such as individual freedom, autonomy and personal growth, would be much more readily associated with countries that have more **individualist** tendencies (e.g. the US). Countries with **collectivist** tendencies emphasise more the needs of the group and interdependence. In such countries, the ideals of humanistic psychology may not be as important as in others (e.g. self-actualisation).

Therefore, it is possible that this approach does not apply universally and is a product of the cultural context within which it was developed.

Evaluation eXtra

Limited application

Critics have argued that humanistic psychology has had relatively little impact in psychology – or little practical application in the real world (in comparison with other approaches, such as behaviourism or the biological approach). The approach has been described, not as a comprehensive theory, but as a loose set of abstract ideas.

On the other hand, Rogerian therapy revolutionised counselling techniques and Maslow's hierarchy of needs has been used to explain motivation, particularly in the workplace.

Consider: *Do you agree with the argument that the humanistic approach has had little impact?*

Counselling psychology

Rogers' client-centred (or latterly, *person-centred*) therapy is an important form of modern-day psychotherapy. It led to the general approach of **counselling** which is applied in many settings today (e.g. Samaritans and other helplines). Rogers referred to those in therapy as 'clients' rather than 'patients' as he saw the individual as the expert on their own condition. Thus, therapy is not directed by the therapist (non-directive), and the client is just encouraged towards the discovery of their own solutions within a therapeutic atmosphere that is warm, supportive and non-judgemental.

For Rogers, an effective therapist should provide the client with three things: genuineness, empathy and unconditional positive regard. The aim of Rogerian therapy is to increase the person's feelings of self-worth, reduce the level of incongruence between the self-concept and the ideal self, and help the person become a more fully functioning person.

Rogers' work transformed psychotherapy and introduced a variety of counselling techniques. In the UK and the US, similar counselling skills are practised, not only in clinical settings, but throughout education, health, social work and industry.

Client-centred therapy has been praised as a forward-looking and effective approach that focuses on present problems rather than dwelling on the past. However, much like psychoanalysis (see previous spread), it is best applied to the treatment of 'mild' psychological conditions, such as anxiety and low self-worth.

Apply it Concepts: Evaluating counselling

Question

Why would counselling be less effective in treating more serious mental disorders such as schizophrenia?

Apply it Concepts: Joyce: teacher or dancer?

Joyce is a successful teacher and is well-liked by her colleagues. However, Joyce has always dreamed of becoming a ballroom dancer. She spends much of her free time with her partner practising elaborate lifts, and can often be seen twirling around the classroom during break times.

Joyce is considering leaving teaching and becoming a professional dancer. Her colleagues have described Joyce's plans as 'ridiculous', and her parents, who are very proud of the fact that their daughter is a teacher, have told Joyce they will not speak to her again if she does. Joyce is beginning to feel sad and miserable.

Question

Referring to features of humanistic psychology, explain how Joyce's situation may affect her personal growth.

Study tip

One of the key influences on behaviour is culture. Psychologists have tried to categorise the main ways in which cultures influence behaviour, such as distinguishing between individualist and collectivist cultures (see left). The UK, the US, Australia and most European countries are regarded as individualist and also often described as industrialised and/or 'Western'. But because 'Western' is a bit of an outdated term, we have preferred to use either 'individualist' or 'industrialised'. However, things are rarely so simple and any attempt to divide the world into polar opposites cannot truly reflect the differences that exist between cultures.

Check it

1. Explain what humanistic psychologists mean by 'conditions of worth'. *[3 marks]*
2. Outline **and** briefly evaluate the influence of humanistic psychology on counselling. *[5 marks]*
3. Discuss Maslow's hierarchy of needs. Refer to self-actualisation in your answer. *[8 marks]*
4. Outline humanistic psychology. Compare humanistic psychology with the psychodynamic approach. *[16 marks AL]*

Comparison of approaches A level only

The specification says...

Comparison of approaches.

In this chapter, we have considered six of the major psychological approaches. Here, we outline some of the areas of agreement, disagreement, contention and overlap between these different ways of viewing and explaining human behaviour. Our discussion is organised around five themes: views on development, nature versus nurture, reductionism, determinism, explanation and treatment of psychological disorders.

We also assess the benefits (and otherwise) of adopting an **eclectic approach** which aims to combine elements from different approaches.

Apply it Concepts

Let's be friends: areas of overlap and agreement between approaches

Although there are many significant differences between the theories and assumptions within each approach, there are some areas of overlap and ways in which approaches complement each other.

You may recall how the social learning theory approach was described as a 'bridge' between the behaviourist and cognitive approaches because it emphasised the importance of learning from the environment as well as the role of mediating cognitive factors.

The fusion of cognitive and biological approaches has led to the development of cognitive neuroscience – a sophisticated field that links mental states to biological structures.

The psychodynamic approach shares much in common with the biological approach as both see biological drives and instincts as crucial determinants of human development.

Finally, humanistic and psychodynamic approaches can both be reasonably described as person-centred in the way that they place subjective experience at the centre of their research.

These are just some of the ways in which psychological approaches overlap.

Question

Select two or three approaches. Draw Venn diagrams (see example below) to show the ways in which these approaches overlap and intersect. Use this page and the rest of the chapter to draw out the features and assumptions that different approaches have in common.

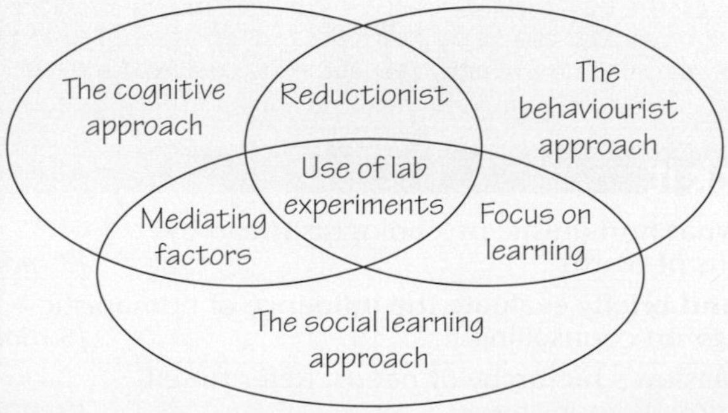
The cognitive approach
Reductionist
The behaviourist approach
Use of lab experiments
Mediating factors
Focus on learning
The social learning approach

An example of a Venn diagram.

Views on development

In terms of child development, the **psychodynamic approach** presents the most coherent theory of development, tying its concepts and processes to specific (psychosexual) stages that are determined by age. That said, Freud saw very little further development once a child enters the genital stage in the teen years.

Stage theories within the **cognitive approach** have contributed to our understanding of child development. For example, as part of their intellectual development, children form increasingly complex concepts (**schema**) as they get older.

Maturation is an important principle within the **biological approach** whereby genetically determined changes in a child's physiological status influence psychological and behavioural characteristics.

Humanistic psychologists see the development of the **self** as ongoing throughout life. However childhood is a particularly important period and a child's relationship with their parents is important in terms of **unconditional positive regard**.

Finally, the **behaviourist approach** and **social learning theory** do not offer coherent stage theories of development but instead see the processes that underpin learning as continuous, occurring at any age.

Nature versus nurture

The debate about whether human behaviour is more influenced by **inherited** biological factors (**nature**) or by the environment and experience (**nurture**) has a long history in psychology. The biological approach and the two learning approaches are furthest apart in this respect. Behaviourists characterised babies as 'blank slates' at birth and suggest that all behaviour comes about through learned associations, **reinforcement** contingencies or, in the case of social learning theory, observation and imitation. In contrast, the biological approach argues from a position that behaviour is the result of a **genetic** blueprint that we inherit from our parents (**genotype**), though the way it is expressed is influenced by the environment (**phenotype**).

Freud thought that much of our behaviour was driven by biological drives and instincts, but he also saw relationships with parents as playing a fundamental role in future development. Similarly, humanistic psychologists regard parents, friends and wider society as having a critical impact on the person's **self-concept**. Finally, although cognitive psychologists would recognise that many of our information processing abilities and schema are **innate**, they are constantly refined through experience.

Reductionism

Reductionism refers to the belief that human behaviour can be most effectively explained by breaking it down into constituent parts. The opposing view is **holism**, that phenomena are best understood by looking at the interplay and interaction of many different factors.

Behaviourism is reductionist in the sense that it breaks up complex behaviour into stimulus–response units for ease of testing in the **lab**. The biological approach is also reductionist in the way that it explains human behaviour and psychological states at the level of the gene or **neuron**. The psychodynamic approach reduces much of our behaviour to the influence of sexual drives and biological instincts, although Freud's argument that personality is a dynamic interaction between the three parts of the personality is often viewed as a more holistic explanation. The cognitive approach has been accused of **machine reductionism** by presenting people as information processing systems and ignoring the influence of emotion on behaviour. Like behaviourists, social learning theorists reduce complex learning to a handful of key processes (imitation, modelling, etc.) though they do at least place emphasis on cognitive factors that mediate learning, and how these interact with external influences.

Finally, and quite distinct from other approaches, is humanistic psychology, which formulates a holistic approach to understanding human behaviour. This involves investigating all aspects of the individual, including the effects of interaction with others and wider society.

Determinism

Determinism is often confused with reductionism but is quite distinct from it – though many determinist explanations are also reductionist. Determinism proposes that all behaviour has an internal or external cause and is thus predictable.

The behaviourist approach sees all behaviour as environmentally determined by external influences that we are unable to control (e.g. operant conditioning). The biological approach advocates a form of **genetic determinism** in its assumption that much of our behaviour is directed by innate influences. **Psychic determinism** is a key feature of the psychodynamic approach insofar as the **unconscious** forces that drive our behaviour are the ultimate cause of behaviour, and that these are simply rationalised by our conscious minds.

The positions described above are known as **hard determinism**, the next two approaches take a less all-or-nothing view (**soft determinism**). The cognitive approach suggests that we are the 'choosers' of our own thoughts and behaviours, yet these choices can only operate within the limits of what we know and have experienced. Social learning theorists, like Bandura, put forward the notion of **reciprocal determinism** – the idea that as well as being influenced by our environment, we also exert some influence upon it through the behaviours we choose to perform. Only humanistic psychology stands alone in its assertion that human beings have **free will** and operate as active agents who determine their own development.

Explanation and treatment of psychological disorders

The behaviourist model sees abnormality as arising from maladaptive or faulty learning in the sense that inappropriate or destructive patterns of behaviour have been reinforced. **Behaviour therapies**, such as **systematic desensitisation**, which aim to condition new, more healthy responses, have been applied successfully to the treatment of **phobias**.

Social learning theory has had relatively little application to treatment, but the principles of **modelling** and **observational learning** have been used to explain how negative behaviours such as aggression may be learned through the influence of dysfunctional **role models**.

Freud saw anxiety disorders as emerging from unconscious conflict, childhood trauma and the overuse of **defence mechanisms**. **Psychoanalysis** has had some success as a therapy but it is not appropriate for everyone because it requires a considerable input from the patient in terms of time and also ability to talk about and reflect on emotions.

Cognitive therapy is much more effective and applicable, especially when combined with behaviour therapy as **CBT** (for example in the treatment of **depression**). It aims to identify and eradicate faulty thinking which is assumed to be the root cause of maladaptive behaviour.

Also effective is humanistic therapy (or **counselling**) based on Rogers' philosophy that closing the gap between the self-concept and the ideal self will increase **self-esteem** and stimulate personal growth.

Finally, many would claim the biological approach has revolutionised the treatment of mental disorders through the development of **drug therapy** which regulates chemical imbalances in the brain.

To what extent is our behaviour dictated by forces beyond our control?

Apply it Concepts: The eclectic approach

Many modern psychologists take a multidisciplinary approach to the study of human behaviour. Eclecticism in psychology refers to the combining of several approaches, methods and/or theoretical perspectives in order to provide a more comprehensive account of human behaviour.

Such an ethos has proved fruitful in the field of mental disorders. Combining treatment options from several different perspectives – such as drugs, cognitive therapy and family therapy – has led to more effective outcomes for people with schizophrenia and lower relapse rates (e.g. Stein and Test 1980).

Many topic areas in psychology have also benefitted from 'interactionist' theories that combine different levels of explanation. The diathesis-stress model in psychiatry accounts for the fact that many mental disorders are a complex interaction of biological predisposition and environmental triggers. Similarly, the biosocial approach rejects the traditional distinction between nature and nurture by explaining how basic biological differences are reinforced by the environment during gender development, for instance.

Question

Although there are obvious advantages associated with eclecticism in psychology, what issues/problems might such an approach present?

Apply it Concepts: Idiographic and nomothetic approaches

The six approaches are also divided in terms of whether they are attempting to establish general laws by studying large groups of people (nomothetic approach) or whether they are aiming to understand what makes individuals unique (idiographic approach). The former generally involves the use of the experimental method whereas the latter tends to be more concerned with in-depth qualitative methods such as case studies and unstructured interviews.

Broadly speaking, the more scientific approaches – behaviourist, social learning theory, cognitive and biological – subscribe to the experimental nomothetic approach. However, the biological and cognitive approaches often draw upon data derived from case studies, especially those involving individuals with unusual abnormalities or deficits (as in the case of HM in memory on page 51) – a more idiographic approach. The person-centred approaches – psychodynamic and humanistic – are idiographic in that they favour the case study method, usually carried out within clinical settings.

Question

What are the strengths and limitations of adopting:

(a) An idiographic approach to human behaviour?

(b) A nomothetic approach to human behaviour?

Study tip

You might enhance your understanding of the information on this spread by drawing a table with the six approaches across the top and the five themes covered on this spread down the side. Then summarise the information on this spread in relation to each approach.

Check it

1. Outline **one** way in which the behaviourist approach and social learning theory approach overlap. *[2 marks]*
2. Explain **two** differences between the cognitive approach and humanistic psychology. *[6 marks]*
3. Outline the biological approach. Compare the biological approach with the cognitive approach. *[16 marks AL]*

Practical corner

The specification says...

Knowledge and understanding of ... research methods, practical research skills and maths skills. These should be developed through ... ethical practical research activities.

This means that you should conduct practical investigations wherever possible. Here, we suggest an idea for an experiment that you might conduct related to the biological approach, as well as a demonstration of electrical transmission in the nervous system. There is also a naturalistic observation linked to your knowledge of learning approaches.

Ethics check

Ethics are discussed in detail on pages 178–179. We strongly suggest that you complete this checklist before collecting data.

1. Do participants know participation is voluntary?
2. Do participants know what to expect?
3. Do participants know they can withdraw at any time?
4. Are individuals' results anonymous?
5. Have I minimised the risk of distress to participants?
6. Have I avoided asking sensitive questions?
7. Will I avoid bringing my school/teacher/psychology into disrepute?
8. Have I considered all other ethical issues?
9. Has my teacher approved this?

Table 1 Results for an experiment on the effects of arousal.

Condition A: Time in seconds to cross out e's without an audience.

Condition B: Time in seconds to cross out e's with an audience.

Participant	Condition A	Condition B
1	56	52
2	63	64
3	60	48
4	72	71
5	57	46
6	62	64
7	70	53
8	81	83
9	50	54
10	66	56
Totals		
Standard deviation	8.9573	11.4450

Practical idea 1: The effect of arousal on performance

Psychological anxiety affects biology, an example of the biological approach. The anxiety of performing in front of an audience causes physiological arousal (activation of the autonomic nervous system) and the release of adrenaline. This can improve performance on a simple or familiar task, which explains why athletes break records in front of an audience rather than in training. On difficult or unfamiliar tasks, however, people tend to become stressed leading to more errors and poorer performance.

The aim of this study is to see whether the physiological arousal caused by an audience affects performance on a simple task. This is a **laboratory experiment**.

The practical bit

Materials and basic design

The task participants will complete is straightforward – crossing out the letter 'e' from a passage of text as quickly as possible. The text needs to be long enough to keep participants occupied for a reasonable period of time, but not so long that they are there all day! There are a number of ways to assess the dependent variable. Probably the easiest way is simply to time how long participants take to complete the task. (You could also take into account any mistakes made, e.g. letter e's that they missed.)

All participants should complete the task alone and then with an audience of about three or four people. As this is a **repeated measures** design, the order of conditions should be **counterbalanced**.

Keep control

The only thing that should affect the **dependent variable** in this experiment (time taken to complete the task) is the **independent variable** (whether an audience is present or not). All other possible **extraneous variables** should be kept constant. For this reason, there should be strict **standardisation** of procedures for all participants. You should write a **briefing** statement, **standardised instructions** (for both conditions of the experiment) and a **debriefing**. These should take account of all relevant **ethical issues** (see left) and participants should be treated with respect.

It might be wise to inform participants at the beginning that they will be placed in a situation where their performance on a task will be observed by others, as some participants may be reluctant to continue. However, revealing the full aim of the investigation may be best left to the end as this could have some influence on how participants approach the tasks.

Which hypothesis?

On the face of it this looks a simple task, and evidence suggests that the arousing effects of an audience lead to improved performance when a task is easy. However, for some people, the distracting effects of the audience may lead to 'over-arousal' and poorer performance as a result (see the **Yerkes-Dodson Law** on page 60). For this reason, we would recommend writing a **non-directional hypothesis** for this study.

Sampling

You will need to consider a suitable **sampling technique** for this study and you need to think about what would make an appropriate sample size.

Analysing your data

Finally, you should present your results in the form of tables and graphs so that the effect of arousal on performance of a task can be clearly seen. You could also use the **sign test** (see page 200) to analyse the data.

Apply it Methods — The maths bit 1

1. In Table 1, what percentage of participants improved their performance with an audience? (*1 mark*)
2. Using the data in Table 1, calculate the **mean** time it took to cross out letter e's in Condition A and B. (*2 marks*)
3. Explain *one* strength and *one* limitation of the mean as a **measure of central tendency**. (*2 marks + 2 marks*)
4. Sketch a suitable graph to represent the mean values calculated in question 2. (*3 marks*)
5. Give each **standard deviation** in Table 1 to one **decimal place**. (*1 mark*)
6. What do the standard deviations tell us about the spread of data in each condition? (*2 marks*)

ʼractical idea 2: Gender differences in ıdult–child play

he aim of this study is to see if there is a difference in the way that adults interact with heir children depending on the child's gender.

Following **social learning theory**, are gender differences in children's play reinforced by ıe ways in which adults interact with children?

This is a **quasi-experiment** because gender is the independent variable. **Observational echniques** are used to collect data.

ʼhe practical bit

Ve have chosen a **naturalistic observation** as the most suitable method to collect data. : may be possible to simply ask parents or guardians, via a **questionnaire** or **interview**, vhat forms of play they prefer to engage in with their children but there may be a **social esirability bias** as parents may not want to appear gender-stereotypical in their answers ɔr look as if they don't play with their children at all!). Similarly, if parents know they are eing observed within a controlled environment – as in a **laboratory** observation – they nay change their normal behaviour due to the **demand characteristics** of the situation. herefore, this study will take the form of a **covert observation** in a natural environment, in his case, a local park.

s it ethical?

overt observations are ethical as long as they involve *public* behaviour that would be appening anyway in the absence of the researcher. If it is not obvious that you are ecording behaviour then there is no need to ask for **consent** or **debrief** your participants on his occasion.

ɔesigning your observation

erhaps you will simply record the type of play that the adults and children are engaged in, or instance 'playing football' or 'hide and seek'. Alternatively, you might want to categorise dult–child interaction as, say, 'active' or 'passive', in which case you will need a list of **ehavioural categories** that specify the difference between the two. For instance, 'active play' nay involve running around whereas 'passive play' may involve sitting and talking. Once hese categories are drawn up, you can then record the **frequency** with which they occur.

You also need to determine the **sampling method** for the observation. Will you record he number of times behaviour occurs (**event sampling**) or record the behaviour of ɔarticipants at specific time intervals (**time sampling**)? This may also affect *how* behaviour is ecorded, that is, through written description or the use of a tally chart.

Vill you work alone or with someone else?

Ve shall see in Chapter 6 how observations conducted by a single researcher may introduce **ias** so it might be a good idea to work with a partner. To this end, you might wish to onduct a **pilot study**, for instance of a family member or friend playing with their children, o you can assess the **reliability** of your observations with your co-researcher.

Whatever you decide, you will need to present your results in the form of tables and raphs to give an instant picture of the gender differences in play.

Try it – The speed of electrical transmission

Stand in a line with a bunch of your friends (or classmates) all holding hands. The person on one end of the line needs a stopwatch and the person on the other end of the line should hold a bicycle horn (the squeezy kind).

On the count of three the person with the watch should start the timer and squeeze the hand of the person next to them. That person then squeezes the hand of the person next to them, and so on. When the person holding the horn's hand is squeezed they should sound the horn and the timer is stopped. Bear in mind that you might need to practise a couple of times to get it right!

Do the same but this time hold the hand of the person on your left and touch the shoulder of the person on your right. Is the time from start to end now different from the holding-hands trial?

Now for the maths bit...

Measure the span from the tip of one person's right hand to the tip of their left hand for all the people in the group and calculate the total distance the signal travelled. Divide the distance travelled by the time the signal travelled to determine the speed in metres per second.

Scientists have estimated that the speed of electrical transmission across a large **myelinated axon** is around 200 metres per second.

How did you compare? Have another go and see if you can beat your time.

ʌpply it ʌethods The maths bit 2

1. Using the data in Table 2, calculate the total number of times active play was observed in adult–boy pairs and in adult–girl pairs. Do the same for passive play. (*2 marks*)
2. Draw a **bar chart** to show the difference in active play and passive play for adult–girl pairs and adult–boy pairs. (*3 marks*)
3. Explain *one* conclusion that can be drawn from the bar chart you have drawn. (*2 marks*)
4. Identify the type of data in Table 2. Explain *one* limitation of using this type of data. (*1 mark + 2 marks*)

Table 2 Data collected for frequency of active and passive play between adult–girl pairs and adult–boy pairs.

	Type of play					
	Active play			Passive play		
	Running	Shouting	Physical contact	Sitting	Talking	No physical contact
Adult–boy pair	11	8	5	3	2	3
Adult–girl pair	4	3	5	5	6	3

Revision summaries

Origins of Psychology

We're going to go back in time.

Wundt and introspection

Wundt's lab
First psychology lab in Leipzig, introduced introspection to study the human mind systematically (scientific).

Standardised procedures
Observations of objects and sounds are recorded.

Structuralism
Consciousness divided into three categories: thoughts, images, sensations (structuralism).

Evaluation

Scientific
Controlled environment, carefully standardised.

Subjective data
General laws not possible as all introspections are different.

Evaluation extra: Wundt's contribution
The founder of modern psychology.

The emergence of Psychology as a science

Science involves systematic and objective measurement to discover general laws.

1900s Behaviourists
Researchers (e.g. Watson and Skinner) conducted controlled experiments on behaviours that were directly observable.

1950s Cognitive approach
Made the study of the mind legitimate and scientific, experiments tested the computer metaphor (e.g. multi-store model).

1980s Biological approach
Observable behaviours studied, using controlled measures e.g. fMRI. Also genetic testing studies relationship between genes and behaviour.

Evaluation

Modern psychology
Learning, cognitive and biological approaches all use scientific methods e.g. lab research.

Subjective data
Humanistic and psychodynamic approaches rely on unscientific case studies. Research hampered by demand characteristics.

Evaluation extra: Paradigm
The question of whether psychology has agreed methods and assumptions is open to debate.

Learning approaches

The behaviourist approach

All behaviour is learned through association or consequences.

The approach

Assumptions
Observable behaviour is all that is needed to be studied.
Basic processes same in all species.

Classical conditioning – Pavlov
Research on salivation in dogs.
Association of UCS with NS to produce new CS and CR.

Operant conditioning – Skinner
Research with rats and pigeons in Skinner box.
Animal operates on the environment, behaviour shaped by consequences.
Reinforcement (positive and negative).
Punishment.

Evaluation

Well-controlled research
Behaviour broken down to stimulus–response units, helps remove extraneous variables.
Counterpoint – reducing behaviour in this way removes important influences on behaviour (e.g. thought).

Real-world application
Token economy systems used in prisons and psychiatric institutions.

Environmental determinism
All behaviour influenced by past experience, no room for free will.

Evaluation extra: Ethical issues
Controlled conditions important for research but not good for animals (e.g. kept hungry).

Social learning theory

All behaviour is learned from observing other people.

The approach

Assumptions
Behaviour is learned from experience.
In contrast with behaviourism, learned through observation and imitation of others (social).

Vicarious reinforcement
Observation leads to imitation if behaviour is vicariously reinforced (Bobo doll experiment).

Mediational processes
Attention, retention, motor reproduction, motivation.

Identification
More likely to imitate role models you identify with (e.g. attractive, high status).

Evaluation

Cognitive factors
More comprehensive account of learning than proposed by the behaviourist approach.
Counterpoint – underestimates influence of biology, social learning involves mirror neurons in the brain.

Contrived lab studies
Demand characteristics (Bobo doll is designed to be hit), so low validity.

Real-world application
SLT can account for development of cultural differences e.g. in gender role.

Evaluation extra: Reciprocal determinism
Less determinist than behaviourism (reciprocal determinism).

The cognitive approach

The study of internal mental processes.

The approach

Assumptions
Internal mental processes can be studied through inference.

The role of schema
Beliefs and expectations affect thoughts and behaviour.
Innate (e.g. sucking schema) or learned.
Mental shortcut, leads to perceptual errors.

Theoretical and computer models
Information processing approach.
Mind is likened to a computer and applied to artificial intelligence.

The emergence of cognitive neuroscience
Scientific study of how brain structures affect mental processes.
Biological structures link to mental states e.g. Broca.
Brain imaging (e.g. fMRI) used to read the brain.

Evaluation

Scientific methods
Lab studies to produce reliable, objective data.
Cognitive neuroscience is scientific.
Counterpoint – use of inference and artificial stimuli lead to low external validity.

Real-world application
Successfully applied to the fields of artificial intelligence, depression and eyewitness testimony.

Machine reductionism
Computer analogy is too simple, it ignores the influence of emotion e.g. effect of anxiety on eyewitness testimony.

Evaluation extra: Soft determinism
Cognitive approach is an example of soft determinism, a middle-ground and more reasonable than behaviourism.

The biological approach

Everything psychological is at first biological.

The approach

Assumptions
The mind and body are one and the same.

The neurochemical basis of behaviour
Thought and behaviour depend on chemicals (neurotransmitters e.g. serotonin).

The genetic basis of behaviour
Concordance between MZ and DZ twins shows genetic basis of psychological characteristics.

Genotype and phenotype
Genes versus expression of genes in environment (nature and nurture).

Evolution and behaviour
Natural selection of genes based on survival value and, ultimately, reproductive success.

Evaluation

Real-world application
Understanding of biochemical processes is associated with the development of psychoactive drugs.

Counterpoint – antidepressants do not work for everyone (Cipriani *et al.*).

Scientific methods
Precise and objective methods e.g. scanning techniques such as fMRI and EEGs.

Biological determinism
Sees human behaviour as governed by internal genetically-determined factors, an oversimplification.

Evaluation extra: Natural selection
Popper claims theory of natural selection can't be falsified, but fossil record is supportive.

Biopsychology

The two major physiological systems that regulate behaviour.

The nervous system

Nervous system
A specialised network of cells, fast-acting and electrical (and chemical) internal communication system.

Central nervous system (CNS)
Brain – divided into hemispheres, cerebral cortex (outer layer), 3 mm thick.

Spinal cord – connects brain to PNS, reflexes.

Peripheral nervous system (PNS)
Autonomic nervous system (ANS) – governs vital functions.

Somatic nervous system (SNS) – muscle movement, sensory information.

The endocrine system

Glands and hormones
Glands produce hormones.

Hormones distributed in bloodstream, e.g. thyroid gland produces thyroxine.

Pituitary is the master gland.

Fight or flight
Sympathetic arousal: hypothalamus + pituitary → adrenal gland → adrenaline.

Adrenaline leads to increased heart rate, faster breathing, sweating, inhibits digestion.

Immediate and automatic.

Parasympathetic state – once threat has passed, body returns to rest and digest.

Structure and function of neurons

Types of neurons
Sensory – PNS to CNS, long dendrites – short axons.

Relay – sensory to motor or other, short – short.

Motor – CNS to effectors, short – long.

Structure of a neuron
Cell body contains nucleus, has dendrites.

Axon covered in myelin sheath divided by nodes of Ranvier.

Electrical transmission
Positive charge leads to action potential.

Synaptic transmission

Synapse
Neurons separated by very tiny gap.

Chemical transmission
Neurotransmitter released from synaptic vesicle into synapse, taken up by postsynaptic receptor site on receiving dendrite.

Neurotransmitters
Specialist functions e.g. acetylcholine for muscle contraction.

Excitation and inhibition
Adrenaline is excitatory, serotonin is inhibitory.

Summation
Impulses are 'added up', net effect is excitatory or inhibitory.

A LEVEL ONLY

The psychodynamic approach

Behaviour is determined by unconscious forces that we cannot control.

The approach

The role of the unconscious
The conscious mind is the 'tip of the iceberg'.

The structure of personality
Id – primitive part, pleasure principle.

Ego – reality principle, protected by defence mechanisms.

Superego – formed age 5, sense of right and wrong, morality principle.

Psychosexual stages
Five stages, a different conflict at each stage leads to fixations.

Defence mechanisms
Used by the Ego to keep the Id 'in check' and reduce anxiety – repression, denial, displacement.

Evaluation

Real-world application
New form of therapy (psychoanalysis), forerunner to 'talking therapies'.

Counterpoint – not suitable for all mental disorders (e.g. not for schizophrenia).

Explanatory power
Influential theories about personality, moral development and gender identity.

Untestable concepts
Much of the theory is unfalsifiable, and based on case studies, thus pseudoscientific.

Evaluation extra: Psychic determinism
All behaviour is driven by the unconscious, leaves no room for free will.

A LEVEL ONLY

Humanistic psychology

Emerged as the third force in psychology.

The approach

Free will
People are active agents who are self-determining.

Maslow's hierarchy of needs
5 levels – physiological, safety and security, love and belongingness, self-esteem, self-actualisation.

Self-actualisation
An innate tendency to want to reach your potential.

The self, congruence and conditions of worth
Personal growth requires congruence between self and ideal self.

Counselling psychology
Counsellor is genuine, empathic, unconditional positive regard (Rogers).

Evaluation

Not reductionist
Emphasis placed on the whole person (holism).

Counterpoint – concepts can't be observed or measured, so approach lacks empirical evidence.

Positive approach
Optimistic approach that sees people as basically good and in control.

Cultural bias
Associated with individualism.

Evaluation extra: Limited application
Critics claim little impact but revolutionised therapy (counselling), Maslow's hierarchy explains motivation.

Practice questions, answers and feedback

Question 1 Explain what Wundt meant by 'introspection'. (*2 marks*)	
Morticia's answer *This is a method that was used by Wundt to investigate the way people thought.*	Morticia's answer is too vague to be of any merit.
Luke's answer *It means to look inwards, specifically to look inside a person's head to understand what they are thinking and the way their mind works. It's a way to access conscious thinking.*	Luke's answer is somewhat better but there remains little reference to what Wundt did or how he did it.
Vladimir's answer *Wundt opened the first lab dedicated to the study of psychology. He wanted to investigate human behaviour and consciousness and used introspection to do this.*	Again, a disappointing answer. Vladimir's reference to the first psychology lab does not help define the term and how Wundt investigated consciousness is not explained properly.

Question 2 Using an example, explain the difference between 'genotype' and 'phenotype'. (*3 marks*)	
Morticia's answer *Genotypes are your genes which determine things like eye colour and many aspects of behaviour. Phenotype is what you actually see in terms of what people are like.*	The phenotype explanation is too vague to be of any value. The genotype definition is marginally better.
Luke's answer *You are born with a set of genes, called your genotype. However, these are expressed through the environment so the outcome is your phenotype which is your genes plus the environment. A good example is PKU, a genetic disorder which can cause later difficulties unless the baby's diet is adjusted (their environment). This adjustment of the environment leads to the baby's phenotype.*	This is an excellent answer from Luke. The definitions are supported by the example that clearly communicates the distinction between the two terms.
Vladimir's answer *Identical twins are a good example of phenotype because they have exactly the same genotype but not necessarily the same phenotype. Their phenotype is affected by their experiences (environment) which may be different.*	Vladimir almost communicates what is meant by 'phenotype' in the last sentence but more explanation is required. The only solid comment is the example of identical twins.

Question 3 Outline the fight or flight response. (*3 marks*)	
Morticia's answer *The fight or flight response describes how a person or animal reacts in an emergency situation. The first thing is that adrenaline is produced and this makes the body ready for physical action. This might mean fighting or fleeing. If there is no danger then the body can go back to the relaxed state.*	Morticia's answer is rather generic but there is relevant content, including reference to adrenaline. Better answers would include detail of physiological changes and the nervous system.
Luke's answer *When stressed the sympathetic branch of the autonomic nervous system is aroused. This leads the hypothalamus and pituitary gland to trigger a response in the adrenal glands, producing adrenaline. It is this hormone that causes the physiological arousal associated with the fight/flight response, e.g. heart rate and breathing increase.*	Luke provides a sophisticated general description of the stress response followed by specific detail of fight or flight and there are examples of relevant physiological changes. Well done.
Vladimir's answer *Adrenaline causes biological changes such as increased heart rate, increased breathing, eye pupils dilate, digestion is inhibited, saliva production is suppressed, the rectum contracts and so on. All of this enables an animal to be able to stand and fight or flee for their life.*	Vladimir's answer is spot on but a little 'list-like' in terms of examples of the various bodily changes. Some additional detail is at the end but there really needs to be a bit more – it's all in the detail.

Question 4 A research report claimed that people who believe in aliens are 17 times more likely to claim that they have seen a UFO compared to people who do not. Explain what cognitive psychologists mean by 'schema'. Refer to the information above in your answer. (*4 marks*)	
Morticia's answer *Schema are packages of ideas that generate expectations. They are part of the way we think. Cognitive psychologists use them to explain thinking. People see UFOs because they believe in aliens and therefore are more likely to report them.*	Morticia gives a brief but accurate definition of schema supported by a similarly brief link to the stem, so neither component amounts to more than a partial answer.
Luke's answer *Schema are used by cognitive psychologists to describe how people think about the world and their experiences. This would explain UFOs because if you don't believe in them you wouldn't see them. This is an example of schema because it shows how people are thinking and it is affected by their schema.*	Luke's definition of schema offered here is not strong, though the link to the stem is partially successful.
Vladimir's answer *In the example the schema would be the belief that some people have that aliens do exist. Such schema are a mental framework for thinking about certain types of things such as UFOs as well as aliens. Having this belief leads to expectations and makes such people more likely to actually interpret something they see as a UFO. Schema may speed up information processing or may make our cognitive system prone to error (the UFO may not be there).*	Vladimir has done well. There is reference within this answer to 'mental framework', 'expectations' and to the idea that schema may speed up or distort processing, all of which show clear understanding of the concept. The application is also thorough and well embedded in the answer.

On this spread we look at some typical student answers to questions. The comments provided indicate what is good and bad in each answer. Learning how to produce effective question answers is a SKILL. Read pages 213–223 for guidance.

Question 5 Describe **and** evaluate the behaviourist approach in psychology. (*12 marks AS, 16 marks AL*)

Morticia's answer *Behaviourists take the view that the only thing that psychologists should concern themselves with is observable behaviour. Behaviourists are also focused on learning. They believe that all behaviour can be explained through learning – the experiences you have after you have been born.* *Learning may involve classical conditioning or operant conditioning. In the case of classical conditioning, first described by the Russian Pavlov, learning begins with a basic stimulus-response link. An unconditioned stimulus causes an unconditioned response. If a neutral stimulus becomes associated with the unconditioned stimulus it eventually predicts the unconditioned response, then it has become a conditioned stimulus producing a conditioned response. Pavlov demonstrated this with dogs and salivation. The dogs eventually salivated when they heard a bell because that became associated with the arrival of food.* *Operant conditioning is about operating on your environment. An animal operates on its environment and this has consequences. If these consequences are rewarding then this reinforces the behaviour that brought about the reward and it will be repeated. A behaviour might lead an animal to avoid a negative experience and this is also reinforcing (negative reinforcement), so the behaviour is likely to be repeated. Punishment decreases the likelihood that behaviour will be repeated.* *One limitation of behaviourist ideas is that they present a rather determinist view of behaviour. They leave out the idea that people can make decisions themselves which is called free will. This is better explained by the cognitive approach. Behaviourists suggest that everything we are can be explained by past conditioning experiences.* *One strength of the approach is that it is very scientific with lots of very controlled studies of animals where there are few extraneous variables so the conclusions are firm. On the other hand there is the question of whether such very controlled artificial research with non-human animals really can be applied to human behaviour in the real world.* *Another strength of the behaviourist approach is that it has been applied usefully. For example, token economy systems are used in prisons where rewards are used to shape prisoner behaviour.* **(393 words)**	**Morticia's essay is an AS response whereas Vladimir's is an A level response.** Morticia's answer is well written and well balanced. The first paragraph is clear enough and followed by accurate, detailed accounts of the two forms of learning. Her descriptive content demonstrates knowledge, accuracy, clarity and organisation as well as use of specialist terminology. There are relevant strengths and a limitation here too. Some of these – such as the point about being a determinist explanation – might have been supported by reference to alternative approaches. This is not a requirement of the question but is just plain good analysis. Morticia could have offered more commentary/analysis in relation to the use of lab studies. Overall the answer is light on evaluation, which is especially important for A level. In order to produce good answers students must give special focus to evaluation and evaluation skills.
Vladimir's answer *The behaviourist approach is to explain all behaviour in terms of classical and operant conditioning, i.e. learning.* *The first demonstration of classical conditioning was by Pavlov. He was investigating salivation in dogs and noticed that they could be trained to salivate to the sound of a bell. He demonstrated this process in controlled lab conditions. If a bell was rung repeatedly at the same time as food was presented, the animal learned to associate the bell with food and eventually salivated to the bell alone.* *Operant conditioning was demonstrated by Skinner with rats and pigeons in a cage called a Skinner box. If the animal pressed a lever a food pellet appeared. This reinforced the lever-press behaviour so that the animal repeated it more and more. Rats (and pigeons) could also be conditioned to avoid a stimulus such as an electric shock.* *Both kinds of learning involve no thought. New connections are formed in the brain but behaviourists are not interested in what goes on in the brain – they just focused on how new behavioural links are formed, i.e. learned. They proposed that everything can be learned in this way.* *Behaviourists suggest that humans are made of the same building blocks as animals and therefore the same laws apply. So all human behaviour too is learned and it is a passive process. Your behaviour is conditioned by things outside you. Of course this suggests that we have no free will yet most people do feel they have a sense of their own will. Skinner would argue that this is just an illusion of having made a decision.* *On the positive side the behaviourist approach has been useful and good because it has led to some good ways to help people such as in prisons where people can be given rewards to encourage different behaviours. Real-world application is a positive for any approach.* **(313 words)**	Vladimir also describes the two forms of learning but with slightly less sophistication than in the answer above. Besides this initial description there is further descriptive detail. He makes points related to the focus on observable behaviour and the link between human and animal learning though these are not always clearly expressed. Evaluation/analysis is present but it is not the main focus of the essay. There is some analytic reference to free will (or lack of it), the qualitative difference between humans and animals, and a very brief comment on the limitations of animal studies at the end. Overall, not as strong on evaluation as the previous answer and an overly descriptive answer. The evaluation content is partly effective but very limited, whereas the description is mostly clear and organised and specialist terminology has been used. The lack of evaluation has a serious impact on the overall worth of the answer. There should always be significantly more evaluation.

Multiple-choice questions

Origins of Psychology

1. From earliest to most recent, which of the following is the correct chronological order of when the following psychological approaches were first established?
   (a) Social learning theory, humanistic, behaviourist, cognitive neuroscience
   (b) Cognitive neuroscience, social learning theory, behaviourist, humanistic
   (c) Humanistic, behaviourist, cognitive neuroscience, social learning theory
   (d) Behaviourist, humanistic, social learning theory, cognitive neuroscience

2. Which of the following is a criticism that Watson made of introspection?
   (a) It can't be replicated.
   (b) It doesn't deal with experience.
   (c) It produces objective data.
   (d) It produces subjective data.

3. Which of the following approaches used a computer metaphor to study the mind?
   (a) The humanistic approach.
   (b) The behaviourist approach.
   (c) The cognitive approach.
   (d) The social learning theory approach.

4. The name of Wundt's pioneering method:
   (a) Introjection.
   (b) Interlocution.
   (c) Interpretation.
   (d) Introspection.

Learning approaches: The behaviourist approach

1. Which is a basic assumption of the behaviourist approach?
   (a) Learning processes in animals cannot be generalised to humans.
   (b) The main influence on behaviour is your genes.
   (c) Learning is influenced by private mental processes.
   (d) Learning should be studied scientifically in a laboratory.

2. Which correctly describes the key steps in classical conditioning?
   (a) UCR + NS = UCS and CS.
   (b) UCS + UCR = CS and CR.
   (c) NS + UCS = UCR + CR.
   (d) UCS + NS = CS and CR.

3. Complete this sentence: Operant conditioning is best described as:
   (a) A form of learning in which behaviour is shaped and maintained by its consequences.
   (b) A form of learning in which a stimulus is associated with a response.
   (c) A form of learning in which an observer imitates the behaviour of a role model.
   (d) A form of learning in which new behaviour is produced that avoids an unpleasant consequence.

4. A Behaviourist researcher carried out a lab experiment. He put a rat in a specially designed box. Every time a light came on, the rat would receive an electric shock to its feet. However, over time, the rat learned that if it pressed a lever when the light came on, it would not receive the shock.
   What aspect of operant conditioning is the Behaviourist researcher investigating?
   (a) Partial reinforcement.
   (b) Positive reinforcement.
   (c) Negative reinforcement.
   (d) Punishment.

Learning approaches: Social learning theory

1. Which one of the following statements about Bandura's Bobo doll experiments is false?
   (a) Children were more likely to imitate aggression that was rewarded (reinforced).
   (b) Children who saw the model punished were more likely to imitate aggression than children who saw no consequences.
   (c) The experiments have been used to support the idea that children may be influenced by what they see in the media.
   (d) The experiments support the idea that learning can often occur indirectly.

2. Which of the following is *not* a mediational process in the social learning approach?
   (a) Motivation.
   (b) Attention.
   (c) Retention.
   (d) Application.

3. Learning through observing the consequences of other people's behaviour is:
   (a) Positive reinforcement.
   (b) Negative reinforcement.
   (c) Operant reinforcement.
   (d) Vicarious reinforcement.

4. Which statement about the social learning theory approach is false?
   (a) Learning and performance always occur together.
   (b) Attention and retention are more likely to be involved in the learning than performance of behaviour.
   (c) Motor reproduction and motivation are more likely to be involved in the performance than learning of behaviour.
   (d) Role models that children identify with need not be real but may be symbolic.

The cognitive approach

1. Which statement about the role of schema is false?
   (a) They allow us to make mental shortcuts.
   (b) They may lead to perceptual errors.
   (c) They are not present at birth.
   (d) They act as a mental framework of interpretation.

2. A cognitive psychologist gave students simple word lists to learn under lab conditions. The students were able to recall an average of seven words within their short-term memory (STM). The psychologist concluded that the capacity of STM is seven items. This is a good example of:
   (a) Inference.
   (b) Interference.
   (c) Implication.
   (d) Illustration.

3. The cognitive approach is a good example of:
   (a) Motor reproduction.
   (b) Mundane realism.
   (c) Mirror reflection.
   (d) Machine reductionism.

4. Which statement about cognitive neuroscience is false?
   (a) It was first identified in the 1970s as an emergent discipline.
   (b) It investigates how biological structures influence mental processes.
   (c) It brings together the fields of cognitive psychology, anatomy and neurophysiology.
   (d) It makes use of advances in brain imaging technology such as fMRI.

The biological approach

1. Which of the following formulas is true?
   (a) Genotype + phenotype = environment.
   (b) Phenotype + environment = genotype.
   (c) Genotype + environment = phenotype.
   (d) Genotype – phenotype = environment.

2. Which is the best definition of natural selection?
   (a) The perpetuation of the best physical and psychological traits.
   (b) The selection of traits that promote successful survival and reproduction.
   (c) The survival of the fittest.
   (d) Choosing the best genes for future generations.

3. Dizygotic twins share approximately what percentage of their genes?
   (a) 100.
   (b) 50.
   (c) 25.
   (d) 0.

4. Which of the following is *not* an assumption of the biological approach?
   (a) The brain and the mind are distinct and separate.
   (b) Psychological characteristics may be genetically determined in the same way that physical characteristics are.
   (c) An imbalance in neurochemical levels may explain mental disorder.
   (d) Human behaviour has adapted to the environment through natural selection.

Biopsychology: The nervous system and the endocrine system

1. Which division of the nervous system is divided into sympathetic and parasympathetic branches?
   (a) The central nervous system.
   (b) The peripheral nervous system.
   (c) The somatic nervous system.
   (d) The autonomic nervous system.

2. Which describes the somatic nervous system?
   (a) Maintains homeostasis by regulating body temperature, heartbeat, etc.
   (b) Made up of the brain and the spinal cord.
   (c) Controls muscle movement.
   (d) Passes messages to and from the brain and connects nerves to the PNS.

3. The master endocrine gland is the:
   (a) Adrenal gland.
   (b) Pituitary gland.
   (c) Thyroid gland.
   (d) Hypothalamus.

4. Which is *not* an action of the parasympathetic branch of the ANS?
   (a) Inhibits digestion.
   (b) Contracts pupils.
   (c) Stimulates saliva production.
   (d) Decreases heart rate.

Biopsychology: Neurons and synaptic transmission

1. Which of the following carries messages from the PNS to the CNS?
   (a) Sensory neuron.
   (b) Motor neuron.
   (c) Relay neuron.
   (d) Synaptic neuron.

2. Which is *not* part of the basic structure of a neuron?
   (a) Cell body.
   (b) Axon.
   (c) Effector.
   (d) Dendrite.

3. Which of the following does *not* occur during synaptic transmission?
   (a) The neuron is in a resting state.
   (b) An electrical impulse triggers the release of neurotransmitter.
   (c) Neurotransmitter diffuses across the synaptic gap.
   (d) The chemical message is converted back into an electrical impulse.

4. The following describes what process?
   'When a neuron is activated by a stimulus, the inside of the cell becomes positively charged for a split second. This creates an electrical impulse that travels down the axon towards the end of the neuron.'
   (a) Synaptic transmission.
   (b) Inhibitory response.
   (c) Presynaptic terminal.
   (d) Action potential.

The psychodynamic approach A LEVEL ONLY

1. Which of the following is *not* a term used by Freud in relation to the structure of the mind?
   (a) Conscious.
   (b) Preconscious.
   (c) Subconscious.
   (d) Unconscious.

2. In which stage does the Oedipus complex take place?
   (a) Oral.
   (b) Anal.
   (c) Phallic
   (d) Genital.

3. Which of the following is 'transferring feelings from the true source of distressing emotion onto a substitute object'?
   (a) Displacement.
   (b) Denial.
   (c) Repression.
   (d) Regression.

4. Freud's theory is most associated with?
   (a) Environmental determinism.
   (b) Biological determinism.
   (c) Reciprocal determinism.
   (d) Psychic determinism.

Humanistic psychology A LEVEL ONLY

1. When it first emerged, humanistic psychology came to be known as:
   (a) The first force.
   (b) The second force.
   (c) The third force.
   (d) May the force be with you.

2. When there is a mismatch between the self-concept and the ideal self, this is referred to as:
   (a) Self-actualisation.
   (b) Conditions of worth.
   (c) Congruence.
   (d) Incongruence.

3. According to Rogers, an effective therapist should provide the client with three things. Which of the following is not one of these?
   (a) Being empathic.
   (b) Being judgemental.
   (c) Being genuine.
   (d) Unconditional positive regard.

4. Which of the following is a 'growth need' in Maslow's hierarchy?
   (a) Self-actualisation.
   (b) Love and belongingness.
   (c) Safety and security.
   (d) Physiological.

MCQ answers

Origins of psychology 1D, 2D, 3C, 4D
Learning approaches: The behaviourist approach 1D, 2D, 3A, 4C
Learning approaches: Social learning theory 1B, 2D, 3D, 4A
The cognitive approach 1C, 2A, 3D, 4A
The biological approach 1C, 2B, 3B, 4A
Biopsychology: The nervous system and the endocrine system 1D, 2C, 3B, 4A
Biopsychology: Neurons and synaptic transmission 1A, 2C, 3A, 4D
The psychodynamic approach 1C, 2C, 3A, 4D
Humanistic psychology 1C, 2D, 3B, 4A

Chapter 5 Psychopathology

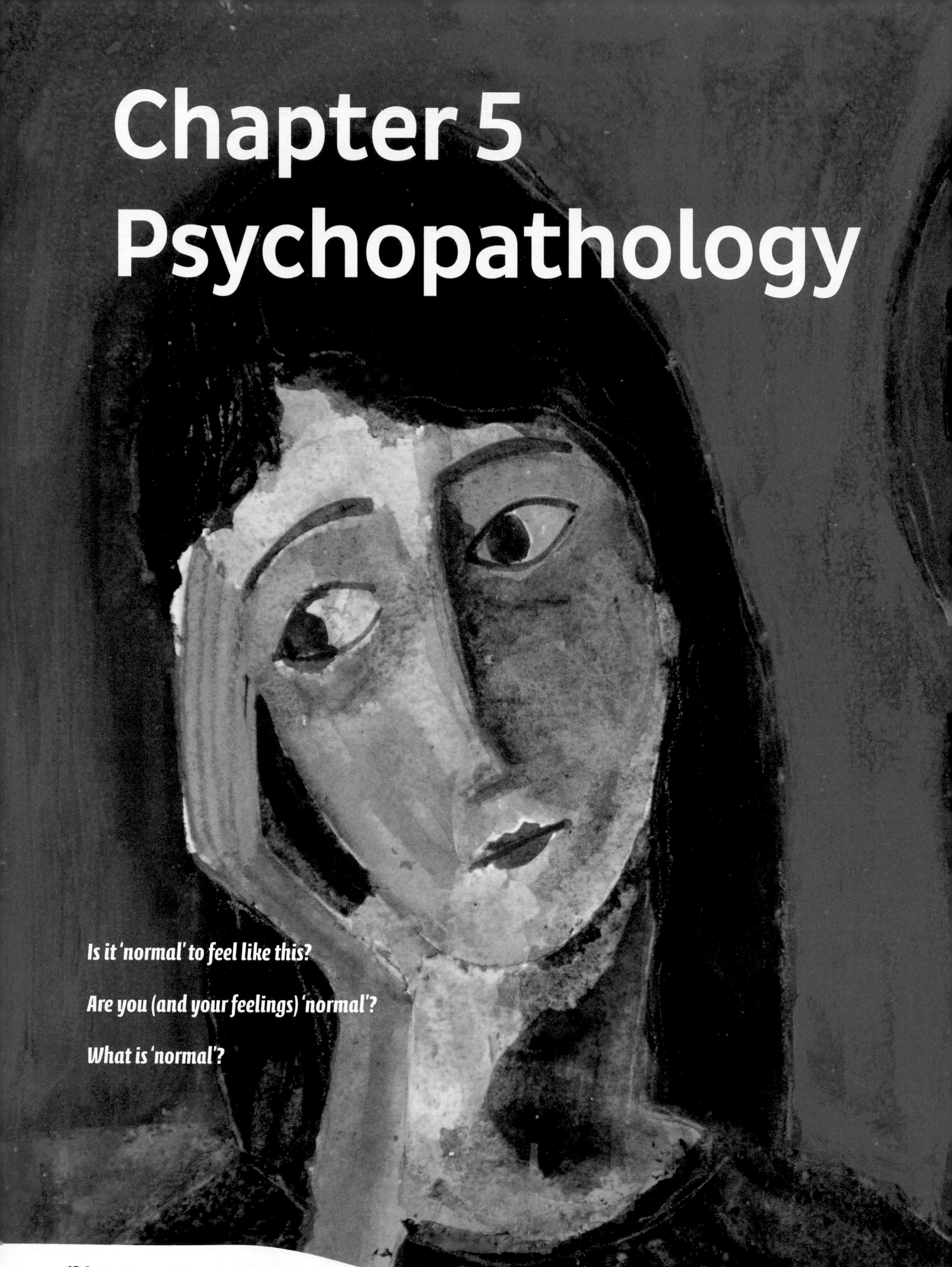

Is it 'normal' to feel like this?

Are you (and your feelings) 'normal'?

What is 'normal'?

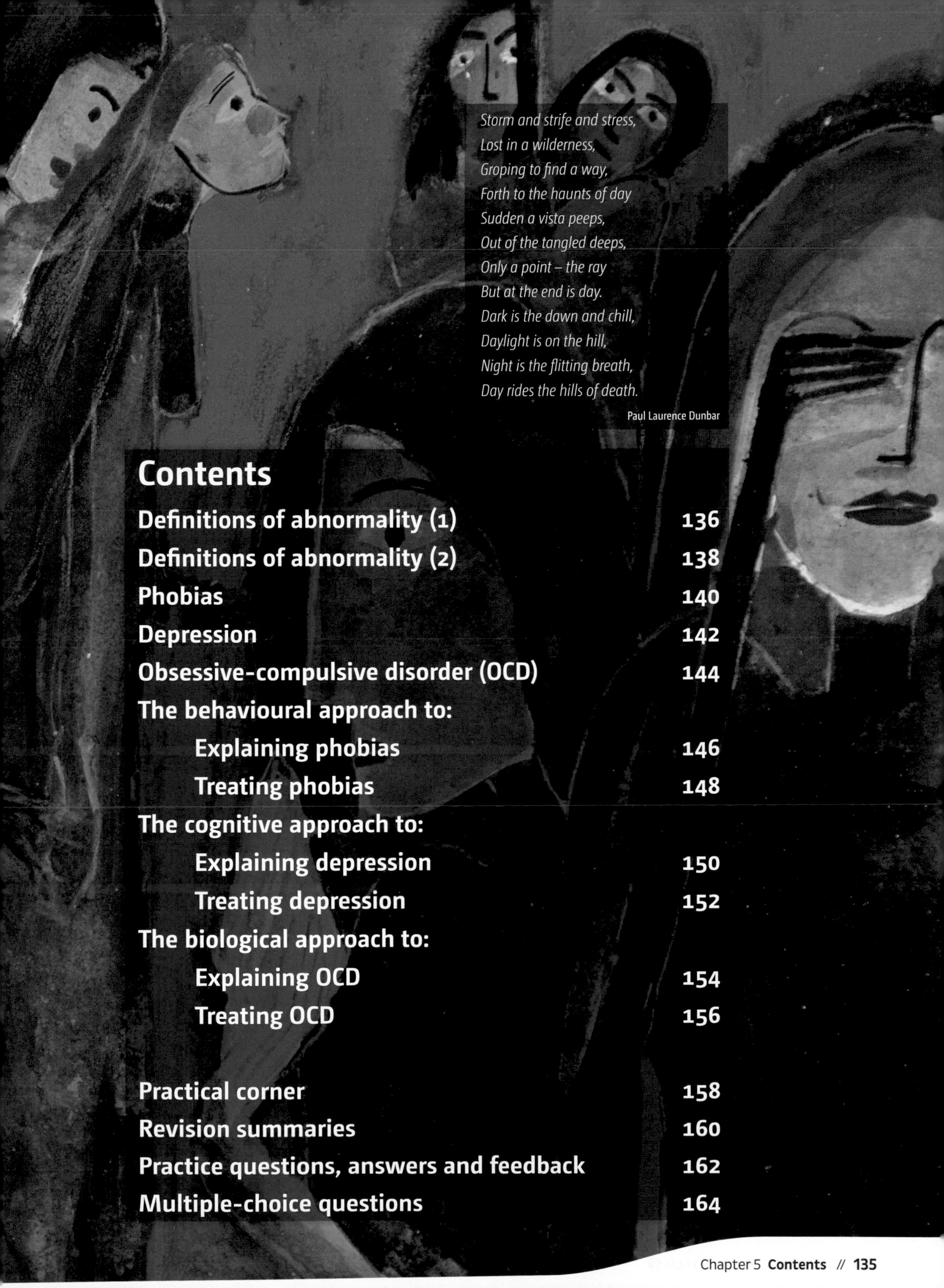

Storm and strife and stress,
Lost in a wilderness,
Groping to find a way,
Forth to the haunts of day
Sudden a vista peeps,
Out of the tangled deeps,
Only a point – the ray
But at the end is day.
Dark is the dawn and chill,
Daylight is on the hill,
Night is the flitting breath,
Day rides the hills of death.

Paul Laurence Dunbar

Contents

Definitions of abnormality (1)

The specification says...

Definitions of abnormality, including statistical infrequency and deviation from social norms.

This chapter is concerned with psychopathology, which is the study of psychological disorder – *psycho* for psychological and *pathology*, which means the study of the causes of diseases.

How can we decide if a person's behaviour and/or psychological state are sufficiently unusual (i.e. abnormal) to justify diagnosing and treating them for a psychological disorder? On this spread we consider two methods used to make this decision: statistical infrequency and deviation from social norms.

Key terms

Statistical infrequency Occurs when an individual has a less common characteristic, for example being more depressed or less intelligent than most of the population.

Deviation from social norms Concerns behaviour that is different from the accepted standards of behaviour in a community or society.

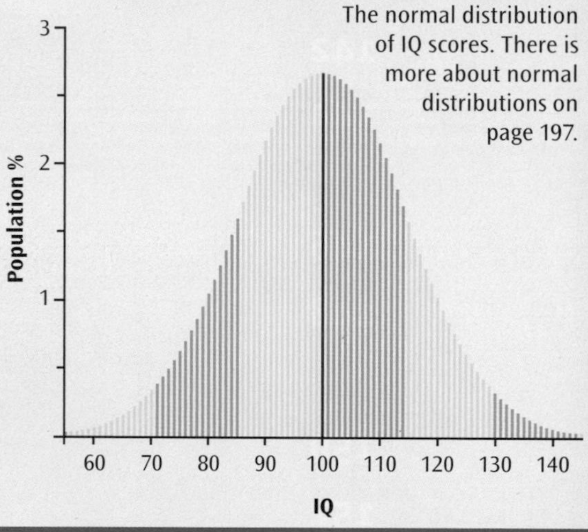

3
2
1
Population %
60
70
80
90
100
110
120
130
140
IQ

The normal distribution of IQ scores. There is more about normal distributions on page 197.

Statistical infrequency

Perhaps the most obvious way to define anything as 'normal' or 'abnormal' is according to how often we come across it. **Statistics** are about numbers. According to the statistical definition any relatively *usual* behaviour or characteristic can be thought of as 'normal', and any behaviour that is unusual is 'abnormal'. This is what is meant by **statistical infrequency**. We can, for example, say that at any one time only a small number of people will have an irrational fear of buttons or believe for no good reason that their neighbours are zombies.

Example: IQ and intellectual disability disorder

This statistical approach comes into its own when we are dealing with characteristics that can be reliably measured, for example intelligence. We know that, in any human characteristic, the majority of people's scores will cluster around the average, and that the further we go above or below that average, the fewer people will attain that score. This is called the **normal distribution**. You can see the normal distribution of **IQ** below left.

The average IQ is set at 100. In a normal distribution, most people (68%) have a score (in this case IQ) in the range from 85 to 115. Only 2% of people have a score below 70. Those individuals scoring below 70 are very unusual or 'abnormal', and are liable to receive a diagnosis of a psychological disorder – **intellectual disability disorder** (IDD).

Deviation from social norms

Most of us notice people whose behaviour represents a **deviation from social norms**, i.e. when a person behaves in a way that is different from how we expect people to behave. Groups of people (hence 'social') choose to define behaviour as abnormal on the basis that it offends their sense of wha is 'acceptable' or the **norm**. We are making a collective judgement as a society about what is right.

Norms are specific to the culture we live in

Of course those social norms may be different for each generation and different in every culture, so there are relatively few behaviours that would be considered *universally* abnormal on the basis that they breach **social norms**. For example, homosexuality was considered abnormal in our culture in the past and continues to be viewed as abnormal (and illegal) in some cultures (e.g. in April 2019, Brunei introduced new laws that make sex between men an offence punishable by stoning to death).

Example: antisocial personality disorder

A person with **antisocial personality disorder** (psychopathy) is impulsive, aggressive and irresponsible. According to the **DSM-5** (the manual used by psychiatrists to diagnose mental disorder) one important symptom of antisocial personality disorder is an 'absence of **prosocial** internal standards associated with failure to conform to lawful and culturally normative ethical behaviour'.

In other words we are making the social judgement that psychopaths are abnormal because they don't conform to our moral standards. Psychopathic behaviour would be considered abnormal in a very wide range of cultures.

Apply it Concepts — Mark

Mark is a practising Pagan (i.e. a follower of a pre-Christian religion). He lives alone and works as an IT consultant, doing most of his work at home and communicating via the Internet. His IQ is 145 (placing him in the top 1% of the population) and measures of depression are around average.

Questions

1. Based on statistical infrequency and deviation from social norms, would you say that there is a case for judging Mark to be abnormal? Explain your answer.
2. Why is there a good case for *not* classifying Mark as abnormal at all?

Apply it Methods — Amanda

Human characteristics are normally distributed, with most people clustering around the mean and small numbers of people at the extremes.

Amanda has poor social skills and is referred to a clinical psychologist. The psychologist assesses her and shows her where her skills fall on the normal distribution. The mean score on this test is 50. Amanda scores 21.

SD stands for standard deviation.

About 68% of the population lies between +1 and −1 SD.

About 95% of the population lies between +2 and −2 SD.

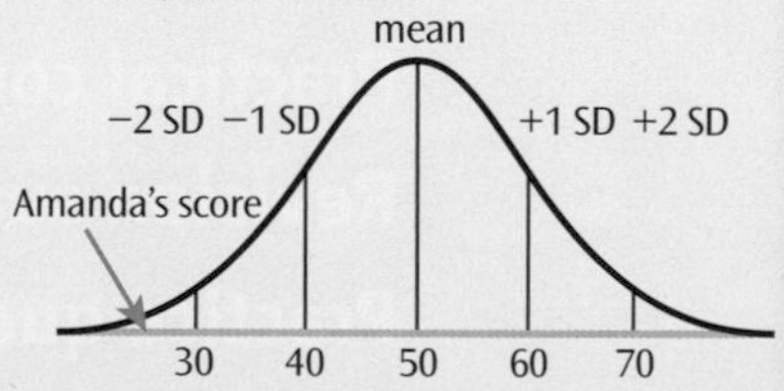

mean
−2 SD −1 SD
+1 SD +2 SD
Amanda's score
30
40
50
60
70

Questions

1. Estimate where Amanda's social skills fall in the population. (*2 marks*)
2. Based on this statistical distribution, should Amanda be considered abnormal? Explain your answer. (*2 marks*)

Evaluation

Practical activity on page 159

Real-world application

One strength of statistical infrequency is its usefulness.

Statistical infrequency is used in clinical practice, both as part of formal diagnosis and as a way to assess the severity of an individual's symptoms. For example a diagnosis of intellectual disability disorder requires an IQ of below 70 (bottom 2%). An example of statistical infrequency used in an assessment tool is the **Beck depression inventory** (BDI). A score of 30+ (top 5% of respondents) is widely interpreted as indicating severe depression.

This shows that the value of the statistical infrequency criterion is useful in diagnostic and assessment processes.

Unusual characteristics can be positive

One limitation of statistical infrequency is that infrequent characteristics can be positive as well as negative.

For every person with an IQ below 70 there is another with an IQ above 130. Yet we would not think of someone as abnormal for having a high IQ. Similarly, we would not think of someone with a very low depression score on the BDI as abnormal. These examples show that being unusual or at one end of a psychological spectrum does not necessarily make someone abnormal.

This means that, although statistical infrequency can form part of assessment and diagnostic procedures, it is never sufficient as the sole basis for defining abnormality.

Evaluation eXtra

Benefits versus problems

Some unusual people benefit from being classed as abnormal. For example someone who has a very low IQ and is diagnosed with intellectual disability can then access support services or someone with a very high BDI score is likely to benefit from therapy.

On the other hand, not all statistically unusual people benefit from labels. Someone with a low IQ who can cope with their chosen lifestyle would not benefit from a label. There is a social stigma attached to such labels.

Consider: *Should we label unusual people as abnormal?*

Evaluation

Real-world application

One strength of deviation from social norms is its usefulness.

Deviation from social norms is used in clinical practice. For example, the key defining characteristic of antisocial personality disorder is the failure to conform to culturally acceptable ethical behaviour i.e. recklessness, aggression, violating the rights of others and deceitfulness. These signs of the disorder are all deviations from social norms. Such norms also play a part in the diagnosis of **schizoptypal personality disorder**, where the term 'strange' is used to characterise the thinking, behaviour and appearance of people with the disorder.

This shows that the deviation from social norms criterion has value in psychiatry.

Cultural and situational relativism

One limitation of deviation from social norms is the variability between social norms in different cultures and even different situations.

A person from one cultural group may label someone from another group as abnormal using their standards rather than the person's standards. For example, the experience of hearing voices is the norm in some cultures (as messages from ancestors) but would be seen as a sign of abnormality in most parts of the UK. Also, even within one cultural context social norms differ from one situation to another. Aggressive and deceitful behaviour in the context of family life is more socially unacceptable than in the context of corporate deal-making.

This means that it is difficult to judge deviation from social norms across different situations and cultures.

Evaluation eXtra

Human rights abuses

Using deviation from social norms to define someone as abnormal carries the risk of unfair labelling and leaving them open to human rights abuses. Historically this has been the case where diagnoses like *nymphomania* (women's uncontrollable or excessive sexual desire) have been used to control women, or diagnoses like *drapetomania* (black slaves running away) were a way to control slaves and avoid debate.

On the other hand it can be argued that we need to be able to use deviation from social norms to diagnose conditions such as antisocial personality disorder.

Consider: *Is the use of deviation from social norms as a criterion for defining abnormality ever justifiable?*

If you are statistically unusual and refuse to conform to social norms, does that make you abnormal or just 'eccentric'?

The ultimate aim of defining abnormality is to use these concepts to help classify mental disorders and diagnose people experiencing mental health problems.

First we have to decide what counts as a mental disorder. Some people can be statistically unusual and deviate from social norms without being thought of as abnormal. Therefore they shouldn't be diagnosed with a mental disorder.

Apply it Concepts — SPD

In the past there were examples of mental disorders that have been invented in order to control how people live. But are any modern diagnoses open to the same criticism?

Schizotypal personality disorder (SPD) is defined largely by deviation from social norms. Individuals are characterised by eccentric behaviour including superstition and beliefs in the supernatural that deviate from their cultural norms. They may also see flashes and shadows that are not seen by others and presumably are not real. This personality type is often found in families where relatives have a diagnosis of schizophrenia.

Question

Is it a reasonable approach to define schizotypal personality as abnormal or is it a human rights abuse?

Check it

1. Explain what is meant by 'statistical infrequency' as a definition of abnormality. *[4 marks]*
2. Outline **one** limitation of the statistical deviation definition of abnormality. *[3 marks]*
3. Explain what is meant by 'deviation from social norms' as a definition of abnormality. *[4 marks]*
4. Describe **and** evaluate **two** definitions of abnormality. *[12 marks AS, 16 marks AL]*

Definitions of abnormality (2)

The specification says...

Definitions of abnormality, including failure to function adequately and deviation from ideal mental health.

On the previous spread we considered ways to identify when a person's behaviour and/or mental state is sufficiently unusual to justify diagnosing them with and treating them for a mental disorder. Two further definitions of abnormality are identified in the specification and explained on this spread – failure to function adequately and deviation from ideal mental health.

Key terms

Failure to function adequately Occurs when someone is unable to cope with ordinary demands of day-to-day living.

Deviation from ideal mental health Occurs when someone does not meet a set of criteria for good mental health.

Failure to function adequately is the most important criterion for abnormality in psychiatric diagnosis.

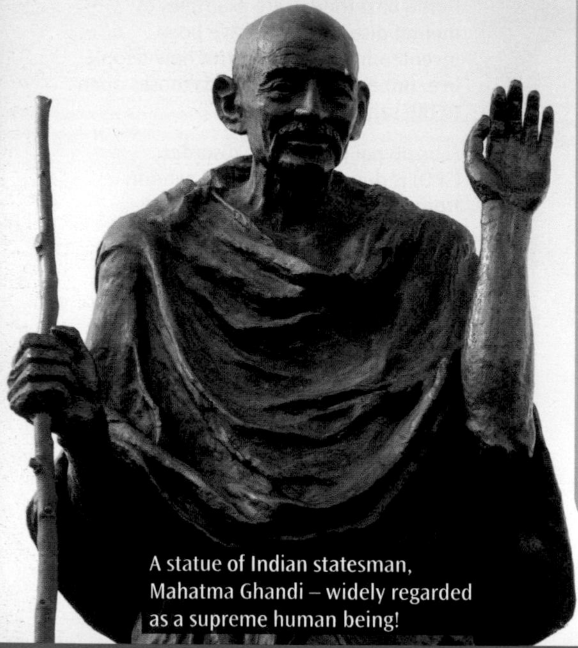

A statue of Indian statesman, Mahatma Ghandi – widely regarded as a supreme human being!

Study tip

We have covered four definitions altogether. It is most important that you know all four of these definitions – and important that you can give a detailed explanation of each one.

One way of providing detail is to use examples so don't ignore these.

One other word of advice – a good way of demonstrating your understanding is being able to apply it to cases like that of Pondlife (facing page), so make sure you can answer our questions on applying it.

Failure to function adequately

A person may cross the line between 'normal' and 'abnormal' at the point when they can no longer cope with the demands of everyday life. This is described as a **failure to function adequately**. We might decide that someone is not functioning adequately when they are unable to maintain basic standards of nutrition and hygiene. We might also consider that they are no longer functioning adequately if they cannot hold down a job or maintain relationships with people around them.

When is someone failing to function adequately?

David Rosenhan and Martin Seligman (1989) have proposed some additional signs that can be used to determine when someone is not coping. These include:

- When a person no longer conforms to standard interpersonal rules, for example maintaining eye contact and respecting personal space.
- When a person experiences severe personal distress.
- When a person's behaviour becomes irrational or dangerous to themselves or others.

Example: intellectual disability disorder

On the previous spread we looked at the example of intellectual disability disorder and saw that one of the criteria for diagnosis was having a very low IQ (a statistical infrequency). However, a diagnosis would not be made on this basis only – an individual must also be failing to function adequately before a diagnosis would be given.

Deviation from ideal mental health

A very different way to look at normality and abnormality is to ignore the issue of what makes someone abnormal but instead think about what makes anyone 'normal'. In other words we consider **deviation from ideal mental health**. Once we have a picture of how we should be psychologically healthy then we can begin to identify who deviates from this ideal.

What does ideal mental health look like?

Marie Jahoda (1958) suggested that we are in good mental health if we meet the following criteria:

- We have no symptoms or distress.
- We are rational and can perceive ourselves accurately.
- We **self-actualise** (strive to reach our potential).
- We can cope with stress.
- We have a realistic view of the world.
- We have good **self-esteem** and lack guilt.
- We are independent of other people.
- We can successfully work, love and enjoy our leisure.

Inevitably there is some overlap between what we might call deviation from ideal mental health and what we might call failure to function adequately. So we can think of someone's inability to keep a job as either a failure to cope with the pressures of work or as a deviation from the ideal of successfully working

Apply it
Concepts Paraphilias

One thing that has changed over time is that psychologists have generally become less inclined to classify people as abnormal simply on the basis of one definition. For example, we used to define *paraphilias* (unusual sexual behaviours) on the basis that they were deviations from social norms. This meant, for example, that when homosexuality was less socially acceptable it was classified as a paraphilia.

This would not happen now. In the DSM-5 system paraphilias are only classified as mental disorders if they involve harm or distress to the person themselves or other people. So exhibitionism (flashing), paedophilia (attraction to children) and frotteurism (rubbing up against people in public) are still considered abnormal because they cause harm and distress *as well as being* deviations from social norms. Consensual sadomasochism and transvestitism (cross-dressing) are no longer classified as abnormal simply because they deviate from social norms.

Question

Explain how our modern understanding of paraphilia is based on several of the definitions considered on this spread and the previous spread.

:valuation

₹epresents a threshold for help

)ne strength of the failure to function criterion is that it represents a sensible threshold for when eople need professional help.

Most of us have symptoms of mental disorder to some degree at some time. In fact, according to the nental health charity Mind, around 25% of people in the UK will experience a mental health problem in ny given year. However, many people press on in the face of fairly severe symptoms. It tends to be at the oint that we cease to function adequately that people seek professional help or are noticed and referred for elp by others.

This criterion means that treatment and services can be targeted to those who need them most.

)iscrimination and social control

)ne limitation of failure to function is that it is easy to label non-standard lifestyle choices as abnormal.

In practice it can be very hard to say when someone is really failing to function and when they have imply chosen to deviate from social norms – consider, for example, the table on the right. Not having a job or ermanent address might seem like failing to function, and for some people it would be. However, people with ternative lifestyles choose to live 'off-grid'. Similarly those who favour high-risk leisure activities or unusual piritual practices could be classed, unreasonably, as irrational and perhaps a danger to self.

This means that people who make unusual choices are at risk of being labelled abnormal and their eedom of choice may be restricted.

:valuation eXtra

ailure to function may not be abnormal

here are some circumstances in which most of us fail to cope for a time e.g. bereavement. It may be unfair to ive someone a label that may cause them future problems just because they react to difficult circumstances.

On the other hand the failure to function is no less real just because the cause is clear. Also, some people eed professional help to adjust to circumstances like bereavement.

:onsider: *Should we call people 'abnormal' when they fail to function following distressing ircumstances?*

:valuation

\ comprehensive definition

)ne strength of the ideal mental health criterion is that it is highly comprehensive.

Jahoda's concept of 'ideal mental health' includes a range of criteria for distinguishing mental health from nental disorder. In fact it covers most of the reasons why we might seek (or be referred for) help with mental ealth. This in turn means that an individual's mental health can be discussed meaningfully with a range of rofessionals who might take different theoretical views e.g. a medically-trained psychiatrist might focus on ymptoms whereas a humanistic counsellor might be more interested in self-actualisation.

This means that ideal mental health provides a checklist against which we can assess ourselves and thers and discuss psychological issues with a range of professionals.

/lay be culture-bound

)ne limitation of the ideal mental health criterion is that its different elements are not equally applicable cross a range of cultures.

Some of Jahoda's criteria for ideal mental health are firmly located in the context of the US and Europe enerally. In particular the concept of self-actualisation would probably be dismissed as self-indulgent 1 much of the world. Even within Europe there is quite a bit of variation in the value placed on personal ndependence, e.g. high in Germany, low in Italy. Furthermore what defines success in our working, social nd love-lives is very different in different cultures.

This means that it is difficult to apply the concept of ideal mental health from one culture to another.

:valuation eXtra

:xtremely high standards

ery few of us attain all of Jahoda's criteria for mental health, and probably none of us achieve all of nem at the same time or keep them up for very long. It can be disheartening to see an impossible et of standards to live up to.

On the other hand having such a comprehensive set of criteria for mental health to work towards night be of practical value to someone wanting to understanding and improve their mental health.

:onsider: *Is it helpful to have a comprehensive set of criteria for mental health?*

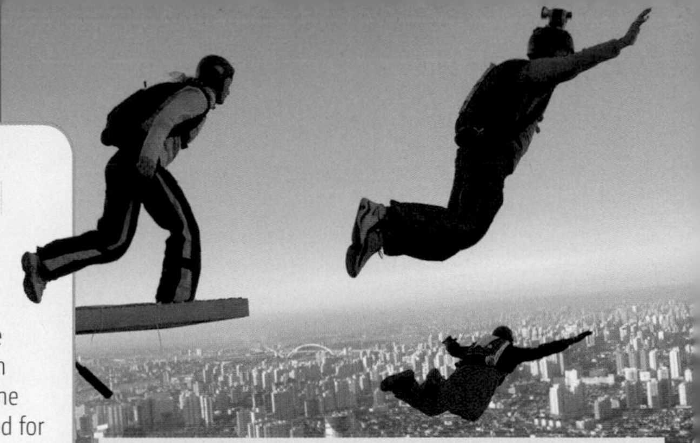

People who live alternative lifestyles may appear to function inadequately or to deviate from ideal mental health. When does a lifestyle choice become abnormal?

Failure to function adequately or lifestyle choice?

Group	Behaviour
New Age Travellers	Do not live in permanent accommodation and may not work.
Base jumpers	Take part in an extreme sport with a high mortality rate.
Spiritualists	Take part in religious rituals, communicating with the dead.

Apply it Concepts — Pondlife

A problem with both failure to function and deviation from ideal mental health definitions is that they may not help us make objective judgements about people who choose a lifestyle outside the mainstream. Some lifestyles can be considered maladaptive because they involve high-risk activities or considered irrational because they involve unusual religious or political beliefs.

Pondlife is a well-qualified 25-year-old software analyst who has chosen to live an alternative lifestyle in a squat. He does not regularly work. He struggles sometimes to keep his hair and clothes clean because his current squat does not have running water. Apart from this inconvenience Pondlife is happy as ... well he is very happy.

Question

According to the failure to function adequately and ideal mental health criteria, should Pondlife be considered abnormal? Explain your answer

Check it

1. Explain what is meant by 'failure to function adequately' as a definition of abnormality. *[4 marks]*
2. Outline **one** strength of the failure to function adequately definition of abnormality. *[4 marks]*
3. Explain what is meant by 'deviation from ideal mental health' as a definition of abnormality. *[4 marks]*
4. Describe **and** evaluate **at least two** definitions of abnormality. *[12 marks AS, 16 marks AL]*

Phobias

The specification says...

The behavioural, emotional and cognitive characteristics of phobias.

In your course you will focus on three examples of mental disorder: phobias, depression and obsessive-compulsive disorder (OCD). This spread is concerned with signs and symptoms of phobias. These include the ways in which people experiencing a phobia behave, think and feel in relation to the phobic stimulus, i.e. the thing they are afraid of.

Key terms

Phobia An irrational fear of an object or situation.

Behavioural Ways in which people act.

Emotional Related to a person's feelings or mood.

Cognitive Refers to the process of 'knowing', including thinking, reasoning, remembering, believing.

The DSM system

There are a number of systems for classifying and diagnosing mental health problems. Perhaps the best known is the DSM. This stands for Diagnostic and Statistical Manual of Mental Disorder and is published by the American Psychiatric Association.

The DSM is updated every so often as ideas about abnormality change. The current version is the 5th edition so it is commonly called the DSM-5. This was published in 2013.

Apply it Concepts — Case study: Padraig

When we think of phobias in everyday life we tend to have in mind fairly mild fears – such as avoiding snakes or spiders. However, where phobias have been diagnosed as a mental disorder (called clinical phobias), it can be disabling and cause tremendous distress. In fact a clinical phobia is only diagnosed if anxiety is considerable and it impacts on the person's life. Consider the case of Padraig.

Padraig is a psychology undergraduate. He experiences *gynophobia* – a phobia of women. This is an unusual condition and one which Padraig finds causes offence to many people he meets. Others don't take it seriously and laugh at Padraig. Padraig finds his studies very difficult because most of the students on his course are women.

His social life is limited because the people he likes best at university all hang out in mixed-gender groups. This causes Padraig severe distress and he feels guilty – he does not dislike women, he is just very anxious around them. His self-esteem is low and this is made worse by the fact that Padraig has no idea where his phobia comes from.

Question

Consider each of the four definitions of abnormality you have studied. For each one explain how Padraig would be judged as abnormal.

DSM-5 categories of phobia

All **phobias** are characterised by excessive fear and anxiety, triggered by an object, place or situation. The extent of the fear is out of proportion to any real danger presented by the phobic stimulus. The latest version of the DSM recognises the following categories o phobia and related anxiety disorder:

- **Specific phobia** – phobia of an object, such as an animal or body part, or a situation such as flying or having an injection.
- **Social anxiety (social phobia)** – phobia of a social situation such as public speaking or using a public toilet.
- **Agoraphobia** – phobia of being outside or in a public place.

On this spread there is an illustration of each of these three types of phobia.

Behavioural characteristics of phobias

We respond to things or situations we fear by **behaving** in particular ways. We respond by feeling high levels of anxiety and trying to escape. The fear responses in phobias are the same as we experience for any other fear even if the level of fear is irrational – out of all proportion to the phobic stimulus.

Panic

A person with a phobia may panic in response to the presence of the phobic stimulus. Panic may involve a range of behaviours including crying, screaming or running away. Children may react slightly differently, for example by freezing, clinging or having a tantrum.

Avoidance

Unless the person is making a conscious effort to face their fear they tend to go to a lot of effort to prevent coming into contact with the phobic stimulus. This can make it hard to go about daily life.

For example, someone with a fear of public toilets may have to limit the time they spend outside the home in relation to how long they can last without a toilet. This in turn can interfere with work, education and a social life.

Endurance

The alternative behavioural response to avoidance is endurance. This occurs when the person chooses to remain in the presence of the phobic stimulus. For example a person with *arachnophobia* might choose to remain in a room with a spider on the ceiling and keep a wary eye on it rather than leaving.

Agoraphobia **is an excessive fear of being outside or in a public place. This can be disabling to the extent that the person cannot leave their home.**

Practical activity on page 158

Social phobias include a fear of public speaking.

:motional characteristics of phobias

‹nxiety

hobias are classed as **anxiety disorders**. By definition then they involve an **emotional** :sponse of anxiety, an unpleasant state of high arousal. This prevents a person relaxing nd makes it very difficult to experience any positive emotion. Anxiety can be long term.

'ear

.lthough in everyday speech we might use the terms 'anxiety' and 'fear' interchangeably ıey do have distinct meanings. Fear is the immediate and extremely unpleasant :sponse we experience when we encounter or think about a phobic stimulus. It is sually more intense but experienced for shorter periods than anxiety.

:motional response is unreasonable

he anxiety or fear is much greater than is 'normal' and disproportionate to any threat osed. For example, a person with *arachnophobia* will have a strong emotional response to tiny spider. Most people would respond in a less anxious way even to a poisonous spider.

:ognitive characteristics of phobias

he **cognitive** element is concerned with the ways in which people process information. eople with phobias process information about phobic stimuli differently from other bjects or situations.

;elective attention to the phobic stimulus

a person can see the phobic stimulus it is hard to look away from it. Keeping our ttention on something really dangerous is a good thing as it gives us the best chance f reacting quickly to a threat, but this is not so useful when the fear is irrational. A erson with *pogonophobia* will struggle to concentrate on what they are doing if there is omeone with a beard in the room.

rrational beliefs

person with a phobia may hold unfounded thoughts in relation to phobic stimuli, e. that can't easily be explained and don't have any basis in reality. For example, social hobias can involve beliefs like 'I must always sound intelligent' or 'if I blush people will ıink I'm weak'. This kind of belief increases the pressure on the person to perform well in ocial situations.

:ognitive distortions

he perceptions of a person with a phobia may be inaccurate and unrealistic. So, or example, someone with *mycophobia* sees mushrooms as disgusting, and an *phidiophobic* may see snakes as alien and aggressive-looking.

Examples of specific phobias

Phobia	Phobic stimulus
Arachnophobia	Spiders
Ophidiophobia	Snakes
Zemmiphobia	Giant mole rats
Coulrophobia	Clowns
Kinemortophobia	Zombies
Lutraphobia	Otters
Mycophobia	Mushrooms
Omphalophobia	Belly buttons
Rectaphobia	Bottoms
Xanthophobia	Yellow
Nomophobia	Lack of a phone signal
Pogonophobia	Beards
Alphabutyrophobia	Peanut butter
Triskaidekaphobia	Thirteen

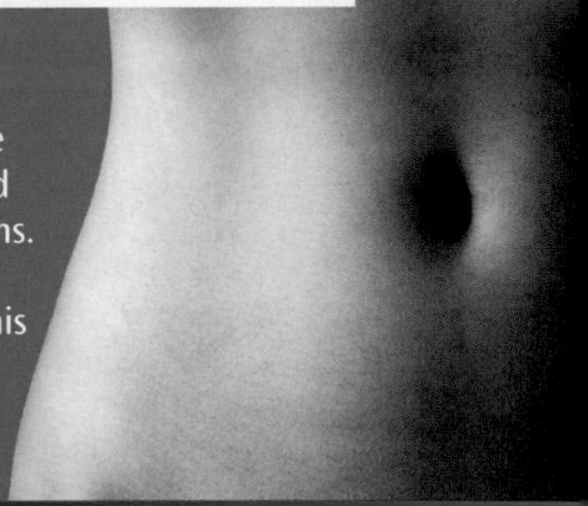
A **specific phobia**. There are people who fear buttons and people who fear belly buttons. To an *omphalophobic*, belly buttons may appear ugly. This is an example of a cognitive distortion.

Apply it Concepts — Eloise and the buttons

Young children are prone to phobias, including some that may appear downright odd to older people. One phobic stimulus is buttons.

Eloise has a phobia of buttons. She refuses to wear any clothes with buttons and she even refuses to go into clothes shops where there are likely to be clothes with buttons. When questioned, Eloise says that this is because of the extreme anxiety that buttons cause her. She also says that she believes that buttons will pinch her skin and that this will leave a bruise.

Questions

1. Identify the behavioural, emotional and cognitive aspects of Eloise's fear.
2. Conduct your own research and find another specific phobia. What behaviours, emotions and cognitions characterise it?

Check it

1. Outline behavioural characteristics of phobias. *[3 marks]*
2. Outline **one** emotional characteristic that may be seen in a person who has a spider phobia. *[2 marks]*
3. Outline cognitive characteristics of phobias. *[3 marks]*
4. Outline what is meant by a 'phobia'. *[2 marks]*

Depression

The specification says...

The behavioural, emotional and cognitive characteristics of depression.

This spread is concerned with signs and symptoms of depression. Where phobias are characterised by anxiety, depression is characterised by a low mood – it belongs to the general category of 'mood disorders'.

Key terms

Depression A mental disorder characterised by low mood and low energy levels.

Behavioural Ways in which people act.

Emotional Related to a person's feelings or mood.

Cognitive Refers to the process of 'knowing', including thinking, reasoning, remembering, believing.

Depression is associated with withdrawal from social and work life.

People with depression may experience reduced sleep (insomnia).

DSM-5 categories of depression

All forms of **depression** and depressive disorders are characterised by changes to mood. The latest version of the DSM recognises the following categories of depression and depressive disorders:

- **Major depressive disorder** – severe but often short-term depression.
- **Persistent depressive disorder** – long-term or recurring depression, including sustained major depression and what used to be called *dysthymia*.
- **Disruptive mood dysregulation disorder** – childhood temper tantrums.
- **Premenstrual dysphoric disorder** – disruption to mood prior to and/or during menstruation.

Behavioural characteristics of depression

Behaviour changes when we experience an episode of depression.

Activity levels

Typically people with depression have reduced levels of energy, making them lethargic. This has a knock-on effect, with people tending to withdraw from work, education and social life. In extreme cases this can be so severe that the person cannot get out of bed.

In some cases depression can lead to the opposite effect – known as **psychomotor agitation**. Agitated individuals struggle to relax and may end up pacing up and down a room.

Disruption to sleep and eating behaviour

Depression is associated with changes to sleeping behaviour. A person may experience reduced sleep (*insomnia*), particularly premature waking, or an increased need for sleep (*hypersomnia*). Similarly, appetite and eating may increase or decrease, leading to weight gain or loss. The key point is that such behaviours are disrupted by depression.

Aggression and self-harm

People with depression are often irritable, and in some cases they can become verbally or physically aggressive. This can have serious knock-on effects on a number of aspects of their life. For example, someone experiencing depression might display verbal aggression by ending a relationship or quitting a job.

Depression can also lead to physical aggression directed against the self. This includes self-harm, often in the form of cutting, or suicide attempts.

Apply it Concepts Sadra

Sadra is a 20-year-old university student. Her parents have been very worried since she returned home for a holiday. They hear Sadra up late into the night and also notice that she appears to have lost quite a lot of weight. She is very sensitive when asked about this and snaps at her parents.

During one argument Sadra says that she hates her parents and herself. In another argument she says that she doesn't enjoy university and also hates visiting her family. She shows no enthusiasm about returning to university after the holiday and has been unable to concentrate on a piece of coursework she has brought home to work on.

Questions

1. Identify the behavioural, emotional and cognitive aspects of Sadra's state.
2. Based on these characteristics, should Sadra's parents be concerned that she may be experiencing depression? Explain your answer.

:motional characteristics of depression

.owered mood

/hen we use the word 'depressed' in everyday life we are usually describing having a)wered mood, in other words feeling sad. As you can see from the rest of this spread there more to **clinical** depression than this.

Lowered mood is still a defining **emotional** element of depression but it is more ronounced than in the daily kind of experience of feeling lethargic and sad. People with epression often describe themselves as 'worthless' and 'empty'.

nger

lthough people with depression tend to experience more negative emotions and fewer ositive ones during episodes of depression, this experience of negative emotion is not mited to sadness. People with depression also frequently experience anger, sometimes xtreme anger. This can be directed at the self or others. On occasion such *emotions* lead) aggressive or self-harming *behaviour* – which is why this characteristic appears under ehavioural characteristics as well.

.owered self-esteem

elf-esteem is the emotional experience of how much we like ourselves. People with epression tend to report reduced self-esteem, in other words they like themselves less ian usual. This can be quite extreme, with some people with depression describing a ense of self-loathing, i.e. hating themselves.

:ognitive characteristics of depression

he **cognitive** aspect of depression is concerned with the ways in which people process iformation. People experiencing depression or who have experienced depression tend to rocess information about several aspects of the world quite differently from the 'normal' /ays that people without depression think.

'oor concentration

epression is associated with poor levels of concentration. The person may find themselves nable to stick with a task as they usually would, or they might find it hard to make ecisions that they would normally find straightforward. Poor concentration and poor ecision-making are likely to interfere with the individual's work.

ttending to and dwelling on the negative

/hen experiencing a depressive episode people are inclined to pay more attention to egative aspects of a situation and ignore the positives. In other words they tend to see a lass as half-empty rather than half-full.

People with depression also have a bias towards recalling unhappy events rather than appy ones – the opposite bias that most people have when not depressed.

bsolutist thinking

/lost situations are not all-good or all-bad, but when a person is depressed they tend to iink in these terms. This is sometimes called 'black-and-white thinking'. This means that /hen a situation is unfortunate they tend to see it as an *absolute* disaster.

Apply it Methods — Oona

Some doctors consider weight change as a result of depression to be significant when a person gains or loses 5% of their body weight.

Oona normally weighs 10 stone exactly. Her current weight is nine stone six pounds.

Questions

1. Approximately what percentage of her body weight has Oona lost? (*1 mark*)
2. Is this weight change likely to be seen as clinically significant? Explain your answer. (*2 marks*)

Apply it Concepts — Case study: Dai

Most of us would describe ourselves as feeling 'depressed' at some point in our lives and possibly may feel depressed relatively frequently. What we are usually describing is a feeling of being 'a bit down', a normal variation in mood. However, clinical depression can be a severe condition, as illustrated in the case of Dai.

Dai is 27. In most cases depression appears between the ages of 20 and 40. He has been experiencing very severe depression for some time. Although depression itself is not particularly unusual, depression as severe as Dai's is rare.

His depression was first diagnosed 18 months ago when he failed to 'bounce back' after the death of his mother. Dai has been unable to work for the last year and he has not felt able to get out of bed for several weeks now.

His doctor prescribed some drugs and arranged for psychotherapy but neither has really made any difference. Although on long-term sick leave, Dai no longer receives sick pay and his employer is about to dismiss him, declaring him unfit to work.

Dai's family is concerned about his reputation in their community if he has to live on benefits. Dai's mood and self-esteem are very low and he experiences periodic anxiety as well.

Question

Consider each of the four definitions of abnormality you have studied. For each one consider in what way Dai would be judged as abnormal.

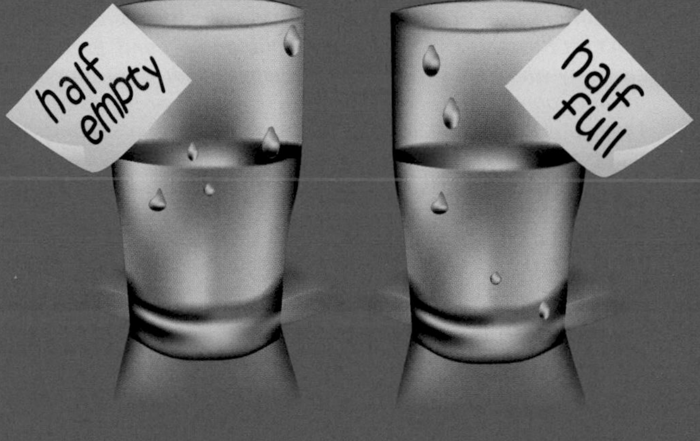
half empty
half full

Most of us see the glass as half-full but when in a depressive episode we are more likely to see it as half-empty.

Check it

1. Outline behavioural characteristics of depression. *[3 marks]*
2. Outline emotional characteristics of depression. *[3 marks]*
3. Outline cognitive characteristics of depression. *[3 marks]*
4. Outline what is meant by 'depression'. *[2 marks]*

Obsessive-compulsive disorder (OCD)

The specification says...

The behavioural, emotional and cognitive characteristics of obsessive-compulsive disorder (OCD).

The third mental disorder in the specification is obsessive-compulsive disorder (OCD). This involves anxiety (similar to phobias) and irrational thinking (similar to depression).

Key terms

OCD (obsessive-compulsive disorder) A condition characterised by obsessions and/or compulsive behaviour. Obsessions are cognitive whereas compulsions are behavioural.

Behavioural Ways in which people act.

Emotional Related to a person's feelings or mood.

Cognitive Refers to the process of 'knowing', including thinking, reasoning, remembering, believing.

Study tip

When describing OCD, students often find it difficult to distinguish between obsessions and compulsions. It may help you to be clear that:

- A compulsion is a behaviour, i.e. it is something you do.
- An obsession is a cognition, i.e. it takes place in the mind.

Apply it Concepts — Jez

Jez experiences OCD. He described his condition as follows:

I'm constantly anxious about catching diseases from other people. I can't get thoughts and pictures of dirt out of my mind. Every day I clean my whole house and wash my hands hundreds of times. When anyone comes to the house I make them wash their hands before I can go near them. I know this is ridiculous but I can't help it – it makes me feel better, but only for a little while.

Questions

1. Identify the behavioural, emotional and cognitive aspects of Jez's state.
2. At the top of the facing page OCD is illustrated as a cycle. Use this to describe Jez's OCD as a cycle.

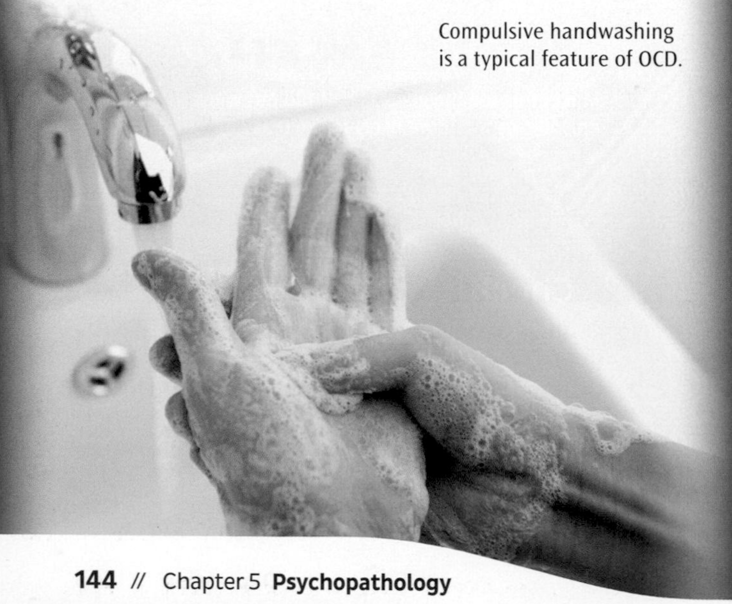

Compulsive handwashing is a typical feature of OCD.

DSM-5 categories of OCD

The DSM system recognises **OCD** and a range of related disorders. What these disorders all have in common is repetitive behaviour accompanied by obsessive thinking.

- **OCD** – characterised by either obsessions (recurring thoughts, images, etc.) and/or compulsions (repetitive behaviours such as handwashing). Most people with a diagnosis of OCD have both obsessions and compulsions.
- **Trichotillomania** – compulsive hair-pulling.
- **Hoarding disorder** – the compulsive gathering of possessions and the inability to part with anything, regardless of its value.
- **Excoriation disorder** – compulsive skin-picking.

Behavioural characteristics of OCD

The **behavioural** component of OCD is *compulsive behaviour*. There are two elements to compulsive behaviours.

Compulsions are repetitive

Typically people with OCD feel compelled to repeat a behaviour. A common example is handwashing. Other common compulsive repetitions include counting, praying and tidying/ordering groups of objects such as CD collections (for those who have them) or containers in a food cupboard.

Compulsions reduce anxiety

Around 10% of people with OCD show compulsive behaviour alone – they have no obsessions, just a general sense of irrational anxiety. However, for the vast majority, compulsive behaviours are performed in an attempt to manage the anxiety produced by obsessions. For example, compulsive handwashing is carried out as a *response* to an obsessive fear of germs. Compulsive checking, for example that a door is locked or a gas appliance is switched off, is in *response* to the obsessive thought that it might have been left unsecured.

Avoidance

The behaviour of people with OCD may also be characterised by their avoidance as they attempt to reduce anxiety by keeping away from situations that trigger it.

People with OCD tend to try to manage their OCD by avoiding situations that trigger anxiety. For example, people who wash compulsively may avoid coming into contact with germs. However, this avoidance can lead people to avoid very ordinary situations, such as emptying their rubbish bins, and this can in itself interfere with leading a regular life.

Apply it Methods — Bar chart

Most people with OCD experience both obsessions and compulsions – 10% experience compulsions alone and 20% experience obsessions alone.

Question

On a bar chart, plot the percentages for those experiencing (a) obsessions only, (b) compulsion only and (c) obsession + compulsion (you have to work this out!).

Make sure that you follow the conventions of bar charts:

- Bars should not touch.
- Axes need to be labelled.
- The graph should have an appropriate scale.
- It should also have a suitable title. *(4 marks)*

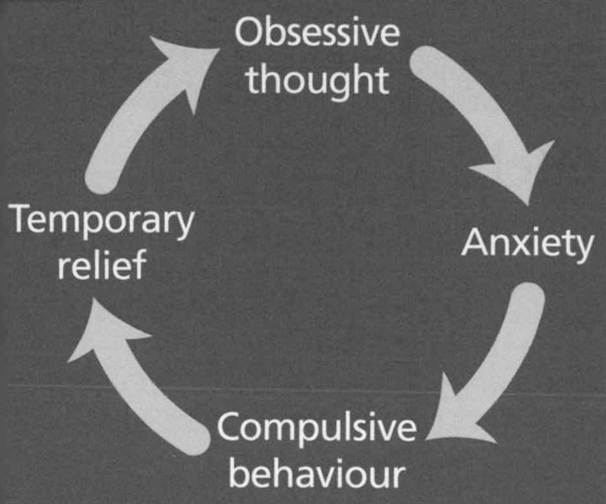
Obsessive thought
Anxiety
Compulsive behaviour
Temporary relief

'he cycle of OCD. Adapted from www.mind.org.uk

For around 90% of people with OCD, the major cognitive feature of their condition is obsessive thoughts.

:motional characteristics of OCD

\nxiety and distress

CD is regarded as a particularly unpleasant **emotional** experience because of the owerful anxiety that accompanies both obsessions and compulsions. Obsessive houghts are unpleasant and frightening, and the anxiety that goes with these can e overwhelming. The urge to repeat a behaviour (a compulsion) creates anxiety.

\ccompanying depression

CD is often accompanied by **depression**, so anxiety can be accompanied by low nood and lack of enjoyment in activities. Compulsive behaviour tends to bring ome relief from anxiety but this is temporary.

;uilt and disgust

s well as anxiety and depression, OCD sometimes involves other negative motions such as irrational guilt, for example over minor moral issues, or disgust, vhich may be directed against something external like dirt or at the self.

:ognitive characteristics of OCD

ne **cognitive** approach is concerned with the ways in which people process nformation. People with OCD are usually plagued with obsessive thoughts but they lso adopt cognitive strategies to deal with these.

)bsessive thoughts

or around 90% of people with OCD the major cognitive feature of their condition obsessive thoughts, i.e. thoughts that recur over and over again. These vary onsiderably from person to person but are always unpleasant. Examples of ecurring thoughts are worries of being contaminated by dirt and germs, or certainty nat a door has been left unlocked and that intruders will enter through it, or npulses to hurt someone.

:ognitive coping strategies

bsessions are the major cognitive aspect of OCD, but people also respond by dopting cognitive coping strategies to deal with the obsessions. For example, religious person tormented by obsessive guilt may respond by praying or neditating. This may help manage anxiety but can make the person appear bnormal to others and can distract them from everyday tasks.

nsight into excessive anxiety

eople with OCD are aware that their obsessions and compulsions are not rational. fact this is necessary for a diagnosis of OCD. If someone really believed their bsessive thoughts were based on reality that would be a symptom of a quite fferent form of mental disorder. However, in spite of this insight, people with OCD xperience catastrophic thoughts about the worst case scenarios that might result if neir anxieties were justified. They also tend to be hypervigilant, i.e. they maintain onstant alertness and keep attention focused on potential hazards.

Apply it Concepts — Case study: Sarita

OCD involves severe anxiety, and any strategies to reduce this anxiety are likely to interfere with living a regular life.

Sarita experiences OCD. She has had OCD on and off since she was a teenager, when her parents separated. Only 1–2% of the population experiences clinical OCD, making it fairly unusual.

Like most people with OCD Sarita has both compulsive behaviours and obsessions. She has obsessive thoughts of dirt and a compulsion to wash her hands every time she touches something that might be dirty.

As a new mother, Sarita experiences difficulty because her obsession with dirt makes it very hard for her to change nappies. She is often alone with her baby as her husband works so, in the daytime, this is a real problem.

The other local mothers find Sarita's OCD hard to understand and she wonders whether they see her as a bad mother. This in turn has led to Sarita experiencing low self-esteem. She is now receiving support from Children's Services.

Question

Consider each of the four definitions of abnormality you have studied. For each one consider in what way Sarita would be judged as abnormal.

Check it

1. Outline behavioural characteristics of OCD. *[3 marks]*
2. Outline emotional characteristics of OCD. *[3 marks]*
3. Outline cognitive characteristics of OCD. *[3 marks]*
4. Outline what is meant by 'OCD'. *[2 marks]*

The behavioural approach to explaining phobias

The specification says...

The behavioural approach to explaining phobias: the two-process model, including classical and operant conditioning.

Psychologists are interested in explaining what leads a person to develop a mental disorder and using such explanations as the basis of treatments. One of the key explanations for phobias is the behavioural approach – that phobias can be learned by classical conditioning and maintained by operant conditioning.

Key terms

Behavioural (behaviourist) approach A way of explaining behaviour in terms of what is observable and in terms of learning.

Two-process model An explanation for the onset and persistence of disorders that create anxiety, such as phobias. The two processes are classical conditioning for onset and operant conditioning for persistence.

Classical conditioning Learning by association. Occurs when two stimuli are repeatedly paired together – an unconditioned (unlearned) stimulus (UCS) and a new 'neutral' stimulus (NS). The neutral stimulus eventually produces the same response that was first produced by the unconditioned (unlearned) stimulus alone.

Operant conditioning A form of learning in which behaviour is shaped and maintained by its consequences. Possible consequences of behaviour include positive reinforcement, negative reinforcement or punishment.

The two-process model

The **behavioural approach** emphasises the role of learning in the acquisition of behaviour. The approach focuses on behaviour – what we can see. On page 140 we identified the key behavioura aspects of phobias – panic, avoidance and endurance. The behavioural approach is geared toward explaining these rather than the cognitive and emotional aspects of phobias.

Orval Hobart Mowrer (1960) proposed the **two-process model** based on the behavioural approach to phobias. This states that phobias are acquired (learned in the first place) by **classical conditioning** and then continue because of **operant conditioning**.

Acquisition by classical conditioning

Classical conditioning involves learning to associate something of which we initially have no fear (called a **neutral stimulus**) with something that already triggers a fear response (known as an **unconditioned stimulus**).

John Watson and Rosalie Rayner (1920) created a phobia in a 9-month-old baby called 'Little Albert'. Albert showed no unusual anxiety at the start of the study. When shown a white rat he tried to play with it. However, the experimenters then set out to give Albert a phobia. Whenever the rat was presented to Albert the researchers made a loud, frightening noise by banging an iron bar close to Albert's ear. This noise is an unconditioned stimulus (**UCS**) which creates an **unconditioned response** (**UCR**) of fear. When the rat (a neutral stimulus, **NS**) and the **UCS** are encountered close together in time the NS becomes associated with the UCS and both now produce the fear response – Albert displayed fear when he saw a rat (the NS). The rat is now a learned or **conditioned stimulus** (**CS**) that produces a **conditioned response** (**CR**).

This conditioning then **generalised** to similar objects. They tested Albert by showing him other furry objects such as a non-white rabbit, a fur coat and Watson wearing a Santa Claus beard made out of cotton balls. Little Albert displayed distress at the sight of all of these.

Maintenance by operant conditioning

Responses acquired by classical conditioning usually tend to decline over time. However, phobias are often long-lasting. Mowrer has explained this as the result of operant conditioning.

Operant conditioning takes place when our behaviour is **reinforced** (rewarded) or **punished**. Reinforcement tends to increase the frequency of a behaviour. This is true of both **negative reinforcement** and **positive reinforcement**. In the case of negative reinforcement an individual *avoids* a situation that is unpleasant. Such a behaviour results in a desirable consequence, which means the behaviour will be repeated.

Mowrer suggested that whenever we avoid a phobic stimulus we successfully escape the fear and anxiety that we would have experienced if we had remained there. This reduction in fear reinforces the avoidance behaviour and so the phobia is maintained.

People may acquire and maintain a phobia of dogs if they have a bad experience with an animal. Both classical and operant conditioning are involved.

Apply it Concepts — Zelda

Zelda has a phobia of dogs. As a child she was once bitten by a dog belonging to a family friend. Now when she thinks about dogs she experiences anxiety and she becomes very afraid whenever she sees a dog near her. This is particularly bad when she is approached by a German Shepherd. Zelda avoids dogs whenever possible.

Question

Using the two-process model explain how Zelda might have acquired her phobia and how it might be maintained. Refer to the processes of classical and operant conditioning in your answer.

Apply it Concepts — Nasim

Agoraphobia is an extreme fear of leaving one's own home. This is a serious problem because it prevents the person going about their regular daily life.

Nasim has agoraphobia. He is a keen A level student but is struggling to attend college because of the acute anxiety he experiences when attempting to leave his house in the morning. His phobia began shortly after being mugged. Actually Nasim finds he can leave his house as long as someone else is with him, but his parents leave for work early and he lives in the opposite direction of college from his friends.

Questions

1. Explain how Nasim's agoraphobia might have been acquired and maintained according to the two-process model.
2. Evaluate the two-process model as an explanation of Nasim's condition.

:valuation

:eal-world application

ne strength of the two-process model is its real-world application in **exposure** **erapies** (such as systematic desensitisation, described on the next spread).

The distinctive element of the two-process model is the idea that phobias e maintained by avoidance of the phobic stimulus. This is important in xplaining why people with phobias benefit from being exposed to the phobic imulus. Once the avoidance behaviour is prevented it ceases to be reinforced / the experience of anxiety reduction and avoidance therefore declines. behavioural terms the phobia *is* the avoidance behaviour so when this voidance is prevented the phobia is cured.

This shows the value of the two-process approach because it identifies a eans of treating phobias.

:ognitive aspects of phobias

ne limitation of the two-process model is that it does not account for the **gnitive** aspects of phobias.

Behavioural explanations, including the two-process model, are geared wards explaining *behaviour*. In the case of phobias the key behaviour is voidance of the phobic stimulus. However, we know that phobias are not mply avoidance responses – they also have a significant cognitive component. or example people hold irrational beliefs about the phobic stimulus (such as inking that a spider is dangerous). The two-process model explains avoidance ehaviour but does not offer an adequate explanation for phobic cognitions.

This means that the two-process model does not completely explain the mptoms of phobias.

hobias and traumatic experiences

further strength of the two-process model is evidence for a link between bad xperiences and phobias.

The Little Albert study (facing page) illustrates how a frightening experience volving a stimulus can lead to a phobia of that stimulus. More systematic idence comes from a study by Ad De Jongh *et al.* (2006) who found that 3% of people with a fear of dental treatment had experienced a traumatic xperience, mostly involving dentistry (others had experienced being the victim violent crime). This can be compared to a **control group** of people with low ental anxiety where only 21% had experienced a traumatic event.

This confirms that the association between stimulus (dentistry) and an nconditioned response (pain) does lead to the development of the phobia.

Counterpoint Not all phobias appear following a bad experience. In fact some common phobias such as snake phobias occur in populations where very few people have any experience of snakes let alone traumatic experiences. Also, considering the other direction, not all frightening experiences lead to phobias.

This means that the association between phobias and frightening experiences is not as strong as we would expect if behavioural theories provided a complete explanation.

:valuation eXtra

earning and evolution

ehavioural models of phobias, such as the two-process model, provide edible individual explanations i.e. they can explain how a particular person evelops and maintains a particular phobia.

However, there are other more general aspects to phobias that may be better xplained by evolutionary theory. For example, we tend to acquire phobias of ings that have presented a danger in our evolutionary past (such as snakes id the dark). This is called **preparedness** (Seligman 1971).

onsider: *In the light of the likely role of evolution in phobias, how ood an explanation is the two-factor model?*

We don't usually develop phobias of cars although many of us have bad experiences with them. The two-process model cannot easily explain this.

Apply it Methods — Treating agoraphobia

A clinical psychologist is interested in whether her clients with agorophobia are able to leave their home with relatively little anxiety provided a safe person is with them. She finds that of her last 15 clients with agoraphobia, 10 benefitted from having a trusted companion with them while five did not.

Questions

1. Express these figures as (a) a ratio, (b) a fraction and (c) a percentage to one decimal place. *(3 marks)*
2. Present this data in a graph. (*3 marks*)
3. This study could be described as a **natural experiment**. Explain in what way this might be a natural experiment.
4. How could you conduct this same study as a **field experiment**? (*2 marks*)
5. Outline *one* **ethical issue** a psychologist would need to consider when carrying out this study. (*2 marks*)

Study tip

Be clear about the difference between the behavioural characteristics of phobias, behavioural explanations and behavioural treatments (covered on the next spread). There are similarities in each of these as they are all focused on behaviours. It is important to avoid a knee-jerk response when you read the word 'behavioural'.

Check it

1. Outline the two-process model of phobias. *[4 marks]*
2. Explain **one** strength of the two-process model. *[4 marks]*
3. Outline how classical conditioning can be used to explain phobias. *[4 marks]*
4. Describe **and** evaluate the behavioural approach to explaining phobias. *[12 marks AS, 16 marks AL]*

The behavioural approach to treating phobias

The specification says...

The behavioural approach to treating phobias: systematic desensitisation, including relaxation and use of hierarchy; flooding.

Psychologists are interested in explaining why phobias develop but also in understanding how to treat them. The specification identifies two behavioural methods used in the treatment of phobias.

Key terms

Systematic desensitisation (SD) A behavioural therapy designed to reduce an unwanted response, such as anxiety. SD involves drawing up a hierarchy of anxiety-provoking situations related to a person's phobic stimulus, teaching the person to relax, and then exposing them to phobic situations. The person works their way through the hierarchy whilst maintaining relaxation.

Flooding A behavioural therapy in which a person with a phobia is exposed to an extreme form of a phobic stimulus in order to reduce anxiety triggered by that stimulus. This takes place across a small number of long therapy sessions.

Dog gone good

Craig Newman and Katie Adams (2004) outlined the anxiety hierarchy they used to treat a phobia of dogs in a teenage boy with learning difficulties.

1. Introduction to dogs in photographs.
2. Dogs introduced without direct access.
3. Dog introduced to the same room.
4. Dog introduced to personal space on lead.
5. Loose dog introduced through a window.
6. Loose dog introduced but blocked by waist-high object.
7. Loose dog in the same room.
8. Repeated with different dogs.
9. Observe loose dogs in a park from a distance.
10. Close proximity to dogs in a park.

Fear of cats could be treated either by systematic desensitisation or flooding.

Systematic desensitisation

Systematic desensitisation (SD) is a **behavioural therapy** designed to gradually reduce phobic anxiety through the principle of **classical conditioning**. If a person can learn to relax in the presence of the phobic stimulus they will be cured.

Essentially a new response to the phobic stimulus is learned (phobic stimulus is paired with relaxation instead of anxiety). This learning of a different response is called **counterconditioning**.

There are three processes involved in SD.

1. **The anxiety hierarchy** is put together by a client with phobia and therapist. This is a list of situations related to the phobic stimulus that provoke anxiety arranged in order from least to most frightening. For example, a person with *arachnophobia* might identify a picture of a small spider as low on their anxiety hierarchy and holding a tarantula at the top of the hierarchy.
2. **Relaxation** The therapist teaches the client to relax as deeply as possible. It is impossible to be afraid and relaxed at the same time, so one emotion prevents the other. This is called **reciprocal inhibition**. The relaxation might involve breathing exercises or, alternatively, the client might learn mental imagery techniques. Clients can be taught to imagine themselves in relaxing situations (such as imagining lying on a beach) or they might learn meditation. Alternatively relaxation can be achieved using drugs such as Valium.
3. **Exposure** Finally the client is exposed to the phobic stimulus while in a relaxed state. This takes place across several sessions, starting at the bottom of the anxiety hierarchy. When the client can stay relaxed in the presence of the lower levels of the phobic stimulus they move up the hierarchy. Treatment is successful when the client can stay relaxed in situations high on the anxiety hierarchy.

Flooding

Flooding also involves exposing people with a phobia to their phobic stimulus but without a gradual build-up in an anxiety hierarchy. Instead flooding involves immediate exposure to a very frightening situation. So a person with *arachnophobia* receiving flooding treatment might have a large spider crawl over them for an extended period. Flooding sessions are typically longer than systematic desensitisation sessions, one session often lasting two to three hours. Sometimes only one long session is needed to cure a phobia.

How does flooding work?

Flooding stops phobic responses very quickly. This may be because, without the option of avoidance behaviour, the client quickly learns that the phobic stimulus is harmless. In classical conditioning terms this process is called **extinction**. A learned response is extinguished when the **conditioned stimulus** (e.g. a dog) is encountered without the **unconditioned stimulus** (e.g. being bitten). The result is that the conditioned stimulus no longer produces the conditioned response (fear).

In some cases the client may achieve relaxation in the presence of the phobic stimulus simply because they become exhausted by their own fear response!

Ethical safeguards

Flooding is not unethical *per se* but it is an unpleasant experience so it is important that clients give fully **informed consent** to this traumatic procedure and that they are fully prepared before the flooding session. A client would normally be given the choice of systematic desensitisation or flooding.

Apply it Concepts — Emily and cats

Emily has a phobia of cats. This is inconvenient as several of her friends have cats and she finds it hard to visit them because of her anxiety.

Questions

1. Consider how Emily could be treated by systematic desensitisation.
2. Explain how she could be treated by flooding.
3. Emily can't decide which therapy might be best for her. What would you advise her about choosing between the two treatments?

:valuation

:vidence of effectiveness

ne strength of systematic desensitisation (SD) is the evidence base for its effectiveness.

Lisa Gilroy *et al.* (2003) followed up 42 people who had SD for spider phobia in three 5-minute sessions. At both three and 33 months, the SD group were less fearful than a **control roup** treated by relaxation without exposure. In a recent review Theresa Wechsler *et al.* (2019) oncluded that SD is effective for specific phobia, social phobia and agoraphobia.

This means that SD is likely to be helpful for people with phobias.

'eople with learning disabilities

further strength of SD is that it can be used to help people with learning disabilities.

Some people requiring treatment for phobias also have a learning disability. However, the ıain alternatives to SD are not suitable. People with learning disabilities often struggle with **ɔgnitive therapies** that require complex rational thought. They may also feel confused and stressed by the traumatic experience of flooding.

This means that SD is often the most appropriate treatment for people with learning isabilities who have phobias.

:valuation eXtra

D in virtual reality

'aditional SD involves exposure to the phobic stimulus in a real-world setting. However there e advantages to conducting the exposure part of SD in virtual reality (VR). Exposure through R can be used to avoid dangerous situations (e.g. heights) and is cost-effective because the sychologist and client need not leave the consulting room.

On the other hand there is some evidence to suggest that VR exposure may be less effective ıan real exposure for social phobias because it lacks realism (Wechsler *et al.* 2019).

onsider: *Should clinical psychologists use VR for exposure?*

:valuation

:ost-effective

ne strength of flooding is that it is highly cost-effective.

Clinical effectiveness means how effective a therapy is at tackling symptoms. However when e provide therapies in health systems like the NHS we also need to think about how much they ɔst. A therapy is cost-effective if it is clinically effective and not expensive. Flooding can work in s little as one session as opposed to say, ten sessions for SD to achieve the same result. Even llowing for a longer session (perhaps three hours) this makes flooding more cost-effective.

This means that more people can be treated at the same cost with flooding than with SD or ther therapies.

'raumatic

ne limitation of flooding is that it is a highly unpleasant experience.

Confronting one's phobic stimulus in an extreme form provokes tremendous anxiety. Sarah chumacher *et al.* (2015) found that participants and therapists rated flooding as significantly more ressful than SD. This raises the **ethical** issue for psychologists of knowingly causing stress to their ients, although this is not a serious issue provided they obtain **informed consent**. More seriously, ıe traumatic nature of flooding means that **attrition** (dropout) rates are higher than for SD.

This suggests that, overall, therapists may avoid using this treatment.

:valuation eXtra

ymptom substitution

limitation of behavioural therapies, including flooding, is that they only mask symptoms and o not tackle the underlying causes of phobias (symptom substitution). For example, Jacqueline ersons (1986) reported the case of a woman with a phobia of death who was treated using ooding. Her fear of death declined, but her fear of being criticised got worse.

However, the only evidence for symptom substitution comes in the form of case studies hich, in this case, may only generalise to the phobias in the study (e.g. phobia of death ıay be different from a phobia of heights).

onsider: *Is symptom substitution only a theoretical problem?*

Apply it Methods: Clinical trial

The bar chart below shows the symptom prevalence for groups of clients treated by flooding, systematic desensitisation and kept on a waiting list (a control condition).

Bar chart showing the effectiveness of treatment for specific phobias.

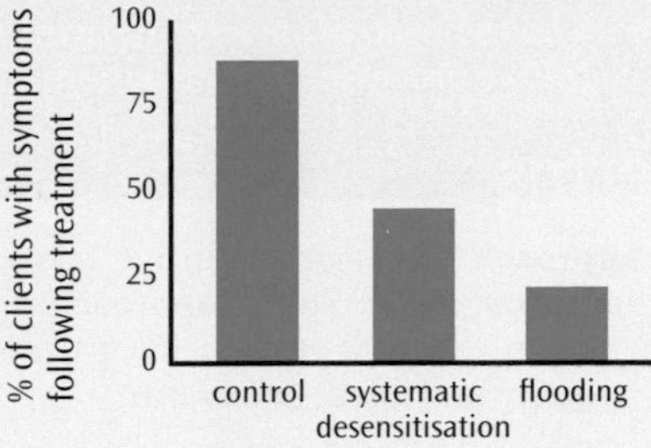
% of clients with symptoms following treatment
100
75
50
25
0
control
systematic desensitisation
flooding

Questions

1. What does the graph tell us about the effectiveness of different treatments for phobias in this study? (*3 marks*)
2. Explain why a **control condition** is necessary. (*2 marks*)
3. Studies comparing different therapies often use an **independent groups design**. Explain what an independent groups design is and why it is preferable for this type of study. (*3 marks*)

Apply it Concepts: Case study: Manish

Manish has a phobia of giant mole rats (*zemmiphobia*). This is a particular problem for him as he works in the mole rat enclosure at a zoo. Imagine you were helping Manish with this problem using systematic desensitisation.

Questions

1. How would you put together an anxiety hierarchy for treating zemmiphobia?
2. How would you teach Manish relaxation?
3. Explain how you would expose Manish to giant mole rats in such a way as to tackle his phobia.

Check it

1. Outline **one** behavioural method for treating phobias. *[4 marks]*
2. Explain how flooding could be used to treat someone with a phobia of dogs. *[2 marks]*
3. Explain **one** limitation of using systematic desensitisation to treat phobias. *[4 marks]*
4. Describe **and** evaluate the behavioural approach to treating phobias. *[12 marks AS, 16 marks AL]*

The cognitive approach to explaining depression

The specification says...

The cognitive approach to explaining depression: Beck's negative triad and Ellis's ABC model.

Another approach to explaining the development of mental disorders is based on the cognitive approach. In particular we are interested in how depression involves negative patterns of thinking and other cognitive processes such as schema.

Key terms

Cognitive approach The term 'cognitive' has come to mean 'mental processes', so this approach is focused on how our mental processes (e.g. thoughts, perceptions, attention) affect behaviour.

Negative triad Beck proposed that there are three kinds of negative thinking that contribute to becoming depressed: negative views of the world, the future and the self. Such negative views lead a person to interpret their experiences in a negative way and so make them more vulnerable to depression.

ABC model Ellis proposed that depression occurs when an activating event (A) triggers an irrational belief (B) which in turn produces a consequence (C), i.e. an emotional response like depression. The key to this process is the irrational belief.

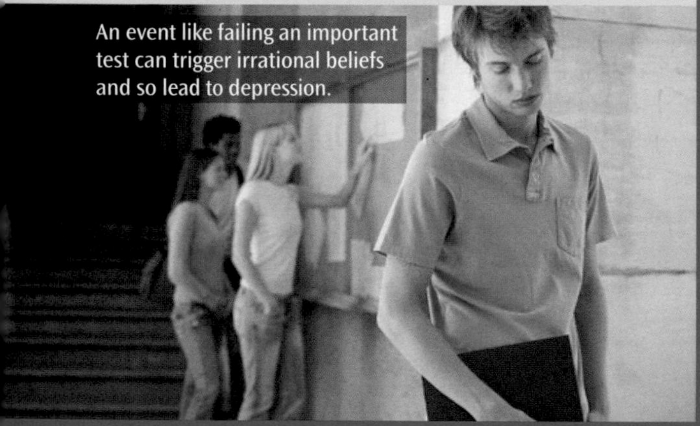

An event like failing an important test can trigger irrational beliefs and so lead to depression.

Apply it Concepts

The cognitive approach

The cognitive approach to understanding depression emerged in the 1960s as psychologists in general changed their emphasis from studying observable behaviour to studying mental processes. The cognitive approach to depression is most concerned with explaining the kinds of thinking and selective attention that characterise depression. The approach does not ignore emotion and behaviour but it sees them as the result of cognition.

Question

Explain in what ways both Beck's and Ellis's explanations are examples of the cognitive approach.

Beck's negative triad

American psychiatrist Aaron Beck (1967) took a **cognitive approach** to explaining why some people are more vulnerable to **depression** than others. In particular it is a person's *cognitions* that create this vulnerability, i.e. the way they think.

Beck suggested three parts to this cognitive vulnerability.

Faulty information processing

This is when depressed people attend to the negative aspects of a situation and ignore positives. For example, if I was depressed and won £1 million on the Lottery, I might focus on the fact that the previous week someone had won £10 million, rather than focus on the positive of all I could do with £1 million. Depressed people may tend towards 'black and white thinking' where something is either all bad or all good (as discussed on page 143).

Negative self-schema

A **schema** is a 'package' of ideas and information developed through experience. They act as mental framework for the interpretation of sensory information. A *self-schema* is the package of information people have about themselves. People use schema to interpret the world, so if a person has a negative self-schema they interpret all information about themselves in a negative way.

The negative triad

Beck suggested that a person develops a dysfunctional view of themselves because of three types of negative thinking that occur automatically, regardless of the reality of what is happening at the time. These three elements are called the **negative triad**. When a person is depressed, negative thoughts about the world, the future and oneself are uppermost.

a) Negative view of the world – an example would be 'the world is a cold hard place'. This creates the impression that there is no hope anywhere.

b) Negative view of the future – an example would be 'there isn't much chance that the economy will really get better'. Such thoughts reduce any hopefulness and enhance depression.

c) Negative view of the self – for example, thinking 'I am a failure'. Such thoughts enhance any existing depressive feelings because they confirm the existing emotions of low **self-esteem**.

Ellis's ABC model

Another American psychiatrist, Albert Ellis (1962) suggested a different cognitive explanation of depression. He proposed that good mental health is the result of rational thinking, defined as thinking in ways that allow people to be happy and free from pain. To Ellis, conditions like anxiety and depression (poor mental health) result from irrational thoughts. Ellis defined **irrational thoughts**, not as illogical or unrealistic thoughts, but as any thoughts that interfere with us being happy and free from pain.

Ellis used the **ABC model** to explain how irrational thoughts affect our behaviour and emotional state.

A Activating event

Ellis focused on situations in which irrational thoughts are triggered by external events. According to Ellis we get depressed when we experience negative events and these trigger irrational beliefs. Events like failing an important test or ending a relationship might trigger irrational beliefs.

B Beliefs

Ellis identified a range of irrational beliefs. He called the belief that we must always succeed or achieve perfection *'musturbation'*. *'I-can't-stand-it-itis'* is the belief that it is a major disaster whenever something does not go smoothly. *Utopianism* is the belief that life is always meant to be fair.

C Consequences

When an activating event triggers irrational beliefs there are emotional and behavioural consequences. For example, if a person believes that they must always succeed and then fails at something this can trigger depression.

Evaluation

Research support

One strength generally of Beck's cognitive model of depression is the existence of supporting research.

'Cognitive vulnerability' refers to ways of thinking that may predispose a person to becoming depressed, for example faulty information processing, negative self-schema and the cognitive triad. In a review David Clark and Aaron Beck (1999) concluded that not only were these cognitive vulnerabilities more common in depressed people but they preceded the depression. This was confirmed in a more recent **prospective** study by Joseph Cohen *et al.* (2019). They tracked the development of 473 adolescents, regularly measuring cognitive vulnerability. It was found that showing cognitive vulnerability predicted later depression.

This shows that there is an association between cognitive vulnerability and depression.

Real-world application

A further strength of Beck's cognitive model of depression is its applications in screening and treatment for depression.

Cohen *et al.* (see above) concluded that assessing cognitive vulnerability allows psychologists to screen young people, identifying those most at risk of developing depression in the future and monitoring them. Understanding cognitive vulnerability can also be applied in **cognitive behaviour therapy** (CBT – see next spread). These therapies work by altering the kind of cognitions that make people vulnerable to depression, making them more resilient to negative life events.

This means that an understanding of cognitive vulnerability is useful in more than one aspect of clinical practice.

Evaluation eXtra

A partial explanation

There seems to be no doubt that depressed people show particular patterns of cognition, and that these can be seen before the onset of depression. It therefore appears that Beck's suggestion of cognitive vulnerabilities is at least a partial explanation for depression.

However, there are some aspects to depression that are not particularly well explained by cognitive explanations. For example, some depressed people feel extreme anger, and some experience hallucinations and delusions.

Consider: *Is cognitive vulnerability a good explanation for depression?*

Evaluation

Real-world application

One strength of Ellis's ABC model is its real-world application in the psychological treatment of depression.

Ellis's approach to cognitive therapy is called *rational emotive behaviour therapy* or REBT for short. The idea of REBT is that by vigorously arguing with a depressed person the therapist can alter the irrational beliefs that are making them unhappy. There is some evidence to support the idea that REBT can both change negative beliefs and relieve the symptoms of depression (David *et al.* 2018).

This means that REBT has real-world value.

Reactive and endogenous depression

One limitation of Ellis's ABC model of depression is that it only explains **reactive depression** and not **endogenous depression**.

There seems to be no doubt that depression is often triggered by life events – what Ellis would call 'activating events'. Such cases are sometimes called reactive depression. How we respond to negative life events also seems to be at least partly the result of our beliefs. However, many cases of depression are not traceable to life events and it is not obvious what leads the person to become depressed at a particular time. This type of depression is sometimes called endogenous depression. Ellis's ABC model is less useful for explaining endogenous depression.

This means that Ellis's model can only explain some cases of depression and is therefore only a partial explanation.

Evaluation eXtra

Ethical issues

The ABC model of depression is controversial because it locates responsibility for depression purely with the depressed person. Critics say this is effectively blaming the depressed person, which would be unfair.

On the other hand, provided it is used appropriately and sensitively, the application of the ABC model in REBT (discussed on next spread) does appear to make at least some depressed people achieve more resilience and feel better.

Consider: *In the end, should REBT be judged as unethical?*

Those who look at the downsides of a situation are more prone to depression.

Apply it
Concepts — Yasmin

Yasmin has just been made redundant. She takes this very hard and is experiencing symptoms of depression. When questioned, Yasmin says that the situation is unfair and that she feels ashamed.

Questions

1. How would you put this sequence of events into the ABC model?
2. In terms of Ellis's theory, what kinds of irrational thinking is Yasmin displaying?
3. Does Yasmin have any symptoms that Ellis's approach would struggle to explain?

Study tip

We have presented two cognitive explanations for depression. You must know both of them as they are named in the specification.

It is very important when discussing these that you do focus on depression rather than giving a more general description of the cognitive approach.

Check it

1. Outline Ellis's ABC model as an explanation for depression. *[4 marks]*
2. Explain **one** limitation of Beck's negative triad as an explanation for depression. *[4 marks]*
3. Describe **and** evaluate the cognitive approach to explaining depression. *[12 marks AS, 16 marks AL]*

The cognitive approach to treating depression

The specification says...

The cognitive approach to treating depression: cognitive behaviour therapy (CBT), including challenging irrational thoughts.

The cognitive approach offers explanations for depression which can then be applied to the treatment of depression. In particular we are interested in cognitive behaviour therapy (CBT), the standard psychological treatment for depression. You are also required specifically to know about the role of challenging irrational thoughts in CBT.

Key terms

Cognitive behaviour therapy (CBT) A method for treating mental disorders based on both cognitive and behavioural techniques. From the cognitive viewpoint the therapy aims to deal with thinking, such as challenging negative thoughts. The therapy also includes behavioural techniques such as behavioural activation.

Irrational thoughts Also called dysfunctional thoughts. In Ellis's model and therapy, these are defined as thoughts that are likely to interfere with a person's happiness. Such dysfunctional thoughts lead to mental disorders such as depression.

CBT begins with a collaborative assessment.

Cognitive behaviour therapy

Cognitive behaviour therapy (CBT) is the most commonly used psychological treatment for **depression** and a range of other mental health issues. It is an example of the cognitive approach to treatment, though it also includes behavioural elements.

Cognitive element CBT begins with an assessment in which the client and the cognitive behaviour therapist work together to clarify the client's problems. They jointly identify goals for the therapy and put together a plan to achieve them. One of the central tasks is to identify where there might be negative or **irrational thoughts** that will benefit from challenge.

Behaviour element CBT then involves working to change negative and irrational thoughts and finally put more effective behaviours into place.

Beck's cognitive therapy

Cognitive therapy is the application of Beck's cognitive theory of depression (see previous spread). The idea behind cognitive therapy is to identify automatic thoughts about the world, the self and the future – this is the **negative triad**. Once identified these thoughts must be challenged. This is the central component of the therapy.

As well as challenging these thoughts directly, cognitive therapy aims to help clients test the reality of their negative beliefs. They might therefore be set homework, such as to record when they enjoyed an event or when people were nice to them. This is sometimes referred to as the 'client as scientist', investigating the reality of their negative beliefs in the way a scientist would. In future sessions if clients say that no one is nice to them or there is no point in going to events, the therapist can then produce this evidence and use it to prove the client's statements are incorrect.

Ellis's rational emotive behaviour therapy

Rational emotive behaviour therapy (REBT) extends the **ABC model** (see previous spread) to an **ABCDE model** – **D** stands for dispute and **E** for effect. The central technique of REBT is to identify and dispute (challenge) irrational thoughts.

For example, a client might talk about how unlucky they have been or how unfair things seem. An REBT therapist would identify these as examples of *utopianism* and challenge this as an irrational belief. This would involve a vigorous argument. The intended effect is to change the irrational belief and so break the link between negative life events and depression.

This vigorous argument is the hallmark of REBT. Ellis identified different methods of disputing. For example, *empirical argument* involves disputing whether there is actual evidence to support the negative belief. *Logical argument* involves disputing whether the negative thought logically follows from the facts.

Behavioural activation

As individuals become depressed, they tend to increasingly avoid difficult situations and become isolated, which maintains or worsens symptoms.

The goal of **behavioural activation** is to work with depressed individuals to gradually decrease their avoidance and isolation, and increase their engagement in activities that have been shown to improve mood, e.g. exercising, going out to dinner, etc. The therapist aims to reinforce such activity.

Apply it Methods — Clinical trial of CBT

The table below right shows the outcomes for a trial of CBT versus the older form of just behaviour therapy without cognitive techniques. A higher score indicates greater depression.

Questions

1. Calculate how much improvement each client showed. Put the data from your calculations in a table. (*2 marks*)
2. On a **scattergram** plot the improvement for each client against the number of CBT sessions they received. (*4 marks*)
3. What would you conclude about the relationship between number of sessions and reduction in symptoms? (*2 marks*)

Condition	Client number	Number of sessions	Depression score before therapy	Depression score after therapy
CBT	1	12	18	6
	2	12	22	10
	3	7	16	8
	4	5	17	10
	5	5	18	12
Behaviour therapy	6	9	21	11
	7	9	16	7
	8	10	18	9
	9	6	18	11
	10	11	17	7

:valuation

:vidence for effectiveness

ne strength of CBT is the large body of evidence supporting its effectiveness for eating depression.

Many studies show that CBT works. For example, John March *et al.* (2007) ompared CBT to **antidepressant drugs** and also to a combination of both eatments when treating 327 depressed adolescents. After 36 weeks, 81% f the CBT group, 81% of the antidepressants group and 86% of the CBT plus ntidepressants group were significantly improved. So CBT was just as effective vhen used on its own and more so when used alongside antidepressants. CBT is sually a fairly brief therapy requiring six to 12 sessions so it is also cost-effective.

This means that CBT is widely seen as the first choice of treatment in public ealth care systems such as the National Health Service.

uitability for diverse clients

ne limitation of CBT for depression is the lack of effectiveness for severe cases and or clients with learning disabilities.

In some cases depression can be so severe that clients cannot motivate themselves) engage with the cognitive work of CBT. They may not even be able to pay attention) what is happening in a session. It also seems likely that the complex rational ninking involved in CBT makes it unsuitable for treating depression in clients with earning disabilities. Peter Sturmey (2005) suggests that, in general, any form of sychotherapy (i.e. any 'talking' therapy) is not suitable for people with learning isabilities, and this includes CBT.

This suggests that CBT may only be appropriate for a specific range of people vith depression.

Counterpoint Although the conventional wisdom has been that CBT is unsuitable for very depressed people and for clients with learning disabilities, there is now some more recent evidence that challenges this. A review by Gemma Lewis and Glyn Lewis (2016) concluded that CBT was as effective as antidepressant drugs and behavioural therapies for severe depression. Another review by John Taylor *et al.* (2008) concluded that, when used appropriately, CBT is effective for people with learning disabilities.

This means that CBT may be suitable for a wider range of people than was once thought.

Relapse rates

further limitation of CBT for the treatment of depression is its high relapse rates.

Although CBT is quite effective in tackling the symptoms of depression, there are ome concerns over how long the benefits last. Relatively few early studies of CBT or depression looked at long-term effectiveness. Some more recent studies suggest nat long-term outcomes are not as good as had been assumed. For example in one tudy, Shehzad Ali *et al.* (2017) assessed depression in 439 clients every month for 2 months following a course of CBT. 42% of the clients relapsed into depression vithin six months of ending treatment and 53% relapsed within a year.

This means that CBT may need to be repeated periodically.

:valuation eXtra

:lient preference

BT for depression focuses on identifying and changing unhelpful patterns of ninking and behaviour. There is a large body of evidence to show that, when sed with appropriate clients, this is highly effective, at least in the short term, in ackling symptoms of depression.

However, not all clients want to tackle their depression this way. Some people ıst want their symptoms gone as quickly and easily as possible and prefer nedication. Others, for example survivors of trauma, wish to explore the origins of neir symptoms. In a study of client preference, Antoine Yrondi *et al.* (2015) found nat depressed people rated CBT as their least preferred psychological therapy.

onsider: *Does it matter what depressed people want from a sychological therapy if it is effective?*

Some clients are too distressed to engage with CBT.

Apply it Concepts — Treating Yasmin

You have read about Yasmin's experience of redundancy on the previous spread and her resulting depression. We are now going to look at Ellis's ideas about challenging irrational beliefs to show how a cognitive behaviour therapist might be able to help Yasmin.

Questions

1. Yasmin experiences irrational thoughts. Explain how these are irrational.
2. How might you go about challenging these thoughts if you were a cognitive behaviour therapist?

Apply it Concepts — Trina

Depression is a common but very debilitating condition. The 'first line' treatment in the National Health Service is CBT.

Trina has been diagnosed with depression. Her symptoms include sadness and lethargy – she struggles to get out of bed each morning – and she is disturbed by automatic thoughts that she is a failure and her future is going to be unhappy.

Questions

1. How might a cognitive behaviour therapist tackle Trina's depression?
2. Trina asks her therapist how useful CBT is. What might the therapist tell her?

Check it

1. Outline cognitive behaviour therapy as a treatment for depression. *[4 marks]*
2. Explain **one** strength of cognitive behaviour therapy as a treatment for depression. *[4 marks]*
3. Outline how a therapist may encourage a client to challenge irrational thoughts when treating depression. *[4 marks]*
4. Discuss the cognitive approach to treating depression. *[12 marks AS, 16 marks AL]*

The biological approach to explaining OCD

The specification says...

The biological approach to explaining OCD: genetic and neural explanations.

We now turn to the third mental disorder in the specification, OCD, and consider explanations for it. In particular we are interested in how an individual's vulnerability to OCD may be affected by their genetic make-up and how the brain functioning of someone with OCD may differ from that of someone without the condition.

Key terms

Biological approach A perspective that emphasises the importance of physical processes in the body such as genetic inheritance and neural function.

Genetic explanations Genes make up chromosomes and consist of DNA which codes the physical features of an organism (such as eye colour, height) and psychological features (such as mental disorder, intelligence). Genes are transmitted from parents to offspring, i.e. inherited.

Neural explanations The view that physical and psychological characteristics are determined by the behaviour of the nervous system, in particular the brain as well as individual neurons.

Apply it Concepts — Jack

OCD is widely believed to be a biological condition with its roots in genetic vulnerability and brain dysfunction.

Jack has OCD. His grandfather and uncle also had OCD, to the extent that his uncle had brain surgery to relieve his symptoms. As a psychology student Jack is curious about what might have caused his condition.

Questions

1. How likely is it that a genetic vulnerability has caused Jack's OCD?
2. How might Jack's symptoms be linked to activity in his brain?

Underview of the brain showing regions implicated in OCD.

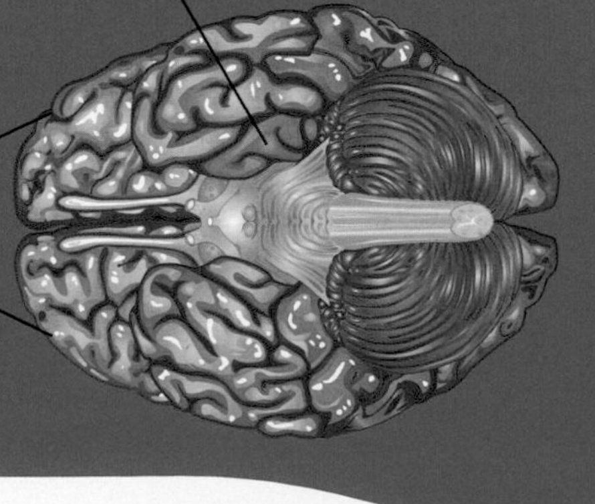
Parahippocampal gyrus
Lateral frontal lobes

Genetic explanations

Some mental disorders appear to have a stronger biological component than others, and **OCD** is a good example of a condition that may be largely understood as biological in nature. One form of biological explanation is the **genetic explanation**.

Genes are involved in individual vulnerability to OCD. In a classic study, Aubrey Lewis (1936) observed that of his OCD patients, 37% had parents with OCD and 21% had siblings with OCD. This suggests that OCD runs in families, although what is probably passed on from one generation to the next is genetic *vulnerability* not the certainty of OCD. According to the **diathesis-stress model** certain genes leave some people more *likely* to develop a mental disorder but it is not certain. Some environmental stress (experience) is necessary to trigger the condition.

Candidate genes

Researchers have identified genes, which create vulnerability for OCD, called *candidate genes*. Some of these genes are involved in regulating the development of the **serotonin** system. For example, the gene 5HT1-D beta is implicated in the transport of serotonin across **synapses**.

OCD is polygenic

However, like many conditions, OCD seems to be **polygenic**. This means that OCD is not caused by one single gene but by a combination of genetic variations that together significantly increase vulnerability.

Steven Taylor (2013) has analysed findings of previous studies and found evidence that up to 230 different genes may be involved in OCD. Genes that have been studied in relation to OCD include those associated with the action of **dopamine** as well as serotonin, both **neurotransmitters** believed to have a role in regulating mood.

Different types of OCD

One group of genes may cause OCD in one person but a different group of genes may cause the disorder in another person. The term used to describe this is *aetiologically heterogeneous*, meaning that the origins (aetiology) of OCD vary from one person to another (heterogeneous).

There is also some evidence to suggest that different types of OCD may be the result of particular genetic variations, such as hoarding disorder and religious obsession.

Neural explanations

The genes associated with OCD are likely to affect the levels of key neurotransmitters as well as structures of the brain. These are **neural explanations**.

The role of serotonin

One explanation for OCD concerns the role of the neurotransmitter serotonin, which is believed to help regulate mood. Neurotransmitters are responsible for relaying information from one **neuron** to another. If a person has low levels of serotonin then normal transmission of mood-relevant information does not take place and a person may experience low moods (and other mental processes may also be affected). At least some cases of OCD may be explained by a reduction in the functioning of the serotonin system in the brain.

Decision-making systems

Some cases of OCD, and in particular hoarding disorder, seem to be associated with impaired decision-making. This in turn may be associated with abnormal functioning of the lateral (side bits) of the **frontal lobes** of the brain. The frontal lobes are the front part of the brain (behind your forehead) that are responsible for logical thinking and making decisions.

There is also evidence to suggest that an area called the left **parahippocampal gyrus** (see diagram on left), associated with processing unpleasant emotions, functions abnormally in OCD.

All the main approaches in psychology are discussed in Chapter 4. The biological approach is on pages 114–119. Psychology grew out of biology, and the study of mental disorder developed largely within the medical profession, so it is no surprise that there are important biological approaches to explaining mental health issues.

:valuation

Research support

)ne strength of the genetic explanation for OCD is the strong evidence base.

There is evidence from a variety of sources which strongly suggests that some people are vulnerable
o OCD as a result of their genetic make-up. One source of evidence is twin studies. In one study Gerald
Jestadt *et al.* (2010) reviewed twin studies and found that 68% of identical twins (MZ) shared OCD as
pposed to 31% of non-identical (DZ) twins. Another source of evidence for a genetic influence on OCD
s family studies. Research has found that a person with a family member diagnosed with OCD is around
our times as likely to develop it as someone without (Marini and Stebnicki 2012).

These research studies suggest that there must be some genetic influence on the development of OCD.

:nvironmental risk factors

)ne limitation of the genetic model of OCD is that there are also environmental risk factors.

There is strong evidence for the idea that genetic variation can make a person more or less vulnerable
o OCD. However, OCD does not appear to be entirely genetic in origin and it seems that environmental
isk factors can also trigger or increase the risk of developing OCD. In one study for example, Kiara Cromer
t al. (2007) found that over half the OCD clients in their sample had experienced a traumatic event in
heir past. OCD was also more severe in those with one or more traumas.

This means that genetic vulnerability only provides a partial explanation for OCD.

:valuation eXtra

Animal studies

t has proved difficult to find candidate genes i.e. genetic variations that are possible causes of OCD. There
s evidence though from animal studies showing that particular genes are associated with repetitive
ehaviours in other species, for example mice (Ahmari 2016).

However, although mice and humans share most genes, the human mind and brain are much more
omplex, and it may not be possible to generalise from animal repetitive behaviour to human OCD.

:onsider: *To what extent do animal studies tell us anything about the genetic basis of OCD?*

:valuation

Research support

)ne strength of the neural model of OCD is the existence of some supporting evidence.

Antidepressants that work purely on serotonin are effective in reducing OCD symptoms (see next
pread for evidence) and this suggests that serotonin may be involved in OCD. Also, OCD symptoms
orm part of conditions that are known to be biological in origin, such as the degenerative brain disorder
'arkinson's disease, which causes muscle tremors and paralysis (Nestadt *et al.* 2010). If a biological
lisorder produces OCD symptoms, then we may assume the biological processes underlie OCD.

This suggests that biological factors (e.g. serotonin and the processes underlying certain disorders)
nay also be responsible for OCD.

No unique neural system

)ne limitation of the neural model is that the serotonin–OCD link may not be unique to OCD.

Many people with OCD also experience **clinical** depression. Having two disorders together is called
o-morbidity. This depression probably involves (though is not necessarily caused by) disruption to the
ction of serotonin. This leaves us with a logical problem when it comes to serotonin as a possible basis
or OCD. It could simply be that serotonin activity is disrupted in many people with OCD because they are
lepressed as well.

This means that serotonin may not be relevant to OCD symptoms.

:valuation eXtra

:orrelation and causality

'here is evidence to show that some neural systems (such as serotonin) do not work normally
n people with OCD. According to the biological model of mental disorder this is most easily
xplained by brain dysfunction *causing* the OCD.

However, this is simply a correlation between neural abnormality and OCD, and such correlations
lo not necessarily indicate a causal relationship. It is quite possible that the OCD (or its accompanying
lepression) causes the abnormal brain function or both are influenced by a third factor.

:onsider: *In the absence of causal data (hard to produce), are correlations enough?*

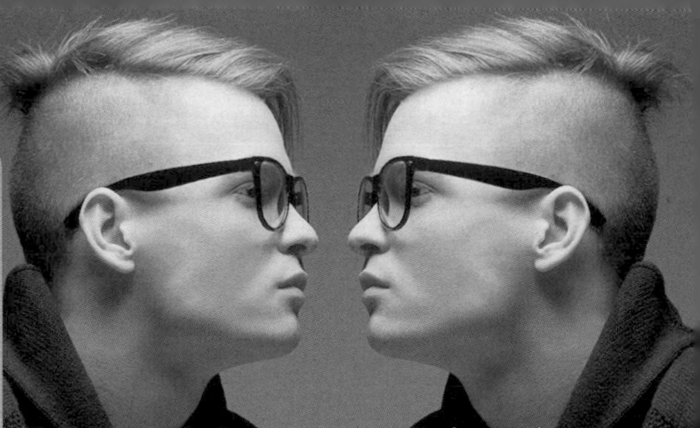

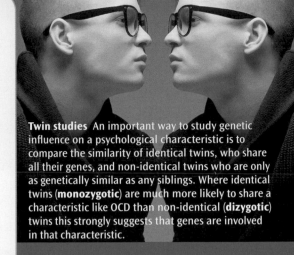

Twin studies An important way to study genetic influence on a psychological characteristic is to compare the similarity of identical twins, who share all their genes, and non-identical twins who are only as genetically similar as any siblings. Where identical twins (**monozygotic**) are much more likely to share a characteristic like OCD than non-identical (**dizygotic**) twins this strongly suggests that genes are involved in that characteristic.

Apply it Methods — Family studies

Lewis (see facing page) assessed 50 people with OCD at the Maudsley Hospital in London, looking for co-occurrence of OCD in the immediate family. He found that 37% of people with OCD had parents with OCD and 21% had siblings with OCD. This suggests there may be a genetic basis to OCD.

Questions

1. Explain why this study might be considered to be a **quasi-experiment**. (*2 marks*)
2. You plan to carry out a similar study on individuals with OCD and their siblings. You have access to a list of all people with OCD in your nearest city. Describe how you would obtain a **random sample** of participants. (*3 marks*)
3. Describe how you would obtain a **stratified sample**. (Strata might include gender, age and socio-economic status.) (*3 marks*)

Study tip

There is quite an overlap in the explanations about the role of genetic and neural factors in the development of OCD. However, you need to be clear what is a neural explanation and what is a genetic explanation because both terms are identified in the specification.

Check it

1. Outline genetic explanations of OCD. *[6 marks]*
2. Evaluate the evidence for a genetic basis to OCD. *[4 marks]*
3. Outline the neural basis of OCD. *[4 marks]*
4. Explain **one** limitation of neural explanations for OCD. *[2 marks]*
5. Outline **and** evaluate the biological approach to explaining OCD. *[12 marks AS, 16 marks AL]*

The biological approach to treating OCD

The specification says...

The biological approach to treating OCD: drug therapy.

The biological explanations of OCD imply that biological treatments may be successful, most obviously through the use of drug treatments that target abnormal neurotransmitter levels.

Key term

Drug therapy Treatment involving drugs, i.e. chemicals that have a particular effect on the functioning of the brain or some other body system. In the case of psychological disorders such drugs usually affect neurotransmitter levels.

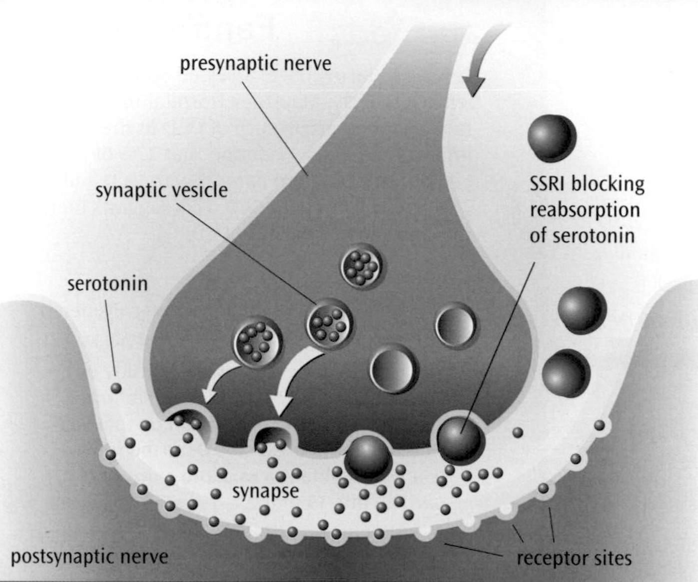
presynaptic nerve
synaptic vesicle
SSRI blocking reabsorption of serotonin
serotonin
synapse
postsynaptic nerve
receptor sites

Drug therapy

Drug therapy for mental disorders aims to increase or decrease levels of **neurotransmitters** in the brain or to increase/decrease their activity. On the previous spread we saw that low levels of **serotonin** are associated with OCD. Therefore drugs to treat OCD work in various ways to increase the level of serotonin in the brain.

SSRIs

The standard medical treatment used to tackle the symptoms of OCD involves a particular type of **antidepressant** drug called a **selective serotonin reuptake inhibitor** (or **SSRI** for short). SSRIs work on the serotonin system in the brain. Serotonin is released by certain **neurons** in the brain. In particular it is released by the **presynaptic neurons** and travels across a **synapse** (see diagram on the left). The neurotransmitter chemically conveys the signal from the presynaptic neuron to the **postsynaptic neuron** and then it is reabsorbed by the presynaptic neuron where it is broken down and reused.

By preventing the reabsorption and breakdown, SSRIs effectively increase levels of serotonin in the synapse and thus continue to stimulate the postsynaptic neuron. This compensates for whatever is wrong with the serotonin system in OCD.

Dosage and other advice vary according to which SSRI is prescribed. A typical daily dose of *fluoxetine* (e.g. brand name Prozac) is 20 mg although this may be increased if it is not benefitting the person. The drug is available as capsules or liquid. It takes three to four months of daily use for SSRIs to have much impact on symptoms.

Combining SSRIs with other treatments

Drugs are often used alongside **cognitive behaviour therapy** (CBT) to treat OCD. The drugs reduce a person's emotional symptoms, such as feeling anxious or depressed. This means that people with OCD can engage more effectively with the CBT.

In practice some people respond best to CBT alone whilst others benefit more when additionally using drugs like *fluoxetine*. Occasionally other drugs are prescribed alongside SSRIs.

Alternatives to SSRIs

Where an SSRI is not effective after three to four months the dose can be increased (e.g. up to 60 mg a day for *fluoxetine*) or it can be combined with other drugs. Sometimes different antidepressants are tried. People respond very differently to different drugs and alternatives work well for some people and not at all for others.

- **Tricyclics** (an older type of antidepressant) are sometimes used, such as *clomipramine*. This acts on various systems including the serotonin system where it has the same effect as SSRIs. *Clomipramine* has more severe side-effects than SSRIs so it is generally kept in reserve for people who do not respond to SSRIs.
- **SNRIs** (serotonin-noradrenaline reuptake inhibitors) have more recently been used to treat OCD. These are a different class of antidepressant drugs and, like *clomipramine*, are a second line of defence for people who don't respond to SSRIs. SNRIs increase levels of serotonin as well as another different neurotransmitter – **noradrenaline**.

Apply it Methods — Symptom severity

The table below shows the symptom severity in people with OCD being treated with SSRIs or a placebo. The scale goes up to 10.

SSRIs	3 6 4 3 6 4 3 1 2 5 4 5 3 5 5
Placebo	6 7 5 8 5 9 5 7 6 7 8 7 8 8 9

Questions

1. Is this data **quantitative** or **qualitative**? Explain your answer. (*2 marks*)
2. Suggest an example of the sort of data that might be gathered to go alongside the data above. (*2 marks*)
3. Suggest a research method that could be used to gather this kind of data. (*2 marks*)
4. Placebos act as a **control condition**. Explain why a control condition is needed in this kind of research. (*3 marks*)

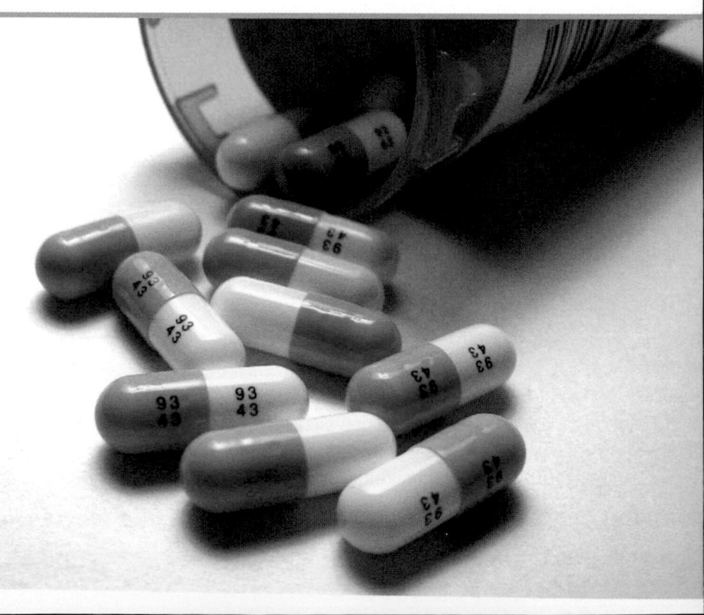

Evaluation

Evidence of effectiveness

One strength of drug treatment for OCD is good evidence for its effectiveness.

There is clear evidence to show that SSRIs reduce symptom severity and improve the quality of life for people with OCD. For example, G. Mustafa Soomro *et al.* (2009) reviewed 17 studies that compared SSRIs to **placebos** in the treatment of OCD. All 17 studies showed significantly better outcomes for SSRIs than for the placebo conditions. Typically symptoms reduce for around 70% of people taking SSRIs. For the remaining 30%, most can be helped by either alternative drugs or combinations of drugs and psychological therapies.

This means that drugs appear to be helpful for most people with OCD.

Counterpoint There is some evidence to suggest that even if drug treatments are helpful for most people with OCD they may not be the most effective treatments available. Petros Skapinakis *et al.* (2016) carried out a systematic review of outcome studies and concluded that both cognitive and behavioural (exposure) therapies were more effective than SSRIs in the treatment of OCD.

This means that drugs may not be the optimum treatment for OCD.

Cost-effective and non-disruptive

One further strength of drugs is that they are cost-effective and non-disruptive to people's lives.

A strength of drug treatments for psychological disorders in general is that they are cheap compared to psychological treatments because many thousands of tablets or liquid doses can be manufactured in the time it takes to conduct one session of a psychological therapy. Using drugs to treat OCD is therefore good value for public health systems like the NHS and represents a good use of limited funds. As compared to psychological therapies, SSRIs are also non-disruptive to people's lives. If you wish you can simply take drugs until your symptoms decline. This is quite different from psychological therapy which involves time spent attending therapy sessions.

This means that drugs are popular with many people with OCD and their doctors.

Serious side-effects

One limitation of drug treatments for OCD is that drugs can have potentially serious side-effects.

Although drugs such as SSRIs help most people, a small minority will get no benefit. Some people also experience side-effects such as indigestion, blurred vision and loss of sex drive. These side-effects are usually temporary, however they can be quite distressing for people and for a minority they are long-lasting. For those taking the tricyclic *clomipramine*, side-effects are more common and can be more serious. For example more than 1 in 10 people experience erection problems and weight gain, 1 in 100 become aggressive and experience heart-related problems.

This means that some people have a reduced quality of life as a result of taking drugs and may stop taking them altogether, meaning the drugs cease to be effective.

Evaluation eXtra

Biased evidence

There is always some controversy over the evidence for the effectiveness of drugs. Some psychologists believe that the evidence for drug effectiveness is biased because researchers are sponsored by drug companies and may selectively publish positive outcomes for the drugs their sponsors are selling (Goldacre 2013).

On the other hand, there is a lack of independent studies of drug effectiveness and also research on psychological therapies may be biased. The best evidence *available* is supportive of the usefulness of drugs for OCD.

Consider: *Should we trust the evidence for the effectiveness of drugs?*

Study tip

This is one of the most technically complex parts of the specification because there are a lot of long and unfamiliar words to get your head around. Use the initials like SSRIs and SNRIs to make it simpler. Don't get bogged down in detail or anxious that you can't imagine serotonin crossing a synapse! That's normal.

Drug therapies are relatively cheap compared with the cost of psychological therapy. They are also easy – people don't have to make much effort, they just have to remember to take the drugs.

Apply it Methods — Olanzapine

SSRIs significantly reduce symptoms in around 70% of patients (Sansone and Sansone 2011). This means that alternative treatments are needed for the remaining 30%.

Filippo Bogetto *et al.* (2000) trialled a drug called *olanzapine* with 23 people with OCD who had not responded to SSRIs. Ten of these people responded to *olanzapine*. The mean symptom rating improved from 26.8 to 18.9 on the Yale Brown Obsessive Compulsion Scale.

Questions

1. State the **aim** of the study. (*2 marks*)
2. Write a **non-directional hypothesis** for this study. (*2 marks*)
3. Briefly explain *one* **ethical issue** the researchers should take into account when carrying out the study, *and* explain how they could deal with this. (*2 marks + 2 marks*)

Apply it Concepts — Akash

SSRIs are the first-line treatment for OCD. They may be taken alone or with a psychological therapy. It may be possible in some cases to just have the psychological therapy.

Akash is a busy entrepreneur with a young family. He has a recent diagnosis of OCD and his doctor prescribes drug treatment – *fluoxetine*. Akash has always been healthy and never thought much about taking drugs for a psychological disorder. He enquires about the possibility of having a psychological treatment instead.

Questions

1. Given Akash's lifestyle can you see any reasons why *fluoxetine* might suit him better than psychological treatment?
2. How else might Akash's doctor advise him to relieve his symptoms of OCD?

Check it

1. Outline the use of drug therapy to treat OCD. *[4 marks]*
2. Explain **one** limitation **and one** strength of using drug therapies to treat OCD. *[6 marks]*
3. Describe **and** evaluate the biological approach to the treatment of OCD. *[12 marks AS, 16 marks AL]*

Practical corner

The specification says...

Knowledge and understanding of ... research methods, practical research skills and maths skills. These should be developed through ... ethical practical research activities.

This means that you should conduct practical investigations wherever possible. Because you cannot carry out research on participants with mental health problems you are limited here to research using a non-clinical population (a quasi-experiment looking at gender differences) or making observations of existing data.

Ethics check

Ethics are discussed in detail on pages 178–179. We strongly suggest that you complete this checklist before collecting data.

1. Do participants know participation is voluntary?
2. Do participants know what to expect?
3. Do participants know they can withdraw at any time?
4. Are individuals' results anonymous?
5. Have I minimised the risk of distress to participants?
6. Have I avoided asking sensitive questions?
7. Will I avoid bringing my school/teacher/psychology into disrepute?
8. Have I considered all other ethical issues?
9. Has my teacher approved this?

Remember not to frighten or upset your participants!

Table 1 People who have an irrational fear.

Gender	Men (*N* = 10)	Women (*N* = 10)
Irrational fear	4	7

Table 2 Severity of fear.

Severity of fear (measured on a scale of 1–5 where 5 = greatest fear)	
Men	**Women**
2	4
4	5
3	5
2	4
2	4
2	3
1	4
1	4
4	5
2	5

Practical idea 1: Gender differences in fears

The **aim** of this study is to explore whether there are gender differences in the extent to which people experience fears. More specifically we are interested in whether men or women are more likely to have an irrational fear, and whether they tend to be afraid of different things.

This is a **quasi-experiment** because gender is the **independent variable**. A **questionnaire** is used to collect data.

The practical bit

There are various ways you could investigate gender differences in irrational fears. For practical and **ethical** reasons we recommend that you do this by self-report. You will need to construct a questionnaire and use it to collect data from men and women about their fears.

Designing your questionnaire

On page 188 we explain key decisions to be made when designing a questionnaire.

For this particular questionnaire the most basic thing you want to know about is how many men and how many women have irrational fears. This can be discovered using a simple yes/no question. Don't forget to have some way of recording whether each participant is a man or a woman.

You will also want to ask about what fears they may have. You need to decide whether to have a tick-list with a selection of fears (**closed question**) or just ask people what fears they have (**open question**). The former will make it easier to analyse results but you may miss unusual fears. You may decide you would also like to collect information about severity of fears. If so you need a way to record this, such as using a 1–5 **rating scale**.

Ethical issues

This study should be ethically acceptable as long as it is conducted well, but there are some issues to be aware of. You are asking people to disclose what may be fairly personal information so be particularly aware of **confidentiality**. You are also discussing an unpleasant emotional experience so it is critical that participants are fully aware that participation is voluntary, that they know exactly what will take place in the study and that they are aware that they have the right to pull out at any time. Most importantly, your survey should just involve people with *sub-clinical* fears, i.e. not people with a **clinical** phobia. You are not allowed to work with people with mental health issues as you may cause real distress. Make sure that you check this with each participant.

Choosing your sample

You will need to consider a suitable **sampling method** for this study (see page 176 for a detailed discussion of sampling). As always there is a trade-off between sampling techniques that allow you to get a large number of participants quickly and those that allow you to obtain participants who are more representative of their **population**. You also need to think about what is an appropriate sample size for this study.

Analysing your data

You will need to present your results in the form of tables and graphs. You will want to be able to show your results so that someone will instantly be able to see whether there are indeed gender differences in fears and what the differences are. Think of how you might display your results in a bar chart – for example, average scores for men and women, or you might show average scores for men and women for different kinds of fear (snakes, heights etc).

Apply it Methods — The maths bit 1

1. In Table 1, *N* = 10. What does this mean? (*1 mark*)
2. What percentages of men and women reported an irrational fear? (*1 mark*)
3. What conclusion would you reach based on the information in Table 1? (*2 marks*)
4. Using the data in Table 2, calculate the **median** severity scores for men and women and present them in a suitable table. (*2 marks*)
5. Identify the **range** of scores for men and women. (*1 mark*)
6. What do these ranges tell us about the fears of the two groups of participants? (*2 marks*)

ʼractical idea 2: ɅIental health in the media

revious studies have found that press coverage of mental health issues was poor. News reports ended to focus on violent incidents or use inappropriate language like 'nutcase' or 'bonkers' to escribe people with a mental health issue. However, there is much better awareness of mental ealth now so it may be that this is much less of a problem than in the past.

The aim of this study is to investigate the language used in press coverage of mental health sing a method of indirect **observation**.

Negative coverage of mental health issues in the media is distressing for people with a mental health issue and their families.

ʼhe practical bit

his study is a kind of observational study. It is a bit different from other kinds of observation in ıat you are not watching live participants. Instead you are studying people indirectly through ıe records they produce (called a **content analysis**). This can be a book, magazine, newspaper, vebsite or film.

ʼhoosing your media

his is very much up to you. You may have a stack of newspapers and magazines in your chool library to work from. Alternatively, many publications keep a free archive that you an access online (see suggestions on right). Past studies have either focused on analysing a articular type of publication over time or instead tried to obtain a snapshot of coverage across range of media. We recommend that you choose a particular publication (or compare two) nd aim to gather a good range of data from it.

ʼour tally chart

efore you start sampling your media for information, you need a good idea of exactly what ou are looking for. There are a number of options here. You could categorise each mention of ıental health according to the overall thrust of the article. Some articles might, for example, be bout the financial pressures on mental health services, others about particular conditions or eatments, others on celebrity mental health issues and yet others about the dangers posed by eople with mental health issues. In essence you are identifying **behavioural categories**.

Another approach is to identify key words such as 'nutcase'. You may well find for example, ıat this kind of derogatory language is used more frequently in tabloid newspapers than in ıe broadsheets. You will need a tally system to count up how many articles contain your argets. You can see an example below.

ʼampling your information

ʼnce you know exactly what you are looking for, you need to sample your media. If you are vorking with hard copies of newspapers or magazines you will need to choose a set of editions nd scan each selected one. If you are searching an online archive then you have two options. ither call up each edition in turn and scan it as you would a hard copy or use the search tool nd input your search terms (e.g. 'mental health') and analyse by the hits you obtain from this.

ʼnalysing your data

ou will need to present your results in the form of tables and graphs. You will want to show our results so that someone will instantly be able to see what sort of coverage the media you ooked at give to mental health. You will collect data in the form of frequencies. These can be resented as tables of percentages or bar charts.

Examples of searchable media archives

Name	Publication type	Web address
BBC News	General News Organisation	www.bbc.co.uk/news
The Daily Mail	Newspaper	www.dailymail.co.uk
The Huff Post	Online newspaper	www.huffpost.com
The Guardian	Newspaper	www.theguardian.com

Getting the best from online searches

When searching online databases for articles you need to think carefully about search terms and in particular about how you combine them. In a study of mental health think about the range of terms a publication might use, e.g. 'mental illness' or 'madness'.

For best results put your search terms in double quotes and capitalise the link word OR.

For example, you might search for:

"mental health" OR "mental illness" OR "madness".

The maths bit

On page 217 we have given a list of the mathematical skills you will be expected to demonstrate.

Overall, at least 10% of the marks in assessments for Psychology will require the use of mathematical skills.

ʼpply it ʼethods

The maths bit 2

. Construct a **bar chart** from the data in the table below. (*3 marks*)

Theme	Danger to the public	Crimes involving mental health	Celebrity with mental health issue	Underfunded services
The Daily Sleaze	10	15	45	1
The Bleeding Heart Liberal	0	5	3	36

2. Outline the conclusions you might draw from this bar chart. (*2 marks*)
3. Is the data in the table **quantitative** or **qualitative**? (*1 mark*)
4. Explain *one* strength and *one* limitation of using this kind of data. (*2 marks + 2 marks*)
5. Given that this is an observational study, suggest what **sampling method** could be used to collect data in this study. Explain your answers. (*2 marks*)

Revision summaries

Definitions of abnormality

How do we decide when someone needs treatment for a mental disorder?

Statistical infrequency

Definition
Numerically unusual behaviour or characteristic.

Example: intellectual disability disorder
IQ below 70 (bottom 2%) is part of the diagnosis of IDD.

Evaluation

Real-world application
Useful in diagnosis (e.g. IDD) and assessment (e.g. BDI for depression).

Unusual characteristics can be positive
Some unusual characteristics would not be judged abnormal e.g. high IQ.

Evaluation extra: Benefits versus problems
Some people with low IQ function adequately and don't benefit from being labelled (social stigma).

Deviation from social norms

Definition
Social judgements about what is acceptable.

Norms are culture-specific
What is thought normal in one culture may not be in another (e.g. homosexuality).

Example: antisocial personality disorder
Impulsive, aggressive, irresponsible behaviour is not socially acceptable in many cultures.

Evaluation

Real-world application
Used to diagnose some disorders e.g. antisocial and schizotypal personality disorder.

Cultural and situational relativism
Different standards, therefore hard to make social judgements (e.g. hearing voices).

Evaluation extra: Human rights abuses
Social norm approach maintains control over minority groups, e.g. women (nymphomania) and slaves (drapetomania), but useful e.g. for antisocial personality disorder.

Failure to function adequately

Definition
Inability to cope with demands of everyday life.

When is someone failing?
Rosenhan and Seligman listed signs e.g. non-conformity to social rules, personal distress, severe distress or danger to self or others.

Example: intellectual disability disorder
Failing to function is part of the diagnosis of IDD as well as low IQ.

Evaluation

Represents a threshold for help
Provides a way to identify when someone needs professional help.

Discrimination and social control
May lead to people living non-standard lifestyles being judged as abnormal.

Evaluation extra: Failure to function may not be abnormal
Most of us experience such failure e.g. bereavement, but still may require help.

Deviation from ideal mental health

Definition
Jahoda considered normality rather than abnormality.

What does ideal mental health look like?
Includes lack of symptoms, rationality, self-actualisation, coping with stress, realistic world-view.

Evaluation

A comprehensive definition
Includes most of the reasons anyone might seek help.

May be culture-bound
Some ideas e.g. self-actualisation are specific to US/European cultures, and independence varies within European cultures (e.g. Germany versus Italy).

Evaluation extra: Extremely high standards
Few people ever meet them, but useful as a goal for mental health.

Phobias

An anxiety disorder.

Characteristics

Behavioural
Panic – scream or run away.
Avoidance – conscious effort to avoid.
Endurance – may stay and bear it.

Emotional
Anxiety – unpleasant state of high arousal, disproportionate to threat.
Fear – short-lasting, more intense.
Emotional response is unreasonable/ disproportionate to threat.

Cognitive
Selective attention – can't look away.
Irrational beliefs – unfounded beliefs.
Cognitive distortions – unrealistic.

Behavioural explanation

Two-process model
Two processes of conditioning (Mowrer).

Acquisition by classical conditioning
UCS linked to NS, then both produce UCR (fear), now called the CR.
E.g. Little Albert played with rat (NS), heard loud noise (UCS), then rat (now CS) produces fear response (now CR).

Maintenance by operant conditioning
Avoidance of phobic stimulus negatively reinforced by anxiety reduction, so the phobia is maintained.

Evaluation

Real-world application
Phobias successfully treated by preventing avoidance, as suggested by the model.

Cognitive aspects of phobias
Fails to account for cognitive aspects of phobias, e.g. irrational fears.

Phobias and traumatic experiences
73% of people with a dental phobia had past trauma, in control group with no phobia only 21% had trauma (De Jongh *et al.*)
Counterpoint – not all cases of phobias follow bad experiences and vice versa.

Evaluation extra: Learning and evolution
Two-process model explains individual phobias, but evolutionary approach explains general aspects of phobias.

Systematic desensitisation (SD)

Anxiety hierarchy
A list of situations ranked for how much anxiety they produce.

Relaxation
Reciprocal inhibition – relaxation and anxiety can't happen at the same time.
Relaxation includes imagery and/or breathing techniques.

Exposure
Exposed to phobic stimulus whilst relaxed at each level of the anxiety hierarchy.

Evaluation

Evidence of effectiveness
More effective than relaxation alone after 33 months (Gilroy *et al.*) and effective for a range of phobias (Wechsler *et al.*).

People with learning disabilities
SD best – cognitive therapy requires complex rational thought, flooding is traumatic.

Evaluation extra: SD in virtual reality
Avoids dangerous situations and cost-effective, but lacks realism (Wechsler *et al.*).

Flooding

What is it?
Exposes clients to a very frightening situation without a build-up.

How does it work?
Works by extinction of the conditioned fear response.

Ethical safeguards
Clients must give informed consent and be prepared for flooding.

Evaluation

Cost-effective
Clinically effective and not expensive, may take only 1–3 sessions.

Traumatic
Rated as more stressful than SD (Schumacher *et al.*), lack of informed consent and higher attrition rates.

Evaluation extra: Symptom substitution
Occurs if cause of phobia is not tackled e.g. women with death phobia (Persons), but only evidence is from case studies, may not generalise.

Depression

A mood disorder.

Characteristics

Behavioural
Activity levels – lethargy or agitation.
Disruption to sleep/eating – increased or decreased
Aggression and self-harm, and irritability.

Emotional
Lowered mood.
Anger towards self and others, leading to behavioural change.
Lowered self-esteem, self-loathing.

Cognitive
Poor concentration – difficulty making decisions.
Attending to and dwelling on the negative – half-empty glass instead of half-full.
Absolutist thinking – 'black-and-white'.

Beck's theory

Faulty information processing
Attending to the negative aspects of a situation.

Negative self-schema
Negative information about ourselves is accessed whenever we encounter a self-relevant situation.

The negative triad
Negative views of the world, the self and the future.

Evaluation

Research support
Research shows cognitive vulnerability precedes depression (Clark and Beck, Cohen *et al.* prospective study of adolescents).

Real-world application
Identify cognitive vulnerability to screen those at risk of depression, then target vulnerabilities in CBT.

Evaluation extra: A partial explanation
Explains patterns of cognition, but cannot easily explain extremes of anger or hallucinations and delusions.

Ellis's ABC model

A Activating event
A negative life event that triggers an irrational response e.g. failing a test.

B Beliefs
Beliefs that lead us to overreact to the activating event, e.g. that life must always be fair ('utopianism'), we must succeed ('musturbation').

C Consequences
Depression results when we overreact to negative life events.

Evaluation

Real-world application
Irrational thoughts can be identified and challenged by a therapist.

Reactive and endogenous depression
Only explains reactive depression, does not explain cases that do not follow an activating event (endogenous depression).

Evaluation extra: Ethical issues
ABC model places responsibility on the depressed person (victim blaming), but the therapy derived from the model (REBT) does create resilience.

Cognitive behaviour therapy

Beck's cognitive therapy
Aims to identify negative thoughts (negative triad) and challenge them (client as scientist).

Ellis's REBT
ABC + D (dispute) and E (effect). Aims to identify and challenge irrational beliefs e.g. by empirical argument.

Behavioural activation
Encouraging the depressed person to engage in enjoyable activities.

Evaluation

Evidence for effectiveness
CBT is as effective as antidepressants, most effective combined (81% vs 86%, March *et al.*).

Suitability for diverse clients
May not be suitable for severe cases of depression or for people with learning disabilities (e.g. Sturmey).
Counterpoint – newer evidence suggests CBT is as effective as drugs or behavioural therapies (Lewis and Lewis) and OK for learning disabilities (Taylor *et al.*).

Relapse rates
Benefits short-term, 42% relapsed after 6 months and 53% within a year (Ali *et al.*). May need regular repeating.

Evaluation extra: Client preference
CBT effective, at least short-term but some clients prefer to take medication or explore past.

OCD

An anxiety disorder.

Characteristics

Behavioural
Compulsions are repetitive.
Compulsions are performed to reduce anxiety.
Avoid situations that trigger anxiety.

Emotional
Anxiety and distress created by compulsions/obsessions.
Accompanying depression.
Guilt and disgust – directed at something such as dirt or oneself.

Cognitive
Obsessive thoughts, e.g. about germs.
Cognitive coping strategies, e.g. meditating.
Insight into excessive anxiety – may include catastrophic thoughts and hypervigilance.

Genetic

Candidate genes
Genes that may be involved in producing symptoms of OCD, e.g. 5HT1-D beta.

OCD is polygenic
Different combinations of up to 230 genetic variations (Taylor).

Different types of OCD
Different combinations of gene variations may cause different kinds of OCD.

Evaluation

Research support
68% MZ twins and 31% DZ twins have OCD (Nestadt *et al.*), OCD 4 times more likely if family member has it (Marini and Stebnicki).

Environmental risk factors
Over half OCD clients in one sample experienced a traumatic event, and OCD was more severe (Cromer *et al.*).

Evaluation extra: Animal studies
Candidate genes have been found in e.g. mice (Ahmari), but can we generalise from animal repetitive behaviour to human OCD?

Neural

The role of serotonin
Low levels of serotonin (lower mood) linked to OCD.

Decision-making systems
Frontal lobes and parahippocampal gyrus may be malfunctioning.

Evaluation

Research support
Antidepressants that work on the serotonin system alleviate OCD, biological conditions (e.g. Parkinson's) have similar symptoms to OCD (Nestadt *et al.*).

No unique neural system
The apparent serotonin–OCD link may just be co-morbidity with depression – the depression disrupts serotonin.

Evaluation extra: Correlation and causality
Dysfunction of neural systems may cause OCD but most evidence is correlational, so could be vice versa.

Drug therapy

SSRIs
Antidepressants that increase levels of serotonin at the synapse e.g. *fluoxetine*.

Combining SSRIs with other treatments
SSRIs plus CBT offers best effectiveness, plus maybe other drugs.

Alternatives to SSRIs
Tricyclics e.g. *clomipramine* (acts on serotonin plus other systems) or SNRIs (noradrenaline).

Evaluation

Evidence of effectiveness
17 studies all showed SSRIs more effective than placebos (Soomro *et al.*).
Counterpoint – psychological therapies alone (e.g. CBT) are likely to be more effective than drugs for OCD.

Cost-effective and non-disruptive
Relatively cheap for NHS and don't involve time spent going to therapy sessions.

Serious side-effects
SSRIs may lead to indigestion, blurred vision and loss of sex drive, worse for *clomipramine* (e.g. weight gain and aggressiveness).

Evaluation extra: Biased evidence
Drug researchers sponsored by drug companies, biased results (Goldacre), but still best available evidence and psychological therapies research may be biased too.

Practice questions, answers and feedback

Question 1 Beck's negative triad consists of three kinds of negative views. One of these negative views is about the self. Identify **one** of the other components of the negative triad and explain how this might lead to depression. (*2 marks*)

Morticia's answer *The world is another negative view. If people think it is always going to be negative then they give up trying and withdraw.*	**Morticia's answer fits the bill. Another point of the triad is identified and the elaboration meets the requirement set out in the question.**
Luke's answer *The triad is the self, the future and the world. Negative worldview makes you just generally feel negative, for example you think the world is a cruel place and this makes you lose hope.*	**Luke takes a slightly different approach and the elaboration this time is communicated via an example, but the overall effect is the same as Morticia's.**
Vladimir's answer *Feeling negative about other people makes you feel depressed because everything seems black and depressing.*	**Not so good for Vladimir. 'Other people' is too vague as is the elaboration.**

Question 2 What is obsessive-compulsive disorder (OCD)? (*3 marks*)

Morticia's answer *OCD has three components. The behavioural component is having compulsions which the person tries to avoid. The emotional component is accompanying anxiety and distress. The cognitive component is the obsessive thoughts that give rise to compulsions.*	**Morticia organises her answer around the three features identified in the specification (behavioural, emotional and cognitive components) but her answer is rather list-like. For example she just says the cognitive component is obsessions - but what are the obsessions?**
Luke's answer *OCD is an anxiety disorder where a person has obsessions and compulsions. Obsessions are recurring intrusive thoughts and compulsions are repetitive actions that the person feels they must complete in order to stop the obsessions.*	**This is a clear and accurate answer from Luke. Both elements of the disorder are outlined and there is additional detail in recognising that OCD is an anxiety disorder. Notice that he wrote less than the other two students but his is the best answer.**
Vladimir's answer *An obsessive-compulsive disorder is a recurring intrusive thought that produces anxiety. In order to reduce this and feel better many people with OCD feel compelled to do certain things. For example, they might wash their hands five times a day. This reduces their anxiety.*	**Vladimir defines the idea of an obsession (though it is not labelled as such). 'Compulsion' is not clearly defined and the example does not work very well – washing your hands five times a day doesn't really qualify as a compulsion! A weak answer.**

Question 3 Rashid has a phobia of balloons. She decides to overcome this phobia using systematic desensitisation. Her therapist teaches her how to relax. Explain another important part of preparing for her treatment. (*3 marks*)

Morticia's answer *Rashid needs to construct the hierarchy. This would go from low to high. At the high level it might be her exposure to the biggest thing she would be frightened of, such as a room with lots of balloons. At the lowest level would be something that creates just a little anxiety, such as a picture of a balloon on the other side of the room.*	**Morticia shows some understanding of an anxiety hierarchy, which is relevant, as is the application to Rashid's fear of balloons. There is engagement with the context beyond just using the word 'balloons' or 'Rashid' occasionally which is all that Vladimir has done. A reasonably good answer from Morticia.**
Luke's answer *Rashid would produce a hierarchy of her anxieties, starting from something that produces very little fear (just a photo of one balloon) up to something that would produce a lot of fear (a room with lots of balloons). Then Rashid starts at the bottom level and practises being relaxed with the photo. When she can do that she does the same for each level until she can cope with a lot of balloons.*	**Luke's answer is even better. It includes implicit reference to the 'stepped approach' in confronting the phobia and is well focused on the scenario. An ace response.**
Vladimir's answer *She produces an anxiety hierarchy working with the psychologist. This hierarchy contains items at the bottom which cause very little anxiety and gradually increases until there is an item which would create maximum anxiety. At each level Rashid practises feeling relaxed until she is finally cured. She also might have homework to do.*	**Vladimir gives some relevant detail of the process but there is no application to Rashid or her balloon fear – just including names doesn't really count as engaging with the stem of the question. The information on systematic desensitisation is relevant but that's it.**

Question 4 Briefly explain **one** limitation of using systematic sensitisation to treat phobias. (*3 marks*)

Morticia's answer *Systematic desensitisation is a reasonably effective method used to treat phobias such as balloon phobia. However, it isn't the most effective therapy as research has found that flooding is more effective but far more scary so clients may drop out. Therefore, overall, systematic desensitisation may be better to use because there is more likelihood of a positive end result.*	**Morticia's answer is somewhat muddled but there is sufficient detail for a 3-mark question. She gets side-tracked a little in the middle part of this answer but the comparison point is made clearly enough by the end.**
Luke's answer *An important limitation of this kind of treatment is that it is not really effective. In fact it results in symptom substitution which makes people worse not better.*	**This is a weak answer because the limitation offered lacks elaboration. Luke should have explained what symptom substitution is and why it is a particular problem for systematic desensitisation. His second sentence is wrong – symptom substitution does not necessarily make the client worse.**
Vladimir's answer *One limitation of systematic desensitisation is that it is based on behaviourism and behaviourism is based on animals. This means we are trying to apply the results from research on animals to human behaviour. Humans are different from animals so this is not really justified. It doesn't make sense to make such assumptions.*	**Vladimir's answer gets nothing because it is more a limitation of the behaviourist approach in general rather than applied to the therapy particularly. Also just saying 'quicker' or 'cheaper' without adequate explanation of why is not sufficient.**

n this spread we look at some typical student answers to questions. The comments provided indicate what is good and bad in each answer. earning how to produce effective question answers is a SKILL. Read pages 213–223 for guidance.

Question 5 Discuss two or more definitions of abnormality. (*12 marks AS, 16 marks AL*)

Morticia's answer *There are four main definitions of abnormality. The first is the statistical infrequency model, the second is deviation from social norms, the third is failure to function and the fourth is deviation from ideal mental health.*

According to the first, statistical infrequency model, people are judged to be abnormal because they do not statistically behave in the same way as others. Most people behave one way but a few people behave differently and therefore are judged abnormal. One problem with this definition is that some desirable traits can be judged as abnormal.

The second definition is also deviation, this time not statistical but from social norms. This means that a person might be judged as abnormal because they behave differently from the group. For example, the group might think that people should not murder other people so anyone who does this is judged as abnormal. A problem with this definition is that social norms change and therefore it isn't a fixed way to judge abnormality. It also is subjective and can lead to human rights abuses.

The third definition is failure to function. What this means is that some people can't do normal everyday things like get up and go to bed at usual times, feed themselves, hold down a job and so on. So they aren't really coping adequately with life and this is a way to judge them as abnormal. This too requires subjective judgements but on the positive side it is more about the client's experience than the other definitions, which is a good thing.

The final definition is deviation from ideal mental health. Jahoda suggested a list of things that could be used to judge mental health. For example, she said having good self-esteem, a job, having no distress, a realistic view of the world, coping with stress, being independent and so on – all of these things are what mentally healthy people have. The trouble with this definition is that very few people actually have all of these things and therefore it isn't a very good definition. **(342 words)**

Morticia's essay is an AS response whereas Luke's is an A level response.

Morticia starts with an introduction listing all the definitions at the beginning. This wastes valuable time when answering a question and is simply repeated later. Introductions rarely make a valuable contribution.

She has managed to cover all four definitions that are named on the specification but that has been at the expense of detail in places. Descriptively though, this is a good response. Although the first definition is a little vague, the other three are well described and include examples to illustrate key points. This essay deals well with description.

The downside of comprehensive description is a lack of time to produce evaluation, which is especially important when writing a timed essay. It would have been better to simply be selective and just cover two definitions (as Luke has done below). In a question such as this full marks are available for just two definitions.

The evaluation in Morticia's answer is placed after each definition. At least one point has been given for each definition but it is a shame Morticia did not elaborate these and develop a more thorough discussion. The point about human rights abuses, particularly, would benefit from further qualification.

This answer is descriptively strong but with only some cursory underdeveloped evaluation. The overall result is weak.

Luke's answer *One of the ways to define abnormality is in terms of social norms. A social norm is how society has defined what is acceptable. A norm is something that is typical in any society not just in terms of how frequent some behaviours are (which is the statistical infrequency definition) but also in terms of what that society has deemed acceptable. An example of this would be antisocial personality disorder which is defined by DSM-5 in terms of a failure to conform to behaviour that is culturally normative. Thus this mental disorder has been specifically defined in terms of social standards.*

In a sense this can be seen as a useful and defendable position. People who behave in an antisocial way, doing things that disrupts the lives of other people and the fabric of our society is abnormal and suggests something is wrong with that person's moral standards. The problem, however, is that this kind of definition is open to abuse. It offers a means for any society to control behaviours that are seen as undesirable by some. For example, women who were sexually promiscuous were diagnosed as nymphomaniacs and put in mental hospitals. By defining abnormality in terms of social norms, societies make moral judgements absolute and allow a small number of people to decide what is right.

A further important issue with the deviation from social norms approach is that it is culturally relative. What is acceptable in one society is not acceptable in another. This means that a person living in the UK from another culture may behave in ways following their own social norms but be judged abnormal by local standards. This clearly creates problems for them because they are behaving normally but are judged as abnormal.

A second definition of abnormality is failure to function adequately. Essentially this is about not being able to cope with day-to-day life. A person should be able to independently maintain basic standards of eating and hygiene. We also expect that people should be able to relate to other people and should be able to do some kind of work. In a sense this definition spills over into the social norms definition because some of these ideas of 'functioning adequately' are socially determined – in some cultures it might not be expected that everyone has to have a job.

Other signs of inadequate functioning have been suggested such as being distressed and being a danger to oneself. From this point of view this definition of abnormality takes the client's perspective and tries to find a way of defining abnormality, which will help the people who need it.

One problem with this is that such judgements may lead to social control. Some people choose alternative lifestyles and may only work when they have to and not be in a relationship or may engage in dangerous leisure activities. Defining such behaviours as abnormal means there is a risk that such people would be treated as having a psychological disorder. **(487 words)**

Luke has taken a very different approach to the question from the one above by focusing on two definitions only. This is arguably the more difficult route as this requires more depth of detail which many find demanding. However, on the positive side it leaves him much more time for evaluation.

Both definitions are clearly and accurately explained. There is a sophisticated level of descriptive detail in both, supported by relevant examples.

The evaluative points are thorough and very well developed (compare these with those above). The answer is rich in analysis and commentary and this makes all the difference to the overall value of the answer. Well done.

Multiple-choice questions

Definitions of abnormality (1)

1. Which of the following is statistically abnormal?
(a) An IQ of 45.
(b) An IQ of 71.
(c) An IQ of 120.
(d) An IQ of 100.

2. What is the main reason why someone with antisocial personality disorder would be judged abnormal?
(a) They are very unusual people.
(b) Their behaviour deviates from social norms.
(c) They can't function effectively.
(d) They don't display ideal mental health.

3. Which of these is a strength/limitation of statistical infrequency?
(a) It has no real-world application in diagnosis and assessment.
(b) All unusual characteristics are a bad thing.
(c) Unusual people need a diagnosis to help them become more normal.
(d) Unusual positive characteristics are just as uncommon as unusual negative characteristics.

4. Which is the best definition of 'cultural relativism'?
(a) Social norms vary between different cultures.
(b) Mental health is more common in some cultures.
(c) Social norms are only useful in some cultures.
(d) Relationships between relatives is the same in all cultures.

Definitions of abnormality (2)

1. According to Rosenhan and Seligman which of these is a sign of failing to cope?
(a) A person no longer conforms to social rules.
(b) A person hears voices.
(c) A person experiences mild distress.
(d) A person's behaviour is unusual.

2. According to Jahoda's ideal mental health criteria, which of the following is a sign of ideal mental health?
(a) Failure to cope with stress.
(b) Good self-esteem.
(c) Being dependent on other people.
(d) Conforming to social norms.

3. Which of these people is failing to function adequately?
(a) Someone who cannot hold down a job.
(b) Someone with an alternative lifestyle.
(c) Someone who has a fairly happy relationship.
(d) Someone with a smallish house.

4. Which of these is a strength of deviation from ideal mental health?
(a) It is usefully narrow.
(b) It applies well to a variety of cultures.
(c) It is comprehensive.
(d) It sets a realistic standard for mental health.

Phobias

1. Which of these is a behavioural characteristic of phobias?
(a) Fear.
(b) Avoidance.
(c) Anxiety.
(d) Aggression.

2. Which of these is an emotional characteristic of phobias?
(a) Fear.
(b) Sadness.
(c) Anger.
(d) Humour.

3. Which of these is a cognitive characteristic of phobias?
(a) Selective attention.
(b) Delusions.
(c) Avoidance.
(d) Endurance.

4. What is the difference between fear and anxiety?
(a) Fear is cognitive, anxiety is emotional.
(b) Fear is emotional, anxiety is cognitive.
(c) Fear is immediate and anxiety is long term.
(d) Fear is long term and anxiety is immediate.

Depression

1. People with depression may experience which of the following behavioural characteristics?
(a) Changes to activity level.
(b) Changes to sleep patterns.
(c) Changes to eating patterns.
(d) All of the above.

2. People with a diagnosis of depression are likely to have:
(a) Lowered mood.
(b) Anger.
(c) Low self-esteem.
(d) All of the above.

3. Which of the following is a cognitive characteristic of depression?
(a) Focusing on the negative aspects of a situation.
(b) Low self-esteem.
(c) Anger.
(d) All of the above.

4. Absolutist thinking is also called:
(a) Half-full, half-empty thinking.
(b) Black-and-white thinking.
(c) Self-harming thinking.
(d) Psychomotor thinking.

OCD

1. Most people with OCD experience:
(a) Obsessions only.
(b) Compulsions only.
(c) Obsessions and compulsions.
(d) Obsessions or compulsions.

2. Which of the following is *not* an emotional characteristic of OCD?
(a) Anxiety
(b) Lowered mood.
(c) Guilt.
(d) Compulsions.

3. People with a diagnosis of OCD are *unlikely* to experience which of these cognitions?
(a) Obsessive thoughts.
(b) Rational thoughts about their obsessive stimulus.
(c) Cognitive coping strategies.
(d) Good insight into their OCD.

4. Maintaining constant alertness is called:
(a) Catastrophic attention.
(b) A behavioural characteristic.
(c) Hypervigilance.
(d) Paranoia.

The behavioural approach to explaining phobias

1. The two-process model of phobias involves:
(a) Classical conditioning only.
(b) Operant conditioning only.
(c) Social learning only.
(d) Classical and operant conditioning.

2. A case study of learning a phobia by classical conditioning involved:
(a) Little Peter.
(b) Little Hans.
(c) Little Albert.
(d) Little Mix.

3. Which is a limitation of the two-process model?
(a) It can't explain how phobias are maintained ove time.
(b) There is no supporting evidence.
(c) It can't explain how fear of dogs might be acquired.
(d) It can't explain preparedness for certain phobias

4. What reinforces avoidance in the two-process model?
(a) Anxiety reduction.
(b) Safety cues.
(c) Preparedness.
(d) Positive reinforcement.

The behavioural approach to treating phobia

1. Which of the following is *not* normally part of systematic desensitisation?
(a) Learning relaxation procedures.
(b) Constructing an anxiety hierarchy.
(c) Massive immediate exposure to the phobic stimulus.
(d) Gradually increasing exposure to the phobic stimulus.

2. Which of these is a good example of flooding?
   (a) Placing a small spider in the next room to a person with arachnophobia.
   (b) Making a person with kinemortophobia watch a zombie film in the front row of a cinema.
   (c) Showing a person with zemmiphobia a giant mole rat through a window.
   (d) Showing a person with lutraphobia a small picture of a book about otters through glass.

3. Which of the following applies to systematic desensitisation?
   (a) It has very limited application.
   (b) It is unsuitable for clients with learning difficulties.
   (c) It has a high dropout rate.
   (d) It is more effective than relaxation alone.

4. Why might flooding be considered to be superior to systematic desensitisation?
   (a) It is less traumatic.
   (b) It is suitable for a wider range of clients.
   (c) It is more cost-effective.
   (d) There are fewer ethical issues.

The cognitive approach to explaining depression

1. Which of the following is *not* part of Beck's cognitive triad?
   (a) Negative view of the world.
   (b) Negative view of the future.
   (c) Negative view of therapy.
   (d) Negative view of the self.

2. Which of these is a type of dysfunctional belief in Ellis's cognitive model?
   (a) Negative self-schema.
   (b) Musturbation.
   (c) Negative view of the world.
   (d) Negative view of the self.

3. Which of the following is a limitation of Beck's model of depression?
   (a) Studies have never found abnormal cognition in depressed clients.
   (b) Depressed clients do not report abnormal cognition.
   (c) It doesn't explain all aspects of depression effectively.
   (d) All of the above.

4. Which of the following is a limitation of the ABC model?
   (a) There is no evidence linking activating events to depression.
   (b) It has no practical application in psychological therapies.
   (c) It doesn't explain cognitive aspects of depression.
   (d) It can't explain hallucinations and delusions in severe depression.

The cognitive approach to treating depression

1. CBT does *not* use techniques from which of the following?
   (a) Behavioural therapies.
   (b) Cognitive therapy.
   (c) Beck's theory of depression.
   (d) Biological treatments.

2. Which is the main technique in REBT?
   (a) Reality testing.
   (b) Disputing irrational beliefs.
   (c) Disputing automatic thoughts.
   (d) Behavioural activation.

3. Which of the following is true of CBT?
   (a) It treats the way people think.
   (b) It treats the way people behave.
   (c) It is reasonably cost-effective.
   (d) All of the above.

4. Which of these is a strength of CBT?
   (a) It only takes several weeks to work.
   (b) It is of benefit for most clients.
   (c) CBT focuses on the circumstances in which clients live.
   (d) Clients choose CBT to explore their past.

The biological approach to explaining OCD

1. Which of these is a true statement concerning OCD?
   (a) OCD does not run in families.
   (b) OCD involves just one gene.
   (c) OCD is caused by one particular combination of genes.
   (d) Twin studies suggest OCD is genetically influenced.

2. Which neural system appears *not* to be involved in OCD?
   (a) The serotonin system.
   (b) The lateral frontal lobes.
   (c) The right parahippocampal gyrus.
   (d) The left parahippocampal gyrus.

3. Which of these applies to neural explanations for OCD?
   (a) There is no supporting evidence.
   (b) The same mechanisms explain all cases of OCD.
   (c) Neural mechanisms may not cause OCD.
   (d) The serotonin system is a complete explanation.

4. Which of these would *not* suggest a genetic basis for OCD in a person?
   (a) OCD runs in their family.
   (b) They have an identical twin with OCD.
   (c) A brain scan shows reduced activity in the lateral frontal lobes.
   (d) They had a recent trauma.

The biological approach to treating OCD

1. Drugs are often used to treat OCD for which of the following reasons?
   (a) No side-effects of drugs.
   (b) The cost of drugs compared to other treatments.
   (c) Drugs have an instant effect.
   (d) The permanent cure offered by a course of drugs.

2. What is the standard biological treatment for OCD?
   (a) SNRIs.
   (b) CBT.
   (c) SSRIs.
   (d) *Clomipramine*.

3. Which of the following is *not* a side-effect of antidepressants?
   (a) Memory loss.
   (b) Reduced sex drive.
   (c) Weight gain.
   (d) Depression.

4. Which of the following statements is true?
   (a) A standard dose of *fluoxetine* is 20 mg a day.
   (b) SSRIs should not be combined with any other treatment.
   (c) SNRIs increase levels of serotonin and dopamine.
   (d) SSRIs can take up to four years to have an effect.

MCQ answers

Definitions of abnormality (1) 1A, 2B, 3D, 4A
Definitions of abnormality (2) 1A, 2B, 3A, 4C
Phobias 1B, 2A, 3A, 4C
Depression 1D, 2D, 3A, 4B
OCD 1C, 2D, 3B, 4C
The behavioural approach to explaining phobias 1D, 2C, 3D, 4A
The behavioural approach to treating phobias 1C, 2B, 3D, 4C
The cognitive approach to explaining depression 1C, 2B, 3C, 4D
The cognitive approach to treating depression 1D, 2B, 3D, 4B
The biological approach to explaining OCD 1D, 2C, 3C, 4D
The biological approach to treating OCD 1B, 2C, 3D, 4A

Chapter 6 Research methods

Contents

Research

noun: research;

the systematic investigation into and study of materials and sources in order to establish facts and reach new conclusions.

Method

noun: method;

a particular procedure for accomplishing or approaching something, especially a systematic or established one.

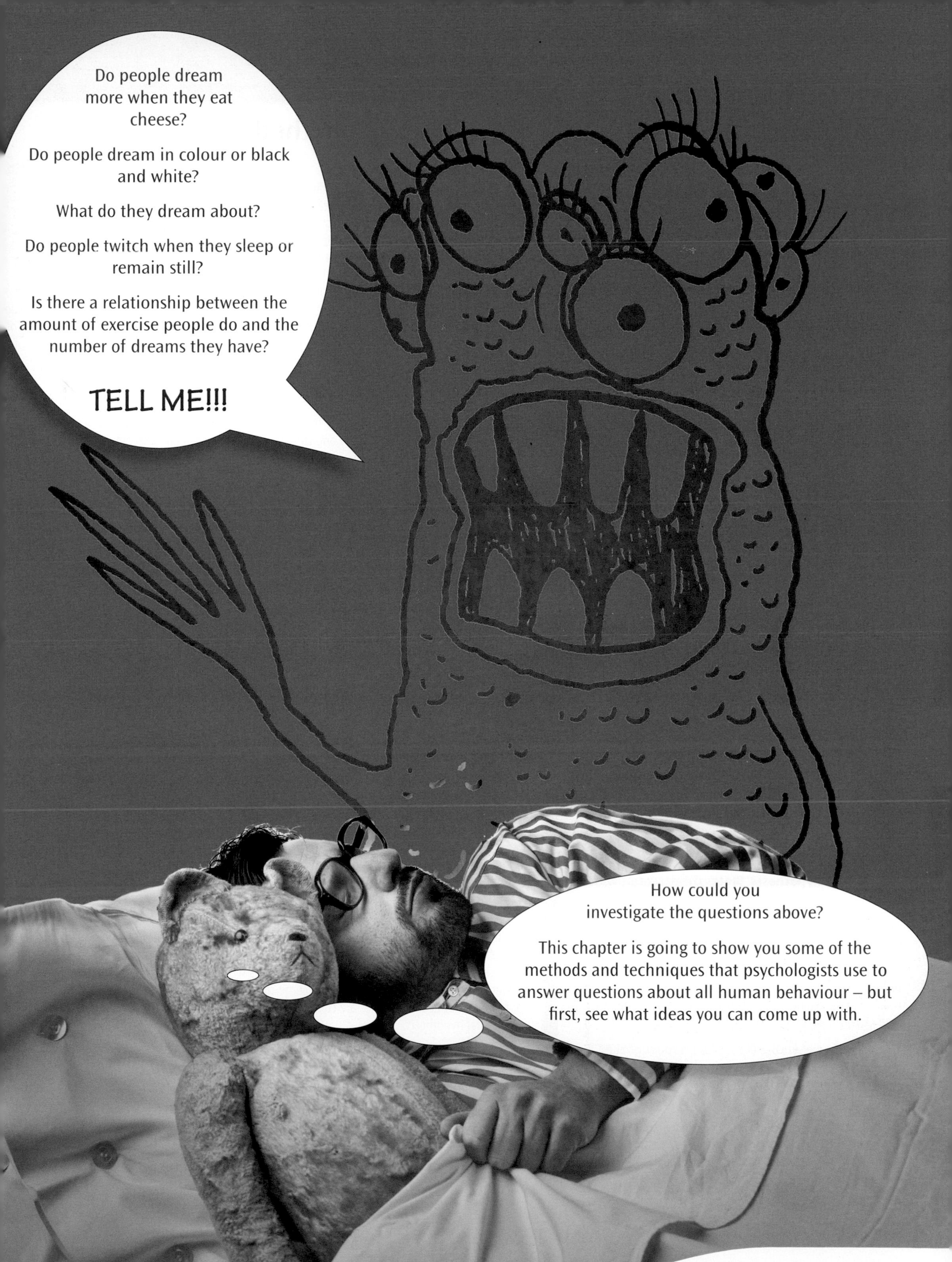
Do people dream more when they eat cheese?
Do people dream in colour or black and white?
What do they dream about?
Do people twitch when they sleep or remain still?
Is there a relationship between the amount of exercise people do and the number of dreams they have?
TELL ME!!!
How could you investigate the questions above?
This chapter is going to show you some of the methods and techniques that psychologists use to answer questions about all human behaviour – but first, see what ideas you can come up with.

Experimental method

The specification says...

Experimental method.

Aims: stating aims, the difference between aims and hypotheses.

Hypotheses: directional and non-directional.

Variables: manipulation of variables including independent and dependent; operationalisation of variables.

Psychologists are able to draw upon a number of different methods as part of their research but one of the most often used is the experimental method.

0.33L
CARBONATED FLAVOR SOFT DRINK
FRESH
ENERGY
DRINK
STORE IN A COOL DRY PLACE

Go on…it might make you more talkative.

Key terms

Experimental method Involves the manipulation of an independent variable (IV) to measure the effect on the dependent variable (DV). Experiments may be laboratory, field, natural or quasi.

Aim A general statement of what the researcher intends to investigate, the purpose of the study.

Hypothesis A clear, precise, testable statement that states the relationship between the variables to be investigated. Stated at the outset of any study.

Directional hypothesis States the direction of the difference or relationship.

Non-directional hypothesis Does not state the direction of the difference or relationship.

Variables Any 'thing' that can vary or change within an investigation. Variables are generally used in experiments to determine if changes in one thing result in changes to another.

Independent variable (IV) Some aspect of the experimental situation that is manipulated by the researcher – or changes naturally – so the effect on the DV can be measured.

Dependent variable (DV) The variable that is measured by the researcher. Any effect on the DV should be caused by the change in the IV.

Operationalisation Clearly defining variables in terms of how they can be measured.

Experimental method

Aims

We have a theory that energy drinks affect how much people talk. This is based on our understanding (having read a few research studies on the Internet) that energy drinks contain sugar and caffeine, and that these substances increase alertness, making people 'chattier'. As luck would have it, a new energy drink – *SpeedUpp* – has come on to the market and we're keen to know whether it might affect the talkativeness of those who drink it.

Now that we have an initial idea, the next step is to narrow the focus of our research to produce an **aim**. In psychological research, aims are developed from **theories**, like our energy drink theory above, except in psychology the theories tend to be much more sophisticated and are based on many more hours of research! Aims are general statements that describe the purpose of an investigation. In the case of our investigation, the aim would be something along the lines of:

To investigate whether drinking energy drinks makes people more talkative.

Hypotheses

Having written an aim, we now need to formulate a **hypothesis**. A hypothesis is a statement that is made at the start of a study and clearly describes the relationship between variables as stated by the theory. In the case of our investigation this might be:

Drinking SpeedUpp *causes people to become more talkative.*

Hypotheses can be directional or non-directional. In a **directional hypothesis** the researcher makes clear the sort of difference that is anticipated between two conditions or two groups of people. For this reason, directional hypotheses include words like more or less, higher or lower, faster or slower, etc.

People who drink SpeedUpp *become more talkative than people who don't.*

People who drink water are less talkative than people who drink SpeedUpp.

A **non-directional hypothesis** simply states that there is a difference between conditions or groups of people but, unlike in a directional hypothesis, the nature of the difference is not specified.

People who drink SpeedUpp *differ in terms of talkativeness compared with people who don't drink* SpeedUpp.

Doing an experiment

We have decided to test our energy drink theory by using the **experimental method**. Firstly, we are going to gather together two groups of people, let's say ten in each group. Then, starting with the first group, we will give each person (or each *participant* – because that's what you call people in studies) a can of *SpeedUpp* to drink. The participants in the other group will just have a glass of water each. We will then record how many words each participant says in a five-minute period immediately after they have had their drink.

Deciding which type of hypothesis to use

Leaving aside the debate about whether or not this is a 'good' experiment (it's not really – but we are taking the whole design process slowly) and the exact details of how it would work (it probably wouldn't), which type of hypothesis should we choose?

Researchers tend to use a directional hypothesis when a theory or the findings of previous research studies suggest a particular outcome. When there is no theory or previous research, or findings from earlier studies are contradictory, researchers instead decide to use a non-directional hypothesis.

Even though *SpeedUpp* is a new energy drink, the effects of caffeine and sugar on talkativeness are well-documented. Therefore we will opt for a directional hypothesis on this occasion.

Study tip

Writing clear and testable hypotheses is not easy.

When you read your hypothesis back to yourself, make sure (1) the IV and DV are clear and measurable, (2) you have stated the relationship between the IV and DV and not stated an aim, (3) you have selected the appropriate hypothesis, i.e. directional or non-directional, based on the information you have been given in the question.

Practical activity on pages 64 and 126

ndependent and dependent variables

ı an experiment, a researcher changes or manipulates the ıdependent variable (IV) and records or measures the effect of ıis change on the **dependent variable** (DV). All other variables that ıight potentially affect the DV should remain constant in a properly run xperiment. This is so the researcher can be confident that any change in the V was due to the IV, and the IV alone.

.evels of the IV

ı order to test the effect of the IV we need different **experimental onditions**. If we simply gave some participants *SpeedUpp*, how would we ıow how talkative they were? We need a comparison. We could either:

- Compare participants' talkativeness before and after drinking *SpeedUpp*.
- Compare two groups of participants – those who drink *SpeedUpp* with those who drink water (which is the way we have described the study on the facing page).

ı either case the two conditions are no *SpeedUpp* or drinking *SpeedUpp*. hese are the two levels of the IV: the **control condition** (no *SpeedUpp* / drink f water) and the experimental condition (energy drink).

A well-written hypothesis should make it easy to tell what the IV and DV re. May we proudly unveil the directional hypothesis we have written for our nergy drink investigation comparing two groups of participants...

The group that drinks an energy drink will be chattier than the group that drinks water.

ote that this is different from the hypothesis on the facing page – ypotheses come in all shapes and sizes but are still correct as long as they tate the operationalised variables and the relationship between them.

)perationalisation of variables

o far, so good – except we have not yet managed to **operationalise** the ariables in the hypothesis in order to make it testable.

Many of the things that psychologists are interested in, such as social ehaviour, intelligence or thinking, are often a little fuzzy and not easy to efine. Thus, in any study, one of the main tasks for the researcher is to nsure that the variables being investigated are as unfuzzy and measurable s possible.

So, a much better hypothesis than the one above would be:

After drinking 300 ml of SpeedUpp, *participants say more words in the next five minutes than participants who drink 300 ml of water.*

ee the difference? Now that our variables are operationalised and our ypothesis is complete, we're free to concentrate on more important things, uch as how on earth we're going to count all the words that twenty people ay in five minutes.

Apply it Methods — Bringing it all together

Questions

For each of the aims of the investigations below, operationalise the IV and DV, and write a directional and non-directional hypothesis. (*4 marks each*)

1. To investigate whether high confidence levels in children affect their level of obedience.
2. To investigate whether a new drug (*Anxocalm*) reduces anxiety in patients with phobias, as compared with having no treatment.
3. To investigate whether yawning is contagious.
4. To investigate whether owning a goldfish has a positive effect on psychological well-being.
5. To investigate whether grey-haired people have more fun than people with other hair colours.

Are two tails better than one? Sometimes the terms 'two-tailed' and 'one-tailed' are used when describing a hypothesis instead of 'non-directional' and 'directional'. (Though strictly speaking they are not the same – directional is not the same as 'two-tailed'. A directional hypothesis requires a two-tailed test of significance ... to be explained later ...)

Apply it Methods — Directional or non-directional?

Questions

Decide whether the following hypotheses are directional or non-directional. What features/words in each hypothesis are important when making your choice? (*2 marks each*)

1. There is a difference in children's reading ability depending on whether they have blue or brown eyes.
2. Dogs that are rewarded with treats sit when told to do so more often than dogs that are not rewarded with treats.
3. There is a difference in the psychology grades of students depending on whether they are men or women.
4. Teenagers who watch horror films have more friends than teenagers who watch romantic comedies.

Apply it Methods — IVs and DVs

Questions

Identify the IVs and DVs in the examples below. (*2 marks each*)

1. Talking to a child will increase their language ability.
2. People are more aggressive on hot days.
3. Students may be late for school because they stayed up late the night before.
4. Watching horror films will make children have nightmares.
5. People will be rated as more attractive if they wear red.

Check it

1. Explain the difference between an aim and a hypothesis. *[2 marks]*
2. Identify **one** way in which each of the following terms could be operationalised: memory, physical aggression and intelligence. *[3 marks]*
3. Suggest **two** reasons why a psychologist might choose to use a non-directional hypothesis. *[2 marks]*

Research issues

The specification says...

Variables: extraneous and confounding.

Demand characteristics and investigator effects.

Control: randomisation and standardisation.

In any experiment, there will always be a number of unwanted factors that can potentially affect the relationship between the independent and dependent variables, spoiling or distorting the results in the process.

Fortunately, psychologists are aware of this issue and have devised several different ways of tackling it, some of which we shall explore here.

Key terms

Extraneous variable (EV) Any variable, other than the independent variable (IV), that may affect the dependent variable (DV) if it is not controlled. EVs are essentially nuisance variables that do not vary systematically with the IV.

Confounding variables A kind of EV but the key feature is that a confounding variable varies systematically with the IV. Therefore we can't tell if any change in the DV is due to the IV or the confounding variable.

Demand characteristics Any cue from the researcher or from the research situation that may be interpreted by participants as revealing the purpose of an investigation. This may lead to a participant changing their behaviour within the research situation.

Investigator effects Any effect of the investigator's behaviour (conscious or unconscious) on the research outcome (the DV). This may include everything from the design of the study to the selection of, and interaction with, participants during the research process.

Randomisation The use of chance methods to control for the effects of bias when designing materials and deciding the order of experimental conditions.

Standardisation Using exactly the same formalised procedures and instructions for all participants in a research study.

Research issues

Extraneous variables

The key to an **experiment** is that an **independent variable** (IV) is manipulated (changed) to see how this affects the **dependent variable** (DV). The only thing that should influence the DV is the IV. Any other variables that might potentially interfere with the IV (or the DV) should be controlled or removed. These additional, unwanted variables are called **extraneous variables** and, where possible, are identified at the start of the study by the researcher, who then takes steps to minimise their influence.

Many extraneous variables are straightforward to control such as the age of the participants, the lighting in the **lab**, etc. These are described as 'nuisance variables' that do not vary systematically with the IV. These may 'muddy' the experimental water so to speak but do not confound the findings of the study. They may just make it harder to detect a result.

Confounding variables

Confounding variables *do* change systematically with the IV. Let us imagine in our energy drink study we have twenty participants in total and decide to use the first ten participants who arrive for the *Speedupp* condition. It happens that these first ten participants are all very excited because they saw Prince William arrive at their school. This meant that there was some delay before further participants arrived and by then people were less excited. This unexpected event means we have ended up with a second unintended IV – being excited or not.

So when we come to analyse our results and find that the *Speedupp* group were chattier we can't be sure if this is because of the drink or the excitement. The problem is that the emotion varied systematically with the IV and this alone could explain changes in the DV.

Demand characteristics

Participants are not passive within experiments and are likely to be spending much of their time trying to make sense of the new situation they find themselves in. As such, **participant reactivity** is a significant extraneous variable in experimental research and one that is very difficult to control.

In the research situation, participants will try to work out what is going on. Certain clues may help them interpret what is going on. These clues (or *cues*) are the **demand characteristics** of the experimental situation and may help a participant to 'second-guess' the experimenter's intentions as well as the aims of the study.

Participants may also look for clues to tell them how they should behave in the experimental situation. They may act in a way that they think is expected and over-perform to please the experimenter (the 'please-U effect'), or, they may deliberately under-perform to sabotage the results of the study (the 'screw-U effect'). Either way, participant behaviour is no longer natural – an extraneous variable that may affect the DV.

Saint or sinner? Some participants try to please the researcher in experiments whereas others try to negatively affect the results. Which type of participant would you be?

Apply it Methods — Extraneous variables

In a properly conducted experiment it is important that potential extraneous variables are identified during the design of the study and appropriate steps are taken to control them.

Questions

1. Come up with *at least ten* extraneous variables that would need to be controlled in the energy drink study. (*10 marks*)
2. Which of the extraneous variables you have listed would be easy to control and which would be more difficult? (*2 marks*)
3. Take *five* of the extraneous variables you have listed and explain what steps you would take to control them. (*5 marks*)

Investigator effects

Participant reactivity also leads to **investigator effects**. Consider this: it is possible that during our energy drink study, as we are recording the words spoken by each participant, we may be inclined to smile more during our interactions with some participants than others. Given that we are *expecting* the energy drink group to speak more than the water group, we may unknowingly – in our unconscious behaviour – *encourage* a greater level of chattiness from the energy drink participants.

This is an example of an investigator effect, which refers to any unwanted influence of the investigator on the research outcome. As Hugh Coolican (2006) points out, this can include expectancy effects and unconscious cues (such as those described above). It might also refer to any actions of the researcher that were related to the study's design, such as the selection of the participants, the materials, the instructions, etc. **Leading questions**, which are discussed in relation to eyewitness testimony on page 58, are a good example of the power of investigator effects.

Randomisation

In any investigation there are simple steps that a researcher can take to minimise the effect of extraneous/confounding variables on the outcome. One of these is **randomisation**, which refers to the use of chance methods to reduce the researcher's unconscious biases when designing an investigation. In short, this is an attempt to control investigator effects.

For example, a memory experiment may involve participants recalling words from a list. The order of the list should be **randomly** generated so that the position of each word is not decided by the researcher.

In an experiment where participants are involved in a number of different conditions, the order of these conditions should be randomly determined. For example, in the energy drink experiment we might want to know what quantity of *SpeedUpp* caused chattiness. We may set up four experimental conditions: drinking water (Condition A), drinking 100 ml of *SpeedUpp* (Condition B), drinking 200 ml of *SpeedUpp* (Condition C), and drinking 300 ml of *SpeedUpp* (Condition D).

If all participants were to take part in all four conditions, the order in which these conditions were completed would need to be randomised for each participant (this is an alternative to **counterbalancing** – discussed on the next spread).

Standardisation

As far as is possible within an investigation, all participants should be subject to the same environment, information and experience. To ensure this, all procedures are **standardised**, in other words there is a list of exactly what will be done in the study. This includes **standardised instructions** that are read to each participant. Such standardisation means that non-standardised changes in procedure do not act as extraneous variables.

The Variable family
Ivy (IV) and Davy (DV) are a happy couple with a good relationship. However, Civy (CV) is often interfering and tries to constantly change Davy much to Ivy's annoyance…

Study tip

Be careful not to refer to ALL investigations as experiments. This is something that students new to psychology tend to do quite often.

If you are not sure whether the piece of research you are talking about involved an experiment then you should use a more general term such as 'investigation' or 'study'.

Note that in research methods, some of the terms and concepts we discuss relate to experiments specifically, but others are also a feature of investigations in general.

Apply it Methods: Participant variables and situational variables

Extraneous variables can be subdivided into participant variables and situational variables. Participant variables are any individual differences between participants that may affect the DV. Situational variables are any features of the experimental situation that may affect the DV.

Question

Decide which of the variables below are participant variables and which are situational variables. *(4 marks)*

Noise	*Age*	*Motivation*	*Weather*
Personality	*Temperature*	*Intelligence*	*Concentration*
Time of day	*Gender*	*Instructions*	

Apply it Methods: Maths test

A teacher wanted to see how the investigator effect would influence performance on a maths test. She gave 20 of her sixth form class the same maths test but told half of the class the test was suitable for year 10 students and the other half that it was suitable for degree students. When the results of the test were analysed, the group that were told it was suitable for year 10s had performed significantly better on average.

Questions

1. Identify the **IV** and the **DV** within this experiment. (*2 marks*)
2. Identify *one* possible **extraneous variable** in this experiment and briefly explain how it may have affected the DV. (*3 marks*)
3. Explain how the results of this experiment could be used to support the investigator effect. (*3 marks*)

Check it

1. Outline what is meant by 'demand characteristics'. *[2 marks]*
2. Explain the difference between an extraneous variable and a confounding variable. *[2 marks]*
3. Suggest **one** example of how randomisation could be used within psychological research. *[2 marks]*
4. Outline what is meant by 'investigator effects' **and** explain why it is important to control for these when conducting research. *[4 marks]*

Experimental designs

The specification says...

Experimental designs: repeated measures, independent groups, matched pairs.

Control: random allocation and counterbalancing.

In order to find out whether the independent variable (IV) affects the dependent variable (DV), we need something to compare it with – a comparison condition – a different level of the IV.

This leads us to three types of experimental design, each with different strengths and limitations.

Key terms

Experimental design The different ways in which participants can be organised in relation to the experimental conditions.

Independent groups design Participants are allocated to different groups where each group represents one experimental condition.

Repeated measures All participants take part in all conditions of the experiment.

Matched pairs design Pairs of participants are first matched on some variable(s) that may affect the dependent variable. Then one member of the pair is assigned to Condition A and the other to Condition B.

Random allocation An attempt to control for participant variables in an independent groups design which ensures that each participant has the same chance of being in one condition as any other.

Counterbalancing An attempt to control for the effects of order in a repeated measures design: half the participants experience the conditions in one order, and the other half in the opposite order.

Study tip

Don't confuse experimental 'designs' with 'types' of experiment (as in lab, field, natural and quasi – covered on the next spread). It's easily done so make sure you're aware of the difference!

Experimental designs

Experimental design refers to the way in which participants are used in **experiments**. By 'used' we do not mean taking them out for dinner and never calling them again, we mean how participants are *arranged* in relation to the different experimental conditions.

Independent groups

An **independent groups design** is when two separate groups of participants experience two different conditions of the experiment. If there are two levels of the **independent variable** (IV) this means that all participants experience one level of the IV only. In our *SpeedUpp* energy drink investigation this would involve:

- One group of participants (group 1) drinking the energy drink (let's call this condition A, the **experimental condition**).
- A different group of participants (group 2) drinking the water (let's call this condition B, the **control condition**).

The performance of the two groups would then be compared. In this case, we would compare the difference in the **mean** number of words spoken in the five-minute period after drinking for each group/condition.

Repeated measures

Another way of carrying out the energy drink investigation would be to use a **repeated measures** design – all participants experience *both* conditions of the experiment.

- Each participant would first, for example, experience condition A (the energy drink condition, the experimental condition).
- Each participant would then later be tested again in condition B (the glass of water condition, the control condition).

Following this, the two mean scores from both conditions would be compared to see if there was a difference.

Matched pairs

In a **matched pairs** design, participants are paired together on a variable or variables relevant to the experiment. For instance, in a memory study participants might be matched on their IQ, as this might be a good indicator of their ability to recall information. The two participants with the first and second highest IQ scores would be paired together, as would the participants with the third and fourth highest, and so on. Then one participant from each pair would be allocated to a different condition of the experiment. This is an attempt to control for the **confounding variable** of **participant variables** and often necessitates the use of a pre-test if matching is to be effective.

So back to our *SpeedUpp* study, we might observe participants interacting in a room before the experiment begins and select the two people that appear to be the chattiest. One of the pair would be placed in condition A and the other in condition B. We would then do the same with the third and fourth most talkative participants, and so on. The experiment would then be run in the same way as an independent groups design (see above).

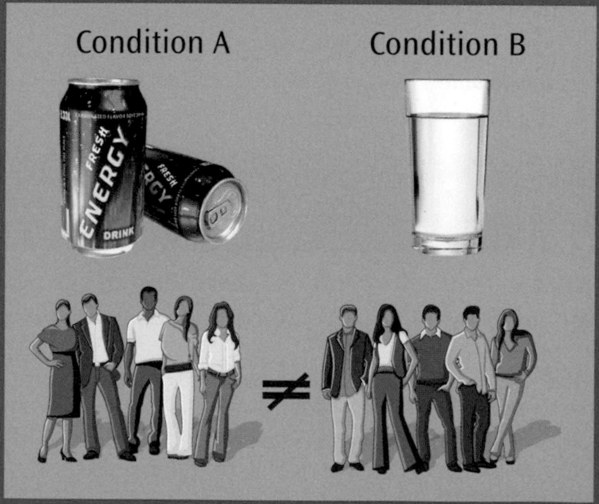
Condition A
Condition B
FRESH ENERGY DRINK
≠

In an independent groups design (left) the participants in each condition are different…but they are the same in a repeated measures design (right).

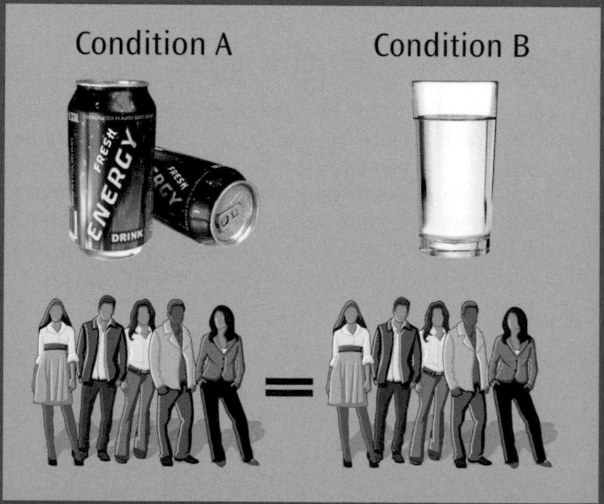
Condition A
Condition B
FRESH ENERGY DRINK
=

Evaluation

Independent groups

The biggest issue with an independent groups design is that the participants who occupy the different groups are not the same in terms of participant variables. If a researcher finds a mean difference between the groups on the **dependent variable** (DV) this may be more to do with participant variables than the effects of the IV. These differences may act as a confounding variable, reducing the **validity** of the findings. To deal with this problem researchers use **random allocation** (see right).

Independent groups designs are less economical than repeated measures as each participant contributes a single result only. Twice as many participants would be needed to produce equivalent data to that collected in a repeated measures design. This increases the time/money spent on recruiting participants.

The strengths of using independent groups are that **order effects** are not a problem whereas they are a problem for repeated measures designs. Participants also are less likely to guess the aims.

Repeated measures

The biggest issue for repeated measures is that each participant has to do at least two tasks and the order of these tasks may be significant (i.e. there are order effects). In the energy drink example, having the energy drink first may have a continuing effect when a participant drinks water afterwards. To deal with this, researchers use **counterbalancing** (see right).

Order effects also arise because repeating two tasks could create boredom or fatigue that might cause deterioration in performance on the second task, so it matters what order the tasks are in. Alternatively, participants' performance may improve through the effects of practice, especially on a skill-based task – in this case participants would perform better on the second task. Order acts as a confounding variable.

It is also more likely that participants will work out the aim of the study when they experience all conditions of the experiment. For this reason, **demand characteristics** tend to be more of a feature of repeated measures designs than independent groups.

The strengths of using repeated measures are that participant variables are controlled (therefore higher validity) and fewer participants are needed (therefore less time spent recruiting them).

Matched pairs

Participants only take part in a single condition so order effects and demand characteristics are less of a problem.

Although there is some attempt to reduce participant variables in this design, participants can never be matched exactly. Even when identical twins are used as matched pairs, there will still be important differences between them that may affect the DV.

Matching may be time-consuming and expensive, particularly if a pre-test is required, so this is less economical than other designs.

Apply it Methods

Which design?

Questions

Which of the following is an independent groups design, a repeated measures design or a matched pairs design? (*1 mark each*)

1. Depressed participants were assigned to receive either cognitive therapy or behaviour therapy for a 12-week period. A standardised test for depression was administered and participants were paired on the severity of their symptoms.
2. A researcher randomly assigned student volunteers to two conditions. Those in condition 1 attempted to recall a list of words that were organised into meaningful categories; those in condition 2 attempted to recall the same words, randomly grouped on the page.
3. To investigate whether students are more alert in the morning or the afternoon, each student is given a hazard perception test before school and at the end of the day.

Apply it Methods

Random allocation

To address the problem of participant variables in an independent groups design, participants should be randomly allocated to the different experimental conditions. Random allocation attempts to evenly distribute participant characteristics across the conditions of the experiment using random techniques – for example pieces of paper with A or B written on them are placed in a 'hat' and the researcher selects them one at a time to assign participants to groups.

Question

Explain *one* way in which we could have randomly allocated participants to the two conditions in the energy drink study. (*3 marks*)

Apply it Methods

Counterbalancing

Counterbalancing is an attempt to control order effects in a repeated measures design. In counterbalancing, half the participants take part in condition A then B, and the other half take part in condition B then A as follows:

Participant 1	A–B
Participant 2	B–A
Participant 3	A–B and so on.

Counterbalancing is sometimes referred to as the ABBA technique for obvious reasons i.e. where every participant does four trials, A, B, B then A.

Note (as with random allocation in relation to participant variables), counterbalancing does not remove or prevent the problem, but *attempts* to balance out the effects.

Question

Explain how, if we had used a repeated measures design in the energy drink study, we could have counterbalanced the two conditions. (*3 marks*)

Apply it Methods

Rat-man

Look at the Bugelski and Alampay rat-man study on page 113. Explain why a repeated measures design would not have been suitable for this investigation. (*2 marks*)

ABBA
ANNUAL 1980
THE WONDERFUL MUSICAL WORLD OF ABBA INSIDE!

It's a little known fact that the Swedish pop group ABBA took their name from a way of reducing order effects in a repeated measures design experiment.

Check it

1. Outline what is meant by 'random allocation' **and** outline **one** way in which this could be carried out. *[3 marks]*
2. Explain **one** limitation of a repeated measures design. *[3 marks]*
3. Outline what is meant by a 'matched pairs design'. *[2 marks]*

Types of experiment

The specification says...

Types of experiment, laboratory and field experiments; natural and quasi-experiments.

All experiments involve a change in an independent variable, with the researcher recording or measuring the subsequent effects on the dependent variable.

How the IV changes, and *under what circumstances*, varies from one type of experiment to another. There are four different types of experiment used in psychology, each with its own strengths and limitations.

Key terms

Laboratory (lab) experiment An experiment that takes place in a controlled environment within which the researcher manipulates the IV and records the effect on the DV, whilst maintaining strict control of extraneous variables.

Field experiment An experiment that takes place in a natural setting within which the researcher manipulates the IV and records the effect on the DV.

Natural experiment An experiment where the change in the IV is not brought about by the researcher but would have happened even if the researcher had not been there. The researcher records the effect on a DV they have decided on.

Quasi-experiment A study that is almost an experiment but lacks key ingredients. The IV has not been determined by anyone (the researcher or any other person) – the 'variables' simply exist, such as being old or young. Strictly speaking this is not an experiment.

Good enough to eat?
If a researcher had deprived you of food for four hours you might perceive this cake as being brighter than if you had just eaten, but would you have been involved in a lab, field, natural or quasi-experiment?

Laboratory experiments

Laboratory experiments are conducted in highly controlled environments. This is not always a laboratory (**lab**) – it could, for example, be a classroom where conditions can be well-controlled.

Strengths

Lab experiments have high control over **confounding** (CVs) and **extraneous variables** (EVs). This means that the researcher can ensure that any effect on the **dependent variable** (DV) is likely to be the result of manipulation of the **independent variable** (IV). Thus, we can be more certain about demonstrating cause and effect (high **internal validity**).

Replication is more possible than in other types of experiment because of the high level of control. This ensures that new extraneous variables are not introduced when repeating an experiment. Replication is vital to check the results of any study to see whether the finding is **valid** and not just a one-off.

Limitations

Lab experiments may lack **generalisability**. The lab environment may be rather artificial and not like everyday life. In an unfamiliar context participants may behave in unusual ways so their behaviour cannot always be generalised beyond the research setting (low **external validity**).

As well as this, participants are usually aware they are being tested in a lab experiment (though they may not know why) and this may also give rise to 'unnatural' behaviour (see **demand characteristics** described on page 170).

Furthermore, the tasks participants are asked to carry out in a lab experiment may not represent everyday experience; for instance, recalling unconnected lists of words as part of a memory experiment (low **mundane realism**).

Field experiments

In **field experiments** the IV is manipulated in a natural, more everyday setting (in *the* field). The researcher goes to the participants' usual environment rather than, in a lab experiment, participants going to a researcher's lab.

Strengths

Field experiments have higher mundane realism than lab experiments because the environment is more natural. Thus field experiments may produce behaviour that is more valid and authentic. This is especially the case as participants may be unaware they are being studied (high external validity).

Limitations

However, there is a price to pay for increased realism due to the loss of control of CVs and EVs. This means cause and effect between the IV and the DV in field studies may be much more difficult to establish and precise replication is often not possible.

There are also important **ethical issues**. If participants are unaware they are being studied they cannot **consent** to being studied and such research might constitute an invasion of **privacy**.

Apply it Methods — Lab, field, natural or quasi? You decide

Questions

Which of the four investigations below is the lab experiment, the field experiment, the natural experiment and the quasi-experiment? (*1 mark each*)

1. Three groups were recruited – autistic children, children with Down syndrome and a control group (*no diagnosis*). The autistic children did significantly worse on a task involving putting a comic strip in the right order (Baron-Cohen *et al.* 1986).
2. An experiment was conducted on a busy New York subway in which a researcher pretended to collapse. It was found more people helped when the victim was carrying a walking stick than when they smelt of alcohol (Piliavin *et al.* 1969).
3. The behaviour of children aged 6–11 in a Canadian town was monitored before and after television was first introduced. Increases in levels of aggression were observed after the children had access to television (Williams 1986).
4. Participants were deprived of food and water for four hours and then shown pictures of food. These participants rated the pictures of food as being brighter than the control group who had not been food-deprived (Gilchrist and Nesburg 1952).

Practical activity on pages 65, 97, 127 and 205

latural experiments

atural experiments are like a lab or field experiment insofar as the researcher measures the effect of ı IV on a DV. However, what distinguishes a natural experiment is the researcher has no control over e IV and cannot change it – someone or something else causes the IV to vary. For example, before and ter a natural disaster or whether a child is in hospital at age 5 or 10.

Note that it is the IV that is natural, not necessarily the setting – participants may be tested in a lab. ıe DV may also be naturally occurring (e.g. exam results) or may be devised by the experimenter and en measured in the field or a lab.

trengths

atural experiments provide opportunities for research that may not otherwise be undertaken for practical ethical reasons, such as the studies of institutionalised Romanian orphans (Rutter *et al.*, see page 92).

Natural experiments often have high external validity because they involve the study of real-world sues and problems as they happen, such as the effects of a natural disaster on stress levels.

imitations

naturally occurring event may only happen very rarely, reducing the opportunities for research. This so may limit the scope for generalising findings to other similar situations.

Another issue is that participants may not be **randomly allocated** to **experimental conditions** (note that is only applies when there is an **independent groups design**). This means the researcher might be less ıre whether the IV affected the DV. For example, in the study of Romanian orphans, the IV was whether ıildren were adopted early or late. However, there were lots of other differences between these groups, such s those who were adopted late may also have been less sociable than some of the other children which ay have made them less appealing for prospective parents.

Such research may be conducted in a lab and therefore may lack realism and demand characteristics ay be an issue.

uasi-experiments

uasi-experiments have an IV that is based on an existing difference between people (for instance, age gender). No one has manipulated this variable, it simply exists and, unlike in a natural experiment, ıe 'independent variable' cannot be changed. For instance, if the anxiety levels of phobic and non-hobic patients were compared, the IV of 'having a phobia' would not have come about through any xperimental manipulation.

As with a natural experiment, the DV may be naturally occurring (e.g. exam results) or may be evised by the experimenter and measured in the field or a lab.

trengths and limitations

uasi-experiments are often carried out under controlled conditions and therefore share some strengths f a lab experiment (e.g. replication).

Quasi-experiments, like natural experiments, cannot randomly allocate participants to conditions and ıerefore there may be **confounding variables**.

In addition, in both quasi-experiments and natural experiments, the IV is not deliberately changed by ıe researcher and therefore we cannot claim that the IV has caused any observed change.

Apply it Methods — 'True' experiments

In a true experiment the IV is under the direct control of the researcher who manipulates it and records the effect on the DV. From this perspective, only lab and field experiments are true experiments as they involve manipulation of the IV by the researcher.

Questions

1. Explain why natural and quasi-experiments cannot be classified as 'true' experiments. (*2 marks*)
2. Decide which of the following studies would be classed as true experiments and which would not. (*1 mark each*)
   a) Comparing the attitudes of psychology and sociology students towards independent study.
   b) Comparing the recall of students who learned a psychology theory in groups and those who learned on their own.
   c) Comparing the exam results of men and women.
   d) Comparing the progress of students who were randomly assigned at the beginning of the year to either a group taught using traditional methods or a group taught using contemporary methods.

We might expect a rise in people's stress levels as a result of a zombie outbreak, but what type of experiment would measure this?

BEWARE
OF
ZOMBIES

Apply it Methods — Experiments with zombies

Questions

1. Identify the type of **experiment** (lab, field, natural or quasi) described below. (*1 mark each*)
   a) Measuring the change in stress levels in the local residents of a town following a zombie invasion.
   b) Comparing the performance of a group of 20 humans and a group of 20 zombies on a video game that requires divided attention and multitasking.
   c) Measuring the physiological response of zombies to a range of stimuli including bright light, loud noise and mild electric shocks.
   d) Recording the number of people who refuse to enter a lift when one zombie is in there compared to when there are three zombies in there.
2. What are the strengths *and* limitations of each of the experiments described above? (*2 marks each*)

Study tip

Internal validity is about what goes on inside an experiment. Was it poorly controlled? Was the task really mundane? If so, the findings are probably meaningless.

External validity is about generalising the findings from a study to other situations, such as everyday life. That's the whole point of doing research!

Students often think that lab studies don't tell us much about everyday life because they are artificial but that's not always true – often it is the task that is artificial (low mundane realism) and this can be true in a field experiment – reducing external validity.

Check it

1. Explain what is meant by a 'laboratory experiment'. *[3 marks]*
2. Explain **one** strength **and one** limitation of a field experiment. *[2 marks + 2 marks]*
3. Explain the difference between a field experiment and a natural experiment. *[4 marks]*

Sampling

The specification says…

Sampling: the difference between population and sample; sampling techniques including: random, systematic, stratified, opportunity and volunteer; implications of sampling techniques, including bias and generalisation.

Psychological investigations require one important ingredient – people!*

Groups of people (participants) that form part of research studies are selected through the process of 'sampling'. There are five important sampling techniques used in psychology and these are discussed on this spread.

*Or sometimes animals

Key terms

Population A group of people who are the focus of the researcher's interest, from which a smaller sample is drawn.

Sample A group of people who take part in a research investigation. The sample is drawn from a (target) population and is presumed to be representative of that population, i.e. it stands 'fairly' for the population being studied.

Sampling techniques The method used to select people from the population.

Bias In the context of sampling, when certain groups are over- or under-represented within the sample selected. For instance, there may be too many younger people or too many people of one ethnic origin in a sample. This limits the extent to which generalisations can be made to the target population.

Generalisation The extent to which findings and conclusions from a particular investigation can be broadly applied to the population. This is possible if the sample of participants is representative of the target population.

Sometimes, researchers will 'take their opportunity' to stop people in the street.

Study tip

Don't confuse opportunity sampling and random sampling. If the word is used in its everyday sense, it could be argued that opportunity sampling involves selecting people 'at random'. In psychology, however, random sampling involves 'proper' random methods.

Population and sample

The term **population** refers to the large group of individuals that a particular researcher is interested in studying, for example students attending colleges in the North West, autistic children under six years old, women in their thirties, etc. This is often called the **target population** because it is a subset of the general population.

For practical and economic reasons, it is usually not possible to include all members of a target population in an investigation so a researcher selects a smaller group, known as the **sample**.

Ideally, the sample that is drawn will be **representative** of the target population so that **generalisation** of findings becomes possible. In practice, however, it is often very difficult to represent populations in any given sample due to the inevitably diverse nature of populations of people (different gender, age, interests, experience, etc.). Inevitably then, the vast majority of samples contain some degree of **bias**.

Samples are selected using a **sampling technique** that aims to produce a representative sample. We will look at the main techniques used by psychologists.

Random sample

A **random sample** is a sophisticated form of sampling in which all members of the target population have an equal chance of being selectec

The first step in selecting a random sample is t obtain a complete list of all members of the target population. Second, all of the names on the list ar assigned a number. Finally, the actual sample is selected through the use of some **lottery method** (a computer/phone randomiser or picking number from a hat).

Systematic sample

A **systematic sample** is when every *n*th member of the target population is selected, for example every 3rd house on a street or every 5th pupil on a school register.

A **sampling frame** is produced, which is a list of people in the target population organisec into, for instance, alphabetical order. A sampling system is nominated (every 3rd, 6th or 8th person, etc.). May begin from a randomly determined start to reduce bias. The researcher then works through the sampling frame until the sample is complete.

Stratified sample

A **stratified sample** is a sophisticated form of sampling in which the composition of the sample reflects the proportions of people in certain subgroups (strata) within the target population or the wider population.

To carry out a stratified sample the researcher first identifies the different *strata* that make up the population. Then, the proportions needed for the sample to be representative are worked out. Finally, the participants that make up each stratum are selected using random sampling. For example, let's say in Manchester, 40% of people support Manchester United, 40% support Manchester City, 15% support Bolton and 5% support Leeds. In a stratified sample of 20 participants there would be eight United fans, eight City, three Bolton fans and one solitary Leeds supporter. Each of these would be randomly selected from the larger grou of fans of their team, e.g. Bolton fans selected from Bolton supporters, if there are enough.

Opportunity sample

Given that representative samples of the target population are so difficult to obtain, many researchers simply decide to select anyone who happens to be willing and available (an **opportunity sample**). The researcher simply takes the chance to ask whoever is around at th time of their study, for example in the street (as in the case of market research).

Volunteer sample

A **volunteer sample** involves participants selecting themselves to be part of the sample; hence, it is also referred to as self-selection.

To select a volunteer sample a researcher may place an advert in a newspaper or on a common room noticeboard. Alternatively, willing participants may simply raise their hand when the researcher asks.

:valuation

:andom sample

random sample is potentially unbiased. This means that confounding or extraneous ıriables should be equally divided between the different groups, enhancing internal ılidity.

However, random sampling is difficult and time-consuming to conduct. A complete ;t of the target population may be extremely difficult to obtain.

Furthermore, you may end up with a sample that is still unrepresentative – the laws of ·obability suggest that random sampling is likely to produce a more representative sample ıan, say, opportunity sampling. However, it is still possible that the random method may ·lect, for example, 20 female psychology teachers from Lancashire called Joyce.

In addition, selected participants may refuse to take part (which means you end up ith something more like a volunteer sample). This particular issue applies to all of the ıethods below.

·ystematic sample

ıis sampling method is objective. Once the system for selection has been established ıe researcher has no influence over who is chosen (this is even more the case if the start randomly selected).

As with random sampling, this method is time-consuming and, in the end, ırticipants may refuse to take part, resulting in a volunteer sample.

·tratified sample

ıis method produces a representative sample because it is designed to accurately reflect ıe composition of the population. This means that generalisation of findings becomes ɔssible.

However, stratification is not perfect. The identified strata cannot reflect all the ways that ·eople are different, so complete representation of the target population is not possible.

)pportunity sample

pportunity sampling is convenient. This method is much less costly in terms of ıme and money than, say, random sampling, because a list of members of the target ɔpulation is not required, and there is no need to divide the population into different ·rata as there is in stratified sampling.

On the negative side, opportunity samples suffer from two forms of bias. First, the ımple is unrepresentative of the target population as it is drawn from a very specific area, ıch as one street in one town, so findings cannot be generalised to the target population.

Second, the researcher has complete control over the selection of participants and, for ıstance, may avoid people they do not like the look of (**researcher bias**).

′olunteer sample

ɔllecting a volunteer sample is easy. It requires minimal input from the researcher :hey come to you') and so is less time-consuming than other forms of sampling. The ·searcher ends up with participants who are more engaged, more so than someone ·ho was stopped in the street.

Volunteer bias is a problem. Asking for volunteers may attract a certain 'profile' of ·erson, that is, one who is curious and more likely to try to please the researcher (which ıight then affect how far findings can be generalised).

Create a stratified sample of 10 Smarties that accurately reflects the proportion of different colours in the whole tube. How would you work it out? You might have to eat a couple to make it simpler!

Hey! Who fancies being in our sample?

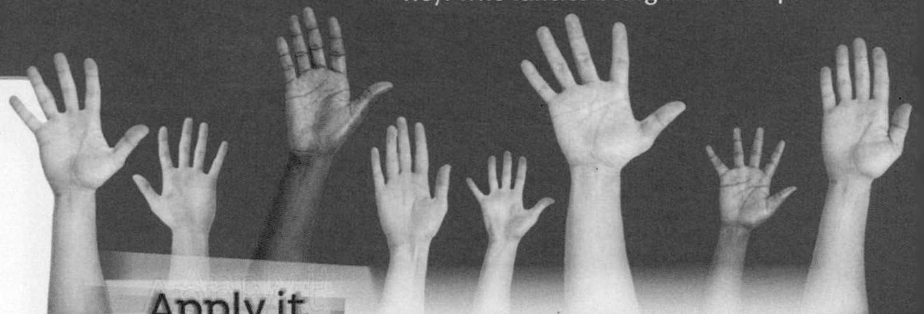

Apply it Methods — Which sampling method?

Questions

Decide which one of the five sampling techniques is being used in the examples below. (*1 mark each*)

1. Students investigating the link between age and attitudes to the legalisation of drugs stop people in the street and ask them their views.
2. An occupational psychologist surveying employees about stress at work selects a sample that reflects the overall staff ratio of management to shop floor workers.
3. A teacher selects a sample of Year 9 students to take part in a test of selective attention by picking every third student from the register.
4. A member of senior management is interested in teachers' opinions regarding their workload. She assigns all the staff a number, places these in a hat and draws out 20 numbers.
5. A university lecturer requests participants for an experiment into how expectation affects perception by placing an advert on the common room noticeboard.

Apply it Methods — Being random

Two psychology students designed a study on conformity. They planned to ask people to fill in a questionnaire. They arranged it so it looked like some other students had already filled in some answers. In fact the student researchers filled in the answers themselves so that most of them were wrong. The student researchers wanted to see if their participants would conform to the wrong answers. They decided to use a random sampling technique.

Questions

1. Explain how they could obtain a random sample of 20 from all the students in their school. (*3 marks*)
2. Explain why they might have found it easier to use an opportunity sample. (*2 marks*)
3. Explain why that might have produced a less representative sample. (*2 marks*)

Check it

1. Outline **one** strength **and one** limitation of random sampling. *[4 marks]*
2. Explain what is meant by 'stratified sampling'. *[3 marks]*
3. Explain the difference between a population and a sample. *[3 marks]*
4. Explain how you would select a stratified sample of all the male and female workers within a sausage factory. *[3 marks]*
5. Explain **one** reason why it might be difficult to make generalisations from a volunteer sample. *[2 marks]*

Ethical issues and ways of dealing with them

The specification says...

Ethics, including the role of the British Psychological Society's code of ethics; ethical issues in the design and conduct of psychological studies; dealing with ethical issues in research.

One of the most important considerations in psychology is how to conduct worthwhile and innovative research whilst at the same time respecting the dignity and well-being of participants.

Here, we discuss the major ethical issues in psychology and how professional psychologists deal with these in accordance with the guidelines set down by their professional organisation - the British Psychological Society.

Key terms

Ethical issues These arise when a conflict exists between the rights of participants in research studies and the goals of research to produce authentic, valid and worthwhile data.

BPS code of ethics A quasi-legal document produced by the British Psychological Society (BPS) that instructs psychologists in the UK about what behaviour is and is not acceptable when dealing with participants. The code is built around four major principles: respect, competence, responsibility and integrity.

PROCEED
WITH
CAUTION

Apply it Methods — Briefing and debriefing

When participants arrive to take part in a study they are given a briefing so they can provide informed consent (told what they will be asked to do, told some or all of the aims of the research, etc.). After the research has taken place, participants will be debriefed (see facing page).

Question

Write a briefing and a debriefing statement that could be read out to each of the participants in the energy drink experiment. You'll need to write separate ones for each of the **experimental conditions**. Try to make sure you include all the details and issues described on these pages to ensure that participants are treated as ethically as possible. (*5 marks*)

Ethical issues in the design and conduct of psychological studies

Ethical issues arise in psychology when a conflict or dilemma exists between participants' rights and researchers' needs to gain valuable and meaningful findings. This conflict has implications for the safety and well-being of participants.

For instance, a researcher may not wish to reveal the true purpose of a research study to participants in order to study more 'natural' behaviour. But is it acceptable to mislead participants in this way – it might involve lying to them? Is it acceptable to tell participants they failed a test in order to study responses to failure? Is causing psychological distress to participants ever justified? What if they were made aware o this beforehand, would that make a difference?

Let us consider four of the major ethical issues that face participants and researchers in psychology.

Informed consent

At a basic level, prospective participants in studies should know what they are getting into before they get into it. **Informed consent** involves making participants aware of the **aims** of the research, the procedures, their rights (including the **right to withdraw** partway through the investigation should they so wish), and also what their data will be used for. Participants should then make an informed judgement whether or not to take part without being coerced or feeling obliged.

From the researcher's point of view, asking for informed consent may make the study meaningless because participants' behaviour will not be 'natural' as they know the aims of the study.

Deception

Deception means deliberately misleading or withholding information from participants at any stage of the investigation. This is linked to the above. Participants who have not received adequate information when they agreed to take part (or worse, have been deliberately lied to) cannot be said to have given informed consen

Despite that, there are occasions when deception can be justified if it does not cause the participant undue distress. For instance, in our energy drink study it would probably be acceptable not to tell participants that there is another group drinking a different substance, as knowing this may affect their behaviour.

Protection from harm

As a result of their involvement, participants should not be placed at any more risk than they would be in their daily lives, and should be protected from physical and psychological harm. The latter includes being made to feel embarrassed, inadequate or being placed under undue stress or pressure. An important feature of protection from harm, as mentioned above, is participants being reminded of the fact that they have the right to withdraw from the investigation at any point.

Privacy and confidentiality

Participants have the right to control information about themselves. This is the right of **privacy**. If this is invaded then confidentiality should be protected. **Confidentiality** refers to our right, enshrined in law under the Data Protection Act, to have any personal data protected.

The right to privacy extends to the area where the study took place such that institutions or geographical locations are not named.

Study tip

Your understanding of ethical issues will be important throughout the whole of your study of psychology. You can use this understanding to present ethical evaluations of the studies you have read about throughout this book and may have an opportunity to discuss cost–benefit issues – can the ethical costs be justified in terms of the benefits?

It is important, when using ethical issues as evaluation, to remember that such issues do not challenge the findings of a study. Just because a study might be judged unethical by today's standards does not mean its findings are meaningless.

:thical issues apply to all the different research methods used in 'sychology – it may seem as if they just apply to experiments but ou have yet to read about the others!

Vays of dealing with ethical issues

3PS code of conduct

ne **British Psychological Society** (BPS), like many other professional bodies, has its wn **BPS code of ethics** and this includes a set of **ethical guidelines**. Researchers have a rofessional duty to observe these guidelines when conducting research – they won't be ent to prison if they don't follow them but they may well lose their job.

The guidelines are closely matched to the ethical issues on the facing page and ttempt to ensure that all participants are treated with respect and consideration during ach phase of research. Guidelines are implemented by **ethics committees** in research nstitutions who often use a **cost–benefit approach** to determine whether particular esearch proposals are ethically acceptable (see Apply it below).

)ealing with informed consent

articipants should be issued with a consent letter or form detailing all relevant information hat might affect their decision to participate. Assuming the participant agrees, this is then gned. For investigations involving children under 16, a signature of parental consent is equired. There are other ways to obtain consent, which are described on the right.

)ealing with deception and protection from harm

t the end of a study, participants should be given a full **debrief**. Within this, participants hould be made aware of the true aims of the investigation and any details they were ot supplied with during the study, such as the existence of other groups or experimental onditions.

Participants should also be told what their data will be used for and must be given the ght to withdraw during the study and the **right to withhold data** if they wish. This is articularly important if retrospective consent is a feature of the study (see right).

Participants may have natural concerns related to their performance within the vestigation, and so should be reassured that their behaviour was typical or normal. In xtreme cases, if participants have been subject to stress or embarrassment, they may quire **counselling**, which the researcher should provide.

)ealing with confidentiality

personal details are held these must be protected. However it is more usual to mply record no personal details, i.e. maintain **anonymity**. Researchers usually refer to articipants using numbers or initials when writing up the investigation. In a **case study**, sychologists often use initials when describing the individual or individuals involved ee the study of HM on page 48).

Finally, it is standard practice that during briefing and debriefing, participants are minded that their data will be protected throughout the process and told that the data ill not be shared with other researchers.

Apply it Methods

Cost–benefit analysis

It is the responsibility of ethics committees to weigh up the costs and benefits of research proposals to decide whether a research study should go ahead. Benefits might include the value or groundbreaking nature of the research. Possible costs may be the damaging effect on individual participants or to the reputation of psychology as a whole. (*3 marks each*)

Questions

Imagine you are sitting on an ethics committee. Should the following investigations go ahead? Do a cost–benefit analysis of each.

1. A teacher actively discriminates against the children who have blue eyes in her Year 5 class (and encourages the non-blue-eyed classmates to do the same) by withholding privileges and giving them more difficult tasks to do. This was a study to demonstrate the evils of ethnic prejudice (Elliott 1968).
2. As a naïve participant sits in a waiting room, (fake) smoke is pumped under the door suggesting that the next room is on fire. A group of **confederates** have been told to remain passive and not raise the alarm. This is an investigation into the factors that influence behaviour in an emergency (Latané and Darley 1968).

Apply it Methods

Alternative ways of getting consent

From a researcher's point of view the problem with asking for informed consent is that it may spoil the research – participants then know what is being studied and alter their behaviour accordingly. Psychologists have tried to address this problem by devising three alternatives:

- **Presumptive consent** – rather than getting consent from the participants themselves, a similar group of people are asked if the study is acceptable. If this group agrees, then consent of the original participants is 'presumed'.
- **Prior general consent** – participants give their permission to take part in a number of different studies – including one that will involve deception. By consenting, participants are effectively consenting to be deceived.
- **Retrospective consent** – participants are asked for their consent (during debriefing) having already taken part in the study. They may not have been aware of their participation or they may have been subject to deception.

Question

None of these methods are considered 'ideal' by researchers. What would you suggest are the main problems with each? (*2 marks each*)

PROS
CONS

Cost–benefit analysis
The role of ethics committees is to make judgements about the costs and benefits involved in carrying out individual pieces of research.

Check it

1. Using an example, explain what is meant by 'ethical issue'. *[3 marks]*
2. Outline **one** ethical issue in psychology. Explain **how** this issue could be dealt with. *[3 marks]*
3. Briefly explain the role of the British Psychological Society's code of ethics in psychological research. *[4 marks]*
4. Discuss ethical issues in psychological research. Refer to **one or more** research studies in your answer. *[12 marks AS, 16 marks A level]*

Pilot studies (and more)

The specification says...

Pilot studies and the aims of piloting.

Pilot studies are an important element of research design. They allow a researcher to test investigation procedures with a small group of participants before the investigation begins.

We shall consider the aims of piloting on this spread as well as some of the other features of experimental design that have not been mentioned elsewhere.

Key term

Pilot study A small-scale version of an investigation that takes place before the real investigation is conducted. The aim is to check that procedures, materials, measuring scales, etc., work. The aim is also to allow the researcher to make changes or modifications if necessary.

Study tip

Many students misunderstand the purpose of pilot studies and often assume they have something to do with testing or finding support for the hypothesis. They don't. 'Piloting', as it is sometimes referred to, is an important part of the design process that makes the researcher aware of problems that can be fixed before data gathering begins.

Apply it Methods Piloting

Remember the energy drink study? How could you forget?

An experienced researcher has taken a look at our proposed design and suggested we conduct a pilot study before carrying out the main investigation.

Question

Explain, in as much detail as you can, how such a pilot study could be done and what, as researchers, we might learn from it. (*4 marks*)

Apply it Methods SpeedUpp

Answer these questions on the energy drink investigation. (*2 marks each*)

Questions

1. Explain why a single-blind procedure may be useful in reducing the effects of demand characteristics.
2. If a single-blind procedure was used, explain what would have to happen at the end of the study.
3. Explain how you might set up a double-blind procedure.
4. Explain how this would be effective in reducing the influence of investigator effects within the experiment.
5. Which condition of the energy drink experiment is the control group? Explain what purpose this group serves.

Pilot studies

The aims of piloting

A **pilot study** is a small-scale trial run of the actual investigation.

A pilot study involves a handful of participants, rather than the total number, in order to 'road-test' the procedure and check the investigation runs smoothly.

It is also important to recognise that pilot studies are not just restricted to experimental studies. When using self-report methods, such as **questionnaires** or **interviews**, it is helpful to try out questions in advance and remove or reword those that are ambiguous or confusing.

In **observational studies**, a pilot study provides a way of checking coding systems before the real investigation is undertaken. This may be an important part of training observers.

In short then, a pilot study allows the researcher to identify any potential issues and to modify the design or procedure, saving time and money in the long run.

Some other things you should know

Single-blind procedure

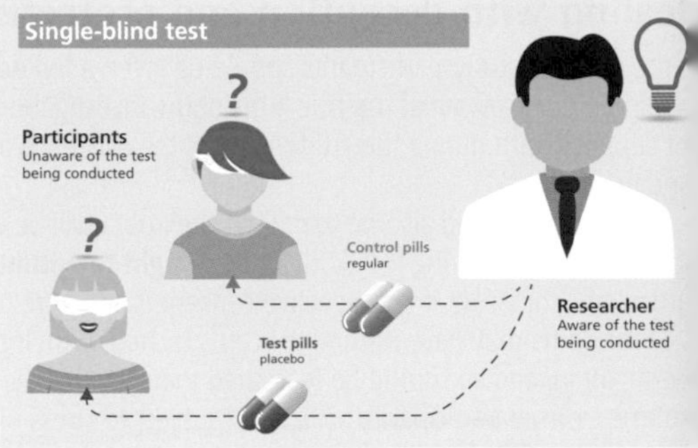
Single-blind test
Participants
Unaware of the test being conducted
Control pills
regular
Test pills
placebo
Researcher
Aware of the test being conducted

We mentioned, when discussing **ethical issues**, that participants will sometimes *not* be told the **aim** of the research at the beginning of a study. As well as this, other details may be kept from participants, such as which condition of the experiment they are in or whether there is another condition at all. This is known as a **single-blind procedure** – any information that might create expectations is not revealed until the end of the study to control for the confounding effects of **demand characteristics** (see page 170).

Double-blind procedure

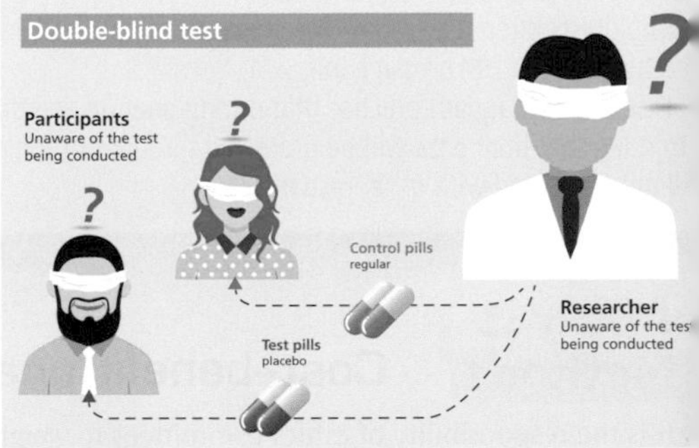
Double-blind test
Participants
Unaware of the test being conducted
Control pills
regular
Test pills
placebo
Researcher

In a **double-blind procedure** neither the participants nor the researcher who conducts the study is aware of the aims of the investigation (often a third party conducts the investigation without knowing its main purpose).

Double-blind procedures are often an important feature of drug trials. Treatment may be administered to participants by someone who is independent of the investigation and who does not know which drugs are real and which are **placebos** ('fake' drugs). If they don't know what each participant is receiving then expectations cannot influence participant behaviour.

Control groups and conditions

In the example of the drug trial above, the group that receives the real drug is the **experimental group** and the group that receives the placebo is the **control group**.

We use the word 'control' in research to refer to the control of variables but we use it here to refer to setting a baseline. Control is used in many experimental studies for the purpose of *comparison*. If the change in behaviour of the experimental group is significantly greater than that of the control group, then the researcher can conclude that the cause of this effect was the **independent variable** (assuming all other possible **confounding variables** have remained constant).

Having two groups in an experiment is an independent groups design, but we can also have **control conditions** in a repeated measures design. Each participant takes part twice – once in the **experimental condition** and then in the control condition.

Apply it Methods

Review of research methods concepts

Fake estimates

A sixth-form psychology student was interested in the effect of social influence on behaviour and decided to conduct an experiment. She approached 40 Year 11 students around her school and presented each of them with a picture of a crowd scene. Each participant was asked to estimate how many people were in the picture.

20 participants (Group A) were shown the picture of the crowd scene only. The other 20 participants (Group B) were shown the picture of the crowd scene alongside five numbers that, they were told, were the estimates of other participants who had guessed before them.

Based on the size of the crowd, these guesses were clearly too high, but the psychology student wanted to know whether these would affect the estimates of the participants in Group B.

Questions

1. What is the **independent variable** in this experiment? (*2 marks*)
2. What is the **dependent variable** in this experiment? (*2 marks*)
3. Identify the **experimental design** used in this experiment. (*1 mark*)
4. Explain *one* advantage of the experimental design you identified in your answer to question 3. Refer to this experiment in your answer. (*3 marks*)
5. Write a suitable **hypothesis** for this experiment. (*2 marks*)
6. Identify the **sampling method** used in this experiment. Justify your answer. (*2 marks*)
7. Explain how **random allocation** could have been used in this experiment. (*2 marks*)
8. Write a **debriefing** statement that could be read out to the participants in Group B. (*4 marks*)
9. Explain why **standardisation** is important when conducting experimental research. (*2 marks*)
10. Explain *one* way in which the procedure of this experiment could have been **standardised**. (*2 marks*)
11. Explain what is meant by 'extraneous variable'. (*1 mark*)
12. Identify *one* extraneous variable in this experiment, explain why it would need to be controlled, and how this could be done. (*3 marks*)

Gender differences in texting

A teacher was interested to know whether there was a difference in the number of mobile phone texts boys and girls send each day.

The teacher selected a random sample of 20 boys and 20 girls from the whole school and got them to record the number of texts they had sent at the end of each day.

After two weeks, the teacher compared the total number of texts for boys and girls and found there was very little difference between them.

Questions

1. This is an example of a **quasi-experiment**. Explain why this is a quasi-experiment. (*2 marks*)
2. Explain *one* disadvantage of a quasi-experiment. Refer to this experiment in your answer. (*3 marks*)
3. The teacher used **random sampling** to select participants. Explain how the teacher may have used random sampling in this experiment. (*3 marks*)
4. Explain *one* strength of using random sampling in this experiment. (*2 marks*)
5. Before the experiment began, the teacher conducted a **pilot study**. Explain why the teacher decided to conduct a pilot study. (*2 marks*)
6. Explain how **social desirability bias** may have affected the outcome of this experiment. (*3 marks*)
7. Identify *one* **ethical issue** that the teacher should have taken account of when conducting this experiment. (*1 mark*)
8. Explain *one* way in which the teacher could have dealt with the ethical issue that you identified in your answer to question 7. (*3 marks*)
9. Explain what is meant by 'operationalisation' when designing experiments. (*2 marks*)
10. Explain how the teacher has operationalised 'difference in texting' within this experiment. (*1 mark*)
11. Explain what is meant by 'confounding variable'. (*2 marks*)
12. Explain *one* way in which **investigator effects** may confound the findings of this experiment. (*3 marks*)

Estimate how many people are here.

If I tell you the previous estimates were 96 and 115, would that influence your answer?

Observational techniques

The specification says...

Observational techniques. Types of observation: naturalistic and controlled observation; covert and overt observation; participant and non-participant observation.

The experimental method may not always provide the most suitable way to study a particular behaviour. There are a number of non-experimental methods available to psychologists, one of which is observation.

On this spread we consider the different types of observational method, as well as the strengths and limitations of each.

Key terms

Naturalistic observation Watching and recording behaviour in the setting within which it would normally occur.

Controlled observation Watching and recording behaviour within a structured environment, i.e. one where some variables are managed.

Covert observation Participants' behaviour is watched and recorded *without* their knowledge or consent.

Overt observation Participants' behaviour is watched and recorded *with* their knowledge and consent.

Participant observation The researcher becomes a member of the group whose behaviour he/she is watching and recording.

Non-participant observation The researcher remains outside of the group whose behaviour he/she is watching and recording.

There's got to be a cat around here somewhere...

On page 168 we describe the 'aims' of an experiment. All research studies have aims – they're not just for experiments.

Types of observation

One important non-experimental method is **observation**. Observations provide psychologists with a way of seeing what people do without having to ask them (as in studies involving **self-report** methods – a joy yet to come). They also allow researchers to study observable behaviour within a natural or controlled setting (see below). This method allows a researcher the flexibility to study more complex interactions between variables.

Note that observation is often used within an experiment as a way, for example, of assessing the **dependent variable**.

Naturalistic and controlled observations

Naturalistic observations take place in the setting or context where the target behaviour would usually occur. All aspects of the environment are free to vary. For instance, it would not make sense to study how senior management and employees in a particular factory interact by dragging the whole of the workforce into an artificial **lab** setting. It is much better to study 'interaction' in the factory environment where it would normally take place.

It is sometimes useful to control certain aspects of the research situation, so a **controlled observation** may be preferred. For example, Mary Ainsworth made use of a controlled observation as part of her **Strange Situation** studies (see page 86). Ainsworth recorded the way in which children reacted to their mothers and how they dealt with the introduction of a stranger within a specially designed playroom environment. Ainsworth and her team recorded their data remotely, via a **two-way mirror**, so as not to disturb the action.

In a controlled observation there is some control over variables, including manipulating variables to observe effects and also control of **confounding/extraneous variables**.

Covert and overt observations

Behaviour may occasionally be recorded without first obtaining the consent of the participants. **Covert observations** are those in which the participants are unaware they are the focus of study and their behaviour is observed in secret (covertly), say from across a room or from a balcony (but rarely from behind a bush). Such behaviour must be public and happening anyway if the observation is to be **ethical**.

In contrast, **overt observations** are when participants know their behaviour is being observed and have given their **informed consent** beforehand.

Participant and non-participant observations

Sometimes it may be necessary for the observer to become part of the group they are studying, as is the case with **participant observations**. For instance, we might have improved the study of factory workers and management (referred to above) by having the researcher actually join the workforce to produce a first-hand account.

Non-participant observations are when the researcher remains separate from those they are studying and records behaviour in a more objective manner. It may often be impractical or even impossible to join particular groups so that non-participation is the only option – such as a middle-aged female researcher observing behaviour amongst Year 10 students at a boys' school!

Apply it Methods — Types of observation

Questions

State whether the following observations are naturalistic or controlled, covert or overt, participant or non-participant. Explain your choices in each case. (*1 mark each*)

1. A researcher secretly joins a religious cult to see if people are being brainwashed.
2. A researcher watches primary school children through a two-way mirror in a playroom to investigate co-operation.
3. A researcher observes the crowd at a football match using footage from CCTV recordings. The crowd do know there are CCTV cameras.
4. A researcher observes student behaviour by enrolling on an AS course and pretending to be a mature student.
5. The head of a psychology department observes an A level class by watching the lesson at an agreed time, sitting at the back of the room.

ɛvaluation

ll observations

ɓbservations of behaviour have the benefit of capturing what people actually do, which ıay be unexpected behaviour. People often do not act the same as they say they would. o observational methods are useful because they give special insight into behaviour.

One limitation of observation is **observer bias**. The observer's interpretation of a ituation may be affected by their expectations. This may be reduced by using more ıan one observer.

Another limitation is observational studies cannot demonstrate causal ɜlationships – though observational techniques may be used in experiments and aid ı detecting cause-and-effect relationships.

ıaturalistic and controlled observations

ɪaturalistic observations tend to have high **external validity** as findings can often e **generalised** to everyday life. This is because the behaviour is studied within the nvironment where it would normally occur. That said, the lack of control over the ɜsearch situation makes **replication** of the investigation difficult. There may also be ıany uncontrolled confounding/extraneous variables that make it more difficult to ıdge any pattern of behaviour.

Controlled observations, in contrast, may produce findings that cannot be as ɜadily applied to everyday life. Confounding/extraneous variables may be less of a ıctor so replication of the observation becomes easier.

;overt and overt observations

ɦe fact that participants do not know they are being watched removes the problem f **demand characteristics** (see page 170) and ensures any behaviour observed will be atural. This increases the **internal validity** of the data gathered.

However, the **ethics** of these studies may be questioned as people, even in public, ıay not wish to have their behaviours noted down (right to privacy). For instance, hopping' would generally be recognised as a public activity, but the amount of ıoney people spend on a shopping trip is probably their own private business!

In this sense, overt observations are more ethically acceptable but the knowledge articipants have that they are being observed may act as a significant influence on ıeir behaviour.

ʾarticipant and non-participant observations

ı participant observations, the researcher can experience the situation as the articipants do, giving them increased insight into the lives of the people being tudied. This may increase the external validity of the findings.

There is a danger, however, that the researcher may come to identify too strongly ʲith those they are studying and lose **objectivity**. Some researchers refer to this s adopting a local lifestyle when the line between being a researcher and being a articipant becomes blurred.

Non-participant observations allow the researcher to maintain an objective sychological distance from their participants so there is less danger of them adopting a ɔcal lifestyle. However, they may lose the valuable insight to be gained in a participant bservation as they are too far removed from the people and behaviour they are studying.

STANFORD
COUNTY
PRISON

eread Zimbardo's Stanford prison xperiment on page 20. Decide which f the three types of observation – escribed on the facing page – it is.

ɪow does this study illustrate ome of the strengths and mitations of observational ɜsearch?

Apply it Methods

On being sane in insane places

A very famous observational study was conducted by David Rosenhan (1973), investigating the problem of defining abnormality.

Rosenhan arranged for eight pseudopatients, one of whom was himself, to present themselves individually to various psychiatric institutions in the US complaining of fake symptoms of mental disorder. These symptoms included hearing voices. All eight pseudopatients were admitted and given a diagnosis of *schizophrenia* except in one case.

Once the pseudopatients had gained access to the psychiatric institution, the observation began. Each pseudopatient stopped pretending to have symptoms and instead observed and recorded the daily life of the patients in the institution – the usual ward routine, interactions with the staff, etc.

One notable finding was the way in which staff at the hospital behaved towards the researchers. Despite the fact that many of the genuine patients quickly realised that the pseudopatients were fake, staff were slower to catch on.

Significant also was the way in which the behaviour of the pseudopatients was regarded by staff. Note-taking by one of the researchers was described as 'repetitive writing behaviour' in their patient notes, and pacing the corridors, which researchers often engaged in to ease their boredom, was interpreted as a sign of anxiety. In short, the 'normal' behaviour of the researchers was seen by staff at the various hospitals as 'symptomatic' of the mental disorder they had been labelled with.

Questions

1. Is Rosenhan's observational study:
   a) Naturalistic or controlled? (*1 mark*)
   b) Covert or overt? (*1 mark*)
   c) Participant or non-participant? (*1 mark*)
2. This study is seen as a powerful example of the influence that the label 'mental disorder' has on the way we view behaviour but how valid is the method used? Identify *two* strengths and *two* limitations of the observational methods used in this study. (*4 marks*)

Study tip

There is a tendency to confuse controlled observations with laboratory experiments, whilst naturalistic observations are often mixed up with natural experiments!

Remember that although there may be variables in an observation there is no independent variable (IV). In an experiment, this IV either exists regardless of the researcher (as in a natural or quasi-experiment) or is manipulated by the experimenter (in a lab or field experiment).

Check it

1. Explain the difference between a naturalistic observation and a controlled observation. *[4 marks]*
2. Outline the difference between a covert and an overt observation. *[2 marks]*
3. Explain **one** strength **and one** limitation of a non-participant observation. *[2 marks + 2 marks]*
4. Briefly evaluate the use of naturalistic observations in psychological research. *[4 marks]*
5. Identify **two** types of observation **and** state **one** limitation of each. *[4 marks]*

Observational design

The specification says...

Observational design: behavioural categories; event sampling; time sampling.

On the previous spread we considered observational techniques – the different types of observation available to psychologists. Here, we focus on how a researcher would actually plan an observational study.

Key terms

Behavioural categories When a target behaviour is broken up into components that are observable and measurable (operationalisation).

Event sampling A target behaviour or event is first established then the researcher records this event every time it occurs.

Time sampling A target individual or group is first established then the researcher records their behaviour in a fixed time frame, say, every 60 seconds.

A level only

Inter-observer reliability

It is recommended that researchers do not conduct observational studies alone. Single observers may miss important details or may only notice events that confirm their opinions or hypothesis. This introduces **bias** into the research process.

To make data recording more objective and unbiased, observations should be carried out by at least two researchers. Then data from different observers is compared to check for consistency i.e. reliability, and this is called **inter-observer reliability**. To do this:

- Observers should familiarise themselves with the behavioural categories to be used.
- They then observe the same behaviour at the same time, perhaps as part of a small-scale **pilot study**.
- Observers should compare the data they have recorded and discuss any differences in interpretations.
- Finally observers should analyse the data from the study. Inter-observer reliability is calculated by **correlating** each pair of observations made and an overall figure is produced.

You can check the inter-observer reliability of a set of observations using the behavioural categories for your observational study (see Apply it on facing page). Pass your list to a friend and ask them to use the list to observe a recording of the same people for five minutes. How does your data compare? Have you established close inter-observer reliability?

Issues in observational design

Ways of recording data

One of the key influences on the design of any observation is how the researcher intends to record their data. The researcher may simply want to write down everything they see. This is referred to as an **unstructured observation** and tends to produce accounts of behaviour that are rich in detail. This method may be appropriate when observations are small in scale and involve few participants. For example, observing interaction between a couple and a therapist within a relationship support counselling session.

Often, however, there may be too much going on in a single observation for the researcher to record it all. Therefore, it is necessary to simplify the target behaviours that will become the main focus of the investigation using behavioural categories (see below). This then becomes a **structured observation**. Although the distinction between 'structured' and 'unstructured' observations is not on the specification, it is useful to know because the information that follows relates to structured observations only.

Behavioural categories

In order to produce a structured record of what a researcher sees (or hears), it is first necessary to break the target behaviour up into a set of **behavioural categories** (sometimes referred to as a **behaviour checklist**). This is very similar to the idea of **operationalisation** that we came across earlier on page 169. Target behaviours to be studied should be precisely defined and made observable and measurable.

For instance, the target behaviour 'affection' may be broken down into observational categories such as hugging, kissing, smiling, holding hands, etc. Each of these behaviours must be observable – there should be no need for inferences to be made, such as 'being loving'. Two observers might interpret this differently and thus it would not be a reliable category.

Before the observation begins, the researcher should ensure that they have, as far as possible, included all the ways in which the target behaviour may occur within their behavioural checklist.

Sampling methods

Continuous recording of behaviour is a key feature of unstructured observations in which all instances of a target behaviour are recorded. For very complex behaviours, however, this method may not be practical or feasible. As such, in structured observations, the researcher must use a systematic way of sampling their observations (note that 'sampling' in this context has a different meaning from that discussed on page 176).

Event sampling involves counting the number of times a particular behaviour (the 'event') occurs in a target individual or group. For instance, event sampling of dissent at a football match would mean counting the number of times players disagree with the referee.

Time sampling involves recording behaviour within a pre-established time frame. For example, in a particular football match we may only be interested in one specific player so we may make a note (using a behavioural checklist) of what our target individual is doing every 30 seconds.

Study tip

It is important you are able to put into practice what you learn by designing and carrying out your own investigations using observational methods. So, on this spread, we discuss how to design observational research, having described and evaluated different types of observation on the previous spread.

What do students do when their teacher leaves the room?

The record sheet below is used to record behaviour. A behaviour checklist is given (across the top) with space below to record the behaviour of a target student. A tally mark is placed each time one of the behaviours is observed – an example of event sampling.

Carries on working	Uses mobile phone	Talks to another student	Listens to music	Leaves the room	Reads a magazine	Falls asleep	Eats
IIII	I	III	II				I

Practical activity on pages 96, 127 and 159

:valuation

'tructured versus unstructured

tructured observations that involve the use of behavioural ategories make the recording of data easier and more ystematic. The data produced is likely to be *numerical* (see the iscussion of **quantitative data** on page 192), which means 1at analysing and comparing the behaviour observed between articipants is more straightforward. In contrast, **unstructured bservations** tend to produce **qualitative data**, which may be 1uch more difficult to record and analyse.

However, unstructured observations benefit from more chness and depth of detail in the data collected. Though 1ere may be a greater risk of **observer bias** with unstructured bservations, as the objective behavioural categories that are feature of structured observations are not present here. The esearcher may only record those behaviours that 'catch their eye' nd these may not be the most important or useful.

3ehavioural categories

lthough the use of behavioural categories can make data ollection more structured and objective, it is important that such ategories are as clear and unambiguous as possible. They must e *observable*, *measurable* and *self-evident*. In other words, they hould not require further interpretation.

Researchers should also ensure that all possible forms of the arget behaviour are included in the checklist. There should not e a 'dustbin category' in which many different behaviours are eposited.

Finally, categories should be exclusive and not overlap. For 1stance, the difference between 'smiling' and 'grinning' would e very difficult to discern.

;ampling methods

vent sampling is useful when the target behaviour or event appens quite infrequently and could be missed if time sampling /as used. However, if the specified event is too complex, the bserver may overlook important details if using event sampling.

Time sampling is effective in reducing the number of bservations that have to be made. That said, those instances vhen behaviour is sampled might be unrepresentative of the bservation as a whole.

Psychologists monitoring a group of people having a meeting.

Apply it Methods: Behavioural categories

Task

Draw up a behavioural checklist of facial expressions that might be observed in a six-month-old baby. Try to observe all the 'rules' of behavioural categories explained on this spread. (*4 marks*)

Apply it Methods: Methods: Observation: Over to you

Observational techniques are often used as a means of assessing the dependent variable (DV) in an experiment.

Task

You could conduct an experiment looking at the differences in the way men or women behave when in same-gender pairs/groups and opposite-gender pairs/groups (it would be a natural experiment if you observe 'self-determined' pairs).

In this study the independent variable (IV) is same-gender or opposite-gender pairs. You need to measure the DV – the differences in the way men or women behave. To measure this you can observe their behaviour.

Follow the steps below in designing your study.

Decisions to make

Aim and hypothesis

- What is the aim of your study?
- If this is an experiment, what is the hypothesis? Is it directional or non-directional?

Decide on design of the observation

- Setting – controlled or naturalistic?
- Observer's status – covert or overt?
- Observer's involvement – participant or non-participant?
- Sampling method – continuous, time sampling or event sampling?

Decide how DV will be recorded

- Unstructured observations or structured ones?
- Fully operationalise the DV into behavioural categories.
- Create a behaviour checklist (record sheet) to record frequency of observations.

Consider ethical issues

- Can covert observations be justified?
- Is this a public behaviour that would be happening anyway?

Analysis of data

- How will you present your results? (For ideas see pages 196–197.)

Check it

1. Explain how you would use time sampling in an observation of children's aggression in the playground. *[4 marks]*
2. Imagine you are conducting an observation of the 'confidence' shown by students in a lesson. Operationalise the behaviour 'confidence' using **three** behavioural categories. *[3 marks]*
3. With reference to your answer to question 2, design a record sheet that could be used to observe the difference in confidence between male and female students in a Year 12 class. *[3 marks]*

Self-report techniques

The specification says...

Self-report techniques: questionnaires, use of open and closed questions; interviews, structured and unstructured.

Sometimes the most straightforward way of understanding why people behave in the way that they do is to ask them. This is the self-report method and it comprises questionnaires and interviews, two separate techniques that we shall consider on this spread.

Key terms

Self-report technique Any method in which a person is asked to state or explain their own feelings, opinions, behaviours and/or experiences related to a given topic.

Questionnaire A set of written questions (sometimes referred to as 'items') used to assess a person's thoughts and/or experiences.

Interview A 'live' encounter (face-to-face or on the phone) where one person (the interviewer) asks a set of questions to assess an interviewee's thoughts and/or experiences. The questions may be pre-set (as in a structured interview) or may develop as the interview goes along (unstructured interview).

See next spread for definitions of **open** and **closed questions**.

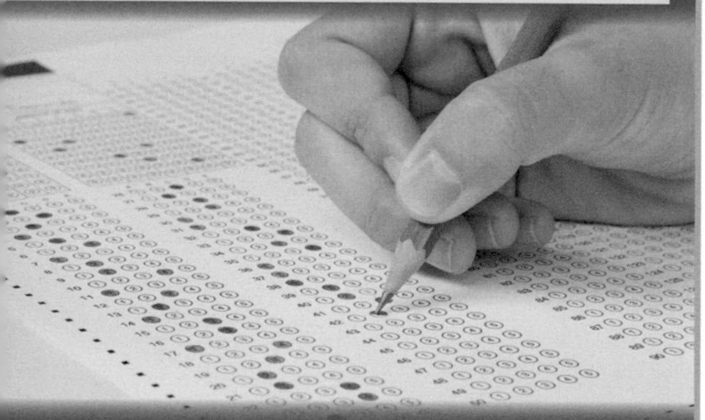

A multiple-choice questionnaire is a good example of using closed, rather than open, questions.

Questionnaires

Questionnaires are probably the most common type of **self-report technique**. They involve (not surprisingly) a pre-set list of written questions (or *items*) to which a participant responds. Psychologists use questionnaires to assess thoughts and/or feelings. A study may simply consist of a question to find out about the kind of dreams people have or a long list of items designed to assess an individual's personality type.

A questionnaire may be used as part of an experiment to assess the **dependent variable**. For example, whether views on the legalisation of specific recreational drugs are different in older and younger people.

Open and closed questions

There are a number of different possible styles of questions in a questionnaire but these can be broadly divided into **open questions** and **closed questions**.

An open question does not have a fixed range of answers and respondents are free to answer in any way they wish. For instance, we might ask participants in our energy drink experiment how they felt during the investigation or why they thought they became more talkative (assuming they did). Open questions tend to produce **qualitative data** that contains a wide range of different responses but may be difficult to analyse.

A closed question offers a fixed number of responses. We might ask our participants if they felt more talkative as a result of the energy drink and restrict them to two options: 'yes' or 'no' (qualitative data). Alternatively we might get them to rate how sociable they felt after consuming the drink on a scale of 1 to 10 (**quantitative data**). Quantitative data like this is usually easy to analyse but it may lack the depth and detail associated with open questions. Note that closed questions that produce qualitative data can be turned into quantitative data by, for example, counting the number of yes and no responses.

Interviews

Although some **interviews** may be conducted over the phone/internet, most involve a face-to-face interaction between an interviewer and an interviewee. There are three broad types of interview.

Structured interviews

Structured interviews are made up of a pre-determined set of questions that are asked in a fixed order. Basically this is like a questionnaire but conducted face-to-face (or over the phone/internet) in real time, i.e. the interviewer asks the questions and waits for a response.

Unstructured interviews

An unstructured interview works a lot like a conversation. There are no set questions. There is a general aim that a certain topic will be discussed, and interaction tends to be free-flowing. The interviewee is encouraged to expand and elaborate their answers as prompted by the interviewer.

Semi-structured interviews

Many interviews are likely to fall somewhere between the two types described above. The sort of interview that one is most likely to encounter in everyday life – a job interview – is a good example of a **semi-structured interview**: there is a list of questions that have been worked out in advance but interviewers are also free to ask follow-up questions based on previous answers.

Apply it Methods — Open and closed questions

Questions

1. Write *one* closed and *one* open question for each of the following scenarios. (*2 marks each*)
   a) A psychologist interviewed PE teachers at a local school to assess the pupils' attitudes towards exercise.
   b) A teacher distributed a questionnaire to her pupils to assess their mood on a Monday morning.
   c) A doctor produced a patient questionnaire to assess whether a new computer system had affected waiting times for appointments.
   d) A scientist designed a questionnaire to assess people's anxiety levels about a zombie apocalypse.

2. Which of the following are associated with open questions and which are associated with closed questions? (*1 mark each*)
   a) Responses tend to include greater depth/detail.
   b) Often involves ticking a box or circling an answer.
   c) Responses are easier to compare.
   d) Respondents can't explain their answers.
   e) Conclusions drawn may be open to bias.
   f) Difficult to collate and summarise data.

:valuation

;trengths

luestionnaires are cost-effective. They can gather large amounts of data quickly ecause they can be distributed to large numbers of people (note that it is ne number of people that is important as this determines the volume of data ollected). A questionnaire can be completed without the researcher being present, s in the case of a postal questionnaire, which also reduces the effort involved.

The data that questionnaires produce is usually straightforward to analyse and his is particularly the case if the questionnaire comprises mainly fixed-choice osed questions (contrast this with interview data, below). The data lends itself to tatistical analysis, and comparisons between groups of people can be made using raphs and charts.

.imitations

. major problem is that the responses given may not always be truthful. espondents may be keen to present themselves in a positive light and this may ifluence their answers. For example, if asked 'How often do you lose your phone?', nost people would underestimate the frequency. This is a form of **demand haracteristic** called **social desirability bias**.

Questionnaires often produce a **response bias**, which is where respondents end to reply in a similar way, for instance, always ticking 'yes' or answering at ne same favoured end of a **rating scale** (discussed on the next spread). This nay be because respondents complete the questionnaire too quickly and fail to ead questions properly. A particular form of response bias, **acquiescence bias**, is iscussed on the right.

Practical activity on pages 37 and 65

:valuation

;tructured interviews

tructured interviews, like questionnaires, are straightforward to **replicate** due to heir standardised format. The format also reduces differences between interviewers.

It is not possible, however, given the nature of the structured interview, for nterviewers to deviate from the topic or explain their questions and this will limit he richness of the data collected as well as limit unexpected information.

Jnstructured interviews

here is much more flexibility in an unstructured than in a structured interview. The nterviewer can follow up points as they arise and is much more likely to gain insight nto the worldview of the interviewee, including eliciting unexpected information.

However, this may lead to an increased risk of **interviewer bias**. In addition, nalysis of data from an unstructured interview is not straightforward. The esearcher may have to sift through much irrelevant information and drawing firm onclusions may be difficult.

As with questionnaires, there is a risk that interviewees may lie for reasons of ocial desirability. However, a skilled and experienced interviewer should be able o establish sufficient rapport with the participant so that even when sensitive and ersonal topics are discussed, any responses given are more truthful.

Apply it Methods: Questionnaires or interviews

Questions

Sort the following points into two categories: those that are more likely to apply to questionnaires, or to interviews, or to both. (*1 mark each*)

1. Responses are easy to analyse.
2. Involves large numbers of participants.
3. Qualitative data.
4. Can create rapport between researcher and participant.
5. More control over responses.
6. Formal structure.
7. The respondent can be encouraged to elaborate.

Apply it Methods: Social desirability bias

The following items appeared in a questionnaire:

1. Have you ever lied to a teacher? YES/NO
2. Do you enjoy homework? YES/NO
3. Have you ever forgotten your mum's/dad's/sibling's birthday? YES/NO
4. Do you regularly recycle? YES/NO

Question

Explain why the items above may produce a social desirability bias. (*2 marks*)

Looks like the interview is going well.

Apply it Methods: Acquiescence bias and the F-scale

Acquiescence bias (or 'yea-saying') is the tendency to agree with items on a questionnaire regardless of the content of the question.

Douglas Jackson and Samuel Messick (1961) demonstrated acquiescence bias using the F-scale, a standard questionnaire that measures *authoritarianism* (see page 29). They created a reversed version of the F-scale where all the items were the opposite in meaning to the original questionnaire. They gave both the original and reversed versions to the same group of respondents and found a strong positive correlation (see page 190) between the two sets of results (which is not what you would expect).

Question

What does this suggest was happening each time participants answered the F-scale questionnaires? (*2 marks*)

Check it

1. Explain **one** strength **and one** limitation of collecting data using a questionnaire. *[3 marks +3 marks]*
2. Explain the difference between a questionnaire and an interview. *[2 marks]*
3. Explain why a researcher may decide to use a structured interview rather than an unstructured interview. *[2 marks]*
4. Briefly evaluate the use of interviews in psychological research. *[4 marks]*

Self-report design

The specification says...

Questionnaire construction; design of interviews.

Having introduced questionnaires and interviews on the previous spread, we now turn to issues involved in the design of these self-report techniques.

Key terms

Open questions Questions for which there is no fixed choice of response and respondents can answer in any way they wish. For example, *Why did you take up smoking?*

Closed questions Questions for which there is a fixed choice of responses determined by the question setter. For example, *Do you smoke?* (yes/no)

Study tip

It is important you are able to put into practice what you learn by designing and carrying out your own self-report investigations on a variety of topics. So, on this spread, we discuss how to design effective questionnaires and interviews, having described and evaluated these methods on the previous spread.

Apply it Methods — Open and closed questions

OPEN
CLOSED

Questions

Indicate which of the following are open questions and which are closed questions. (*1 mark each*)

1. Do you think recycling is important? (*YES/NO*)
2. Explain your answer to question 1.
3. How often is your rubbish bin collected? (*tick the option that applies*)
   once a week — once a fortnight
   once a month — other
4. How likely are you to recycle the following items in an average week?
   Plastic bottles
   Very likely 1 2 3 4 5 Not at all likely
   Cans
   Very likely 1 2 3 4 5 Not at all likely
5. How old are you?

Designing questionnaires

On the previous spread we explained that **questionnaires** could include two types of question **open questions** and **closed questions**. It is also the case that closed questions can be further divided into different types. It makes sense to refer to the following examples as 'items' as these are not really questions in the traditional sense.

Likert scales

A **Likert scale** is one in which the respondent indicates their agreement (or otherwise) with a statement using a scale of usually five points. The scale ranges from *Strongly agree* to *Strongly disagree*, for example:

Statement: Zombie films can have educational value.

1	2	3	4	5
Strongly agree	Agree	Neutral	Disagree	Strongly disagree

Rating scales

A **rating scale** works in a similar way but gets respondents to identify a value that represents their strength of feeling about a particular topic, for example:

Question: How entertaining do you find zombie films?
(Circle the number that applies to you.)
Very entertaining 1 2 3 4 5 Not at all entertaining

Fixed-choice option

A **fixed-choice option** item includes a list of possible options and respondents are required to indicate those that apply to them, for example:

Question: For what reasons do you watch zombie films? *(Tick all those that apply.)*

- ☐ Entertainment
- ☐ To escape
- ☐ To be frightened
- ☐ Amusement
- ☐ Education
- ☐ To please others

Designing interviews

Most interviews involve an **interview schedule**, which is the list of questions that the interviewer intends to cover. This should be **standardised** to reduce the contaminating effect of **interviewer bias** (see facing page). Typically, the interviewer will take notes throughout the interview, or alternatively, the interview may be recorded and analysed later.

Interviews usually involve an interviewer and a single participant, though **group interviews** may be appropriate especially in **clinical** settings. In the case of a one-to-one interview, the interviewer should conduct the interview in a quiet room, away from other people, as this will increase the likelihood that the interviewee will open up. It is good practice to begin the interview with some neutral questions to make the interviewee feel relaxed and comfortable, and as a way of establishing rapport. Of course, interviewees should be reminded on several occasions that their answers will be treated in the strictest confidence (see ways of dealing with **ethical issues** on page 179). This is especially important if the interview includes topics that may be personal or sensitive.

Rapport is important in an interview, but this might be judged as slightly too much…

Vriting good questions

arity is essential when designing questionnaires and interviews. If spondents are confused by or misinterpret particular questions, this will ave a negative impact on the quality of the information received. With is in mind, the following are common errors in question design that nould be avoided where possible.

)veruse of jargon

rgon refers to technical terms that are only familiar to those within a oecialised field or area. For instance, the following question includes rgon:

Do you agree that maternal deprivation in early childhood inevitably leads to affectionless psychopathy in later life?

f course as psychology specialists who have read Chapter 3 you know l about **maternal deprivation** but to the layperson this would be onfusing. It is also unnecessarily complex – the best questions are mple and easily understood.

:motive language and leading questions

ometimes, a researcher's attitude towards a particular topic is clear from ne way in which the question is phrased, as in the following examples:

Boxing is a barbaric sport and any sane person would want it banned.

Is it not obvious that student fees should be abolished?

When did you last drive over the speed limit?

n the first example, the words 'barbaric' and 'sane' are emotive and hould be replaced with more neutral alternatives. The second example s a **leading question** as it guides the respondent towards a particular nswer. The third example is also leading as it assumes that the person eing questioned has broken the speed limit at some point!

)ouble-barrelled questions and double negatives

double-barrelled question contains two questions in one, the issue being hat respondents may agree with one half of the question and not the other.

Do you agree with the following statement?

Premier league footballers are overpaid and should have to give twenty per cent of their wages to charity.

inally, questions that include double negatives can be difficult for espondents to decipher.

I am not unhappy in my job. (Agree / Disagree)

here is a much more straightforward way of asking this question – see if ou can work it out!

Apply it Methods: Interviewer bias

Standardisation of questions within an interview is one way of controlling for the possible effects of interviewer bias. However, this may not remove bias entirely. This is especially true if the interview is unstructured because the interviewer controls the way the discussion develops and the lines of enquiry followed.

Question

Read back through this chapter and identify *at least four* forms of bias in psychological research – and the steps taken to minimise these (*hint: there are lots!*). (*2 marks for each form of bias and how to minimise it*)

Apply it Methods: Self-report: Over to you

Task:

Design a questionnaire that could be distributed to students at school or college. Perhaps you could investigate some aspect of school life that people may have strong views about such as how much homework students receive or whether school uniform should be worn.

You might conduct this as a quasi-experiment and compare the views of boys and girls or students across different year groups. In this case the questionnaire is being used to assess a dependent variable.

Follow the steps below in designing your study.

Decisions to make

Aim and hypothesis

- What is the aim of your study?
- If an experiment, what is the hypothesis, is it directional or non-directional?

Decide items for your questionnaire

- Open questions?
- Closed questions (Likert scale, rating scale, fixed-choice option)?

Pilot the questionnaire

- Remove/reword questions that are too complex, leading, double-barrelled, etc.

Sampling

- What is your target population?
- How will you select participants?

Consider ethical issues

- How will you gain informed consent?
- How will you ensure anonymity/confidentiality?

Analysis of data

- How will you present your results? (For ideas see pages 196–197.)

Apply it Methods: The importance of a pilot study

Before the study begins, questionnaire and interview questions should always be piloted. Reread the discussion on the aims of piloting on page 180 and answer the following questions.

Questions

1. Briefly explain what is meant by a pilot study. (*2 marks*)
2. Describe how a pilot study of a questionnaire or interview would be carried out. (*3 marks*)
3. Explain what would be gained from conducting the pilot study and what the researcher might do as a result. (*3 marks*)

Check it

1. Using the example of a questionnaire that measures stress in the workplace, explain the difference between closed and open questions. *[4 marks]*
2. Explain **two** issues that should be considered when designing interviews. *[4 marks]*
3. Explain **two** issues that should be considered when designing questionnaires. *[4 marks]*

Correlations

The specification says...

Correlations. Analysis of the relationship between co-variables. The difference between correlations and experiments. Positive, negative and zero correlations.

We now turn to the fourth main research method in the Year 1 specification - correlation. Properly speaking, correlation is a method of analysis not a research method but it is easier to just say 'correlation' rather than 'studies using correlational analysis'.

Key terms

Correlation A mathematical technique in which a researcher investigates an association between two variables, called co-variables.

Co-variables The variables investigated within a correlation, for example height and weight. They are not referred to as the independent and dependent variables because a correlation investigates the association between the variables, rather than trying to show a cause-and-effect relationship.

Positive correlation As one co-variable increases so does the other. For example, the number of people in a room and noise tend to be positively correlated.

Negative correlation As one co-variable increases the other decreases. For example, the number of people in a room and amount of personal space tend to be negatively correlated.

Zero correlation When there is no relationship between the co-variables. For example, the association between the number of people in a room in Manchester and the total daily rainfall in Peru is likely to be zero.

Correlations

Correlation illustrates the strength and direction of an association between two or more **co-variables** (things that are being measured). Correlations are plotted on a **scattergram** (see examples below). One co-variable is represented on the *x*-axis and the other the *y*-axis. Each point or dot on the graph is the x and y position of each co-variable.

Types of correlation

Let's consider two things that might be correlated. Frequent use of caffeine is correlated with high anxiety. We might get people to work out how many caffeine drinks they consume over a weekly period. We could then ask these same people to **self-report** their level of anxiety (let's say on a 20-point scale) at the end of the week. We might expect to see a **positive correlation** between the two variables if we plotted the data on a scattergram – a positive correlation means the more caffeine people drink, the higher their level of anxiety.

Perhaps we could also get these same people to record how many hours sleep they have over the same period. Drinking a lot of caffeine often disrupts sleep patterns, so perhaps the *more* caffeine someone drinks the *less* sleep they have. This would be a **negative correlation** – as one variable rises the other one falls.

Finally, we might also persuade our intrepid participants to record the number of dogs they see in the street within the same week. As far as we are aware, there is no relationship between the number of caffeine drinks someone has and the number of dogs they see in the street. For this reason, we might expect to find something close to a **zero correlation** between these two variables.

The difference between correlations and experiments

In an **experiment** the researcher controls or manipulates the **independent variable** (IV) in order to measure the effect on the **dependent variable** (DV). As a result of this deliberate change in one variable it is possible to infer that the IV caused any observed changes in the DV.

In contrast, in a correlation, there is no such manipulation of one variable and therefore it is not possible to establish cause and effect between one co-variable and another. Even if we found a strong **positive correlation** between caffeine and anxiety level we cannot assume that caffeine was the cause of the anxiety.

Apply it
Methods

Positive and negative correlations

Questions

Are the following positive or negative correlations? (*1 mark each*)

1. The more aggressive the parents, the more aggressive their children are.
2. The hotter the temperature, the fewer clothes people wear.
3. The fewer sweets eaten, the fewer fillings needed.
4. The colder the weather, the higher people's fuel bills.
5. The more people exercise, the less their risk of heart disease.
6. More sociable people have more friends.
7. The fewer hours of daylight, the more depressed people there are.
8. The more films you watch, the more interesting you are.

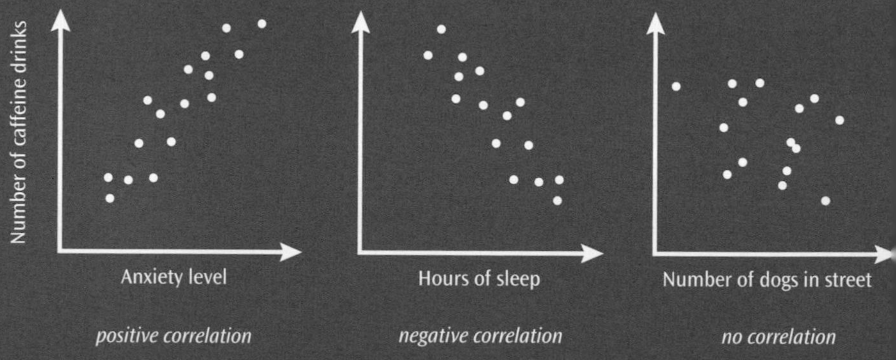

Number of caffeine drinks
Anxiety level
positive correlation
Hours of sleep
negative correlation
Number of dogs in street
no correlation

Scattergrams to show the relationships between number of caffeine drinks and anxiety level (left), number of caffeine drinks and hours of sleep (middle) and number of caffeine drinks and number of dogs seen in the street (right).

Practical activity on pages 36, 158 and 205

:valuation

;trengths

orrelations are a useful preliminary tool for research. By assessing ıe strength and direction of a relationship, they provide a precise and uantifiable measure of how two variables are related. This may suggest ideas ɔr possible future research if variables are strongly related or demonstrate n interesting pattern. Correlations are often used as a starting point to ssess possible patterns between variables before researchers commit to an xperimental study.

Correlations are relatively quick and economical to carry out. There is no need ɔr a controlled environment and no manipulation of variables is required. Data ɔllected by others (**secondary data** such as government statistics) can be used, 'hich means correlations are less time-consuming than experiments.

.imitations

s a result of the lack of experimental manipulation and control within a ɔrrelation, studies can only tell us *how* variables are related but not *why*. ɔrrelations cannot demonstrate cause and effect between variables and ıerefore we do not know which co-variable is causing the other to change. For ıstance – in the example on the facing page – we cannot conclude that drinking affeine causes anxiety. It may be that people who are already anxious drink more affeine as a result. So, establishing the direction of the effect is an issue.

It may also be the case that another untested variable is causing the elationship between the two co-variables we are interested in – an **intervening ariable** (also known as the **third variable problem**). Perhaps people who have igh-pressured jobs – and hence spend a lot of their time feeling anxious – drink lot of caffeine because they work long hours and need to remain alert. Thus, ıe key unaccounted-for variable here is job type which, in effect, is causing the elationship between the other two co-variables.

Largely because of the issues above, correlations can occasionally be misused r misinterpreted. Relationships between variables are sometimes presented s causal when they aren't – especially by the media. Consider the claim that eople from 'broken' homes are more likely to become criminals. This is often nisinterpreted to mean that the broken home is what caused the criminality and ıerefore people from broken homes will inevitably become criminals.

Such conclusions are absurd. There are many intervening or 'third' variables t work here, such as poverty being a cause of the broken home and also the key actor in criminality. This might explain the apparent link between a broken home nd criminality.

Yeah it tastes great obviously – but is it worth the money?

Apply it Methods — Correlation: Over to you

Is there a correlation between the price of chocolate and how tasty it is? Why not test this on your friends? This might be one of the more expensive investigations you carry out but, chances are, your friends will like you a lot more afterwards!

Buy five bars of chocolate ranging from cheap to, well, not so cheap! Get a friend to try each one – blindfolded – and rate them for tastiness on a scale, say, out of twenty.

Questions

1. Analyse the data by sketching a scattergram of the data for each co-variable (*price of chocolate plotted against tastiness rating*) to see if there is a relationship between the two. (*3 marks*)
2. Then try it again with another two or three participants to see if results are similar – assuming your chocolate budget will stretch that far! Remember, it's all in the name of science… (*3 marks*)

Apply it Methods — Curvilinear relationships

Some relationships are more complex than positive or negative correlations. The Yerkes-Dodson law of arousal states that performance is at its best when there is a moderate (optimal) level of arousal and will deteriorate if the arousal level is too low or too high.

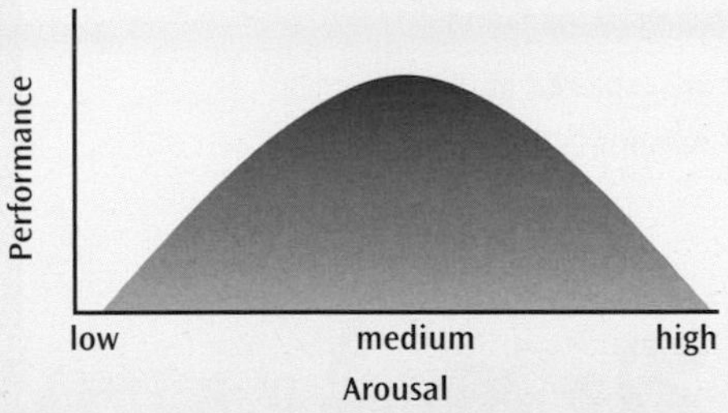
Performance
low
medium
high
Arousal

Question

Can you think of any co-variables that might demonstrate such a relationship? (*1 mark for each pair of co-variables*)

Apply it Methods — Correlational hypotheses

Hypotheses written for correlations are not the same as those for experiments. There is no IV or DV in a correlation. The hypothesis still has to clearly state the expected relationship between variables – but co-variables in this case, which must be clearly operationalised.

Also, as with experimental hypotheses, correlational hypotheses can be directional or non-directional. A directional hypothesis for the chocolate correlation (above right) could be:

> *There is a positive correlation between the price of a chocolate bar and its tastiness rating (out of 20).*

Whereas the equivalent non-directional hypothesis would be:

> *There is a correlation between the price of a chocolate bar and its tastiness rating (out of 20).*

Question

Write directional and non-directional hypotheses for the caffeine and anxiety level study, and the caffeine and sleep study, described on this spread. (*2 marks for each hypothesis*)

Check it

1. Explain what is meant by a 'correlation'. [*2 marks*]
2. Explain **one** strength **and one** limitation of the use of correlations in psychological research. [*6 marks*]
3. Using an example for each, explain the difference between a positive and a negative correlation. [*4 marks*]

Types of data

The specification says...

Qualitative and quantitative data; the distinction between qualitative and quantitative data collection techniques. Primary and secondary data, including meta-analysis.

When an investigation is conducted, data is collected. This may be words, numbers, images, sounds etc. There are different ways to describe types of data.

Key terms

Qualitative data Data that is expressed in words and non-numerical (although qualitative data may be converted to numbers for the purposes of analysis).

Quantitative data Data that can be counted, usually given as numbers.

Primary data Information that has been obtained first-hand by a researcher for the purposes of a research project. In psychology, such data is often gathered directly from participants as part of an experiment, self-report or observation.

Secondary data Information that has already been collected by someone else and so pre-dates the current research project. In psychology, such data might include the work of other psychologists or government statistics.

Meta-analysis The process of combining the findings from a number of studies on a particular topic. The aim is to produce an overall statistical conclusion (the effect size) based on a range of studies. A meta-analysis should not be confused with a *review* where a number of studies are compared and discussed.

A qualitative perspective

How must the soldiers be feeling?

What themes are explored in the picture?

What style of painting is this?

A quantitative perspective

How many soldiers are there?

What time of day is it?

How many soldiers are wearing hats?

Qualitative and quantitative data

Qualitative data

Qualitative data is expressed in words, rather than numbers or statistics, and may take the form of a written description of the thoughts, feelings and opinions of participants (or a written account of what the researcher saw in the case of an observation). Thus, a transcript from an **interview**, an extract from a diary or notes recorded within a **counselling** session would all be classed as qualitative data. (Note that yes/no answers are also classed as qualitative though they lack the detail that is usually provided by qualitative data.)

Qualitative methods of data collection are those that are concerned with the interpretation of language from, for example, an interview or an **unstructured observation**.

Quantitative data

Quantitative data is expressed numerically. Quantitative data collection techniques usually gather numerical data in the form of individual scores from participants such as the number of words a person was able to recall in a memory **experiment**. Data is open to being analysed statistically and can be easily converted into graphs, charts, etc.

Which one is best?

Neither really, it depends upon the purpose and aims of the research. Also there is significant overlap between the two: researchers collecting quantitative data as part of an experiment may often interview participants as a way of gaining more qualitative insight into their experience of the investigation. Similarly, there are a number of ways in which qualitative information can be converted to numerical data.

Primary and secondary data

Primary data

Primary data (sometimes called field research) refers to original data that has been collected specifically for the purpose of the investigation by the researcher. It is data that arrives first-hand from the participants themselves. Data which is gathered by conducting an experiment, **questionnaire**, interview or **observation** would be classed as primary data.

Secondary data

Secondary data is data that has been collected by someone other than the person who is conducting the research. In other words, this is data that already exists before the psychologist begins their research or investigation. Data such as this is sometimes referred to as 'desk research' and it is often the case that secondary data has already been subject to **statistical testing** and therefore the **significance** is known.

Secondary data includes data that may be located in **journal articles**, books or websites. Statistical information held by the government (such as that obtained in the Census), population records or employee absence records within an organisation are all examples of secondary data.

Apply it Methods — Qualitative and quantitative data

Questions

Which of the following would produce qualitative data and which quantitative data? (*1 mark each*)

1. Students rate their enjoyment of research methods on a scale of 1–10.
2. An individual describes his experience of schizophrenia.
3. A researcher asks passers-by their views on litter in the town centre (using a series of 'yes' and 'no' questions).
4. Students give feedback on their teacher using a questionnaire made up of open questions.
5. A researcher categorises the social behaviour of children into one of three types.
6. Students record the number of hours they spend revising and the number of hours they spend on social network sites.
7. A teacher interviews Year 10 students about their ideas of what psychology is.
8. A girl writes a diary describing what daily life is like for a child.

:valuation

ualitative data

ualitative data offers a researcher much more richness of detail than uantitative data. It is much broader in scope and gives the participant/ spondent the opportunity to more fully report their thoughts, feelings and pinions on a given subject.

For this reason, qualitative data tends to have greater **external validity** an quantitative data; it provides the researcher with a more meaningful sight into the participant's worldview.

That said, qualitative data is often difficult to analyse. It tends not to lend self to being summarised statistically so that patterns and comparisons ithin and between data may be hard to identify.

As a consequence, conclusions often rely on the subjective interpretations the researcher and these may be subject to bias, particularly if the searcher has preconceptions about what he/she is expecting to find.

uantitative data

ssentially the evaluations of quantitative data are the *opposite* of iose above – quantitative data is relatively simple to analyse, therefore mparisons between groups can be easily drawn. Also, data in numerical rm tends to be more objective and less open to bias. On the other hand, uantitative data is much narrower in meaning and detail than qualitative ata. It thus may fail to represent 'real life'.

:valuation

rimary data

ne main strength of primary data is that it fits the job. Primary data is uthentic data obtained from the participants themselves for the purpose of particular investigation. Questionnaires and interviews, for instance, can be esigned in such a way that they specifically target the information that the searcher requires.

To produce primary data, however, requires time and effort on the part of ne researcher. Conducting an experiment, for instance, requires considerable anning, preparation and resources, and this is a limitation when compared ith secondary data, which may be accessed within a matter of minutes.

econdary data

contrast to primary data above, secondary data may be inexpensive and asily accessed requiring minimal effort. When examining secondary data ne researcher may find that the desired information already exists and so iere is no need to conduct primary data collection.

The flip side is that there may be substantial variation in the quality and curacy of secondary data. Information might at first appear to be valuable nd promising but, on further investigation, may be outdated or incomplete. ne content of the data may not quite match the researcher's needs or bjectives. This may challenge the **validity** of any conclusions.

Apply it Methods — What data?

Questions

Of the methods listed below, which would produce qualitative data and which quantitative? (*1 mark each*)

1. An experiment.
2. An interview.
3. A questionnaire (*mainly closed questions*).
4. A questionnaire (*mainly open questions*).
5. A correlation.
6. A structured observation.
7. An unstructured observation.

Meta-analysis

A form of research method that uses secondary data is **meta-analysis**. This refers to a process in which a number of studies are identified which have investigated the same aims/hypothesis. The results of these studies can be pooled together and a joint conclusion produced. In the case of experimental research, where the independent variable has been measured in the same way, it is possible to perform a statistical analysis and calculate an effect size – basically the dependent variable of a meta-analysis – which gives an overall statistical measure of difference or relationship between variables across a number of studies.

On the plus side, meta-analysis allows us to create a larger, more varied sample and results can then be generalised across much larger populations, increasing validity.

However, meta-analysis may be prone to **publication bias**, sometimes referred to as the file drawer problem. The researcher may not select all relevant studies, choosing to leave out those studies with negative or non-significant results. Therefore the conclusions from the meta-analysis will be biased because they only represent some of the relevant data.

Apply it Methods — Meta-analysis

Questions

1. Find an example of a meta-analysis within this book. (*1 mark*)
2. Explain how this study was conducted. (*3 marks*)
3. Was there an effect size? If so, what is it? (*1 mark*)

Apply it Methods — Primary and secondary data

Questions

Which of the following would be classed as primary and which secondary data? (*1 mark each*)

1. A researcher searches through newspapers to see if there is a relationship between daily temperature and the total number of violent incidents.
2. An interview with people with obsessive-compulsive disorder about their experiences.
3. An observation of how primary school children negotiate rules during a game of marbles.
4. A comparison of crime statistics in inner city and rural areas to see if there is a difference.
5. A researcher assesses how the GCSE results of schools in her local area compare with national averages.
6. A lab study to see if men or women are more susceptible to visual illusions.
7. A researcher examines the transcript of a trial to see if there were inconsistencies in eyewitness accounts.
8. A researcher asks cinemagoers leaving a horror movie if they feel more murderous after seeing the film.

Check it

1. Explain the difference between primary data and secondary data. [*4 marks*]
2. Explain **one** strength **and one** limitation of qualitative data. [*6 marks*]
3. Explain why a 'meta-analysis' is used in psychological research. [*3 marks*]

Measures of central tendency and dispersion

The specification says...

Descriptive statistics: measures of central tendency – mean, median, mode; calculation of mean, median and mode; measures of dispersion – range and standard deviation; calculation of range.

We have seen how data may come in two forms: qualitative or quantitative. Here we shall focus on the latter. There are various ways of summarising and analysing numerical data in order to draw meaningful conclusions. These are collectively known as descriptive statistics – which include measures of central tendency, measures of dispersion and also graphs (on the next spread).

Key terms

Descriptive statistics The use of graphs, tables and summary statistics to identify trends and analyse sets of data.

Measures of central tendency The general term for any measure of the average value in a set of data.

Mean The arithmetic average calculated by adding up all the values in a set of data and dividing by the number of values.

Median The central value in a set of data when values are arranged from lowest to highest.

Mode The most frequently occurring value in a set of data.

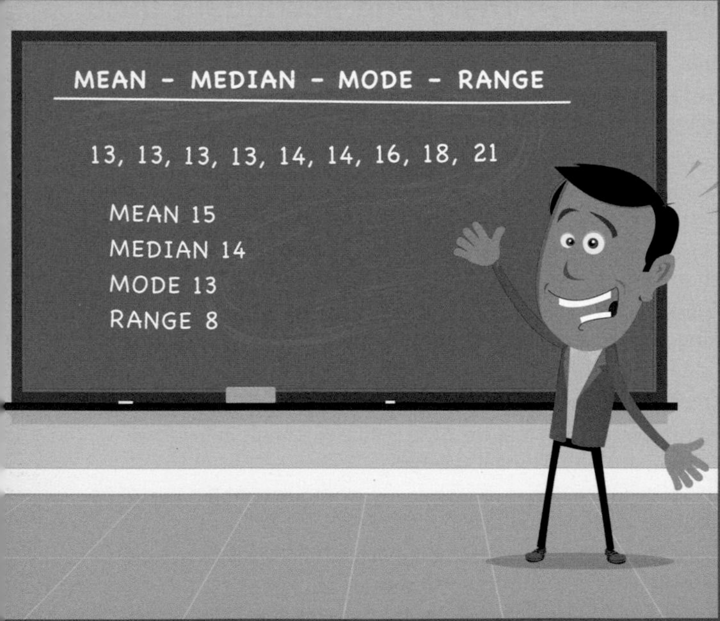
MEAN – MEDIAN – MODE – RANGE
13, 13, 13, 13, 14, 14, 16, 18, 21
MEAN 15
MEDIAN 14
MODE 13
RANGE 8

Study tip

If you have to decide what method of central tendency should be used with a particular set of data, consider whether there are any extreme scores – a score that is significantly lower or higher than the others. If there are no extreme scores then the mean is the best option as it is the most sensitive measure of the three. However, if there is an extreme score, the median is most suitable as the mean would become distorted. Note that the mode is never the best option, except if the data is in categories.

Measures of central tendency

Descriptive statistics include **measures of central tendency**. These measures are 'averages' which give us information about the most *typical* values in a set of data. There are three of these to consider: the **mean**, the **median** and the **mode**.

Mean

The mean is what most of us will recognise as the average. It is calculated by adding up all the scores or values in a data set and dividing this figure by the total number of scores there are.

For instance, in the following data set of scores:

5, 7, 7, 9, 10, 11, 12, 14, 15, 17

The total is 107 divided by the number of scores (10), which gives us a mean value of 10.7

The mean is the most sensitive of the measures of central tendency as it includes all of the scores/values in the data set within the calculation. This means it is more representative of the data as a whole.

However, the mean is easily distorted by extreme values. If we replace 17 in the data above with the number 98, the mean becomes 18.8 which does not really seem to represent the data overall!

Median

The median is the middle value in a data set when scores are arranged from lowest to highest. In an odd number of scores, the median is easily identified. In an even number of scores (just as the ten numbers above) the median is halfway between the two middle scores. These are 10 and 11, so the median is 10.5.

The strength of the median, unlike the mean, is that extreme scores do not affect it, so whether 98 replaces 17 in the data above or not, the median remains the same. It is also easy to calculate (once you have arranged the numbers in order). However, it is less sensitive than the mean as the actual values of lower and higher numbers are ignored and extreme values may be important.

Mode

The mode is the most frequently occurring score/value within a data set. In some data sets there may be two modes (**bi-modal**) or no mode if all the scores are different.

Although the mode is very easy to calculate, it is a very crude measure. Notice how in the set of scores above, the mode is 7, which is quite different from the mean and the median (and not representative of the whole data set). Additionally, when there are several modes in a data set, this is then not a very useful piece of information.

For some data – data in categories – the mode is the only method you can use. For example, if you asked your class to list their favourite dessert, the only way to identify the most 'typical' or average value would be to select the **modal group**.

Apply it Methods

And the results are in...

The table below shows the results of our energy drink experiment using a repeated measures design (as suggested on page 172). The score for each participant is the number of words said in the five minutes after consuming each drink (participants were filmed and the number of words spoken after each drink were counted).

	P1	P2	P3	P4	P5	P6	P7	P8	P9	P10
SpeedUpp	110	59	206	89	76	141	152	98	198	57
Water	122	45	135	90	42	87	131	113	129	62

Questions

1. Calculate the **mean**, **median** and **mode** for the *SpeedUpp* condition and the water condition above. Give all answers rounded up to the nearest whole number. (*3 marks*)
2. What can you conclude from these calculations? (*2 marks*)

Measures of dispersion

Measures of dispersion are based on the *spread* of scores. That is, how far scores vary and differ om one another. We shall focus on two of these – the **range** and the **standard deviation**.

Range

he range is a simple calculation of the spread of scores and is worked out by taking the lowest alue from the highest value and (usually) adding 1.

Thus, the range for the data on the left is (17 – 5) + 1 = 13.

dding 1 is a mathematical correction that allows for the fact that raw scores are often rounded p (or down) when they are recorded within research. For instance, someone may complete simple task (such as crossing out all the letter e's in a paragraph) in 45 seconds. However, it unlikely they took *exactly* 45 seconds to complete this task (in fact it may have taken them nywhere between 44.5 and 45.5 seconds), so the addition of 1 accounts for this margin of error.

The advantage of the range is that it is easy to calculate. However, it only takes into account e two most extreme values, and this may be unrepresentative of the data set as a whole. For stance, pupils in a maths class achieved the following test scores:

0, 47, 49, 50, 50, 50, 51, 53, 54, 56, 56, 57, 100

he range here is 101: one student was ill during the test and scored nothing, the top-scoring udent had been given the test to study for homework by mistake! This example illustrates the ct that the range may not give a fair representation of the general distribution of scores. Most udents achieved around half marks in the test – if we exclude the two outliers (scores of 1 nd 100) then the range would be 11. This shows how the range is influenced by outliers.

The range also does not indicate whether most numbers are closely grouped around the ean or spread out – whereas the standard deviation does show this aspect of dispersion.

Standard deviation

much more sophisticated measure of dispersion is the standard deviation. This is a single alue that tells us how far scores deviate (move away) from the mean.

The larger the standard deviation, the greater the dispersion or spread within a set of data. If we e talking about a particular condition within an experiment, a large standard deviation suggests at not all participants were affected by the IV in the same way because the data is quite widely read. It may be that there are a few **anomalous** results.

A low standard deviation value reflects the fact that the data is tightly clustered around the ean, which might imply that all participants responded in a fairly similar way.

The standard deviation is a much more precise measure of dispersion than the range as it cludes all values within the final calculation. However, for this reason – like the mean – it can e distorted by a single extreme value. Also, extreme values may not be revealed, unlike with e range.

No, not that kind of spread.

Key terms

Measures of dispersion The general term for any measure of the spread or variation in a set of scores.

Range A simple calculation of the dispersion in a set of scores which is worked out by subtracting the lowest score from the highest score and adding 1 as a mathematical correction.

Standard deviation A sophisticated measure of dispersion in a set of scores. It tells us by how much, on average, each score deviates from the mean.

To calculate the standard deviation the difference between each score and the mean is calculated and squared. All the differences squared are then added up and divided by the number (N) of scores (or N – 1 is used). This gives the variance. The standard deviation is the square root of the variance. You can see the formula for this on page 199.

Study tip

Look carefully at the wording of the specification (at the top left of the facing page). This means you must know how to calculate the mean, median, mode or range (and can use a calculator for this).

There is no requirement to calculate the standard deviation, though it will enhance your understanding if you play around with different data sets and see how changing the numbers leads to different standard deviations. You can do this on various online websites or use a spreadsheet (e.g. Excel) or a scientific calculator.

Apply it Methods: Drawing conclusions from a table of results

The table below includes a summary of the results gained from an experiment. The experiment compared the number of words recalled when words were learned in silence compared to when words were learned whilst music was playing in the background.

Table showing the means and standard deviations for the number of words recalled when learned in silence and when learned with music playing.

	Condition A (learned in silence)	Condition B (learned with music playing)
Mean number of words recalled	21.2	14.6
Standard deviation	1.1	4.6

Questions

1. What conclusion can be drawn from the **mean** values above? (*2 marks*)
2. What do the **standard deviations** tell us about the scores in each condition? (*2 marks*)

Check it

1. Explain what is meant by the 'standard deviation'. *[2 marks]*
2. State **one** strength **and one** limitation of the median as a measure of central tendency. *[3 marks]*
3. The following data was collected in an experiment:
   23, 24, 26, 28, 29, 29, 30, 31, 32, 32, 33
   What is the most appropriate measure of central tendency for the data above? Justify your answer. *[3 marks]*

Presentation of quantitative data

The specification says...

Presentation and display of quantitative data: graphs, tables, scattergrams, bar charts, histograms.

Distributions: normal and skewed distributions; characteristics of normal and skewed distributions.

On this spread, we continue our discussion of descriptive statistics and look at some of the ways in which data can be presented and how it may be distributed.

Key terms

Scattergram A type of graph that represents the strength and direction of the relationship between co-variables in a correlational analysis.

Bar chart A type of graph in which the frequency of each variable is represented by the height of the bars.

Histogram A type of graph which shows frequency but, unlike a bar chart, the area of the bars (not just the height) represents frequency. The x-axis must start at a true zero and the scale is continuous.

Bar chart showing the mean number of words spoken in five minutes for the *SpeedUpp* condition and the water condition.

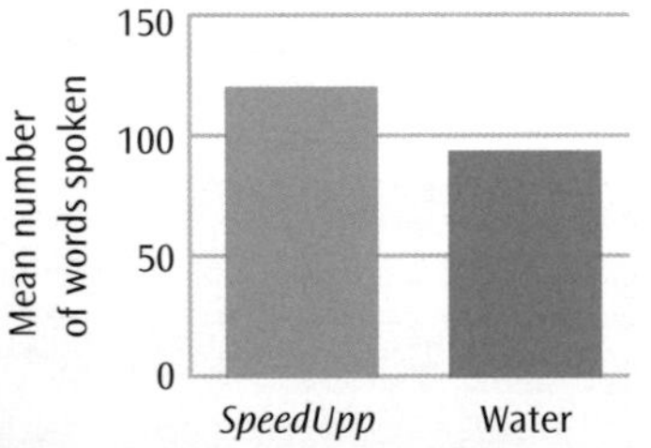
150
100
50
0
Mean number of words spoken
SpeedUpp
Water

Histogram showing percentage scores in a maths test.

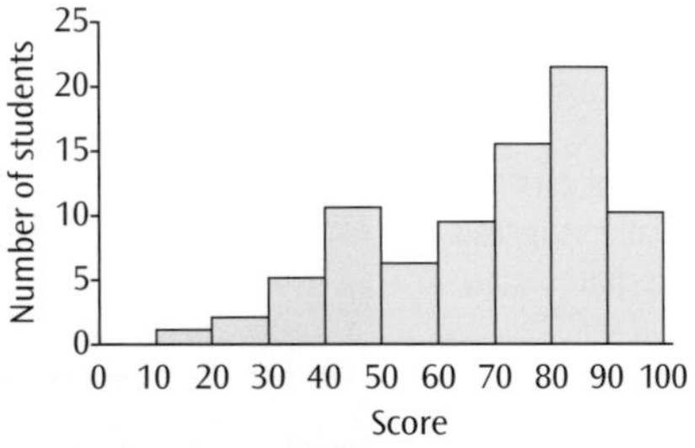
25
20
15
10
5
0
Number of students
0 10 20 30 40 50 60 70 80 90 100
Score

Apply it Methods

Other types of graphs: Line graphs

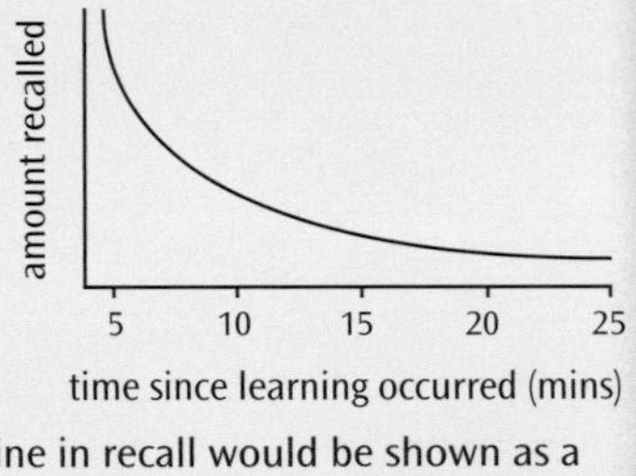
amount recalled
5 10 15 20 25
time since learning occurred (mins)

Line graphs, like histograms, represent continuous data and use points connected by lines to show how something changes in value, for instance, over time. Typically, the IV is plotted on the *x*-axis and the DV on the *y*-axis. For instance, in an investigation of how the passage of time affects our ability to remember information, the decline in recall would be shown as a continuous line.

Questions

What graphical display would be most appropriate to represent the following: a bar chart, a scattergram, a histogram or a line graph? (*1 mark each*)

1. The change in a person's body temperature over the course of a day.
2. The difference in average annual rainfall between Manchester and Paris.
3. The relationship between daily temperature and people's ratings of how happy they are.
4. The frequency of people who chose 'snow' as their favourite weather condition broken down into subcategories of age.

Tables and graphs

Summarising data in a table

There are various ways of representing data. One of these is in the form of a summary table. It is important to note that when tables appear in the results section of a report they are not merely **raw scores** (like the example seen at the bottom of page 194) but have been converted to **descriptive statistics**.

Table showing the mean number of words spoken in five minutes and standard deviations for the *SpeedUpp* condition and the water condition.

	SpeedUpp condition	Water condition
Mean	119	96
Standard deviation	53.8	35.8

It is standard practice to include a summary paragraph beneath a table explaining the numbers and drawing conclusions, for example:

We can see from the mean values that there were more words spoken, on average, in the five minutes following the consumption of the energy drink (119 mean words) than the water drink (96 mean words). This suggests that drinking an energy drink makes people more talkative than drinking water.

The standard deviation is higher in the SpeedUpp *condition (53.8) suggesting that there was a larger spread of scores than in the water condition (35.8). This suggests that not all participants were equally affected by the energy drink. In the water condition, scores were clustered around the mean to a greater degree.*

Bar charts

Data can be represented visually using a suitable graphical display so the difference in mean values can easily be seen. The most suitable **graph** in this case is a **bar chart** (see top left). Bar charts are used when data is divided into categories, otherwise known as **discrete data**. In the example above, the categories are our two conditions (the *SpeedUpp* condition and the water condition) and these occupy the horizontal *x*-axis. The frequency or amount of each category is plotted on the vertical *y*-axis (effectively the height of the bar). Bars are separated on a bar chart to denote that we are dealing with separate conditions.

Histograms

In a histogram (see middle left), the bars touch each other, which show that *x*-axis data is **continuous** rather than discrete (as in a bar chart). The *x*-axis is made up of equal-sized intervals of a single category, for instance, percentage scores in a maths test broken down into intervals such as 0–9, 10–19, 20–29, etc. The *y*-axis represents the frequency (number of people who scored a certain mark) within each interval. If there was a zero frequency for one of the intervals, the interval remains but without a bar.

Scattergrams

We came across **scattergrams** earlier in this chapter, during our discussion of **correlations** on page 190. Unlike the other forms of graph on this spread, scattergrams do not depict differences but *associations* between **co-variables**. Either of the co-variables occupies the *x*-axis and the other the *y*-axis (it does not matter which) and each point on the graph corresponds to the x and y position of the co-variables.

Study tip

When presenting a table or graph, always have a title and clearly label columns or axes.

)istributions

Normal distribution

you measure certain variables, such as the height of all the people in your school/college, ne frequency of these measurements should form a bell-shaped curve similar to the equency graph at the bottom left of the page. This is called a **normal distribution** which is ymmetrical.

Within a normal distribution, most people (or items) are located in the middle area f the curve with very few people at the extreme ends. The **mean**, **median** and **mode** all ccupy the same midpoint of the curve. The 'tails' of the curve, which extend outwards, ever touch the horizontal *x*-axis (and therefore never reach zero) as more extreme scores re always theoretically possible.

This normal distribution is discussed on page 136 with reference to defining abnormality.

kewed distributions

ot all distributions form such a balanced symmetrical pattern. Some data sets derived om psychological scales or measurements may produce **skewed distributions**, that is, istributions that appear to lean to one side or the other, as in the examples below right.

A **positive skew** is where most of the distribution is concentrated towards the left of ne graph, resulting in a long tail on the right (see illustration bottom right). Imagine a ery difficult test in which most people got low marks with only a handful of students at ne higher end. This would produce a positive skew. It is interesting to note how the various **easures of central tendency** are affected by this situation. The mode (as we would expect) emains at the highest point of the peak, the median comes next, but the mean is dragged cross towards the 'tail'. Remember how extreme scores affect the mean. Here, the very high-coring candidates in the test have had the effect of pulling the mean to the right, whereas the nedian and mode – neither of which include all the scores when they are calculated – remain ss affected by this.

The opposite occurs in a **negative skew**. A very easy test would produce a distribution here the bulk of the scores are concentrated on the right, resulting in the long tail of nomalous scores on the left. The mean is pulled to the left this time (due to the lower corers who are in the minority), with the mode dissecting the highest peak and the median the middle.

Did you know?
78% of statistics are made up on the spot?
Or is it 87%?!
Err...hang on ...

Key terms

Normal distribution A symmetrical spread of frequency data that forms a bell-shaped pattern. The mean, median and mode are all located at the highest peak.

Skewed distribution A spread of frequency data that is not symmetrical, where the data clusters to one end.

Positive skew A type of frequency distribution in which the long tail is on the positive (right) side of the peak and most of the distribution is concentrated on the left.

Negative skew A type of frequency distribution in which the long tail is on the negative (left) side of the peak and most of the distribution is concentrated on the right.

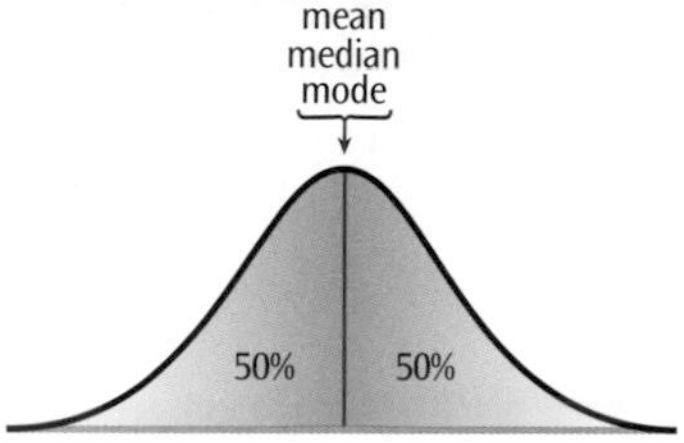
mean
median
mode
50%
50%

Above: The normally distributed bell curve. Note the position of the mean, median and mode.

Below: Skewed distributions, negative and positive skew. This time see how the median and mean shift with the change in distribution.

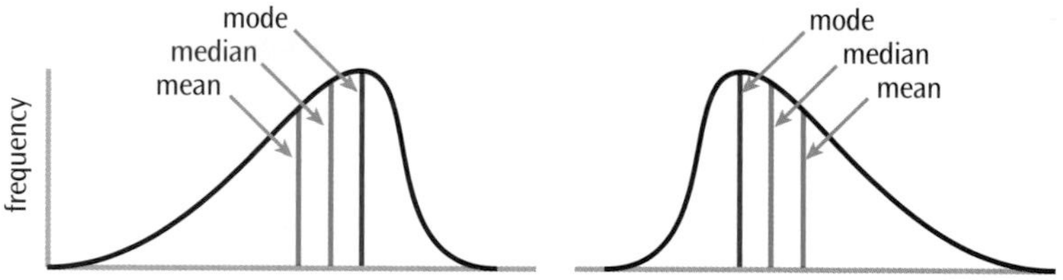
mode
median
mean
frequency
mode
median
mean

Negatively skewed (longer tail to the left, in a negative direction)

Positively skewed (longer tail to the right, in a positive direction)

Apply it Methods — The area under the curve

There are certain statistical facts in relation to the normal distribution and the standard deviation.

As can be seen from the graph below, 68.26% of the population fall between one standard deviation above and one standard deviation below the mean value (the light yellow section).

Two standard deviations above and below the mean include 95.44% of the population, and 99.73% are three standard deviations above and below the mean.

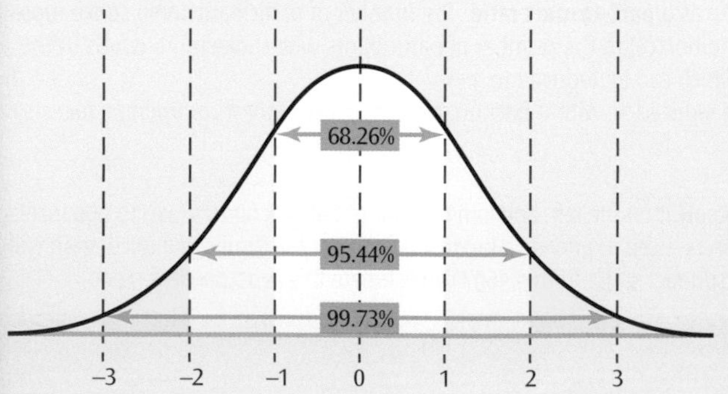
68.26%
95.44%
99.73%
–3
–2
–1
0
1
2
3

Question

Using the graph above, work out what percentage of the population would be between the mean and one standard deviation below average. Note that the answer is the same in the case of one standard deviation above average. (*2 marks*)

Check it

1. Identify **three** features of a 'normal distribution'. *[3 marks]*
2. Explain the difference between a positive and a negative skew. *[2 marks]*
3. You are comparing means across two independent groups. Explain why a histogram would **not** be an appropriate way of displaying the means for these groups. *[2 marks]*

Mathematical content

The specification says...

There is a list of the required mathematical skills on page 217.

On this spread, we cover some of the mathematical skills identified in the specification. No – don't run away! Many of you may be concerned about the maths content in psychology – some of you may be excited! For the worried ones, rest assured that we have already covered, on other spreads, a number of the mathematical skills. These include working out the mean, median and mode, drawing conclusions from tables and graphs, recognising different forms of data, etc.

Here we cover much more, so, take a deep breath – there's nothing to be scared of...

PLEASE
NO SWIMMING !

Maths. Officially not as scary as being chased by an alligator.

Apply it Methods

Estimate results

It may be necessary to comment on the average or dispersion of a set of data, which may require estimating the answer.

The most words spoken in the *SpeedUpp* condition was 206 and the lowest was 59 (this data is at the bottom of page 194).

What would you estimate the range would be? (Use rounded figures such as 200 – 60.) See answer on facing page.

Question

Now do the same for the water condition. (*1 mark*) (Data also in table at bottom of page 194.)

Mathematical content

Percentages

With reference to the raw data at the bottom of page 194, what percentage of participants spoke more words in the *SpeedUpp* condition than the water condition?

There were 6 participants whose word score was higher for the *SpeedUpp* condition than the water condition out of a total of 10 participants.

To calculate the percentage we use the following formula:

$$\frac{\text{Number participants who spoke more after } \textit{SpeedUpp}}{\text{Total number of participants}} \times 100 = \frac{6}{10} \times 100 = 60\%$$

Converting a percentage to a decimal

To convert a percentage to a decimal, remove the % sign and move the decimal point two places to the left. For example:

37% is 37.0 then move the decimal point two places to left = 0.37

So, for the percentage of participants who spoke more words in the *SpeedUpp* condition: 60% is 60.0, move the decimal point two places to the left = 0.60 (0.6).

Decimal places

The term **decimal places** refers to the number of digits to the right of the decimal point.

Converting a decimal to a fraction

Start by working out the number of decimal places in your number. For example, 0.81 has two decimal places (two digits after the decimal point) and 0.275 has three decimal places.

If there are two decimal places then you divide by 100, if there are three decimal places you divide by 1,000. The number of decimal places equals the number of zeros.

The fractions you get are 81/100 and 275/1000

Sometimes you can reduce the fraction by finding the *highest common factor*, the biggest number that divides evenly into both parts of the fraction.

In the case of 275/1000 you can divide both by 25 and get 11/40

In the energy drink experiment, 0.6 of the total group spoke more words in the *SpeedUpp* condition. There is only one decimal place here, so we divide by 10. The fraction is 6/10.

The biggest number that will divide into both parts of the fraction is 2 therefore, after dividing both parts of the fraction by 2, we are left with 3/5 (or three-fifths).

Ratios

We can also express the information above as a **ratio**. Considering the *SpeedUpp* example, we could calculate a **part-to-whole ratio**, that is, the ratio of the number of participants who spoke more words in the *SpeedUpp* condition (6) to the total number of participants (10) = 6:10 (which can be reduced to 3:5).

This could also be written as a **part-to-part ratio**. The number of participants who spoke more words in the *SpeedUpp* condition (6) to the number of participants who spoke more words in the water condition (4) = 6:4 (which can be reduced to 3:2).

Ratios should always be reduced as with a fraction, by finding the *highest common factor*.

Estimates

These are discussed in the Apply it on the left, and aim to produce ballpark figures (e.g. 10,000 instead of 9,569). Such estimates can be used to provide a broad idea of what the results of a calculation will be, for example if I want to subtract 5,492 from 9,569 I can estimate this as 10,000 less 5,000.

Apply it Methods — Percentages, decimals, fractions, ratios

Task:

For further practice, why not work through all the calculations in the main text (above), this time using the number of participants who spoke more words in the water condition. Make sure you always show all your workings for any calculation so your teacher can assess the method(s) you used.

›ignificant figures

'Vhen we are faced with a long number, for the sake of clarity, we might round it off o the nearest thousand, or nearest million. This is the basis of making an estimate – ısing a specific number of significant figures. So, for example 432,765 to 2 **significant igures** (s.f.) is 430,000. Similarly, when there are many digits coming after a decimal oint (as there often are when we have used a calculator to work out, say, a percentage) ve may round this off to 1, 2 or 3 significant figures. For example:

0.002047 would be:
- 0.002 (1 s.f.)
- 0.0020 (2 s.f.)
- 0.00205 (3 s.f., note that we round up or down if necessary)

305,620 would be:
- 300,000 (1 s.f.)
- 310,000 (2 s.f.)
- 306,000 (3 s.f.)

(Sometimes a zero is just a placeholder and sometimes it counts as one of the significant figures as in the last example above.)

›tandard form

›tandard form is a shorthand used to express very large or very small numbers. The ormula to use is:

number between 1 and 10] × 10 [to the power of x]

'he number between 1 and 10 is called the *mantissa*. The power of 10 is called the *xponent*.

3.2×10^5 is 320,000 (move decimal point 5 places to right).

If the number was 323,000 we could use 3.2 or 3.23 (round up) or just 3 as the mantissa.

If the number was 327,000 we could use 3.3 or 3.27 or 3 as the mantissa.

3.2×10^{-5} is 0.000032 (move decimal point 5 places to left).

Or we could just use 3 as the mantissa.

)rder of magnitude calculations

)rder of magnitude calculations are another kind of estimate, this time using tandard form and comparing the exponents. You can then say how many times igger or smaller one number is than another.

Λathematical symbols

'ou will need to be able to understand and use the following mathematical symbols:

Symbol	Symbol name	Meaning / definition	Example
=	equals sign	equality	4 = 3+1
>	strict inequality	greater than	3 > 2
<	strict inequality	less than	2 < 3
>>	inequality	much greater than	3000 >> 0.02
<<	inequality	much less than	0.02 << 3000
∝	proportional to	proportional to	$f(x) \propto g(x)$
≈	approximately equal	weak approximation	11 ≈ 10

ɔply it Estimate results: ıe range from 59 to)6 is 147 (or 148 with ıe correction of +1).

ɔw close was your timate?

I
ma²th/s

HAVE WE CONVINCED YOU YET?

Maths at school should just be one lesson... how to divide a restaurant bill between three people.

A level only

Substituting values

You may be required to substitute numerical values into algebraic equations. All this means is:

1. You are given an equation, such as $a = b + c$.
2. You are given values for b and c (for example, $b = 4$ and $c = 7$).
3. What is a? (answer: $a = 11$).

Let's try a slightly more difficult equation, the one for standard deviation – which gives you the opportunity to understand standard deviation better.

The formula is $\sqrt{\frac{\sum(x-\bar{x})^2}{N-1}}$ — x represents each value in the data set. $\bar{x}$ is the symbol for the mean for the data set.

Calculate the difference between the mean and each value, and then square this difference.

$\sum$ is the symbol for 'sum of', so we add all the squared differences.

N means 'number' (how many numbers did we have?).

$\sqrt{\ }$ means square root (we press that key on our calculator).

If you are told $\sum(\bar{x} - x)^2 = 56$ and $n = 12$, you can work out the standard deviation:

Square root (56 / 11) = 2.26 (to 2 decimal places).

Japan's Akira Haraguchi holds the current world record for reciting decimal places of pi from memory. He managed 100,000 decimal places in 6 hours in October 2006.

π

Check it

1. Steve scored 18 out of 20 in a memory test as part of a psychology experiment.
   - (a) Express Steve's mark as a percentage. *[1 mark]*
   - (b) Express Steve's mark as a decimal. *[1 mark]*
   - (c) Express Steve's mark as a fraction of the maximum mark. *[1 mark]*
2. Express the value 0.01678365 to 3 decimal places. *[1 mark]*
3. Write out the following equation in words: 1 << 1,000,000 *[1 mark]*

Statistical testing: The sign test

The specification says...

Introduction to statistical testing; the sign test. When to use the sign test; calculation of the sign test.

Our final mathematical challenge is an overview of the processes involved in statistical testing including the concepts of probability and significance.

Then we see how these ideas are applied to the calculation of a simple statistical test: the sign test.

Key terms

Statistical testing Provides a way of determining whether hypotheses should be accepted or rejected. By using a statistical test we can find out whether differences or relationships between variables are significant (meaningful) or are likely to have occurred by chance.

Sign test A statistical test used to analyse the difference in scores between related items (e.g. the same participant tested twice). Data should be nominal or better.

When expressing the 5% probability level (described on the right), students will often not include the appropriate number of decimal places. Remember that 5% is not equivalent to 0.5 (this is 50%) but should be written as 0.05.

Be careful, this is an easy mistake to make!

Table of critical values of the sign test (*S*)

Level of significance for a **one-tailed test**	0.05	0.025	0.01	0.005
Level of significance for a **two-tailed test**	0.10	0.05	0.02	0.01
N = 5	0			
6	0	0		
7	0	0	0	
8	1	0	0	0
9	1	1	0	0
10	1	1	0	0
11	2	1	1	0
12	2	2	1	1
13	3	2	1	1
14	3	2	2	1
15	3	3	2	2
16	4	3	2	2
17	4	4	3	2
18	5	4	3	3
19	5	4	4	3
20	5	5	4	3
25	7	7	6	5
30	10	9	8	7
35	12	11	10	9

Calculated value of *S* must be EQUAL TO or LESS THAN the critical value in this table for significance to be shown.

Statistical testing

The concept of significance

It turned out we found a difference in the level of chattiness after participants drank *SpeedUpp* compared to when they drank water. Fantastic! We can now market *SpeedUpp* as a scientific cure for shyness and make millions. Or can we?

Just because we found a difference in the **mean** number of words spoken in the two conditions, we do not yet know if this is what psychologists refer to as a **significant** difference. The difference we found may have been no more than that which could have occurred by **chance**, that is, by coincidence or a fluke. To find this out, we need to use **statistical testing**.

The sign test

To determine whether the difference we have found is significant, we can use a simple statistical calculation called the **sign test**. There are a number of statistical tests in psychology, each of which have their own conditions of use. To use the sign test:

1. We need to be looking for a *difference* rather than an association (which we are).
2. We need to have used a **repeated measures design** (which we did).
3. We need data that is organised into categories, known as **nominal data**. Our data isn't nominal (yet) but we can convert it for the purposes of this test.

The concept of probability

Probability (*p*) refers to the likelihood that certain events will occur. This is applied to understanding the findings from a study. The findings we obtain come from a **sample** of participants. What we want to know is 'how likely are these findings if the **null hypothesis** is true?'. The null hypothesis states there is no difference/association in the population. If we find a difference/association in our sample, can we say that this is 'true' for the population (i.e. accept the **alternative hypothesis**)?

The accepted level of probability (level of significance) in psychology is 0.05 (which is 5% when written as a percentage). This is the level at which a researcher decides that the findings are significant (meaningful) and will reject the null hypothesis. In some circumstances, researchers need to be even more confident that findings were not due to chance and so employ a stricter, more stringent significance level such as 0.01 (the 1% level). This is in cases when research may involve a human cost, such as when new drugs are being trialled, or when a particular investigation is a one-off, and there is no possibility that it can be repeated in future.

Even though researchers may find statistically significant differences/associations within data, they can never find statistical certainties. This is why psychologists use phrases such as 'this suggests' rather than 'this proves'. In the absence of proof or certainty, psychologists have decided that 5% will generally be sufficient.

The critical value

When the statistical test has been calculated (see the worked example on the right) the researcher is left with a number – the **calculated value**. This needs to be compared with a **critical value** to decide whether the result is significant or not. The critical values for a sign test are given in a **table of critical values** (see left).

You need the following information to use the table:

1. The significance level (generally 0.05 or 5%).
2. The number of participants in the investigation (the *N* value or sometimes degrees of freedom, *df*).
3. Whether the hypothesis is **directional** (**one-tailed test**) or **non-directional** (**two-tailed test**) (see page 168).

These pieces of information allow you to locate the critical value for your data. For the sign test, the calculated value has to be equal to or lower than the critical value for the result to be significant.

Sign test anyone? Who ordered a sign test?

7.5T
20
40
GIVE WAY

'he sign test: a worked example

/e analyse the data from our energy drink experiment to illustrate the use of the sign test (for ie purpose of this example, 10 participants have been added), to make 20 participants in total.

tep 1 We need to convert the data to nominal data by working out which participants roduced a higher word count after the energy drink, and which produced a lower word count.

/e do this by subtracting the score for water from the score for *SpeedUpp*. If the answer is egative we record a negative sign, if the answer is positive we record a plus sign.

Participant	*SpeedUpp*	Water	Sign of difference
1	110	122	–
2	59	45	+
3	206	135	+
4	89	90	–
5	76	42	+
6	141	87	+
7	152	131	+
8	98	113	–
9	198	129	+
10	57	62	–
11	267	176	+
12	282	240	+
13	134	157	–
14	167	103	+
15	88	108	–
16	201	121	+
17	267	231	+
18	322	200	+
19	249	207	+
20	90	104	–

tep 2 From the table we add up the pluses and the minuses. The total number of pluses 13) is the number of participants who spoke more words in the five minutes after drinking *peedUpp* than they did after drinking water. The total number of minuses (7) is the number f participants who spoke more words in the five minutes after drinking water than they did fter drinking *SpeedUpp*.

tep 3 We take the less frequent sign (in this case it is the total number of minuses) and call nis *S*. Therefore $S = 7$ (this is our calculated value of *S*).

Note that if there had been any participants who spoke the same number of words in both conditions (Participant 4 got pretty close!) this data would be ignored and the total number (*N*) would be adjusted.

tep 4 Now we must compare our calculated value with the critical value (see facing page, ar left).

The hypothesis was: *Participants speak significantly more words in the five minutes after drinking* SpeedUpp *than in the five minutes after drinking water.*

The hypothesis is directional, so we are looking for a one-tailed test.

We will use the 5% (0.05) level of significance. This determines the column.

$N = 20$. This determines the row.

The point where the column and row meet gives us the critical value. The critical value for the sign test is 5 when *N* is 20 at 0.05 level of significance for a one-tailed test.

The calculated value of S must be *equal to or less than* (≤) the critical value at the 0.05 level of significance.

Ve can see that for our investigation, the calculated value of S (7) is *more than* the critical value of (5). This can be expressed as $7 > 5$. Therefore, the difference is not significant at the 0.05 level. So, even though there was a difference in the mean number of words spoken between the wo conditions, it was *not* a statistically significant difference on this occasion. So, it's back to he drawing board for possible ways to make a million. I wonder if coffee would work...

Apply it
Methods

The sign test: over to you

A teacher wanted to know whether his psychology students thought they had benefitted from reading a chapter on research methods he had produced in a textbook.

After 15 of the teacher's students had read the chapter, they simply had to indicate whether they thought their understanding of research methods was better (+), worse (–) or had stayed the same (=).

The results of the investigation were as follows:

Student	Better	Worse	Same
1	+		
2			=
3		–	
4	+		
5	+		
6	+		
7		–	
8		–	
9			=
10	+		
11		–	
12	+		
13	+		
14		–	
15			=

At the beginning of the investigation, the teacher wrote a directional (one-tailed) hypothesis stating that the students' understanding of research methods would be improved after reading the chapter.

Questions

1. Using the critical values table on the facing page, decide whether the result of the teacher's investigation is significant or not. (*1 mark*)
2. Explain how you arrived at your answer. (*2 marks*)

Check it

1. Identify **three** conditions that would need to be met in order to use the sign test. *[3 marks]*
2. What is the generally accepted level of probability in psychological research? Explain why. *[3 marks]*
3. Outline **two** circumstances in which a researcher might employ the 1% level of significance. *[2 marks]*
4. Identify **three** pieces of information that are required when reading a table of critical values. *[3 marks]*

Peer review and psychological research and the economy

The specification says...

The role of peer review in the scientific process.

The implications of psychological research for the economy.

This spread has a dual purpose: first, we investigate and evaluate the role that peer review plays in the scientific process.

Second, we discuss some of the ways in which psychological research may impact upon, and be of benefit to, the economy.

Key terms

Peer review The assessment of scientific work by others who are specialists in the same field, to ensure that any research intended for publication is of high quality.

Economy The state of a country or region in terms of the production and consumption of goods and services.

PAPER
ACCEPTED!

Apply it Methods

Fraudulent research

In 2011, an intriguing Dutch study reported that when there's a lot of rubbish in the street we are more likely to stereotype other people.

The following year it was revealed that the co-author, Diederik Stapel, had made up the data. It turned out that Stapel had been manipulating and fabricating data for a number of years and he was forced to return his PhD qualification.

Questions

1. Fraud in psychological research is not unheard of. Do some research of your own and try to find **two** other examples of fraudulent research in psychology. (*4 marks*)
2. Explain how the process of peer review is an attempt to guard against fraud in psychology. (*3 marks*)

The role of peer review

The aim of science is to produce a body of knowledge based on the results of research. In addition to carrying out the research what matters is how this knowledge is communicated within the scientific community, and to the wider public. In psychology, research findings are publicised through conferences, textbooks, but most often via academic journals (such as *Journal of Experimental Social Psychology* or *American Psychologist*).

Before a piece of research can become part of a journal, however, it must be subject to a process of **peer review**. This involves all aspects of the written investigation being scrutinised by a small group of usually two or three experts ('peers') in the particular field. These experts should conduct an objective review and be unknown to the author or researcher.

The main aims of peer review

1. *To allocate research funding*. Independent peer evaluation also takes place to decide whether or not to award funding for a proposed research project. This may be co-ordinated by government-run funding organisations such as the *Medical Research Council*, who have a vested interest in establishing which research projects are most worthwhile.
2. *To validate the quality and relevance of research*. All elements of research are assessed for quality and accuracy: the formulation of hypotheses, the methodology chosen, the statistical tests used and the conclusions drawn.
3. *To suggest amendments or improvements*. Reviewers may suggest minor revisions of the work and thereby improve the report. In extreme circumstances, they may conclude that the work is inappropriate for publication and should be withdrawn.

Evaluation of peer review

Whilst the benefits of peer review – in establishing the **validity** and accuracy of research – are clear, certain features of the process are open to criticism.

Anonymity

It is usual practice that the 'peer' doing the reviewing remains anonymous throughout the process as this is likely to produce a more honest appraisal. However, a minority of reviewers may use their anonymity as a way of criticising rival researchers who they perceive as having crossed them in the past! This is made all the more likely by the fact that many researchers are in direct competition for limited research funding. For this reason, some journals favour a system of open reviewing whereby the names of the reviewer(s) are made public.

Publication bias

It is a natural tendency for editors of journals to want to publish significant 'headline-grabbing' findings to increase the credibility and circulation of their publication. They also prefer to publish positive results (see **file drawer problem**, page 193).

This could mean that research which does not meet these criteria is ignored or disregarded. Ultimately, this creates a false impression of the current state of psychology if journal editors are being selective in what they publish.

Burying groundbreaking research

The peer review process may suppress opposition to mainstream theories, wishing to maintain the status quo within particular scientific fields. Reviewers tend to be especially critical of research that contradicts their own view and much more favourable to that which matches it.

Established scientists are the ones more likely to be chosen as reviewers, particularly by prestigious journals and publishers. As a result, findings that chime with current opinion are more likely to be passed than new and innovative research that challenges the established order.

Thus, peer review may have the effect of slowing down the rate of change within a particular scientific discipline.

mplications of psychological ·esearch for the economy

)ne of the wider concerns for psychology, as well as science in general, is what the mplications of research are for the **economy**. By 'implications' we mean – how does vhat we learn from the findings of psychological research influence, affect, benefit or levalue our financial prosperity?

We will revisit two examples of research discussed elsewhere in this book, the ndings of which have implications for the nation's financial well-being.

\ttachment research into the role of the father

\ttachment research has come a considerable way since John Bowlby first asserted hat a child can only ever form a secure and lasting monotropic bond with its mother see page 84). Thus, at the time Bowlby was writing, childcare was seen as a mother's esponsibility, and hers alone, whilst the father was free to carry out his 'natural' role as rovider for the family.

More recent research suggests that the father may fulfil a qualitatively different role rom the mother. Crucially, this role is no less *valuable* in the child's upbringing.

Psychological research has shown that *both* parents are equally capable of providing he emotional support necessary for healthy psychological development, and this nderstanding may promote more flexible working arrangements within the family. It is ow the norm in lots of households that the mother is the higher earner and so works onger hours, whilst many couples share childcare responsibilities across the working veek. This means that modern parents are better equipped to maximise their income nd contribute more effectively to the economy.

The development of treatments for mental disorders

\bsence from work costs the economy an estimated £15 billion a year. A recent ;overnment report revealed that a third of all absences are caused by mild to moderate nental health disorders such as **depression**, anxiety and stress (*The Telegraph* 2014). 'sychological research into the causes and treatments of mental disorders therefore has n important role to play in supporting a healthy workforce.

In Chapter 5 we looked at treatment of mental disorders. Patients are able to be ssessed quickly and gain swift access to treatment. Many conditions are treated hrough the use of **psychotherapeutic drugs** such as **SSRIs** for depression and **OCD** (see)age 156). **Antianxiety drugs** are used for stress conditions.

Referrals can also be made by GPs for psychotherapies such as **systematic lesensitisation** (see page 148) or **CBT** (see page 152). Individuals can also engage in ,elf-treatment using similar methods.

This means that, in many cases, people with mental disorders are able to nanage their condition effectively and return to work. Thus, the economic benefit of)sychological research into disorders such as depression is considerable.

Research into psychological conditions such as depression may benefit the economy.

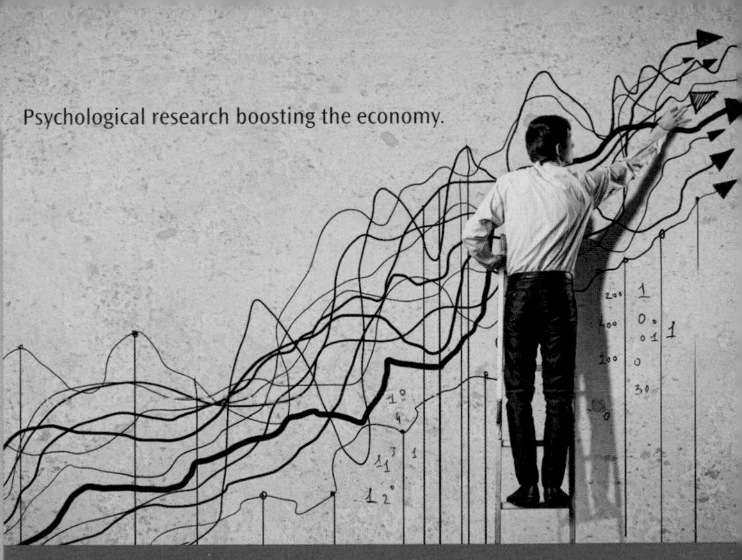

Psychological research boosting the economy.

Apply it Methods

The Nudge Unit

In our Introduction to this book we described the Nudge Unit (see page 13). The 'Nudge Unit' is the name given to the Behavioural Insights Team, an organisation that used to be part of the UK government. It was formed to change behaviour using psychological principles (in small steps, or 'nudges').

The work of the Nudge Unit has been wide-ranging (and controversial) but much of it has focused on gains for the economy and preventing financial waste.

Questions

1. Do some research and find **three** policies the Nudge Unit has introduced. How successful have they been in saving money for the economy? (*6 marks*)
2. Do you have any (*ethical or moral*) concerns with the use of psychological research to influence people's behaviour? (4 marks)

Apply it Methods

Psychological research and the economy

On the left we have described two examples of psychological research that may have implications for the economy but can you find any other similar examples elsewhere in this book?

Questions

1. How might research into eyewitness testimony and the cognitive interview (see pages 58 and 62) lead to economic benefits in the long run? (*2 marks each*)
2. How might research into the processes that influence social change benefit the economy (page 34)? (*2 marks*)

Check it

1. Explain how the peer review process is conducted. *[2 marks]*
2. Explain **two** roles of peer review in the scientific process. *[4 marks]*
3. Briefly discuss the implications of psychological research for the economy. *[6 marks]*

Practical corner

The specification says...

Knowledge and understanding of ... research methods, practical research skills and maths skills. These should be developed through ... ethical practical research activities.

This means that you should conduct practical investigations wherever possible. Within the Research methods chapter there have been a number of suggestions as to how you might go about conducting your own practical investigations. Here, right at the end, are a couple of others. First up, a field experiment based on research from the Social influence topic and secondly, a correlational analysis based on data collected from a lab study. Good luck carrying out both!

Ethics check

Ethics are discussed in detail on pages 178–179. We strongly suggest that you complete this checklist before collecting data.

1. Do participants know participation is voluntary?
2. Do participants know what to expect?
3. Do participants know they can withdraw at any time?
4. Are individuals' results anonymous?
5. Have I minimised the risk of distress to participants?
6. Have I avoided asking sensitive questions?
7. Will I avoid bringing my school/teacher/psychology into disrepute?
8. Have I considered all other ethical issues?
9. Has my teacher approved this?

She who must be obeyed (hard hat optional).

Practical idea 1: The influence of uniform on obedience

The aim of this study is to investigate whether the wearing of a uniform affects levels of obedience.

More specifically we are interested in whether an official-looking uniform (in the form of a high visibility jacket) will increase the likelihood that people will carry out simple 'orders' such as picking up litter. A **field experiment** is used to investigate this.

The practical bit

Based on obedience studies, such as those by Stanley Milgram (see page 22) and Leonard Bickman (see page 25), we suggest that you investigate the power of a uniform in a social setting. Electric shocks are out (apparently that's not very ethical) but it might be acceptable to encourage younger students to perform some simple tasks to see if they obey.

Setting up the experimental situation: the 'uniform'

In a field experiment many variables cannot be controlled. However, there are some steps you can take to ensure the procedure is as **standardised** as possible. First: the uniform. Let's not be too ambitious here – you need not scour the local fancy dress shop shelves and arrive at school looking like a police officer, fire fighter or prison guard. A high visibility jacket will do the job nicely. The uniform need not look very technical just as long as it makes you stand out from other students. Perhaps combine it with a Milgram-style clipboard for extra authenticity.

The 'order'

You should not use students under the age of 16 in your study and should not ask your participants to do anything that will cause them undue embarrassment. You might simply ask them to pick up a piece of litter. On the other hand, if you attend a school that is exceptionally tidy (!) you might just order them to stand by a wall for no particular reason or to remain still for a short period. Make a note of whether the student obeys your order or not in each case. Whatever you decide to do, check with your teacher first to make sure it is acceptable.

Choosing your sample

It may be a good idea to conduct the study during a break or lunchtime as stopping students in the corridor may elicit higher levels of obedience during free time. Either way, this constitutes an **opportunity sample** as you are using participants who happen to be available. Approach students on their own or in pairs otherwise the experiment is likely to become a study of collective rebellion – people in groups are more likely to resist orders to obey (see page 30)!

Ethical issues

Aside from issues already mentioned, it is also essential that you offer participants a full **debrief** not least because they have not actually consented to be part of a research study. Explain the aim of the research, record whether the student obeyed – but do not take their name – and ask whether you can use their data.

Control group

Finally do not forget to repeat the study (with different students) *without* the jacket to establish a **control group** so you can make effective comparisons between how students behaved when the person issuing the order was wearing a uniform and when they weren't wearing the uniform.

Table 1 Number of students who obeyed and disobeyed in the uniform and non-uniform conditions.

	Uniform	Non-uniform
No. of students who obeyed	22	19
No. of students who disobeyed	8	11

Apply it Methods

The maths bit 1

1. In Table 1 the total number of participants tested is shown. What **percentage** obeyed in the uniform condition? (*1 mark*)
2. Of the total number of participants tested, what **fraction** obeyed in the uniform condition? (*1 mark*)
3. Which **graphical display** would be most suitable to show the difference in levels of obedience between the uniform and non-uniform conditions? Explain your answer. (*2 marks*)
4. What are the **independent** and **dependent variables** in this experiment? Make sure your answers are **operationalised**. (*2 marks*)

⁾ractical idea 2: ESP and extraversion

he aim of this study is to see if there is a relationship between ESP (**extrasensory** **erception**) and the personality trait of **extraversion**.

In other words, is there a **correlation** between how extrovert you are (sociable, confident, utgoing, etc.) and your ability to mind-read?

The practical bit

arapsychology is a branch of psychology that is concerned with all things supernatural. ccording to psychological research, a high score on an extraversion scale (that measures ersonality traits such as sociability and confidence) is **positively correlated** with telepathic ower – in other words, the ability to receive information from the minds of others. Your task s to test this.

;etting up the experimental situation

'our role (as well as being the researcher) is to act as the 'sender' – the person who transmits he message to the 'receiver' (your participants). You will do this by first constructing a set f 25 Zener cards (see bottom of the page). These can be purchased from specialist shops or ver the Internet but to save time and money it's easier to make your own, five of each type.

The Zener test

t is your decision but probably the best and most controlled method is to test each articipant individually. Testing all participants at once may cause sensory leakage where the houghts of others present in the room may influence or affect the ESP abilities of others. 'ou should also minimise other influences, such as background noise, which may affect oncentration.

The pack of 25 cards should be shuffled by a third party before the test begins. The ender (you) should look at the card and think only of the image on the card. The receiver the participant) who cannot see the card should write the name – or draw – the image that omes into their mind. This process is repeated for all 25 cards. The probability of correctly dentifying cards is 5 out of 25 (or 1 in 5). Higher scores may indicate telepathic powers.

The extraversion scale

'our participants also need to complete an extraversion scale, for example use tinyurl.com/5bfr8f. There are others you can find online.

Once you have an ESP score and an extraversion score for each participant you can nalyse your findings using a correlation.

Ethical issues

Jnlike the investigation on the facing page, it is not necessary to deceive participants about he aim of this study until the end. They will not be able to influence their own performance n the ESP test (unless their powers of mind control are phenomenally good!). They may, owever, want to present themselves in a good light on the extraversion scale and give **ocially desirable** answers. You might guard against this by not telling them what the uestionnaire measures until debriefing.

As ever, keep all data you collect **confidential**. Participants may need some reassurance hat the score they achieved on either of the two tests is 'normal'. Of course, if someone does core much higher on the Zener card test than would be predicted by chance, you might get hem to make a quick prediction of next week's lottery numbers before they leave...

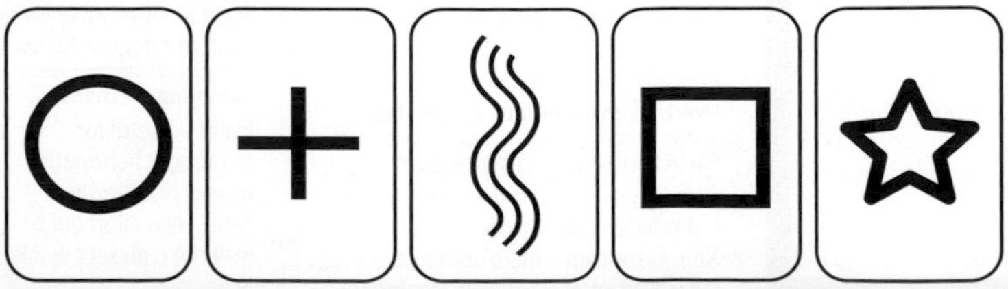

Apply it Methods — The maths bit 2

1. In Table 2, what percentage of participants scored 10 or above on the ESP test and the extraversion scale? (*2 marks*)
2. Which graphical display would be most suitable to show the relationship between ESP score and extraversion score in Table 2? Explain your answer. (*2 marks*)
3. Sketch a suitable graphical display to show the relationship between ESP score and extraversion score in Table 2. (*3 marks*)
4. Referring to Table 2 and the display you have drawn, explain the relationship between ESP scores and extraversion scores in this investigation. (*2 marks*)
5. Explain why, from this investigation, it is not possible to conclude that there is a causal relationship between ESP score and extraversion. (*1 mark*)
6. The chance probability score on a set of 25 Zener cards is 1 in 5. Express this figure as a **decimal**. (*1 mark*)

Participant	ESP score	Extravert score
1	3	6
2	14	20
3	8	10
4	9	9
5	11	16
6	2	7
7	4	9
8	9	12
9	13	17
10	10	10

Here's one we did before ...

Table 2 ESP score and extraversion score for each participant.

The maths bit

On page 217 we have given a list of the mathematical skills you will be expected to demonstrate.

Overall, at least 10% of the marks in assessments for Psychology will require the use of mathematical skills.

Revision summaries

Experiments

Experimental method

Aims
Purpose of the investigation.

Hypotheses
Testable, operationalised statement.

Directional or non-directional
Identifying a difference/correlation or not. Choice depends on previous theory/research.

Variables

IVs and DVs
IV manipulated, DV measured.

Levels of the IV
Experimental and control conditions.

Operationalisation
Defining variables so they can be measured.

Research issues

Extraneous variables
Nuisance variables but randomly distributed.

Confounding variables
Vary systematically with IV.

Demand characteristics
Participants second guess the aims, alter their behaviour.

Investigator effects
Influence of researcher on DV/design decisions.

Randomisation
Chance methods to reduce researcher's bias.

Standardisation
Ensuring all participants have the same experience.

Experimental designs

Independent groups
Participants in each condition of experiment are different.

Repeated measures
All participants take part in all conditions.

Matched pairs
Similar participants paired on participant variables, allocated to condition A or B.

Evaluation

Independent groups
Participant variables not controlled (use random allocation).
Less economical. No order effects.

Repeated measures
Order effects (use counterbalancing). Demand characteristics. Participant variables controlled. More economical.

Matched pairs
No order effects. Cannot match participants exactly. Time-consuming.

Types of experiment

Lab experiments
IV is manipulated in a controlled setting. Participants go to researcher.

Field experiments
IV is manipulated in a natural setting. Researcher goes to participants.

Natural experiments
IV changes naturally. DV/setting may be natural or in a lab.

Quasi-experiments
IV based on an existing difference between people, effect on DV is recorded.

Evaluation

Lab experiments
High internal validity (control CVs/EVs, cause and effect shown), replication more possible (support for findings). However low external validity (generalisability, mundane realism), low internal validity (demand characteristics).

Field experiments
Higher external validity (more authentic, realism). Lower internal validity (less control). Ethical issues (consent not possible).

Natural experiments
Only option for practical/ethical reasons, high external validity (real-world problems). Limited opportunities, no random allocation (CVs), low realism in a lab, no manipulation of IV (can't claim cause and effect).

Quasi-experiments
If in a lab, issues as for lab experiment. No random allocation, no manipulation of IV (can't claim cause and effect).

Sampling

Population and sample

Random sample
Equal chance of selection, lottery.

Systematic sample
Selecting every *n*th person from list.

Stratified sample
Sample reflects the proportion of people in different population strata.

Opportunity sample
Choosing whoever is available.

Volunteer sample
Participants 'self-select' e.g. advert.

Evaluation

Random sample
Potentially unbiased, control CVs/EVs. Time-consuming, may not work.

Systematic sample
Objective method, but time-consuming, those selected may refuse (= volunteer sample).

Stratified sample
Representative. Cannot account for all subgroups.

Opportunity sample
Convenient. Unrepresentative.

Volunteer sample
Easy and participants engaged. Volunteer bias, responsive to cues.

Ethical issues

The issues

Conflict between rights of participants and aims of research.

Informed consent
Advise participant what is involved. Reveals research aims.

Deception
Misleading participants/withholding information. OK if not distressing.

Protection from harm
Psychological/physical risk should be 'normal'.

Privacy and confidentiality
Right to control and protect personal data.

How to deal with them

Informed consent
Signed consent form. Presumptive, prior general, retrospective.

Deception / protection from harm
Debriefing, right to withdraw/withhold data, counselling.

Privacy and confidentiality
Use numbers not names. Data not shared with other researchers.

Pilot studies (and more)

Research techniques

Pilot studies
Check procedures and techniques, make changes.

Single-blind
Participants aren't aware of aims/conditions until end.

Double-blind
Neither participants nor individual conducting research know the aim/condition.

Control groups and conditions
Used as a comparison or baseline.

Observation

Types of observation

Naturalistic observations
Behaviour observed where it would normally occur. No control over variables.

Controlled observations
Some control over environment, e.g. manipulation of variables.

Covert and overt observations
Observing without or with participants' knowledge.

Participant and non-participant
Join the group or remain an outsider.

Evaluation

All observations
Capture what people do. Observer bias and no causal relationships shown.

Naturalistic observations
Low internal validity (control difficult). High external validity (everyday life).

Controlled observations
High internal validity – extraneous variables may be controlled.
Low external validity (except if covert).

Covert and overt observations
Covert – low demand characteristics but ethically questionable.
Overt – behaviour may be affected.

Participant and non-participant
Participant – increased external validity but may lose objectivity.
Non-participant – more objectivity (increased internal validity), less insight.

Observational design

Ways of recording data
Record everything (unstructured) or categories (structured).

Behavioural categories
Target behaviours broken down into observable components.

Sampling methods
Continuous.
Event sampling: count events.
Time sampling: count at timed intervals.

Evaluation

Structured versus unstructured
Structured – numerical, easier to analyse.
Unstructured – may just be eye-catching information, qualitative data harder to analyse. Observer bias.

Behavioural categories
Must be observable. Avoid dustbin category. No overlap.

Sampling methods
Event – useful for infrequent behaviour, misses complexity.
Time – less effort but may not represent whole behaviour.

Self-report

Questionnaires

Questionnaires
Pre-set list. Can use to measure DV in experiments.

Closed and open questions
Fixed-choice or not. Quantitative data or not.

Evaluation

Questionnaires
Distribute to many people.
Fixed-choice, easy to analyse.
Social desirability response bias.

Closed and open questions
Quantitative or qualitative data, affects ease of analysis.

Interviews

Structured interviews
Pre-set questions, fixed order, face-to-face.

Unstructured interviews
No formula, just general topic.
Questions based on responses.

Semi-structured interviews
Some pre-set questions with follow-ups.

Evaluation

Structured interviews
Easy to replicate. Interviewer can't elaborate/explain.

Unstructured interviews
Flexible. Increased interviewer bias. Analysis more difficult. Social desirability bias reduced by rapport.

Designing self-report

Questionnaires
Likert scale, rating scale, fixed choice.

Interviews
Standardised schedule, avoids interviewer bias. Comfortable setting for rapport. Ethical issues.

Good questions

Overuse of jargon
Don't be too technical.

Emotive language and leading questions
Replace 'loaded' phrases with neutral ones.

Double-barrelled questions and double negatives
Ask one question only.

Correlations

The method

Types of correlation
Positive, negative and zero.

Difference between correlations and experiments
No manipulation of variables, no cause and effect.

Evaluation

Strengths
Useful starting point. Quick and economical, using secondary data.

Limitations
Can't demonstrate cause and effect. Intervening variables. May be misinterpreted.

Data analysis

Qualitative and quantitative data

Qualitative data
Written, non-numerical description of participants' thoughts, feelings etc.

Quantitative data
Expressed numerically rather than words.

Evaluation

Qualitative data
Rich in detail. Greater external validity. Difficult to analyse. May be subjective.

Quantitative data
Easy to analyse (e.g. graphs). Less biased. Narrower in meaning.

Primary and secondary data

Primary data
Collected firsthand for purpose of investigation.

Secondary data
Collected by someone other than researcher.

Evaluation

Primary data
Fits the job, targets relevant information. Requires time.

Secondary data
Inexpensive and easy to access. Variation in the quality, e.g. outdated.

Meta-analysis

Type of secondary data
Statistical analysis of large number of studies. Produces effect size.

Evaluation

Large sample, high validity. Publication bias/file drawer problem.

Measures of central tendency

Mean
Add up, divide by the number.

Median
The middle value.

Mode
Most frequently occurring.

Evaluation

Mean
Most sensitive and representative. Easily distorted by extreme values.

Median
Less affected by extremes but not sensitive.

Mode
Relevant to categorical data. Crude, unrepresentative.

Measures of dispersion

Range
Subtract the lowest from the highest (add 1).

Standard deviation
How much scores (on average) deviate from mean.

Evaluation

Range
Easy to calculate. Unrepresentative if there are extremes.

Standard deviation
More precise than range. Distorted by extreme values.

Presentation of quantitative data

Tables
Raw scores summarised in a grid.

Bar charts
Discrete categorical data. Frequency = height of bar.

Histograms
Continuous data rather than discrete, so no space between bars. True zero.

Scattergrams
Shows strength and direction of relationship between co-variables.

Normal distribution
Bell curve. Mean, median and mode at same point. Tails never touch zero.

Skewed distributions
Negative leans right. Positive leans left.

Mathematical content

What you need to know

Percentages and fractions
Out of 100, part of a whole.

Decimal places
Digits to right of decimal point 10ths, 100ths etc.

Ratios
Part-to-whole. Part-to-part.

Estimates and order of magnitude calculations
Ballpark figures to check calculations.

Significant figures
Count non-zero figures, except zero place holders.

Standard form
[number between 1 and 10] × 10 [to the power of x]

Mathematical symbols
=, >, <, >>, <<, ∝, ≈

Statistical testing: The sign test

Statistical testing

The concept of significance
Research findings have not occurred by chance.

The sign test
Difference. Repeated measures. Nominal data.

The concept of probability
Likelihood the sample would occur if the null hypothesis were true.
Usually use the 5% significance level ($p < 0.05$).
Sometimes more stringent 1% level ($p < 0.01$).

The critical value
Comparison with calculated value for significance.

Steps
1. Convert to nominal data.
2. Add up pluses, add up minuses.
3. S = less frequent sign.
4. Compare calculated value of S with critical value. If $S \leq$ critical value, the difference is significant.

Peer review

Aims

Main aims of peer review
1. Allocate funding.
2. Validate quality of research.
3. Suggest amendments/improvements.

Evaluation

Anonymity
May permit unjustified criticisms by rivals.

Publication bias
File drawer problem, creates false impression of current knowledge.

Burying groundbreaking research
Maintains status quo.

Psychological research and the economy

Examples

Attachment research
Role of father – equal care from mother and father, means more effective contribution to economy.

Mental health
Absenteeism due to e.g. depression has a cost, psychological research reduces mental disorder (e.g. new drugs, CBT).

Practice questions, answers and feedback

Question 1 A teacher was interested to know whether there was a gender difference in the time spent doing homework between students at his school. The teacher selected a random sample of 20 boys and 20 girls from the whole school and got them to record the time (in minutes) they spent doing homework at the end of each day. After four weeks the teacher compared the total time for boys and girls and found there was very little difference in the time boys and girls spent doing homework.

(a) This is an example of a quasi-experiment. Explain why this is a quasi-experiment. (*2 marks*)

Morticia's answer *It is a quasi-experiment because it was done in a natural setting.*	Morticia's answer does not distinguish a quasi-experiment, many quasi-experiments are actually done in labs.
Luke's answer *It is a quasi-experiment because participants were not randomly allocated to conditions and the variables were natural.*	Luke gives half a good answer but the 'variables were natural' is too vague for more than a basic answer.
Vladimir's answer *Participants were not randomly allocated to conditions and the independent variable was pre-existing categories (gender), not something manipulated.*	Helpfully, Vladimir supplies the missing element to Luke's answer! This is clear and accurate with a relevant link to the study described.

(b) Explain **one** limitation of a quasi-experiment. Refer to the experiment above in your answer. (*3 marks*)

Morticia's answer *One limitation is that you can't draw cause and effect conclusions about boys and girls.*	Morticia's answer could be made into a relevant limitation that applies to this study but is too poorly expressed for any value.
Luke's answer *One limitation of quasi-experiments is that there may be confounding variables because we can't randomly allocate the participants to conditions, for example it might be that girls were smarter and that's why they spent more time on homework.*	This is a good answer from Luke. The limitation is brief but clearly stated and explained in the context of the investigation described in the stem.
Vladimir's answer *In this example a limitation would be that the girls and boys were aware of what the teacher was investigating and shaped their answer to suit the aims.*	Vladimir's answer is focused on the stem and is plausible but is not really a limitation of quasi-experiments as much as experiments in general so only some value in this answer.

(c) The teacher used random sampling to select participants. Explain how the teacher may have used random sampling in this experiment. (*2 marks*)

Morticia's answer *You do this by using the lottery method where you select their names from a hat.*	It's not clear who 'they' are in Morticia's answer and reference to the lottery method alone is not sufficient. Little of merit here.
Luke's answer *First you get a list of everyone in the school, then you put all the names in a large bowl and select 20 girls and 20 boys.*	Luke's is a better answer – there is some application to the stem – but the girls and boys would be selected separately (as described below). This is a reasonable response.
Vladimir's answer *If you first divide the list of everyone in the school into girls' names and boys' names and number every name you can then use a computer randomiser to select 20 of each.*	An excellent answer from Vladimir that is clearly focused on the stem and recognises the importance of the girls and boys as separate groups.

(d) Before the experiment began, the teacher conducted a pilot study. Explain **one** reason why the teacher decided to conduct a pilot study. (*2 marks*)

Morticia's answer *The teacher would do this because he wants to see if his hypothesis is right and not waste time on the real study if it isn't.*	Morticia makes a common error – pilot studies do not test hypotheses, they 'road-test' procedures and materials.
Luke's answer *A pilot study is a small-scale trial run of the study itself where you can test procedures and see if there are any problems.*	Luke's answer reads more like a definition of a pilot study rather than a reason to conduct it. There is reference to testing procedures though, so there is something of value here.
Vladimir's answer *This is a good way to make sure you don't waste time later.*	Quite a weak, generic answer but Vladimir has cited a reason why pilot studies are conducted and thus the answer has some value but not perfect.

(e) Explain how demand characteristics may have affected the outcome of this experiment. (*2 marks*)

Morticia's answer *The students may have guessed what the study was about and changed their behaviour.*	Morticia has given a generic answer and not focused on the stem. This is a weak answer.
Luke's answer *If they guess the aims then they might give the answer the teacher wants such as the girls might have exaggerated the time they spent because that's what the teacher expected.*	Luke demonstrates understanding of the concept and there is some context in the answer suggested by the stem. This question is only worth 2 marks so his answer is sufficient.
Vladimir's answer *They would have made the experiment less valid because the teacher would not have got honest answers.*	Vladimir's use of validity is relevant but, unlike above, the understanding of demand characteristics is not sufficiently conveyed to go beyond being 'partial'.

On this spread we look at some typical student answers to questions. The comments provided indicate what is good and bad in each answer. Learning how to produce effective question answers is a SKILL. Read pages 213–223 for guidance.

Question 2 Following the experiment described on the facing page, the teacher selected a smaller sample of girls and boys from the original study to take part in an interview. The interview was made up of a list of pre-set questions that the teacher read out to the students one after the other. The topic was whether students felt they received too much homework, too little, or the right amount.

(a) Identify the type of interview the teacher conducted. Justify your answer. (*2 marks*)	
Morticia's answer *It's a structured interview because there were pre-set questions.*	Morticia has given the bare minimum but enough! The correct interview is identified and there is application, albeit brief.
Luke's answer *It's structured rather than unstructured which suits this task.*	Luke has identified the type correctly but the application to this context is too minimal.
Vladimir's answer *The questions were fixed in advance and therefore it is called a structured interview.*	Vladmir's answer is short but accurate.

(b) Write **one** closed question that the teacher could have asked as part of the interview. (*1 mark*)	
Morticia's answer *Why is homework important?*	Morticia's example is not a closed question as it would not restrict the respondent to a fixed range of answers, so no good.
Luke's answer *Do you mind doing homework – yes or no?*	In Luke's example the choice is restricted, so spot on.
Vladimir's answer *How many nights a week do you do homework?*	Vladmir's question has a fixed range of answers (between 1 and 7) so it is also fine.

(c) Explain **one** limitation of interviews in the context of this study. (*3 marks*)	
Morticia's answer *It may be difficult to analyse the answers if there are a lot of open questions. This is a limitation.*	A relevant limitation is identified here but not developed further, a weak answer.
Luke's answer *Since the topic is homework it might be better to adapt the questions as you go along to get more information from the students instead of having fixed questions. Further questions depend on how much homework they actually get and how much they do.*	Luke's answer is entirely focused on the context of the study and is well elaborated, a perfect answer.
Vladimir's answer *Structured interviews ensure that different interviewers don't behave differently.*	Unfortunately Vladimir has given a strength of structured interviews rather than a limitation.

(d) Identify **one** ethical issue that the teacher should have taken account of when designing this follow-up investigation and explain **one** way the teacher could have dealt with this ethical issue. (*3 marks*)	
Morticia's answer *Informed consent. Asked them to sign a consent form.*	Morticia has identified an appropriate issue but the rest of her answer isn't complete because, as the children are of school age, consent would also need to be sought from the parents.
Luke's answer *Protection from harm. Told them beforehand about any potential harm such as revealing personal information or feeling upset.*	Luke again has an appropriate issue but the rest is a brief attempt at the second half of the question (protection from harm is quite a difficult issue to discuss anyway) that would only partially deal with the issue. However, this answer is obviously a bit better than Morticia's.
Vladimir's answer *Confidentiality. Told the students before that no names would be stored with the answers and all answers would be confidential.*	Finally Vladimir has selected a different but creditworthy issue. His method of dealing with it would only partly deal with the issue. The students might also be reminded of this during debriefing and the teacher should not share their data with others. This answer is on a par with Luke's because he has identified an issue and given some (but not sufficient) information about dealing with it.

Multiple-choice questions

Experimental method

1. Which statement is the non-directional hypothesis?
   (a) To investigate whether there is a gender difference in judging the speed of a car.
   (b) Men are more accurate in judging the speed of a car than women.
   (c) There is a difference in accuracy of judging the speed of a car between men and women.
   (d) Women are more accurate in judging the speed of a car than men.

2. An experiment investigated whether close proximity to strangers increased heart rate. The DV would be:
   (a) Proximity of strangers.
   (b) The strangers.
   (c) Heart rate.
   (d) The participants.

3. Which would *not* be an effective way of operationalising aggression?
   (a) Number of punches thrown.
   (b) Number of expletives used.
   (c) Distance someone stood from someone else.
   (d) Facial expressions.

4. An effective experimental hypothesis should include:
   (a) A clearly operationalised co-variable.
   (b) A clearly operationalised DV.
   (c) A clearly operationalised EV.
   (d) A clear aim.

Research issues

1. Which best describes a 'confounding variable'?
   (a) Any variable, other than the IV, that may have systematically affected the DV.
   (b) Any variable that may potentially affect the IV or DV.
   (c) Any cue from the researcher or research situation that may reveal the aims of the study.
   (d) Any effect of the investigator's behaviour that may influence the outcome of research.

2. 'Individual differences between participants that may affect the DV' is specifically described as:
   (a) Extraneous variables.
   (b) Confounding variables.
   (c) Situational variables.
   (d) Participant variables.

3. The use of chance in order to control for the effects of bias best describes which of the following?
   (a) Situational variables.
   (b) Demand characteristics.
   (c) Standardised instructions.
   (d) Randomisation.

4. Standardisation is useful when it comes to investigations being...
   (a) Reinterpreted.
   (b) Replicated.
   (c) Complicated.
   (d) Estimated.

Experimental designs

1. Which is *not* a type of experimental design?
   (a) Repeated measures.
   (b) Independent groups.
   (c) Matched pairs.
   (d) Participant design.

2. Which is *not* a type of order effect?
   (a) Fatigue.
   (b) Concentration.
   (c) Practice.
   (d) Boredom.

3. Which of these is an attempt to control for order effects in a repeated measures design?
   (a) Random allocation.
   (b) Control condition.
   (c) Demand characteristics.
   (d) Counterbalancing.

4. Which of these is an attempt to control for participant variables in an independent groups design?
   (a) Random allocation.
   (b) Control condition.
   (c) Demand characteristics.
   (d) Counterbalancing.

Types of experiment

1. An experiment that measured the effects of an earthquake on stress levels (measured before and after) would be a:
   (a) Quasi-experiment.
   (b) Lab experiment.
   (c) Natural experiment.
   (d) Field experiment.

2. Which would *not* be classed as a 'true' experiment?
   (a) Field experiment.
   (b) Lab experiment.
   (c) Quasi-experiment.
   (d) Controlled experiment.

3. Which one is *not* usually a strength of a lab experiment?
   (a) High external validity.
   (b) Establishes cause and effect.
   (c) Precise control of variables.
   (d) Replication is possible.

4. Which is *not* possible in a quasi-experiment?
   (a) Operationalisation.
   (b) Random allocation.
   (c) Standardisation.
   (d) Replication.

Sampling

1. Which is *not* a feature of random sampling?
   (a) Obtain a complete list of the target population.
   (b) Identify subgroups/strata within the population.
   (c) Assign all the names on the list a number.
   (d) Generate a sample using a lottery method.

2. Choosing every 4th house on a street is an example of:
   (a) Opportunity sampling.
   (b) Volunteer sampling.
   (c) Systematic sampling.
   (d) Stratified sampling.

3. Which is most likely to produce a representative sample?
   (a) Opportunity sampling.
   (b) Volunteer sampling.
   (c) Systematic sampling.
   (d) Stratified sampling.

4. Standing in a busy shopping centre and picking people 'at random' to be part of the sample is:
   (a) Opportunity sampling.
   (b) Volunteer sampling.
   (c) Systematic sampling.
   (d) Stratified sampling.

Ethical issues and ways of dealing with them

1. Which is *not* an alternative way of gaining consent?
   (a) Affirmative consent.
   (b) Presumptive consent.
   (c) Prior general consent.
   (d) Retrospective consent.

2. Anonymity is a way of dealing with:
   (a) Informed consent.
   (b) Confidentiality.
   (c) Deception.
   (d) Harm.

3. Which is *not* a major principle of the BPS code of ethics?
   (a) Respect.
   (b) Incompetence.
   (c) Responsibility.
   (d) Integrity.

4. Which would *not* typically be part of a debriefing?
   (a) Informing participants of the aim of the investigation.
   (b) Informing participants of the right to withhold data.
   (c) Thanking participants for their involvement.
   (d) Allocating participants to different conditions.

Appendix: A level and AS skills

Question styles

I
EXAMS

On the following spreads we look at how short-answer questions and essay questions can be answered and how they may be marked.

t both A level and AS you may have multiple-choice, short-answer and/or extended writing/essay uestions. How do you know how to answer these? There are clues:

- The command word (see list on right).
- The number of marks.
- Extra information in the question.

Multiple-choice questions

Select the type of attachment where infants, in the Strange Situation, show high levels of stranger and separation anxiety and show resistance to being comforted at reunion.

A Secure attachment ☐

B Insecure–resistant attachment ☐

C Insecure–avoidant attachment ☐ (1 mark)

Short-answer questions

Such questions may require description, application and/or evaluation. These questions are worth 8 marks or less.

Short-answer questions involving description

Outline **two** definitions of abnormality. (4 marks)

Name **three** types of long-term memory. (3 marks)

Explain what is meant by 'informational social influence'. (2 marks)

Describe the learning theory of attachment. (6 marks)

Short-answer questions involving evaluation

Briefly evaluate the multi-store model of memory. (4 marks)

Explain **one** strength **and one** limitation of unstructured interviews. (4 marks)

Compare participant and non-participant observation. (4 marks)

Discuss **two** limitations of the cognitive approach. (6 marks)

Short-answer questions with describe and evaluate

Briefly outline **and** evaluate informational social influence as an explanation for conformity. (4 marks)

Outline **and** evaluate research into the Authoritarian Personality. (6 marks)

Discuss research into proactive **and** retroactive interference as an explanation of forgetting. (8 marks)

Examples of application questions are shown on page 216.

Longer essay questions

Discuss what research has shown about the features of short-term memory. (12 marks AS)

Describe **and** evaluate research (theories and/or studies) on types of attachment. (12 marks AS)

Describe **and** evaluate the effects of institutionalisation. Include Romanian orphan studies in your answer. (16 marks AL)

Discuss how the cognitive approach has contributed to understanding **and** treating depression. (16 marks AL)

Command words

The following command words are used in exam questions. The definitions given here are from AQA (see tinyurl.com/yx7jqjy5).

Analyse	Separate information into components and identify their characteristics.
Calculate	Work out the value of something.
Choose	Select from a range of alternatives.
Comment	Present an informed opinion.
Compare	Identify similarities and/or differences.
Complete	Finish a task by adding to given information.
Consider	Review and respond to given information.
Describe	Give an account of.
Design	Set out how something will be done.
Discuss	Present key points about different ideas or strengths and weaknesses of an idea.
Distinguish	Explain ways in which two things differ. Provide detail of characteristics that enable a person to know the difference between ...
Draw	Produce a diagram.
Evaluate	Judge from available evidence.
Explain	Set out purposes or reasons.
Explain how	Give a detailed account of a process or way of doing something.
Explain why	Give a detailed account of reasons in relation to a particular situation.
Give	Produce an answer from recall or from given information.
Identify	Name or otherwise characterise.
Justify	Provide reasons, reasoned argument to support, possibly provide evidence.
Label	Provide appropriate names on a diagram.
Name	Identify using a recognised technical term.
Outline	Set out main characteristics.
Select	Choose or pick out from alternatives.
State	Express in clear terms.
Suggest	Present a possible case/solution.
What is meant by	Give a definition.
Which is	Select from alternatives.
Write	Provide information in verbatim form.

Understanding description (AO1)

There are three main skills that you need to develop:

- **Description** of psychological knowledge, assessment objective 1 – aka AO1.
- **Application** of psychological knowledge (AO2).
- **Evaluation** of psychological knowledge (AO3).

When we say 'psychological knowledge' we are referring to the concepts, research studies, therapies and theories/explanations used and developed by psychologists.

This spread starts by looking at *description skills*. What is it you have to do when you *describe* something?

Think of describing an orange. You might say – it is round and orange – which is true but that is a rather *limited* description.

A better description would include more *detail* – The skin is a little squishy and pockmarked. The remains of the green stalk are set in a dimple.

To produce good descriptions you need to grasp this concept of *detail*.

Describing concepts

One of the first concepts in this book is *internalisation*.

This is what we have written on page 18:

Internalisation occurs when a person genuinely accepts the group norms. This results in a private as well as a public change of opinions/behaviour. This change is usually permanent because attitudes have been internalised, i.e. become part of the way the person thinks. The change in opinions/behaviour persists even in the absence of other group members.

If you were asked to **outline** this concept you might write:

'Internalisation is when someone takes on another person's views'.

This is a *basic* answer.

A good answer needs to be **accurate**, **detailed** and have **clarity** and **coherence**.

'Internalisation is when someone takes on the same views as the other person. They don't simply agree in public, but they have a personal and private change of their views.'

If you were asked to **explain** this concept you might include an example:

'Internalisation is when someone takes on the same views as the other person. For example, when you listen to a politician talking about capital punishment and decide to change your view.'

Describing research studies

Psychology is a science and therefore psychologists seek evidence to support their views. This evidence comes from research studies.

In some questions you may decide to use a research study as part of your answer, for example:

Explain how psychologists have investigated the duration of short-term memory.

Describe what research has shown about conformity.

Sometimes you are being asked to provide details of what researcher(s) did ('how' questions) and sometimes to provide details about what was found (the findings – 'show' questions).

A good answer should be **accurate**, **detailed** and have **clarity** and **coherence**.

A special note about research studies

When describing a research study you do not have to include researchers' names but it does provide useful detail. It also ensures that the reader knows which study you are describing – otherwise you might not perform so well because your answer does not appear to apply to a specific study.

Don't worry too much about exact dates.

Another special note about research studies

Research studies may also be used as evaluation – when they are being used in this way you will not be credited for details of the procedure. More about this on page 218.

Timing

On the AS exam there are 72 marks for each paper and you have 90 minutes.

On A level exams, there are 96 marks for each paper and 120 minutes.

That means you have 1¼ minutes per mark. This gives you a sense of how much time you should spend on each exam question.

Don't forget that this timing is not just about writing but you should spend time thinking too.

Description questions use these command words:

Outline

Describe

Explain

Identify

Name

State

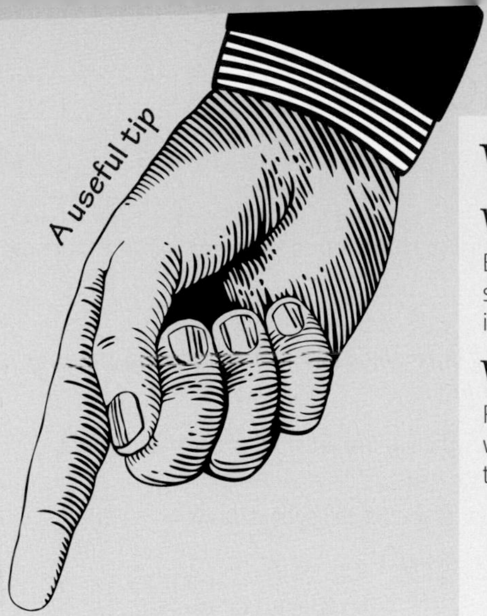
A useful tip

Every time you make a point, make sure you also explain it.

Describing theories/explanations

Such questions look like this:

Outline explanations for conformity. (4 marks)

Describe the multi-store model of memory. (6 marks)

In these questions, as with all other questions, there is no *one* answer. A good answer is one that is **accurate**, **detailed** and **has clarity** and **coherence**.

In addition, for longer answer questions **organisation** and **use of specialist terminology** are important.

Marks for longer answer questions are determined by which *descriptors* (in the table below) best represent what a student has written (bearing in mind the amount of time available to write your answer). The appropriate *level* can then be determined.

A student does not have to fulfil *all* the criteria in a particular level – it is the level that best describes the answer.

Once the level is identified, the mark is determined by considering whether the assessor is tempted by the level above or below.

AO1 Mark scheme

In this mark scheme you can see the key descriptors that we identified above (e.g. accuracy, clarity, coherence).

Level	Marks	Description
3	5–6	Knowledge is generally accurate and generally well-detailed. The answer is clear and coherent. Specialist terminology is used effectively.
2	3–4	Knowledge is evident and focused. There are some inaccuracies. The answer is mostly clear and coherent. There is some appropriate use of specialist terminology.
1	1–2	Knowledge is limited and lacks detail. The answer lacks clarity, accuracy and organisation in places. Specialist terminology is either absent or inappropriately used.
	0	No relevant content.

The mark scheme is presented as an illustration of the AQA mark scheme. Always check the AQA website for the latest version of mark schemes as these may have been amended.

Research

f asked to 'Describe research related to conformity' then you can either describe esearch studies or concepts or theories.

Concepts and theories are derived from the research process and therefore constitute research.

What do these terms mean?

What is *accuracy*?

Being correct. You are not *necessarily* penalised for inaccuracy but you should avoid muddled or confused answers. Aim to present material that is correct.

What is *detail*?

Providing specific pieces of information. This does not always mean writing lots. Instead it means including the small pieces of information that really bring your answer into focus. For example:

Internalisation is when a person changes their opinions in their own mind.

Internalisation is when a person changes their private as well as public opinions.

The second answer is more detailed but not much longer.

What is *organisation*?

You know what an organised bedroom looks like. No doubt some of you do not have very organised bedrooms and often have to search high and low to find things. Teachers reading student answers often feel like this.

Put the information in your answer so that each point follows the previous one in a systematic way rather than just dumping everything you know onto the page – a teacher can see the mess.

In longer answer questions it is important to have a plan and a structure (see page 222–223).

What is *clarity* and *coherence*?

One of the major issues for people who read what you write is that it doesn't always make sense. Lack of clarity is when you don't quite understand what the person is trying to say.

One useful way to ensure clarity (and coherence) is to always try to explain what you have just written, for example:

Internalisation is when a person changes their private as well as public opinions. In other words they actually believe the views they are expressing.

What is *specialist terminology*?

This is linked to 'detail' – using psychologists' specialist terms provides specific information for your answers.

What are these specialist terms? They are the vocabulary used by psychologists for their concepts and theories, such as the term *identification*.

Specialist terms may be words that are used in ordinary English – but they have been given a specific meaning in psychology – like *identification*.

Or they may be terms that are new to you, such as *normative* or *nAffiliator*. Get used to using these.

nAffiliators – just using my specialist terms (see page 19).

Understanding application (AO2)

We will now move on to the second skill – *application*.

The trick of the application questions is that you are required to *apply* what you have learned about psychological concepts, studies and theories – to a **scenario**.

Imagine the following scenario ...

> *... it is a dark night, a thin sliver of moon and ink black clouds, the wind is starting to get stronger. You walk home down a street with no lights and suddenly ...*

A scenario is a scene – it is context. You now have a chance to put your psychology into action. This kind of question is intended to be something that tests your real understanding of psychology.

You should become brilliant at this because we have supplied lots and lots of practice throughout this book.

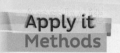

Wrong sort of dark night!
A different scenario altogether ...

Apply it Concepts

In Chapter 2 we discuss eyewitness testimony.

> Each year a small village holds a cycling event which attracts hundreds of cyclists and also hundreds of people come to watch the event. This spring at the event there was an accident where one of the race leaders seemed to collide with another cyclist and ended up in the crowd, to the horror of the onlookers. A number of people were seriously injured. Police interviewed eyewitnesses to see what might have caused the accident.

Explain how anxiety may affect the eyewitnesses' memory of what happened. (*6 marks*)

The description of the event is the 'scenario' (also sometimes referred to as the 'stem'). It provides a context for you to answer the question. When doing this you must include:

1. **CONCEPT** You must describe how anxiety affects eyewitness testimony.
2. **CONTEXT** You must relate your description to the specific issue of how anxiety might affect the recall of the events described here.

Some scenarios (and questions) are shorter. For example, in Chapter 5 we discussed phobias.

> Tomas has a phobia of cats. Outline how Tomas's phobia of cats could be treated using systematic desensitisation. (*3 marks*)

1. **CONTEXT** You must focus on treating a phobia of cats.
2. **CONCEPT** You must describe how systematic desensitisation is done.

AO2 Mark scheme

These are the levels that may be used when marking an application question. Identify the key descriptors.

Level	Marks	Description
3	5–6	Knowledge related to psychological topic is clear and generally well-detailed. Application is mostly clear and effective. The answer is generally coherent with appropriate use of terminology.
2	3–4	Knowledge is evident. Application is appropriate but not explained. The answer lacks clarity in places. Terminology is used appropriately on occasions.
1	1–2	Knowledge is limited. Application is either absent or inappropriate. The answer as a whole lacks clarity and has inaccuracies. Terminology is either absent or inappropriately used.
	0	No relevant content

The mark scheme is presented as an illustration of the AQA mark scheme. Always check the AQA website for the latest version of mark schemes as these may have been amended.

Apply it Methods

About 25% of your exam questions will assess skills in relation to research methods. These questions are mainly application questions that begin with a scenario as shown below:

> A psychologist wanted to investigate the memory of older and younger children. He tested memory by giving the children a list of 50 words to memorise.
>
> 1. Explain why this study would be considered to be a quasi-experiment. (*2 marks*)
> 2. Write a suitable hypothesis for this study. (*2 marks*)
> 3. The research found that the mean score for older children was 20.3 and for younger children was 15.7. What would you conclude from this? (*1 mark*)
> 4. The mean scores are given to 1 decimal place. Explain what this means. (*1 mark*)

The description of the research study is the scenario. It again provides the context for your answer.

For example, when studying research methods you will learn about quasi-experiments. You now use that knowledge in the context of this research study.

In the case of question 1 above this is likely to be marked as:

- 1 mark for explanation of the concept.
- 2 marks for an explanation of the concept plus content related to the stem.

There are marked examples on pages 208–9.

Remember:

Concept Context

or

Context Concept

CC

Mathematical content for A level and AS

A minimum of 10% of marks across the whole qualification will involve mathematical content. (This content is listed on the right.) This 10% is included in the total 25% (or more) for research methods questions.

Some of the mathematical content requires the use of a calculator, which is allowed in the exam. In the specification it states that calculations of the mean, median, mode and range may be required, as well as percentages, fractions and ratios. You may also be asked to apply the sign test to a set of data and calculate the statistic.

Content in the table on the right that is shaded in grey is A level only but it is covered in this Year 1 book.

Other research methods questions

Many research methods questions are application. But not all.

Description

Some research methods questions are just description. For example:

Explain how you would collect a volunteer sample. (2 marks)

If the question said 'Explain how you would collect a volunteer sample in this study' then it would be application.

Evaluation

Some research methods questions are evaluation. For example:

Give **one** strength of using a volunteer sample. (2 marks)

If the question said 'Give **one** strength of using a volunteer sample in this study' then it would be application.

Mathematical content

There is a special focus on mathematical content in each chapter on the 'Practical corner' spreads.

	Mathematical concepts	Tick here when you are confident you understand this concept.
Arithmetic and numerical computation	Recognise and use expressions in decimal and standard form.	
	Use ratios, fractions and percentages.	
	Estimate results.	
Handling data	Use an appropriate number of significant figures.	
	Find arithmetic means.	
	Construct and interpret frequency tables and diagrams, bar charts and histograms.	
	Understand simple probability.	
	Understand the principles of sampling as applied to scientific data.	
	Understand the terms mean, median and mode.	
	Use a scattergram to identify a correlation between two variables.	
	Use a statistical test.	
	Make order of magnitude calculations.	
	Distinguish between levels of measurement.	
	Know the characteristics of normal and skewed distributions.	
	Select an appropriate statistical test.	
	Use statistical tables to determine significance.	
	Understand measures of dispersion, including standard deviation and range.	
	Understand the differences between qualitative and quantitative data.	
	Understand the difference between primary and secondary data.	
Algebra	Understand and use the symbols: $=$ $<$ $\ll$ $\gg$ $>$ $\propto$ $\approx$	
	Substitute numerical values into algebraic equations using appropriate units for physical quantities.	
	Solve simple algebraic equations.	
Graphs	Translate information between graphical, numerical and algebraic forms.	
	Plot two variables from experimental or other data.	

Understanding evaluation (AO3)

We finally move onto the third skill – *evaluation*.

What is it you have to do when you *evaluate* something?

Think of the orange again (picture on right to help you). How can you evaluate an orange? Most people are puzzled by such a question.

Evaluation means 'consider its value' (eVALUatE). No, the answer is not 30 p.

You might say – it is great to take an orange in your bag for lunch because it doesn't get damaged.

That's an advantage/strength of an orange.

You might also say – I don't like to eat oranges because my hands get all sticky.

That's a disadvantage/limitation of an orange.

You could *elaborate* your answer by making a comparison – I don't like oranges because my hands get all sticky whereas they don't get so sticky with a banana.

Understanding elaboration is what it is all about.

AO3 is a bit more than evaluation. It also means to analyse and interpret. To analyse an orange you might consider what it is made of.

Beginner level evaluation: State the point

There are many different kinds of evaluation, as you will discover in this book. For example, research support for a theory is a strength whereas lack of research support is a limitation. High validity is a strength and low validity is a limitation.

To evaluate a concept, study or theory you might say:

This concept is supported by research.

This study has been supported by other studies.

This study was well-controlled.

This study had a limited sample.

This theory lacks validity.

You have identified the evaluation, which is a beginning! Some students don't ever get much beyond this – and have to rely on their AO1 marks.

It's too easy just to state these rather *generic* evaluations, i.e. comments that can be used anywhere. But it is a beginning. So don't feel too bad if that is all you can do for a while.

Intermediate level evaluation: Make it relevant

The next step is to make your evaluation relevant to the particular concept/study/theory. You need to say something to make your evaluation unique rather than generic.

For example:

- *This concept is supported by research. Elliott et al. also found that men were more conformist than women.*
- *This study had a limited sample. The investigation only involved five people and they were friends of the researcher.*

Look at the evaluation below – it may look good but it is still generic (and therefore not worth much):

This study was well-controlled. All important extraneous variables were monitored so that only the independent variable affected the dependent variable.

You can drop that evaluation in almost anywhere and it will make sense.

Higher level evaluation: Explain it well

When you have mastered intermediate level, it is time to move on – but don't do this until you have mastered the intermediate level. Don't run before you can walk.

There are many ways to explain your evaluation point:

- You can use examples.
- You can elaborate on what you have said already.
- You can end by explaining why your point is a strength or limitation.

ENDINGS

Always finish with a conclusion – this is not a summary, it is a judgement. It is useful to use phrases such as:

This suggests ... This shows that ... This means ... Therefore ...

Always end with a sentence beginning with T (of course it doesn't have to be a T but that is a useful prompt, just start writing 'This shows ...').

Look at any of the critical points in this book. We have tried to ensure that all our critical points follow the same rule:

State the point.

Make it relevant and explain the point with reference to theories or research studies.

End with a conclusion (This suggests that ...).

Some marked examples

Evaluation questions mainly use these command words:
Evaluate
Discuss

There are other command words that also indicate evaluation, such as analyse, compare, justify, comment on.

Question: Discuss **one** limitation of social learning theory. (2 marks)

One limitation is that it used artificial evidence. A lot of the studies were done in laboratories and are very artificial. This means the theory may not be relevant because people don't behave like that.

Teacher comment: For 2 marks you would first be expected to identify the problem, which has been done here. For a further mark there should be additional information about the limitation, for example an explanation about why this is a limitation. There has been some attempt to do this ('done in laboratories') but it is very generic so not very effective. This is a very weak answer.

Question: Briefly evaluate the use of non-human animal studies in attachment research. (4 marks)

Such studies are used because it would not be ethical to use humans and separate them from their parents, so this is a strength of such studies.

On the other hand, it is difficult to generalise from research using animals, such as the studies by Lorenz where he demonstrated imprinting by arranging for some goslings to see him when they hatched. The research on imprinting led to attachment theory but maybe is not relevant.

Teacher comment: If a question just asks for evaluation you can present strengths and/or limitations. There is no requirement for balance and no specific number of evaluations is required – you could receive full marks for just one point of evaluation. The answer above covers two points of evaluation that are both relevant but not very effective – the descriptive content about Lorenz's research is not an explanation of the evaluation point. In this way the answer has lost focus. The explanations are limited and no specialist terminology has been used. This answer would get some credit but is not very effective.

AO3 Mark scheme

The descriptors that may be used to mark a 4-mark AO3 question:

Level	Marks	Description
2	3–4	Evaluation is relevant, well-explained and focused, rather than generic criticism. The answer is generally coherent with effective use of specialist terminology.
1	1–2	Evaluation is relevant although there is limited explanation and/or limited focus. Specialist terminology is not always used appropriately. Award one mark for answers consisting of a single point briefly stated or muddled.
	0	No relevant content.

The mark scheme is presented here as an illustration of the AQA mark scheme. Always check the AQA website for the latest version of mark schemes as these may have been amended.

Question: Evaluate the multi-store model of memory. (6 marks)

Case studies have been used to show that there is a distinct difference between short- and long-term memory. For example, the study of HM who sustained damage to his hippocampus found that his long-term memory was still intact but he couldn't form new short-term memories. This shows that the two kinds of memory have different physical locations in the brain, supporting the multi-store model.

One limitation of the multi-store model is that it is probably too simple. Subsequent research has shown that short-term memory has several sub-stores (e.g. visual and verbal stores as in the working memory model) and the same is true for long-term memory (e.g. episodic and procedural memory). This means that the multi-store model was quite restricted in what it told us about memory.

Teacher comment: In an evaluation question worth 6 marks you probably need to present more than one evaluation. Two evaluations, well explained, could be enough. Three evaluations might be better but once you try to cover more than two evaluations you don't have time to explain them sufficiently, which jeopardises your overall mark. The two evaluations covered here are both effective, well-explained, focused, organised and there is evidence of specialist terminology. This is altogether an impressive answer.

AO3 Mark scheme

The descriptors that may be used to mark a 6-mark AO3 question:

Level	Marks	Description
3	5–6	Evaluation is clear and effective. The answer is coherent and well-organised with effective use of specialist terminology.
2	3–4	Evaluation is mostly effective. The answer is mostly clear and coherent, with some appropriate use of specialist terminology.
1	1–2	Discussion lacks detail/explanation. The answer lacks clarity, accuracy and organisation in places. Specialist terminology is either absent or inappropriately used.
	0	No relevant content.

The mark scheme is presented here as an illustration of the AQA mark scheme. Always check the AQA website for the latest version of mark schemes as these may have been amended.

What do these terms mean?

What is *effective*?

Essentially 'effective' means something that works, such as 'an effective treatment for malaria'.

An effective evaluation point is therefore one that works – it should not be generic.

What is *generic*?

The word 'generic' means 'general'. In the context of making evaluations it refers to that nice little list of all-purpose comments 'This study lacked validity', 'This theory is culturally-biased', etc.

Such all-purpose evaluations can be scattered everywhere and require little understanding. Anyone can do that.

Some generic evaluations can be quite lengthy. For example, 'One problem with this research is that it is quite artificial. It was conducted in a laboratory where things are not like they are in everyday life. This makes it difficult to generalise the findings to everyday experience and makes the research worthless.'

Such a comment can be put in many essays with no attempt to make it specifically relevant – and therefore it doesn't count for much.

What is *explanation*?

'Explain' means offer some further information to help the reader understand what you are saying. This may include providing more relevant facts, offering an interpretation ('This means that...'), justifying the point you are trying to make, and so on.

Maybe think of the difference between someone asking you to tell them what you did last night and them asking you to *explain* what you did last night. Hmm.

What is *focus*?

If you focus on an image, you concentrate your attention on that one thing. The same is required for good evaluation. You need to pay attention just to the study or theory you are evaluating rather than making general comments.

One issue related to focus is that students often *describe* material (such as describing the procedures of a study) instead of explaining the evaluation point. They lose focus.

Using research studies as evaluation

On page 214 we noted that you may present information about a research study as part of your descriptive content – but you can also use research studies as evaluation.

If you do this then it is really only the findings/conclusion that will be creditworthy as AO3. Description of procedure *might* be credited as description (AO1).

Essay questions

The final kind of question for us to examine is the essay question (AKA an *extended writing question* when worth 12 or 16 marks) – where you are required to include both description (AO1) and evaluation (AO3) and sometimes also application (AO2).

Examples of such questions are shown on the right.

Notice:

- The command words vary.
- The number of marks varies. Essay questions at AS level are a maximum of 12 marks where AO1 and AO3 are likely to be equally divided.
- Essay questions at A level are a maximum of 16 marks – on such questions the balance of marks is likely to be 6 marks for AO1 and 10 marks for AO3 except if there is application.
- One of the questions on the right includes some application material.
- One question asks specifically for studies, others concern theories/explanations and there is also one that just mentions research (so a theory or studies would be acceptable).
- Questions sometimes say 'one or more'. This means that you could produce an effective answer if you only discuss one study/theory but you can do more if you wish.

At the end of each chapter in this book are some student answers to practice questions, including answers for essay questions.

- *Briefly outline* ***and*** *evaluate the Authoritarian Personality as an explanation of obedience to authority.* *(8 marks AS, 8 marks AL)*
- *Discuss* ***one or more*** *definitions of abnormality.* *(8 marks AS, 8 marks AL)*
- *Outline* ***and*** *evaluate* ***two*** *studies of social influence.* *(10 marks AS, 8 marks AL)*
- *Discuss what psychological research has told us about why people conform.* *(12 marks AS, 16 marks AL)*
- *Describe* ***and*** *evaluate explanations of forgetting.* *(12 marks AS, 16 marks AL)*
- *Discuss the contribution of Lorenz* ***and*** *Harlow to our understanding of attachment.* *(12 marks AS, 16 marks AL)*
- *Maria and Sam were both abandoned at birth and spent the first few months of their lives in an institution. Sam was adopted by a loving family at the age of two months whereas Maria was not finally adopted until she was just over one year of age.*

  Discuss the influence of early attachment on childhood and adult relationships. Refer to the experiences of Maria ***and*** *Sam as part of your discussion.* *(12 marks AS, 16 marks AL)*

Some useful phrases for AO3
An application is ...
This means that ...
On the other hand ...
One strength is ...
One limitation is ...
This shows that ...
In contrast ...
However ...
LESS IS MORE
Fewer studies/evaluation points.
More time for detail/elaboration.

Essays on research studies

In an AS question on research studies that is worth 12 marks, half of the marks are available for a description of the studies. If you try to describe too many studies you won't have time to include details of the studies – and it is the details that show your understanding. Less is more – cover fewer studies but give lots of detail. Just one or two studies may be enough. It's about quality rather than quantity.

Essays with application material

Such questions include application in addition to the usual describe and evaluate elements of an essay question.

You are required to make appropriate links between the theory and the scenario (stem) presented. If you do not do this you will not have fully answered the question.

Partial performance

Some questions ask for two things. For example, 'Outline **and** evaluate **two** definitions of abnormality. (12 marks)'

In such an essay if you only describe and evaluate one definition, this is called 'partial performance'. You have only answered half of the question.

What do students do wrong in essays?

- Students give too much description, not enough well-explained evaluation.
- Students fail to make their evaluation effective – use the lead-in phrases on the left to make it clear when you are presenting evaluation.
- Students fail to answer the question – take time to plan your answer to focus on what will be creditworthy. If you just start writing your answer you may forget the focus of the question so it pays to do some planning. It may also help, as you start each new paragraph, to go back to the title to remind yourself what the essay should be about.
- Students do not use paragraphs – which makes the essay very difficult to read. 'Organisation' is one of the criteria by which you are assessed so it will affect the overall impression of the essay.

Discuss drug therapy as a treatment for obsessive-compulsive disorder. Refer to evidence in your answer. (*12 marks AS, 16 marks AL*)	
Student answer	**Teacher comments**
OCD is seen to be mainly biological in origin and therefore drug treatments are an obvious solution. OCD has been linked to low serotonin and obsessive thoughts. Therefore SSRIs are used to treat OCD. SSRIs (they are called selective serotonin reuptake inhibitors) slow down the reuptake of serotonin at the synapse and calm people down. This calming down means that their thoughts and rituals become less frequent and they can lead a more normal life.	On the positive side this essay is well-organised. The student has put all the descriptive material first followed by all the evaluation. This would help a reader to identify these components of the essay. The paragraphs make the essay easy to read, which contributes to the organisation of the essay.
A typical dose of the drug is 20 mg given as capsules or in liquid form which they take daily. The drugs often take 3–4 months before any effect is noticed which is something that may put people off. Then they stop taking the drugs and then they obviously don't benefit from them.	The descriptive content has used specialist terminology and is accurate and well-detailed in places but this is not always true. For example, the action of SSRIs has not been explained.
If people do keep on but still the SSRIs do not work there are other alternatives. First the dosage can be increased to 60 mg but that might lead to side effects. There is another drug Clomipramine that also affects the serotonin system but it has more side-effects and therefore is not the first line treatment. SNRIs are also used. These target another neurotransmitter, noradrenaline as well as serotonin.	Four evaluative points are discussed, none of which are thorough. The effectiveness is spoiled by the lack of precision, for example the study on effectiveness has not been cited.
Research suggests that such drugs can be very effective. One study reviewed a number of other studies and found that SSRIs performed better than placebos in about 70% of cases. SSRIs were most effective when combined with psychological therapies such as CBT. *However, recently researchers have drawn attention to the fact that some of the drug evidence may be unreliable. It is mainly funded by drug companies who may be biased about what evidence they publish as they make a lot of money from drugs.*	In the evaluation section of the essay specialist terms have not been used, the study on effectiveness was a meta-analysis so that term might have been included. The account of drug companies conducting biased research is rather superficial (lacks focus). The final paragraph repeats what has already been said so adds nothing to the answer.
Some people and doctors prefer drug therapy to psychological therapy because it is cost effective and easy. From the individual's perspective very little effort is required. From the doctor's perspective giving drugs is cheaper than psychological therapies.	Altogether the evaluation is mostly effective but not thorough.
One considerable problem is that drugs have side-effects though these tend to be minimal for SSRIs. Typical side-effects are indigestion, blurred vision and reduced sex drive. If they do occur, they may be temporary but it could be enough to put someone off taking the drugs.	The student's final attainment is calculated by working out the best fit for all these different assessments to see what level best describes the answer. The actual mark will be determined by whether one is drawn to the level above or below.
There are many other issues with drug treatments but overall people like them because they require no effort and they often appear to be doing some good, though that could be a placebo effect. They generally don't have bad effects. **404 words**	For an A level essay more rigour and evaluation is expected and therefore, for that standard, this essay would be assessed less well than as an AS response.

Mark scheme used for essay questions

You can use the mark scheme below to mark extended writing questions:

12-mark essay (6 marks AO1 and 6 marks AO3).

16-mark essay (6 marks AO1 and 10 marks AO3).

Note, in an application essay the marks are distributed differently and the mark scheme includes criteria related to application:

12-mark essay (6 marks AO1, 2 marks AO2, 4 marks AO3).

16-mark essay (6 marks AO1, 4 marks AO2, 6 marks AO3).

Level	Marks for AS level	Marks for A level	Description
4	10–12	13–16	Knowledge is accurate and generally well-detailed. Evaluation/discussion is thorough and effective. Minor detail and/or expansion of argument is sometimes lacking. The answer is clear, coherent and focused. Specialist terminology is used effectively.
3	7–9	9–12	Knowledge is evident. There are occasional inaccuracies/omissions. Evaluation/discussion is mostly effective. The answer is mostly clear and organised but occasionally lacks focus. Specialist terminology is mostly used effectively.
2	4–6	5–8	Limited knowledge is present. Focus is mainly on description. Any evaluation/discussion is of limited effectiveness. The answer lacks clarity, accuracy, organisation and focus in places. Specialist terminology is used inappropriately on occasions.
1	1–3	1–4	Knowledge is very limited. Evaluation/discussion is limited, poorly focused or absent. The answer as a whole lacks clarity, has many inaccuracies and is poorly organised. Specialist terminology is either absent or inappropriately used.
	0	0	No relevant content.

To decide on a mark identify the level that best describes the essay, and then consider whether you are more tempted by the level above or below to determine the exact mark to award. Always check the AQA website for the latest version of mark schemes as these may have been amended.

AS versus A level standard

It may look like the A level standard is simply the same as the AS standard but just more marks (for more evaluation). That's not quite true:

1. The essay questions themselves may be more challenging.
2. By the end of Year 2 it will be expected that a student will be able to make use of their wider understanding of issues, debates, approaches and research methods and thus produce more mature discussions.

Applying Psychology to successful studying

Start by considering the descriptive component of your essay. The most you will need is 6 marks' worth of description (AO1). If you identify about six key points this will help you structure your answer. We have done this below for an essay on locus of control.

Select any essay title in this book, produce an empty frame like the one below and fill it in for the description component. You may decide to add a few more rows but don't add many more or you'll end up with too much for 6 marks (you won't need more ... ever ... even for A level).

There are probably two big challenges ahead for you:

1. Writing essays.
2. Learning all the material in this book.

The suggestions on this spread are informed by psychological research – after all, we are psychologists.

Writing frame for an essay

AO1 Key point	Description
Locus of control (LOC)	Rotter suggested people have a sense of what controls their behaviour.
Internals	Some people believe that the things that happen to them are largely controlled by themselves. For example, if you do well in an exam it is because you worked hard.
Externals	Other people believe that things happen without their control. If they did well in an exam they might say it was good luck or the textbook. If they fail it was bad luck or the questions were hard.
Continuum	There is a continuum with high internal LOC at one end and high external LOC at the other end of the continuum, with low internal and low external lying in-between.
Explanation 1	People who have an internal LOC are more likely to be able to resist pressures to conform or obey.
Explanation 2	People with a high internal LOC tend to be more self-confident, more achievement-oriented, have higher intelligence and have less need for social approval.

There are just over 150 words here, which is about right for the AO1 content of an essay.

Now do the same for the evaluation (AO3). To plan your evaluation the organisation of the writing frame is a bit different. On page 218 we explained that good evaluation points start with the basics, and then you may add further elaboration (intermediate and higher level). The table below will help you plan this.

AO3 Key point	Intermediate level evaluation	Higher level evaluation
There is research support for the link between LOC and resistance to obedience.	Holland measured levels of LOC in a repeat of Milgram's study. 37% of internals did not continue whereas only 23% of externals did not continue.	So internals showed a greater level of resistance than externals.
There is counter-evidence, challenging the link.	Twenge *et al*. analysed 40 years of research from the 1960s and found people were more resistant to being obedient.	But they also found people were more external. If resistance is linked to an internal locus of control, we would expect people to have become more internal.

There are about 100 words in these two rows – each point also needs a conclusion to finish it off (this would give you almost 150 words, enough for the AO3 content). You shouldn't need to write down your conclusion in the writing frame.

The psychology behind writing frames is called scaffolding. Psychologists use this term to describe the process where a person needs support in the early stages of learning to do something new.

The idea is that, when you are ready, you kick away the scaffold, and – hey presto – you can do it on your own.

Not a good idea if you are standing on a real scaffold.

Some AS students and A level students may consider some further evaluation points, and even offer a discussion.

LOC may be less important than Rotter suggested.	Many studies (e.g. Holland) show that internal LOC is linked to being able to resist social influence.	However Rotter pointed out that the situation may be more important because LOC only seems important in new situations. Otherwise you just do what you did before, regardless of your LOC.

Some essays also involve some application (AO2), for example:

Mavis didn't do so well in her exams. She blames her teacher, she blames the textbook, and she blames the fact that none of her friends worked. In fact she blames everything but herself.

Describe **and** evaluate research relating to the role of locus of control in resisting social influence. Refer to Mavis in your answer. (12 marks AS, 16 marks AL)

If you are answering an essay like this you must remember to make links to the context.

Remember: CC

Believe in the power of psychology

Revision cards

'Ve have divided this book into spreads. Each spread represents one chunk of the pecification as indicated at the top left of each spread. For each topic you should roduce a revision card.

or some spreads you might decide to have two revision cards.

he big secret is that you hould do this **NOW**. ?evision is meant to be e-vision – seeing it again.

When you study a opic, prepare a card like he one below. It will elp you understand the pread.

But the joy is that you vill have a set of revision ards all ready for the end f year exams.

A cue

There are snooker cues and there are other cues – a cue is a thing that serves as reminder of something else. An actor knows she must come in on cue – a reminder or signal.

Psychologists have investigated the value of cues in remembering. They act as a reminder of what else you know.

The revision card on the left has **cue words**. Cover the text in the middle column and see if the cue word can help you remember what is there.

If you can't remember anything, then look at the middle column. If you need further prompting look at the writing frame on the facing page.

Tomorrow repeat the same sequences and see if you can remember more. And so on. Eventually all you need to remember are the cue words and the rest will pop into your mind.

Psychological research shows that people often have much more in their heads than they can recall – they just need the right cue (see page 56).

Topic: Locus of control		Cue words
Describe	A sense of what controls your behaviour.	Rotter LOC
Describe	Own control, e.g. poor exam mark due to lack of effort.	Internal
Describe	Outside our control, e.g. bad luck, bad teacher.	External
Describe	High low low high.	Continuum
Describe	Internal LOC → resist conform or obey.	Can resist
Describe	Internal LOC → less need for social approval.	Confidence
Evaluate	37% internals, 23% externals.	Holland
	Internals more resistance.	
Evaluate	40 years, more resistance.	Twenge
	More external, not expected.	
Optional		
Evaluate	LOC linked to resistance.	Familiar situations
	Past matters, LOC matters in new situations.	

There are two spaces for each evaluation point in order to record the levels of elaboration.

Try writing an essay just using your revision card.

Mnemonics

Here is a final bit of psychology – we psychologists know what techniques work! And the main answer is ... *processing*. The more you play around with and discuss the ideas, the better you will remember them. Just making the revision card will give you an opportunity to process the new ideas.

Here are two further thoughts:

Method of loci

This is a method used by stage performers who wow audiences with memory feats. Say, for example, the performer is trying to memorise the names of every member of the audience. He mentally walks around his house (or down a street) and places each name somewhere, forming a link between the name and place – for example he puts 'Mary' in a bowl of berries (Mary Berry, the cookery expert). Later, when trying to recall names he just takes a mental walk and finds the items where he left them. Try it out – it really works for things you are finding difficult to remember.

Test your recall

Most students revise by reading things over and over (**maintenance rehearsal** in the lingo of psychologists). But this doesn't work *that* well. What works much better is to read something, then close your book, and write down everything you can remember. *The act of trying to recall the information* strengthens the **memory trace**.

References

Festinger, L. and Carlsmith, J. M. (1959). Cognitive consequences of forced compliance. *Journal of Abnormal and Social Psychology, 58*, 203–210. ▶ **page 7**

Zajonc, R. B. (1968). Attitudinal effects of mere exposure, *Journal of Personality and Social Psychology (Monograph), 9*, 1–29. ▶ **pages 8, 9**

Dolcos, S. and Albarracin, D. (2014). The inner speech of behavioral regulation: Intentions and task performance strengthen when you talk to yourself as a you. *European Journal of Social Psychology*, DOI: 10.1002/ejsp.2048 ▶ **page 13**

Chapter 1

Adorno, T. E., Frenkel-Brunswik, E. and Levinson, D. (1950). *The authoritarian personality*. New York: Harper. ▶ **page 28**

Albrecht, S. A., Caruthers, D., Patrick, T., Reynolds, M., Salamie, D., Higgins, L. W., *et al.* (2006). A randomised controlled trial of a smoking cessation intervention for pregnant adolescents. *Nursing Research*, 55(6), 402–10. ▶ **page 31**

Allen, V. L. and Levine, J. M. (1971). Social support and conformity: the role of independent assessment of reality. *Journal of Experimental Social Psychology, 7*, 48–58. ▶ **page 31**

Aronson, E. (2011). *The social animal*. New York: Worth/Freeman. ▶ **page 16**

Asch, S. E. (1951). Effects of group pressure upon the modification and distortion of judgements. In H. Guetzkow (Ed.), *Groups, leadership and men*. Pittsburgh: Carnegie Press. ▶ **pages 16, 17**

Asch, S. E. (1955). Opinions and social change. *Scientific American, 193*, 31–35. ▶ **pages 16, 17**

Banuazizi, A. and Movahedi, S. (1975). Interpersonal dynamics in a simulated prison: a methodological analysis. *American Psychologist, 30*, 152–160. ▶ **page 21**

Bashir, N. Y., Lockwood, P., Chasteen, A. L., Nadolny, D. and Noyes, I. (2013). The ironic impact of activists: negative stereotypes reduce social change influence. *European Journal of Social Psychology, 43*, 614–626. ▶ **page 35**

Baumrind, D. (1964). Some thoughts on ethics of research: after reading Milgram's 'Behavioural study of obedience'. *American Psychologist, 19*, 421–423. ▶ **page 23**

Beauvois, J. L., Courbet, D. and Oberlé, D. (2012). The prescriptive power of the television host: A transposition of Milgram's obedience paradigm to the context of TV game show. *European Review of Applied Psychology*, 62(3), 111–119. ▶ **page 23**

Bickman, L. (1974). The social power of a uniform. *Journal of Applied Social Psychology, 85*, 87–92. ▶ **page 25**

Bond, R. and Smith, P. B. (1996). Culture and conformity: a meta-analysis of studies using Asch's line judgement task. *Psychological Bulletin, 119*, 111–137. ▶ **page 17**

British Psychological Society (2009). *Code of ethics and conduct*. Leicester: British Psychological Society. ▶ **page 22**

Christie, R. and Jahoda, M. (Eds.). (1954). *Studies in the scope and method of 'The authoritarian personality': continuities in social research*. Glencoe, Illinois: Free Press. ▶ **page 29**

Deutsch, M. and Gerard, H. B. (1955). A study of normative and informational social influences upon individual judgment. *Journal of Abnormal and Social Psychology, 51*, 629–636. ▶ **page 18**

Elms, A. C. and Milgram, S. (1966). Personality characteristics associated with obedience and defiance toward authoritative command. *Journal of Experimental Research in Personality, 1*, 282–289. ▶ **page 29**

Fiske, S. T. (2014). *Social beings: core motives in social psychology*. New York: Wiley. ▶ **page 17**

Foxcroft, D. R., Moreira, M. T., Santimano, N. M. A. and Smith, L. A. (2015). Social norms information for alcohol misuse in university and college students. *Cochrane database of systematic reviews, (12)*. ▶ **page 35**

Fromm, E. (1973). *The anatomy of human destructiveness*. Harmondsworth: Penguin Books. ▶ **page 21**

Gamson, W. B., Fireman, B. and Rytina, S. (1982). *Encounters with unjust authority*. Hounwood, Illinois: Dorsey Press. ▶ **page 31**

Greenstein, F. I. (1969). *Personality and politics: problems of evidence, inference and conceptualisation*. Chicago: Markham. ▶ **page 29**

Haslam, S. A., Reicher, S. D. and Birney, M. E. (2014). Nothing by mere authority: Evidence that in an experimental analogue of the Milgram paradigm participants are motivated not by orders but by appeals to science. *Journal of Social Issues*, 70(3), 473–488. ▶ **page 23**

Holland, C. D. (1967). Sources of variance in the experimental investigation of behavioural obedience. *Dissertation Abstracts International, 29*, 2802A. ▶ **page 31**

Kelman, H. (1958). Compliance, identification, and internalization: three processes of attitude change. *Journal of Conflict Resolution, 1*, 51–60. ▶ **page 18**

Kelman, H. C. and Hamilton, V. L. (1989). *Crimes of obedience: toward a social psychology of authority and responsibility*. New Haven, Connecticut: Yale University Press. ▶ **page 27**

Kilham, W. and Mann, L. (1974). Level of destructive obedience as a function of transmitter and executant roles in the Milgram obedience paradigm. *Journal of Personality and Social Psychology, 29*, 692–702. ▶ **page 27**

Lucas T., Alexander, S., Firestone, J. and Baltes, B. B. (2006). Self-efficacy and independence from social influence: discovery of an efficacy–difficulty effect. *Social Influence, 1*, 58–80. ▶ **page 17**

Mackie, D. M. (1987). Systematic and nonsystematic processing of majority and minority persuasive communications. *Journal of Personality and Social Psychology, 53*, 41–52. ▶ **page 35**

Mandel, D. R. (1998). The obedience alibi: Milgram's account of the Holocaust reconsidered. *Analyse & Kritik, 20*, 74–94. ▶ **pages 25, 27**

Mantell, D. (1971). The potential for violence in Germany. *Journal of Social Issues, 27*, 101–112. ▶ **page 27**

Martin, R., Martin, P. Y., Smith, J. R. and Hewstone, M. (2003). Majority versus minority influence and prediction of behavioural intentions and behaviour. *Journal of Experimental Social Psychology, 43*, 763–771. ▶ **page 33**

McDermott, M. (2019). Evaluating the criticisms of the Stanford Prison Experiment. *Psychology Review, 24*. ▶ **page 21**

McGhee, P. E. and Teevan, R. C. (1967). Conformity behaviour and need for affiliation. *The Journal of Social Psychology, 72*, 117–121. ▶ **page 19**

Meeus, W. H. J. and Raaijmakers, Q. A. W. (1986). Administrative obedience: Carrying out orders to use psychological-administrative violence. *European Journal of Social Psychology, 16*(4), 311–324. ▶ **page 25**

Milgram, S. (1963). Behavioural study of obedience. *Journal of Abnormal and Social Psychology, 67*, 371–378. ▶ **page 22**

Milgram, S. (1974). *Obedience to authority: an experimental view*. New York: Harper and Row. ▶ **page 26**

Moscovici, S., Lage, E. and Naffrechoux, M. (1969). Influence of a consistent minority on the responses of a majority in a colour perception task. *Sociometry, 32*, 365–380. ▶ **page 32**

Nemeth, C. J. (1986). Differential contributions of majority and minority influence. *Psychological Review, 93*, 1–10. ▶ **page 32**

Nemeth, C. J. (2009). Minority influence theory. In P. Van Lange, A. Kruglanski and T. Higgins (Eds.), *Handbook of theories of social psychology*. New York: Sage. ▶ **page 35**

Neto, F. (1995). Conformity and independence revisited. *Social Behaviour and Personality, 23*, 217–222. ▶ **page 17**

Nolan, J. M., Schultz, P. W., Cialdini, R. B., Goldstein, N. J. and Griskevicius, V. (2008). Normative social influence is underdetected. *Personality and Social Psychology Bulletin, 34*, 913–923. ▶ **page 35**

Orlando, N. J. (1973). The mock ward: a study in simulation. In O. Milton and R. G. Wahler (Eds.), *Behaviour disorders: perspectives and trends*. Philadelphia: Lippincott. ▶ **page 20**

Orne, M. T. and Holland, C. H. (1968). On the ecological validity of laboratory deceptions. *International Journal of Psychiatry, 6*, 282–293. ▶ **page 23**

Perry, G. (2013). *Behind the shock machine: the untold story of the notorious Milgram psychology experiments*. New York: The New Press. ▶ **page 23**

Rank, S. G. and Jacobson, C. K. (1977). Hospital nurses' compliance with medication overdose orders: a failure to replicate. *Journal of Health and Social Behaviour, 18*, 188–193. ▶ **page 23**

Reicher, S. and Haslam, S. A. (2006). Rethinking the psychology of tyranny: the BBC prison study. *British Journal of Social Psychology, 45*, 1–40. ▶ **page 21**

Rotter, J. B. (1966). Generalized expectancies for internal versus external control of reinforcement. *Psychological Monographs: General & Applied, 80*, 1–28. ▶ **page 30**

Rotter, J. B. (1982). *The development and applications of social learning theory: selected papers*. Englewood Cliffs, New Jersey: Prentice Hall. ▶ **page 31**

Schultz, P. W., Khazian, A. M., and Zaleski, A. C. (2008). Using normative social influence to promote conservation among hotel guests. *Social Influence, 3*, 4–23. ▶ **page 19**

Sheridan, C. L. and King, R. G. (1972). Obedience to authority with an authentic victim. *Proceedings of the Annual Convention of the American Psychological Association, 80*, 165–166. ▶ **page 23**

Smith, P. B. and Bond, M. H. (1998). *Social psychology across cultures*. London: Prentice Hall Europe. ▶ **page 25**

Twenge, J. M., Zhang, L. and Im, C. (2004). It's beyond my control: a cross-temporal meta-analysis of increasing externality in locus of control. *Personality and Social Psychology Review, 8*, 308–319. ▶ **page 31**

Wood, W., Lundgren, S., Ouellette, J. A., Busceme, S. and Blackstone, T. (1994). Minority influence: a meta-analytic review of social influence processes. *Psychological Bulletin, 115*, 323–345. ▶ **page 33**

Zimbardo, P. (2007). *The Lucifer effect: understanding how good people turn evil*. New York: Random House. ▶ **pages 21, 34**

Zimbardo, P. G., Banks, W. C., Haney, C. and Jaffe D. (1973). Pirandellian prison: The mind is a formidable jailer. *New York Times Magazine*, 8 April, 38–60. ▶ **page 20**

Chapter 2

Aggleton, J. P. and Waskett, L. (1999). The ability of odours to serve as state-dependent cues for real world memories: can Viking smells aid the recall of Viking experiences? *British Journal of Psychology, 90*, 1–8. ▶ **page 56**

Atkinson, R. C. and Shiffrin, R. M. (1968). Human memory: a proposed system and its control processes. In K. W. Spence (Ed.), *The psychology of learning and motivation: advances in research and theory, Vol. 2* (pages 89–195). New York: Academic Press. ▶ **page 48**

Atkinson, R. C. and Shiffrin, R. M. (1971). The control of short-term memory. *Scientific American, 224*, 82–90. ▶ **page 48**

Baddeley, A. D. (1966a). Short-term memory for word sequences as a function of acoustic, semantic and formal similarity. *Quarterly Journal of Experimental Psychology, 18*, 362–365. ▶ **page 46**

Baddeley, A. D. (1966b). The influence of acoustic and semantic similarity on long-term memory for word sequences. *Quarterly Journal of Experimental Psychology, 18*, 302–309. ▶ **page 46**

Baddeley, A. D. (1997). *Human memory: theory and practice*. Hove, UK: Psychology Press. ▶ **page 57**

Baddeley, A. D. (2000). The episodic buffer: a new component of working memory? *Trends in Cognitive Sciences, 4*, 417–423. ▶ **page 52**

Baddeley, A. D. (2003). Working memory: Lookin back and looking forward. *Nature Reviews Neuroscience, 4*, 829–839. ▶ **pages 52, 53**

Baddeley, A. D. (2012) Working memory: theories, models and controversies. *Annual Review of Psychology, 63*, 1–29. ▶ **page 52**

Baddeley, A. D. and Hitch, G. (1974). Working memory. In G. Bower (Ed.), *Recent advances in learning and motivation, Vol. 8*. New York: Academic Press. ▶ **page 52**

Baddeley, A. D. and Hitch, G. (1977). Recency re-examined. In S. Dornic (Ed.), *Attention and performance VI* (pages 647–667). Hilsdale, N. Lawrence Erlbaum Associates. ▶ **page 55**

Baddeley, A. D., Grant, S., Wight, E. and Thomas, N. (1975). Imagery and visual working memory. In P. M. A. Rabbitt and S. Dornic (Eds), *Attention and performance V* (pages 205–217). London: Academic Press. ▶ **page 53** ahrick, H.P., Bahrick, P.O. and Wittlinger, R.P. (1975). Fifty years of memory for names and faces: a cross-sectional approach. *Journal of Experimental Psychology: General, 104*, 54–75. ▶ **pages 46–48**

aker, J.R., Bezance, J.B., Zellaby, E, and Aggleton, J.P. (2004). Chewing gum can produce context-dependent effects upon memory. *Appetite, 43*, 207–210. ▶ **page 57**

elleville, S., Gilbert, B., Fontaine, F., Gagnon, L., Menard, E. and Gauthier, S. (2006). Improvement of episodic memory in persons with mild cognitive impairment and healthy older adults: Evidence from a Cognitive Intervention Program. *Dementia and Geriatric Cognitive Disorders, 22*, 486–499. ▶ **page 51**

odner, G. E., Musch, E. and Azad, T. (2009). Re-evaluating the potency of the memory conformity effect. *Memory and Cognition, 37*, 1069–1076. ▶ **page 59**

opp, K. L. and Verhaeghen, P. (2005). Aging and verbal memory span: A meta-analysis. *The Journals of Gerontology Series B: Psychological Sciences and Social Sciences, 60*(5), pp.P223–P233. ▶ **page 47**

uckner, R. L. and Petersen, S. E. (1996). What does neuroimaging tell us about the role of prefrontal cortex in memory retrieval? *Seminars in the Neuroscience, 8*(1), 47–55. ▶ **page 51**

urke, R. and Skrull, T. (1988). Competitive Interference and Consumer Memory for Advertising. *Journal of Consumer Research, 15*, 55–68 ▶ **page 54**

arter, S. J. and Cassaday, H. J. (1998). State-dependent retrieval and chlorpheniramine. *Human Psychopharmacology, 13*, 513–523. ▶ **page 56**

hristianson, S.Å. and Hübinette, B. (1993). Hands up! A study of witnesses' emotional reactions and memories associated with bank robberies. *Applied Cognitive Psychology, 7*(5), pp.365–379. ▶ **page 61**

fasefi, S. L., Bernstein, D.M., Mantonakis, A. and Loftus, E.F (2013). Queasy does it: false alcohol beliefs and memories may lead to diminished alcohol preferences. *Acta Psychologica, 143*, 14–19. ▶ **page 58**

enen, A. M. L. and van Luijtelaar, E. L. J. M. (1997). Effects of benzodiazepines, sleep and sleep deprivation on vigilance and memory. *Acta Neurologica Belgica, 97*, 123–129. ▶ **page 55**

wan, N. (2001). The magical number four in short-term memory: a reconsideration of mental short-term capacity. *Behavioural and Brain Sciences, 24*, 87–114. ▶ **page 47**

aik, F.I.M. and Watkins, M.J (1973). The role of rehearsal in short-term memory. *Journal of Verbal Learning and Verbal Behaviour, 12*, 599–607. ▶ **page 49**

ffenbacher K. (1983). The influence of arousal on reliability of testimony. In S.M.A. Lloyd-Bostock and B.R. Clifford (Eds), *Evaluating witness evidence: recent psychological research and new perspectives* (pages 235–251). Chichester, UK: Wiley. ▶ **page 60**

senck, M. and Keane, M. (2010). *Cognitive psychology: a student's handbook*. Hove, UK: Psychology Press. ▶ **page 57**

sher, R. P. and Geiselman, R. E. (1992). *Memory-enhancing techniques in investigative interviewing: the cognitive interview*. Springfield, IL: C.C. Thomas. ▶ **page 62**

Fisher, R. P., Geiselman, R. E. and Raymond, D. S. (1987). Critical analysis of police interviewing techniques. *Journal of Police Science and Administration, 15*, 177–185. ▶ **page 62**

Foster, R.A., Libkuman, T.M., Schooler, J.W. and Loftus, E.F. (1994). Consequentiality and eyewitness person identification. *Applied Cognitive Psychology, 8*, 107–121. ▶ **page 59**

Gabbert, F., Memon, A. and Allen, K. (2003). Memory conformity: can eyewitnesses influence each other's memories for an event? *Applied Cognitive Psychology, 17*, 533–543 ▶ **page 58**

Godden, D. and Baddeley, A.D. (1975). Context-dependent memory in two natural environments: on land and under water. *British Journal of Psychology, 66*, 325–331. ▶ **page 56**

Godden, D. and Baddeley, A.D. (1980). When does context influence recognition memory? *British Journal of Psychology, 71*, 99–104. ▶ **page 57**

Hitch, G. and Baddeley, A.D. (1976). Verbal reasoning and working memory. *Quarterly Journal of Experimental Psychology, 28*, 603–621. ▶ **page 64**

Hodges, J. R. and Patterson, K. (2007). Semantic dementia: A unique clinicopathological syndrome. *The Lancet Neurology, 6*(11), 1004–1014. ▶ **page 51**

Jacobs, J. (1887). Experiments of prehension. *Mind, 12*, 75–79. ▶ **page 46**

Johnson, C. and Scott, B. (1976). Eyewitness testimony and suspect identification as a function of arousal, sex or witness, and scheduling of interrogation. Paper presented at the American Psychological Association Annual Meeting, Washington, D.C. ▶ **page 60**

Kebbell, M.R. and Wagstaff, G.F. (1997). Why do the police interview eyewitnesses? Interview objectives and the evaluation of eyewitness performance. *The Journal of Psychology, 131*, 595–601. ▶ **page 63**

Köhnken, G., Milne, R., Memon, A. and Bull, R. (1999). The cognitive interview: A meta-analysis. *Psychology, Crime and Law, 5*, 3–27. ▶ **page 63**

Loftus, E.F. (1975). Leading questions and the eyewitness report. *Cognitive Psychology, 7*, 560–572. ▶ **page 59**

Loftus, E.F. and Palmer, J.C. (1974). Reconstruction of automobile destruction: an example of the interaction between language and memory. *Journal of Verbal Learning and Verbal Behaviour, 13*, 585–589. ▶ **page 58**

Logie, R.H. (1995). *Visuo-spatial working memory*. Hove, UK: Erlbaum. ▶ **page 52**

McGeoch, J.A. and McDonald, W.T. (1931). Meaningful relation and retroactive inhibition. *American Journal of Psychology, 43*, 579–588. ▶ **page 54**

Miller, G.A. (1956). The magical number seven plus or minus two: some limits on our capacity for processing information. *Psychological Review, 63*, 81–97. ▶ **page 46**

Milne, R. and Bull, R. (2002). Back to basics: A componential analysis of the original cognitive interview mnemonics with three age groups. *Applied Cognitive Psychology, 7*, 743–755. ▶ **page 63**

Parker, J.F., Bahrick, L.E., Fivush, R. and Johnson, P. (2006) The impact of stress on mothers' memory of a natural disaster. *Journal of Experimental Psychology: Applied, 12*, 142–154. ▶ **page 60**

Peterson, L.R. and Peterson, M.J. (1959). Short-term retention of individual verbal items. *Journal of Experimental Psychology, 58*, 193–198. ▶ **page 46**

Pickel, K.L. (1998). Unusualness and threat as possible causes of "weapon focus." *Memory, 6*, 277–295. ▶ **page 61**

Shallice, T. and Warrington, E.K. (1970). Independent functioning of verbal memory stores: A neuropsychological study. *Quarterly Journal of Experimental Psychology, 2*, 261–273. ▶ **page 49**

Shepard, R.N. (1967) Recognition memory for words, sentences and pictures. *Journal of Verbal Learning and Verbal Behaviour, 6*, 156–163. ▶ **page 47**

Skagerberg, E. M. and Wright, D. B. (2008). The co-witness misinformation effect: Memory blends or memory compliance? *Memory, 16*(4), 436–442. ▶ **page 59**

Sperling. G. (1960). The information available in brief visual presentations, *Psychological Monographs, 74* (Whole no. 498), 1–29. ▶ **page 49**

Sutherland, R. and Hayne, H. (2001). The effect of post-event information on adults' eyewitness reports. *Applied Cognitive Psychology, 15*(3), 249–263. ▶ **page 59**

Tulving, E. (1983). *Elements of episodic memory*. Oxford: OUP. ▶ **page 56**

Tulving, E. (1985). How many memory systems are there? *American Psychologist, 40*, 385–398. ▶ **page 50**

Tulving, E. (2002) Episodic memory and common sense: How far apart? In A. Baddeley, J. P. Aggleton and M. A. Conway (Eds.), *Episodic memory: New directions in research*. Oxford: Oxford University Press. ▶ **page 51**

Tulving, E. and Psotka, J. (1971) Retroactive inhibition in free recall: Inaccessibility of information available in the memory store. *Journal of Experimental Psychology, 87*, 1–8. ▶ **page 55**

Tulving, E., Kapur, S., Craik, F.I.M., Moscovitch, M. and Houle, S. (1994). Hemispheric encoding/retrieval asymmetry in episodic memory: positron emission tomography findings. *Proceedings of the National Academy of Sciences USA, 91*, 2016–2020. ▶ **page 51**

Valentine, T. and Mesout, J. (2009). Eyewitness identification under stress in the London Dungeon. *Applied Cognitive Psychology, 23*, 151–161. ▶ **page 61**

Wixted, J. T. (2004). The psychology and neuroscience of forgetting. *Annual Review of Psychology, 55*, 235–269. ▶ **page 55**

Yerkes R.M. and Dodson J.D. (1908). The relation of strength of stimulus to rapidity of habit-formation. *Journal of Comparative Neurology and Psychology*, 18, 459–482. ▶ **page 60**

Yuille, J.C. and Cutshall, J.L. (1986). A case study of eyewitness memory of a crime. *Journal of Applied Psychology, 71*, 291–301. ▶ **page 60**

Zaragoza, M.S. and McCloskey, M. (1989). Misleading post-event information and the memory impairment hypothesis: comment on Belli and reply to Tversky and Tuchin. *Journal of Experimental Psychology: General, 118*, 92–99. ▶ **page 59**

Chapter 3

Ainsworth, M.D.S. and Bell, S. M. (1970). Attachment, exploration and separation: illustrated by the behaviour of one-year-olds in a Strange Situation. *Child Development, 41*, 49–65 ▶ **page 86**

Ainsworth, M.D., Blehar, M.C., Waters, E., and Wall, S. (1978). *Patterns of attachment: Assessed in the strange situation and at home*. New Jersey: LEA. ▶ **page 86**

Bailey, H.N., Moran, G., Pederson, G.R. and Bento, S. (2007). Understanding the transmission of attachment using variable- and relationship-centred approaches. *Development and Psychopathology, 19*, 313–343. ▶ **pages 85, 94**

Becker-Stoll, F., Fremmer-Bombik, E., Wartner, U., Zimmermann, P. and Grossmann, K. E. (2008). Is attachment at ages 1, 6 and 16 related to autonomy and relatedness behavior of adolescents in interaction towards their mothers? *International Journal of Behavioural Development, 32*(5), 372–380. ▶ **page 95**

Beckett, C., Castle, J., Rutter, M. and Sonuga-Barke, E.J. (2010). Institutional deprivation, specific cognitive functions and scholastic achievement: REA study findings. *Monographs of the Society for Research in Child Development, 75*, 125–142. ▶ **page 92**

Bick, J., Dozier, M. and Perkins, E. (2012). Convergence between attachment classifications and natural reunion behaviour among children and parents in a child care setting. *Attachment and Human Development, 14*, 1–10. ▶ **page 87**

Bowlby, J. (1944). *Forty-four juvenile thieves*. London: Balliere, Tindall and Cox. ▶ **page 90**

Bowlby, J. (1953). Some pathological processes set in train by early mother-child separation. *Journal of Mental Science, 99*, 265–272. ▶ **page 90**

Bowlby, J. (1958). The nature of the child's tie to his mother. *International Journal of Psychoanalysis, 39*, 350–373. ▶ **page 84**

Bowlby, J. (1969). *Attachment and loss vol I*. London: Pimlico. ▶ **page 94**

Bowlby, J. (1975). *Attachment and Loss, vol 2*. Harmondsworth: Penguin. ▶ **page 84**

Brazelton T.B., Tronick, E., Adamson, L., Als, H. and Wise, S. (1975). Early mother-infant reciprocity. Parent-infant Interaction. *Ciba Symposium, 33*, 137–154. ▶ **pages 74, 85**

Burman, E. (1994). *Deconstructing developmental psychology*. London: Routledge. ▶ **page 85**

Clarke, A.D.B. and Clarke, A.M. (1998). Early experience and the life path. *The Psychologist, 11*, 433–436. ▶ **page 95**

Crotwell, R. M., Hernandez-Reif, M. and Curtner-Smith, M. E. (2013). Five skills to help improve caregiver-child interaction during play. *Dialog, 16*(3), 178-182. ▶ **page 75**

Dollard, J. and Miller, N. E. (1950). *Personality and psychotherapy*. New York: McGraw-Hill. ▶ **page 82**

Fearon, R. P. and Roisman, G. I. (2017). Attachment theory: progress and future directions. *Current Opinion in Psychology, 15*, 131–136. ▶ **page 95**

Feldman, R. (2007). Parent-infant synchrony: Biological foundations and developmental outcomes. Current *Directions in Psychological Science 16* 340–345. ▶ **page 74**

Feldman, R. (2012). Parent-infant synchrony: a viobehavioural model of mutual influences in the formation of affiliative bonds. *Monographs of the Society for Research in Child Development, 75*, 125–142. ▶ **page 75**

Feldman, R. and Eidelman, A.I. (2007). Maternal postpartum behavior and the emergence of infant–mother and infant–father synchrony in preterm and full-term infants: The role of neonatal vagal tone. *Developmental Psychobiology, 49*, 290–302. ▶ **page 74**

Field, T. (1978). Interaction behaviors of primary versus secondary caretaker fathers. *Developmental Psychology, 14*, 183–184. ▶ **page 78**

Finegood, E. D., Blair, C., Granger, D. A., Hibel, L. C., Mills-Koonce, R., & Family Life Project Key Investigators (2016). Psychobiological influences on maternal sensitivity in the context of adversity. *Developmental Psychology, 52*(7), 1073–1087. ▶ **page 74**

Gao, Y., Raine, A., Chan, F. and Venables, P. H. (2010). Early maternal and paternal bonding, childhood physical abuse and adult psychopathic personality. *Psychological Medicine 40*(6), pp. 1007–1016. ▶ **page 91**

Goldfarb, W. (1943) The effects of early institutional care on adolescent personality. *Journal of Experimental Education, 12*(2), 106–129. ▶ **page 91**

Goldfarb, W. (1947). Variations in adolescent adjustment of institutionally-reared children. *American Journal of Orthopsychiatry, 17(3)*, 449. ▶ **page 90**

Goldfarb, W. (1955). Emotional and intellectual consequences of psychologic deprivation in infancy: a re-evaluation. In P. Hoch and J. Zubin (Eds) *Psychopathology of childhood.* New York: Grune and Stratton. ▶ **page 91**

Grossmann, K., Grossmann, K. E., Fremmer-Bombik, E., Kindler, H., Scheuerer-Englisch, H. and Zimmermann, A. P. (2002). The uniqueness of the child–father attachment relationship: Fathers' sensitive and challenging play as a pivotal variable in a 16-year longitudinal study. *Social development, 11*(3), 301–337. ▶ **page 78**

Grossmann, K. E., Grossmann, K., Huber, F. and Wartner, U. (1981). German children's behavior towards their mothers at 12 months and their fathers at 18 months in Ainsworth's Strange Situation. *International Journal of Behavioral Development, 4*(2), 157–181. ▶ **page 89**

Harlow, H. (1958). The nature of love. *American Psychologist, 13*, 673–685. ▶ **page 80**

Hay, D.F. and Vespo, J.E. (1988). Social learning perspectives on the development of the mother-child relationship. In Burns, B. and Hay, D.F. (Eds). *The Different Faces on Motherhood.* New York: Springer. ▶ **page 83**

Hazan, C. and Shaver, P.R. (1987). Romantic love conceptualised as an attachment process. *Journal of Personality and Social Psychology, 52*, 511–524. ▶ **pages 94, 97**

Howe, D. (1998) *Patterns of adoption: nature, nurture and psychosocial development.* Oxford, Blackwell. ▶ **page 81**

Isabella, R.A., Belsky, J. and von Eye, A. (1989). Origins of infant-mother attachment: An examination of interactional synchrony during the infant's first year. *Developmental Psychology, 25*, 12–21. ▶ **pages 74, 75, 78, 83**

Jin, M.K., Jacobvitz, D., Hazen, N. and Jung, S.H. (2012). Maternal sensitivity and infant attachment security in Korea: Cross-cultural validation of the Strange Situation. *Attachment and Human Development, 14*, 33–44. ▶ **page 88**

Kagan, J. (1982). The construct of difficult temperament: a reply to Thomas, Chess and Korn. *Merrill-Palmer Quarterly, 28*, 21–24. ▶ **page 87**

Kagan, J., Reznick, J. S., and Snidman, N. (1986). *Temperamental inhibition in early childhood. The study of temperament: Changes, continuities and challenges.* Hove: Psychology Press, 53–67. ▶ **page 87**

Kennedy, M., Kreppner, J., Knights, N., Kumsta, R., Maughan, B., Golm, D., ... & Sonuga-Barke, E. J. (2016). Early severe institutional deprivation is associated with a persistent variant of adult attention-deficit/hyperactivity disorder: clinical presentation, developmental continuities and life circumstances in the English and Romanian Adoptees study. *Journal of Child Psychology and Psychiatry, 57*(10), 1113–1125. ▶ **page 92**

Kerns, K.A. (1994). A longitudinal examination of links between mother-infant attachment and children's friendships. *Journal of Personality and Social Relationships, 11*, 379–381. ▶ **page 94**

Kokkinos, C. M. (2007). Elementary school children's involvement in bullying and victimisation: the role of attachment style and internalising and externalising symptomatology. *Scientia Paedigogia Experimentalis, XLIV*, 49–60. ▶ **page 87**

Koluchová, J. (1976). The further development of twins after severe and prolonged deprivation: a second report. *Journal of Child Psychology and Psychiatry, 17*, 181–188. ▶ **page 91**

Kornienko, D. S. (2016). Child temperament and mother's personality as predictors of maternal relation to child. *Procedia – Social and Behavioral Sciences, 233*, 343–347. ▶ **page 85**

Langton, E.G. (2006). Romania's children. *The Psychologist, 19*, 412–413. ▶ **page 93**

Lévy, F., Melo, A. I., Galef, B. G., Madden, M. and Fleming, A. S. (2003). Complete maternal deprivation affects social, but not spatial, learning in adult rats. *Developmental Psychobiology, 43*(3), 177–191 ▶ **page 91**

Lewis, H. (1954). *Deprived children: the Mersham experiment, a social and clinical study.* London: Oxford University Press. ▶ **page 91**

Lorenz, K. (1952). *King Solomon's ring.* London: Methuen. ▶ **page 80**

Main, M. and Solomon, J. (1986). Discovery of a disorganised disoriented attachment pattern. In *Affective development in infancy.* Norwood: Ablex. ▶ **page 87**

McCallum, F. and Golombok, S. (2004). Children raised in fatherless families from infancy: a follow-up of children of lesbian and single heterosexual mothers at early adolescence. *Journal of Child Psychology and Psychiatry, 45*, 1407–1419. ▶ **page 79**

McCarthy, G. (1999). Attachment style and adult love relationships and friendships: a study of a group of women at risk of experiencing relationship difficulties. *British Journal of Medical Psychology, 72*, 305–321. ▶ **page 94**

McCormick, M. P., O'Connor, E. E. and Barnes, S. P. (2016). Mother–child attachment styles and math and reading skills in middle childhood: The mediating role of children's exploration and engagement. *Early Childhood Research Quarterly, 36*, 295–306. ▶ **page 87**

Meltzoff, A.N. and Moore, M.K. (1977). Imitation of facial and manual gestures by human neonates. *Science, 198*, 75–78. ▶ **page 74**

Morelli, G. A. and Tronick, E. Z. (1991). Efe multiple caretaking and attachment. In J. L. Gewirtz, W. M. Kurtines and J. L. Lamb (Eds) *Intersections with attachment*, pp. 41–51. Hove, Sussex: Psychology Press. ▶ **page 89**

Myron-Wilson, P. and Smith, P.K. (1998). Attachment relationships and influences on bullying. *Proceedings of the British Psychological Society, 6(2)*, 89–90. ▶ **page 94**

Regolin, L. and Vallortigara, G. (1995). Perception of partly occluded objects by young chicks. *Perception & Psychophysics, 57*(7), 971–976 ▶ **page 81**

Rutter, M. (1981). *Maternal deprivation reassessed.* 2nd edition. Penguin: Harmondsworth. ▶ **page 91**

Rutter, M. (2006). Attachment from infancy to adulthood. The major longitudinal studies. *Journal of Child Psychology and Psychiatry, 47*, 974–977. ▶ **page 92**

Rutter, M., Sonuga-Barke, E.J., Beckett, C., Castle, J., Kreppner, J., Kumsta, R., Bell, C.A. (2011) Deprivation-specific psychological patterns: Effects of institutional deprivation. *Monographs of the Society for Research in Child Development. 75(1)*, 1–250. ▶ **page 92**

Schaffer, H.R. and Emerson, P. (1964). The development of social attachments in infancy. *Monographs of the Society for Research in Child Development, 29*, 1–77. ▶ **pages 76, 77**

Sears, R. R., Maccoby, E.E. and Levin, H. (1957). *Patterns of child-rearing.* Evanston, Ill: Peters and Row. ▶ **page 82**

Seebach, P. (2005). Baby duck syndrome: Imprinting on your system makes change a very hard thing. *IBM Developerworks.* ▶ **page 81**

Simonelli, A., de Palo, F., Moretti, M. Baratter, P.M. and Porreca, A. (2014). The strange situation procedure: The role of the attachment patterns in the Italian culture. *American Journal of Applied Psychology, 3*, 47–56. ▶ **page 88**

Takahashi, K. (1986). Examining the strange-situation procedure with Japanese mothers and 12-month-old infants. *Developmental Psychology, 22*(2), 265–270. ▶ **pages 87, 89**

Takahashi, K. (1990). Affective relationships and their lifelong development. In Baltes, P.B. (ed) *Lifespan development and behaviour* vol 10. Hillsdale: Lawrence Erlbaum. ▶ **page 87**

van IJzendoorn, M.H. (1993). Multiple caregiving among African Americans and infant attachment: The need for an emic approach. Commentary. *Human Development, 36*, 103–105. ▶ **page 77**

van IJzendoorn, M.H. (1995). Adult attachment representations, parental responsiveness, and infant attachment: a meta-analysis on the predictive validity of the Adult Attachment Interview. *Psychological Bulletin, 117*(3), 387. ▶ **page 84**

van IJzendoorn, M.H., and Kroonenberg, P.M. (1988) Cross-cultural patterns of attachment: A meta-analysis of the Strange Situation. *Child Development, 59*, 147–156. ▶ **page 88**

Vincent, J. (2006). Emotional attachment and mobile phones. *Knowledge, Technology and Policy, 19*, 39–44. ▶ **page 97**

Ward, M.J., Lee, S.S. and Polan, I. (2006). Attachment and psychopathology in a community sample. *Attachment and Humar Development, 8*, 327–340. ▶ **page 87**

Zeanah, C.H., Smyke, A.T., Koga, S.F. and Carlson, E. (2005). Attachment in institutionalised and community children in Romania. *Child Development, 76*, 1015–1028. ▶ **page 92**

Chapter 4

Bandura, A. (1977). Self-efficacy: Toward a unifying theory of behavioural change. *Psychological Review, 84*, 191–215. ▶ **page 111**

Bandura, A. and Walters, R.H. (1963). *Social Learning and Personality Development.* New York: Holt, Rinehart and Winston. ▶ **page 110**

Bandura, A., Ross, D. and Ross, S. (1961). Transmission of aggression through imitation of aggressive role models. *Journal of Abnormal and Social Psychology, 63*, 575–582. ▶ **page 110**

Braver, T. S., Cohen, J. D., Nystrom, L. E., Jonides, J., Smith, E. E. and Noll, D. C. (1997). A parametric study of prefrontal cortex involvement in human working memory. *Neuroimage, 5*, 49–62. ▶ **page 112**

Bugelski, B.R. and Alampay, D.A. (1962). The role of frequency in developing perceptual sets. *Canadian Journal of Psychology, 15*, 205–211. ▶ **page 113**

Cipriani, A., Furukawa, T. A., Salanti, G., Chaimani, A., Atkinson, L. Z. ...and Geddes, J. R. (2018). Comparative efficacy and acceptability of 21 antidepressant drugs for the acute treatment of adults with major depressive disorder: a systematic review and network meta-analysis. *The Lancet, 391*(10128), 1357–1366. ▶ **page 115**

Cumberbatch, G., Wood, G. and Littlejohns, V. (2001). *Television: The Public's view 2000.* London: ITC. ▶ **page 111**

Freud, S. (1909/1977) *Analysis of a phobia in a five year old boy (Little Hans) The Pelcian Freud Library, Volume 8*, Hammondsworth: Penguin. ▶ **pages 106, 120, 121, 123**

Pavlov, I. P. (1927). *Conditioned Reflexes.* Londo Oxford University Press. ▶ **page 108**

Skinner, B.F. (1953). *Science and Human Behaviour.* New York: MacMillan. ▶ **pages 108, 109**

Stein, C.J. and Test, M.A. (1980). Alternative to mental hospital treatment program and clinical evaluation. *Archives of General Psychology, 37*, 392–397. ▶ **page 125**

Watson, J.B. (1913). Psychology as the Behaviourist views it. *Psychological Review, 20*, 158–177. ▶ **pages 106, 108**

Wong, D. (2008). *Five creepy ways video games are trying to get you addicted:* http://www.cracked.com/article_18461_5-creepy-ways-video-games-are-trying-to-get-you-addicted.html [Accessed July 2014] ▶ **page 109**

Chapter 5

hmari, S. E. (2016). Using mice to model obsessive compulsive disorder: from genes to circuits. *Neuroscience, 321*, 121–137. ▶ **page 155**

li, S., Rhodes, L., Moreea, O., McMillan, D., Gilbody, S., Leach, C., ... and Delgadillo, J. (2017). How durable is the effect of low intensity CBT for depression and anxiety? Remission and relapse in a longitudinal cohort study. *Behaviour research and therapy, 94*, 1–8. ▶ **page 153**

eck, A. T. (1967). *Depression: clinical, experimental and theoretical aspects.* Pennsylvania: University of Pennsylvania Press. ▶ **page 150**

ogetto, F., Bellino, S., Vaschetto, P. and Ziero, S. (2000). Olanzapine augmentation of fluvoxamine-refractory obsessive–compulsive disorder (OCD): a 12-week open trial. *Psychiatry Research, 96*, 91–98. ▶ **page 157**

ark, D.A., and Beck, A.T. (1999). *Scientific foundations of cognitive theory and therapy of depression.* New York: John Wiley and Sons. ▶ **page 151**

ohen, J. R., So, F. K., Hankin, B. L. and Young, J. F. (2019). Translating cognitive vulnerability theory into improved adolescent depression screening: a receiver operating characteristic approach. *Journal of Clinical Child & Adolescent Psychology, 48*(4), 582–595. ▶ **page 151**

omer, K.R., Schmidt, N.B. and Murphy, D.L. (2007). An investigation of traumatic life events and obsessive-compulsive disorder. *Behaviour Research and Therapy, 45*, 1683–1691. ▶ **page 155**

avid, D., Cristea, I. A. and Beck, A. T. (2018). Varieties of Psychotherapy for Major Depressive Disorder in Adults. In D. David, S. J. Lynn and G. H. Montgomery (Eds.) *Evidence-Based Psychotherapy: The State of the Science and Practice*, pp.11–35. ▶ **page 151**

e Jongh, A., Fransen, J., Oosterink-Wubbe, F. and Aartman, I. (2006). Psychological trauma exposure and trauma symptoms among individuals with high and low levels of dental anxiety. *European Journal of Oral Sciences, 114*(4), 286–292. ▶ **page 147**

is, A. (1962). *Reason and emotion in psychotherapy.* Michigan: L Stuart. ▶ **page 150**

Gilroy, L.J., Kirby, K.C., Daniels, B.A., Menzies, R.G. and Mongomery, I.M. (2003). Long-term follow-up of computer-aided vicarious exposure versus live graded exposure in the treatment of spider phobia. *Behaviour Therapy, 34*, 65–76. ▶ **page 149**

Goldacre, B. (2013). *Bad Pharma: How medicine is broken and how we can fix it.* London: Fourth Estate. ▶ **page 157**

Jahoda, M. (1958). *Current concepts of positive mental health.* New York: Basic Books. ▶ **page 138**

Lewis, A. (1936). Problems with obsessional illness. *Proceedings of the Royal Society of Medicine, XXIX*, 525–336. ▶ **page 154**

Lewis G. & Lewis, G. (2016). No evidence that CBT is less effective than antidepressants in moderate to severe depression. *Evidence-based mental health, 19*(4), 125. ▶ **page 153**

March, J.S., Silva, S., Petrycki, S., Curry, J., Wells, K., Fairbank, J., Burns, B., Domino, M., McNulty, S., Vitiello, B. and Severe, J. (2007). The treatment for adolescents with depression study (TADS): long-term effectiveness and safety outcomes. *Archives of General Psychiatry, 64(10)*, 1132–1143. ▶ **page 153**

Marini, I. and Stebnicki, M. A. (2012). *The Psychological and Social Impact of Illness and Disability.* New York: Springer. ▶ **page 155**

Mowrer, O.H. (1960). *Learning theory and behaviour.* New York: Wiley. ▶ **page 146**

Nestadt, G., Grados, M. and Samuels, J.F. (2010). Genetics of OCD. *Psychiatric Clinics of North America, 33*, 141–158. ▶ **page 155**

Newman, C. and Adams, K. (2004). Dog gone good: managing dog phobia in a teenage boy with a learning disability. *British Journal of Learning Disabilities, 32*, 35–38. ▶ **page 148**

Persons, J. B. (1986). Generalization of the effects of exposure treatments for phobias: A single case study. *Psychotherapy: Theory, Research, Practice, Training, 23*(1), 160. ▶ **page 149**

Rosenhan, D.L. and Seligman, M.E.P. (1989). *Abnormal Psychology* (Second edition). New York: W.W. Norton. ▶ **page 138**

Sansone, R.A. and Sansone, L.A. (2011). SNRIs Pharmacological Alternatives for the Treatment of Obsessive Compulsive Disorder? *Innovations in Clinical Neuroscience, 8*. 10–14. ▶ **page 157**

Schumacher, S., Miller, R., Fehm, L., Kirschbaum, C., Fydrich, T. and Ströhle, A. (2015). Therapists' and patients' stress responses during graduated versus flooding in vivo exposure in the treatment of specific phobia: *A preliminary observational study. Psychiatry Research, 230*(2), 668–675. ▶ **page 149**

Seligman, M.E.P. (1971). Phobias and preparedness. *Behaviour Therapy, 2*, 307–320. ▶ **page 147**

Skapinakis, P., Caldwell, D., Hollingworth, W., Bryden, P., Fineberg, N., Salkovskis, P., ... and Lewis, G. (2016). A systematic review of the clinical effectiveness and cost-effectiveness of pharmacological and psychological interventions for the management of obsessive-compulsive disorder in children/adolescents and adults. *Health technology assessment, 20*(43), 1–392. ▶ **page 157**

Soomro, G.M., Altman, D.G., Rajagopal, S. and Oakley Browne, M. (2009). *Selective serotonin re-uptake inhibitors (SSRIs) versus placebo for obsessive compulsive disorder (OCD).* Chichester: Wiley. ▶ **page 157**

Sturmey, P. (2005). Against psychotherapy with people who have mental retardation. *Mental Retardation, 43*(1), 55–57. ▶ **page 153**

Taylor, J. L., Lindsay, W. R. and Willner, P. (2008). CBT for people with intellectual disabilities: emerging evidence, cognitive ability and IQ effects. *Behavioural and Cognitive Psychotherapy, 36*(6), 723–733. ▶ **page 153**

Taylor, S. (2013). Molecular genetics of obsessive-compulsive disorder: a comprehensive meta-analysis of genetic association studies. *Molecular Psychiatry 18*, 799–805. ▶ **page 154**

Watson, J.B. and Rayner, R. (1920). Conditioned emotional responses. *Journal of Experimental Psychology, 3*, 1–14. ▶ **page 146**

Wechsler, T. F., Mühlberger, A. and Kümpers, F. (2019). Inferiority or even superiority of virtual reality exposure therapy in phobias? A systematic review and quantitative meta-analysis on randomized controlled trials specifically comparing the efficacy of virtual reality exposure to gold standard in vivo exposure in agoraphobia, specific phobia and social phobia. *Frontiers in psychology, 10*, 1758. ▶ **page 149**

Yrondi, A., Rieu, J., Massip, C., Bongard, V. and Schmitt, L. (2015). Depressed patients' preferences for type of psychotherapy: a preliminary study. *Patient preference and adherence, 9*, 1371–1374. ▶ **page 153**

Chapter 6

Baron-Cohen, S., Leslie, A.M. and Frith, U. (1986). Mechanical, behavioural and intentional understanding of picture stories in autistic children. *British Journal of Developmental Psychology, 4*, 113–125. ▶ **page 174**

Bugelski, B.R. and Alampay, D.A. (1961). The role of frequency in developing perceptual sets. *Canadian Journal of Psychology, 15*, 205–211. ▶ **page 173**

Coolican, H. (2006). *Introduction to research methods in Psychology.* London: Hodder Arnold. ▶ **page 171**

Elliott (1968). See http://www.pbs.org/wgbh/pages/frontline/shows/divided/etc/script.html ▶ **page 179**

Gilchrist, D.T. and Nesburg, L.S. (1952). Need and perceptual change in need-related objects. *Journal of Experimental Psychology, 44*, 369–376. ▶ **page 174**

Jackson, D.N. and Messick, S. (1961). Acquiescence and the factorial interpretation of the MMPI. *Psychological Bulletin, 58(4)*, Jul 1961, 299–304. ▶ **page 187**

Latané, B. and Darley, J.M. (1968). Group inhibition of bystander intervention in emergencies. *Journal of Personality and Social Psychology, 10*, 215–221. ▶ **page 179**

Piliavin, L.M., Rodin, J.A. and Piliavin, J.A. (1969). Good samaritanism: an underground phenomenon? *Journal of Personality and Social Psychology, 13*, 289–299. ▶ **page 174**

Rosenhan, D.L. (1973). On being sane in insane place. *Science, 179(4070)*, 250–258. ▶ **page 183**

The Telegraph (2014). One in three absences at work due to anxiety and stress, official Government survey finds, 19 September. See http://www.telegraph.co.uk/health/healthnews/10143915/One-in-three-absences-at-work-due-to-anxiety-and-stress-official-Government-survey-finds.html (Accessed September 2014) ▶ **page 203**

Williams, T.M. (Ed.). (1986). *The impact of television: A natural experiment in three communities.* New York: Academic Press. ▶ **page 174**

Index/Glossary

44 thieves study 90–91, 103

ABC model Ellis proposed that depression occurs when an activating event (A) triggers an irrational belief (B) which in turn produces a consequence (C), i.e. an emotional response like depression. The key to this process is the irrational belief. **150–152, 161, 165**

ABCDE model Extends Ellis's explanation of depression (ABC model) to a therapy – D stands for disputing irrational thoughts and E for the effect of disputing. **152**

Acetylcholine A neurotransmitter. In the central nervous system, acetylcholine plays a role in attention and arousal. In the peripheral nervous system, it works by causing muscles to contract. **119, 129**

Acoustically Refers to sounds or the sense of hearing. **46, 48**

Acquiescence bias Tendency for a person to respond to any questionnaire/interview item with agreement regardless of the actual content. **187, 211**

Action potential A short increase and decrease of electrical activity in the membrane of a neuron, transmitting a signal away from the cell body. **118–119, 129, 133**

Adaptive Any physical or psychological characteristic that enhances an individual's survival and reproduction, and is thus likely to be naturally selected. Such characteristics are passed on to future generations. **114, 125, 139**

Adorno, Theodor 28–29, 39, 43

Adrenal glands Small glands located on top of each kidney that are part of the endocrine system. Various hormones are produced including adrenaline and noradrenaline and corticosteroids, including cortisol. **117, 129, 130, 133**

Adrenaline A hormone produced by the adrenal glands. These are part of the human body's immediate stress response. Adrenaline has a strong effect on the cells of the cardiovascular system – stimulating the heart rate, contracting blood vessels and dilating air passages. **116–117, 119, 126, 129–130, 156, 161**

Adult relationships Those relationships the child goes on to have later in life as an adult. These include friendships and working relationships but most critically relationships with romantic partners and the person's own children. **94–95**

Affectionless psychopathy A behaviour disorder in which the individual has no ability to experience shame or guilt and lacks a social conscience. This means that they may find it 'easier' to commit crimes. **90–91, 99, 103, 189**

Agentic shift Changing from being in an autonomous state to being in an agentic state, i.e. moving from taking personal responsibility for one's actions to believing one is acting on behalf of an authority figure. **26–27, 39**

Agentic state A mental state where we feel no personal responsibility for our behaviour because we believe ourselves to be acting for an authority figure, i.e. as their agent. This frees us from the demands of our consciences and allows us to obey even a destructive authority figure. **26–27, 39, 42–43**

Agoraphobia Intense fear of being in public places where you feel escape might be difficult. **140, 146–147, 149**

Aim A general statement of what the researcher intends to investigate, the purpose of the study. **23, 65, 81, 86, 92, 96–97, 103, 126–127, 157–159, 168–170, 173, 178, 180, 185, 189, 204–205, 210–211**

Ainsworth, Mary 86–88, 103, 182

Amnesia A loss of memory due to brain damage, disease, or psychological trauma. **34, 49, 50–51, 66**

Animal studies In psychology these are studies carried out on non-human animal species rather than on humans, either for ethical or practical reasons – practical because animals breed faster and researchers are interested in seeing results across more than one generation of animals. **73, 80–81, 83, 98, 100–103, 131, 155, 161**

Anomalous results Data that does not fit in with the pattern of the other data. **195**

Anonymity An important aspect of confidentiality; a participant remains anonymous, i.e. their name is withheld or simply not recorded. **36, 179, 189, 202, 207, 210**

Antidepressant A group of drugs which increase the production of serotonin and/or noradrenaline, and reduce symptoms of depression. **115, 129, 153, 155–156, 161, 165**

Antianxiety drugs 203

Anti-Semitism Hatred or discrimination of Jews as a religious or cultural group. **28**

Antisocial personality disorder A mental health condition where a person has a repeated pattern of behaviour manipulating or violating the rights of others. Often leads to crimes against people. **90, 136–137, 160, 163, 164**

Anxiety A state of emotional and physical arousal. The emotions include having worried thoughts and feelings of tension. Physical changes include an increased heart rate and sweatiness. Anxiety is a normal reaction to stressful situations, but it can affect the accuracy and detail of eyewitness testimony. **23, 26, 36, 39, 45, 58, 60–62, 65, 67–68, 71, 74, 76–77, 79, 85–87, 92, 97–100, 102–103, 113, 123, 125, 128–129, 140–150, 160–162, 164, 169, 175, 183, 186, 190–191, 196, 203**

Anxiety disorders A group of mental disorders characterised by levels of fear and apprehension which are disproportionate to any threat posed. **125, 140–141, 160–162**

Anxiety hierarchy 148–149, 160, 162, 164

Approach A way to explain behaviour; a general perspective or mode of thinking. **29, 32, 34–35, 60, 63–65, 67, 82, 86, 100, 104–116, 118, 120–126, 128–133, 135–137, 145–157, 159–160, 162–166, 179, 181, 204**

Armchair psychology 8

Articulatory process A component of the phonological loop which acts as an 'inner voice', i.e. words/sounds are verbally repeated. **52, 66, 70**

Artificial intelligence Machines showing human-like reasoned behaviour. **112–113, 128**

Asch, Solomon 16–19, 30–31, 33–34, 38–43

Asocial stage 76–77, 98, 100, 102

Association 22, 74, 82–83, 91, 94–95, 98–99, 103, 108, 124, 128, 140, 146–147, 151, 190, 196, 200

Attachment An emotional bond between two people that endures over time. Leads to certain behaviours such as clinging and proximity-seeking. Serves the function of protecting an infant. **72–103, 114, 203, 207**

- **Definition of** 74
- **Figures** 76, 78–79, 81–85, 89–92, 94, 98–99, 102–103
- **Multiple** 76–77, 85, 98, 100, 102
- **Stages** 76–78, 92, 98, 102–103

Attachment type Refers to whether a person is securely or insecurely attached, i.e. the way you relate to others in the context of intimate relationships. **86–89, 92, 94–95, 97, 99, 103**

Augmentation principle If a person performs an action when there are known constraints, their motive for acting must be stronger. **32, 34, 43**

Authoritarian Personality (AP) A type of personality that Adorno argued was especially susceptible to obeying people in authority. Such individuals are also thought to be submissive to those of higher status and dismissive of inferiors. **28, 39, 43**

Authority 22–31, 39–40, 42–43

Autonomic nervous system (ANS) Transmits information to and from internal bodily organs. It is 'autonomic' as the system operates involuntarily (i.e. automatic). It has two main divisions: the *sympathetic* and *parasympathetic* nervous systems. **116–117, 126, 129–130, 133**

Autonomous state Being aware of the consequences of one's own actions and therefore taking voluntary control of one's own behaviour. This explains why some individuals act independently rather than obediently, as in an agentic state. **26, 39**

Avoidance 86, 108, 140, 144, 146–148, 152, 160, 164

Axon The long projection of the neuron from the cell body. **118–119, 127, 129, 133**

Bandura, Albert 107, 110–111, 125, 132, 211

Bar chart A type of graph in which the frequency of each variable is represented by the height of the bars. **32, 37, 50, 57, 65, 96–97, 127, 144, 149, 158–159, 196, 207, 212**

Baseline study 16–17, 22, 24–25, 31

Behaviour 16, 18–35, 37–39, 41–42, 50, 61, 66, 74–87, 89, 92–94, 96–116, 120–125, 127–133, 135–157, 159–167, 169–171, 173–174, 178–186, 192, 203, 206, 208, 210–211

- **Controlling** 12
- **Describing** 12
- **Explaining** 12
- **Maladaptive** 125, 139
- **Predicting** 12

Behaviour checklist In an observational study, dividing the behaviour(s) to be observed into individual components. A form of operationalisation. Each component should be an observable behaviour. **184–185**

Behavioural Ways in which people act. **19, 21, 61, 79, 96, 99, 108, 114, 124, 127, 131, 135, 140–150, 152–153, 157, 159–161 162, 164–165, 184–185, 203, 206, 211**

Behavioural activation A therapy for depression focusing on encouraging individuals to engage in those activities they are avoiding. The goal of the intervention is to increase environmental reinforcement. **152, 161, 165**

Behaviourist (behavioural) approach A way of explaining behaviour in terms of what is observable and in terms of learning. **82, 105–113, 124–125, 128, 131–133, 135, 146–149, 160, 162, 164–165**

Behavioural categories When a target behaviour is broken up into components that are observable and measurable (operationalisation). **19, 21, 79, 96, 127, 159, 184–185, 206, 21**

Behavioural characteristics 124, 140–145, 147, 164

Behavioural explanation 147, 160

Behavioural Insights Team 13, 203

Behavioural therapy Any form of therapy derived from the behaviourist model, for example systematic desensitisation. **148**

Bias In the context of sampling, when certain groups may be over- or under-represented within the sample selected. For instance, there may be too many younger people or too many people of one ethnic origin in a sample. This limits the extent to which generalisations can be made to the target population. **29, 36, 39, 58, 67, 71, 77, 79, 89, 91, 98–99, 102–103, 106–107, 109, 115, 121, 123, 125, 127, 129, 135, 140–144, 146–149, 157, 160–162, 164–165, 169–171, 176–17 181, 183–189, 193, 202, 206–207, 210–212**

Binding factors 26, 39

Biological A perspective that emphasises the importance of physical processes in th body such as genetic inheritance and neural function. **105–107, 114–115, 123–126, 128–129, 132–133, 135, 154–157, 165**

Biological explanation 154, 156, 161

Biological preparedness The ability of some organisms to associate significant (i.e. in terms of survival) combinations of stimuli, responses and reinforcers. **14 164**

iological structure An arrangement or organisation of parts to form an organ, system or living thing. **107, 112, 114–115, 118, 124, 128, 132**

iosocial **125**

owlby, John **73, 84–86, 88–92, 94, 99–103, 114, 203**

PS *See* British Psychological Society. **22, 178–179, 210**

PS code of ethics A quasi-legal document produced by the British Psychological Society (BPS) that instructs psychologists in the UK about what behaviour is and is not acceptable when dealing with participants. The code is built around four major principles: respect, competence, responsibility and integrity. **178–179, 210**

rain fingerprinting' **112**

rain scan A technique used to investigate the functioning of the brain by taking images of the living brain. This makes it possible to match regions of the brain to behaviour by asking participants to engage in particular activities while the scan is done. Brain scans are also used to detect brain abnormalities such as tumours. Examples: CAT scan, PET scan, MRI scan, fMRI scan. **10, 12, 106, 112, 114–115, 129, 165**

riefing **23, 64–65, 126, 178–179, 181, 205–206, 209–210**

ritish Psychological Society (BPS) Professional association for psychologists in Britain, governing and guiding the behaviour of psychologists. **22, 83, 178–179**

roca's area An area of the brain in the frontal lobe, usually in the left hemisphere, associated with production of language. **112, 128**

lculated value The value of a test statistic calculated for a particular data set. **200–201, 207**

ndidate genes **154–155, 161**

pacity The amount of information that can be held in a memory store. **45–49, 52, 66, 70–71, 101, 122, 132**

se study A research method that involves a detailed study of a single individual, institution or event. Case studies provide a rich record of human experience but are hard to generalise from. **48, 53, 68, 70, 80, 107, 121, 125, 140, 143, 145, 149, 164, 179**

ll body The part of a cell that contains the nucleus. **118, 129, 133**

ntral executive (CE) The component of the WMM that co-ordinates the activities of the three subsystems in memory. It also allocates processing resources to those activities. **52–53, 64, 66, 70, 112–113, 199**

ntral nervous system (CNS) Consists of the brain and the spinal cord and is the origin of all complex commands and decisions. **116, 118–119, 129, 133**

rebral cortex The surface layer of the forebrain (the two hemispheres). It is grey in colour and it is highly folded to make it possible to fit the massive amount of material inside the skull. **70, 116, 129**

Chance The extent to which something occurs randomly, i.e. in the absence of a discoverable cause. **9, 21, 200, 205, 207**

Charts **32, 37, 50, 57, 65, 96–97, 104, 106, 127, 144, 149, 158–159, 187, 192, 196, 207, 212**

Childhood experiences **28, 95**

Childhood relationships Affiliations with other people in childhood, including friends and classmates, and with adults such as teachers. **94**

Chunking Grouping sets of digits or letters into units or 'chunks'. **46–47, 66**

Classical conditioning Learning by association. Occurs when two stimuli are repeatedly paired together – an unconditioned (unlearned) stimulus (UCS) and a new 'neutral' stimulus (NS). The neutral stimulus eventually produces the same response that was first produced by the unconditioned (unlearned) stimulus alone. **82, 98, 102, 108–109, 128, 131–132, 146–148, 160, 164**

Client-centred therapy A method of treatment for mental disorders where the focus is on the problem from the client's viewpoint rather than any diagnosis from the therapist. *See* counselling. **122–123**

Clinical Refers to a condition that has been medically diagnosed. **49–51, 53, 66, 81, 115, 123, 125, 136–137, 140, 143, 145, 147, 149, 151–152, 155, 158, 160, 188**

Closed questions Questions for which there is a fixed choice of responses determined by the question setter. For example, *Do you smoke?* (yes/no) **27, 37, 61, 65, 94, 186–189, 193, 207, 209, 211–212**

Coding The format in which information is stored in the various memory stores. **45–48, 52, 56–57, 62, 66–67, 70–71, 180**

Cognitive Refers to the process of 'knowing', including thinking, reasoning, remembering, believing. **18, 28, 39, 45, 50, 52–53, 61–63, 67, 71, 92, 105–107, 109–114, 121–125, 128, 130–133, 135, 140–147, 149–153, 156–157, 160–162, 164–165, 173, 203**

Cognitive approach The term 'cognitive' has come to mean 'mental processes', so this approach is focused on how our mental processes (e.g. thoughts, perceptions, attention) affect behaviour. **105–107, 109–110, 112–114, 121–125, 128, 131–133, 135, 145, 150–153, 165**

Cognitive behaviour therapy (CBT) A method for treating mental disorders based on both cognitive and behavioural techniques. From the cognitive viewpoint the therapy aims to deal with thinking, such as challenging negative thoughts. The therapy also includes behavioural techniques such as behavioural activation. **125, 151–153, 156, 161, 165, 203, 207**

Cognitive characteristics **140–145, 164**

Cognitive dissonance **7**

Cognitive distortion **141, 160**

Cognitive explanation **150–151, 161**

Cognitive interview (CI) A method of interviewing eyewitnesses to help them retrieve more accurate memories. It uses four main techniques, all based on evidence-based psychological knowledge of human memory – report everything, reinstate the context, reverse the order and change perspective. **45, 62–63, 67, 71, 75, 203**

Cognitive neuroscience The scientific study of biological structures that underpin cognitive processes. **107, 112–113, 124, 128, 132**

Cognitive style An individual's characteristic way of thinking. **28, 39**

Cognitive therapy A form of psychotherapy which attempts to change a client's thoughts and beliefs as a way of treating maladaptive behaviour. It differs from cognitive behaviour therapy because the latter involves some element of behavioural techniques. **125, 151–152, 160–161, 165, 173**

Collectivist A group of people who place more value on the 'collective' rather than on the individual, and on interdependence rather than on independence. The opposite is true of individualist culture. **17, 77, 88, 98, 123**

Commitment Minority influence is more powerful if the minority demonstrates dedication to their position, for example, by making personal sacrifices. This is effective because it shows the minority is not acting out of self-interest. **32–34, 38, 43**

Common sense **40**

Co-morbidity The presence of two or more coexisting unhealthy conditions or diseases. **155, 161**

Compliance A superficial and temporary type of conformity where we outwardly go along with the majority view, but privately disagree with it. The change in our behaviour only lasts as long as the group is monitoring us. **18, 37–38, 41–43**

'Computer metaphor' **128, 132**

Computer models **112–113, 128**

Concordance rate A measure of similarity (usually expressed as a percentage) between two individuals or sets of individuals on a given trait. **114–115, 129**

Conditioned response (CR) In classical conditioning, an unconditioned stimulus (UCS) naturally produces the unconditioned response (UCR). The UCS is repeatedly paired with a neutral stimulus (NS) so that eventually the NS produces the UCR which is now called the conditioned response (CR) and the NS becomes a conditioned stimulus (CS). **82, 102, 108, 128, 131–132, 146–148, 160**

Conditioned stimulus (CS) *See* Conditioned response (CR). **82, 93, 98, 102, 108, 131–132, 146, 148, 160, 175, 193**

Conditions of worth When a parent places limits or boundaries on their love of their children. For instance, a parent saying to a child, 'I will only love you if... you study medicine' or 'if you split up with that boy'. **122–123, 129, 133**

Confederate An individual in a study who is not a real participant and has been instructed how to behave by the researcher. **16–17, 22, 24–25, 30–32, 34, 38–43, 179**

Confidentiality An ethical issue concerned with a participant's right to have personal information protected. **36–37, 64, 158, 178–179, 189, 206, 209–210**

Conformity 'A change in a person's behaviour or opinions as a result of real or imagined pressure from a person or group of people' (Aronson 2011). **15–21, 30–32, 34–43, 58–59, 67, 71, 160, 177**

Explanations of **18**

Types of **18**

Confounding variables A kind of EV but the key feature is that a confounding variable varies systematically with the IV. Therefore we can't tell if any change in the DV is due to the IV or the confounding variable. **47, 53, 55, 61, 67, 89–91, 93, 95, 99, 170–175, 180–181, 206, 208, 210–211**

Congruence The aim of Rogerian therapy, when the self-concept and ideal self are seen to broadly accord or match. **122–123, 129, 133**

Consent **22, 36–37, 39, 64–65, 96, 127, 148–149, 160, 174, 178–179, 182, 189, 204, 206, 209–210**

Consistency Minority influence is most effective if the minority keeps the same beliefs, both over time and between all the individuals that form the minority. Consistency is effective because it draws attention to the minority view. **32–35, 38, 43, 184**

Consonant syllable Three-letter chunks with no vowels, also called a trigram. **46–47, 49, 54, 66**

Content analysis A kind of observational study in which behaviour is observed indirectly in pictorial or verbal material. A detailed analysis is made of, for example, books, diaries or TV programmes. May involve an initial qualitative analysis to produce categories, which then can be represented with qualitative data (examples from each category) or quantitative data analysis (counting the frequency of particular instances in each category). **159**

Context-dependent forgetting **56, 62, 67, 69, 71**

Continuous data Data that is not in categories, can take any value within a range. **196, 207**

Continuous recording Making a note of everything without pause. **184, 211**

Control condition The condition in a repeated measures design that provides a baseline measure of behaviour without the experimental treatment (IV). **54, 64, 149, 156, 169, 172, 180, 206, 210–211**

Control group In an experiment with an independent groups design, a group of participants who receive no treatment. Their behaviour acts as a baseline against which the effect of the independent variable (IV) may be measured. **31–32, 51, 55, 58, 80, 90, 92, 102, 110, 147, 149, 160, 174, 180, 204, 206**

Controlled observation Watching and recording behaviour within a structured environment, i.e. one where some variables are managed. **86 87, 99, 102–103, 182–183, 206**

Conversion explanation **32**

Correlation A mathematical technique in which a researcher investigates an association between two variables, called co-variables. **28, 36, 92, 96, 103, 117, 155, 161, 166, 187, 190–191, 193, 196, 204–207, 211–212**

Cost-benefit analysis Making a decision by weighing up costs (in terms of time, money, harm) against gains (in terms of value to society). **178–179**

Counselling A form of therapy that aims to increase a client's self-esteem through unconditional positive regard from the therapist. This is based on the concept that maladjusted behaviour or unhappiness occurs as a result of receiving conditional love in childhood and, as a result, continuing to strive for acceptance. Such striving blocks the ability to self-actualise. **95, 121–123, 125, 129, 179, 184, 192, 206, 212**

Counterbalancing An attempt to control for the effects of order in a repeated measures design: half the participants experience the conditions in one order, and the other half in the opposite order. **126, 171–173, 206, 210**

Counterconditioning Being taught a new association that is the opposite of the original association, thus removing the original association. **148**

Co-variables The variables investigated within a correlation, for example height and weight. They are not referred to as the independent and dependent variables because a correlation investigates the association between the variables, rather than trying to show a cause-and-effect relationship. **36, 117, 190–191, 196, 207, 210–211**

Covert observation Participants' behaviour is watched and recorded *without* their knowledge or consent. **127, 182, 185, 211**

Critical period The time within which an attachment must form if it is to form at all. Lorenz and Harlow noted that attachment in birds and monkeys had critical periods. Bowlby extended the idea to humans, proposing that human babies have a sensitive period after which it will be much more difficult to form an attachment. **80, 84–85, 90–92, 98–100, 102–103**

Critical value The value that a test statistic must reach in order for the null hypothesis to be rejected. **200–201, 207, 212**

Cross-cultural research A kind of natural experiment in which the IV is different cultural practices and the DV is a behaviour such as attachment. **25, 39, 89, 99, 103**

Cue A 'trigger' of information that allows us to access a memory. Such cues may be meaningful or may be indirectly linked by being encoded at the time of learning. Indirect cues may be external (environmental context) or internal (mood or degree of drunkenness). **55–57, 60, 67, 69–71, 75, 80, 164, 170–171, 206, 210**

Cued recall test A method of testing memory where participants are given material to be learned, and then when recall is tested, they are given cues (such as category names) to enhance recall. This permits one to discover all the words that are available not just those that are currently accessible. **55**

Cultural relativism **164**

Cultural variations 'Culture' refers to the norms and values that exist within any group of people. Cultural variations then are the differences in norms and values that exist between people in different groups. In attachment research we are concerned with the differences in the proportion of children of different attachment types. **73, 88–89, 99, 103**

Culture-bound Restricted to a particular culture, i.e. group of people defined by their shared practices. **87, 99, 139, 160**

Curvilinear relationship **16, 191, 212**

Darwin, Charles **108, 114–115**

Data **22–23, 28, 31, 36–37, 46, 48, 52, 59, 61, 63–66, 75–77, 83, 88–89, 93, 96–99, 106–107, 113, 115, 125–128, 132, 147, 152, 155–156, 158–159, 166, 173, 178–180, 182–187, 189–202, 204–207, 209–212**

- **Primary** **192–193, 207, 211–212**
- **Qualitative** **22–23, 37, 185–187, 192–193, 206–207, 211–212**
- **Quantitative** **23, 37, 185–186, 192–193, 196, 207, 212**
- **Secondary** **191–193, 207, 211–212**

Debrief A post-research interview designed to inform the participants of the true nature of the study and to restore them to the state they were in at the start of the study. **22–23, 64–65, 126–127, 178–179, 181, 204–206, 209–210**

Deception An ethical issue, most usually where a participant is not told the true aims of a study (e.g. what participation will involve) and thus cannot give truly informed consent. Occasionally deception may involve the provision of false information. **22–23, 25, 39, 178–179, 206, 210**

Decimals **32, 126, 147, 198–200, 205, 207, 212**

Decision-making **33, 52, 109, 143, 154, 161**

Deeper processing **32–35, 38, 43**

Defence mechanisms Unconscious strategies that the Ego uses to manage the conflict between the Id and the Superego. **120–121, 125, 129**

Demand characteristics Any cue from the researcher or from the research situation that may be interpreted by participants as revealing the purpose of an investigation. This may lead to a participant changing their behaviour within the research situation. **17, 23, 25, 38, 57, 59, 67, 107, 111, 127–128, 170–171, 173–175, 180, 183, 187, 206, 208, 210**

Dendrite Branching projections from the end of a neuron carry nerve impulses from neighbouring neurons towards the cell body. **118–119, 129, 133**

Denial An ego defence mechanism whereby anxiety is reduced simply by denying that there is a problem. **120, 129, 133**

Dependent variable (DV) The variable that is measured by the researcher. Any effect on the DV should be caused by the change in the IV. **31, 49, 64–65, 90, 96–97, 115, 123, 126–127, 158, 168–170, 172–175, 180–183, 185–186, 189–190, 193, 204, 208, 211**

Depression A mental disorder characterised by low mood and low energy levels. **113, 115, 119, 125, 128, 135–137, 140, 142–145, 150–153, 155, 160–162, 164–165, 173, 203, 207**

Descriptive statistics The use of graphs, tables and summary statistics to identify trends and analyse sets of data. **64, 194, 196**

Determinism The view that an individual's behaviour is shaped or controlled by internal or external forces rather than an individual's will to do something. **109, 111, 113, 115, 121, 124–125, 128–129, 133**

Deviation from ideal mental health Occurs when someone does not meet a set of criteria for good mental health. **138–139, 160, 163–164**

Deviation from social norms Concerns behaviour that is different from the accepted standards of behaviour in a community or society. **136–137, 160, 163**

Diachronic consistency Consistency over time. **32**

Diagnosis **136–138, 144–145, 157, 160, 164, 174, 183**

Diathesis-stress model **125, 154**

Digit span A way of measuring the capacity of short-term memory in terms of the maximum number of digits that can be recalled in the correct order. **46–47, 66**

Directional hypothesis States the direction of the difference or relationship. **31, 81, 126, 157, 168–169, 191, 210**

Discrete data Data that can only take certain values, for example the number of children in a class – you can't have half a child. **196**

Disinhibited attachment A type of insecure attachment where children do not form close attachments. Such children will treat strangers with inappropriate familiarity (overfriendliness) and may be attention-seeking. **92–93, 99, 103**

Disorganised attachment Characterised by a lack of consistent patterns of social behaviour. Such infants lack a coherent strategy for dealing with the stress of separation. For example, they show very strong attachment behaviour which is suddenly followed by avoidance or looking fearfully towards their caregiver. **95**

Displaced A form of ego defense where the individual unconsciously redirects the threatening emotion from the person or thing that has caused it onto a third party. For example, you might kick your dog after having a row with your girl/boyfriend. **28, 39, 121**

Displacement Same as displaced. **69, 120–121, 129, 133**

Dispositional explanation Any explanation of behaviour that highlights the importance of the individual's personality (i.e. their disposition). Such explanations are often contrasted with situational explanations. **15, 28–29, 39–40, 43**

Disruptive mood dysregulation disorder **142**

Distributions **88, 136, 195–197, 207, 212**

Dizygotic twins Non-identical twins formed from two fertilised eggs (or zygotes). **114–115, 129, 132, 155, 161**

Dopamine A neurotransmitter that generally has an excitatory effect and is associated with the sensation of pleasure. Unusually high levels are associated with schizophrenia and unusually low levels are associated with Parkinson's disease. **114, 154, 16**

Double-barrelled questions **189, 207**

Double-blind procedure Neither the participant nor researcher conducting the study are aware of the research aims or other important details of a study, and thus have no expectations that might alter a participant's behaviour. **180, 206, 211**

Double negatives **189, 207**

Drawing attention **34, 38, 121**

Dream interpretation **11, 121**

Drive reduction An animal is motivated to act in order to satisfy biological needs; once satisfied, the result is drive reduction. **82**

Drug therapy Treatment involving drugs, i.e. chemicals that have a particular effect on the functioning of the brain or some other body system. In the case of psychological disorders such drugs usually affect neurotransmitter levels. **125, 156–157, 161**

DSM-5 The Diagnostic and Statistical Manual of Mental Disorders. This is a classification system of mental disorders published by the American Psychiatric Association. It contains typical symptoms of each disorder and guidelines for clinicians to make a diagnosis. The most recent version is DSM-5. **136, 138, 140, 142, 144, 163**

Dual-task performance Refers to a research procedure where an individual is askec to perform two tasks simultaneously. If participants are slower doing these tasks at the same time than when doing them separately, it is assumed that both tasks compete for the same resources in the brain. For example, reading out loud and walking are two tasks that can be performed just as we separately as simultaneously. However reading out loud while writing a letter at the same time leads to reduced performance on each task. **53, 64, 66, 68**

Duration The length of time information can b held in memory. **45–49, 66, 70–71, 9**

DV *See* dependent variable. **168–175, 185, 190–191, 196, 206–207, 210**

Echoic memory The sensory register that store auditory information. **48, 70**

Eclectic **124–125**

Economy The state of a country or region in terms of the production and consumption of goods and services. **109, 128, 131, 150, 166, 202–203, 207, 212**

EEGs Electroencephalograph (EEG). A method of detecting activity in the living brain, electrodes are attached to a person's scalp to record general levels of electrical activity. **106, 115, 129**

ffect size A measure of the strength of the relationship between two variables. **192–193, 207**

go The 'reality check' that balances the conflicting demands of the Id and the Superego. **120–121, 123, 129**

laborative rehearsal **49, 66, 70**

lectra complex **120–121**

motional Related to a person's feelings or mood. **18, 20–21, 60–61, 74, 78–79, 81, 85, 90–95, 99, 103, 113, 140–146, 150, 156, 158, 160–162, 164, 191, 203, 211**

mpirical evidence **8–9, 121, 123, 129, 152, 161**

ncoding *See* coding. **56–57, 62, 67, 71**

ncoding specificity principle Recall is best when there is a large overlap between the information available at the time of retrieval (cues) and the information in the memory trace. **56–57, 67, 71**

ndocrine system One of the body's major information systems that instructs glands to release hormones directly into the bloodstream. These hormones are carried towards target organs in the body. **105, 116–117, 129, 133**

nhanced cognitive interview (ECI) **62–63, 67, 71**

nvironment **24, 34–35, 48, 52, 56–57, 62, 67, 80, 89, 99–100, 107–112, 114–116, 124–125, 127–133, 154–155, 161, 171, 174, 182–183, 191, 206**

pilepsy A disorder which causes occasional storms of electrical activity in the brain (a fit) leading to convulsions and loss of consciousness. **48**

pisodic buffer (EB) The component of the WMM that brings together material from the other subsystems into a single memory rather than separate strands. It also provides a bridge between working memory and long-term memory. **52–53, 66, 70, 151–152, 161, 165**

pisodic memory A long-term memory store for personal events. It includes memories of when the events occurred and of the people, objects, places and behaviours involved. Memories from this store have to be retrieved consciously and with effort. **50–51, 66, 70**

timating Obtaining an approximate answer. **198**

hical behaviour **136–137**

hical guidelines A set of principles designed to help professionals behave honestly and with integrity. **179**

hical issues These arise when a conflict exists between the rights of participants in research studies and the goals of research to produce authentic, valid and worthwhile data. **17, 21–24, 36, 38–39, 59, 64–65, 79, 81, 83, 96–98, 101, 109, 126, 128, 147, 149, 151, 157–158, 161, 165–166, 174, 178–181, 185, 188–189, 204–207, 209–210, 212**

hics committee A group of people within a research institution that must approve a study before it begins. **179**

hologists Researchers who promote the use of naturalistic observation to study animal behaviour. They focus on the importance of innate capacities and the adaptiveness of behaviour. **80**

Event sampling A target behaviour or event is first established then the researcher records this event every time it occurs. **19, 87, 127, 184–185, 206, 211**

Evolution The changes in inherited characteristics in a biological population over successive generations. **84, 92, 106, 113–115, 123, 125, 129, 147, 160**

Evolutionary theory An account for the changes in species over millions of years; characteristics that enhance survival and reproduction are naturally selected. **147**

Excitation When a neurotransmitter, such as adrenaline, increases the positive charge of the postsynaptic neuron. This increases the likelihood that the neuron will fire and pass on the electrical impulse. **118–119, 129**

Excoriation disorder **144**

Experimental condition The condition in a repeated measures design containing the independent variable as distinct from the control. **65, 169–173, 175, 178–180, 211**

Experimental design The different ways in which participants can be organised in relation to the experimental conditions. **31, 49, 63, 83, 115, 166, 172–173, 180–181, 206, 210, 212**

Experimental group The group in an independent groups design containing the independent variable as distinct from the control. **80, 90, 102, 180**

Experimental method Involves the manipulation of an independent variable (IV) to measure the effect on the dependent variable (DV). Experiments may be laboratory, field, natural or quasi. **125, 166, 168–169, 182, 206, 210, 212**

Experimental philosophy A field of psychology that uses empirical data as distinct from rational argument. **106**

External validity The degree to which a research finding can be generalised to, for example, other settings (ecological validity), other groups of people (population validity) and over time (temporal validity). **33, 47, 66, 77, 98, 113, 128, 174–175, 183, 193, 206–207, 210–211**

Externals Individuals who feel that their behaviour and/or thoughts are controlled by factors other than their personal decisions and/or action, such as being controlled by luck, fate or the behaviour of other people. **30–31, 36, 43**

Extinction In conditioning theory, the disappearance of a learned response when stimuli stop being paired (classical conditioning) or no reinforcement occurs (operant conditioning). **109, 148, 160**

Extraneous variable (EV) Any variable, other than the independent variable (IV), that may affect the dependent variable (DV) if it is not controlled. EVs are essentially nuisance variables that do not vary systematically with the IV. **100, 107, 109, 126, 128–129, 131, 133, 170–171, 174, 177, 181–183, 206, 210–211**

Extra-sensory perception (ESP) The ability to acquire information without the direct use of the five known physical senses. **56–57, 67, 205**

Extraversion A personality trait where the individual is outgoing and impulsive. **170, 205**

Eyewitness testimony (EWT) The ability of people to remember the details of events, such as accidents and crimes, which they themselves have observed. Accuracy of EWT can be affected by factors such as misleading information and anxiety. **45, 58–63, 65, 67–68, 71, 113, 128, 171, 203**

Failure to function adequately Occurs when someone is unable to cope with ordinary demands of day-to-day living. **138–139, 160, 163**

False memory **58**

Family studies Research where close relatives (parents and their children) are compared on certain traits such as IQ or mental disorder in order to determine whether genetic factors underlie these traits. **155**

Falsification Proving the truth of a research hypothesis by demonstrating that the null version is false. Scientific theories cannot be proved to be true; they can only be subjected to attempts to prove them false. **121**

Father In attachment research the father is anyone who takes on the role of the main male caregiver, this can be but is not necessarily the biological father. **21, 29, 73, 78–79, 85, 87, 98, 100, 102–103, 107, 121, 128, 154, 203, 207**

Field experiment An experiment that takes place in a natural setting within which the researcher manipulates the IV and records the effect on the DV. **25, 39, 147, 174–175, 183, 204, 206, 210**

Fight or flight response The way an animal responds when stressed. The body becomes physiologically aroused in readiness to fight an aggressor or, in some cases, flee. **60, 116, 117, 130**

File drawer problem Bias created because the results of some studies are not published (filed away), for example studies with negative results. **193, 202, 207, 212**

Fixation In psychoanalytic theory, a focus on a particular stage of psychosexual development because of over- or under-gratification during that stage. **120, 129**

Fixed choice option Question with a predetermined number of answers. **207, 211**

Flexibility Relentless consistency could be counter-productive if it is seen by the majority as unbending and unreasonable. Therefore minority influence is more effective if the minority show flexibility by accepting the possibility of compromise. **32–33, 38, 43, 67, 182, 187**

Flooding A behavioural therapy in which a person with a phobia is exposed to an extreme form of a phobic stimulus in order to reduce anxiety triggered by that stimulus. This takes place across a small number of long therapy sessions. **148–149, 160, 162, 165**

fMRI Functional magnetic resonance imaging. A method used to scan brain activity while a person is performing a task. It enables researchers to detect those regions of the brain which are rich in oxygen and thus are active. **106, 112, 115, 128–129, 132**

Fraction Indicates parts of a whole. **17, 96–97, 147, 198–199, 204, 207, 212**

Free recall A method of testing memory. Participants are given a list of to-be-remembered items, one at a time. Later the participant is asked to recall the items (e.g. by writing down as many items from the list as possible in any order they choose). **46, 66**

Free will The notion that humans can make choices and are not determined by internal biological or external forces. **106, 109, 111, 113, 121–122, 125, 128–129, 131**

Frequency **35, 127, 136–138, 146, 160, 163–164, 185, 187, 196–197, 207**

Freud, Sigmund **106, 120–125, 133**

Frontal lobes Responsible for logical thinking and making decisions. **48, 112, 154, 161, 165**

F-scale A test of tendencies towards fascism, used to assess the Authoritarian Personality. **28–29, 39, 40, 187**

Gender roles **21, 111, 121, 128**

Generalisation In conditioning, the tendency to transfer a response from one stimulus to another which is quite similar. **17, 39, 69, 77, 81–82, 93, 98, 100–101, 132, 146, 149, 155, 160–161, 174–177, 183, 193, 206**

Generalisation In relation to research findings, the extent to which findings and conclusions from a particular investigation can be broadly applied to the population. This is possible if the sample of participants is representative of the population. **17, 39, 69, 77, 81–82, 93, 98, 100–101, 132, 146, 149, 155, 160–161, 174–177, 183, 193, 206**

Genes Genes make up chromosomes and consist of DNA which codes the physical features of an organism (such as eye colour, height) and psychological features (such as mental disorder, intelligence). Genes are transmitted from parents to offspring, i.e. inherited. **99, 106, 113–115, 128–130, 132, 154–155, 161, 165**

Genetic explanations *See* Genes

Genetic determinism **125**

Genetic explanation **154–155**

Genotype The particular set of genes that a person possesses. **114–115, 124, 129–130, 132**

Gland An organ in the body that synthesises biochemical substances such as hormones. **88, 116–119, 129–130, 133**

Gradual commitment When you start with a small commitment, but this gradually increases and before you know it you have made more of a commitment than you intended. **34, 38, 43**

Introspection The first systematic experimental attempt to study the mind by breaking up conscious awareness into basic structures of thoughts, images and sensations. **106–108, 128, 130, 132**

Inverted-U theory **60–61, 67, 71**

Investigator effects Any effect of the investigator's behaviour (conscious or unconscious) on the research outcome (the DV). This may include everything from the design of the study to the selection of, and interaction with, participants during the research process. **63, 170–171, 180–181, 206**

IQ Stands for intelligence quotient because it was originally calculated by dividing test score by age. More recent tests use norms to work out a person's IQ based on their score and age. **90–92, 99, 136–138, 160, 164, 172, 212**

Irrational thoughts Also called dysfunctional thoughts. In Ellis's model and therapy, these are defined as thoughts that are likely to interfere with a person's happiness. Such dysfunctional thoughts lead to mental disorders such as depression. **150, 152–153, 161**

IV *See* independent variable. **168–175, 183, 185, 190–191, 195–196, 206, 210, 212**

Jargon **189, 207, 211**

Journal articles Report of a research study or group of studies related to a similar aim, published in an academic magazine (journal). **192**

Lab Any setting (room or other environment) specially fitted out for conducting research. A lab is not the only place where scientific experiments can be conducted. It is, however, the ideal place for experiments because it permits maximum control. Labs are not used exclusively for experimental research, for example controlled observations are also conducted in labs. **22, 24, 53, 55, 57, 59–60, 67, 69, 106–109, 111, 113, 115, 124, 128, 130–132, 170, 172, 174–175, 182–183, 193, 204, 206, 210**

Laboratory (lab) experiment An experiment that takes place in a controlled environment within which the researcher manipulates the IV and records the effect on the DV, whilst maintaining strict control of extraneous variables. **64–65, 69, 103, 124, 126, 132, 174–175, 183, 206, 210**

Laboratory (lab) studies Any research conducted in a lab, such as a controlled observation. Lab research is not always experimental. **55, 59–60, 67, 69, 107–108, 111, 113, 128, 131, 175, 193, 204**

Leading question A question which, because of the way it is phrased, suggests a certain answer. For example: 'Was the knife in his left hand?' leads a person to think that's where the knife was. **58–59, 65, 67–68, 71, 171, 189, 207**

Learning approach The explanation of behaviour using the principles of classical and operant conditioning. The view that all behaviour is learned, a position held by behaviourists. **105, 107–111, 124, 126, 128, 132–133**

Learning theory A set of theories from the behaviourist approach to psychology, that emphasise the role of learning in the acquisition of behaviour. Explanations for learning of behaviour include classical and operant conditioning. **82–84, 89, 98, 101–103, 107, 110, 127;** *also see* **Social learning theory**

Legitimacy of authority An explanation for obedience which suggests that we are more likely to obey people who we perceive to have authority over us. This authority is justified (legitimate) by the individual's position of power within a social hierarchy. **26–27, 39, 42–43**

Lifestyle choices **37, 78, 139**

Likert scale Respondents can indicate the extent to which they agree or disagree with a statement. There are usually five levels ranging from 'strongly agree' through 'neutral' to 'strongly disagree'. **36, 188–189, 207, 211**

Line graph A graph displaying continuous variables shows information as a series of data points connected by straight line segments. **196, 212**

Location The place where an order is issued. The relevant factor that influences obedience is the status or prestige associated with the location. **24–26, 37, 39, 40, 42**

Locus of control (LOC) Refers to the sense we each have about what directs events in our lives. Internals believe they are mostly responsible for what happens to them (internal locus of control). Externals believe it is mainly a matter of luck or other outside forces (external locus of control). **19, 30–31, 36, 39, 43**

Long-term memory (LTM) The permanent memory store. In LTM, coding is mainly semantic (meaning), it has unlimited capacity and can store memories for up to a lifetime. **45–52, 54, 56, 66, 68, 70–71, 112**

Longitudinal study **78, 95, 99, 103**

Lorenz, Konrad **80–84, 98, 101–102**

LTM *See* long-term memory. **46–52, 54–55, 57, 66, 69–70**

Machine reductionism Explanations which liken human behaviour to that of a machine. This means that such explanations tend to overlook the influence of emotional and social factors. **113, 124, 128, 132**

Maintenance rehearsal Verbally repeating an item to keep it in memory. **48, 52–53, 66, 70**

Major depressive disorder **142**

Majority influence The influence of the majority i.e. more than 50% of the people. *See* conformity. **32, 35, 38, 43**

Maladaptive The extent to which a behaviour is not adaptive (literally 'badly adapted'). Something that is adaptive increases an individual's well-being and survival. **125, 139**

Maslow, Abraham **106, 122–123, 129, 133**

Matched pairs design Pairs of participants are first matched on some variable(s) that may affect the dependent variable. Then one member of the pair is assigned to Condition A and the other to Condition B. **172–173, 211–212**

Maternal deprivation The emotional and intellectual consequences of separation between a child and his/her mother or mother substitute. Bowlby proposed that continuous care from a mother is essential for normal psychological development, and that prolonged separation from this adult causes serious damage to emotional and intellectual development. **73, 80, 90–92, 99–100, 103, 189**

Mathematics **198–199**

Mean The arithmetic average calculated by adding up all the values in a set of data and dividing by the number of values. **37, 46, 50, 58, 63–64, 92, 97, 112, 126, 136, 157, 172, 194–201, 212**

Measures of central tendency The general term for any measure of the average value in a set of data. **166, 194–195, 197, 207, 212**

Measures of dispersion The general term for any measure of the spread or variation in a set of scores. **194–195, 207**

Media **110–111, 122, 132, 159, 191**

Median The central value in a set of data when values are arranged from lowest to highest. **36, 158, 194–195, 197–198, 207, 212**

Mediational processes Cognitive factors (i.e. thinking) that influence learning and come between stimulus and response. **110–111, 128**

Memory conformity **58–59, 67, 71**

Memory trace The physical record or 'trace' of a memory. **223**

Meta-analysis The process of combining the findings from a number of studies on a particular topic. The aim is to produce an overall statistical conclusion (the effect size) based on a range of studies. A meta-analysis should not be confused with a *review* where a number of studies are compared and discussed. **33, 38, 63, 84, 88–89, 192–193, 212**

Milgram, Stanley **22–31, 34, 38–40, 42–43, 204, 211**

Minority influence A form of social influence in which a minority of people (sometimes just one person) persuades others to adopt their beliefs, attitudes or behaviours. Leads to internalisation or conversion, in which private attitudes are changed as well as public behaviours. **15, 32–35, 38, 43**

Misleading information Incorrect information given to an eyewitness usually after the event (hence often called '*post*-event information'). It can take many forms, such as leading questions and post-event discussion between co-witnesses and/or other people. **45, 58–59, 65, 67–68, 71**

Mnemonic techniques **56, 223**

Modal group Related to the mode, the most commonly occurring group. **194**

Mode The most frequently occurring value in a set of data. **119, 194, 197, 212**

Modelling From the observer's perspective, modelling is imitating the behaviour of a role model. From the role model's perspective, modelling is the precise demonstration of a specific behaviour that may be imitated by an observer. **83, 98, 110–111, 124–125, 194**

Models May refer to role models but term also used to refer to a representation of an aspect of behaviour, such as the multi-store model. **30, 34, 38, 48, 61, 85, 94–95, 102–103, 110, 112–113, 122, 125, 128, 132, 147**

Monotropic A term sometimes used to describe Bowlby's theory. Mono means 'one' and tropic means 'leaning towards'. This indicates that one particular attachment is different from all others and of central importance to a child's development. **84–85, 90, 100, 203**

Monozygotic twins Identical twins formed from one fertilised egg (or zygote). **114–115, 129, 155, 161**

Morality principle **120, 129**

Motivating **13**

Motor neurons These connect the CNS (central nervous system) to effectors such as muscles and glands. They have short dendrites and long axons. **118–119, 133**

MRI Magnetic resonance imaging (MRI) produces a three-dimensional image of the static brain which is very precise. A magnetic field causes the atoms of the brain to change their alignment when the magnet is on and emit various radio signals when the magnet is turned off. A detector reads the signals and uses them to map the structure of the brain. **106, 112, 115, 128–129, 132**

Multiple attachments Attachments to two or more people. Most babies appear to develop multiple attachments once they have formed one strong attachment to one of their carers. **76–77, 85, 98, 100, 102**

Multi-store model (MSM) A representation of how memory works in terms of three stores called the sensory register, short-term memory (STM) and long-term memory (LTM). It also describes how information is transferred from one store to another, what makes some memories last and what makes some memories disappear. **45, 47–50, 52–53, 66, 68, 70–71, 106, 112, 128**

Mundane realism Refers to how an experiment mirrors the real world. The simulated task environment is realistic to the extent to which experiences encountered in the simulated environment will occur in the real world. **132, 174–175, 206**

Myelin sheath **118, 129**

Myelinated axon **127**

nAffiliators People who have a need for affiliation, i.e. association with others; preferring the company of others. **19, 38, 41**

Natural experiment An experiment where the change in the IV is not brought about by the researcher but would have happened even if the researcher had not been there. The researcher records the effect on a DV they have decided on. **90, 147, 174–175, 183, 185, 206, 210**

Natural selection The major process that explains evolution whereby inherited traits that enhance an animal's reproductive success are passed on to the next generation and thus 'selected', whereas animals without such traits are less successful at reproduction and their traits are not selected. **114–115, 129, 132**

Naturalistic observation Watching and recording behaviour in the setting within which it would normally occur. **19, 77, 103, 126–127, 182–183, 206, 211**

Nature Those aspects of behaviour that are innate and inherited. Nature does not simply refer to abilities present at birth but to any ability determined by genes, including those that appear through maturation. **114, 124–125, 129**

Negative correlation As one co-variable increases the other decreases. For example, the number of people in a room and amount of personal space tend to be negatively correlated. **92, 103, 190–191, 196, 211**

Negative reinforcement In operant conditioning, a stimulus that increases the probability that a behaviour will be repeated because it leads to escape from an unpleasant situation and is experienced as rewarding. **82, 102, 108, 131–132, 146**

Negative skew A type of distribution in which the long tail is on the negative (left) side of the peak and most of the distribution is concentrated on the right. **197, 212**

Negative thinking **150**

Negative triad Beck proposed that there are three kinds of negative thinking that contribute to becoming depressed: negative views of the world, the future and the self. Such negative views lead a person to interpret their experiences in a negative way and so make them more vulnerable to depression. **150–152, 161–162**

Nervous system Consists of the central nervous system and the peripheral nervous system. Communicates using electrical signals. **105, 116–119, 126, 129–130, 133, 154**

Neural explanations The view that physical and psychological characteristics are determined by the behaviour of the nervous system, in particular the brain as well as individual neurons. **154–155, 165**

Neural networks A structure of interconnected neurons, each with multiple connections. **119**

Neurochemistry Relating to chemicals in the brain that regulate psychological functioning. **114**

Neurological Related to neurons/nervous system. **112**

Neuron The basic building blocks of the nervous system, neurons are nerve cells that process and transmit messages through electrical and chemical signals **105, 111, 116, 118–119, 124, 128–129, 133, 154, 156**

Neuroses A personality or mental disturbance characterised by anxiety but where the individual has not lost touch with reality, as distinct from psychosis. **121**

Neurotransmitter Brain chemicals released from synaptic vesicles that relay signals across the synapse from one neuron to another. Neurotransmitters can be broadly divided in terms of whether they are excitatory or inhibitory. **114–115, 118–119, 129, 133, 154, 156**

Neutral stimulus (NS) *See* Conditioned response (CR). **18–19, 38, 41, 82, 98, 108, 116–119, 128–129, 131–133, 146, 160**

Nodes of Ranvier The gaps in the myelin sheath that protect the axon of a neuron. **118, 129**

Nominal data Data that is in separate categories. **200–201, 207, 212**

Nomothetic An approach to research that focuses more on general laws of behaviour rather than on the individual, possibly unique case (the idiographic approach). **125**

Non-directional hypothesis Does not state the direction of the difference or relationship. **81, 126, 157, 168–169, 191, 210**

Non-participant observation The researcher remains outside of the group whose behaviour he/she is watching and recording. **87, 182–183, 211**

Noradrenaline A hormone and a neurotransmitter that generally has an excitatory effect, similar to the hormone adrenaline. The hormone is produced by the adrenal gland. **156, 161**

Normal distribution A symmetrical spread of frequency data that forms a bell-shaped pattern. The mean, median and mode are all located at the highest peak. **136, 197, 207, 212**

Normative social influence (NSI) An explanation of conformity that says we agree with the opinion of the majority because we want to gain social approval and be liked. This may lead to compliance. **18–19, 34–35, 38, 41–43**

Norms Something that is standard, usual or typical of a group. **18, 35, 38, 40, 43, 77, 88, 99, 111, 136, 139, 160, 163–164, 203**

Nucleus The control centre of a cell containing genetic material. **118, 129**

Nudge Unit **12–13, 203**

Nurture Those aspects of behaviour that are acquired through experience, i.e. learned from interactions with the physical and social environment. **114, 124–125, 129**

Obedience A form of social influence in which an individual follows a direct order. The person issuing the order is usually a figure of authority who has the power to punish when obedient behaviour is not forthcoming. **15, 22–31, 34, 36–40, 42–43, 169, 204, 211**

'Obedience alibi' **27, 39**

Objectivity Being uninfluenced by personal opinions or past experiences, being free from bias. As distinct from subjectivity. **108, 183, 206**

Observation A research study where only observational techniques are used. **19, 21–22, 46, 75–77, 79–80, 86–87, 96, 98–99, 102–103, 106, 110–111, 113, 124–128, 158, 159, 166, 180, 182–185, 192–193, 206, 211–212**

Observational design An overall plan for conducting observational research. **166, 184–185, 206, 211**

Observational learning **111, 125**

Observational study **21, 76, 159, 183–184**

Observational techniques A set of systems to increase the objectivity and validity of data collected when a researcher watches or listens to participants engaging in whatever behaviour is being studied. Observational techniques may be used in an experiment as a method of assessing the dependent variable. **96, 127, 166, 182–185, 211–212**

Observer bias In observational studies there is a danger that observers' expectations affect what they see or hear. This reduces the validity of the observations. **79, 98, 183, 185, 206, 211**

Obsessive-compulsive disorder *See* OCD. **135, 144–145, 162, 193**

OCD (obsessive-compulsive disorder) A condition characterised by obsessions and/or compulsive behaviour. Obsessions are cognitive whereas compulsions are behavioural. **112, 114, 135, 140, 144–145, 154–157, 161–162, 164–165, 203**

Oedipus complex Freud's explanation of how a boy resolves his love for his mother and feelings of rivalry towards his father by identifying with his father. **121, 133**

One-tailed test Form of test used with a directional hypothesis. **200–201**

Open questions Questions for which there is no fixed choice of response and respondents can answer in any way they wish. For example, *Why did you take up smoking?* **27, 37, 61, 65, 158, 186, 188–189, 192–193, 207, 209, 211**

Operant conditioning A form of learning in which behaviour is shaped and maintained by its consequences. Possible consequences of behaviour include positive reinforcement, negative reinforcement or punishment. **82–83, 98, 108–111, 125, 128, 131–132, 146, 160, 164;** *also see* **Reinforcement**

Operationalisation Clearly defining variables in terms of how they can be measured. **60, 90, 168–169, 181, 184–185, 191, 204, 206, 210**

Opportunity sampling A sample of participants produced by selecting people who are most easily available at the time of a study. **36, 37, 64, 176–177, 204, 206, 210**

Order effects In a repeated measures design, a confounding variable arising from the order in which conditions are presented, e.g. a practice effect or boredom effect. **173, 206, 210–211**

Orphan studies These concern children placed in care because their parents cannot look after them. An orphan is a child whose parents have either died or have abandoned them permanently. **73, 92–93, 99, 103**

Overt observation Participants' behaviour is watched and recorded *with* their knowledge and consent. **75, 77, 127, 182–183, 185, 206, 211**

Parahippocampal gyrus An area of the cerebra cortex (grey matter) that surrounds the hippocampus. Involved in memory. **112, 154, 161, 165**

Paraphilias **138**

Parapraxes A Freudian slip, a minor error in action, such as slips of the tongue, due to repressed emotions. **120**

Parapsychology **205**

Parasympathetic nervous system A division of the autonomic nervous system (ANS) which controls the relaxed state (rest and digest), conserving resources and promoting digestion and metabolism. The parasympathetic branch works in opposition to the sympathetic branch of the ANS. One or the other is active at any time. **116–117**

Parkinson's disease **155**

Participant observation The researcher becomes a member of the group whose behaviour he/she is watching and recording. **77, 87, 182–183, 211**

Participant reactivity The tendency for participants to react to cues from the researcher or the research environment. **170–171**

Participant variables Characteristics of individual participants (such as age, intelligence, etc.) that might influence the outcome of a study. **171–173, 206, 210**

Part-to-part ratio A comparison of one part of a whole to another part. A ratio is a comparison of two things. **198, 212**

Part-to-whole ratio A comparison of one part of a whole to the total number of parts in the whole. **198, 212**

Pavlov, Ivan **108, 128, 131**

Peer review The assessment of scientific work by others who are specialists in the same field, to ensure that any research intended for publication is of high quality. **166, 202–203, 207, 212**

Pelmanism **47**

Penis envy **121**

Percentages **31, 37, 144, 158–159, 198, 207**

Peripheral nervous system (PNS) Sends information to the CNS from the outside world, and transmits messages *from* the CNS to muscles and glands in the body. **116, 118–119, 129, 133**

Persistent depressive disorder **142**

PET scan Positron emission tomography. A brain-scanning method used to study activity in the brain. Radioactive glucose is ingested and can be detected in the active areas of the brain. **112**

Phallic stage In psychoanalytic theory, the third stage of psychosexual development when the organ-focus is on the genitals. **120–121**

Phenotype The characteristics of an individual determined by both genes and the environment. **114–115, 124, 129, 130, 132**

Phenylketonuria (PKU) An inherited disorder that prevents metabolism of phenylalanine, resulting in a build-up of poisonous substances that cause brain damage. If the disorder is detected at birth, the individual can be given a diet that avoids phenylalanine and thus prevents the potential brain damage. **115**

hobia An irrational fear of an object or situation. **109, 121, 125, 135, 140–142, 144, 146–149, 158, 160, 162, 164–165, 169, 175**

honological loop (PL) The component of the WMM that processes information in terms of sound. This includes both written and spoken material. It's divided into the phonological store and the articulatory process. **52–53, 64, 66, 68, 70**

honological store (PS) A component of the phonological loop which acts as an 'inner ear', i.e. storing sounds. **22, 52, 66, 70, 178–179, 210**

hysical harm **22**

ilot study A small-scale version of an investigation that takes place before the real investigation is conducted. The aim is to check that procedures, materials, measuring scales, etc., work. The aim is also to allow the researcher to make changes or modifications if necessary. **21, 25, 63, 65, 88, 96, 127, 180–181, 184, 189, 208, 211**

ituitary gland Called the master gland of the body's hormone system because it directs much of the hormone activity. **117, 130, 133**

KU *See* phenylketonuria. **114–115, 130**

lacebo A treatment that should have no effect on the behaviour being studied, it contains no active ingredient. Therefore it can be used to separate out the effects of the IV from any effects caused merely by receiving *any* treatment. **55, 115, 156–157, 161, 180, 211**

leasure principle In psychoanalytic theory, the drive to do things which produce pleasure or gratification, and to avoid pain. **120, 129**

olygenic **154, 161**

opulation A group of people who are the focus of the researcher's interest, from which a smaller sample is drawn. **22, 29, 34, 65, 77, 88–89, 96, 114, 136, 145, 147, 158, 176–177, 189, 192–193, 197, 200, 206, 210, 212**

NS *See* peripheral nervous system. **116, 118–119, 129, 133**

ositive correlation As one co-variable increases so does the other. For example, the number of people in a room and noise tend to be positively correlated. **28, 103, 117, 187, 190–191, 196, 212**

ositive reinforcement In operant conditioning, a stimulus that increases the probability that a behaviour will be repeated because it is pleasurable. **102, 108, 132, 146, 164**

ositive skew A type of distribution in which the long tail is on the positive (right) side of the peak and most of the distribution is concentrated on the left. **197, 212**

ost-event discussion (PED) Occurs when there is more than one witness to an event. Witnesses may discuss what they have seen with co-witnesses or with other people. This may influence the accuracy of each witness's recall of the event. **58–59, 61, 67–68**

ostsynaptic neuron **119, 156**

Postsynaptic receptor site A receptor on the neuron that is receiving the information at the synapse. A neurotransmitter locks into a specific receptor on the receiving neuron and this triggers an electrical signal in the receiving neuron. **119, 129**

Preconscious Consists of information and ideas that could be retrieved easily from memory and brought into consciousness. **120, 133**

Prefrontal cortex **51, 66, 70, 112**

Premenstrual dysphoric disorder **142**

Presumptive consent A method of dealing with lack of informed consent or deception, by asking a group of people who are similar to the participants whether they would agree to take part in a study. If this group of people consents to the procedures in the proposed study, it is presumed that the real participants would agree as well. **179, 210**

Presynaptic neuron The transmitting neuron, before the synapse. **119, 156**

Presynaptic terminal The end of the transmitting neuron, ending at a synapse. **119, 133**

Primary attachment figure The person who has formed the closest bond with a child, demonstrated by the intensity of the relationship. This is usually a child's biological mother but other people can fulfil the role. **76, 78–79, 83–85, 89–91, 94, 98, 102–103**

Primary data Information that has been obtained first-hand by a researcher for the purposes of a research project. In psychology, such data is often gathered directly from participants as part of an experiment, self-report or observation. **192–193, 207, 211–212**

Primary drive Innate drives (motivators) such as for food, water and sex. **82, 102**

Prior general consent Prospective participants in a research study are asked if they would take part in certain kinds of research, including ones involving deception. If they say yes they have given their general consent to taking part in such research. **179, 210**

Privacy An ethical issue that refers to a zone of inaccessibility of mind or body and the trust that this will not be 'invaded'. Contrasts with confidentiality. Can be dealt with in some situations by providing anonymity. **37, 65, 174, 178, 183, 206**

Privation The failure to develop any attachments during early life. This is contrasted with 'deprivation' or 'disruption' where attachment bonds have formed but may be disrupted either through physical or simply emotional separation (the *loss* of attachments). **73, 80–81, 90–92, 99–100, 102–103, 111, 189**

Proactive interference (PI) Forgetting occurs when older memories, already stored, disrupt the recall of newer memories. The degree of forgetting is greater when the memories are similar. **54–55, 67, 69–70**

Probability (*p*) A numerical measure of the likelihood or chance that certain events will occur. **177, 200–201, 205, 207**

Procedural memory A long-term memory store for our knowledge of how to do things. This includes our memories of learned skills. We usually recall these memories without making a conscious or deliberate effort. **50–51, 66, 68, 70**

Prosocial **136**

Protection from harm **178–179, 206, 209**

Proximity The physical closeness or distance of an authority figure to the person they are giving an order to. Also refers to the physical closeness of the teacher to the victim (learner) in Milgram's studies. **24–26, 39–40, 42, 74, 86–87, 89, 99–100, 148, 210**

Proximity-seeking Wishing to remain in close contact with a caregiver/attachment figure. **86–87, 89, 99**

Psychic determinism **121, 125, 129, 133**

Psychoactive drugs A chemical substance that alters one's mental processes. **115, 119, 129**

Psychoanalysis A form of psychotherapy, originally developed by Sigmund Freud, that is intended to help individuals become aware of long-repressed feelings and issues by using techniques such as free association and dream analysis. **106, 121, 123, 125, 129**

Psychodynamic A perspective that describes the different forces (dynamics), most of which are unconscious, that operate on the mind and direct human behaviour and experience. **28, 105–107, 120–125, 128–129, 133**

Psychodynamic explanation **28**

Psychological development **90–91, 203**

Psychological harm **36–37, 64–65, 178**

Psychology The scientific study of the mind, behaviour and experience. **6, 12, 106**

  Goals of **12**

Psychomotor agitation Unintentional and purposeless motions associated with high levels of distress. **142**

Psychosexual stages Five developmental stages that all children pass through. At each stage there is a different conflict, the outcome of which determines future development **120, 129**

Psychotherapeutic drugs **203**

Publication bias The tendency for academic journals to publish only positive findings, or findings that agree with existing theory. **193, 202, 207, 212**

Punishment Any procedure that decreases the likelihood that a behaviour will be repeated because the overall experience is unpleasant. **20, 28–29, 40, 82, 102, 108, 128, 131–132, 146**

Qualitative data Data that is expressed in words and non-numerical (although qualitative data may be converted to numbers for the purposes of analysis). **22–23, 37, 185–187, 192–193, 206–207, 211–212**

Qualitative data analysis Any means of extracting meaning from data that focuses more on words (i.e. what participants say) than on forms of numerical data. Qualitative analyses interpret the meaning of an experience to the individual(s) concerned. **22–23, 37, 185–187, 192–193, 206–207, 211–212**

Qualitative methods **125, 192**

Quantitative data Data that can be counted, usually given as numbers. **23, 37, 166, 185–186, 192–193, 196–197, 207–212**

Quantitative data analysis Any means of extracting meaning from data that uses numerical data as the basis for investigation and interpretation (e.g. descriptive or inferential statistics). **23, 37, 166, 185–186, 192–193, 196–197, 207–212**

Quasi-experiment A study that is almost an experiment but lacks key ingredients. The IV has not been determined by anyone (the researcher or any other person) – the 'variables' simply exist, such as being old or young. Strictly speaking this is not an experiment. **61, 96–97, 115, 127, 155, 158, 174–175, 181, 183, 189, 206, 208, 210**

Questionnaire A set of written questions (sometimes referred to as 'items') used to assess a person's thoughts and/or experiences. **22, 27, 36, 58–59, 61, 64–65, 94, 96–97, 117, 127, 158, 177, 180, 186–189, 192–193, 205, 207, 211–212**

Random allocation An attempt to control for participant variables in an independent groups design which ensures that each participant has the same chance of being in one condition as any other. **172–173, 181, 206, 210**

Random sampling A sample of participants produced by using a random technique such that every member of the target population being tested has an equal chance of being selected. **82, 89, 176–177, 181, 208, 210**

Random technique A method that ensures that each item has an equal chance of being selected. This can be achieved with random number tables or numbers drawn from a hat. **173**

Randomisation The use of chance methods to control for the effects of bias when designing materials and deciding the order of conditions. **170–171, 206, 210**

Randomly generated list **171**

Range A simple calculation of the dispersion in a set of scores which is worked out by subtracting the lowest score from the highest score and adding 1 as a mathematical correction. **36, 64, 158, 195, 198–199, 212**

Rating scale A means of assessing attitudes or experiences by asking a respondent to rate statements on a scale of 1 to 3 or 1 to 5, etc. Produces ordinal data. **158, 187–189, 207, 211**

Ratio A comparison of two things. **109, 147, 177, 198, 212**

Rational choices **11**

Raw scores Original data that has not been transformed in any way, for example by working out an average. **195–196, 207**

Reactive depression Depression that can be attributed to a reaction to a life event such as the death of a loved one. **151, 161**

Real-world studies **60**

Reality principle In psychoanalytic theory, the drive to accommodate to the demands of the environment in a realistic way. **120, 129**

REBT (Rational emotive behaviour therapy) An example of cognitive behavioural therapy (CBT) where maladaptive behaviour is attributed to faulty thinking. Therefore the therapy aims to change this faulty thinking, making it rational. REBT acknowledges the importance of emotions as well as thinking. The outcome is behavioural change, thus R + E + B. **151–152, 161, 165**

Recall **46–51, 53–63, 65–71, 94, 124, 132, 143, 171–175, 190, 192, 195–196**

Reciprocal determinism A person's behaviour both influences and is influenced by personal factors and the social environment. **111, 125, 128, 133**

Reciprocal inhibition In the case of opposing muscles, one is inhibited by the other's action. **148, 160**

Reciprocity A description of how two people interact. Caregiver–infant interaction is reciprocal in that both caregiver and baby respond to each other's signals and each elicits a response from the other. **74–75, 78, 83, 98, 102**

Reductionism **113, 123–125, 128, 132**

Rehearsal **46, 48–49, 52–53, 66, 70**

Reinforcement A consequence of behaviour that increases the likelihood of that behaviour being repeated. Can be positive or negative. **82, 102, 108–111, 124, 128, 131–132, 146, 164;** *also see* **Operant conditioning**

Relay neurons These connect the sensory neurons to the motor or other relay neurons. They have short dendrites and short axons. **118–119, 133**

Reliability Refers to how consistent a measuring device is – and this includes psychological tests or observations which assess behaviour. **75, 87, 98–99, 102–103, 113, 127, 184**

Repeated measures All participants take part in all conditions of the experiment. **126, 172–173, 180, 194, 200, 206–207, 210, 212**

Replication The opportunity to repeat an investigation under the same conditions in order to test the validity and reliability of its findings. **21, 23, 25, 39, 47, 57, 66, 81, 91, 103, 132, 174–175, 183, 187, 206–207, 210**

Repression A form of ego defence whereby anxiety-provoking material is kept out of conscious awareness as a means of coping. **120, 129, 133**

Research **16–17, 19–25, 27–40, 42–43, 46–52, 54–69, 71, 74–85, 87–96, 98–102, 106–113, 115, 117, 122, 124, 126–128, 130–132, 141, 146, 151, 154–158, 161–162, 166, 168–196, 198–208, 210–212**

- **Hypothesis** **21, 31, 53, 62, 64, 81, 96, 126, 157, 168–169, 180–181, 184–185, 189, 191, 193, 200–201, 207–208, 210–212**
- **Limitations** **49, 52, 75, 79, 131, 174–175, 182–183**
- **Methods** **168–212**
- **Support** **17, 19, 23, 25, 27, 29, 31, 33, 35, 38–39, 43, 49, 57, 60, 66–67, 81, 84, 95, 98–99, 151, 155, 161**

Also see **Validity**

Researcher bias **177**

Resistance to obedience **31**

Resistance to social influence Refers to the ability of people to withstand the social pressure to conform to the majority or to obey authority. This ability to withstand social pressure is influenced by both situational and dispositional factors. **15, 30–31, 39, 43**

Response bias A tendency for interviewees to respond in the same way to all questions, regardless of context. This would bias their answers. **29, 36, 39, 67, 187, 207, 211**

Retrieval Recall of information previously stored in memory. **45, 48, 55–57, 66–67, 69, 70–71, 112**

Retrieval failure A form of forgetting. It occurs when we don't have the necessary cues to access memory. The memory is available but not accessible unless a suitable cue is provided. **45, 55–57, 67, 69–71**

Retroactive interference (RI) Forgetting occurs when newer memories disrupt the recall of older memories already stored. The degree of forgetting is again greater when the memories are similar. **54–55, 69–70**

Retrospective consent Obtaining permission after a study or event. **179, 210**

Review A consideration of a number of studies that have investigated the same topic in order to reach a general conclusion about a particular hypothesis. **35, 47, 51, 56, 60, 67, 84, 89, 95, 99, 149, 151, 153, 155, 157, 166, 181, 192, 202–203, 207, 212**

Right to withdraw An ethical issue; participants should have the right to withdraw from participating in a research study if they are uncomfortable with the study. **22, 36–37, 64–65, 96, 178–179, 206**

Right to withhold data **179, 210**

Rogers, Carl **106, 122–123, 125, 129, 133**

Role model People who have qualities we would like to have and we identify with, thus we model or imitate their behaviour and attitudes. **34, 38, 110, 125, 128, 132**

Sample A group of people who take part in a research investigation. The sample is drawn from a (target) population and is presumed to be representative of that population, i.e. it stands 'fairly' for the population being studied. **27, 29, 35–37, 64–65, 69, 77, 82, 88–92, 96, 99, 107, 126, 155, 158–159, 161, 176–177, 181, 185, 193, 200, 204, 206–210**

Sampling frame The source material from which a sample is drawn. **176**

Sampling techniques The method used to select people from the population. **89, 126, 158, 176–177**

Scanning Scanning is used for research purposes and also used to record the structure and action of the brain and body, such as PET scans and MRI scans. This is done for research and also to detect abnormalities such as tumours. **106, 112, 114–115, 129**

Scattergram A type of graph that represents the strength and direction of the relationship between co-variables in a correlational analysis. **36, 92, 96, 152, 190–191, 196, 207, 212**

Schema A mental framework of beliefs and expectations that influence cognitive processing. They are developed from experience. **62, 67, 112–113, 124, 128, 130, 132, 150–151, 161, 165**

Schizophrenia A severe mental disorder where contact with reality and insight are impaired, a kind of psychosis. **114, 121, 123, 129, 137, 183, 192**

Schizotypal personality disorder (SPD) A personality disorder characterised by difficulties with relationships, and being emotionally and socially withdrawn. **137, 160**

Science A means of acquiring knowledge through systematic and objective investigation. The aim is to discover general laws. **23, 26, 29–30, 39, 43, 90, 106–107, 112–113, 115, 121, 123–124, 128, 132, 191, 202–203**

Scientific method An objective means of testing hypotheses in order to develop empirically-based explanations/theories. **107, 113, 115, 128–129**

Secondary attachment figure The closest emotional bond is with a primary attachment figure; additional support is available from secondary attachment figures who provide an emotional safety net. **78–79**

Secondary data Information that has already been collected by someone else and so pre-dates the current research project. In psychology, such data might include the work of other psychologists or government statistics. **191–193, 207, 211–212**

Secondary drive Learned drives (motivators) acquired though association with a primary drive, such as money that enables primary drives to be satisfied. **82, 98**

Secure attachment Generally thought of as the most desirable attachment type, associated with psychologically healthy outcomes. In the Strange Situation this is shown by moderate stranger and separation anxiety and ease of comfort at reunion. **84, 86–88, 92, 94–95, 97, 99–100, 103**

Secure-base behaviour Secure attachment provides a sense of safety to enable exploration and independence. **74, 86**

Selective serotonin reuptake indicator (SSRI) An antidepressant group of drugs that increase available amounts of serotonin by preventing their reabsorption by the transmitting neuron. **119, 156–157, 161, 165, 203**

Self The ideas and values that characterise 'I' and 'me' and includes perception and valuing of 'what I am' and 'what I can do'. **122–124, 129, 142–143, 145, 150, 152, 161–162, 165**

Self-actualisation The desire to grow psychologically and fulfill one's full potential – becoming what you are capable of. **122–123, 129, 133, 139, 160**

Self-concept The self as it is currently experienced, all the attitudes we hold about ourselves. **122–125**

Self-esteem The feelings that a person has about their self-concept. **122, 125, 129, 138, 140, 143, 145, 150, 161, 163–164**

Self-harm **142–143, 161, 164**

Self-report technique Any method in which a person is asked to state or explain their own feelings, opinions, behaviours and/or experiences related to a given topic. **77, 94, 97, 99, 103, 107, 158, 180, 182, 186–189, 192, 199, 207, 211–212**

Self-reporting **94, 107**

Self-talk **13**

Semantic memory A long-term memory store for our knowledge of the world. This includes facts and our knowledge of what words and concepts mean. These memories usually also need to be recalled deliberately. **50–51, 66, 70, 112**

Semantically The meaning of something, such as a word. **46, 48**

Semi-structured interview An interview that combines some predetermined questions (as in a structured interview) and some questions developed in response to answers given (as in an unstructured interview). **37, 186, 207, 211**

Sensory neurons These carry messages from the PNS (peripheral nervous system) to the CNS. They have long dendrites and short axons. **118–119, 133**

Sensory register The memory stores for each of our five senses, such as vision (iconic store) and hearing (echoic store). Coding in the iconic sensory register is visual and in the echoic sensory register it is acoustic (sounds). The capacity of sensory registers is huge (millions of receptors) and information lasts for a very short time (less than half a second). **46, 48–49, 66, 70**

Separation anxiety Distress shown by an infant when separated from an attachment figure. **76–77, 86–87, 98–100, 102–103**

Serotonin **81, 114–115, 119, 129, 154–157, 161, 165**

Serotonin-noradrenaline reuptake inhibitor (SNRI) **156–157, 161, 165**

Sexual imprinting Acquiring a template of the characteristics of a desirable mate. **80, 98, 102**

Short-term memory (STM) The limited-capacity memory store. In STM, coding is mainly acoustic (sounds), capacity is between 5 and 9 items on average, duration is about 18 seconds. **46–48, 52, 56, 66, 68, 70, 132**

Sign test A statistical test used to analyse the difference in scores between related items (e.g. the same participant tested twice). Data should be nominal or better. **126, 166, 200–201, 207, 212**

Significance A statistical term indicating that the research findings are sufficiently strong to enable a researcher to reject the null hypothesis under test and accept the research hypothesis. **78, 169, 192, 200–201, 207, 212**

Significance level The level of probability (p) at which it has been agreed to reject the null hypothesis. **200, 207, 212**

ignificant figures Giving a rough idea of a number by substituting zeros as place holders. In a number with two significant figures we keep the two most important digits and replace others with zeros, rounding up if necessary. **199, 207**

ingle-blind procedure A type of research design in which a participant is not aware of research aims and/or of which condition of the experiment they are receiving. **180**

ituational variables Features of the immediate physical and social environment which may influence a person's behaviour (such as proximity, location and uniform). The alternative is dispositional variables where behaviour is explained in terms of personality. **15, 17, 24–26, 28, 39–40, 42–43, 171, 210**

kewed distribution A spread of frequency data that is not symmetrical, where the data clusters at one end. **196–197, 207**

kinner, BF **106, 108–109, 128, 131**

LT *See* social learning theory. **110–111, 128**

nowball effect A process that starts from an initial state of small significance and increasingly becomes larger, such as starting with only a small group of people supporting an idea and gradually more and more people are supportive. **32, 34, 38, 43**

NRIs Serotonin–norepinephrine reuptake inhibitors, a group of antidepressant drugs. **156–157, 161, 165**

NS *See* somatic nervous system. **116, 129**

ocial anxiety (social phobia) **140**

ocial approval **18, 30, 43, 58, 67**

ocial change This occurs when whole societies, rather than just individuals, adopt new attitudes, beliefs and ways of doing things. Examples include accepting that the Earth orbits the Sun, women's suffrage, gay rights and environmental issues. **15, 34–35, 38, 43, 203**

ocial cryptomnesia When social change occurs, the new attitude becomes an integral part of the society's culture, and the source of the minority influence that led to it is often forgotten. 'Cryptomnesia' refers to the experience that an idea is new and original whereas in fact it is a memory from the past. For example, a person writes a song they believe is their own but in fact they heard it before. **34, 38, 43**

ocial desirability bias A tendency for respondents to answer questions in such a way that presents themselves in a better light. **127, 181, 187, 207, 211**

ocial hierarchy A structure with a few people at the top having power over those at lower levels of the structure. **26**

ocial identity theory (SIT) The theory that suggests your behaviour is motivated by your social identity. A person's self-image has two components: personal identity and social identity. Personal identity is based on your characteristics and achievements. Social identity is determined by the various social groups to which you belong, your 'ingroups'. **21, 23, 29, 38–39**

Social influence The process by which individuals and groups change each other's attitudes and behaviours. Includes conformity, obedience and minority influence. **14–16, 18–20, 22, 24, 26, 28, 30–43, 181, 204**

Social learning theory A way of explaining behaviour that includes both direct and indirect reinforcement, combining learning theory with the role of cognitive factors. **83, 98, 105, 107, 109–111, 124–125, 128, 132–133**

Social norms Something that is standard, usual or typical of a group. **35, 136–139, 160, 163–164**

Social phobia (social anxiety) An excessive fear of social situations such as leaving the house or speaking in public. **140–141, 149**

Social releasers A social behaviour or characteristic that elicits a caregiving reaction. **84–85, 99, 102**

Social roles The 'parts' people play as members of various social groups. Everyday examples include parent, child, student, passenger and so on. These are accompanied by expectations we and others have of what is appropriate behaviour in each role, for example caring, obedient, industrious, etc. **15, 20–21, 38, 40, 42–43**

Social support The presence of people who resist pressures to conform or obey can help others to do the same. These people act as models to show others that resistance to social influence is possible. **18–19, 30–31, 39, 43**

Soft determinism The view that behaviour may be predictable (caused by internal/external factors) but there is also room for personal choice from a limited range of possibilities (restricted free will). **113, 125, 128**

Somatic nervous system (SNS) Transmits information from receptor cells in the sense organs to the CNS. It also receives information from the CNS that directs muscles to act. **116, 129, 133**

Specific phobia One type of phobia where fear is linked to a particular class of objects such as spiders or heights. **140–141, 149**

Spinal cord Part of the central nervous system, a bundle of nerves from the brain transmitting nervous signals between the brain and the rest of the body. **116, 118–119, 129, 133**

SSRI *See* selective serotonin reuptake inhibitor. **119, 156–157, 161, 165, 203**

Stages of attachment Many developmental theories identify a sequence of qualitatively different behaviours linked to specific ages. In the case of 'stages of attachment' qualitatively different infant (baby) behaviours are linked to specific ages, and all babies go through them in the same order. **73, 76–78, 92, 98, 102–103**

Standard deviation A sophisticated measure of dispersion in a set of scores. It tells us how much scores deviate from the mean by calculating the difference between the mean and each score. All the differences are added up and divided by the number of scores. This gives the variance. The standard deviation is the square root of the variance. **126, 136, 194–197, 199, 207, 212**

Standard form Shorthand used to express very large or very small numbers. The formula to use is: [number between 1 and 10] $\times 10^{\text{[to the power of x]}}$ **199, 207**

Standard police interview **63, 71**

Standardisation Using exactly the same formalised procedures and instructions for all participants in a research study so as to avoid investigator effects caused by different procedures/instructions. **57, 106–107, 126, 128, 170–171, 173, 181, 187–189, 204, 206–207, 210–211**

Standardised instructions A set of instructions that are the same for all participants so as to avoid investigator effects caused by different instructions. **126, 171, 210–211**

Stanford prison experiment **20, 38, 42, 183**

State-dependent forgetting **56–57, 67**

Statistical analysis **187, 193, 207**

Statistical infrequency Occurs when an individual has a less common characteristic, for example being more depressed or less intelligent than most of the population. **136–138, 160, 163–164**

Statistical test (Inferential test) Procedures for drawing logical conclusions (inferences) about the population from which samples are drawn. **166, 192, 200–202, 207, 212**

Statistical testing Provides a way of determining whether hypotheses should be accepted or rejected. By using a statistical test we can find out whether differences or relationships between variables are significant (meaningful) or are likely to have occurred by chance. **166, 192, 200–201, 207, 212**

Statistics A method of collecting, summarising and analysing data for the purpose of drawing some conclusions about the data. **64, 136, 191–194, 196–197**

Stereotypes A perception of an individual in terms of some readily available feature, such as their group membership or physical attractiveness, rather than their personal attributes. **21, 28, 38–39, 79, 89–90, 98, 202**

STM *See* short-term memory. **46–49, 52–53, 56, 66–68, 70–71, 132**

Strange Situation A controlled observation designed to test attachment security. Babies are assessed on their response to playing in an unfamiliar room, being left alone, left with a stranger and being reunited with a caregiver. **86–89, 92, 94, 99, 103, 182**

Stranger anxiety Distress shown by an infant when approached by an unfamiliar person. **76–77, 86–87, 92, 98, 100, 102**

Stratified sampling A sampling technique in which groups of participants are selected in proportion to their frequency in the population in order to obtain a representative sample. The aim is to identify sections of the population, or strata, that need to be represented in the study. Individuals from those strata are then selected for the study using a random technique. If the sample is not randomly selected from the stratum, it is then a quota sample. **177, 210–211**

Structuralism Any theory that aims to study the relationship among phenomena rather than the phenomena themselves, and the systems formed by these relations. **106, 128**

Structured interview Any interview where the questions are decided in advance, basically a questionnaire delivered by a person. **23, 37, 94, 125, 186–187, 207, 209**

Structured observations The researcher uses various 'systems' to organise observations, such as a sampling technique and behavioural categories. **184–185, 192–193, 211–212**

Summation The process that determines whether or not an action potential will be triggered, based on the combined effects of the excitatory and inhibitory signals of the neurotransmitters. **119, 129**

Superego The moralistic part of our personality which represents the ideal self – how we ought to be. **120–121, 123, 129**

Survival of the fittest **132**

Sympathetic nervous system A division of the autonomic nervous system (ANS) which activates internal organs for vigorous activities and emergencies, such as the 'fight or flight' response. It consists of nerves that control, for example, increased heart rate and breathing, and decreased digestive activity. The sympathetic branch works in opposition to the parasympathetic branch of the ANS. **116–117**

Symptom severity **156–157**

Symptom substitution **149, 160, 162**

Synapse **115, 118–119, 129, 154, 156–157, 161**

Synaptic transmission The process by which neighbouring neurons communicate with each other by sending chemical messages across the gap (the synapse) that separates them. **105, 114, 118–119, 129, 133**

Synaptic vesicles Small sacs on the end of a presynaptic neuron that contain neurotransmitters that will be released into a synapse. **119, 129, 156**

Synchronic consistency Consistency between group members. **32, 43**

Systematic desensitisation (SD) A behavioural therapy designed to reduce an unwanted response, such as anxiety. SD involves drawing up a hierarchy of anxiety-provoking situations related to a person's phobic stimulus, teaching the person to relax, and then exposing them to phobic situations. The person works their way through the hierarchy whilst maintaining relaxation. **125, 136, 147–149, 160, 162, 164–165, 203**

Systematic sample A method of obtaining a representative sample by selecting every 5th, 7th, 10th or whatever person. This can be random if the first person is selected using a random method; then you select every 5th, 7th, 10th person after this. **176–177, 206**

The back page

The authors would like to thank our fantastic support team at Illuminate Publishing – first and foremost **Rick Jackman** who managed the superhuman task of bringing this project to fruition and with good humour! We would also like to thank the rest of the team at Illuminate – **Peter Burton**, **Clare Jackman**, **Saskia Burton** and **Adrian Moss.**

The second enormous thanks goes to the world's most fabulous editor **Nic Watson**, aided by the supremely efficient team of **Sarah Clifford** and **Stephanie White** who set out the text and illustrations with great care and inventiveness, guided by the book's design guru **Nigel Harriss**. In addition the book has benefitted from the watchful eye of **Dr Tracey Elder** who took a lot of time and great care to check and refine our advice.

Finally the authors and publisher also wish to thank the following teachers and their students for their invaluable suggestions: Veena Bhandal, Tom Buxton-Cope, Anthony Curtis, Sara Dryburgh, Deb Gajic, Jo Haycock, Mark Jones, Ruth Jones, Zoe Johnson, Jane McGee, Andy Rayner, Claudia Stevens, Dan Vernon, Faye Whiteley.

Cara has written many books for A level psychology and is senior editor of *Psychology Review*. She speaks at and organises student conferences. In a previous life she was a teacher probably for more years than you have been alive. Her spare time (what there is of it) involves her husband and children (now over 20 years old), pubs and mountains, preferably on the same day.

Rob was an A level teacher for more than 20 years and would like to give a big shout out to his ex-colleagues at Winstanley College in Wigan. In his spare moments, he likes nothing more than to pluck away tunelessly at his guitar, ideally in the Lake District. He plans to ask Matt how you become a Chartered Psychologist. In an eerie echo of the first edition of this book, he still hasn't seen *Frozen 2*.

Matt is a Chartered Psychologist and Associate Fellow of the British Psychological Society. He taught psychology for 25 years and is currently Learning Technology and Innovation Manager for a Social Justice and Education charity. Matt is also an editor of *Psychology Review*. When not working or writing, Matt DJs and loves live music and festivals.

About the cover:

Madeline Rae Mason is the model gracing the front of our cover once more. **Jason Duda** took this incredible photo. They both live and work in Sydney, Australia and we thank them both for helping to give this series such a strong and memorable identity.

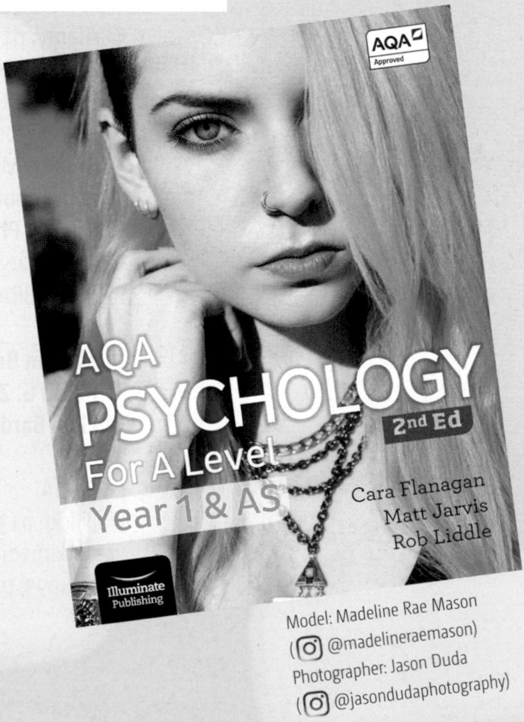
AQA Approved
AQA
PSYCHOLOGY
2nd Ed
For A Level
Year 1 & AS
Cara Flanagan
Matt Jarvis
Rob Liddle
Illuminate Publishing

Model: Madeline Rae Mason
(@madelineraemason)
Photographer: Jason Duda
(@jasondudaphotography)